M. Schuman, Mr. Acheson and Mr. Bevin at the Waldorf Astoria Hotel for the opening of the New York Conference of Foreign Ministers on 12 September 1950.

HMSO publications are available from:

HMSO Publications Centre
(Mail and telephone orders only)
PO Box 276, London, SW8 5DT
Telephone orders 01-873 9090
General enquiries 01-873 0011
(queuing system in operation for both numbers)

HMSO Bookshops
49 High Holborn, London, WC1V 6HB   01-873 0011 (Counter service only)
258 Broad Street, Birmingham, B1 2HE   021-643 3740
Southey House, 33 Wine Street, Bristol, BS1 2BQ   (0272) 264306
9–21 Princess Street, Manchester, M60 8AS   061-834 7201
80 Chichester Street, Belfast, BT1 4JY   (0232) 238451
71 Lothian Road, Edinburgh, EH3 9AZ   031-228 4181

HMSO's Accredited Agents
(see Yellow Pages)

and through good booksellers

DOCUMENTS ON BRITISH POLICY OVERSEAS

EDITED BY

ROGER BULLEN, Ph.D.

(*London School of Economics*)

AND

M.E. PELLY, M.A.

ASSISTED BY

H.J. YASAMEE, M.A. AND G. BENNETT, M.A.

SERIES II

Volume III

LONDON

HER MAJESTY'S STATIONERY OFFICE

DOCUMENTS ON BRITISH POLICY OVERSEAS

Series II, Volume III

German Rearmament
September – December 1950

ROGER JOHN BULLEN 1944–1988

Roger Bullen died on 21 September 1988, when work on all but the Preface to this book had been completed. The three volumes of Series II that he edited, *The Schuman Plan 1950–1952*, *The London Conferences 1950* and the present volume, together stand as an enduring monument to an exact scholar, an endearing colleague and a staunch friend.

PATRICIA M. BARNES

PREFACE

The documents in this volume were selected and edited by Dr. Roger Bullen, who was, unfortunately, unable to write a preface before he died. He had, however, begun to map it out and continued to give directions until overtaken by illness. This preface therefore follows his instructions and has been written on the basis of his own notes and the many conversations we enjoyed during the editing of this volume.

Volume III documents the negotiations for German rearmament between the North Atlantic Treaty powers in the autumn of 1950. These negotiations were part of the Western drive to rearm after the outbreak of hostilities in Korea in June. The Korean war itself will be covered in Volume IV. The present volume deals with the impact of the war on Europe and develops the themes, explored in Volumes I and II, of Britain's rôle in Europe and 'special relationship' with the United States of America. Volume III begins in September 1950 with the surprise American initiative for the creation of an Atlantic unified force and ends in December with the decision of the North Atlantic Council to seek a military contribution from the Federal Republic of Germany.

The hard bargaining between the Western Allies which preceded this decision, only five years after the end of the Second World War, was conducted on a number of levels at a series of tripartite and North Atlantic Treaty conferences in New York (September), Washington (October) and Brussels (December). The negotiations, set in motion by the American proposal, itself composed of several parts but presented as a single package, took several directions: political, military and economic. They ran alongside separate negotiations for the financing, supply and equipment of new European defence programmes and for the continuing transformation of N.A.T.O. into 'a living reality' (Volume II, No. 74.i). From the end of October the question of German rearmament, increasingly linked to Occupation issues, was further complicated by rival initiatives from France and the Soviet Union: the Pleven plan for a European Army and the Soviet proposal for a Council of Foreign Ministers on Germany. Allied discussions on all these issues brought into sharp focus their divisions on Europe, at the heart of which lay the unresolved question of the future of Germany. Throughout, Mr. Bevin's main objective was to secure Western Europe within an Atlantic rather than a purely European framework. This depended on British partnership with the United States, the cementing of which was the fundamental aim of Mr. Attlee's visit to Washington in December.

In the summer of 1950 European member countries of N.A.T.O. responded quickly to U.N. appeals for rearmament after the outbreak of the Korean war. By September, rearmament in Western Europe was proceeding on two fronts. Firstly, all countries were taking steps to increase their own national defence programmes. Mr. Bevin had taken the lead in persuading the Brussels Treaty powers to follow the British example of extending national service and stationing more troops in Germany. Secondly, European N.A.T. members were cooperating in a high priority defence production programme, proposed by the Americans in July, which supplemented the main N.A.T. defence programme, the Medium Term Plan. Overall the British government proposed to double its defence budget at a cost of £3,600 millions over three years. This budget had been worked out on the assumption of a contribution from the United States of £550 millions. Progress was dependent on at least a first instalment of American aid, which, though promised in principle, had yet to materialise as a specific offer. Mr. Bevin spoke for all European countries when he told Mr. Acheson, U.S. Secretary of State, on 2 September that it was not fair to expect commitments to new defence programmes without a corresponding American commitment to help pay for them (No. 1).

At the same time Mr. Bevin was aware that the planned defence programmes were not enough to guarantee western defence. This had suddenly become a matter of urgency. The Medium Term Plan was based on the assumption that war was unlikely to break out in Europe before 1954. However, by September 1950 reports of substantial increases in the numbers and level of equipment of the military police force (Bereitschaften) in the Soviet zone of Germany indicated that it was being turned into a regular army, capable of overrunning Berlin and invading the Federal Republic of Germany within eighteen months (see Nos. 12 and 40.i). This led Mr. Bevin to fear 'that next year the Soviet Government will seek to repeat in Germany what they have done in Korea' (No. 3.i: D.O. (50) 66).

British concern about the defence of Western Europe was intensified by the Chiefs of Staff's new view of global strategy, accepted by Ministers in May, which maintained that 'our defence lies along a land line in Europe, as far east as we can make it' (No. 73: see also Volume II, No. 43, note 2). It was acknowledged that such a line was indefensible without the military help of Germany. The Chiefs of Staff therefore put forward in August a long term plan for the gradual rearmament of the Federal Republic of Germany (No. 3.i). On 1 September the Defence Committee of the Cabinet, chaired by Mr. Attlee, agreed with Mr. Bevin that this was not practicable at the present time, but that some form of German contribution to defence was essential. Ministers therefore endorsed Mr. Bevin's alternative solution for, *inter alia*, mobile police forces in the F.R.G. and in Berlin and authorised him to seek agreement at the forthcoming tripartite and N.A.C. meetings in New York, beginning on 12 September (see Nos. 3.i and 8).

On 4 September Mr. Bevin was informed in London by the U.S. Chargé d'Affaires of Mr. Acheson's intention to propose at New York the formation of an Atlantic unified force under an American Supreme Commander into which German units would be integrated (No. 2). Other features of the plan, which took concrete shape in U.S. draft resolutions at New York and Washington (Nos. 33 and 72.i), included an industrial contribution to defence from the F.R.G. and some structural reorganisation within N.A.T.O., thereby complicating existing N.A.T.O. plans for rationalising the overlap with the Brussels Treaty Organisation (cf. No. 3.ii).

Britain welcomed the plan for a unified force as firm evidence of American willingness to supply men, money and machinery to the defence of Europe. Mr. Attlee expressed 'warm satisfaction at this development' (No. 2, note 11). Mr. Bevin saw no harm in discussing the plan at New York, provided that the American government gave prior assurances on finance and agreed that the German contribution could take the form of a police force rather than military units. At New York the proposals for German police forces and military units were pursued as separate questions. Agreement was soon reached for the formation of police forces (Nos. 16, note 2, and 26.ii). Mr. Bevin agreed that they should be formed on a Land rather than a Federal basis, even though this was regarded by the British Chiefs of Staff as militarily unsound (No. 44, note 4).

The question of German military units proved much more difficult. Mr. Acheson made it plain that U.S. offers for a unified force, more troops in Europe and aid for European defence programmes were all dependent on agreement to the principle of German military units. He conceded that once this principle was accepted, the actual implementation could take its time. Under these conditions Mr. Bevin, who was anxious to make a start with the unified force before bringing in the F.R.G., was prepared to agree (Nos. 18 and 20). His Cabinet colleagues were more reluctant, but were eventually brought round when persuaded by Mr. Bevin that the Americans were not bluffing when they threatened to withdraw their new found commitment to Europe, if no agreement was reached on the principle of German units. The French delegation led by M. Schuman, Minister for Foreign Affairs, was more sceptical (cf. Nos. 42 and 71) and resolutely refused to give way.

French arguments against German rearmament, advanced by M. Schuman at New York, were fairly persuasive and by no means entirely negative (see No. 32). German rearmament, while not ruled out for the future, was said to be premature, unduly provocative to the Soviet Union and hardly welcome to the Germans themselves. M. Schuman readily agreed to a German contribution to defence in the form of police, labour battalions and industrial production, but insisted that the raising of military units must wait until European defences were stronger and able to contain the dangers inherent in a revival of German military power. German participation in a unified force was regarded as a potential source of weakness. The effort of controlling the German element would be disproportionate to the added strength, and there was always the risk of becoming embroiled in a European war for the recovery of Königsberg (see No. 63), to say nothing of internal French political difficulties. At one point M. Schuman suggested he would have no difficulty in agreeing, if only it could be kept secret (No. 28). Fundamentally, however, French objections to German rearmament derived from a greater fear of Germany than of the Soviet Union (cf. Nos. 38, 46, note 4, 73 and 84).

In Mr. Bevin's eyes there was no doubt that the Soviet Union posed the greater threat. This view was shared by Mr. Acheson who in any case 'did not accept the argument that training Germans would provoke the Russians to attack' (No. 21). Mr. Bevin was less certain but felt that 'the risks inherent in any strengthening of the German defence forces must be faced sometime, unless we are to run the greater risk of losing Germany to the Soviets' (No. 3). The French did not agree and maintained that German rearmament would so increase the risk of war as to have dangers disproportionate to the immediate advantages to be gained (No. 41). The differences between the Allies were later summed up by Mr. Bevin when he told the Belgian Foreign Minister, M. van Zeeland: 'One of the troubles seemed to him to be that, whereas the other North Atlantic Treaty countries were thinking in terms of building up powerful forces to act as a deterrent, the French were inclined to think more of what might happen if fighting began' (No. 83).

Although tripartite discussions at New York essentially revolved around tripartite fears and concerns, the Western Occupying powers were aware that at some stage German attitudes would have to be taken into account. German unwillingness to rearm was one of the reasons why the British Cabinet had been reluctant on 14 September to accept the principle of German rearmament (No. 19). When brought to agree on the next day, the Cabinet warned that 'the United States Government were apt to talk as though it was for the North Atlantic Treaty Powers to determine the extent and form of German participation in Western defence, whereas an entirely new situation would be created if any endeavour were made to go beyond what the Germans were themselves prepared to do' (No. 27). No-one, not least the Cabinet, which had not been kept informed of previous German offers on defence, was quite sure how far the Germans would willingly go.

In the autumn of 1950 German opinion on rearmament was known to be fairly well divided between concern to safeguard internal security and unwillingness to rearm, especially against fellow-countrymen in the east. No serious problem was anticipated by the Western Occupying Powers with their proposal to raise armed police forces. The Federal Chancellor, Dr. Adenauer, had himself been pressing for measures along these lines since April (Volume II, No. 45), and even the die-hard opponents of rearmament in the S.P.D., led by Dr. Schumacher, were thought unlikely to object to measures primarily designed to protect internal security (see No. 3.iii). Military units were, however, a different matter and the British government shared French concern as to the price the Federal government might make them pay. At the end of August, Dr. Adenauer had indicated his readiness to discuss a German military contribution to a European army, provided it was on the basis of military equality: a point insisted upon by the S.P.D. At the same time Dr. Adenauer had pressed for further Occupation concessions.

Mr. Bevin quickly appreciated the wider implications for Allied policy in Germany of a decision to seek a German military contribution to defence. On 12 September, he warned Mr. Acheson and M. Schuman of the 'embarrassing demands' the Federal government was liable to make. He did not think, for example, that 'it was possible to separate this question of German participation in defence from the problem of the control of German foreign policy' (No. 15). Mr. Bevin, whose Occupation policy was consistently liberal (see Nos. 4–5), was not averse to making more concessions, provided they were made on Allied terms after proper consideration and not hastily given away as a bargaining chip. He therefore stated: 'We were very ready to examine how far we should go, but we should not consider the problem from the narrow angle of the extent to which the Germans could help us to defend ourselves against Russia. We should constantly bear in mind that it was our objective to establish Germany as a permanent and responsible member of the Western comity of nations' (No. 15).

Nevertheless, apart from following up Mr. Bevin's suggestion of asking the Allied High Commissioners to study German attitudes to rearmament, Ministers did not really get to grips with the problem. They confined themselves to considering the tactics of an approach on defence to the Federal government, without worrying too much as to where that approach might lead. Everyone agreed that there must be no bargaining with the Federal government. Allied tactics, proposed by Mr. Bevin, were therefore 'to avoid any suggestion that the defence of Europe was in any way dependent on the Germans', thereby avoiding the chance of 'blackmail' (No. 10). Quite how this was to be achieved, when even the Rhine–Ijssel line could not be defended without German help and new N.A.T. plans aimed at defending a line still further east, was never addressed by Ministers at New York, other than to agree with Mr. Bevin that the Germans must be very carefully handled (see Nos. 15 and 83).

N.A.C. discussions, which began on 15 September at New York, followed the pattern of the preceding tripartite talks. Only the French remained unimpressed by the 'historic decision' of the United States to be 'in the fighting in Europe from the first day' (No. 25, cf. also No. 73). Hopes of avoiding a complete impasse by temporary adjournments and the summoning of the three Defence Ministers to New York seemed ill-founded when M. Moch, French Defence Minister, took up a much more inflexible position than M. Schuman (Nos. 41 and 46). On 22 September a mistake on the part of the new American Defence Secretary, General Marshall, opened the way for an interim agreement, which all were thankful to conclude (see Nos. 42 and 52). In addition to the new mobile police forces, measures were agreed for the strengthening of existing police and auxiliary forces and some industrial contribution to defence (No. 43).

Steps were taken immediately by the Allied High Commissioners to implement these measures beginning with a meeting on 23 September with Dr. Adenauer, who welcomed the New York decisions (see No. 45). Subsequent negotiations were complicated by a tendency among the military staffs to regard the new police forces, particularly in Berlin, as an alternative route to rearmament (cf. Nos. 12, 40 and 60). This tendency was not helped by a genuine confusion as to what had been agreed at New York regarding police weapons (No. 113). Mr. Bevin was quick to block any move to turn the police forces into a covert army (No. 60, note 17) and was equally insistent that measures in Berlin 'where we are so vulnerable' should not get out of step with those taken in the F.R.G. (No. 113).

There was no disagreement at New York about a German industrial contribution. Although pursued as a subsidiary question, the economic side was regarded by British officials as equally important and they regretted the way it was overshadowed by manpower questions (No. 92, note 4). The main point of concern, shared by all N.A.T.O. countries, was that if the F.R.G. were left out of the new defence production effort, she would gain an unfair advantage in non-defence export markets. For once no one quarrelled with M. Moch when he said 'it would be wrong that Germany should be allowed to concentrate on building tractors or consumer goods while the allied countries were devoting their resources to production of armaments' (No. 41). As a first step to making sure that this did not happen, the tripartite study group on Germany (I.G.G.) was directed in September to review the Prohibited and Limited Industries Agreement. The intention was to ease restrictions which impeded the common defence effort, but I.G.G. progress between October and December was frustrated by French reluctance to lift controls before the Schuman Plan treaty was signed (cf. No. 140). Negotiations on the Schuman Plan reached a delicate stage in October when German enthusiasm began to evaporate. The New York conferences had raised expectations that the F.R.G. might soon be asked to rearm, which could enable her 'to recover her place in European society' independently of the Schuman Plan (Volume I, No. 170).

British officials were also instructed to look more closely at the possibilities of a German financial contribution. Areas of study, commissioned by Mr. Attlee and senior Ministers, included 'getting the water out of Occupation costs' so as to enable Germany to bear a heavier defence burden (Nos. 61 and 112).

No agreement on the plan for a unified force was reached at New York, other than to refer it to the military arm of N.A.T.O. for further study. An outline of the plan was included in the final N.A.C. resolution (No. 47), but the plan itself was held in suspense, pending agreement to the principle of German rearmament. It was hoped that this might be reached at the next meeting of the North Atlantic Committee of Defence Ministers which was being held in Washington on 28 October.

Returning from New York at the beginning of October, Mr. Bevin and his advisers reflected on the successes and failures of the New York conferences (Nos. 55–6). On the whole the British delegation was well satisfied with the position reached on finance. Mr. Acheson had not given anything away but he had at least been constructive (see No. 11). His suggestion of pursuing claims for aid outside as well as inside the North Atlantic Treaty forum was particularly welcome to the British, who thought they had more chance in bilateral negotiation of staying out of the 'European queue' (see Nos. 14 and 22). On his return voyage to England, Mr. Bevin read a long memorandum of 27 September from the British Ambassador in Washington, Sir O. Franks, which revived old Cabinet differences (No. 49, cf. also Volume II, Nos. 57, 62–3). By the autumn of 1950 the British economy was doing well enough to suggest that 'we were becoming able for the first time since the war to sustain our world-wide commitments' (No. 49, cf. also No. 11, note 7). According to Sir O. Franks, this economic independence had brought about a corresponding measure of political independence, particularly in relation to the United States. The projected increases in British defence expenditure after Korea threatened to plunge Britain once more into such debt as to jeopardize 'the position we were just attaining, the partner in world affairs of the United States. We shall be back again in the European Queue' with unpalatable consequences for British leadership not only in Europe but also in the Commonwealth (Nos. 49 and 79).

Although Sir O. Franks' political analysis was accepted by Ministers, his solution of asking the United States to write off the 1945 loan was rejected in favour of working towards an American formula for the equitable sharing of burdens (Nos. 53 and 79). Mr. Bevin attached importance to this getting away from the idea of givers and receivers towards 'the fundamental North Atlantic Treaty conception of a common effort between partners' (No. 33, note 2). Even so, the United States remained the largest paying partner: a point of concern to some Cabinet members, headed by the Minister of Health, Mr. Aneurin Bevan (see Nos. 108 and 143).

The main failures of the New York conferences undoubtedly related to defence. As far as the British delegation was concerned, the main casualty of tripartite clashes on defence had been Anglo-American hopes of accelerating the integration of the F.R.G. into the west. British officials regretted that clumsy American tactics on the defence issue had led to unsatisfactory compromises on Occupation questions and placed Anglo-French relations under strain (see No. 62). British disappointment at American readiness to support the French in postponing certain Occupation decisions tended to obscure the fact that a good many others were still taken. In particular Ministers agreed to end the state of war with

Germany, to give the Federal government, now recognised as the only German government entitled to speak for Germany, control of foreign policy and to revise the Occupation statute (see Nos. 26.ii and 55).

Anglo-French relations were clouded by events at New York. Only M. Schuman remained unperturbed as recriminations abounded (see Nos. 35, note 4, and 64). M. Pleven, President of the Council of Ministers, was said to be 'pained by the rapidity with which we had changed our position on the question of German rearmament in New York and had come round to the United States view. If we had stood with the French rather longer than we did, we might have brought the Americans to change their attitude. It would have been more in keeping with the relationship of one Brussels Power to another, if we had not parted company with them quite so quickly' (No. 71, note 2). British officials shared French resentment at being hustled by the Americans (Nos. 57 and 94, note 3), but felt there was now no time to waste, since American offers, though genuine enough, would not remain indefinitely on the table.

British preparations for the next meetings in Washington concentrated on how to bring the French round. On the military side, safeguards for keeping German rearmament under control were worked out by the Chiefs of Staff in conjunction with the Foreign Office (No. 54.ii). The main difficulty was how to draw up safeguards which would be militarily effective and yet politically acceptable to the Federal government (No. 67). Sir I. Kirkpatrick, U.K. High Commissioner in Germany, was influential in striking a fair balance (see Nos. 70 and 74). From the end of October safeguards took shape in N.A.T.O., passing on 18 November from the Standing Group to the Military Committee and on to the political Deputies of the N.A.C., before reaching the N.A.C. itself on 18 December. The least contentious point was that there should be no German Army or General Staff, while the most contentious was the level at which German units would be integrated into the unified force. The French insisted successfully that the level should be brought down from division to brigade level (see No. 136).

On the diplomatic side, pressure was exerted in October on the French government and Socialist party (see Nos. 50, note 2, 63–4 and 94). Although the Americans were anxious 'to "keep the heat on" the French' (No. 66), Mr. Bevin was reluctant to press the divided French government too hard, paying heed to warnings that its fall would benefit French Socialists and Communists, who were taking the lead in opposing rearmament (see Nos. 46.i and 75). On 12 October he decreed a period of silence so as to 'leave the French and Americans to fight this out between them for a time' (No. 65, note 3).

On the next day the Foreign Office received its first hint that the French government, encouraged by the American Embassy in Paris, was preparing an alternative plan for a European Army (No. 66). This hint was apparently not pursued in the immediately following period of discreet silence imposed by Mr. Bevin. On 24 October British Ministers and officials, distracted by the first signs of a Soviet response to Western plans for rearmament (No. 78), were therefore unprepared for the announcement of the Pleven Plan for a European Army. The French government proposed to invite the Federal government to participate in negotiations for a European army, which would begin in Paris only when the Schuman Plan treaty was signed (see Nos. 80–1).

Immediate British reactions to the Pleven Plan were mixed. In so far as the plan represented French acceptance of the principle of German rearmament, it was welcomed. The way seemed clear for reaching agreement on the American plan after all. M. Pleven himself maintained that negotiations for a European Army need not interfere with the constitution of a unified force: 'European nations, apart from Germany, could make their contribution to this force at once' (No. 81). Mr. Bevin and his advisers were less optimistic. They foresaw endless complications and said that their main objection to the plan was the delay it would cause not only to German rearmament, but also to the formation of an Atlantic unified force (No. 89). The Pleven plan was also disliked as a move away from the Atlantic conception of defence towards a European federal solution. Mr. Bevin made it clear that 'if the French are trying to create a federated European force, including the British, as a sort of makeweight to the power of the new world on one side and the Soviet Union on the other, then he is utterly and irrevocably opposed to the proposals' (No. 85, note 5). On balance, however, Mr. Bevin thought that once the French were stronger themselves and surrounded by sufficient safeguards, 'they would probably not die in the last ditch for their specifically federal solution' (No. 89). On military grounds, the plan was regarded as unsound. The size of the proposed European army was considered too small to be militarily effective. Encouraged by the French Embassy in London, the Foreign Office concluded that the Plan was primarily designed to help M. Pleven through a parliamentary emergency and need not be taken 'too seriously' (No. 89).

British participation in the Pleven plan was never really an issue. The French sent clear signals that they neither wished nor expected the British to join (Nos. 80, note 3 and 88) and the Cabinet took an early opportunity of rejecting participation in favour of observer status (Nos. 92 and 148, note 6). At the same time, following Mr. Acheson's lead, Mr. Bevin was careful not to reject the plan outright. By agreeing to study the French plan further, it was hoped that the French would respond by taking a more constructive line on the American plan for a unified force: a policy of 'little steps for little feet' (No. 82). When briefing the Minister of Defence, Mr. Shinwell, on 26 October before his departure for Washington, Mr. Attlee and Mr. Bevin emphasised the importance of not allowing the French proposal to deflect attention away from the more pressing need to make progress with the unified force, the reorganization of N.A.T.O. and the appointment of a Supreme Commander (No. 85).

In Washington these hopes were confounded by M. Moch's unequivocal refusal to discuss any ideas other than French ones. The Americans responded by tightening their own package, so that the formation of a unified force was made dependent on the simultaneous formation of German units rather than, as allowed in New York, agreement merely to the principle of their being formed (cf. No. 136). This tougher requirement was harder for all to swallow and N.A.T. members, who had joined with their Anglo-American colleagues in dismissing the Pleven Plan, began to have second thoughts (cf. Nos. 91.i and 98).

Nonetheless at the end of the Washington meetings, at which some progress was made on subsidiary issues, such as the reorganization of N.A.T.O. (see Nos. 85, note 3, and 91.i), the French remained in a minority of one. On 6 November the U.K. Deputy on the N.A.C., Sir F. Hoyer Millar, warned Mr. Bevin that 'If the French persist in this attitude they may not only delay the rearmament of the West indefinitely but wreck the whole N.A.T.O. organisation' (No. 98). Reports from early November confirming Chinese intervention in Korea and difficulties over a reply to the Soviet invitation of 3 November to a four-power conference on Germany exacerbated tensions and intensified the pressure for European rearmament. Mr. Bevin was worried by the slow progress of N.A.T.O. and feared that 'if the French were not careful, they might cause the Americans in exasperation to look to Germany rather than to France as the mainstay of Western Europe' (No. 83).

Mr. Bevin's own exasperation took the form of an increasingly violent antipathy to the Pleven plan, which he came to regard as 'a sort of cancer in the Atlantic body' and 'we must nip it in the bud' (No. 115). British objections to the Pleven plan reveal the fundamentally Atlanticist outlook of Mr. Bevin and his advisers (cf. Nos. 84–5, 110, 115). At New York Mr. Bevin had warned that 'it was a mistake to lay too much emphasis on the word "Europe"' (No. 14). He later told Dr. D. Stikker, the Netherlands Foreign Minister, that 'We must face the French quite frankly with the question whether it was to be Europe or the Atlantic. On which basis were we going to build? In our opinion, the answer was the Atlantic, and I thought that in giving this answer I was speaking not only for my own party but also for the Opposition. I had reached this conclusion not because I was anti-European, but because I did not believe Europe alone could ever be strong enough to defend itself' (No. 114, cf. also Nos. 20, note 3, and 50). French policy on the other hand was believed to be not only directed towards keeping Germany out of N.A.T.O., but against N.A.T.O. itself: a fact freely admitted by M. Schuman when he told delegates at the Council of Europe that the Atlantic pact was temporary whereas Europe was permanent (see Nos. 111, note 3, and 117).

Mr. Bevin's disquiet at the way French policy and the whole defence situation was developing surfaced in his conversation with M. van Zeeland on 25 October, when he complained that 'every time one French demand was met they came forward with another . . . His fear now was that the French were going to behave in such a way as to give the Russians a great deal of encouragement. He must admit that there was grave disquiet in Great Britain about the French attitude, and people did not understand all the party manoeuvring which went on when vital questions of defence were at stake' (No. 83). British opinion of French policy deteriorated further after the intransigence displayed by M. Moch at Washington led to a complete stalemate in November. At this point Mr. Bevin and his officials, despite a feeling that the French had 'behaved badly', thought they ought to try to help them out of their difficulties. In the same way as with the Schuman plan in May they had looked for a way 'to get them [the French] out of the mess into which they have landed themselves' (Volume I, No. 31, Annex B), British officials began to consider how to dispose of the Pleven plan so as 'to make things easier for them and to help them to find a way out of the present impasse' (No. 98).

On 8 November the Cabinet Defence Committee invited the Chiefs of Staff and the Foreign Office to search for a way of breaking the deadlock. Mr. Attlee complained that the present 'dangerous situation was the direct result of the French attachment to an unworkable and unsound plan' and asked 'were the French in fact intending to fight, or had they already made up their minds to give in?' (No. 101). The Chiefs of Staff were instructed to see how the original American plan could be modified to meet the French (No. 101), while in the Foreign Office Sir P. Dixon, a Deputy Under-Secretary of State on whom Mr. Bevin heavily relied, began to look for other alternatives. On 21 November Mr. Bevin reviewed all possibilities and decided to adopt a new plan, which took both American and French plans a stage further. The French had proposed that the European Army should eventually form part of the Atlantic integrated force. Mr. Bevin's plan was to develop the whole integrated force into a single Atlantic Army. This was rejected on 27 November by the Cabinet Defence Committee on both military and political grounds. The idea of an Atlantic Confederate force was considered as unsound as the Pleven plan itself, while Mr. Attlee thought that 'it was quite likely that the French would fail to create this European Federated Force, but he could not see why they should not make the attempt' (No. 118, cf. also No. 131). It was therefore agreed that Britain should support the American compromise solution suggested by Mr. Spofford to the N.A.C. Deputies on 20 November, whereby the U.S. plan for a unified force, now with a reduced level of German units, and the Pleven plan for a European Army should proceed in parallel (No. 109).

The Soviet proposal of 3 November for a four-power Council of Foreign Ministers on Germany marked the beginning of a new phase in which the future of the Occupation of Germany, founded on quadripartite agreements, was firmly tied to tripartite defence plans. The Soviet government had been unexpectedly quiet about Western plans for rearmament. The first signs of a Soviet response did not appear until 19 October when the Soviet government at last responded to Allied notes of 23 May on the Bereitschaften. In a note, delivered on 20 October, the

Soviet government countered Allied protests against the military character of the Bereitschaften with allegations that the Western Powers were rebuilding a German Army in the Federal Republic (see No. 78). This was followed by the issue of a communiqué from an Eastern European conference held in Prague on 20–21 October, which proposed the resumption of quadripartite negotiations for the demilitarization of Germany as a prelude to a peace treaty and reunification. These proposals were confirmed in the specific invitation to a four-power conference contained in a further Soviet note of 3 November (see No. 86, note 5).

British reactions to the Soviet initiative were cautious (see Nos. 78 and 86). Uncertainty prevailed as to whether it was a propaganda move in the cold war, a preliminary to a Soviet attack in Germany or an attempt to drive a wedge between the Western Powers, whose differences over rearmament were becoming the subject of public speculation. The immediate motive was thought to be the exploitation of Allied differences so as to delay if not prevent German rearmament (see No. 122). With sure timing the Soviet proposal caught the Western Powers at a moment of maximum disarray. The launch of the Pleven plan had thrown Western rearmament plans into confusion (cf. No. 80, note 4). The positions taken up by the French and Americans at Washington gave little hope of any immediate end to the deadlock. French fears about being left by the Americans to deal with renewed German aggression began to seem more real as the escalation of the war in Korea in November increased doubts about the arrival of American reinforcements in Europe and strengthened concern not to provoke the Russians too far (cf. Nos. 121 and 126).

The question of a reply to the Soviet government became the source of considerable embarrassment and prolonged negotiation between the Western Occupying powers as they endeavoured to find a formula which would reconcile their own differences and satisfy public opinion. Although British Ministers and officials agreed with Mr. Acheson that the Soviet proposals were only 'eye-wash' (No. 86), they had to take account of a groundswell of public opinion which, at a time of acute international tension, did not want to see any genuine Soviet offer for negotiation refused (Nos. 110, note 3, 122 and 146).

British policy was directed towards finding a sound basis for discussion before making a commitment to four-power talks (see Nos. 86, 97 and 122). Mr. Bevin did not want to risk a damaging breakdown, but was concerned to restrain the Americans from attaching so many conditions to talks as to reject the Soviet proposal outright (Nos. 97, 110, note 3, and 138). British and French officials were at one in agreeing that 'we should fall into a trap if we simply said yes, or if we simply said no' (No. 97, note 6). The French were more attracted to the Soviet initiative since it offered them a way out of their rearmament difficulties, by enabling them to say that it was not sensible to come to any decision on defence until the Soviet olive branch had been fully explored (Nos. 78, note 8, and 86). Mr. Bevin thought this line dangerous and was resolute in holding out for Western agreement on defence before any meeting with the Soviet Union (Nos. 86, note 5, and 110).

Soviet pressure intensified at the end of November as reports emanated from Moscow that German rearmament, on which the Allies were at last reaching agreement by way of the Spofford compromise, would provoke the Soviet Union to war in Europe (see Nos. 125, note 2, and 142). On the eve of Mr. Attlee's visit to Washington, at the height of the Korean crisis, Mr. Bevin's own resolution on German rearmament wavered. On 6 December he recommended to Mr. Attlee in Washington that Allied plans for German rearmament should be postponed in view of greater uncertainties as to the arrival of U.S. troops in Europe and the violence of Soviet reactions (No. 128). Mr. Bevin's advice ran contrary to that of Mr. Shinwell, Mr. Herbert Morrison, Lord President of the Council, and the Chiefs of Staff (Nos. 125–6, 128). It coincided on 6 December with French agreement to the Spofford plan and American agreement to proceed with their plan for a unified force and the appointment of a Supreme Commander. In these new circumstances, Mr. Attlee decided that it was 'unthinkable . . . to pause and draw back. To have done so would, in the opinion of everyone here, have killed the present talks and dealt a body blow at the renewed Anglo-American partnership which seems to be developing' (No. 131).

In this volume coverage of Mr. Attlee's talks in Washington with President Truman from 4–8 December is concerned with topics relating to western defence, on which Mr. Attlee was subjected to renewed pressure (see Nos. 132 and 134). Fuller consideration of the rest of the agenda, including use of the atomic bomb and Korea, will be given in Volume IV. It is, however, clear from the present volume that President Truman's remark on 7 December that in the event of war in Europe, only the Americans and the British could be relied upon to fight (No. 131, note 4), strengthened Mr. Attlee in the belief that at Washington he had 'persuaded the Americans to accept Anglo-American partnership as the mainspring of Atlantic defence' (No. 143). Mr. Attlee's success in reaching agreements for the tripartite control of raw materials and resumption of closer Anglo-American military cooperation along the lines of the wartime Combined Boards further boosted British confidence in the 'special relationship' and in their ability to safeguard Commonwealth interests (Nos. 124.i, 131–2).

Meanwhile in London Mr. Bevin continued to apply the brake to Allied plans for German rearmament. On 7 December British agreement to the Spofford plan was conveyed to the Deputies of the N.A.C. with two reservations. Firstly, Mr. Bevin insisted that the approval of the Spofford plan by the Deputies should not commit governments as to the timing of an approach to the Federal government. Secondly, he wished to prevent the Deputies from taking immediate steps to obtain the formal approval of the North Atlantic Defence Committee and Council (see No. 133). Against a background of continued Soviet pressure, Mr. Bevin was anxious to retain control of strategy and was determined to resist American pressure for forcing the pace on Germany. 'Everyone', he complained, 'seems in such a hurry' (No. 133.i).

Mr. Bevin's concern about the timing of German rearmament derived from uncertainty not only about Soviet reactions but also about German ones. Not surprisingly the Allied High Commissioners had not got very far with exploratory talks on defence with the Federal government, conducted in October on the basis 'that the Germans appeared to be neither begged, coerced nor bought' (No. 60, note 11). When assessing likely German reactions to rearmament, the A.H.C. had come up against 'a large and active body of opinion in Germany, probably most widespread among the younger generation, which is not engaged on considering how and when and under what conditions Germany should make her contribution but which simply does not want to make any contribution at all' (No. 103). Despite initial hostility to the Pleven plan, the Federal government had come to prefer it to the American plan for a unified force (see Nos. 81, note 5, 96 and 120.i). On 8 November Dr. Adenauer officially welcomed the Pleven plan in the Bundestag (No. 103.i). A week later he presented the A.H.C. with a long list of Occupation requests, evoking comment in the Foreign Office that 'we may be forced to concede the maximum of political equality in order to bring about even the minimum of military equality' (No. 103.ii). It was recognised that: 'It will not be pleasing or easy to treat Germany as a partner and equal, but we cannot have it both ways. If we need Germany's help and want Germany to form part of our Western bloc, we must make her a full member of the club and reconcile ourselves to seeing her smoking a large cigar in a big chair in front of the fire in the smoking room. Otherwise, Germany will not pay the subscription we are asking; she may even join another club where she will be better treated' (No. 105). Nevertheless when facing up to the prospect of a rapid end to Occupation, even the most forward-looking in the Foreign Office stopped short of restoring full sovereignty (see Nos. 105, note 2, and 111).

Attitudes in the Federal Republic about Occupation and rearmament hardened significantly in December (see No. 136.i). On 1 December, 'rattled' by political difficulties and events in the Far East, Dr. Adenauer pushed the price of a German military contribution to defence up to contractual agreements and the promise of ultimate political equality (No. 120.i). On the same day the head of the German government in the Soviet zone, Herr Grotewohl, invited Dr. Adenauer to begin discussions towards reunification (No. 135.i). On 11 December the Federal Chancellor publicly stated that if the Spofford Plan was presented to him formally 'he would be in the unhappy position of having to reject it' (No. 135). This confirmed Mr. Bevin in the view that the pace towards German rearmament must be slowed down until progress had been made with the unified force, so as to build up 'our strength in Europe, while not courting a collision with the Russians or a rebuff from the Germans' (No. 139).

Much to Mr. Bevin's dismay, the Americans showed no signs of slowing down. Although the Deputies had, at Mr. Bevin's insistence, left the door open as regards formal N.A.C. approval of the Spofford plan, by 9 December Mr. Acheson had succeeded in fixing a date for an N.A.C. meeting in Brussels and was pressing for tripartite talks on Germany as well (No. 133, note 3).

The N.A.T. and tripartite conferences held in Brussels on 18–20 December were approached with a good deal of concern by Mr. Bevin and his advisers. On 17 December, Sir P. Dixon warned that the atmosphere was likely to be very difficult (No. 141). The Soviet diplomatic offensive had been particularly successful in France and Italy. The Russians were believed 'to be offering inducements to the French in return for French opposition to German rearmament, and we know that the Italian Government have been frightened into believing that a Russian attack on Europe is a serious possibility'. In addition Dr. Adenauer 'has been brought to believe that the potential effect upon German opinion of Grotewohl's offer to meet him to discuss the unification of Germany must be considered very seriously' (No. 141). In this delicate situation Mr. Bevin's primary objective at Brussels was to rally European morale and calm fears. He hoped to do this by exhorting European countries to concentrate on strengthening their own defence and by inducing the Americans to establish a unified force and Supreme Commander, without insisting on immediate German participation. Although opposed to any revision of the commitment to rearm Germany, Mr. Bevin hoped to persuade his colleagues on the N.A.C. to delay a formal approach to the Federal government until European defences were stronger. In this way he hoped to avoid going 'cap in hand' to the Germans and 'putting them in a position where they could bargain with us' (No. 136).

The Foreign Office was also concerned to slow the Americans down on German Occupation questions. Mr. Acheson's intention of launching at Brussels a new package of far-reaching Occupation concessions tied to German defence was thought likely 'to jeopardize what agreement has been reached since New York and to start another period of deadlock with the French' (No. 141). Mr. Bevin had been informed on 15 December of Mr. Acheson's new ideas for bringing the Occupation to a rapid end. While not disagreeing with the principle, Mr. Bevin was opposed to either rushing ahead too quickly or tying Occupation issues too tightly to the defence question. He hoped it would be possible to arrive gradually at some looser formula, whereby 'the progress of German rearmament was linked to the relaxation of the remaining controls, thus enabling Germany to "work her passage" according to her performance and ability to play her part in Western Europe' (No. 139).

In December 1950 Anglo-American differences with the French over industrial controls were standing in the way of making more progress with the Allied programme of associating the F.R.G. more closely with the West. An 'unbridgeable gap' had opened up between tripartite representatives on the Intergovernmental Study Group in their review of the Prohibited and Limited Industries agreement. The French were continuing to refuse to lift controls until the Federal government joined the Schuman plan. Mr. Bevin hoped to find some way at Brussels of closing the gap, without getting drawn into the question of British attitudes towards European integration, then under hard appraisal in the Foreign Office (see Nos. 140–1 and Volume I, No. 196).

French agreement to the Spofford compromise had been bought in the first week of December at the price of written assurances from Mr. Acheson to M. Schuman of American support for French schemes for European integration. M. Schuman was 'deeply gratified' (No. 132, note 4) by Mr. Acheson's letter, which had been sent in the face of strong British representations (Nos. 120 and 129). Mr. Bevin objected to the issue of 'a declaration on a fundamental issue on which, as the Americans well know, we and the French hold radically different views' (No. 129). Mr. Bevin was concerned that Mr. Acheson's message could 'encourage the French to take the line that further relaxation of our Occupation controls over Germany can only be effected when progress has been made with European integration on the lines of the Pleven Plan' (No. 120). Mr. Bevin thought that this could lead to Occupation questions being taken out of British hands. He complained that it was 'highly dangerous' and refused to be mollified by American dismissal of the letter as only words (see Nos. 129 and 132). He reminded Mr. Acheson that 'we cannot allow our whole future policy towards Europe to be settled merely on the basis of temporary expedients' (No. 129).

Allied plans for Europe were overshadowed by the unresolved question of a reply to the Soviet invitation to quadripartite talks on the demilitarization and eventual reunification of Germany. Tripartite official talks in Paris in early December had failed to produce an agreed reply and the question was referred to Ministers at Brussels (see Nos. 138 and 142). The Americans were holding out for a tough answer, whereas the British and the French wished to keep their options open by sending a less uncompromising reply to the Soviet government. The British position was explained on 18 December by Sir William Strang, Permanent Under-Secretary of State at the Foreign Office, when he told the French Ambassador, M. Massigli, 'We did not really think, any more than did the Americans, that Four-Power talks were likely to succeed. But so long as one was talking, one was talking . . . This was not appeasement, but common prudence. Diplomacy still had a beneficent part to play in the world' (No. 142, note 6).

Sir P. Dixon summed up British objectives at Brussels as: '(1) Putting flesh on our skeleton defences (2) Keeping an area of negotiation open with the Russians (3) Providing for an unprovocative evolution of Germany towards further participation in the benefits and responsibilities of the Western world' (No. 141). Mr. Bevin did not expect that the achievement of these objectives would be easy, and it was with some apprehension that the British delegation assembled in Brussels on 18 December.

In the event British policy at Brussels was unexpectedly successful. At the first meeting on 18 December the N.A.C. approved 'almost without discussion' recommendations from the North Atlantic Military Committee and Deputies for German participation in western defence. Rather to Mr. Bevin's surprise 'no one raised the question of the manner and timing of an approach to the German Federal Government', which was left to the discretion of the western Occupying powers (see No. 144). The North Atlantic Council proceeded to approve proposals for the immediate establishment of an integrated force, whereupon Mr. Acheson announced the appointment of General Eisenhower as Supreme Commander and the imminent increase of U.S. forces in Europe (see No. 145). At the same time it was understood that the French government would now proceed to convene a conference in Paris to begin negotiations for a European Defence Community. In tripartite talks on 19 December it was agreed that the A.H.C. should inform Dr. Adenauer of N.A.C. decisions on defence 'with an indication that they were ready to discuss the matter with him further but without handing him any document and without conveying the impression that he was expected to take hasty decisions' (No. 147).

Mr. Bevin was surprised that the Americans did not step up the pressure for acceleration of national defence efforts, applied during Mr. Attlee's visit to Washington (see Nos. 134, 139 and 145). He was therefore able to take the initiative by announcing British plans for further increasing the British defence programme which had been agreed by the Cabinet on 18 December (No. 143). Mr. Acheson was helpful over raw materials and aid for defence production and accepted the change in British defence policy whereby 'we are going to put the requirement horse before the financial cart – i.e. work out larger programmes and see later how we pay for them' (No. 145, note 5).

Satisfactory progress was made in tripartite discussions of German Occupation questions. Ministers agreed to move slowly towards contractual agreements, while taking steps to speed up the review of the P.L.I. agreement (see No. 147). Discussion on Germany was followed by agreement on the terms of a reply to the Soviet proposal for a Council of Foreign Ministers. As a first step towards a full C.F.M. meeting, the western powers suggested to the Soviet government in notes of 22 December that a preliminary quadripartite meeting of officials should be held 'with a view to finding a mutually acceptable basis for a meeting of the Foreign Ministers of the four countries and recommending to their Governments a suitable agenda' (No. 146).

The British delegation returned from Brussels well pleased with their success. Mr. Acheson had been noticeably subdued, whereas Mr. Bevin's leadership of the inner European group had been enhanced (No. 148). The Cabinet was informed that 'from the purely United Kingdom point of view, we were able to reassert our leadership in Europe' (No. 148, note

6). With renewed confidence therefore the Foreign Office looked ahead to the New Year and the implementation of a commitment 'to the difficult policy of hoeing two rows at once – negotiating with the Federal Republic about rearming the Germans and with Moscow about disarming them' (No. 146, note 5: cf. also Nos. 147.ii, and 149).

The main sources for this volume have been the archives of the Foreign and Commonwealth Office, especially the Foreign Office political files (F.O. 371). Within this class extensive use has been made of papers from the files of German Political department and Western Organizations department, which took the lead on Atlantic pact questions. The file designations of these and other departments used in this volume are listed on page xx of Volume II. Additional documentation has been drawn from the Private Office papers of Mr. Bevin (F.O. 800) and also from the files of the Cabinet Office (CAB), Prime Minister (PREM), Ministry of Defence (DEFE) and Treasury (T).

The photograph in the frontispiece is reproduced with the kind permission of Associated Press.

In accordance with the Parliamentary announcement, cited in Volume I, the Editors have had the customary freedom in the selection and arrangement of documents, including access to special categories of material such as records retained in the Department under Section 3(4) of the Public Records Act of 1958. They have followed customary practice in not consulting personnel files or specifically intelligence material. In the present volume there have been no exceptional cases, provided for in the parliamentary announcement, where it has been necessary on security grounds to restrict the availability of particular documents, editorially selected in accordance with regular practice.

I should like to thank the Head of Library and Records Department of the Foreign and Commonwealth Office, Dr. P.M. Barnes, and her staff for all facilities and help in the preparation of this volume. Kind assistance has also been received from the Records Branches of the Cabinet Office, the Ministry of Defence, No. 10 Downing Street and the Treasury. The staffs of Her Majesty's Stationery Office and the Public Record Office have been helpful at all times. To all members of Historical Branch I am grateful for general assistance and I would like to thank Mrs. M.E. Pelly, M.A., for advice and encouragement in the final stages. I am indebted to Miss K.E. Crowe, B.A., for valuable help towards preparing the manuscript and to Miss K.L. Jones, B.A. for an eagle eye on the proofs. My greatest debt is to Dr. Roger Bullen, whose enlightened and inspiring Editorship of Series II has led to three volumes of distinction in six years of happy collaboration.

H.J. YASAMEE

November 1988

CONTENTS

Volume

		PAGES
CHAPTER I	German Rearmament at the New York Conference. 2 September–10 October 1950	1
CHAPTER II	British reactions to the Pleven Plan and Soviet proposal for a Council of Foreign Ministers. 11 October–20 November 1950. . . .	154
CHAPTER III	Breaking the deadlock: the Spofford Plan, Mr. Attlee's visit to Washington and the Brussels Conference. 20 November–22 December 1950 . . .	274
APPENDIX	Guide to N.A.T.O. and Brussels Treaty Organisation. 1 January 1951	400
INDEX	. . . .	405

Microfiches

FICHE	DOCUMENT NUMBERS	FICHE	DOCUMENT NUMBERS
1	1.i–3.iv	6	110.i–114.i
2	4.i–24.i	7	119.i–131.i
3	26.i–46.i	8	133.i–145.ii
4	47.i–80.i	9	147.i–iii
5	84.i–109.i		

ABBREVIATIONS FOR PRINTED SOURCES

B.F.S.P.	*British and Foreign State Papers* (London, 1841–1977).
Cmd./Cmnd.	Command Paper to 1956/from 1956.
C. of E. *Official Report*	*Council of Europe, Consultative Assembly: Reports* (Strasbourg, 1949–50), subsequently: *Official Report of Debates* (Strasbourg, 1951f.).
D.B.F.P.	*Documents on British Foreign Policy 1919–1939* (H.M.S.O., London, 1946–86).
D.G.O.	*Documents on Germany under Occupation 1945–1954* edited by B.R. von Oppen (London, 1955).
D.S.B.	*Department of State Bulletin* (Washington).
F.R.U.S.	*Foreign Relations of the United States: Diplomatic Papers* (Washington, 1861f.).
Parl. Debs., *5th ser.,* *H. of C.*	*Parliamentary Debates (Hansard), Fifth Series, House of Commons, Official Report* (London, 1909f.).

ABBREVIATED DESIGNATIONS

A.H.C.	Allied High Commission	E.S.C.	Economic Steering Committee
A.O.C.	Atlantic (Official) Committee	F.R.G.	Federal Republic of Germany
AWT/DEF/ZO	Telegram series between B.J.S.M. and Ministry of Defence	G.D.R.	German Democratic Republic
		I.G.G.	Intergovernmental Study Group on Germany
B.J.S.M.	British Joint Services Mission (Washington)	Intel	Foreign Office series of Information Telegrams
C.D.U.	German Christian Democratic Union	J.P.S.	Joint Planning Staff
C.E.P.S.	Central Economic Planning Staff, Treasury	M.D.A.P.	Mutual Defence Assistance Programme
C.F.M.	Council of Foreign Ministers	M.P.S.B.	Military Production and Supply Board
C.I.G.S.	Chief of the Imperial General Staff	M.T.P.	Medium Term Plan
C.O.	Colonial Office	N.A.C.	North Atlantic Council
COJA/JACO	Telegram series between M.O.D. delegation in New York and Chiefs of Staff	N.A.T.	North Atlantic Treaty
		O.E.E.C.	Organisation for European Economic Cooperation
C.O.M.I.S.C.O.	Committee of the International Socialist Conference	P.L.I.	Prohibited and Limited Industries
C.O.S.	British Chiefs of Staff	P.U.S.C.	Permanent Under-Secretary's Committee
C.R.O.	Commonwealth Relations Office		
E.C.A.	American Economic Co-operation Administration	S.H.A.P.E.	Supreme Headquarters of the Allied Powers in Europe
E.P.U.	European Payments Union	S.P.D.	German Social Democratic Party
E.R.P.	European Recovery Programme	U.N.	United Nations

CHAPTER SUMMARIES

CHAPTER I

German Rearmament at the New York Conference
2 September–10 October 1950

NAME	DATE	MAIN SUBJECT	PAGE
1 To Sir O. Franks Washington Tel. No. 3946	2 Sept.	Message from Mr. Bevin to Mr. Acheson asking for confirmation of U.S. aid for U.K. defence programme. *Calendars:* **i–iii** German contribution.	1
2 Mr. Bevin and U.S. Charge d'Affaires: Meeting Foreign Office	4 Sept.	Transmission of U.S. proposal for unified force including German units. *Calendar:* **i** origins.	*4*
3 To Sir O. Harvey Paris No. 921	5 Sept.	U.K. proposals for police force in F.R.G. *Calendars:* **i–iv** D.O. (50) 65–8	9
4 Mr. Mallet Foreign Office	5 Sept.	Note of policy towards Germany. *Calendar:* **i** Cabinet.	14
5 To Sir O. Franks Washington	6 Sept.	Letter from Mr. Bevin asking for pre-conference discussion with Mr. Acheson on Germany.	18
6 Sir O. Harvey Paris Tel. No. 242	7 Sept.	M. Schuman's reactions to U.K. proposals for Federal police force. *Calendar:* **i** Parliamentary debate.	20
7 Air Marshal Sir W. Elliot Ministry of Defence	8 Sept.	Reactions of Chiefs of Staff to proposals for unified force and gendarmerie. *Calendar:* **i** meetings.	22
8 To U.K. High Commissioners Commonwealth Tel. Y No. 249	9 Sept.	Statement of British plans for German defence.	24
9 Sir G. Jebb New York Tel. No. 981	12 Sept.	Bevin-Acheson meeting: U.S. position on European defence. *Calendar:* **i** French common fund.	*26*
10 Sir G. Jebb New York Tel. No. 982	12 Sept.	Bevin-Acheson meeting: Mr. Bevin's concern to avoid German 'blackmail' over defence.	*28*

	NAME	DATE	MAIN SUBJECT	PAGE
11	SIR G. JEBB New York Tel. No. 983	12 Sept.	Bevin-Acheson meeting: finance of defence. *Calendar:* i U.K. economy.	29
12	MR. MALLET Foreign Office	12 Sept.	Minute warning that Chiefs of Staff view police force as first step towards German military units.	32
13	SIR G. JEBB New York Tel. No. 987	13 Sept.	Private tripartite meeting on 12 Sept: M. Schuman asks for time.	35
14	SIR G. JEBB New York Tel. No. 988	13 Sept.	Private meeting contd: Mr. Bevin anxious to consolidate European defence but 'a mistake to lay too much emphasis on the word "Europe"'.	36
15	SIR G. JEBB New York Tel. No. 989	13 Sept.	Private meeting contd: Mr. Bevin represents the need to handle a German contribution to defence with caution.	38
16	SIR G. JEBB New York Tel. No. 990	13 Sept.	1st open Tripartite meeting on 12 Sept: future procedure to include consultation with High Commissioners and eventually Benelux.	39
17	SIR G. JEBB New York Tel. No. 991	13 Sept.	1st meeting contd: N.A.T. medium term plan; unified force; raw materials.	40
18	SIR G. JEBB New York Tel. No. 996	13 Sept.	2nd meeting and request from Mr. Bevin to Mr. Attlee for authority to accept U.S. proposals for unified force including German units.	43
19	To SIR G. JEBB New York Tel. No. 1238	14 Sept.	Cabinet reluctant to abandon proposal for police force in favour of U.S. proposal for unified force.	44
20	SIR G. JEBB New York Tel. No. 1005	14 Sept.	Message from Mr. Bevin to Mr. Attlee: presses for agreement to U.S. proposal.	45
21	SIR G. JEBB New York Tel. No. 1009	14 Sept.	Private Tripartite meeting with High Commissioners: statements from M. Schuman and Mr. Bevin, but no decision.	47
22	SIR G. JEBB New York Tel. No. 1011	14 Sept.	Private meeting contd. U.S. agree to proceed with bilateral discussions on finance.	50
23	MR. RICKETT 10 Downing Street	14 Sept.	Message for Mr. Attlee from Mr. Bevin, who is 'very much disturbed' at Cabinet reluctance to back U.S. proposal.	51
24	SIR W. STRANG Foreign Office	14 Sept.	Minutes his concern at prospect of German rearmament. *Calendar:* i Soviet reactions.	52

NAME	DATE	MAIN SUBJECT	PAGE
25 Sir G. Jebb New York Tel. No. 1018	15 Sept.	2nd Tripartite meeting on 13 Sept. French objections to German participation in Western defence, without which U.S. unwilling to commit more forces.	54
26 Sir G. Jebb New York Tel. No. 1021	15 Sept.	3rd Tripartite meeting on 13 Sept: German Occupation questions. *Calendars: i–ii* decisions.	55
27 Cabinet Conclusions House of Commons C.M. (50) 59th	15 Sept.	U.K. agreement to principle of German participation in Western defence. *Calendar: i* Lord Pakenham.	58
28 Sir G. Jebb New York Tel. No. 1050	16 Sept.	Mr. Bevin informs Mr. Acheson on 15 Sept. of British agreement to U.S. plan.	61
29 U.K. Delegation New York Tel. COJA 115	16 Sept.	Military aspects of U.S. proposals. *Calendar: i* N.A.C. meetings.	63
30 Sir G. Jebb New York Tel. No. 1062	16 Sept.	Mr. Bevin reviews 'curious' situation in New York and the need for caution.	66
31 Sir G. Jebb New York Tel. No. 1065	16 Sept.	Summoning of Defence Ministers to New York.	67
32 Sir G. Jebb New York Tel. No. 1066	17 Sept.	N.A.C. meeting (16 Sept.). Statement by M. Schuman of French objections to German rearmament.	68
33 Sir G. Jebb New York Tel. No. 1069	17 Sept.	Text of U.S. plan for unified force with German units.	70
34 Sir G. Jebb New York Tel. No. 1070	17 Sept.	Intervention from Mr. Bevin to avoid breakdown by securing temporary adjournment of N.A.C.	74
35 Sir G. Jebb New York Tel. No. 1108	19 Sept.	Statement by Mr. Bevin of British position on German rearmament. *Calendar: i* N.A.C. statements.	76
36 To Sir G. Jebb New York Tel. No. 1321	19 Sept.	Information from French Ambassador of position in French Cabinet and warning from F.M. Montgomery on German rearmament.	78
37 U.K. Delegation New York Tel. COJA 122A	20 Sept.	Briefing for Mr. Shinwell at New York.	79
38 Mr. Shuckburgh Foreign Office	21 Sept.	Conv. with M. Massigli, who thinks U.S. insistence on German rearmament is disastrous. Implications for Brussels treaty.	84
39 Mr. Barclay New York	22 Sept.	Letter to Sir R. Makins explaining Mr. Bevin's anxieties at New York.	85

	NAME	DATE	MAIN SUBJECT	PAGE
40	SIR D. GAINER Foreign Office	22 Sept.	Minute to Mr. Attlee asking for authority to agree to new defence measures in Berlin. *Calendar:* **i** Bereitschaften.	87
41	SIR G. JEBB New York Tel. No. 1167	23 Sept.	Tripartite meeting of Defence and Foreign Ministers: arguments for and against German rearmament.	89
42	SIR G. JEBB New York Tel. No. 1168	23 Sept.	Tripartite meeting contd. Compromise offered by Marshall during adjournment is accepted by French.	93
43	SIR G. JEBB New York Tel. No. 1171	23 Sept.	Text of tripartite agreement on defence.	97
44	U.K. DELEGATION New York Tel. COJA 129	23 Sept.	Reviews agreement reached and future procedure.	99
45	SIR I. KIRKPATRICK Wahnerheide Tel. No. 1418	23 Sept.	Dr. Adenauer's reactions to New York decisions on Germany. *Calendars:* **i** A.H.C., **ii** Lord Henderson.	101
46	SIR G. JEBB New York Tel. No. 1204	26 Sept.	Mr. Bevin considers how 'to stop this ugly drift'. *Calendar:* **i** tactics.	103
47	SIR G. JEBB New York Tel. No. 1222	27 Sept.	Text of N.A.C. resolution for unified force. *Calendars:* **i–ii** meeting.	106
48	To SIR I. KIRKPATRICK Wahnerheide Tel. No. 1575	27 Sept.	Invites comment on options for German defence contribution.	109
49	SIR O. FRANKS Washington	27 Sept.	Memo. on U.S. aid for defence: how to remain a partner and not rejoin 'European queue'. *Calendar:* **i** Treasury criticisms.	111
50	SIR G. JEBB New York Tel. No. 1255	29 Sept.	Bevin-Acheson meeting: Mr. Acheson reaffirms U.S. commitment to German participation in defence.	119
51	SIR I. KIRKPATRICK Wahnerheide Tel. No. 1448	30 Sept.	Reply to No. 48. Explains why German military contingent is preferable to police force on either a Land or Federal basis.	121
52	MR. BARCLAY *Queen Mary*	3 Oct.	Explains U.S. confusion over Gen. Marshall's compromise.	122
53	MR. GAITSKELL Treasury	3 Oct.	Criticisms of No. 49. *Calendar:* **i** Gaitskell in Washington.	123
54	SIR R. MAKINS Foreign Office	4 Oct.	Memo. to Mr. Bevin of action taken by Sir O. Harvey to keep sustained but gentle pressure on French. *Calendars:* **i–ii** Safeguards.	126

	NAME	DATE	MAIN SUBJECT	PAGE
55	MR. BEVIN Foreign Office C.P. (50) 222	6 Oct.	Cabinet paper recording New York decisions on Germany.	128
56	MR. BEVIN Foreign Office C.P. (50) 223	6 Oct.	Cabinet paper reviewing position reached at New York on German defence.	133
57	SIR O. HARVEY Paris Tel. No. 408 Saving	7 Oct.	French attitudes and resentment of U.S. 'hustling methods'.	136
58	CABINET CONCLUSIONS 10 Downing Street C.M. (50) 63rd	9 Oct.	Discussion of Nos. 55 and 56. Agree further pressure should be applied to French govt.	137
59	To SIR O. HARVEY Paris Tel. No. 1008	9 Oct.	Instructions for representations to M. Schuman.	140
60	SIR D. GAINER Foreign Office	10 Oct.	Memo. reporting implementation of defence measures agreed at New York e.g. police.	143
61	MR. STEVENS Foreign Office	10 Oct.	Memo. outlining measures for German economic contribution to defence.	147
62	MR. PENSON Washington	10 Oct.	Letter to Mr. Stevens regretting New York concessions to French on German occupation questions.	150

CHAPTER II

British reactions to the Pleven Plan and Soviet proposal for a Council of Foreign Ministers
11 October–20 November 1950

	NAME	DATE	MAIN SUBJECT	PAGE
63	SIR O. HARVEY Paris Tel. No. 267	11 Oct.	Mr. Shinwell fails to move M. Moch from inflexible position on German rearmament. *Calendar:* i Brief.	154
64	SIR O. HARVEY Paris Tel. No. 268	11 Oct.	Search by M. Schuman for formula 'somewhere between "yes" and "no"'.	156
65	SIR O. HARVEY Paris Tel. No. 269	11 Oct.	Sir O. Harvey thinks French are looking for a compromise and should be left to work one out.	158
66	B.J.S.M Washington Tel. AWT 68	12 Oct.	U.S. plans for meeting of special representatives and hint from Mr. Lovett that French cabinet are preparing a military 'Schuman Plan'.	160

NAME	DATE	MAIN SUBJECT	PAGE
67 To Sir I. Kirkpatrick Wahnerheide	13 Oct.	Letter from Mr. Gilchrist giving F.O. reactions to C.O.S. safeguards. *Calendar:* **i** U.K./U.S. comparison.	161
68 Mr. Shinwell Ministry of Defence D.O. (50) 80	13 Oct.	Reviews position and asks for instructions at Defence Ministers' meeting in Washington on 28 Oct.	163
69 Sir R. Makins Foreign Office	14 Oct.	Minute to Mr. Bevin on Mr. Gaitskell's plans for joint paper on finance of defence.	166
70 Sir I. Kirkpatrick Wahnerheide Tel. No. 1499	15 Oct.	Suggestions for safeguards on German rearmament.	167
71 Sir O. Harvey Paris Tel. No. 433 Saving	18 Oct.	French attitude and complaints of Anglo-American behaviour at New York. *Calendar:* **i** U.K. rebuttal.	170
72 Sir O. Franks Washington Tel. No. 2825	19 Oct.	French refuse to discuss U.S. plan at meeting of Personal Representatives. *Calendar:* **i** Text.	172
73 Air Marshal Sir W. Elliot Ministry of Defence	19 Oct.	Reflections on the present deadlock. *Calendar:* **i** German generals.	174
74 Chiefs of Staff Ministry of Defence D.O. (50) 89	20 Oct.	Extract from brief explaining the urgent military necessity for German rearmament.	180
75 Mr. Young Foreign Office	20 Oct.	Effect of constitutional position in France on progress towards German rearmament.	186
76 Informal Ministerial Meeting 10 Downing Street	20 Oct.	Discussion of line Mr. Shinwell should take at Washington meeting of Defence Ministers.	187
77 To Sir O. Harvey Paris Tel. No. 3015 Saving	23 Oct.	Message from Mr. Bevin to M. Schuman dissociating H.M.G. from Labour Party statement on rearmament by Mr. Morgan Phillips.	190
78 To Mr. Attlee 10 Downing Street	23 Oct.	F.O. brief on Soviet reactions to rearmament and developments at Prague conference.	191
79 Mr. Bevin and Mr. Gaitskell London D.O. (50) 91	23 Oct.	Memo. on the finance of defence. *Calendars:* **i–ii** Nitze Plan.	194
80 Sir O. Harvey Paris Tel. No. 286	24 Oct.	Announcement of Pleven Plan for a European Army. *Calendar:* **i** Text.	206
81 Sir O. Harvey Paris Tel. No. 290	25 Oct.	Despite objections to Pleven Plan, Sir O. Harvey warns against outright rejection.	208

NAME	DATE	MAIN SUBJECT	PAGE
82 SIR O. FRANKS Washington Tel. No. 2883	25 Oct.	Preliminary reactions of Mr. Acheson to Pleven Plan are non-committal.	211
83 MR. BEVIN & M. VAN ZEELAND: MEETING Foreign Office	25 Oct.	Mr. Bevin discusses France, finance, German contribution, Pleven Plan and future of Brussels treaty.	213
84 MR. SHUCKBURGH Foreign Office	26 Oct.	Notes for Mr. Bevin of F.O. objections to Pleven Plan. *Calendar:* **i** French doubts.	217
85 INFORMAL MINISTERIAL MEETING 10 Downing Street	26 Oct.	Instructions for Mr. Shinwell at Defence meeting in Washington: reorganisation of N.A.T.O. and Pleven Plan.	220
86 SIR D. GAINER Foreign Office	28 Oct.	Submission to Mr. Bevin, recommending rejection of Soviet proposal for a C.F.M. on Germany.	225
87 B.J.S.M. Washington Tel. ZO 378	28 Oct.	Conv. between Mr. Shinwell and Gen. Marshall: U.S. disappointed with Pleven Plan. *Calendar:* **i** Moch-Marshall meeting.	227
88 SIR I. KIRKPATRICK Wahnerheide Tel. No. 1548	28 Oct.	Meeting of Mr. McCloy with MM. Monnet, Pleven and Schuman: McCloy impressed with Pleven Plan; only Pleven hoping for U.K. participation.	228
89 To SIR O. FRANKS Washington Tel. No. 4786	28 Oct.	F.O. consider Pleven Plan should not be taken too seriously.	230
90 To SIR O. FRANKS Washington Tel. No. 4801	29 Oct.	Belgian suggestion for referral of rearmament problem to N.A.C.	232
91 B.J.S.M. Washington Tel. ZO 384	29 Oct.	Refusal of M. Moch at Defence meeting on 28 Oct. to discuss any proposal other than Pleven Plan. *Calendar:* **i** meetings.	234
92 CABINET CONCLUSIONS 10 Downing Street C.M. (50) 69th	30 Oct.	Cabinet agree (i) cannot join Pleven Plan but will not oppose it (ii) German economic contribution to defence.	237
93 SIR O. HARVEY Paris	31 Oct.	Letter to Sir P. Dixon recording hope of U.S. Ambassador that Pleven Plan will be accepted in principle.	239
94 SIR O. FRANKS Washington Tel. No. 2963	1 Nov.	State Department suggest pressure on French government outside diplomatic channels.	241
95 B.J.S.M. Washington Tel. ZO 410	2 Nov.	Mr. Shinwell reviews situation and suggests new approach to M. Schuman.	242

	NAME	DATE	MAIN SUBJECT	PAGE
96	Sir O. Harvey Paris	3 Nov.	Letter to Sir P. Dixon reporting information from M. de Margerie on French time-table, origins of Pleven Plan, German attitude and Brussels treaty.	243
97	Cabinet Conclusions 10 Downing Street C.M. (50) 71st	6 Nov.	Discussion of reply to Soviet proposal for C.F.M.	246
98	Sir F. Hoyer Millar London	6 Nov.	Reviews limited achievements of Defence Ministers' meeting and future procedure. *Calendar:* i Spofford conv.	248
99	To Sir O. Franks Washington Tel. No. 4911 Saving	7 Nov.	Indications from U.S. Ambassador in Paris that MM. Pleven and Schuman are less rigid than M. Moch and could be susceptible to pressure.	252
100	To Sir O. Franks Washington Tel. No. 4505 Saving	8 Nov.	U.S. suggestion for Commonwealth contribution to defence is 'a non-starter'. *Calendar:* i Global war planning.	253
101	Defence Committee Meeting House of Commons D.O. (50) 21st	8 Nov.	Discussion of impasse. Mr. Attlee asks whether French intend to fight or surrender in event of war. *Calendar:* i D.O. (50) 95.	255
102	Cabinet Conclusions 10 Downing Street C.M. (50) 72nd	9 Nov.	U.S. aid for defence.	259
103	Sir I. Kirkpatrick Wahnerheide Tel. No. 623 Saving	11 Nov.	Bundestag debate on German rearmament. Statements from Drs. Adenauer and Schumacher. *Calendars:* i–ii A.H.C.	261
104	Cabinet Conclusions 10 Downing Street C.M. (50) 74th	16 Nov.	Acceptance of U.S. offer of interim aid. *Calendar:* i Text.	263
105	Mr. Mallet Foreign Office	16 Nov.	Considers the consequences of German rearmament for Occupation regime.	266
106	To B.J.S.M. Washington Tel. No. C.O.S. (W) 900	17 Nov.	Chiefs of Staff suggest how U.S. plan could be redrafted so as to make it acceptable to French. *Calendar:* i C.O.S. (50) 474.	268
107	Sir P. Dixon Foreign Office	17 Nov.	Submission to Mr. Bevin: F.O. ideas for counter-plan. *Calendar:* i alternatives.	270
108	To Sir O. Franks Washington Tel. No. 5167	20 Nov.	No truth in U.S. press rumours that H.M.G. intend to refuse U.S. aid.	272

Breaking the deadlock: the Spofford Plan, Mr. Attlee's visit to Washington and the Brussels Conference
20 November–22 December 1950

	NAME	DATE	MAIN SUBJECT	PAGE
109	Sir F. Hoyer Millar London	20 Nov.	Compromise plan announced by Mr. Spofford. *Calendar:* **i** Text.	274
110	To Sir O. Harvey Paris Tel. No. 1242	22 Nov.	Importance attached by Mr. Bevin to reaching tripartite agreement on German rearmament before negotiation with Soviet Union. *Calendar:* **i** C.F.M. agenda.	277
111	Mr. Mallet Foreign Office	22 Nov.	Minutes on the need to secure German agreement to rearmament even at the price of German equality. *Calendar:* **i** legal aspects.	280
112	Economic Steering Committee Meeting Cabinet Office E.S. (50) 6th	23 Nov.	Discusses how to secure greater German industrial contribution to western defence. *Calendars:* **i–iv** E.S. (50) 12.	282
113	To Sir I. Kirkpatrick Wahnerheide	23 Nov.	Letter from Sir D. Gainer explaining confusion over various proposals for German police forces in F.R.G. and Berlin. *Calendar:* **i** Berlin security.	286
114	To Sir P. Nichols The Hague No. 386	23 Nov.	Conv. between Mr. Bevin and M. Stikker. Dutch reservations about Pleven Plan and hopes of compromise. *Calendar:* **i** N.A.T.O. High Commissioner.	289
115	Mr. Bevin Foreign Office D.O. (50) 100	24 Nov.	Suggests formation of an Atlantic Confederate Force as a counter to Pleven Plan.	291
116	Air Marshal Sir W. Elliot Ministry of Defence	25 Nov.	Brief for Mr. Attlee on military objections to No. 115.	296
117	Sir P. Dixon Foreign Office	25 Nov.	Brief for Mr. Bevin on the political advantages of No. 115.	299
118	Defence Committee Meeting 10 Downing Street D.O. (50) 22nd	27 Nov.	Rejection of Bevin Plan. U.K. should let Pleven Plan take its course.	301
119	To Sir O. Franks Washington Tel. No. 5318	29 Nov.	U.K. will accept Spofford compromise but still view Pleven plan as 'a sort of cancer in the Atlantic body'. *Calendar:* **i** Deputies.	305

NAME	DATE	MAIN SUBJECT	PAGE
120 To Sir O. Franks Washington Tel. No. 5377	1 Dec.	Mr. Bevin's concern at Mr. Acheson's message of support for European integration to M. Schuman. *Calendar:* **i** German stiffening.	307
121 Mr. Attlee and M. Pleven: Meeting 10 Downing Street	2 Dec.	Discussion of French position on German rearmament and reply to Soviet proposal for a C.F.M.	310
122 Mr. Bevin Foreign Office C.P. (50) 294	2 Dec.	Puts forward six alternative courses for dealing with Soviet proposal for C.F.M. *Calendars:* **i–ii** draft reply and spheres of interest.	319
123 Sir W. Strang Foreign Office	3 Dec.	Conv. with M. Massigli, who explains renewed French interest in Dutch solution of N.A.T.O. High Commissioner.	324
124 Sir N. Brook Cabinet Office	4 Dec.	Note of pre-Washington meeting between Mr. Attlee, Mr. Bevin, Sir S. Cripps: rearmament, higher direction of cold war and raw materials. *Calendar:* **i** Economics and liaison.	325
125 To Sir O. Franks Washington Tel. No. 5438	4 Dec.	Mr. Bevin now doubts wisdom of proceeding with German rearmament.	327
126 Staff Conference House of Commons C.O.S. (50) 197th	5 Dec.	Mr. Bevin and Mr. Shinwell discuss with Chiefs of Staff whether to proceed with German rearmament.	328
127 Sir O. Franks Washington Tel. No. 3289	5 Dec.	Further message to M. Schuman welcoming European integration is proposed by Mr. Acheson.	334
128 To Sir O. Franks Washington Tel. No. 5485	6 Dec.	Mr. Bevin represents the case for delaying German rearmament despite objections from Chiefs of Staff, Mr. Shinwell and Mr. Morrison.	337
129 To Sir O. Franks Washington Tel. No. 5486	6 Dec.	British objections to proposed U.S. statement on European integration.	341
130 To Sir O. Franks Washington Tel. No. 5487	6 Dec.	Reviews position reached by Deputies. *Calendar:* **i** N.A.T.O. High Commissioner.	342
131 Sir O. Franks Washington Tel. No. 3309	6 Dec.	Message from Mr. Attlee to Mr. Bevin explaining why it was 'unthinkable' to draw back on German rearmament. *Calendar:* **i** Raw materials.	345
132 Sir O. Franks Washington Tel. No. 3311	7 Dec.	4th Attlee-Truman meeting: Spofford Plan; letter on European integration; U.K. defence effort.	348

	NAME	DATE	MAIN SUBJECT	PAGE
133	To Sir O. Franks Washington Tel. No. 5524	7 Dec.	British acceptance of Spofford Plan with two reservations. *Calendars:* **i–ii** Deputies and doubts.	351
134	Mr. Attlee and Mr. Harriman: Meeting Washington	7 Dec.	Frank speaking from Mr. Harriman: U.S. expect greater U.K. defence effort.	353
135	Sir I. Kirkpatrick Wahnerheide Tel. No. 1759	12 Dec.	Public insistence by Dr. Adenauer on German equality in a unified force. German soldiers are not 'cannon fodder'. *Calendar:* **i** reunification.	354
136	Mr. Bevin Foreign Office C.P. (50) 311	12 Dec.	Summary of Deputies' report on German contribution to defence and the extent to which H.M.G. is committed. *Calendar:* **i** German opposition.	356
137	Cabinet Conclusions 10 Downing Street C.M (50) 86th	14 Dec.	Discussion of No. 136: reaffirm commitment to German rearmament and agree tactics.	367
138	Sir O. Harvey Paris Tel. No. 372	15 Dec.	Failure of tripartite officials to agree reply to Soviet government on C.F.M.	370
139	To Sir O. Franks Washington No. 1605	15 Dec.	Mr. Bevin is informed by U.S. Chargé d'Affaires of proposed U.S. line at Brussels on Western defence and Germany. *Calendar:* **i** Occupation.	371
140	Mr. Stevens Foreign Office	16 Dec.	Brief for Mr. Bevin on difficulties over revision of P.L.I. agreement.	375
141	Sir P. Dixon Brussels	17 Dec.	Brief for Mr. Bevin: warns that atmosphere at Brussels will be 'very difficult'.	376
142	To Sir J. Le Rougetel Brussels Tel. No. 455	18 Dec.	F.O. briefing for Mr. Bevin on Soviet note of 15 Dec. on German rearmament.	379
143	Cabinet Conclusions 10 Downing Street C.M. (50) 87th	18 Dec.	Agree to increase U.K. defence effort.	381
144	Sir J. Le Rougetel Brussels Tel. No. 313	19 Dec.	Approval by N.A.C. of Deputies report and proposals for immediate establishment of integrated force under Gen. Eisenhower.	386
145	Sir J. Le Rougetel Brussels Tel. No. 316	19 Dec.	N.A.C. discussion of increased defence efforts 'went off satisfactorily'. *Calendars:* **i** Brussels meetings **ii** N.A.T.O. reorganisation.	387
146	Tripartite Ministerial Meeting Brussels	19 Dec.	Terms of reply to Soviet proposal for C.F.M. are agreed.	390

NAME	DATE	MAIN SUBJECT	PAGE
147 SIR J. LE ROUGETEL Brussels Tel. No. 323	20 Dec.	Summary of tripartite meeting on Germany. *Calendars:* **i–iii** decisions, Adenauer, future policy.	393
148 SIR P. DIXON Foreign Office	21 Dec.	Reviews surprising success of Brussels meetings.	396
149 SIR I. KIRKPATRICK Wahnerheide Tel. No. 1823	22 Dec.	Reflections on German attitude to rearmament: 'a long row to hoe'.	398
	1951		
APPENDIX	1 Jan.	Guide to N.A.T.O. and Brussels Treaty Organisation.	400

CHAPTER I

German Rearmament at the New York Conference

2 September – 10 October 1950

No. 1

Mr. Bevin to Sir O. Franks[1] *(Washington)*

No. 3946 Telegraphic [*WU 1195/306*]

Immediate. Secret   FOREIGN OFFICE, *2 September 1950, 6.10 p.m.*

Please pass following personal message to Mr. Acheson.[2]

(Begins).

I think we are on the verge of making real progress in our defence measures and in the restoration of confidence on the mainland of Europe. Our own decision to extend national service has been followed by the Belgian Government[3] and I think the Dutch in their own time will do the same. The French say they can produce 5 new divisions by next summer without increasing the training period, but that if this proves impossible they will make the increase. Our decision to bring our forces in Germany up to 3½ Divisions fully up to strength and ready for battle has been very well received by the French[4] and I am now considering what more we can

---

[1] Mr. E. Bevin was Secretary of State for Foreign Affairs. Sir O. Franks was H.M. Ambassador at Washington.

[2] This message for Mr. D. Acheson, American Secretary of State, is printed in *F.R.U.S. 1950*, vol. iii, pp. 271–2.

[3] The raising of compulsory national service from eighteen months to two years and new pay awards for the armed forces were announced by the Prime Minister, Mr. C.R. Attlee, in a broadcast on the evening of 30 August (Cmd. 8026–7). In the following week similar announcements were made by the governments of France, Belgium and Luxembourg while the Netherlands government declared its preparedness to follow suit should the need arise.

[4] French criticisms in August of British plans to bring the strength of existing 2⅓ divisions in Germany up to just under 3 divisions were scarcely modified at the new figure of 3⅓ divisions given in a British statement to the N.A.C. Deputies (see note 5) on 31 August of the proposed expansion of British combat forces in Europe. Although the U.K.

do by way of putting units on to the Continent for training. At the same time the Deputies, under the very able leadership of Mr. Spofford, have made good progress with the plans for coordinated defence production and should have concrete results to report to the Atlantic Council.[5]

2. But I am worried about the financial side. When you asked us to say what we could undertake over the next 3 years, given United States aid, we examined our capacity, both productive and financial, with the utmost care, and the answer[6] we gave you represented the most our economy could bear without resort to war-time measures of manpower mobilisation, requisitioning etc., or a serious set-back in our recovery. But we made it clear that this programme was dependent on the aid which your

statement was well received by the Deputies, the French Minister of Defence, M.J. Moch, represented to Mr. Bevin on 4 September that '3⅓ divisions were not enough, and that we should bring the number up to four. This, he claimed, would make our contribution a fair one, having regard to what the French were proposing to do, and it would have a very good effect not only in France but with the Americans' (minute by Mr. R.E. Barclay, Private Secretary to Mr. Bevin, on WU 1195/330).

[5] The N.A.C. Deputies, based in London, were appointed by the North Atlantic Council, composed of the twelve foreign ministers of the signatory governments of the North Atlantic Treaty of 4 April 1949 (*B.F.S.P.*, vol. 154, pp. 479–83), as agreed at the N.A.C. meeting in London on 15–18 May (see Volume II, No. 113 and the Appendix to this volume for N.A.T. structure in 1950). The U.K. Deputy was Sir F. Hoyer Millar. At the first meeting of the Deputies in London on 25 July–4 August the chairman, Mr. C.M. Spofford, launched an American offer of aid for an increased defence effort. The nine European member countries (U.K., France, Belgium, the Netherlands, Luxembourg, Italy, Portugal, Denmark and Norway) were asked to say what increases in forces and military production they would be prepared to make, if given more U.S. aid. Replies were required by 5 August for use in support of President Truman's request to Congress on 1 August for an appropriation of $4 billion for the provision of military assistance to foreign nations (*D.S.B.*, vol. xxiii, pp. 247–8). This supplemented the foreign aid programme already in being under the terms of the Mutual Defence Assistance Act of October 1949. The Deputies were charged with the coordination of these replies with the aim of working out a High Priority Defence Programme for presentation to the N.A.C. at its next meeting in New York on 15–26 September. The Deputies met again on 22nd August–2 September and reconvened in New York on 13 September to prepare for the N.A.C. meeting.

[6] The British response to the American enquiry of 25 July was transmitted in a general memorandum of 3 August (published in *The Times* on 4 August) followed by a confidential annex of 4 August (both texts at calendar i below). These memoranda contained proposals for a three year national defence programme amounting to £3,400 millions (increased to £3,600 millions by the new measures announced at the end of August—see note 3). The current annual expenditure on defence was £780 millions plus an extra £100 millions authorized at the end of July. In the confidential annex it was stated that £2,850 millions over three years was the most Britain could afford and therefore American assistance of £550 millions was required in order that the full programme could be undertaken. No American reply on this request was forthcoming in subsequent Anglo-American official talks in Washington. Following representations from Mr. Bevin on 23 August (see calendar ii) it was agreed that bilateral talks, this time in London, should continue on the question of Britain's national programme but that at the same time the Deputies should proceed with the question of a coordinated multi-national defence effort. Only the main outline of the lengthy and technical bilateral official talks on aid is traced in this volume e.g. see calendar i and No. 79. For the full F.O. correspondence, see F.O. 371/82873–8 (UE 11914) and F.O. 371/86983–5 (UR 1027).

Government had indicated would be available. We now find that we are being pressed to commit ourselves to this vast productive programme, and to start placing the orders, before receiving any firm commitment on your side as to the extent or the form of the aid we shall receive. I know your difficulties, but I think this is not fair to us having regard to what went before. We have already made commitments for new defence production up to £100 million over our expected defence budget for this year, without any firm assurance of aid and are now contemplating a further commitment of the same order. This is the limit of what our present resources will stand, and if we are to get on with anything more we must have an instalment of the aid from you. I want to get this production started. Time is short and there is a lot to do. Public opinion in this country is seized of the importance of this problem, and I do not want to lose the momentum as a result of the delays on the financial issue. I believe the 8 million trade unionists in this country will back us fully on this matter.

3. The other point on which I want to ask your help is on this matter of forces stationed in Europe. We were all greatly encouraged to hear of the large increases in your armed forces which you expect to make before July next year.[7] Douglas told me about them and said that subject to the Far East situation the greater part of the 22 Divisions which you will have will be available for North Atlantic defence. The question I asked him was how many can you station on the Continent *before* aggression takes place. This is now the key question. If you too can increase your forces in Germany I believe it will be decisive for morale in Europe, and we shall be able to hold France and Germany firm. We are going to do our best, and I shall have various ideas to discuss with you when we meet, especially in regard to training our men on the Continent.

4. As I am bothering you about money, give my regards to John.[8]

CALENDARS TO No. 1

i *3 Aug.–7 Sept. 1950   U.K. 3 year defence programme.* Results of bilateral talks in

[7] On 25 August the American Ambassador in London, Mr. L.W. Douglas, gave Mr. Bevin advance notice of the American statement, tabled in the Deputies on 28 August, of proposed increases in American combat forces totalling 900,000 men, most of whom would be available for North Atlantic Treaty defence by July 1951 (WU 1198/319). These increases were confirmed, though not specified, in a public announcement by President Truman on 9 September (*D.S.B.*, vol. xxiii, p. 468).

[8] Mr. J.W. Snyder, U.S. Secretary of the Treasury. In a separate message to Mr. Acheson of even date, Mr. Bevin referred to Mr. Acheson's intention of discussing in New York the possibility of raising German industrial levels as a contribution to a common defence programme: 'I want you to know that personally I am entirely sympathetic with your approach to this problem and hope to be in a position to arrive at substantial agreement with you over these matters in New York' (F.O. telegram to Washington No. 3949 on F.O. 1013/1190). Mr. Bevin went on in this telegram to explain the problem of scrap: cf. Volume I, No. 162, note 2.

London (30 Aug.–5 Sept.) on U.K. £3,600m. plan (texts of mema. of 3 and 4 Aug. transmitted in F.O. tels. to Washn. Nos. 3527 and 3191 Saving) are 'very disturbing' (Washn. tel. 3580 Saving). Additional defence production programmes proposed by European N.A.T. powers 'fall substantially below American expectations ... The contribution of £550 million which the United Kingdom has asked for goes far beyond anything that the United States had contemplated.' U.S. unlikely to give any reply on aid 'for some months'. U.S. constitutional difficulties on aid explained in F.O. brief of 4 Sept. [UE 11914/8, 48, 60].

ii   *23 Aug. 1950   Conv. between Mr. Bevin and Mr. Spofford.* Representations from Mr. Bevin at 'unsatisfactory attitude of the United States in regard to military production' and in particular Mr. Spofford's proposal of 22 Aug. that replies of European N.A.T. countries on defence be discussed by the Deputies. Mr. Bevin 'quite saw the American desire to see the picture as a whole, but it must be realised that Great Britain was not part of Europe; she was not simply a Luxembourg.' U.K. programme depended on U.S. aid 'and unless we got a favourable answer, there was a risk that the momentum would be lost. Moreover there was the following wider consideration. The people in this country were pinning their faith on a policy of defence built on a Commonwealth–U.S.A. basis—an English-speaking basis. People here were frankly doubtful of Europe. How could he go down to his constituency—Woolwich—which had been bombed by Germans in the war, and tell his constituents that the Germans would help them in a war against Russia? Londoners would not rely on the Germans.' As regards France: 'the man in the street, coming back from a holiday there, was almost invariably struck by the defeatist attitude of the French' [F.O. 800/517].

iii   *1–6 Sept. 1950   German economic contribution to defence.* Following Treasury meeting, F.O. minutes discuss options for some German financial contribution to defence—linked perhaps to lifting of certain industrial controls. Economic considerations point to desirability of German entry into N.A.T.O. [CE 4363/45/181].

No. 2

Record by Sir P. Dixon[1] of a meeting between Mr. Bevin and the U.S. Chargé d'Affaires[2]

[WU 1198/362]

Top secret   FOREIGN OFFICE, *4 September 1950*

Defence of Europe

The United States Chargé d'Affaires called this morning on the Secretary of State in order to deliver a message from the United States

---

[1] Sir P. Dixon was a Deputy Under-Secretary of State at the Foreign Office and Acting U.K. Deputy on the N.A.C. in the temporary absence of Sir F. Hoyer Millar in Washington.

[2] Mr. J. Holmes, Minister, was in charge of the U.S. Embassy in London, during the absence in Washington of the Ambassador, Mr. L.W. Douglas.

Government based on a telegram[3] of which, after the meeting, I made a summary (see Annex). Mr. Spofford and I were also present.

It will be seen that the proposal amounts to the creation of a unified force for the defence of Europe in which United States forces would participate, and entails the establishment of a Supreme Commander with a combined staff. The proposal contemplates the integration in the unified force of a German unit.

The United States Chargé d'Affaires asked for replies, today if possible, on two questions:

(a) Do we agree to this question being discussed between the three Foreign Ministers at the forthcoming Tripartite talks in New York?[4] and

(b) Do we agree that the question should thereafter be discussed at the meeting of the North Atlantic Council, and that for this purpose the other Ministers should be informed of the position?

In the course of discussion the following points arose.

Participation of a German unit. The Secretary of State explained his reasons for believing that it would be dangerous to go further at present than to raise a German Federal Police Force of 100,000 volunteers. French fears of Germany must constantly be borne in mind, and any suggestion that we were aiming at the creation of a German national army would be likely to have a dangerous effect on the French. It was, moreover, doubtful whether German public opinion would accept anything more than a force of the nature of a Gendarmerie. Mr. Bevin had conveyed his thinking on this point privately to M. Schuman; the effect seemed to have been salutary since Mr. Pleven had gone some way in a public speech to accepting the idea of a German Federal Police Force.[5]

Mr. Holmes said that United States thinking was much in line with the Secretary of State's. The message which he had just read clearly showed that the United States had not favoured the creation of a German national army. In their view it was essential that the Western European countries should be strong themselves before the Germans could be safely attracted

[3] The parallel American telegram of instructions of 2 September to the American Ambassador in Paris, Mr. D. Bruce, is printed in *F.R.U.S. 1950*, vol. iii, pp. 261–2.

[4] Tripartite talks between Mr. Bevin, Mr. Acheson and M. R. Schuman, French Minister for Foreign Affairs, were scheduled to take place in New York from 12–14 September before the opening of the N.A.C. meeting on 15 September, and fifth session of the U.N. General Assembly on 19 September.

[5] For a record of conversation between Mr. Bevin and M. R. Massigli, French Ambassador in London, on 31 August in which Mr. Bevin gave his views on the need for a Federal gendarmerie for the personal information of M. Schuman only, see WF 1051/13 (extract relating to the Schuman Plan printed as No. 161 in Volume I). In a speech at Strasbourg on 2 September, M.R. Pleven, President of the French Council of Ministers, said that when considering suggestions for increasing police forces in the F.R.G. (see No. 3, note 3), account must be taken of growing para-military forces (Bereitschaften) in the Soviet Zone of Germany (proclaimed the German Democratic Republic in 1949: cf. Volume II, No. 31).

to any European defence system; nor was it proposed that the Germans should participate in the command structure.

The Secretary of State read out, and Mr. Holmes noted, the Foreign Office recommendations on German association with the defence of the West (D.O. (50) 66) which had been approved by the Defence Committee on September 1st.[6] It had indeed been Mr. Bevin's intention to let Mr. Acheson (and the French Government) know the views of H.M. Government on this question before the forthcoming Ministerial meeting in New York.

Establishment of a Supreme Commander with a combined staff. The Secretary of State explained that, as I had already told Mr. Spofford, we had been considering the reorganisation of inter-allied defence machinery. The Defence Committee had just approved a plan (D.O. (50) 65)[7] which Mr. Bevin was proposing to raise at the North Atlantic Council meeting. A feature of this plan was the proposal that the Fontainebleau Organisation[8] should now assume command of the allied land and air forces stationed in Germany and Austria. It was important to give the Western European Commanders-in-Chief Committee practical responsibilities for the organisation and training of forces under their own command. The Fontainebleau Organisation might thus form the nucleus of the staff now proposed by the Americans.

United States troops in Europe. Mr. Holmes drew attention to the passage in the message which made it clear that the United States were now contemplating entering into greater commitments than they had been willing to consider up to now, in that they were thinking of greater participation in the defence of Europe.

Summing up, the Secretary of State said that, after consultation with his colleagues, he would give Mr. Holmes an answer as soon as possible to the two specific procedural questions. He would like to make it clear that he might wish to have consultations on the United States proposals with the Brussels Treaty Powers who might be able to give a helpful lead. (Earlier in the conversation, the Secretary of State had described the efforts he had made to persuade the other Brussels Treaty Powers to increase the length of military service; the French had now increased the period by 6

[6] See No. 3.i. The Defence Committee of the Cabinet was reconstituted in 1947 '(*a*) To handle current defence problems. (*b*) To coordinate departmental action and plans in preparation for war' (terms of reference on CAB 131/3). The Defence Committee was chaired by the Prime Minister with the Minister of Defence as his Deputy. The other members of the committee were the Lord President of the Council, Secretary of State for Foreign Affairs, Chancellor of the Exchequer, Minister of Labour and National Service, First Lord of the Admiralty, Secretaries of State for War and Air and the Minister of Supply.

[7] See No. 3.ii.

[8] The military organization at Fontainebleau, established under the Brussels Treaty of 1948, signed by the U.K., Netherlands, France, Belgium, and Luxembourg (*B.F.S.P.*, vol. 150, pp. 672–7), was directed by the Western Europe Commanders-in-Chief Committee under the chairmanship of Field-Marshal Lord Montgomery.

months, the Belgians by 12, and there was hope that the Dutch would come along).[9]

ANNEX TO NO. 2

Summary of United States Government's Message as read by the U.S. Chargé d'Affaires

Secret

Suggestions made in Europe for speeding up its defence by the creation of a unified force, has been closely followed by the United States Government. Creation of such a force would entail the establishment of a Supreme Commander with a combined staff. In that event it should be possible for German unit in a controlled status to be integrated without entailing creation of a German national army. United States have noted the feeling that there should be larger participation by them both in troops in Europe and in the direction of the unified force, if such steps are to be effective.

It is suggested that these important ideas should be discussed in the Tripartite meetings in New York and proposed to raise them there.

The United States has not taken a final position on any point above, but will be prepared to discuss them at New York.

The following additional explanation of United States thinking was offered.

Thinking: A unified force for the defence of Europe seems to imply a Supreme Commander presumably receiving directions from the Standing Group[10] and being served by a combined staff. While decision that such a Supreme Commander would be appointed might be made now, actual appointment could be delayed until a European defence force is in being. A combined staff with a Chief could be established now with the object of directing perfection of defence plans and steps for a formation of a unified force. This staff would become the Supreme Commander's staff on appointment.

Ways and means of integrating German military units into unified

---

[9] Cf. No. 1, note 3. Further to this record Sir P. Dixon added on 4 September: 'The Secretary of State also gave an indication of our plans for the stationing of British forces in France and possibly also in Belgium for the purpose of training, together with the possible use of the Royal Navy for the carriage of such troops across the Channel to the beaches' (WU 1198/362).

[10] The North Atlantic Standing Group of representatives of British, American and French Chiefs of Staff was established in Washington as part of the N.A.T. military structure agreed at the first N.A.C. Meeting on 17 September 1949. This consisted of (*a*) Defence Committee of N.A.T. Defence Ministers served by (*b*) Military Committee of N.A.T. Chiefs of Staff (*c*) Standing Group (*d*) five Regional Planning Groups. This structure was expanded by the end of 1949 to include a Defence Financial and Economic Committee of N.A.T. Finance Ministers and a Military Production and Supply Board both with permanent working staffs in London. For further details, see the Appendix.

defence force should be considered and a common structure and supply system arranged in such a way as not to create a national German army.

As regards production and supply, United States is ready to consider steps which would be necessary to enable the M.P.S.B. to direct effectively supply and production questions concerned with equipment of European defence force.

It was made clear that greater participation by the United States in the defence of Europe and direction of a unified force would involve commitments greater than they had been willing to consider up to now. Whether the United States actually enter into such additional commitments will depend on willingness of the Europeans themselves to make substantially greater efforts resulting in adequate steps to increase their actual force. It will not be possible to succeed collectively in building sufficient strength in time to defend Europe in the event of aggression, unless there are comparable commitments of greater effort on the part of the Europeans. Unless the totality of the effort was sufficient to ensure success, the greater United States effort would be wasted and would indeed result in a dissipation of United States strength to the detriment of the free world.

Procedure: It is suggested that these questions should be discussed first in the Tripartite Ministerial meeting. United States Government would like to know whether Mr. Bevin would be prepared to discuss them. Thereafter it seems very important that the questions should be discussed by the North Atlantic Treaty Council and for that purpose it is proposed that the other Ministers attending the Council meeting should be informed as early as possible, in order that they may take guidance from their Governments before departure from their capitals. The United States Government would therefore like to know at the earliest possible moment, whether Mr. Bevin agrees that the other Ministers should be informed of the position.[11]

[11] Mr. Bevin discussed these American proposals with Mr. Attlee after lunch on 4 September. Mr. Attlee agreed that the answer to Mr. Holmes' questions could be in the affirmative and 'expressed warm satisfaction at this development' (Private Office note of 5 September on WU 1198/362). At a Cabinet meeting that afternoon, Mr. Bevin informed the Cabinet of the American approach and 'said that he was disposed to agree that this proposal should be discussed in the forthcoming meetings in New York, subject to his stipulation about the contribution from Western Germany [of a gendarmerie not exceeding 100,000 men], and on condition that the United States Government had first given some more definite assurances about the extent of the financial assistance which they would provide towards increased defence expenditure by the Western European Governments. No further commitment to send United Kingdom troops to fight in Europe in the event of war would be accepted without prior reference to the Cabinet. *The Cabinet* . . . authorised the Foreign Secretary to discuss, on the conditions stated, the proposal of the United States Government for the creation of an integrated defence force in Europe' (CAB 128/18). When informing Mr. Holmes later that day of British agreement to both questions of procedure Sir P. Dixon 'asked Mr. Holmes whether any thought had been given to the terminology which would be used to describe the proposed unified force. He replied that he had seen the force referred to in messages from Washington as "European Defence Force". I remarked that, speaking personally, it seemed important, from the point of view of public

It was explained that the French Government were being similarly approached.[12]

CALENDAR TO No. 2

i *6 Sept. 1950 Origins of U.S. proposal for unified force* explained in message from Lord Tedder, Chairman of the British Joint Services Mission in Washington and U.K. rep. on N.A.T. Standing Group, for British Chiefs of Staff (transmitted in B.J.S.M. tel. AWT 54). U.S. military now coming round to idea of German rearmament, without which 'it will be impossible to provide sufficient forces on the continent'. French govt. to be pressed. State Dept. is now ahead of the military as regards belief in psychological importance of actual appointment of a Supreme Commander of a unified force [C 5371/27/18].

opinion, to find the right term and particularly to avoid any term which would suggest that what was now proposed was the same thing as the "European Army" thrown up by the Council of Europe' (WU 1198/379).

[12] The substance of Sir P. Dixon's record and the text of the annex were transmitted to Washington in Foreign Office telegrams Nos. 3969-70 of 5 September. At a meeting with Mr. Bruce on 5 September, M. Schuman agreed to tripartite discussion in New York of the American proposal but objected to discussion by the N.A.C. 'because of the dangers of leakage from so numerous a body and because of the unfortunate impression which would be caused by divergences of view between the Big Three' (Paris telegram No. 237 on WU 1198/357: cf. *F.R.U.S. 1950*, vol. iii, pp. 267–8). On 8 September Mr. Holmes informed the Foreign Office that in further representations to the French government, the U.S. government had reserved the right to raise its proposal at the N.A.C. meeting.

No. 3

Mr. Bevin to Sir O. Harvey[1] *(Paris)*

No. 921 [C 5541/27/18]

Top secret   FOREIGN OFFICE, *5 September 1950*

Sir,

You will recall that at the meeting which you attended here on 21st August [*ib*] I expressed my anxiety lest the Soviet Government should, perhaps in six months' time, threaten our position in Berlin or West Germany. I said that in my view such a threat might develop without direct Russian participation through use of the Bereitschaften. You saw the report of the meeting of the High Commission on 17th August [*ib*] when Dr. Adenauer gave his views on the menace which this force constitutes.[2] Dr. Adenauer has now made proposals to the High

[1] H.M. Ambassador at Paris.
[2] The report of this meeting between the High Commissioners, who formed the Council of the High Commission in Germany (*U.K.* Sir I. Kirkpatrick, *U.S.* Mr. J.J. McCloy, *France* M. A. François-Poncet) and Dr. K. Adenauer, Chancellor of the Federal Republic of Germany, was annexed to D.O. (50) 66 calendared at i below.

Commission in writing in which he asks both for the strengthening of the allied garrisons and for the creation of a Federal police force.[3] I understand that the Chancellor is satisfied that a sufficient majority in the Bundestag will support this latter proposal. You also saw the Chiefs of Staff paper of 18th August,[4] which recommended that immediate steps be taken to seek the consent of the French and United States Governments to the initiation of a measure of German rearmament which would eventually lead to the inclusion of a German contingent in the forces of Western Europe. The Chiefs of Staff further recommended that certain preliminary steps should be taken at once, including the formation in the Federal Republic of an armed gendarmerie similar to the Bereitschaften. There are, as was indicated at the meeting on 21st August, certain reasons which, in my view, make it impracticable at present to adopt the main recommendation of the Chiefs of Staff. In the first place it is very doubtful whether public opinion in this country, in France or in the United States is prepared today to see a revival of German military strength. Secondly, there is a very strong feeling in Germany itself, especially in the Socialist Party, against the re-creation of the German Army. Thirdly, there is the fact that without massive American aid, finance and equipment, the rearmament of Germany would be impossible. Finally, there is the danger that a decision to re-create a German Army might provoke just that action by the Soviet which it is our aim to prevent.

2. For these reasons I decided that it was necessary for the present to concentrate on certain preliminary measures short of the re-creation of a German Army, some of which had been recommended by the Chiefs of

[3] These proposals were contained in a memorandum of 29 August with amplifications in two shorter memoranda of 2 September (not printed from C 5573, 5668/3333/18). Dr. Adenauer estimated the current strength of the Bereitschaften as between 45,000 and 70,000 and likely to rise to between 150,000 and 300,000 (as compared with British estimates of 52,500 rising to 100,000). He therefore renewed his appeal of 17 August for more Allied forces in the F.R.G. to guarantee external security and declared his readiness to contribute a German contingent to any European army which might be formed. On 2 September Dr. Adenauer asked for a formal undertaking that the Allied governments would defend the Federal Republic from an attack by the Bereitschaften whether or not the attack was supported by the Soviet government. As regards internal security the Chancellor proposed that his government should be authorized to proceed immediately with the creation of a Federal police force (Schutzpolizei), initially of 25,000 men rising to 60,000, as opposed to the 10,000 Land gendarmerie authorized in July (see Volume II, No. 104, note 5). In discussion with the High Commission on 31 August, Dr. Adenauer was informed that his proposals would have to be referred to Ministers. When assuring the Foreign Office on 3 September that no commitment had been made thereby, Sir I. Kirkpatrick commented: 'Nevertheless McCloy has told the Chancellor that he personally favours a Federal Force. At our meetings with the Chancellor none of the three High Commissioners has declared himself to be fundamentally opposed to a Federal Force. Accordingly I believe that the Chancellor hopes and expects that if he can secure the necessary parliamentary support the Western powers will not veto his proposals' (C 5586/3333/18).

[4] See calendar i. The three Chiefs of Staff were Chief of the Imperial General Staff, Field Marshal Sir W. Slim; First Sea Lord and Chief of the Naval Staff, Admiral of the Fleet Lord Fraser of North Cape; Chief of the Air Staff, Marshal of the R.A.F. Sir J. Slessor.

Staff. My recommendations, and the arguments supporting them, are contained in the paper of which I enclose a copy.[5] This and the Chiefs of Staff paper of 18th August were considered by the Defence Committee on 1st September [ic], when I was authorised to raise at the New York meeting the question of the defence of Germany on the lines suggested in my paper, and to give an advance indication of my views to the French and United States Governments.

3. I shall accordingly be glad if you will seek an early interview with the Minister of Foreign Affairs, or, if he is absent, with the President of the Council, and will inform him of the recommendations made in my paper and of my reasons in reaching them. In so doing, you should explain that I am giving this advance indication of my views to the French and United States Governments in order that we may be able profitably to discuss in New York a matter which, in the view of His Majesty's Government can no longer be ignored.

4. In speaking to the French Minister you should say that although, for the reasons given in paragraph 2 above, His Majesty's Government are not prepared at present to contemplate the re-creation of a German Army, they do not rule out the possibility of eventually discussing the incorporation of a German contingent in the defence forces of the West. In the meanwhile there are certain minimum steps which are in any case necessary. These steps should not be delayed while the possibilities of a German contingent in the western forces are explored. The steps referred to are set out in paragraph 3 of my paper. Most important of them are the re-organisation of the auxiliary forces serving with the British and American troops in Germany, the strengthening of the frontier police, the creation of a Federal police force and the formation of a smaller armed force of police in Berlin. The first of these measures is necessary to ensure the mobility of the allied forces in an emergency. The proposal is to re-organise on a disciplined basis the auxiliary German services which are employed to save allied manpower. Some of these men are employed as drivers and others as watchmen. The frontier police at present number

[5] The appended text of D.O. (50) 66, calendared at i below, was for Sir O. Harvey's information only. An edited version of the paper (C 5541/27/18) omitting certain passages dealing with the recommendations of the Chiefs of Staff and feeling in France, was sent to the French Ambassador in London, M. R. Massigli, at his request, following his interview with Mr. Bevin on the afternoon of 5 September when he was shown a copy of the present despatch. Sir O. Harvey was informed of these omissions and instructed to leave a similarly edited version with M. Schuman, if required. At his meeting with Mr. Bevin, 'M. Massigli said that the French Government had certainly come along in their thinking about the German gendarmerie and were prepared to countenance larger numbers than they had envisaged previously. They doubted, however, whether the gendarmerie should be placed under Federal authority so long as (a) this was not agreeable to the Länder; (b) it would require constitutional amendment; (c) there was division on the subject within the Federal Government.' As regards the new American initiative, 'M. Massigli at once noted the reference to German units and suggested that this might be too high a price to pay even for the remarkable advance in America's willingness to be involved in European affairs' (C 5679/27/18).

17,000, and it is desirable that they should be strengthened and slightly expanded. The ordinary police in the three zones number under 100,000 and are unfitted either in numbers, in training, in equipment or in organisation to deal with an emergency in addition to their ordinary police duties. The creation of a Federal police force has become urgent for two reasons. First, because unless we create a force which will enable the Federal Government to deal with Communist-inspired disturbances and sabotage, and to cope with an emergency, such as would arise in a mass movement of refugees, the allied forces would find it difficult to cope with an attack even by the Bereitschaften. Secondly, because unless the Western Powers show their resolution to meet the threat from the East, which is very plain to the West Germans, morale in the Federal Republic, which, as Wahnerheide telegram No. 1253[6] shows, is shaky, will crumble, and when the crisis comes, Western Germany may well disintegrate beneath our feet.

5. I do not share the view that there is no risk of action by the Bereitschaften unless the Russians are prepared to march. I do not believe that the Russians would have taken the trouble to reconstitute a German armed force except with the idea of using it to stage a movement in which the Western Powers, if they refused to abandon Germany, would be made to appear as fighting Germans to prevent the re-unification of the country and its liberation from occupation.

6. I have given much anxious thought to the question whether the creation of a Federal police force would be likely to provoke an attack. In this connexion I am bound to take account of the views of the Chiefs of Staff to the effect that there is no way of providing the forces necessary to defend the territories of the North Atlantic Treaty Powers without German assistance. The fact that we cannot today begin to rearm Germany is no reason for doing nothing. On the contrary, if we are eventually to secure the German contribution that is essential for defence, we must take all possible steps now to ensure that Germany is not lost before the Western Powers are able to build up their forces to a state at

[6] In this telegram of 23 August Sir I. Kirkpatrick reported the damaging effect of the outbreak of hostilities in Korea on German morale: 'In the first place it demonstrated that the Russians were prepared to use force. Secondly in a war for the unity of Korea the Germans saw a disquieting parallel with their own situation. Thirdly the North Korean victories have greatly lowered American prestige and dispelled confidence in American military might. The result has been a notable deterioration in German morale all along the line. It is not too much to say that defeatism is general.' Sir I. Kirkpatrick went on to specify the attitude of various sections of the population concluding: 'the above is a gloomy picture of German morale. But the German people is volatile and the situation could very quickly change . . . If the Western forces in Germany were strengthened, if the Western Germans apprehended that we had resolutely embarked on a coherent programme for Western defence, it is likely that there would be a heartening recovery of morale, and provided we sustain the Federal Government we should receive effective German cooperation. In the contrary event morale is likely to sink still further to a point which may endanger our whole position' (C 5380/5380/18). Mr. Bevin minuted on this telegram: 'U.S.A. should see this. We ought to move quickly.'

which a German contribution could be contemplated. In fact, the risks inherent in any strengthening of the German defence forces must be faced sometime, unless we are to run the greater risk of losing Germany to the Soviets. It is clearly better that the first steps should be taken while the Bereitschaften is still, we believe, unready to act, and that they should be in a form which, being similar to action the Soviet have themselves taken, is least likely to provoke preventive action. Finally, you may say that I am influenced by the fact that Dr. Adenauer has himself asked for such a force. It would be a great mistake to reject this unconditional proposal if there is a possibility that we may later wish for German co-operation.

7. The size and armaments of a federal force are for discussions, but it is essential that this force should be on a sufficiently centralised basis to ensure that swift and effective action can be taken in an emergency. The problem of the defence of Berlin may prove to be more urgent, and to need separate action in advance of the other measures I propose.[7]

I am, &c.,

(For the Secretary of State)

D. ALLEN[8]

CALENDARS TO No. 3

i *Aug.–Sept. 1950 U.K. proposals for German rearmament* (a) *Chiefs of Staff* submit detailed proposals for gradual rearmament of F.R.G. in C.O.S. (50) 305 of 18 Aug. (here reproduced as D.O. (50) 67 of 30 Aug.) (b) *Mr. Bevin* and H.M. Representatives in W. Europe discuss possibilities of German rearmament at meeting on 21 Aug. when strength of morale and forces in Europe is reviewed. Sir I. Kirkpatrick instructed to prepare draft of D.O. (50) 66 of 29 Aug. (to which appended A.H.C. meeting with Adenauer on 17 Aug.). D.O. (50) 66 dismisses scale of C.O.S. proposals as currently impracticable but proposes measures for strengthening internal security of F.R.G., principally by creation of a 100,000 Federal police force and 3,000 force in Berlin. In separate paper, D.O. (50) 68 of 30 Aug., Mr. Bevin recommends the ending forthwith of demolition programme in Germany. (c) *Defence Committee* discuss D.O. (50) 66–8 on 1 Sept. Mr. Bevin authorized to seek tripartite agreement for his proposals [CAB 131/8, 9; C 5425/27/18].

ii *30 Aug. 1950 Reorganisation of Inter-Allied defence machinery.* Proposals from Chiefs of Staff in D.O. (50) 65 for rationalisation of inter-allied defence machinery includes establishment of a Supreme Command for whole European theatre. Outline approved by Defence Committee on 1 Sept. for discussion by N.A.C. in New York [CAB 131/9].

iii *5–18 Sept. 1950 S.P.D. views on German rearmament* reported in Wahnerheide tels. 1312, 1316, 1383. Dr. Schumacher, S.P.D. Leader, favours Federal police

[7] Similar instructions for informing the United States government of Mr. Bevin's proposals were transmitted to Sir O. Franks in F.O. telegram No. 3962 to Washington, in the form of a message from Mr. Bevin to Mr. Acheson (printed in *F.R.U.S. 1950*, vol. iii, pp. 264–5) enclosing a memorandum embodying the substance of D.O. (50) 66 (*ibid.*, pp. 265–6).

[8] Head of F.O. German Political department.

force but as regards re-militarisation: 'no weapons without equal rights' [C 5664/3333/18; C 5676/9/18; C 5935/57/18].

iv *6 Sept. 1950   U.K. brief for New York on defence questions*. Recommends should seek Allied agreement to (*a*) British proposals for gendarmerie, Berlin force and German industrial contribution to defence, contained in D.O. (50) 66; (*b*) coordination of military plans for repelling Bereitschaften attack; (*c*) Security assurance to F.R.G.; (*d*) measures (e.g. coal and food stockpiles) for guarding against renewed blockade of Berlin. Position on suspension of demolition and disarmament programme is explained [ZP 5/57].

No. 4

Note by Mr. Mallet[1] for Mr. Bevin

[C 5712/20/18]

FOREIGN OFFICE, *5 September 1950*

Policy towards Germany

The Defence Committee on September 1st[2] 'took note that the Secretary of State would expound the whole of his policy towards Germany' to the Cabinet. The Private Secretary has suggested that it might be convenient to the Secretary of State if a Note were prepared for this meeting [i].

The Secretary of State told the Defence Committee that he wished to link the consideration of his proposals for associating Germany with the defence of the West with the general re-orientation of our policy towards Germany which he hoped to be able to persuade the Americans and French to accept. The Secretary of State's idea is therefore, I assume, to lay before Mr. Acheson and M. Schuman a general plan under which the Allies on one side and the Federal Republic on the other would each make contributions towards the common object of the closer association of the Republic with the Western Powers.

The matter can therefore be considered under the two headings—What we can do for Germany, and what we want Germany to do.

I *What we can do for Germany*

1. Terminate the programme of demolition.[2]
2. Revise the Prohibited and Limited Industries Agreement.[3]

[1] Mr. W.I. Mallet was an Assistant Under Secretary of State in F.O. German Section.
[2] See No. 3.i.
[3] The tripartite Prohibited and Limited Industries (P.L.I.) Agreement of 14 April 1949 (*B.F.S.P.*, vol. 155, pp. 495–503) had already been partially modified e.g. shipbuilding in the Protocol of Agreements relating to the incorporation of Germany into the European Community of Nations signed at the Petersberg Hotel (seat of the A.H.C.) on 22 November 1949 by the three Allied High Commissioners and Dr. Adenauer (*op. cit.*, vol. 156, pp. 584–8). In discussions in London, July–August, of the Intergovernmental Study Group

3. Revise the Occupation Statute.[4]

(a) *Foreign Affairs*

The Study Group report recommends that the Federal Government should be authorised to establish a Ministry of Foreign Affairs and to conduct diplomatic relations with foreign countries over as wide a field as possible. It also says that the three Governments should support the Federal Republic for membership in as many international organisations as possible under the terms of whose charters the Federal Republic would be eligible for membership. The Study Group recommends that the High Commission should have the right of previous disapproval of the establishment of diplomatic relations, though it is not contemplated that it would disapprove of such relations with friendly countries. The Study Group also recommends that the High Commission should retain the right of previous disapproval of international agreements. There is a disagreement between the French and the Americans who consider that controls over foreign affairs should be reserved and the Federal Republic given certain concessions, and ourselves who feel that the Republic should be free to conduct its foreign affairs subject to certain rights which the High Commission would retain. There is also disagreement as to whether the Federal Government should be allowed to appoint Ambassadors to the capitals of the occupying Powers. It is no doubt these two matters which are referred to when the minutes of the Defence Committee meeting record the Secretary of State as saying that if freedom to conduct her own foreign policy were given to Western Germany, it should be given completely.

(b) *Internal*

The Study Group recommend that controls over internal action be terminated, and that all amendments of constitutions and of legislation other than those affecting the Basic Law[5] should be effective without review by the occupation authorities, though they would be subject to repeal or nullification by those authorities.

4. Status of Federal Republic.

The Study Group has agreed on a formula defining the attitude of the three Governments vis-à-vis the Federal Republic which is drafted in a

on Germany (I.G.G.), commissioned by the three Foreign Ministers in May (see Volume II, No. 95, note 9), the U.S. delegation proposed that the Foreign Ministers at their conference in New York should authorize the Study Group to review the P.L.I. Agreement before the end of 1950 and indicated that they might seek at New York the immediate raising of the level of German steel production fixed at an annual output of 11.1 million tons under article ix of the P.L.I. agreement. For these proposals, supported by the U.K. delegation, see calendar i and *F.R.U.S. 1950*, vol. iii, pp. 1275–6.

[4] Proposals for the revision of the Occupation Statute of 8 April 1949 (*B.F.S.P.*, vol. 155, pp. 490–2), headed the recommendations in the I.G.G. report, concluded on 4 September and printed in *F.R.U.S. 1950*, vol. iii, pp. 1248–1276 (British text on C 5683/3780/18).

[5] The Basic Law for the Federal Republic of Germany promulgated on 23 May 1949, is printed in *B.F.S.P.*, vol. 155, pp. 503–46.

way calculated to reinforce the authority of the Federal Government while avoiding difficulties with the U.S.S.R., and which would enable the Federal Republic to assume on a provisional basis, and with due regard to the limited territorial scope of its authority, the rights and obligations of the former Reich.

5. Termination of the state of war.

The Study Group agrees that the various allied countries should take the necessary action in municipal law to terminate the state of war in their territories, and that any parallel action that is necessary be taken by the Federal Government.

II *What we want Germany to do*

1. To create a Federal police force.

(This the Federal Government are only too anxious to do)

2. To enlarge and improve the frontier police force.

(This the Federal Government are also unlikely to object to)

3. To agree to the British and American plans for reorganising the German auxiliaries with their forces.

(This does not require the express concurrence of the Federal Government)

4. A counterpart to the revision of the Occupation Statute. This takes two forms:

(*a*) matters involving specific action by the Federal Government as a necessary condition for the termination of corresponding reserved powers. Such action will be necessary in the fields of restitution, decartelisation and deconcentration, D.P.s and Refugees, respect for the Basic Law, and foreign trade and exchange.

(*b*) The Study Group also recommends that the Germans should give concrete proof of their goodwill by giving certain undertakings, e.g. for equitable treatment of foreign nationals and with respect to claims and debts.

There is therefore not a very great deal that we want from the Germans that they are not ready to do. It may, however, later prove that we want them to make a further contribution to Western defence. This question would have to be given careful consideration in the light of various factors, such as:

(*a*) The increase in the occupation costs which would result from any increase of the allied forces in Germany;

(*b*) The cost to the Federal budget and economy of the creation of a Federal police force, and improvement of the frontier police;

(*c*) The need of the Western Powers for non-military supplies and equipment from Germany;

(*d*) The need of the Western Powers, either now for their own rearmament or later for rearmament in Germany, to allow Germany to recreate an arms industry, having regard to the economic and military factors which would be involved.

(*e*) The question whether, if Germany contributes equipment or supplies to the Western Powers, she should be paid for them, or should contribute them to a common N.A.T.O. pool.

One might draw the conclusion from the above that it is unnecessary, in order to get what we want, to make too many concessions to the Germans e.g. on the occupation statute or the Prohibited and Limited Industries. If so, the answer would be that they should not be regarded as concessions to the Germans so much as steps that we take in our own interest, because if Western Germany is to be on our side, we must treat her as an equal, make it economically advantageous for her and show that we intend to defend her. Whatever form Germany's defence contribution takes, whether it is a Federal Police or includes a contribution to the equipment of the Western Powers, the Federal Government will renew their request for an increase in the allied forces of occupation in Germany.[6]

I. MALLET

CALENDAR TO No. 4

i *6 Sept. 1950   Cabinet discussion on Germany (C.M. (50) 56th Conclusions, items 6–7* General agreement with Mr. Bevin's proposed line on policy towards Germany for New York: (*a*) support U.S. proposals for revision of P.L.I. agreement as recommended in *C.P.* (*50*) *199* of 4 Sept. (with F.O. brief) on German industrial controls; (*b*) agree establishment of police force, expansion frontier police and reorganisation auxiliary forces; (*c*) end demolition programme; (*d*) revise occupation statute to include full powers for Federal govt. to conduct foreign relations and reduce Allied interference in German internal administration; (*e*) move towards termination state of war; (*f*) formulate policy on Displaced Persons; (*g*) make interim settlement of claims against Germany as proposed in *C.P.* (*50*) *198* of 4 Sept. [CAB 128/18; CAB 129/41; CJ 3874/91/182].

[6] With regard to the Cabinet meeting at i below, the U.S. Chargé d'Affaires informed his government on 11 September that he had learned 'from unimpeachable source' that as regards Germany 'the Cabinet is prepared to go very far and move rapidly with respect to arming German police and raising German military formations within framework of an allied army. Only two Ministers held out on this, one of whom was Dalton [Minister of Town and Country Planning], who is emotionally anti-Germany. In our opinion, Bevin can be pressed very hard on this point' (*F.R.U.S. 1950*, vol. iii, pp. 1186–7).

No. 5

Letter from Mr. Bevin to Sir O. Franks (Washington)

[C 5713/20/18]

Secret   FOREIGN OFFICE, *6 September 1950*

Dear Oliver,

I have been giving much thought to the subject of Germany in connection with the meetings which I shall shortly be having with Mr. Acheson and M. Schuman in New York. I have read the report of the Inter-Governmental Study Group[1] just completed and have noted the developments proposed at the official level in order to bring Germany more definitely into the Western community and thus into the sphere of our defence arrangements.

I am glad that there has been comparatively little disagreement at the official level on the main issues. This is very satisfactory particularly from the point of view of carrying the French with us. At the same time I am doubtful if the recommendations, particularly with the American reservations, go far enough to enable us to achieve our object of assuring the Germans that we mean to have them on our side and we intend to treat them as one of our company. I am told that the American representatives in preparing the plans which will come before us in New York seemed unwilling to take bold measures and hampered by the many administrative details which are apt to hinder the sort of developments we have in mind. The result may be that our advance in Germany will be half-hearted and fail to have the psychological effect which we desire. Soviet Russia would quickly note this and take advantage of it.

In view of the above, I think it would be well for me to see Acheson before the tripartite meetings begin and express my views to him. I have an impression that he may well be more responsive than his officials and would be inclined to see things as I do. I would like you, therefore, to see him if possible before he leaves for New York, and express in general words my views on this subject, and say I would like to have a talk with him before the tripartite talks.

The points to which attention might especially be drawn are the need for taking a bold step now in giving the German Federal Government control of its own foreign affairs, subject to security safeguards. I think the American reservation as to holding back this power but delegating it to the Germans in certain fields is psychologically a mistake. The prestige of the Federal Government will be closely bound up with the authority they have in foreign affairs and the idea of delegation will be hard for them to swallow; whilst it does not add anything to our effective control. Similarly, the American unwillingness to accept a German Ambassador at this stage is unfortunate. I do not see how we can ask other countries to receive

[1] See No. 4, note 4.

Ambassadors if the United States does not. No doubt there may be difficulties in Washington, as elsewhere, but these are just the risks of a secondary order which we must take.

In the field of internal affairs I am sure that we should reduce to a minimum the reserve powers which we retain other than those relating to security. We may have to look at this again in New York to see if we cannot remove from the list one or two of the powers recommended for retention as a transitional step, and I would like this also suggested for Acheson's consideration.

My thought is definitely that about the turn of the year we should have a new Occupation Statute. Not only would this be much clearer than adding an instrument of revision to the present statute, but I believe it would give less opportunity to the Germans to extract further modifications by negotiation during the time when we are bringing the changes into force, and also subsequently I would like to put this point very strongly to Acheson before our meetings open and I should be grateful if you could get his mind thinking on the lines I have expressed.

On the subject of the Prohibited and Limited Industries I have been thinking much, particularly in relation to the help which we might secure from the Germans in our general defence programme. I understand from the United States Ambassador that Acheson is thinking on similar lines. I should be grateful if you would assure him that I hope to be able to meet him generally on this matter. I have already asked you to speak to him about steel scrap[2] and will leave it to you whether to raise that point again. I shall mention this to him also when I see him as it is vitally important that we should have an understanding on the matter.

There is one other point about Germany on which I should wish to have a word with Acheson shortly after I arrive in New York. This is the settlement of the German debt problem. I am very glad that the Americans are thinking in the positive way they are about getting a settlement plan and I am prepared to make very great sacrifices from our original view point to bring about an agreement. I would ask you, however, to indicate to him that it would be almost impossible for me politically to agree to a settlement plan that would provide for pre-war debts only. I realise at the same time the practical difficulty for the United States in any repayment of the post-war economic assistance whilst they are still providing aid to Germany. I believe it is essential, however, that we should reach an understanding on this subject giving mutual recognition to our difficulties, and I hope we could make progress before our formal talks commence.

I am sending this letter via Penson[3] to whom I have spoken. I would be grateful if, as a result, you would express my views to Acheson on the lines suggested above. I have an impression that in several respects at any rate he will be sympathetic to them. I would like him in any case to have in

[2] See No. 1, note 8.

[3] Mr. J.H. Penson was Adviser on German Affairs at H.M. Embassy in Washington.

mind the lines on which I am viewing this important part of our mutual problem.[4]

Yours sincerely,
ERNEST BEVIN

[4] On 9 September Sir O. Franks reported in Washington telegram No. 2447 that when giving Mr. Bevin's message to Colonel H.A. Byroade, Director of the Bureau of German Affairs at the State Department, Mr. Penson was assured that Mr. Acheson 'would undoubtedly make every effort to arrange a preliminary talk with Mr. Bevin. Further he was likely to be highly sympathetic to the views expressed in the message . . . Byroade went on to say that more serious matter of difference between their own views and those of His Majesty's Government arose as to the proposed centralised police force.' State Department feared this 'would tend to be undistinguishable except in name from an army' and if organised by a German general staff might 'place too great a concentration of political power in the hands of one man whoever he might be who controlled the force and would thus tend to repeat the errors which followed 1918. 3. The State Department Byroade said believed that the solution lay in incorporating the German defensive units in the combined forces of the North Atlantic Treaty powers. Assuming that a central N.A.T. Organisation would be set up speedily, German units could be raised for this force with no more delay than in the case of a central police force and any Headquarters Organisation in Germany would have strictly limited functions' (C 5757/3333/18). In Washington telegram No. 2433 of even date Sir O. Franks gave further confirmation of State Department's attitude adding that 'The Pentagon also favour the early creation of German armed forces in the proper sense, also as part of a wider whole' (C 5756/27/18). As regards the I.G.G. report, Mr. Penson was informed on 11 September that the State Department 'were generally satisfied' with it, though they 'wanted to hold out strongly for no Ambassadors to occupying powers, mainly for the sake of maintaining the authority of the High Commission.' On a debt settlement, 'the State Department would press that not only occupation costs, but also compensation for war damage for United Nations property in Germany, be postponed to the peace treaty' (Washington telegram No. 2460 on C 5806/3780/18).

No. 6

Sir O. Harvey (Paris) to Mr. Younger[1]
(Received 7 September, 12.25 p.m.)

No. 242 Telegraphic [C 5691/27/18]

Priority. Secret   PARIS, *7 September 1950, 12.11 p.m.*

Repeated Saving to Washington, The Hague, Brussels, Wahnerheide, Luxembourg, New York.

Your despatch No. 921:[2] Germany and defence.

[1] Mr. K.G. Younger, Minister of State at the Foreign Office, was in charge of the Office during Mr. Bevin's absence in New York. Mr. Bevin embarked on the *Queen Mary* at Southampton on the evening of 6 September and arrived in New York on 12 September for meetings of the three Foreign Ministers, the N.A.C., and the U.N. General Assembly. On 20 September Mr. Younger left London to take over from Mr. Bevin as head of the U.K. delegation at the U.N. Mr. Attlee then took charge of the Foreign Office until Mr. Bevin's return on 6 October.

[2] No. 3.

M. Schuman received me this evening.[3] He had already seen M. Massigli and had had a first account of your views.[4] I went through these again, leaving with him an amended copy of your paper as already handed to M. Massigli.[4]

2. M. Schuman agreed about the danger from the East, but was relieved that you were not in favour of German rearmament, at any rate at present. As regards the general rearmament of Germany, he repeated his view that the time for this would come when the Western Allies had been rearmed and were strong.

3. As regards the preliminary measures you propose, M. Schuman did not raise objection to the reorganisation of the auxiliary forces serving with the British and American troops, but asked that he might be furnished with further particulars of these.[5] Nor did he seem to mind the strengthening of the frontier police. As regards the Federal Police Force he observed that the French view differed from ours in its insistence hitherto upon Land control. It was most important that we should not recreate a German taste for arms. He was in agreement with your objective in constituting such a force to cope with civil disturbance fifth column activities and refugees, thus liberating the Allied forces for purely military action. He had in fact said so in a press interview today.[6] We must not allow our troops, he said, to do police work. On the other hand, he was nervous of centralising control, although he saw no objection to a common organisation, common training and common uniform. What he feared was a German general of the old school like Seekt[7] getting command of the police force and then some future Minister of the Interior giving way to him. His mind did not, however, seem absolutely set and he admitted that he was himself seeking a way to ensure the police force being unified and effective for action. I suggested that Dr. Schumacher would be likely to insist on adequate safeguards as the price for his agreement to the

[3] This telegram was evidently drafted on 6 September.

[4] See No. 3, note 5.

[5] Details of British proposals for reorganising the two auxiliary German bodies, the German Civil Labour Organisation of 35,000 men and the Civil Mixed Watchmen's Service of 10,000, into a single force called the German Service Organisation were accordingly transmitted to Mr. Bevin for M. Schuman at New York in F.O. telegram No. 1143 to New York (not printed from C 5691/27/18).

[6] M. Schuman's remarks on Germany at a press conference on 6 September also included reference to the possibilities of the creation of a German Ministry of Foreign Affairs in advance of a peace treaty, some German industrial contribution to defence and the raising of the steel level. With reference to this and a similar press conference held by Mr. Acheson that day, at which he spoke positively on the question of some German contribution to defence, Sir I. Kirkpatrick commented on 7 September: 'These reports convey the impression that French and Americans are ready for far-reaching concessions to Germany and that Britain is lagging behind. The positive interpretation of French policy, which we know to be the most restrictive of all, is somewhat galling, and there is danger that the blame will fall on us if the results of the Foreign Ministers' conference should not come up to expectation' (Wahnerheide telegram No. 1327 on C 5693/20/18).

[7] Colonel-General H. von Seeckt was Chief of the German Army Command from 1920–1926.

necessary constitutional amendment. M. Schuman, who was thinking aloud, observed that perhaps the police force might in some way be brought under the control of the Bundesrat. He did not challenge your view that it was necessary to take some risks at once in view of the danger of the situation, especially as the Bereitschaft[en] were not yet ready.[8]

CALENDAR TO NO. 6

i *7–9 Sept. 1950   Franco-American suggestions for Prime Minister's Parliamentary statement on defence measures on 12 Sept.* include request from M. Pleven on 7 Sept. for reference to increase of British forces in Germany and Washington concern lest statement should prejudice New York discussions. Detailed comments from Mr. Acheson reported in Washn. tel. No. 2431 [PREM 8/1207; C 5746, 5753–5/27/18; C 5760/20/18].

[8] Sir O. Harvey reported separately in Paris telegram No. 241 of even date some general remarks, from M. Schuman during this conversation, about the forthcoming conference in New York: 'He was dismayed by the heavy agenda prepared for the Three-Power talks. 2. He was dissatisfied at the lack of results produced by the deputies of the Atlantic Council, through no fault of their own, because of American dilatoriness. He felt that the Americans were under considerable nervous strain because of the course of events in Korea. He was particularly anxious that decisions should be reached regarding the standardisation of weapons and the consequent distribution of manufacture among the different countries. Armament was now threatening to hold up all our preparations' (WU 10727/137). In a conversation with Sir W. Strang, Permanent Under-Secretary of State at the Foreign Office, on 7 September M. Massigli referred to the pressures in Korea and the speed with which the Americans were moving towards German rearmament: 'It was clear that they wished to fill the gaps in the European defence forces with Germans and put the whole under an American supreme commander. His own view was that no supreme commander, especially an American, should be appointed until after the Korean affair was over. The Americans were impulsive and imprudent and there was no telling what trouble they might not land themselves into in the Far East. It would be safer not to have an American supreme commander in Europe while the Far East was in turmoil. In any event there was no hurry. Above all it would be desirable not to do anything to provoke the Russians needlessly' (WU 1198/375).

No. 7

Brief by Air Marshal Sir W. Elliot[1] for Mr. Bevin

[CAB 21/1896]

Top secret   MINISTRY OF DEFENCE, *8 September 1950*

Creation of Atlantic Defence Force for Western Europe

The Chiefs of Staff have considered the American plan for the creation

[1] Chief Staff Officer to the Minister of Defence. This text is the draft prepared by the C.O.S. Secretariat, directed by Brigadier C.R. Price, on the basis of discussion by the Chiefs of Staff earlier that day (calendar i) of the American proposal for German units in a unified force, as outlined in No. 2. No further text has been traced.

of an integrated Defence Force in Europe, including possibly a contingent from Western Germany; and they have invited me to submit to you their views.

2. It appears from the United States Government's message, as read to you by the U.S. Chargé d'affaires on the 4th September, and from information which has been received by the Chiefs of Staff from Lord Tedder,[2] that the Americans are now thinking more on the lines of the Chiefs of Staff's original proposals[3] for the formation of fully equipped German military units as opposed to the Gendarmerie which you have visualised. The Chiefs of Staff do not feel, however, that the two conceptions are contradictory. The formation of the Gendarmerie remains a sound initial step in achieving a measure of German re-armament.

3. A point of difference between the American plan and the British plan as adopted by the Defence Committee, is that the Americans visualise that the German military units would be integrated in a unified defence force under the Supreme Commander, whereas we propose that the Gendarmerie should be controlled by the German Federal Government. The Chiefs of Staff prefer our plan, though largely on account of its political advantages: but they do not consider the point to be of such importance that they should advise you to take an uncompromising attitude in discussing it with the Americans.

4. Our plan provides, in fact, for three distinct types of German military organisation. First, there is the proposed Gendarmerie of 100,000 men under Federal control; secondly, there is the expanded Frontier Police Force; and thirdly, there is the re-organisation of the auxiliary forces serving with the Occupation Armies as properly constituted military formations. Both the Frontier Police Force and the re-organised auxiliary forces will be under the control of the occupying powers. At a later stage it would be a simple matter to adjust the relative strengths of the three separate organisations, and the Chiefs of Staff do not feel that it is necessary to lay down now rigid conditions as to where control should lie.

5. The object of establishing the Gendarmerie is to provide a counterpart in Western Germany to the Bereitschaften in Eastern Germany, and so to prevent the repetition in Germany of the type of aggression which has occurred in Korea. The Chiefs of Staff consider, therefore, that the Gendarmerie should be armed on a scale which will enable it to meet the Bereitschaften on approximately equal terms. The heavier types of armament, such as artillery and tanks, can be provided by the Occupation Forces; but the Gendarmerie itself must be armed up to the standard of an infantry battalion with small arms, machine guns, mortars and anti-tank weapons. The Chiefs of Staff's conception is that the initial brunt of an attack by the Bereitschaften would be borne by the

---

[2] See No. 2 and No. 2.i.   [3] See No. 3.i(a).

Occupation Forces. It would be quite unreasonable to expect the Gendarmerie to fulfil this role if it was not equipped with anti-tank weapons. On the other hand, the Chiefs of Staff appreciate that there may well be objections both from the French and the Germans themselves, to arming the Gendarmerie initially on such a scale. It is of great importance that the creation of the force should not be delayed by such objections; and the Chiefs of Staff suggest, therefore, that the right course would be to form the force initially with light weapons only. Anti-tank weapons and other heavier types could be added subsequently without difficulty, although it is important that the necessity for them at the earliest possible moment should be kept clearly in mind.

CALENDAR TO No. 7

i *8–12 Sept. 1950 Extracts from Chiefs of Staff meetings* on (*a*) U.S. plan for integrated defence force to include Germany (*b*) reorganisation of N.A.T.O.—further discussed by C.O.S. on 9 and 12 Sept. leading to revision of D.O. (50) 65 (No. 3.ii), as explained in C.O.S. (W) 866 and F.O. tel. to N. York 1199. Main change is swing towards idea of immediate appointment of a Supreme Commander (as favoured by Pentagon, see No. 2.i), probably an American—problem of rôle for F.M. Montgomery [C 5937/27/18; WU 11915/40, 42–3, 46; DEFE 4/35].

No. 8

Mr. Gordon Walker to U.K. High Commissioners[1]

Y No. 249 Telegraphic [*C 5807/27/18*]

COMMONWEALTH RELATIONS OFFICE, *9 September 1950, 3.14 a.m.*
Top secret

My telegram 31st August A No. 114.[2]

German Defence

As result of German Chancellor's request referred to in my telegram under reference we have been giving careful consideration to question of security of Western Germany.

[1] This telegram from the Secretary of State for Commonwealth Relations was sent to Canada, Australia, New Zealand, South Africa, India, Pakistan and Ceylon.
[2] This telegram informed Commonwealth governments of Dr. Adenauer's proposal for a Federal Police force (see No. 3, note 3) and stated that this was 'a separate issue from very much broader question of German rearmament on which United Kingdom Government's attitude remains as stated by Minister of Defence in House of Commons on 26th July, namely (1) we have repeatedly and in conjunction with our Allies, declared our opposition to rearmament of Germany and any change in this policy must necessarily be result of a joint allied decision; (2) priority in supply of arms must be given to members of North Atlantic Treaty Organisation' (C 5432/3333/18).

24

2. There is little doubt that Bereitschaften, or People's Police, in East Zone of Germany, with a planned total of 150,000 men, armed with tanks and artillery, already contains nucleus of an East German army which could in near future present serious threat to both Western Sectors of Berlin and Western Zones of Germany. Danger therefore exists that we may be faced, possibly in a few months time, with a crisis in Germany similar to but more dangerous than that in Korea, arising from an attempt by Russians, acting through East Zone Police, to drive us out of Berlin or to secure unity of Germany within Soviet orbit by means of aggressive action under guise of civil war.

3. In light of foregoing there are in our view certain minimum measures which should be taken without delay. Furthermore reports from our High Commissioner in Germany indicate that morale of population in Western Germany is at present at a low ebb, and we consider that unless we face up now to danger which confronts the West Germans, we shall lose their confidence and their morale may crack in an emergency.[3] We have therefore decided to put forward following recommendations to United States and French Governments:

(i) German Federal Chancellor should be told in reply to his request that, in view of threat of invasion by East German Army he may as a first step raise federal force of 100,000 volunteers trained and equipped on model of Bereitschaften, the arms to be supplied by Western Allies.

(ii) Similar force of 3,000 men should be raised in Berlin.

(iii) Proposal to create gendarmerie on a *Land* basis (my telegram 21st August A No. 153 saving)[4] should be abandoned.

(iv) Auxiliary forces serving with United Kingdom and United States Occupation Forces in Germany should be improved and re-organised in units.

(v) German Frontier Customs Police Force should be improved and slightly expanded.

(vi) Germany should make an industrial contribution to Western strength.

(vii) Allied High Commissioners in Germany should be empowered to discuss implementation of these steps with German Federal Chancellor and with German representatives nominated by him.

4. Above recommendations have been communicated to United States and French Governments[5] and Mr. Bevin hopes to discuss them with his United States and French colleagues during their forthcoming consultations in New York.

5. Please communicate substance of above to Commonwealth authorities emphasising its secrecy.

[3] Cf. No. 3, note 6.   [4] Not printed: cf. No. 3, note 3.   [5] See No. 3 and note 7 *ibid.*

No. 9

Sir G. Jebb[1] *(New York) to Mr. Younger*
(Received 13 September, 1.4 a.m.)

No. 981 Telegraphic [WU 1198/406]

Immediate. Top secret   NEW YORK, *12 September 1950, 10.16 p.m.*

Repeated to Washington, Wahnerheide, Paris.

Tripartite talks.
Following from Secretary of State.
Acheson came for a preliminary talk with me this morning at which His Majesty's Ambassador was also present. He began by making a statement on the North Atlantic Treaty problems with which we were confronted. He said that with the President's authority the United States Government were now in a position to go a long way on most of the problems confronting us the exception being finance on which sufficient information was not yet available. Firstly the United States would increase their forces in Europe by a substantial amount and at an early date. The exact amount and the precise date were dependent on what happened in Korea. Secondly the United States Government favoured the creation of an integrated staff something on the lines of S.H.A.E.F.[2] When sufficient forces were available the United States would be prepared to provide a Supreme Commander. In the meanwhile they thought there should be a Chief of Staff working under the Standing Group. Thirdly the United States Government considered that the Military Production and Supply Board should be turned into a full time body to ensure that the maximum use was made of the available productive capacity.

2. As regards the financing of production the United States Government thought that agreement should be reached that the high priority programme[3] should go forward as fast as possible. He believed it should be possible to facilitate the granting of United States financial assistance for this programme by simplified procedural methods. The next step would be to consider long term production plans. When it had been established how much the European countries could produce and how much American assistance was required concrete proposals would have to be submitted to Congress for further financial assistance and this might be done either in December or in January. He thought that the arrangements for extending help from the existing four million dollars available for the Military Aid Programme[3] were not sufficiently flexible.

3. Mr. Acheson said that he thought that the French proposals for a

[1] U.K. Permanent Representative to the United Nations.
[2] Supreme Headquarters, Allied Expeditionary Force for the invasion of Europe, 1944–1945.
[3] See No. 1, note 5.

common defence budget[4] would tend to slow things up and while he did not wish to reject the idea he would take the line that this was a matter which might perhaps usefully be considered at a later stage.

4. The United States Government were convinced that it was necessary to build up effective military forces which could defend Europe as far east as possible. The Russians must not be allowed to overrun all Western Germany at the outset. The United States Government did not believe that it would be possible to avoid this without German participation in some form and they therefore considered that German units should be included in the common defence force under the unified command. The German units would have to be supplied with equipment produced outside Germany (though it might be possible for example to make use of Ruhr steel) and their numbers would have to be considerably less than those of the French forces.

Please repeat Priority to Paris and Wahnerheide as my telegrams Nos. 22 and 2.

CALENDAR TO NO. 9

i *5 Sept. 1950 Treasury Brief on French Plan for a Common Defence Budget* without enclosures [UE 11914/49].

[4] French proposals of July–August for a common defence financed from a common fund are explained in the brief at calendar i. These proposals were circulated to the Deputies in a memorandum of 17 August (*F.R.U.S. 1950*, vol. iii, pp. 220–4), which supplemented French plans for a new 3-year defence programme, announced earlier that month (WF 1193/7, 11). French ideas for a common defence fund etc. were referred by the Deputies to a sub-committee of seven (Canada, France, Italy, Norway, the Netherlands, U.K., U.S.A.) with instructions to report back by 18 October. Suggestions from the French Deputy, M. H. Alphand, that the French proposals should also be discussed at New York by both Ministers and officials were received by the British and American Deputies without commitment. In a message to Sir F. Hoyer Millar in Washington on 6 September Sir P. Dixon (then Acting Deputy) warned: 'Although nothing specific was agreed between Mr. Spofford, M. Alphand and myself, I think it very likely that the French will come to New York with a body of experts determined to press for detailed discussions of their proposal . . . There is no enthusiasm here for the suggested exchange of views'. The referral to a sub-committee 'would seem a good reason for suggesting to the French that there is no utility in the three Ministers discussing it. Moreover, since this question was discussed with M. Alphand, the United States have themselves put forward far-reaching proposals for the future of N.A.T.O. which will be in the forefront of all the discussions in New York' (F.O. telegram to Washington No. 3570 Saving on WU 1112/130).

No. 10

Sir G. Jebb (New York) to Mr. Younger
(Received 13 September, 12.49 a.m.)

No. 982 Telegraphic [C 5851/27/18]

Immediate. Top secret   NEW YORK, *12 September 1950, 10.57 p.m.*

Repeated to Washington, Paris, Wahnerheide.

Tripartite talks.
Following from Secretary of State.
My immediately preceding telegram.[1]

I said that I welcomed the decision of the United States Government to send more troops to Europe. This would be especially helpful from the point of view of Germany, since I had always been anxious about the risks involved in bringing the Germans into our defence plans before we had sufficient troops to offer effective resistance. I quite agreed with Mr. Acheson's view that we should try to fight as far east as possible, and I mentioned that Dr. Stikker had spoken to me on the boat about his anxieties concerning the effect on the Netherlands of the plan to defend the line of the Rhine and the Ijssel.[2]

2. As far as Germany was concerned, I thought we must be careful to avoid any suggestion that the defence of Europe was in any way dependent on the Germans. I thought that our first step should be to

[1] No. 9.

[2] The concern voiced by M. D. Stikker, Netherlands Minister for Foreign Affairs, to Mr. Bevin on board the *Queen Mary* that a Western Union plan to defend the Rhine—Ijssel line should be revised so as to provide for a defence line further east which would protect the whole of the Netherlands was the subject of New York telegram No. 364 Saving of 12 September from Mr. Bevin to the Foreign Office. M. Stikker had acknowledged that more troops would be required for a line further east commenting that 'if the United States and Great Britain cannot themselves make up the deficiency, German units must be brought in. In any case, the Dutch view was that the defence of Europe was unrealistic without the participation of German armed forces . . . In subsequent conversations on the same subject, Sir P. Dixon told Mr. Stikker that it was our view that the defence line should be as far east as military considerations allowed it to be placed . . . The question of the rearmament of Germany was difficult and dangerous. Our view was that it was essential that Western European powers should be rearmed first, and our present thinking did not go beyond the question of a German Federal Police Force' (WU 1195/332). As regards complaints from M. Stikker on the *Queen Mary* that Benelux countries had been insufficiently consulted by the Study Group on Germany, Mr. Bevin remarked to F.O. officials travelling with him that 'he had not been altogether happy about the manner in which the Benelux countries had been associated with the discussions on German questions at Paris last November, in London last May and since. He had himself felt somewhat embarrassed at having to bring them in merely in order to tell them of decisions already taken. He said that, while obviously nothing could be done about the past, he thought it important that some rather closer measure of cooperation should be worked out with the Benelux countries in future discussions on German affairs. He considers it important that we should bring the Benelux countries along with us in these German matters' (letter from Mr. Allen to Mr. Mallet of 12 September on C 6032/3780/18).

agree that Adenauer should have a German police force of 25,000 men rising to 60,000 for which he had asked,[3] and which would be an answer to the East German police. I also thought that we ought to go ahead quickly with the reforming of the German auxiliaries with the Allied armies.

3. Mr. Acheson interjected that he agreed. I did however see difficulties about the formation of actual German army units. The feeling in the United Kingdom was that we should not proceed too fast with this. We had to bear in mind the psychological effect both in our country and in France, and we did not wish to give the Germans a chance to blackmail us by making ourselves too dependent on their good will.

4. In response to an enquiry from me Mr. Acheson said that the United States view was that on the whole it was unlikely that the Russians would be provoked to aggression by a decision to form German fighting units.

Please pass priority to Paris and Wahnerheide as my telegrams 23 and 3 respectively.

[3] See No. 3, note 3.

No. 11

Sir G. Jebb (New York) to Mr. Younger
(Received 13 September, 3.20 a.m.)

No. 983 Telegraphic [*UE 11914/58*]

Immediate. Top secret   NEW YORK, *12 September 1950, 11.20 p.m.*

Repeated to Washington, Paris.

Tripartite talks.
Following from Secretary of State. My immediately preceding telegrams.[1]

I then turned to the question of finance. I said that His Majesty's Government now had the full support of public opinion in the United Kingdom for what they were doing with regard to lengthening military service and their general rearmament programme. I was most anxious that we should not lose momentum by any hold-up on finance. We had already made a beginning and placed some orders for new production but we did not yet know quite where we stood about United States help. It was difficult for us to plan unless we had some sort of commitment going beyond July 1951.

2. I agreed with Acheson that the French proposal for a common defence budget should not be followed up[2] and I thought there would be advantage in having bilateral talks between the United States and the United Kingdom. We were after all the biggest producers in Europe. Various possibilities might be considered. It might for example be

[1] Nos. 9 and 10.   [2] See No. 9, note 4.

practicable to arrange for some of our production to be put at the disposal of the United States Government. We might also be able to help in harnessing the resources of some of the Commonwealth countries.

3. Mr. Acheson said that he thought it should be possible for the United States Government to give some sort of assurance going beyond July 1951 as had been done with E.C.A.[3] It might be useful to begin with bilateral talks on this issue but there would also have to be general consideration of the common problems between all the countries concerned. It might ultimately prove desirable to have a sort of general staff for finance.[4]

4. He then referred to the considerable United States losses of gold in recent months which were a factor which would have to be taken into account.

5. Mr. Acheson then repeated that he thought that our objective should be to push ahead with the high priority programme and as regards our 3-year programme to try to work out during the next few weeks how the problems involved could be solved. It occurred to me that Mr. Harriman[5] and Mr. Spofford might organise a group including E.C.A. and Treasury representation which could discuss the problems involved either on a bilateral or multilateral basis with a view ultimately to establishing what assistance was needed so that a definite proposal could be submitted to Congress.

6. His Majesty's Ambassador then intervened to explain that as far as the United Kingdom was concerned the problem was not purely one of dollar aid. Our whole economy as a trading nation was involved. United Kingdom resources were already pretty fully engaged and if more had to

---

[3] The American Economic Co-operation Administration administered the Marshall Aid Programme for the economic recovery of Europe, launched in 1947 and due to end on 1 July 1952.

[4] The necessity for new machinery for finance and supply was acknowledged by the Foreign Office on 13 September, when briefing Mr. Bevin on the possibility of a combined supply and finance programme being considered at New York in pursuance of French proposals for common defence (see No. 9, note 4). Mr. Bevin was informed that: 'while on some aspects of the supply problem our views may not be so far separated from those of the French, the sort of financial arrangement for which they have lately been pressing is unacceptable to us. Our object must therefore be to try to get the initiative away from the French and to get the discussion going on less ambitious but still constructive lines' (telegram to New York No. 1214 on WU 11911/206). Mr. Bevin was also advised to resist any attempt to place new finance and supply machinery within the O.E.E.C. rather than in N.A.T.O.: 'It must be in our interest to push ahead with strengthening and simplifying the N.A.T.O. organisation, though of course not necessarily on the lines of French proposals . . . One of the main advantages of the N.A.T.O. organisation is that the Americans are in on an equal basis' (ibid.). In view of all these considerations the Foreign Office suggested that any proposal for new machinery should be referred to the Deputies for more detailed study. For the establishment of the O.E.E.C. in Paris in 1948, see Volume I, No. 1, note 5, and for F.O. concern at O.E.E.C./N.A.T.O. developments in May 1950, see Volume II, No. 91.

[5] Mr. W.A. Harriman, Special Assistant to the President, had been until June the Special Representative in Europe of the E.C.A.

be devoted to defence this would involve a diversion of effort which would probably mean the cutting down of exports. At the moment we were about on the balance but His Majesty's Government were very concerned at the prospect that they might find themselves running up new sterling debts all over the world. The problem was to make the necessary diversion of effort without bringing about an unbalance in our economy and that was why we had asked for free dollars. The sum of £550 million for which His Majesty's Government had asked[6] was our best guess of what we needed in order to maintain the present somewhat precarious stability to which we had won our way back with American help during the last few years. The problem was now somewhat different from that with which E.C.A. had been confronted and it was no longer mainly a matter of providing dollars in order to purchase dollar goods. His Majesty's Government believed that it was in the United States interest as well as in their own that the United Kingdom should be strong and stable and they had therefore asked for free money to help to balance an anticipated overall deficit. Our problem was somewhat different from that of the French whose economy was less dependent on overseas trade.

7. Mr. Acheson agreed that this aspect of the problem needed further examination and that it might be desirable to begin on a bilateral basis.[7]

Please repeat Priority Paris as my telegram No. 24.

[6] See No. 1, note 6.

[7] On 15 September Mr. Bevin informed the Foreign Office that at Mr. Acheson's suggestion a tripartite group led by Mr. P. Nitze, Director of the Policy Planning Staff in the State Department, Sir O. Franks and M. Alphand had begun discussions on 13 September to identify the main questions holding up progress on the financial side of the rearmament programme. Discussion included Anglo-American objections to the French common fund, British claims for American aid and American concern at the inadequacy of defence programmes proposed by European N.A.T. countries (New York telegram No. 1025 on UE 11914/64). Later discussion focused on proposals originally put forward by Mr. Nitze on 17 September based on the principle of an equitable distribution of economic burdens in carrying out the medium term plan (see No. 17, note 2. For text of Nitze memorandum, as revised on 4 October, see No. 79.i). Bilateral talks conducted by Mr. Nitze and Sir L. Rowan, Economic Minister at H.M. Embassy in Washington, began in New York on 14 September with the object of finding some immediate arrangement for assistance to the U.K. towards an initial instalment of the high priority programme. These talks, continued in Washington from 3 October, superseded those being held in London (see No. 1, note 6). Meanwhile in London, Ministers considered on 8 September Treasury warnings that, in the light of more detailed calculations, showing a more favourable balance of payments, the original bid for £550 millions could no longer be justified and should be reduced to approximately £350 millions. However, it was agreed that: 'It would be undesirable at the present juncture to modify in any way the request for assistance totalling £550 millions. Any suggestion that this figure had been unduly high and was not justified by subsequent detailed investigations, would weaken the position of the Foreign Secretary in the discussions which would now take place in New York. Moreover, the Americans should be held to the promises they had made to assist in maintaining the general balance of payments and not simply the dollar balance': see further calendar i.

i *7–8 Sept. 1950   Effect of U.K. defence programme on national economy* analyzed by Sir E. Bridges, Permanent Secretary, Treasury, in memo. of 7 Sept. (GEN 331/1). Balance of payments more favourable than expected. Even so defence programme will lead to a deficit of £70 m. in 1951 as compared with current surplus of £100 m. Measures to minimise disturbing effects to rest of U.K. industrial production include maximum use of German industrial capacity to meet the additional defence production needs. F.O. brief argues case for U.S. aid and considers basis on which it could be available given tight U.S. legislation. On 8 Sept. (GEN 333/1st Meeting) Ministers agree importance of bringing Germany into industrial side of rearmament programme and need to press on with claims for U.S. aid. Control of exports to E. Europe and communist Asia and general arms exports also discussed [CAB 130/63; UE 11914/62].

No. 12

Minute by Mr. Mallet

[C 6004/3333/18]

Top secret   FOREIGN OFFICE, *12 September 1950*

The postscript to Mr. Shuckburgh's minute alarms me.[1] It will be recalled that the Defence Committee and the Cabinet itself[2] have recently rejected the recommendations of the Chiefs of Staff in favour of immediate action with our Allies with a view to making an early start with the re-creation of German armed forces, and have instead adopted the Secretary of State's recommendations that such action would be premature, and that we should confine ourselves to certain minimum measures, including the creation of a federal gendarmerie, the strengthening of the frontier police and the reorganisation of the auxiliaries in the British and American forces.

I cannot but be surprised that the C.I.G.S. should have suggested at the Chiefs of Staff meeting on 8th September that a German contingent to a combined army might be built up from these three bodies.

[1] Mr. Mallet was here referring to a minute by Mr. C.A.E. Shuckburgh, Head of F.O. Western Organizations department in which he summarized discussion by the Chiefs of Staff on 8 September (see No. 7.i) on the reorganization of N.A.T.O. In a postscript Mr. Shuckburgh summarized their discussion on the question of including German units in a combined Allied force. Field-Marshal Sir W. Slim 'pointed out that there are two sources from which such units could be built up apart from the gendarmerie, namely (*a*) the frontier police, who are already under Allied control; (*b*) the administrative tail of the Allied forces . . . The Chiefs of Staff think we should point out to the Americans the advantages of drawing in fighting units from the first two sources mentioned. If, however, the Secretary of State should feel disposed to agree with the Americans that the gendarmerie should eventually come under the Allied defence forces, the Chiefs of Staff, for their part, would not object' (WU 1198/413).

[2] See No. 3.i and No. 4.i.

The Chiefs of Staff have, for several months, been pressing that steps be taken for the reconstitution of the German armed forces, and, recognising that this proposal would meet with opposition, they have advised, as a first step, the creation of a gendarmerie, for which an excuse could be found in the existence of the People's Police. To the Chiefs of Staff, therefore, the federal gendarmerie has always been nothing more than a first step towards a German armed force, and it is clear from what they said on the 8th September that their minds are still running on the same lines.

These lines seem to me to be all wrong. If you are going to have an army, the men composing it will have to be trained and organised in such a way that they can fill the companies, battalions and divisions of that army. It is true that we used the Guards to test the ventilation in the new House of Commons,[3] but if the German army is to be built up from the frontier police you might just as well expect to commission an aircraft carrier with coastguards. Similarly, if you are going to use the auxiliaries as a basis for a German army, the British and American forces in Germany will become immobile, and will thus cease to be armies.

The same arguments apply to the proposal to build a German army out of the gendarmerie. Just as there is a job for the frontier police and the auxiliaries, so there is a job for the gendarmerie. There is at present in Germany no body capable of dealing with widespread disturbances and sabotage except the allied forces. The local police, who are organised and equipped on the lines of our own local police forces and have similar duties, would not be able to deal with nationwide disturbances. This has already been proved to be a fact. If the allied forces have to act as riot squads, or to control mass movements of refugees, they would not be able to resist an aggressor. Moreover, the Federal Government has no force at its command and is therefore unable to take any central action for the suppression of disturbances or the control of disorders. There is therefore a genuine need for a centrally-controlled, armed and mobile gendarmerie in Germany, just as there is in France and in Italy.

This need has become urgent since Korea opened our eyes to the danger that the Russians will use the Bereitschaften to stage a civil war in Germany for the avowed purpose of reuniting the country and freeing it from foreign occupation. It is doubtful whether the allied forces, as at present constituted, would be able to hold the western sectors of Berlin against the Bereitschaften by the end of the year, or whether they would be able to hold Western Germany by the end of next year if the Bereitschaften continue to develop as they are doing. It is true that we and the Americans and the French are now planning to send reinforcements to Germany, but it still remains most undesirable that the allied armies should be in danger of having to deal with disorders or control refugees.

Furthermore, and this is very important, all the proposals for the creation of a German contingent in a European army would take many

---

[3] For an account of this episode, see C. Jones, *The Great Palace: the Story of Parliament* (London, 1983) p. 123.

months, at best, to realise. Until they are realised the Germans will continue to be and to feel exposed to attack, and the greatest importance of the gendarmerie lies in the fact that its creation will give the Federal Government and the West Germans visible evidence of the fact that we are alive to the danger which threatens them and are taking steps to meet it. Therefore there is a definite need for the gendarmerie and it is needed at once.

If we now take the line that the gendarmerie should eventually form part of the western defence forces, we destroy the whole basis of our argument for the gendarmerie. The fact is that, although two months ago the Americans were telling us officially that they would not hear any talk of German rearmament, they have, in the last two or three weeks, swung completely round, owing, I think, largely to the influence of Mr. McCloy, and are now obsessed with the idea of a European army with a German contingent. The result of this obsession is that they won't even think seriously about a gendarmerie. They argue that such a force is open to all sorts of objections: that being completely under German control it might eventually lead to an uncontrolled German army: that needing some sort of organisation it might eventually lead to the re-creation of a General Staff: that needing some central control it might eventually lead to the overthrow of the Republic and to the suppression not only of the Laender but of democracy itself. The American objections to centralised police forces may come natural to an American but they are not relevant to conditions in Germany today, and the real reason why the Americans object to a gendarmerie is because they fear that if it was once constituted people would say there was no longer any need for a German army. And since the strongest argument for a European army is that it would enable a German contribution to be made to defence, there would then no longer be the same arguments in favour of a European army.

It is, no doubt, the case that we shall need a German contribution before we can fill the gap in the western defences, and that such a contribution will have to be made as part of an integrated western force. But the Cabinet's decision was against the constitution of such a force, at any rate until the other western forces had been built up sufficiently to deter the Russians from taking preventive action. The Chiefs of Staff seem still to ignore that decision, just as they seem to ignore the fact that the Germans are not yet ready to be armed. The line they were taking on September 8 is not only contrary to Cabinet policy but likely to defeat the objects which the Secretary of State was instructed to attain.[4]   I. MALLET

[4] Following discussion with Sir W. Strang and Mr. Shuckburgh, Mr. Mallet sent a copy of his minute to Mr. Bevin's Private Secretary, Mr. Barclay, in New York commenting in his covering letter of 13 September: 'Although Evelyn Shuckburgh is inclined to think that I am being a little unfair to the Chiefs of Staff, and William [Strang] agreed that the Secretary of State has, of course, clearly in mind what the decision of the Defence Committee and of the Cabinet was, he none-the-less thought that it was as well that you should have in mind the possibility that our military may take the line that the gendarmerie is only the first step towards a German army.'

Sir G. Jebb (New York) to Mr. Younger
(Received 13 September, 2.10 p.m.)

No. 987 Telegraphic [WU 1071/179]

Priority. Secret   NEW YORK, *13 September 1950, 3.41 a.m.*

Repeated to Wahnerheide, and Saving to Paris, Washington.

Following from Secretary of State.
Tripartite talks.
After a short formal opening session this afternoon [12 September][1]
Mr. Acheson suggested that the three Ministers might meet in private
session accompanied only by their Private Secretaries, and this was agreed.

2. Mr. Acheson opened the private session by making a statement on
the same lines as that which he made to me this morning, (see my telegram
No. 981[2]). The only additional point he made was that he was confident
that the policy of increased United States participation in the defence of
Europe was fully supported by United States public opinion and by
Congress. The only condition was that there must be a really adequate
defence programme which was sufficient to inspire confidence in its
effectiveness. He dealt with the French proposals for a common finance
budget[3] in the way he had indicated to me, that is to say, he did not reject
the French proposal but said that clearly this would require long and
careful study, and that while it might prove valuable at a later stage, it
would only delay matters if it was debated at the present stage.

3. M. Schuman, who spoke next, said he was glad to note that on most
points the attitude of the French Government was in full agreement with
what Mr. Acheson had said. In particular the French Government
welcomed his statement about the increase of American forces in Europe
and the setting up of a combined command organisation. He thought that
the American ideas for the reorganisation of the Military Production and
Supply Board were excellent.[4] The only two questions on which there
were some difficulties were

(1) finance, and
(2) the problem of German participation in European defence.

4. As regards (1) he agreed that it was very important to get on at once
with the high priority programme, and he thought that this could be done
without awaiting a final decision on the financial principles which were to

---

[1] For this opening meeting on procedural matters, see *F.R.U.S. 1950*, vol. iii, p. 1191. The
full British records of the Foreign Ministers' conference at New York, held in the Waldorf
Astoria Hotel, are entered on F.O. 371/124931–4: ZP 5. Coverage in this volume of the
New York conference is restricted to the discussions on Western European defence and
Germany. Discussions at New York on the Far East will be documented in Volume IV.
[2] No. 9.   [3] See No. 9, note 4.   [4] See No. 17, note 7.

be applied. Nevertheless, long-term programmes could not be put into operation without some agreement on how the cost of defence was going to be shared. He was very glad that this was going to be examined forthwith. The French Government had put forward a proposal of their own,[3] but they would be very ready to consider other solutions.

5. As regards Germany and defence, M. Schuman said he recognised that it was not possible to accept a situation in which the Allies had to defend Germany without the Germans making any contribution to the common cause. There was however a psychological problem to be faced, particularly in France. He did not think this was an obstacle to all action and it was really only a question of timing. If however the French Government were forced to take a stand on this issue before French public opinion was ready everything might go wrong. Since the available resources were limited the French Government took the view that the first step was to divide them out between the Atlantic countries. When their forces had been brought up to a certain level it would be easier to reach a decision on German participation. If in the meanwhile a joint staff and command organisation, under whom the Germans would serve, had been set up, it would further facilitate matters. He thought that the difficulties confronting the French Government would then largely have been removed. He wished to make it clear that it was in his opinion only a question of a few months, and it was possible that events would further accelerate the evolution of French opinion. He therefore asked his two colleagues to be patient.

Please repeat to Wahnerheide as my telegram No. 5 and to Paris as my telegram No. 139 saving.

No. 14

Sir G. Jebb (New York) to Mr. Younger
(Received 13 September, 3.25 p.m.)

No. 988 Telegraphic [WU 1198/389]

Priority. Secret   NEW YORK, *13 September 1950, 4.09 a.m.*

Repeated Saving to Paris, Washington.

Following from Secretary of State.
Tripartite talks.
My immediately preceding telegram.[1]
I followed M. Schuman and after referring to the critical nature of our discussions said I would like to refer to two recent developments (1) the great announcement of President Truman about sending United States troops to Europe;[2] and (2) the steps recently taken by most of the Brussels powers with regard to lengthening military service.[3] I thought that we

---

[1] No. 13.   [2] See No. 1, note 7.   [3] See No. 1, note 3.

were going to get much nearer to meeting our man-power requirements than seemed likely a few months ago, particularly if the Dutch soon came into line.

2. I then said that I thought it was a mistake to lay too much emphasis on the word 'Europe' and to speak in terms of a European army. The United States and Canada, together with other members of the British Commonwealth would all be involved and the issue at stake would be the defence of the whole free world. It was therefore important that we should not imply that the problem was a purely European one.

3. As regards the American proposal for the creation of a combined staff, His Majesty's Government would be very ready to consider any arrangements which were acceptable to our respective military authorities.

4. I then said that His Majesty's Government were most anxious to press on with military production. A start had already been made but it was essential to get the question of finance settled in order that there should be no check to the present momentum. If there was a hold-up and we were unable to go ahead with the placing of orders, it would have a bad psychological effect on our people and particularly in the trade unions. There would be much heart searching if it was found that there was not enough equipment to match the man-power which would be mobilised. Many of our people had bitter memories of the early days of the last war, and it was in my view essential that equipment should keep pace with man-power.

5. As regards finance, I thought it would be a mistake to get involved in arguments on long-term principles. I did not much like the suggestion of a common defence budget, and it seemed to me that in view of the different problems confronting the different countries, it might be better to start talking on a bi-lateral basis. I thought we should avoid excessive rigidity, though it would of course be necessary for all countries to be informed of the position and to be satisfied with the general principles which were being applied. I suggested that it might simplify matters if the question of United States financial assistance could be dealt with in two stages – (1) for the period up to July 1951, and (2) for the subsequent period for which we hoped it would be possible for the United States Government to give us some moral commitment to match the commitments which we should be entering into with regard to production.

Please repeat to Paris as my telegram No. 140 saving.

No. 15

Sir G. Jebb (New York) to Mr. Younger
(Received 13 September, 1.22 p.m.)

No. 989 Telegraphic [C 5843/27/18]

Priority   NEW YORK, 13 September 1950, 4.25 a.m.

Repeated to Wahnerheide, and Saving to Paris, Washington.

Following from Secretary of State.

Tripartite talks. My immediately preceding telegram.[1]

I then turned to the question of Germany. I said I thought we must be very careful how we handled the Germans over the question of a German contribution to Western defence. I did not want to see them put in a position where they could bargain with us. They might make embarrassing demands, e.g. with regard to the future of the High Commission. I thought we ought to ask our High Commissioners to report on how they thought the Germans would respond to a request to form German military units. According to my information, the Germans would not be likely to favour the formation of German units in a combined army unless they were given almost complete freedom from controls.[2] I did not think it was possible to separate this question of German participation in defence from the problem of the control of German foreign policy.

2. There was also the question about which M. Schuman had spoken of how opinion in our countries would react to a decision to invite the Germans to participate in Western defence. I did not think there would be a strong reaction in the United Kingdom, though there would certainly be some feeling particularly among those who had fought against the Germans in the last war.[3]

3. His Majesty's Government had reached the conclusion that it was desirable to proceed cautiously. They favoured the immediate organisation of a gendarmerie. This would have the advantage that we should be acceding to a German request which would put the Allies in a much stronger position. We should have at the same time to consider the question of German foreign relations, the ending of the dismantling programme and the limitations on the German industry. It really seemed to me that we should do better to consider this problem of a German

---

[1] No. 14.

[2] Cf. No. 3.iii and No. 3, note 3. On 14 September Mr. C.E. Steel, U.K. Deputy High Commissioner in Germany then acting for Sir I. Kirkpatrick during his absence in New York, reported that at a dinner party the previous evening Dr. Adenauer had emphasised 'that present meeting in New York was more vital for Germany than any either in the past or future. He made no secret of his deep anxiety that some real psychological tonic should emerge from the discussions. He is indeed in deep water internally. While he is trying to galvanise opinion into acceptance of some kind of effective defence force, his Cabinet is in no state to support him' (Wahnerheide telegram No. 1362 on C 5861/5587/18).

[3] Cf. No. 1.ii.

contribution to defence in the context of these other German problems, rather than as a separate military problem.

4. We were very ready to examine how far we should go, but we should not consider the problem from the narrow angle of the extent to which the Germans could help us to defend ourselves against Russia. We should constantly bear in mind that it was our objective to establish Germany as a permanent and responsible member of the Western comity of nations.

5. I also referred to the danger of Communist-provoked disorders in Western Germany which might create a serious situation. The German police at the moment were weak and their morale was low.

6. I suggested that there might be some advantage in bringing the Benelux countries into our consultations.[4] They were naturally extremely concerned with the German problem and the wider the area of agreement on how to handle it the better.

Please repeat to Wahnerheide as my telegram No. 6 and to Paris as my telegram No. 141 Saving.

[4] Cf. No. 10, note 2.

No. 16

Sir G. Jebb (New York) to Mr. Younger
(Received 13 September, 2.29 p.m.)

No. 990 Telegraphic [C 5844/27/18]

Priority. Secret   NEW YORK, 13 September 1950, 5.41 a.m.

Repeated to Wahnerheide and Saving to Paris, Washington.

Following from Secretary of State.
Tripartite talks. My immediately preceding telegram.[1]
When the meeting resumed in open session, Mr. Acheson began by giving a summary of our private discussions and proposed certain action as result of them.

Germany

2. Mr. Acheson first proposed that we should try to reach tripartite agreement on three points.

(*a*) what was the best way to associate Germany with European defence?
(*b*) how this problem should be discussed with our other allies, especially Benelux and the other North Atlantic Treaty countries, and
(*c*) what we should say in public.

3. I accepted this proposal. So did M. Schuman, but only after

[1] No. 15.

39

repeating the French Government's fears about German rearmament. We must take care to see that by allowing the creation of an enlarged German police force we did not put Germany in a position to exert pressure on us as regards the peace treaty or to play us off against the Soviet Union. Nothing must be done which might permit the growth of a German professional army; the proposed police force must not therefore be too centralised or too large. He had no objection to discussing this question with the Benelux countries, but thought that the time was not yet ripe for informing the other North Atlantic Treaty countries. It was also important that we should try to form a picture of the state of German public opinion on this subject. He proposed therefore that the three High Commissioners should be asked to give their views.

4. It was agreed to ask the three High Commissioners to report by tomorrow on the state of public opinion and on the three points raised by Mr. Acheson.[2]

Please repeat to Wahnerheide as my telegram No. 7 and to Paris as my telegram No. 142 Saving.

[2] In their report, submitted accordingly on 13 September, the High Commissioners recommended (a) increase in strength of Allied forces in F.R.G. (b) security guarantee (c) visible steps towards organization of unified force (d) authority for F.R.G. to ensure its own internal security (e) encouragement to German people for acceptance of German participation in western defence (text of report is printed in *F.R.U.S. 1950*, vol. iii, pp. 1278–9). When this report was considered by Ministers at their Second meeting on 13 September 'Recommendations (a) and (b) were accepted and it was agreed that (c) should be actively examined. 3. Recommendation (d) was approved in principle and led to a discussion on the formation of a Federal Police Force. After both Mr. Acheson and M. Schuman had made it plain that they could not accept my [Mr. Bevin's] proposal for a fully federal force it was agreed that the High Commissioners should draw up recommendations for a force on a land basis but subject to federal control . . . Consideration of recommendation (e) led to inconclusive discussion on German participation in defence summarized in my telegram No. 1018 [see No. 25]' (New York telegram No. 1097 of 18 September on C 5991/27/18).

No. 17

Sir G. Jebb (New York) to Mr. Younger
(Received 13 September, 4.50 p.m.)

No. 991 Telegraphic [WU 1198/390]

Priority. Secret   NEW YORK, *13 September 1950, 6.1 a.m.*

Repeated Saving to Paris, Washington.

Following from Secretary of State.
Tripartite talks.
My immediately preceding telegram.[1]

[1] No. 16.

On this point Mr. Acheson said that the object was to reach agreement so that the three powers could go to the Council with a common view. The Military Organisation were at work on a revision of the medium-term plan.[2] He proposed that the Council should instruct the Defence Committee to have this revised plan ready by October: it should show not only the forces which had to be raised, but also their allocation between the different countries: the Council should then give advance approval to the plan so that it would enter into force as soon as it had been approved by the Defence Committee at its meeting in October. The target which we were aiming at would thus at last be clear and there would be no more waste of time. He suggested that the three deputies should prepare a draft resolution on these lines for eventual submission to the Council.

2. I pointed out that the medium-term plan was based on 1954 . . . ?[3] There was no plan for the next year, when the danger might come, especially if the Soviet Union regarded our plans for Germany as an act of provocation. What we had to know was what forces would be available next year and what equipment would be available for them. It was essential to synchronise the raising of forces with the production of equipment.

3. Mr. Acheson agreed that we had to know what forces were immediately required for the defence of Europe in 1951, and he hoped by tomorrow to have a report from the Defence Committee on this point compiled in the light of the various national replies to the Deputies' enquiries on increases in combat forces. He also agreed that production and finance were essential elements in building up an effective defence but he thought it was first necessary to settle our needs in terms of manpower as a firm starting point for deciding what equipment should be produced and how to finance its production.

4. It was agreed to ask the three Deputies to produce by tomorrow a draft resolution for the Council on the lines proposed by Mr. Acheson, but taking into account also our immediate needs for 1951 and also for 1952.[4]

[2] The Medium Term Plan was a N.A.T. plan for defending Europe as far east as possible in 1954. Estimates of the forces required for the defence of their area, to be achieved in phases between 1951 and 1954, were drawn up by four of the Regional Planning Groups on the basis of a Strategic Concept, approved on 1 December 1949 (*F.R.U.S. 1949*, vol. iv, pp. 353–6). These were attached to an outline strategic plan for 1954: the whole of which constituted the medium term plan presented to the North Atlantic Defence Committee on 1 April (see Volume II, No. 33.i). At this meeting the Defence Committee gave instructions for the rationalisation of the overlapping regional requirements. Revised requirements were sought from the Regional Groups with a view to their collation into a single requirement plan by the Standing Group based on the principle of 'balanced collective forces' as directed by the N.A.C. in May (Volume II, No. 113).

[3] The text is here uncertain.

[4] A draft resolution on the medium term plan was accordingly prepared and approved by Ministers at their Third meeting on 13 September (see No. 26, note 3 and *F.R.U.S. 1950*, vol.

5. It was also agreed to ask the three Deputies to prepare, in the light of the Ministers' private discussion, a scheme for a unified force and unified command for the defence of Western Europe.[5]

6. Mr. Acheson also proposed that the Deputies should be instructed to examine what unified organisation was necessary on the supply side in order to produce the equipment necessary for a unified force. At my request it was agreed to defer this question until tomorrow, when Mr. Gough[6] will have arrived. An attempt is being made to discover what precisely the Americans have in mind.[7]

iii, pp. 1277–8 for the drafts). A final text was agreed by the N.A.C. on 18 September (see No. 35, note 2) in which the Defence Committee was invited to consider the revision of the force levels required for the medium term plan as a matter of urgency so that the Plan could be finalized at the Defence Committee's next meeting on 16 October (later postponed to 28 October). The resolution recommended that when member governments were advised by the N.A.C. of the provisions of the final Plan and the contributions required they should, as a matter of urgency, accept it and take steps to enable them to make their contribution.

[5] Protracted discussions between Sir F. Hoyer Millar, Mr. Spofford and M. Alphand on the evening of 12 September resulted in a draft resolution for a unified force (printed in *F.R.U.S. 1950*, vol. iii, p. 1280) in which the question of whether a Supreme Commander would be appointed immediately instead of the proposed American measure of an interim appointment of a Chief of Staff was left unresolved. When the draft was considered by Ministers at their Third meeting on 13 September, Mr. Bevin pressed for the immediate appointment of a Supreme Commander. This was resisted by Mr. Acheson on the grounds that the U.S. government did not wish to appoint a Commander until there were sufficient forces in Europe to command. The question was referred back to the three Deputies who produced on 14 September a revised draft (*ibid.*, pp. 1281–2), whereby the British dropped the idea of the immediate appointment of a Supreme Commander in return for American agreement to the appointment of a representative of the Supreme Commander. This draft was agreed by Mr. Bevin and M. Schuman on 14 September and awaited Mr. Acheson's signature before circulation to the N.A.C. Reporting these developments in a telegram to the Chiefs of Staff on 15 September Air Marshal Elliot pointed out that the governing consideration, agreed by the Chiefs of Staff and Lord Tedder, was 'the importance of not losing the opportunity of drawing the Americans further into Europe – and this view has been strongly endorsed here by the Foreign Secretary and the Ambassador. In the light of our conversations here this opportunity would have been in grave danger of being lost had we gone on pressing for the immediate appointment of a Supreme Commander.' In any case the fact that the powers of the representative of the Supreme Commander remained open to be defined by the Standing Group 'will give us the opportunity of shaping him and his organisation as we would like and in particular of ensuring that he will be something more than a mere Chief of Staff' (COJA 109 on WU 1198/402).

[6] Assistant Secretary in the Ministry of Defence.

[7] On 14 September Sir F. Hoyer Millar informed the Foreign Office in New York telegram No. 1013 that as regards American proposals for a North Atlantic Treaty Production Board: 'We have on two or three occasions pressed the Americans to let us have their proposals in writing so that we could see exactly what they had in mind. So far however they have failed to do so and our conversations with them have suggested that their ideas on the subject were in fact very far from clear' (WU 11911/205). The question of new supply and production machinery was not pursued in detail at ministerial level at New York but referred to the sub-committee of 7 set up to consider the French proposals for common defence (see No. 9, note 4). American proposals (text on UE 11914/92) were circulated to this sub-committee, now known as the Working Group on Production and Finance, for a meeting in New York on 25 September. The Working Group agreed to nominate experts to pursue the question in London in October.

7. In the course of the discussion I asked Mr. Acheson whether the United States' promise to send more troops to Europe was conditional on a favourable outcome of the Korean war and if so, how long that condition would stand. Mr. Acheson replied categorically that the United States had decided to send more forces to Europe anyway and that the Korean situation would merely affect the speed with which forces could be sent. If forces were not available from Korea, it would be necessary to raise new units to send to Europe.

8. The only other point raised was M. Schuman's suggestion that the Deputies should examine the problem of the supply and price of raw materials essential to war production. (See separate telegram on this question).[8]

Please repeat to Paris as my telegram No. 143 Saving.

[8] In New York telegram No. 986 of 13 September Mr. Bevin recorded that when M. Schuman suggested some N.A.T.O. price control on raw materials, Mr. Bevin asked for time to consider further. Mr. Bevin told the Foreign Office that he did not think this was a suitable matter for N.A.T.O. since major producing countries e.g. Australia, were not members. Mr. Bevin therefore preferred that the question should be dealt with through diplomatic channels rather than by the Deputies. M. Schuman pursued his proposal at the N.A.C. on 16 September. Mr. Bevin stated his objections but agreed that the Deputies could study the question against the widest possible background. On 18 September the N.A.C. agreed a resolution instructing the Deputies to study the short supply and rising prices of raw materials and to make recommendations for dealing with the problem 'bearing in mind that the interests of both producer and consumer countries are involved' (New York telegram No. 1106).

No. 18

Sir G. Jebb (New York) to Mr. Younger
(Received 13 September, 8.20 p.m.)

No. 996 Telegraphic [C 5845/27/18]

Emergency. Secret   NEW YORK, 13 September 1950, 6.48 a.m.

Following for Prime Minister from Secretary of State. Tripartite discussions. German participation in western defence.

At today's meeting[1] Dean Acheson made it quite clear that the President's undertaking to station troops in Europe is dependent on the assembly of a sufficient force to make the whole enterprise successful. He stated that in the United States view this could not be achieved without some German participation in the defence of Europe. Whilst recognising that opinion in Germany and elsewhere is not yet ripe for this development he invited us to agree in principle to envisage the incorporation of German units in a western force under unified command.

[1] i.e. Second meeting of Foreign Ministers at 10.30 a.m. on 13 September which mainly concerned consideration of a report from the High Commissioners (see No. 16, note 2). For general discussion at this meeting of German participation in western defence see No. 25.

2. He also made it clear that if this principle were accepted he would be ready to leave over for further discussion question of timing, method etc. and in meantime to avoid publicity.

3. His general approach is substantially that in Defence Committee paper D.O. (50) 66 of August 29th last. (In particular see paragraph 2).[2] Consequently in view of stakes involved I propose to give general concurrence.[3]

[2] See No. 3.i. Paragraph 2 of this paper read: 'If the premise is accepted that the threat from the East is real and urgent and without Germany cannot be met, the problem is to find the best method of associating Germany, so far as this is politically and economically practicable, with the defence of the West.'

[3] Further to this telegram Mr. Bevin sent a message to Mr. Attlee transmitted in New York telegram No. 998 of even date: 'In view of this development it seems important that problem of eventual German participation should be left open by Government spokesmen in debate' (C 5845/27/18). When the Cabinet considered these two telegrams on the morning of 14 September (C.M. (50) 58th Conclusions, minute 3 on CAB 128/18), it was agreed that German participation in western defence should be left open in the debate on defence in the House of Commons on 12–14 September (*Parl. Debs., 5th ser., H. of C.*, vol. 478, cols. 951–1085, 1103–1240, 1257–1397). However, Mr. Bevin was informed in Foreign Office telegram to New York No. 1233 of 3.30 p.m. on 14 September that 'Cabinet have agreed that although you might continue to discuss Mr. Acheson's proposal you should not agree to it in principle without further reference back to London' (C 5845/27/18).

No. 19

Mr. Younger to Sir G. Jebb (New York)

No. 1238 Telegraphic [C 5845/27/18]

Emergency. Secret   FOREIGN OFFICE, *14 September 1950, 5.35 p.m.*

My telegram No. 1233[1] (of 14th September).

Following for Secretary of State from Minister of State.

It may be useful to you to know the main reasons which made your colleagues reluctant to approve of an agreement even in principle at the present time to the incorporation of German Units in a Western Force under unified command.

2. If any such agreement is registered the likelihood of leakage is so considerable that we must base our policy on the assumption that the decision will become known.[2]

3. Since it is agreed that German opinion is not ready for this step and since United Kingdom Delegation New York telegram No. 987[3] (of the 13th September) shows clearly that French opinion is equally unready, the disadvantage of an agreement on these lines is considerable. Nor does it

[1] See No. 18, note 3.

[2] Further to this point the Cabinet minutes stated 'and it was important to keep in mind possible Russian reactions to proposals for German rearmament, at a time when western defence was still very weak' (CAB 128/18).

[3] No. 13.

seem likely that the decision could have any practical effect on speeding up western rearmament unless military supplies were to be diverted from the North Atlantic powers to Germany.

4. It was appreciated that these arguments might be outweighed if the United States undertaking to station troops in Europe were really dependent upon agreement about German participation. Your colleagues, however, while recognising that only you could form a final judgement on this point felt very doubtful whether the American decision really depended upon this at all.

5. Your colleagues were anxious to adhere to the policy which they had already approved before your departure. The hope was expressed that the proposal to form German military units would not in any event be regarded as an alternative to the creation of adequate police forces.

No. 20

Sir G. Jebb (New York) to Mr. Younger
(Received 14 September, 9.56 p.m.)

No. 1005 Telegraphic [C 5865/27/18]

Emergency. Secret   NEW YORK, *14 September 1950, 8.1 p.m.*

My telegram 996.[1]

Following personal for Prime Minister from Foreign Secretary.

I feel it is absolutely essential we should take a comprehensive review of the whole situation regarding the defence of Europe and not deal with Germany in isolation.

2. The situation as it has developed here is as follows. As far as the United States is concerned they have made it clear that they will play their full part in the defence of the West. They would provide their quota towards a strong integrated force and would be in the struggle from the first day. This is in keeping with our general objectives. In conjunction with that they would be ready to work out supply, finance and other matters which are giving us anxiety, and create the machinery for doing it. When we have all made our contribution they add up the total force available and they argue with force that it will still not be adequate to defend the vital point in Europe which is the heart of Germany. If this is left as a vacuum Russia will walk in and get resources which will be of tremendous gain in carrying on the conflict. That is the situation which the U.S.A. cannot contemplate facing with their public and their Congress. On the other hand, they say that Adenauer has offered to take steps to organise a force, and is willing to discuss it with our representatives. They consider that we ought not to reject in principle a contribution by the West German Republic; but the timing, announcement and method are matters to be worked out.

[1] No. 18.

3. A following telegram will give you the French reaction to all this.[2] It is quite clear that this matter will have to be discussed in the Atlantic Council tomorrow. Our country is a leading power and I cannot take part in discussions without giving some opinion. We must either reject the U.S.A. thesis or accept it and cooperate with them. Otherwise Great Britain will look weak and indecisive. I realise your difficulties at the moment what with the debate and the attitude of Churchill[3] but that in my view is not influencing the U.S.A. Government. The proposal is really based on a calculation of what we need in production and manpower to save Europe.

4. We have made some progress about a unified command and other things generally seem to be taking shape. The positive proposal before us at the moment is will we accept the participation of German units not as a German National Army but as a section of an integrated force which would be a quota contribution to the defence of freedom in Europe.

5. I must urge you give me a reply by 10.30 (New York time) tomorrow morning because the Atlantic Powers are meeting then. I would propose giving general support to the U.S.A. proposal and do not anticipate that in that form it would cause serious trouble for our country.

[2] See Nos. 21 and 25.

[3] In the defence debate (see No. 18, note 3) on 12 September Mr. W.S. Churchill, leader of H.M. Opposition, indicated his support for the inclusion of German forces in a European Army (*Parl. Debs., 5th ser., H. of C.*, vol. 478, col. 985). This followed his motion for a European Army under a unified command proposed to the Consultative Assembly of the Council of Europe on 11 August and subsequently pressed by fellow Conservative M.P., Mr. D. Sandys (Volume I, No. 158, note 5). On the evening before the defence debate Sir W. Strang, acting on instructions from Mr. Attlee and Mr. Bevin, briefed Mr. Anthony Eden, deputy leader of H.M. Opposition, on recent developments in foreign affairs with particular reference to the American proposal for an integrated force. 'He did not express dissent from any of your [Mr. Bevin's] policies. He thought it reasonable that we should try to find out the extent and character of U.S. assistance before finally committing ourselves to our defence programme. He attaches weight, as we do, to the Cairo declaration about Formosa and to the transfer of the administration on a *de facto* basis to the Chinese by MacArthur after the Japanese capitulation. He shares your misgivings about the dangers which American rashness and inexperience may land us into. He is much troubled about the problem of German rearmament and did not express a view. He assures you that Mr. Churchill's advocacy at Strasbourg of a European army was not intended to be embarrassing and hinted that Duncan Sandys had gone too far. He is unhappy about recent party asperities and is confident that if you and he had had the handling of affairs they would not have occurred' (letter from Sir W. Strang to Mr. Bevin of 12 September on F.O. 800/456).

No. 21

Sir G. Jebb (New York) to Mr. Younger
(Received 15 September, 9.40 a.m.)

No. 1009 Telegraphic [C 5873/27/18]

Immediate. Secret   NEW YORK, 14 September 1950, 8.58 p.m.

Repeated to Wahnerheide and Saving to Paris, Washington.

Tripartite talks: following from Secretary of State.

At further restricted meeting this morning at which Ministers were accompanied only by High Commissioners and Private Secretaries we pursued further our discussion of German contribution to Western defence.[1]

2. After an opening statement by Mr. Acheson substance of which is contained in my immediately following telegram[2] he said he thought we were all agreed on following points:

(1) that it was necessary that we should have an integrated force for the defence of the west

(2) that we should all make our contribution to this common defence force and should state as soon as possible what we could put into the pool

(3) that we should require a central command organisation

(4) that there should be machinery for ensuring the most efficient production of the necessary equipment

(5) that financial assistance from the United States would be necessary to enable the other Atlantic powers to make their contribution. (Discussion on this financial issue is recorded in my telegram No. 1011).[3] There remained the problem of the association of Germany with this defence effort.

3. M. Schuman said that the question was essentially one of using German manpower. Germany was not allowed to produce armaments though France was ready to agree that she should contribute indirectly and that some of the restrictions on German steel production should be lifted. The French also agreed that Germany could not remain entirely outside the common effort but the available supplies of arms were limited

---

[1] Mr. Acheson had asked for this private meeting owing to the failure of previous discussion to get 'to grips with the central problem of the defense of Europe ... The purpose of this talk was to get away from minor difficulties of language and really reach the essence of the problem' (telegram from Mr. Acheson for President Truman: *F.R.U.S. 1950*, vol. iii, pp. 1229–1231; *ibid.*, pp. 293–301, for minutes of meeting).

[2] Not printed from WU 1198/404. Mr. Acheson here recapitulated the American position as stated on 13 September (see No. 25) which aimed at building a unified force within eighteen months to include German units for the defence of a line as far east of the Rhine as possible.

[3] No. 22.

and it would take some time for production really to get going. It was essential that Allied troops should have first priority and it was clearly no good mobilising Germans until equipment for them was available. We should also take care not to give provocation to Russia. If this were admitted we could only safely rearm Germany when we already possessed a sufficient force to constitute a deterrent to Russia. Moreover we should not move too fast because he must have time to prepare French opinion. Otherwise there was a serious danger of a hostile reaction in France with great embarrassment to our common plans for defence. He would therefore conclude that we must choose the best moment – and this should be as soon as possible – to take and announce our decision in favour of German participation.

4. M. Schuman continued that Mr. Acheson had referred to the danger constituted by the deterioration of German morale. He would reply that in order to raise German morale what was required was conviction that the Allies were making a real effort. This would have a greater effect than the participation of Germany in Western defence.

5. Finally M. Schuman said that the French Government thought it premature to take any decision regarding German participation before:

(1) Our defence organisations had been created.
(2) The Allies had attained a minimum of defensive strength. He had proposed to his Government that he should be given authority to envisage the participation of Germany in Western Defence at the appropriate moment and subject to certain conditions but he had as yet had no reply. He hoped to be in a position in two or three days to give that reply on behalf of his Government.

6. M. Schuman added that he thought we should avoid making requests to Germany. The High Commissioners had told us[4] that German opinion would have to be prepared for German participation . . .[5] He thought that the Germans would not in fact be ready for this until the Allies were stronger than at present. He therefore concluded that the immediate steps to be taken were (1) to increase the police force (and the French Government were prepared to go some way as regards numbers) (2) to press on with German labour units and (3) create an international legion in which Germans might volunteer.

7. I then said that I similarly had not yet got authority from my Government to reach a definite decision on the formation of German army units. Like the French we had originally thought that the first step might be to go ahead with a police force or gendarmerie and with labour units. We had however certainly not decided against having German military units at a later stage. I thought it would be very useful if we could get agreement on the police which was a matter which could be readily understood by public opinion in all our countries and which would be

---

[4] See No. 16, note 2.   [5] The text is here uncertain.

regarded as a counter to the East German militarised police. I agreed with M. Schuman that there should be no bargaining with the Germans and that we should make ourselves as strong as possible before giving arms to the Germans.

8. Mr. Acheson said that he sympathised with much of what M. Schuman had said. We did not want to go to the Germans as suppliants. We must be careful about the question of timing and the preparation of public opinion. He did not however agree with the argument that we should wait until equipment was available before taking any action. It would no doubt be some time before equipment was available in considerable quantities but in the meanwhile if much time was not to be wasted we should make a beginning with training. He did not accept the argument that training Germans would provoke the Russians to attack. He thought the Kremlin would only be influenced by the relative strength of the Allies and the ability of the Russians to protect themselves against bombing. The sooner we could make ourselves strong the greater the deterrent effect. He equally did not think it really mattered whether the men you trained were called police or military units. He agreed that the labour units were important but they were no real solution to our problem. He doubted whether the foreign legion idea would yield any useful results. In his view what was essential was that in response to the enquiry addressed to the High Commissioners by Adenauer about German participation[6] we should not adopt a negative attitude but should say that we were very ready to discuss what Germany could do. He emphasised that it would take a great deal of time before any material results could ensue. He therefore hoped it could be agreed that we should take a decision in principle now which would not be put into effect for some time.

9. M. Schuman said that it might be possible to agree that the High Commissioners should discuss the issue with Adenauer. They could not however inform him that the three Governments had decided in favour of German participation. He believed that French opinion might come to accept the need for German units when France herself was stronger but if he were to go further now and agree that it should be publicly announced that a decision to this effect had been taken the French Parliament would reject what he had done.

10. There followed some discussion as to what could be said in the Atlantic Council. M. Schuman said he thought that an exchange of views would be very useful. Mr. Acheson . . .[5] he thought it was scarcely possible to contemplate that at the close of these talks we should say nothing more than that a useful exchange of views had taken place. Public opinion was keenly interested in the subject and expected some sort of decision even if it were only in principle and subject to reservations. He thought the minimum we could reasonably say was that we had considered Adenauer's

---

[6] See No. 3, note 3.

communication about German participation in defence and that we were favourably disposed to this though further discussion with the Germans and among ourselves would be necessary before we could say exactly how or when this would be achieved. M. Schuman said he thought something on these lines might be possible and he would like time for reflection.

11. Mr. Acheson said he realised that he could not press either of us to give an immediate decision on this problem since we both awaited further instructions from our Government.[7]

Please repeat Wahnerheide as my telegram No. 8 and Paris No. 144 Saving.

[7] In his telegram on this meeting for President Truman (note 1) Mr. Acheson concluded 'All this was useful, but the discussion ended with one situation quite clear: that they were prepared to accept what we offered but they were not prepared to accept what we asked. In this situation I am taking the attitude, not that we are imposing specific conditions, but that we are unable to proceed with the discussion until their attitude is made more clear . . . The result is that no agreed papers on the matters on which they are ready to agree will issue from our delegation. We have ended the first part of our tripartite meeting with a communiqué which cannot announce decisions and, therefore, says merely that we are continuing our discussions in the Council and will resume them next week' (*F.R.U.S. 1950*, vol. iii, p. 1230).

No. 22

Sir G. Jebb (New York) to Mr. Younger
(Received 15 September, 7.7 a.m.)

No. 1011 Telegraphic [*UE 11914/72*]

Immediate. Secret   NEW YORK, *14 September 1950, 8.40 p.m.*

Repeated Saving to Washington and Paris.

Tripartite talks.
Following from Secretary of State.
My telegram No. 1009.[1]
As regards finance, M. Schuman said he understood that it was agreed that there must be a sharing of the burden, though it was not yet possible to have detailed figures or firm commitments. He welcomed the idea of proceeding by stages and starting with the high priority programme. It was however also urgent to know what we could count on for the second stage. In France it was necessary to establish a budget by 1st January and it would be of great assistance if further information could be available by November.

2. Mr. Acheson said that it was not possible now for the United States Government to say just how much they could contribute to the French or United Kingdom effort. He thought it would first be necessary to establish what efforts the countries concerned could make and then to see what

[1] No. 21.

difficulties would be caused for their economies by these efforts. It would be for the other countries to demonstrate to the United States that without financial help from the United States their economies would go to pieces, and to explain what their problems were. It would then be for the United States Government to say to what extent they could help.

3. M. Schuman said he gathered that the United States Government needed more information beyond what had already been provided, and Mr. Acheson replied in the affirmative. Mr. Acheson said he thought that each Government should have preliminary talks with the United States financial experts to establish what their difficulties were likely to be. He thought that on the United States side they would be ready immediately.

4. I said that I warmly welcomed this method. His Majesty's Government were seriously concerned about the maintenance of economy, which after all their efforts in the war was still in a somewhat precarious state. They had to consider the effect on their people, who had had a lot to put up with in recent years.

5. In conclusion Mr. Acheson confirmed that he was anxious to proceed as quickly as possible with talks on a bilateral basis.[2]

Please pass to Paris as my telegram No. 146 Saving.

[2] See No. 11, note 7 and No. 54, note 4.

No. 23

Minute from Mr. Rickett[1] to Mr. Attlee

[*PREM 8/1429*]

10 DOWNING STREET, *14 September 1950*

Sir William Strang rang up this evening to give the following messages to you from Mr. Bevin.[2]

The first was that, while he did not know what line would be taken by the Government speaker in the Debate tonight about our production programme, it would be unfortunate if Parliament were given the impression that there was a deadlock between us and the Americans on the amount of assistance we are to get from them. There is no call for any impression of pessimism about the possibility of finding a satisfactory solution.

I understand that this message is based on statements made to Mr. Bevin by Mr. Acheson. While these are encouraging, the Foreign Office say that the matter is not of course finally settled yet.

Would you like me to have a word with the Private Secretary to the

[1] Mr. D.H.F. Rickett was Principal Private Secretary to Mr. Attlee.
[2] These messages were conveyed by telephone from Sir P. Dixon in New York (WU 1197/227).

Minister of Defence to make sure that this point is properly covered?[3]

The second message was that Mr. Bevin was very much disturbed about the conclusions of this morning's Cabinet about Germany, a summary of which had been telegraphed to him.[4]

He felt that these conclusions would make matters very difficult for him in New York. He may wish to telephone to you about it this evening.

I understand from Sir Norman Brook[5] that the Cabinet were not inflexibly opposed to Mr. Acheson's proposal but thought that it was too soon to agree to it and that they based this view on the assumption that the matter had not yet been much discussed in New York; that it was by no means certain that M. Schuman would agree, nor was it clear that the President's undertaking to send troops to Europe was linked with the idea of German participation. Brook gave it as his personal opinion that if Mr. Bevin told you that these three assumptions were not in fact justified (that is to say that the matter had in fact been fully discussed, that the American proposal was a firm condition of the President's undertaking to station troops in Europe and that M. Schuman was likely to come round) then you might wish to give Mr. Bevin authority to agree and report afterwards to the Cabinet that you had done so.

D.H.F.R.

[3] Mr. Rickett noted below: 'I have done this. The Minister is not proposing to speak on this, unless of course he were questioned on it.'

[4] See No. 18, note 3.   [5] Secretary of the Cabinet.

No. 24

Minute from Sir W. Strang to Mr. Younger

[C 5999/27/18]

FOREIGN OFFICE, 14 September 1950

New York telegram No. 996[1]

I assume that the Secretary of State will receive from his colleagues the authority for which he asks to agree to the rearmament of Germany. We are being irresistibly carried down the stream of events. Many and great voices are raised in favour of this course. Against it, I can raise nothing but an unreasonable prejudice, some wishful thinking and what will be called an unwillingness to face unpleasant realities.

I was, under instructions, one of the architects of that Four-Power agreement[2] upon which, not so many years ago, it was hoped to establish the peace of Europe. It is not we but the Russians who have progressively broken it. One of the foundations upon which it rested was the

[1] No. 18.

[2] For the political and economic principles for the post-war treatment of Germany agreed at the Potsdam Conference, July–August 1945, see Series I, Volume I, No. 603, Section II.

demilitarization of Germany. I had hoped against hope that we at least might have preserved this as a token of our willingness to rebuild the agreement should the Russians ever make this possible. By now openly conforming to a breach of this principle which the Russians have already committed by subterfuge, we abandon almost the last remnant of the agreement.

By this decisive and fateful act, I think that we confess to ourselves that we believe war to be inevitable. Indeed, I fear that we make it inevitable, for a Russian reaction must sooner or later be expected, which will force us to make war.

If this is so, certain consequences follow. If we think that war is inevitable, we must prepare for it in earnest. Even the measures we are now taking will not suffice. I trust that H.M.G. will draw the necessary conclusion from the decision which they are about to reach.[3]

W. STRANG

CALENDAR TO NO. 24

i *15 and 18 Sept. 1950   Likely Soviet reaction to German rearmament* considered in minutes by (*a*) Mr. Mallet: Russians will claim Allies have broken Potsdam agreement and proceed to back formation of an all-German govt. with capital in Berlin and (*b*) Sir D. Gainer (P.U.S. of F.O. German Section): importance of Federal Govt. being able to safeguard own internal security in period before unified force is built to strength; U.K. should press for gendarmerie and raise question of Berlin at New York [C 5855/65/18; C 6052/27/18].

[3] After conversation with Mr. Younger on the morning of 15 September, Sir W. Strang addressed a further minute to the Minister of State in which he made the following points: (i) 'By agreeing to German rearmament in principle now, subject to no matter what conditions, we start a process which will almost certainly be continuous. That is to say, sooner or later there will be a German Army and a German High Command and General Staff, with the appropriate Ministry. The demand for equality of rights will become more and more insistent. This process will not only be continuous; it will also not be reversible.' (ii) 'We are being driven to this because (as Mr. Churchill says) the American people are angry', but they are also 'volatile' and 'readier than we are to scrap one policy and start a new one.' Their decision to station troops in Europe 'unlike the decision to rearm Germany, is easily reversible. We may one day, if the Russian peril appears to recede, be left with a German Army and no Americans.' (iii) Given recent history it would be 'a mistake to put arms into German hands for purposes of war . . . The right course is for the Atlantic Powers to put themselves more nearly upon a war footing than they at present propose to do, whether or not they rearm the Germans at the same time.' Both minutes were initialled by Mr. Younger and copies sent to New York for the Secretary of State.

No. 25

Sir G. Jebb (New York) to Mr. Younger
(Received 15 September, 3.15 p.m.)

No. 1018 Telegraphic [C 5882/27/18]

Immediate. Secret   NEW YORK, 15 September 1950, 3.47 a.m.

Tripartite talks. German participation in western defence.
My telegram No. 996.[1]
Following is a brief summary of discussion on this question at full meeting on morning of 13th September.

2. After some discussion of question of German Police M. Schuman outlined his difficulties in regard to Mr. Acheson's suggestion for formation of German national units. In addition to psychological difficulties in Germany and parliamentary difficulties in France[2] he felt grave doubt whether the integration of German national units in a force under the North Atlantic Treaty Organisation was legally compatible with provisions of North Atlantic Treaty. He suggested that the Standing Group of North Atlantic Treaty Organisation should make a juridical study of this question.[3] Secondly he doubted whether from the technical military point of view European defence could be organised on a basis of national armies and proposed that the Standing Group should also make a military study of how a contribution from nations not signatories of the North Atlantic Treaty might be organised on a basis of supra-national contingents.

3. This led Mr. Acheson to explain at some length his proposal for the formation of German national units. He emphasised that these units would not form a German national army but would be fully integrated into the European defence force and would have no separate existence outside it.

They should be recruited, paid, fed and uniformed by the German Government and would be officered by Germans up to level of say Divisional Commander but they would draw all their ordnance from non German sources and would be placed under Allied High Command. He rejected the idea of an international army as impracticable.

4. After the intervention by M. Schuman, Mr. Acheson said that he felt it essential, if German opinion was not to be allowed to drift and the present opportunity be lost, to reach an agreement in principle at the present meeting to proceed on the basis he proposed on the understand-

---

[1] No. 18.

[2] M. Pleven's coalition government, formed in July after a prolonged political crisis, had survived by the deferral of contentious Parliamentary issues e.g. electoral reform until after the summer recess. It was considered doubtful whether the government would continue to command a majority once these issues came before the National Assembly after its recall on 17 October.

[3] Apparently not pursued: see further No. 32, paragraph 2(3).

ing that matters of timing and procedure might be left on one side for the time being. The United States had taken an historic decision to commit itself to station forces in Europe as part of a combined European force so that the United States would be in the fighting in Europe from the first day. It would however be impossible for the United States to undertake such a commitment without some assurance that the common effort was likely to be a successful one. The United States Government could at present see no prospect of achieving this aim without German participation in the European defence force.

5. I limited myself to seeking elucidation of Mr. Acheson's point of view and in reply to a question he confirmed that in his view the decision as to United States participation in the defence of Europe would be influenced by the hope of organising a successful defence for which German participation was indispensable. Meanwhile the western powers must make every effort to build up their own strength. But the two lines of progress must be complementary and he urged that decisions be taken at the present meetings to enable parallel progress to be made along both of them.

No. 26

Sir G. Jebb (New York) to Mr. Younger
(Received 15 September, 5.11 p.m.)

No. 1021 Telegraphic [C 5884/3780/18]

Secret   NEW YORK, 15 September 1950, 11.8 a.m.

Repeated Saving to Wahnerheide.

Tripartite talks. Germany.

Apart from discussion on German participation in European defence which have been reported separately the three Foreign Ministers have not been able to devote much time to German questions. At a meeting on the afternoon of the 13th September they gave preliminary consideration to the study group's report.[1] No final decisions were reached but it became evident that the future programme in regard to revision of the occupation statute was closely affected by the United States proposals on defence. The United States Government have in fact made up their minds, rather as we ourselves were disposed to do, that the modifications in the occupation regime proposed in the study group's report will not be far reaching enough to capture public imagination in Germany and effect a considerable improvement in the morale. At any rate, to fit the new situation that will arise when German participation in European defence

[1] See No. 4, note 4. A fuller record of discussion on the I.G.G. report at the Third meeting on 13 September is calendared at i. For other items on the agenda that afternoon, see note 3.

has been secured something more will be required. They therefore propose that the study group's recommendations be put into effect at once on an interim basis and without revision of the occupation statute, on the understanding that more radical and definitive revision will take place as soon as Germany enters the defence picture.

2. On this basis and without prejudice to the eventual decision on defence working parties have been trying to adapt the study group's recommendations to this new conception and at the same time to eliminate outstanding differences. In some cases this has meant concessions on our part in regard to immediate programme. For instance in regard to appointment of German Ambassadors to capitals of occupying powers it is plain that American pre-occupations about risk of undermining position of High Commission derive largely from the fact that, if their plan goes through, particularly delicate discussions will have to be undertaken in the next few months by the High Commission with the German Federal Government on the role Germany is to play in the defence sphere. In these circumstances recommendation to Ministers is likely to be that we should agree not to receive Ambassadors for the present on the tacit understanding that this and other concessions will be made when the time comes for the final revision of the occupation statute.

3. The chief difficulty at present about these plans, and the only important point of difference among the three delegations, is that the French are so far reluctant to commit themselves, even on assumption that United States defence plans go through, to principle of a final more radical revision of the statute some months hence and are clinging to the original ideas of immediate revision on the hope of staving any further concessions thereafter for as long as possible.

4. Because of uncertainty of present position as well as pressure of other business Foreign Ministers have not been able to give any further consideration to these German problems today. Their communiqué accordingly contains only a brief reference to German questions.[2]

[2] An interim communiqué was agreed by Ministers at the Fourth tripartite meeting on 14 September when the Far East largely comprised the agenda (see Volume IV). The interim communiqué published in *The Times* on 15 September indicated the range of discussion so far and stated that Ministers would resume their discussions on 18 September after the N.A.C. meeting (later postponed to 22 September: see No. 41). In this interim Mr. Steel reported from Wahnerheide that 'German comment over the weekend on the New York discussions in regard to rearmament has been in a singularly moderate vein and indeed has taken a decidedly second place to events in Korea. This is however due, I think, to a growing confidence that something nice for Germany is going to come out of the Foreign Ministers deliberations and the underlying view is undoubtedly very close to that represented by Schumacher's statement . . . that equality in the bearing of the burdens of defence must sooner or later involve equality in other spheres . . . Owing to the large scale publicity of the American point of view, that of His Majesty's Government has tended to be somewhat misrepresented as being almost as negative as the French. We are even suspected of opposing German rearmament for fear of a continental bloc which would upset the balance of power. This is however only the result of the usual German search for a motive and it has no responsible backing' (Wahnerheide telegram No. 1384 of 18 September on C 5939/27/18).

Ministers will meet again on Monday next [18 September] to take final decisions. Meanwhile a full communiqué on Germany is being prepared for issue, if approved, after that meeting.

5. Study has also been given to questions of German police and revision of prohibited and limited industries agreement with a view to submission of recommendations to Ministers on Monday. (Please see my two immediately following telegrams).[3]

Please repeat to Wahnerheide as my No. 1 Saving.

CALENDARS TO NO. 26

i *13 Sept. 1950 U.K. Record of discussion of German problems at 3rd Tripartite Meeting.* Position on I.G.G. report summarized in appended U.S. brief – circulated as basis for discussion by Mr. Acheson, who was 'repelled by the complexity' of report itself. Refugees referred to experts. Other questions where disagreement (Restitution; External trade; Foreign relations) referred to High Commissioners. Ministers agree intention to terminate state of war. High Commissioners instructed to draft communiqué on Germany [C 6302/20/18].

ii *18 Sept. 1950 U.K. Record of 5th Tripartite Meeting* with related documents annexed.

    (*a*) *East–West Trade* Difficulties over principles of control resolved by officials on 19 Sept. (Annexes A–B: Message from Mr. Bevin to Mr. Attlee and Agreed Minute)

    (*b*) *Economic Assistance to Yugoslavia* (U.S. proposals at Annex C).

    (*c*) *European Migration* experts' report agreed.

    (*d*) *I.G.G. Report on Germany* Ministers approve:

        (i) *Instruction to A.H.C.* for relaxing certain occupation controls (Annex E) subject to German assurances on debts (Annex H) and raw materials.

        (ii) *Directive to I.G.G.* for resumption of work in October e.g. further revision of P.L.I. and tripartite controls.

[3] The telegrams were in fact Nos. 1023 and 1024, the texts of which are included in calendar ii from the Confidential Print record of the New York meetings prepared by the British Secretariat. The A.H.C. formula for a mobile police force contained in New York telegram No. 1023 was prepared in accordance with instructions from the Foreign Ministers at their Second meeting on 13 September (see No. 16, note 2). Instructions for a recommendation to review the P.L.I. agreement were given at the Third meeting on the afternoon of 13 September after the discussion on the I.G.G. report summarized above. Ministers went on to consider at this meeting: a draft communiqué and security agreement on Berlin (final text at calendar ii); N.A.C. directive rejecting Turkish application to join N.A.T.O. in favour of associating Greece and Turkey with N.A.T.O. military planning for the defence of the Mediterranean (*F.R.U.S. 1950*, vol. iii, pp. 1284–5); draft resolutions for N.A.C. on the medium term plan and a unified force (see Nos. 17, notes 4–5). The decisions reached on Germany at the Fifth tripartite meeting on 18 September were communicated by the three Foreign Ministers to the Foreign Ministers of Belgium, the Netherlands and Luxembourg at a special meeting on 19 September (cf. No. 10, note 2). M. Stikker later expressed to his Ministry his dissatisfaction that 'Benelux was still only being told afterwards what decisions had been taken and not being allowed to participate in the actual taking of the decision' (C 6167/3780/18).

(iii) *Additional recommendations* regarding I.G.G. report e.g. restitution and reparations, conduct of foreign affairs, claims, state of war (Annex G).

(iv) *Communiqué on Germany* records all decisions except that A.H.C. is authorised to explore possibility of German contribution to defence with Dr. Adenauer. This omitted from public communiqué, issued on 19 Sept., at request of M. Schuman. Included in communiqué is reference to authorisation of mobile police force with light arms (text of recommendation in New York telegram No. 1023). Also statement of Allied intention to strengthen forces in F.R.G. and to 'treat any attack against the Federal Republic of Berlin from any quarter as an attack upon themselves'. Measures for strengthening economic and military security of Berlin listed in Annex D together with withdrawn paragraph, proposed by Mr. Acheson, directed towards holding Soviet Union responsible for any Bereitschaften attack whether or not Soviet Union dissociates from it. This withdrawn on understanding that will be considered further [F.O. 371/124934: ZP 5/129].

No. 27

Extract from the Conclusions of a Meeting of the Cabinet held in the Prime Minister's Room at the House of Commons on Friday, 15 September 1950, at 10.30 a.m.[1]

C.M. (50) 59th Conclusions [CAB 128/18]

Secret

Germany: Rearmament

(Previous Reference: C.M. (50) 58th Conclusions, Minute 3).[2]

1. The Cabinet considered three telegrams from the Foreign Secretary (New York telegrams 1005, 1009 and 1010[3] of 14th September, 1950) reporting further discussions of German participation in Western defence which had taken place in the tripartite talks in New York. The United States Secretary of State had stressed the need for conducting a successful defence of Europe as far to the East as possible, to avoid German potential falling into Russian hands. For this purpose he sought acceptance of the

[1] *Present* at this meeting were Mr. Attlee (*in the Chair*); Mr. H.S. Morrison, Lord President of the Council; Mr. H. Dalton; Viscount Alexander of Hillsborough, Chancellor of the Duchy of Lancaster; Mr. J. Chuter Ede, Secretary of State for the Home Department; Mr. E. Shinwell, Minister of Defence; Mr. G.A. Isaacs, Minister of Labour and National Service; Mr. A. Bevan, Minister of Health; Mr. T. Williams, Minister of Agriculture and Fisheries; Mr. G. Tomlinson, Minister of Education; Mr. J.H. Wilson, President of the Board of Trade; Mr. J. Griffiths, Secretary of State for the Colonies, Mr. H. McNeil, Secretary of State for Scotland; Mr. Gordon Walker. *Also present* were Mr. H.T.N. Gaitskell, Minister of State for Economic Affairs and Mr. Younger. *Secretariat*: Mr. A. Johnston and Mr. O.C. Morland.

[2] See No. 18, note 3 and No. 19, note 2.

[3] No. 20, No. 21 and note 2 *ibid.*

participation of German units, not as a German National Army, but as a section of an integrated force for the defence of freedom in Europe. In paragraph 8 of New York telegram 1009 Mr. Acheson was reported as emphasising that the three Governments should not adopt a negative attitude to the German Chancellor's enquiry about Western defence, but should say that they were ready to discuss what Germany could do; and that accordingly a decision in principle should be taken, which could not, however, be put into effect for some time. Mr. Acheson was anxious (paragraph 10 of New York telegram 1009) to be able to state at the meeting of the North Atlantic Council which would be held later on the same day (Friday) that the three Foreign Ministers had considered the German Chancellor's communication about German participation in defence, and that they were favourably disposed to this, though discussion with the Germans and between the United States, Great Britain and France would be necessary before any indication could be given how and when German participation would be achieved. The French Foreign Minister had stressed the point that North Atlantic rearmament should reach a sufficient scale before German rearmament began, and had suggested that the immediate steps to be taken were to increase the German police force, to press on with German labour units and to create an international legion in which Germans might volunteer.

In discussion the following points were made:

(*a*) Little difficulty was seen in reaching in present circumstances an agreement in principle that at some future time, under conditions which had still to be worked out, German units should be included in a Western European force to be built up to meet the threat of Russian aggression. The real difficulties were concerned with the timing of any announcement and the form which German participation in defence should take. It was clearly desirable that the Western European countries other than Germany should build up their forces before substantial German military assistance was recruited. Only in this way could French public opinion be brought to accept the idea of German rearmament. It was also important to avoid any suggestion that the North Atlantic Treaty countries were wooing the Germans and so enable the Germans to impose conditions. The reply to be sent to the Foreign Secretary should stress the need for French agreement to what was to be said.

(*b*) It appeared to be clear from the terms of the telegrams that United States agreement on financial assistance to the United Kingdom defence programme would be linked with the attitude which this country adopted to German participation in Western defence. An early decision was required about the form of United States assistance, in order that adequate progress could be made with the United Kingdom defence programme.

(*c*) It was also important to secure German participation in the supply programme since, if she were not substantially engaged on productive work in connection with rearmament, Germany might very well capture many of the export markets which this country was having to drop under present circumstances.

(d) Although the United States Administration were only seeking at this stage agreement in principle to the creation of German military units, it was clear that there would be great pressure for further practical measures to be taken within the next few months. A good deal of the discussion between the three Foreign Ministers had already appeared in the American press, and the United States Secretary of State had made it clear that Congress would expect steps to be taken at the earliest possible moment.

(e) The proposal that German units should participate in Western defence, not as a German National Army, but as a section of an integrated force, raised problems of law and organisation which had still to be worked out. It might not be found practicable to proceed otherwise than through the creation of German forces responsible to German authorities.

(f) The details of the German Chancellor's communication to the three Foreign Ministers about German participation in defence were not yet available to the Cabinet,[4] although the details were clearly important since the extent to which Germany was prepared to co-operate in these arrangements vitally affected the final form which they could take. The United States Government were apt to talk as though it was for the North Atlantic Treaty Powers to determine the extent and form of German participation in Western defence, whereas an entirely new situation would be created if any endeavour were made to go beyond what the Germans were themselves prepared to do.

(g) To some extent the United States Government appeared to be endeavouring once more to commit this country to firm commitments without a clear indication of the extent of the commitments which the United States was prepared to undertake. Not only was the financial position still unsettled, but it was not clear to what extent the United States were in fact prepared to participate in the land defence of Western Europe.

The Cabinet—
Invited the Prime Minister to inform the Foreign Secretary that the United Kingdom Government—
    (i) Were in general agreement to an acceptance in principle of

---

[4] That afternoon, Mr. Johnston asked the Foreign Office to circulate to the Cabinet the precise terms of the approach from Dr. Adenauer since 'several Ministers felt unhappy about reaching decisions on the subject in the absence of an exact indication of what the German Chancellor had proposed' (C 5950/27/18). Dr. Adenauer's memoranda of 29 August and 2 September (see No. 3, note 3) were accordingly circulated to the Cabinet with a covering note by Lord Henderson, Parliamentary Under-Secretary of State for Foreign Affairs, on 18 September as C.P. (50) 210 (CAB 129/42).

German participation in Western defence, on the lines and subject to the conditions outlined by Mr. Acheson in the last three sentences of paragraph 8 of New York telegram 1009, viz., that the next stage was exploration with the German Government. Importance was attached to the greatest practicable extent of French concurrence. The first development should be the enlargement of the gendarmerie.

(ii) Considered that in any statement in the Atlantic Council about German armed forces, on the lines outlined by Mr. Acheson in paragraph 10 of New York telegram 1009, the subject should not be presented in such a way as to suggest that the Atlantic countries were wooing the Germans.[5]

CALENDAR TO NO. 27

i *18 Sept. 1950   Minute from Lord Pakenham, Minister of Civil Aviation, to Mr. Attlee* representing urgency of German rearmament: 'a French veto cannot be allowed to stand in the way' [C 6053/27/18].

[5] These conclusions of the Cabinet and summary of points made in discussion were transmitted to Mr. Bevin that afternoon in telegrams to New York Nos. 1252 and 1253 (C 5865/27/18).

No. 28

Sir G. Jebb (New York) to Mr. Younger
(Received 16 September, 2.42 p.m.)

No. 1050 Telegraphic [C 5900/27/18]

Immediate. Secret   NEW YORK, *16 September 1950, 3.29 a.m.*

Repeated to Wahnerheide, and Saving Paris, Washington.

Following from Secretary of State.
I was grateful for your telegram No. 1252.[1]
I arranged to see Mr. Acheson before the afternoon session of the Atlantic Council today [15 September] in order to inform him of the attitude of His Majesty's Government on German participation in Western Defence.

I explained why there was a good deal of hesitation in the United Kingdom on the subject. I said we were most anxious to avoid a position in which we seemed to be appealing to the Germans. I then referred to the great importance which His Majesty's Government attached to a solution of the problem of a German police force. Our decided preference was for a Federal police force, but the main thing was to ensure that the Federal Government were in a position to maintain law and order. We did not wish to run any risk of a Communist-organised rising in the factories with which the Germans could not themselves deal. I then explained that

[1] See No. 27, note 5.

61

subject to the conditions referred to in your telegram under reference His Majesty's Government were prepared to agree in principle to German participation in Western defence.

2. Mr. Acheson said that he thought that this would meet the United States Government. He explained that he did not want to see action only on parts of the general programme for the defence of the West which he had outlined at previous meetings. He had had great difficulty in getting the United States defence authorities to agree that he should discuss these matters with his Atlantic colleagues. Their position was that they could not commit United States divisions unless there was agreement on a programme which, taken as a whole, seemed to offer reasonable prospects of success. Equally, they were not prepared to put forward a United States Supreme Commander unless they were satisfied that there were going to be reasonable sized forces for him to command. The United States military authorities were convinced that it would not be feasible to stop the Russians without German participation. What was necessary therefore was that the United States Government should have an assurance that there was general agreement on a programme which would lead ultimately to the incorporation of German units. All they wanted was a decision in principle. It was impossible to decide at this stage exactly how or when the decision would become effective, since for one thing this depended on the attitude of the Germans themselves. What he contemplated was that after some discussion with the Germans the point would be reached where the High Commissioners would tell them to begin to make preparations for the constitution of German units. These preparations would take some months. By the time any young Germans were available for training, the rearmament of the French should have made good progress and the United States and other Allied forces in Europe would have been increased. It would require at least another year from the beginning of training before any German soldiers were available.

3. Mr. Acheson then explained that his idea was that the Atlantic Council should have a general discussion on the German issue at their afternoon meeting, as a result of which he hoped that a general view might emerge. If, as he hoped, the consensus of opinion was that the participation of the Germans at some stage and in some form was part of the general programme (and he did not think that this would be asking too much of Mr. Schuman) he for his part would be willing to announce that the United States Government on their side were prepared to play their full part in the programme for the development of powerful integrated forces, including the appointment of a Supreme Commander.

4. I subsequently saw M. Schuman and informed him of the conclusions reached by His Majesty's Government. I said that I thought I would have to make a statement on the subject in the Council meeting and I hoped that this would not embarrass him. He said that he quite understood and did not wish to raise any objection. As far as he was concerned however he had no authority to commit his Government to an

immediate decision. He had not yet had a reply from Paris, but he rather feared that when it came it would be unfavourable. He would not have found it so difficult to agree to a decision in principle being taken now if it could have been kept secret. He feared however that this would not be possible.[2]

5. As I had spoken again about the question of the German police he wished to say that he thought it should be possible to go some way further towards meeting the United Kingdom position. He would be prepared to agree that as a first stage the Germans should be allowed to have 25,000 additional police, and that this number might later be raised to 50,000. He was further prepared to agree that in some way they should be under the control of the Central Government. The difficulty was to achieve this without necessitating a change in the constitution, which he thought would only delay matters. He believed however that it should be possible to find some formula to get round this.

6. I subsequently made a statement in the Atlantic Council N.A.C. report of which is contained in my immediately following telegram.[3]

Please repeat to Wahnerheide as my telegram No. 10 and to Paris as my telegram No. 149 Saving.

[2] On 15 September M. Massigli informed Mr. Attlee that the French Cabinet were meeting that afternoon to reach a decision but that 'the French Government would not be able to accept any mention in a public communiqué of the principle of German rearmament. As to the principle itself, their attitude was not totally negative, but they were trying to find a possible solution' (F.O. telegram to New York No. 1270 on C 5909/27/18). The following morning M. Massigli reported that 'after long deliberation the opinion of the French Cabinet had hardened on the question of German participation in Western defence. They were now reluctant to agree to this, even in principle and even if the agreement was kept secret for the time being . . . Instructions were being sent to M. Schuman accordingly' (*ibid*).

[3] See No. 29.i.

No. 29

U.K. Delegation (New York) to Ministry of Defence[1]
(*Received 16 September, 10.15 a.m.*)

COJA 115 Telegraphic [*WU 1198/402*]

Top secret. Immediate   NEW YORK, *16 September 1950, 12.37 a.m.*

For Price from Elliot.
For Chiefs of Staff.

[1] Telegrams in the COJA/JACO series between Air Marshal Elliot, then with the Ministry of Defence delegation in New York, and the Chiefs of Staff Secretariat in London, were transmitted and received through the Foreign Office cypher room. This gave rise to some inconsistency in the decyphered typed texts which were variously headed up as 'Foreign Office' or 'Ministry of Defence'. In this volume COJA/JACO headings have been standardized to 'Ministry of Defence'.

My Tel. COJA 109.[2]

It had been hoped that a resolution the terms of which were contained in my COJA 110[3] which had been readily agreed by the S. of S. and by M. Schuman, would likewise be agreed by Mr. Acheson and then tabled over their three signatures at to-day's meeting of the Atlantic Council. Late last night[4] however we learnt that the Americans were not prepared to do this. Their reason which became apparent today was that they did not wish to subscribe to one part only of what we can now see is a new and comprehensive U.S.A. policy for the defence of Western Europe.

2. This policy was outlined with great clarity and vigour by Mr. Acheson this afternoon.[4] His speech concluded today's session of the council which had consisted for the most part of a series of speeches devoted to the question of European defence and German participation therein made by Mr. Bevin and by the Foreign Ministers of most of the other NATO Powers. A full account of the course of the proceedings will be found in telegrams from the Foreign Secretary to the F.O.[5]

3. Mr. Acheson referred to the President's announcement that large numbers of U.S. forces would be made available for Europe in addition to those that were there already and then elaborated his ideas about the integrated and unified force of which they would form a part. The phrase 'integrated force' was not merely a form of word. Specific units of National Forces should be earmarked by Governments to form part of this integrated force and they should be identified as such.

4. Obviously in Mr. Acheson's view this integrated force must have at an early date some command and staff organisation to control, train and administer it.

It was not however his function to elaborate the command structure except to say that as an integrated and unified force it should have one commander and one integrated staff. Although time was pressing it would in his view be premature to appoint an actual Supreme Commander until he had troops to command.

5. It was against this background that Mr. Acheson outlined his proposals on Germany. These proposals are set out in detail in F.O. telegrams.[6] As regards the provision of German military forces Mr. Acheson emphasised that these should be fitted into the framework of the integrated European Force. The Americans were fully alive to the evils of German militarism and did not envisage the creation of a national army with a German commander and general staff. The proposal was that specific German units which would be raised, paid for and uniformed by the German Government, should be incorporated as units in the European force. As an additional safeguard ordnance for the German units should be produced outside Germany. On the other hand there

---

[2] See No. 17, note 5.
[3] Not here printed: see *F.R.U.S. 1950*, vol. iii, pp. 1281–2.
[4] This telegram was drafted on 15 September.
[5] See calendar i.   [6] See No. 33.

would be no question of Germans serving in the European force as mercenaries. They would play an honourable part as specific German units in the force.

6. As regards timing Mr. Acheson recognised that there was much work to be carried out before any such proposal reached fruition. Legal and administrative difficulties were plentiful and even if satisfactory, administrative arrangements could be made. A training period of at least two years would be required before German units would be produced in any strength.

7. I have outlined the specifically military side of the American proposals as they were presented to the Council this afternoon. F.O. telegrams will make clear the political and psychological issues which are involved. The problem is to be discussed in the Council again tomorrow on the basis of the American proposals.

8. Clearly all this represents a revolutionary departure in American policy and one which is of almost immeasurable value in the defence field. Against this background it should be possible to obtain agreement to a resolution on the command structure for the integrated force on the lines set out in COJA 111.[7]

CALENDAR TO No. 29

i *15 Sept. 1950 N.A.C. 5th Session*: chaired by Mr. Acheson, who states at opening meeting that the main work should be to consider further organizational developments in military and economic fields (N.Y. tel. 1046). W.E.U. plan for defence of Rhine–Ijssel line and civilian evacuation described by M. Stikker as 'raving lunacy'. His concern to reconcile defence plans with available resources is shared by Mr. Bevin, who points out that before making a new plan, 'we should have to decide how the bill was to be met' (N.Y. tel. 1047). Afternoon statement by Mr. Bevin includes: German participation in Western defence not party issue in U.K. Important to treat Germany as part of the wider whole rather than in isolation. Presses for immediate consideration of German police force as a separate question from German participation in defence (N.Y. tel. 1051). Views of Portuguese, Norwegian, Belgian, Luxembourg, Danish, Italian and Canadian reps. summarized in N.Y. tels. 1052–3. Mr. Acheson emphasises that U.S. proposals (as contained in No. 33) 'must be taken as a whole' [WU 1071/182; WU 11910/86; C 5901–3/27/18].

[7] This is presumably an error for COJA 110 (note 3). COJA 111 transmitted the text of a draft resolution on the Medium Term Plan as agreed by Ministers on 13 September (see No. 17, note 4).

No. 30

Sir G. Jebb (New York) to Mr. Younger
(Received 17 September, 1.1 a.m.)

No. *1062 Telegraphic* [*C 5912/27/18*]

Immediate. Secret   NEW YORK, *16 September 1950, 10 p.m.*

Following for Prime Minister from Secretary of State.
Your telegram 1270.[1]
The situation here is developing in a very curious manner. Having regard to the general attitude of the Continental countries and the danger they find themselves in I came to the conclusion—and I felt I had the support of the Cabinet after receiving your telegram 1252[2]—that I could accept the principle of German participation. In doing so I made it clear that I thought the first step should be the organisation of the integrated force in order that a position of strength might be established on the Continent before the German units were brought in. Once agreement had been reached on the integrated force the way was open to start discussions with the Germans with a view to their participation. It is quite clear from a further analysis of the situation that the whole morale of Europe and of the Dutch in particular will be jeopardised if it is decided to defend the present Rhine–Ijssel line and thus in effect sacrifice so many people. The United States is seized with this and they have three main considerations in mind. Firstly that if trouble should come it should be met as far east as possible; secondly that it would have to be fought on German soil; and thirdly that if the Germans are not to be antagonised they should be brought in and so strengthen our position.

2. I think my telegrams have made this position clear. I have at the meeting this morning 16th September adhered to the position I took up yesterday.[3] As far as I can see Holland, Belgium, Luxembourg, Italy and Canada all subscribe to the American point of view on this issue. Norway and Denmark will probably make their position clearer this afternoon.

3. From the French and American point of view the situation is this: the whole proceedings on defence might be jeopardised unless care is used. The French had advanced the argument that they would not do anything unless there were United States Canadian and British forces in Europe. We have done all we can to add to our strength in particular by increasing the period of military service and we have tried to carry the Brussels Powers with us. Moreover at the meetings in London last May both M. Schuman and I emphasised to the Americans that it would be no use trying to defend Europe unless the Western Hemisphere troops were in Europe from the moment war broke out.[4]

4. These two factors seem to have influenced the United States

---

[1] See No. 28, note 2.
[3] See No. 29.i.

[2] See No. 27, note 5.
[4] See Volume II, Nos. 89–90 and 113.

administration and are at the back of what they have accepted. They are now ready to proceed provided that the principle of German participation is accepted. Now we are met with another stalemate because as shown in your telegram 1270[1] the French are not prepared to agree even in principle to German participation in Western defence. This is the position we are faced with at the time of adjournment.

5. I feel that whatever the French attitude in the end I must stick to what I said yesterday: that is that we accept in principle German participation and leave the details to be worked out later.

6. As regards the German police force we seem to be getting nearer to agreement and it may be possible to find a formula.[5]

[5] See No. 26, note 3. With reference to the present telegram, and New York telegrams Nos. 1050–1 (Nos. 28 and 29.i) Mr. Barclay suggested to Sir R. Makins, Deputy Under-Secretary of State, that a word of general approval from Mr. Attlee might have 'a very comforting effect' (PREM 8/1429). Mr. Attlee agreed and sent the following message to Mr. Bevin on 18 September: 'I should like you to know that I fully realise the difficulties with which you are faced on this question and entirely support the line you are taking' (F.O. telegram to New York No. 1300 on C 5912/27/18).

No. 31

Sir G. Jebb (New York) to Mr. Younger
(Received 17 September, 10.25 a.m.)

No. 1065 Telegraphic [C 5887/27/18]

Immediate. Top Secret   NEW YORK, 16 September 1950, 11.39 p.m.

Following for Prime Minister from Secretary of State.

It is clear that Schuman is convinced that best hope of being able to reach agreement with the Americans on the German issue is for him to get Moch over here, and the Americans have accepted his suggestion that the three Ministers of Defence should come to New York for talks in the hope that this (. . .? may)[1] facilitate progress. I have accordingly agreed to recommend to you that Mr. Shinwell should come here for talks which might begin on afternoon of 21st September or the morning of 22nd September. I very much hope that this will be possible.

2. Schuman appears fairly hopeful that if he can once get Moch out here and talking with the other Ministers of Defence it will be possible for the French to make some advance on their present attitude, which is more rigid today than yesterday. I gather that Moch himself and the French Socialists have hitherto been the chief obstacles.[2]

[1] The text is here uncertain.
[2] Sir O. Harvey warned Mr. Bevin from Paris on 20 September that 'I fear that you may find Moch stiffer as regards German rearmament than Schuman with whose policy he has not always been in agreement. The latter as a devout catholic brought up in the German part of Lorraine has points of contact with Western Germans, whereas Moch has none except through German Socialists in whom he has little confidence . . . On the other hand,

3. The Americans attach great importance to keeping the matter completely secret until they have thought out some satisfactory explanation for the advent of the three Ministers. It is clearly important that it should not be thought that they are coming purely to discuss the German issue. I undertook to impress on you the importance of keeping the matter secret until they are ready to make an announcement.

4. I should be grateful to know at the earliest possible moment whether Shinwell can come and if so when I may expect him.

5. The decision this coming week will be vital in the world's history. In view of the position of Marshall[3] here and of Moch in France and in view of the confidence which has grown up between Moch and Shinwell I shall warmly welcome the latter's assistance. He will appreciate that I have accepted the principle of German participation on behalf of His Majesty's Government but that unanimity is essential.[4]

Moch . . . is by far the best Minister of Defence we could get here and he has already galvanised the services. What he undertakes he will perform . . . he is outstanding, both as a Socialist and as a Frenchman' (Paris telegram No. 256 on C 6027/27/18).
[3] The appointment of General G.C. Marshall, U.S. Secretary of State 1947–9, as U.S. Secretary for Defence in succession to Mr. L. Johnson was announced on 12 September. The appointment was confirmed on 20 September and General Marshall was officially sworn in on 21 September.
[4] It was subsequently agreed that Mr. Shinwell would leave for New York on 20 September. The press were informed that he was going to discuss defence questions with Mr. Bevin since 'the Americans are averse to any suggestion in public that the British and French Defence Ministers are coming here to act in a corporate capacity with General Marshall' (New York telegram No. 1117 on C 5988/27/18).

No. 32

Sir G. Jebb (New York) to Mr. Younger
(Received 17 September, 3.56 p.m.)

No. 1066 Telegraphic [C 5904/27/18]

Priority. Secret   NEW YORK, 17 September 1950, 3.14 a.m.

Repeated to Wahnerheide, and Saving to Paris and Washington.

Following from Secretary of State.
My telegram 1053:[1] North Atlantic Council.

The third meeting this morning [16 September] was spent in continued discussion of the question of German association with the defence of Western Europe. The Americans had previously circulated a paper setting out their proposals (text in my telegram No. 1069[2]) but this was not discussed.

2. M. Schuman (France) spoke first. He said that there was general agreement on our objective which was to achieve European security by

[1] No. 29.i.   [2] No. 33.

creating common forces. In pursuit of the objective it was proposed to ask Germany to raise, equip and support troops (who would not be volunteers as had at one time been suggested) to serve under a unified command in which Germany would be represented. M. Schuman then proceeded to indicate the main French objections to this proposal.

(1) Whether we liked it or not we should be putting ourselves in the position of petitioners.

(2) He was not sure that German opinion would accept the proposal and quoted a message from the official agency of the Christian Democratic Union which described it as premature and unacceptable.

(3) It was not certain that we had the right under the terms of the Atlantic Treaty to use German troops for Atlantic defence without German membership of the Treaty.

(4) Even if we had such a right he doubted whether Germany would for long accept such a subordinate position.

(5) A decision of this sort could not fail to come as a shock to the peoples of Europe and might provoke disastrous reactions from the point of view of the European defence effort. Public opinion must first be carefully prepared.

(6) The proposal was also likely to have serious reactions in the Soviet satellite countries which were not at present entirely trusted by Russia but whose attitude might change as a result of the fear which German rearmament would inspire in them. Soviet propaganda would certainly represent the German units in the unified forces as being manned by refugees from Eastern Europe.

(7) There were also dangers as far as Germany herself was concerned. He believed in the need to bring Germany back into the European fold and in the good faith of the present German leaders. Nevertheless there had been a stiffening in the German attitude ever since the question of German rearmament had been broached. Germany was still only convalescing from militarism and was not yet cured. As regards German morale M. Schuman agreed that there was a danger of Germany drifting into 'neutralism' but thought that the best way of preventing this was to increase our own strength.

3. M. Schuman then said that the French Government were not irrevocably opposed to a solution of the German problem on the lines proposed: but certain necessary conditions must first be fulfilled. The unified European force must be created before German units were raised. Our own defences must be built up before we could begin building up Germany. Germany was not in a position at present to produce arms and equipment for us or for herself. The Atlantic forces must themselves be properly equipped and have reached an acceptable minimum degree of preparedness before anything was done about German participation in them. His experience of Germany led him to believe that when the time came it would not take as long as the two years suggested by Mr. Acheson

for the Germans to make the necessary administrative arrangements and train the necessary men.

4. On the other hand the attitude of the French Government was not entirely negative. They thought it just that Germany should contribute to her own defence and there were various ways in which she could do this at once. German police could take a load off the troops of occupation. German production could make a much larger contribution than at present to our own war effort. German labour battalions could be used in building a defence line in the East.

5. In conclusion M. Schuman said that the problem had been defined. The French Government agreed that it should be studied. They could not however agree at this stage to take a definite decision of principle.[3]

Please repeat Wahnerheide as my telegram No. 14 and Paris No.153 Saving.

[3] In his immediately following telegram Mr. Bevin summarized reactions to M. Schuman's statement: Count Sforza, Italian Minister for Foreign Affairs, though impressed by M. Schuman's arguments could not accept them since 'Europe was in mortal peril'. M. Stikker 'said that Holland too had suffered from the Germans and had no reason to love them . . . The Dutch people believed in the principle of the common defence of Europe but did not believe that there was any adequate defence at present or that Europe herself was in a position to provide one. It was essential to change this situation at once if European morale was to be supported and strengthened'. M. van Zeeland, Belgian Minister for Foreign Affairs 'doubted whether the divergence of opinion was really as great as it appeared. There was agreement that we must strengthen our defences to the utmost. The question of Germany had been defined and it was agreed in principle that Germany must at some time and in some form or other be associated with European defence' (New York telegram No. 1067 on C 5905/27/18: cf. further No. 73).

No. 33

Sir G. Jebb (New York) to Mr. Younger
(Received 17 September, 5.14 p.m.)

No. 1069 Telegraphic [WU 1198/397]

Priority. Top secret NEW YORK, 17 September 1950, 4 a.m.

North Atlantic Council.

My immediately preceding telegram.[1]

Following is text of United States Memorandum.

The Government of the United States believes that further measures must be taken to provide an effective defence in the European area. The United States Government believes that it is essential that there be an increase in the forces in Europe at the earliest feasible date and that firm

[1] In this telegram of even date (WU 1198/396) Mr. Bevin gave his comments on the U.S. memorandum below which was circulated as a written statement of the American position outlined by Mr. Acheson to the N.A.C. on 15 September (see No. 29.i). Mr. Bevin considered that 'the memorandum seems generally acceptable to us subject to the following important points': for which see notes 2, 4 and 5 below.

commitments should be made promptly of the forces to be devoted to the defence of the Western European area. To this end the United States Government is prepared to participate in the immediate establishment of an integrated force in Europe, within the framework of the North Atlantic Treaty adequate to insure the successful defence of Western Europe, including Western Germany, against possible aggression. The basic concepts involved in the establishment of this force in the view of the United States Government are as follows:

Principles governing the establishment of the force.

1. The force should be subject to political and strategic guidance exercised through the existing N.A.T.O. structure or such modifications therein as may be required.

2. The force should have a Supreme Commander who would be provided with sufficient delegated authority to insure that the separate national forces are organised and trained into one effective force in time of peace and who would be prepared to exercise the full powers of the Supreme Allied Commander over that force in time of war.

3. The Supreme Commander should be appointed when firm assurances have been received that sufficient forces will be provided to constitute a command reasonably capable of fulfilling its responsibilities.

4. The Supreme Commander should be provided with an international staff drawn from the nationals of all of the contributing nations. This staff, which should be appointed immediately, should perform the functions indicated below as well as serve the Commander with all necessary staff support. A priority mission of the combined staff would be to plan and implement the organisation of the unified force.

5. The Chief of Staff of the combined staff should, from the very outset, be endowed by the Standing Group with the consent of the North Atlantic Council, pending the appointment of a Supreme Commander, with the necessary authority for directing the organisation and training of the forces into a unified force and of prescribing the specifications for and the training of units in process of being formed.

6. The terms of reference of the Standing Group should be amended to confer upon it greater authority. It should gradually be transformed into a combined military organisation for higher strategic direction in areas where combined N.A.T.O. forces are operating. As such it would be the superior military body to which the Supreme Commander and pending his appointment, the Chief of Staff of the combined staff would be responsible.

7. The field forces of the force should, in general, be composed of national units operating under N.A.T.O. control and under immediate officers of their own nationalities. The nations concerned should make firm commitments as to the forces that would pass immediately to the control of the Supreme Commander and additional commitments as to the forces which would be placed under his command in the event of war.

8. The United States Government also believes that greater central

71

direction should be provided in the fields of military production and procurement of major items of supply to obtain the timely and effective use of European resources for increased defence and for the most effective utilisation of American assistance. This should be provided by necessary changes in the terms of reference of the present Military Production and Supply Board and by establishing a director with staff which shall provide the necessary guidance for military production and supply, he should direct a group highly qualified in the production field and should be supported by an integrated staff.[2]

9. The force referred to above involves the participation of German units and the use of German productive resources for its supply.

Principles governing German participation in the force.

The United States firmly believes that the recreation of a German national army would not serve the best interests of either Europe or Germany. It is strongly opposed to the creation of a national German army which would be under the control of the Federal Government, have its own general staff and command system, and be supplied independently by its own industry. The United States will not abandon the basic purposes of occupation or its efforts to attain the development of a democratic Germany free of the military tradition. This is the view of the great majority of the German people. In this connexion the United States has taken note of the Chancellor's statement[3] of the willingness of Germany to participate in a unified defence force in Europe and recognises the anomaly of refusing the German people any part in that defence providing a solution can be found which would allow German participation to be attended with certain safeguards. The United States believes these safeguards are contained in its proposal to create a unified defence on the continent of Europe. With these safeguards it believes that:

A. The Federal Republic of Germany should contribute units to the force for the defence of freedom in Europe.

B. The German unit contemplated is the balanced ground division. These German divisions would be integrated with non-German units in corps and higher units, but should be nationally generated and so integrated as not to impair their morale or effectiveness.

C. The creation of a German General Staff is undesirable and will not be considered.

D. The United States Government also considers that German indust-

[2] Mr. Bevin commented in New York telegram No. 1068 that this paragraph 'seems objectionable in that it restricts the operation to European resources and instead of regarding the operation as a common one as in the case of the armed forces treats Europe as one region and the United States as another, thus perpetuating the idea of givers and receivers instead of bringing out the fundamental North Atlantic Treaty conception of a common effort between partners'. Mr. Bevin went on to suggest a complete revise (not here printed): cf. No. 17, note 7.

[3] See No. 3, note 3.

rial resources should contribute to the defence of Europe, including Western Germany. While the maximum contribution would be expected of Germany in the production field, German forces should be dependent upon other nations for vital military equipment which should not be produced by German industry.[4]

Footnote: the above does not go into many details which will have to be resolved by the Deputies, the Defense Committee and other appropriate N.A.T. bodies.[5] It is believed that these details can be worked out in a manner which will:

(A) Avoid the dangers of recreating a German national army.
(B) Gain the strength of the German people in the defence effort.
(C) Definitely tie the Germans to the West,
(D) Satisfy public opinion on the above points.[6]

[4] With regard to sub-paragraph D, Mr. Bevin thought it 'desirable that a provision should be inserted to ensure that increases in German production are directly related to the requirements of the common defence effort. This might be achieved by inserting after the first sentence a new sentence somewhat on the following lines: "The Occupation Powers will exercise suitable control over the character and extent of this contribution and ensure its coordination with the effort of other North Atlantic Treaty Powers". The phrase "vital military equipment" in the second sentence seems rather dangerously vague and it might be desirable to insert after it words such as "and offensive weapons"'.

[5] Mr. Bevin here thought it 'desirable to safeguard the position of the Occupation Powers who will have the responsibility of securing acceptance of the scheme within Germany and to ensure that adequate attention is paid to considerations of German opinion and morale etc. This might be achieved by amending the first sentence to read as follows: "The above does not go into many details which will have to be resolved by the appropriate North Atlantic Treaty bodies in close consultation with the three Occupation Powers"'.

[6] The Chiefs of Staff in London were asked by Air Marshal Elliot to brief Mr. Shinwell on paragraphs 1–7 of this memorandum before his departure for New York. In discussion on 20 September the Chiefs of Staff committee agreed that the proposals in paragraphs 1–7 were at first sight acceptable subject to reservations on the proposed timing of the appointment of a Supreme Commander and the extent of his authority. 'The Committee were strongly of the opinion that it would be a serious mistake to delay the appointment of a Supreme Commander and to expect a Chief of Staff to function satisfactorily in the interim period. It would be very difficult to define the functions and responsibilities of such an officer and we should not be prepared to place our forces in Germany under command until the Supreme Commander had been appointed . . . Very careful study would have to be given to the authority to be delegated to the Supreme Commander for the unified forces. The suggestion that he might "prescribe the specifications for the training of units in process of being formed" was probably unacceptable . . . Some concern was expressed at the fact that reports and telegrams received from Washington gave no indication that the setting up of S.H.A.P.E. and the strengthening of the Standing Group would be accompanied by the dissolution of the three European Regional Planning Groups and of the Western Union Chiefs of Staff Organization. It was important that there should be no misunderstanding on this point, and that there should be no attempt to superimpose the new Supreme Headquarters on the existing Planning Organizations instead of it being a substitute for them' (C.O.S. (50) 152nd meeting on DEFE 4/36).

No. 34

Sir G. Jebb (New York) to Mr. Younger
(Received 17 September, 2.7 p.m.)

No. 1070 Telegraphic [C 5906/27/18]

Priority. Secret   NEW YORK, 17 September 1950, 4.38 a.m.

Repeated to Wahnerheide, and Saving to Paris and Washington.

Following from Secretary of State.
My telegram No. 1067:[1] North Atlantic Council.

At fourth meeting this afternoon [16 September] we continued to discuss question of German association with Western European defence.

2. Mr. Acheson said that it was clearly fruitless to continue the discussion of substance for the moment. We must therefore consider the question of procedure. The Council could not very well break up without referring to this question. On the other hand it could not give out that it had reached a deadlock. He therefore suggested that the Deputies should be instructed to prepare the best possible statement which could be made to the public. This statement might indicate that we had gone to the roots of the problem and that there was a large area of agreement, but many questions had been raised on which the Council needed further advice from other bodies particularly with regard to military production and financial questions. Several Ministers were in favour of another meeting of the Council in the near future. But Mr. Acheson indicated that he did not think it worth while in present circumstances to fix a date for a further meeting.

3. Impression left on me by Mr. Acheson's statements was that there was a danger of the Council adjourning tonight for good I therefore intervened to say that I was not at all happy about Mr. Acheson's proposal. I thought only the Russians would be pleased with a communiqué on the lines he had suggested. The press were experts at reading between the lines of official communiqués and would only draw the conclusion that the Council had failed to reach agreement and was a body which could not function properly. This would cause grievous disappointment among our peoples who expected so much from our deliberations. We must not give the impression that we were throwing in our hand. We had been asked to solve in two days a problem of centuries. We were at an historic moment. What we were trying to do was to build not merely a European army but a world force for peace. We could not afford to throw away that idea and let our peoples lose faith in this great institution to which they clung as the only organised hope for peace. I was therefore most reluctant to agree to an inadequate communiqué. I understood the point of view of France and of the other European countries, but I did not believe the divergences

_____
[1] See No. 32, note 3.

between the two different points of view was really so profound. If it was, then Governments must face the fact and say so. But we should reflect long and deeply before doing that. We should take more time. We could not afford to be driven by our time-table into wrong decision.

4. Mr. Pearson[2] (Canada) supported me. A reference to 'an area of agreement' might imply an area of disagreement. We had only had two meetings and had already gone a long way towards reaching agreement. He therefore proposed we should think things over during the weekend and see if we could not produce a better answer on Monday [18 September].

5. Mr. Acheson said he had no intention of proposing a communiqué which would produce the effects Mr. Pearson and I feared. He agreed nevertheless that there should be another meeting of the Council on Monday, and suggested that the Deputies should meanwhile meet and draw up a statement to show extent of general agreement reached so far as well as dealing with various outstanding subjects. M. Schuman (France) accepted this proposal and it was agreed that the Deputies should meet tomorrow [17 September] and Council on Monday morning.[3]

Please repeat to Wahnerheide as my telegram No. 16 and to Paris as my telegram No. 155 Saving.

[2] Canadian Secretary of State for External Affairs.
[3] The N.A.C. went on at this meeting to hear a Portuguese appeal for the association of Spain with the military work of N.A.T.O., to approve a report on the North Atlantic Planning Board for Ocean Shipping and the directive to the Defence Committee on Turkey and N.A.T.O. (see No. 26, note 3). The control of price and supply of raw materials was raised (see No. 17, note 8). M. Stikker expressed his concern to rationalize overlapping economic functions of N.A.T.O. and O.E.E.C., without reducing O.E.E.C. 'to a mere façade like the Council of Europe' (New York telegram No. 1076 on UR 1020/39). When the Deputies met on 17 September 'It at once became apparent that the Danish, Norwegian and Portuguese delegations were not able without reference to their governments to accept even in principle the idea of an integrated force in Europe and of the appointment of a Supreme Allied Commander'. Since therefore neither these principles nor a decision on German armed forces could be reached by the N.A.C. on the following day, it was agreed that each Minister should be asked to make a short statement indicating so far as they could the attitude of their respective governments on these two questions. 'The Deputies also recommended that after meeting tomorrow the Council should adjourn for about a week. During this interval it was hoped that further progress might be made outside the Council on the matter of the German forces and that those Ministers who needed them would get instructions from their governments on the question of the integrated force and the Supreme Allied Commander' (New York telegram No. 1086 on WU 1198/399).

No. 35

Sir G. Jebb (New York) to Mr. Younger
(Received 19 September, 2.39 p.m.)

No. 1108 Telegraphic [*C 5982/27/18*]

Priority. Secret   NEW YORK, *19 September 1950, 3.33 a.m.*

Repeated to Wahnerheide, and Saving to Paris and Washington.

Following from Secretary of State.
North Atlantic Council.
My telegram No. 1086[1] paragraph 2.

At today's (September 18th) meeting each Minister was asked to make a short statement indicating the attitude of his Government on the two questions of an integrated force and the use of German forces.[2]

2. When it came to my turn I said that I could recapitulate the position of His Majesty's Government as follows.

3. His Majesty's Government agreed on the necessity for an integrated force for the defence of the West. They also agreed that this force should be under a supreme Commander with an integrated staff. I did not think it was proper to the functions of the Council to elaborate the manner in which the integrated force should be constituted or the central command system organised; these in my view were questions the details of which should be worked out by the Defence Committee.

4. As regards Germany, His Majesty's Government generally agreed to accept the principle of German participation in western defence subject to agreed conditions, some of which had already been indicated by Mr. Acheson. We agreed with him however that this would inevitably take time and implied a period of planning, and that it did not imply that we should proceed immediately to the constitution of German armed units. We agreed with Mr. Acheson's statement on September 15th that the next stage should be the examination of the details by the Defence Committee and other appropriate North Atlantic Treaty bodies and exploration of the matter with the German Government in order to ascertain what part Germany should play.[3]

5. As regards procedure, I said I thought that we should reply to Dr. Adenauer that we were prepared in principle to consider German

[1] See No. 34, note 3.

[2] These statements, apart from Mr. Bevin's which is summarized below, are calendared at i. These statements were the last item on the agenda. The meeting had begun by adopting a resolution presented by M. Stikker on the relationship between N.A.T.O. and O.E.E.C. (see No. 34, note 3). The Council recognised the need to avoid duplication between the two organisations and instructed the Deputies to consider asking the O.E.E.C. to help with the collection and assessment of data required for the achievement of N.A.T.O. aims. The Council also approved the resolutions on raw materials (see No. 17, note 8) and on the medium term plan (see No. 29, note 7).

[3] See No. 33 and note 1 *ibid.*

participation in European defence and invite him to discuss the question further with the High Commissioners. The High Commission should then be instructed to study the matter and to find out the views of the German Government.[4] I felt that the High Commission were best placed to handle this problem and to judge what were the possibilities of German collaboration. Only in this way could we obtain a clear picture of the German position.

6. In conclusion I said that this was politically an extremely difficult question, but my Government were determined to face it. Nevertheless there were still many steps to be taken before German participation in European defence could become an accomplished fact.[5]

Please repeat to Wahnerheide as my telegram 21 and to Paris as my telegram 168 Saving.

CALENDAR TO NO. 35

i *18 Sept. 1950 Ministerial statements at N.A.C. Meeting* (Belgium, Canada, France, Iceland, Italy, Luxembourg, Netherlands, Norway, Denmark and Portugal) summarized in N.Y. tels 1120–1. Suggestion from M. Schuman that High Commissioners be asked to study possible use of German manpower for building defence fortifications and airfields in Germany viewed with 'serious misgivings' by Mr. Bevin [C 6006–7/27/18].

[4] This suggestion followed a conversation between Mr. Bevin and M. Schuman on the afternoon of 17 September: 'M. Schuman did not seem in any way perturbed by the way things were going in the Atlantic Council. We had some discussion about how far the French were prepared to go in public on the issue of German participation in western defence. It emerged that he would be willing to accept a formula for publication stating that the Ministers had agreed that in reply to the communication from the Federal Chancellor the Allied High Commissioners should be authorised to ascertain from him in what way Germany could best contribute to the defence of the free world against aggression. I said that I was sure that before we finally parted the Americans would hope to have obtained agreement in principle that German units should be incorporated in the integrated defence force. There could no doubt be conditions as regards timing etc. M. Schuman said he could not give way any further on this pending the arrival of M. Moch but he seemed to think that some understanding should then be possible' (New York telegram No. 1095 on C 5940/27/18).

[5] At the end of this N.A.C. meeting a communiqué was issued to the press (*The Times*, 19 September, p. 4) which made no mention of Germany but stated that the Council 'was determined to proceed with the necessary measures' to strengthen collective defence and that the Council was now recessed for two weeks in order to permit consultations with Governments as to the way in which a plan for an integrated military force could be put into effect. At a meeting of the Deputies on 21 September it was agreed that the Deputies would prepare a draft resolution embodying the decisions which it was hoped the N.A.C. would take with regard to the establishment of an integrated force for the defence of Europe and German participation in that defence: 'As regards future procedure on this question Mr. Spofford said the United States Government envisaged three stages: first there would be a general statement of principles by the Council. This was the paper which the Deputies would try to draft. Secondly plans would be worked out by the Defence Committee for the integrated force and by the three Occupying Powers for the participation of Germany. Finally the action proposed by these bodies would be submitted for final approval to the Council' (New York telegram No. 397 Saving on WU 1198/426).

No. 36

Mr. Younger to Sir G. Jebb (New York)

No. 1321 Telegraphic [C 6002/27/18]

Immediate. Top secret   FOREIGN OFFICE, 19 September 1950, 2.45 p.m.

Repeated to Washington and Saving to Paris.

Tripartite Talks

French Ambassador has given me further information about the attitude of his Government to German participation in Western European defence. He was present yesterday at a meeting of Ministers in Paris which included M. Pleven, M. Moch and M. Queuille.[1] The full Council of Ministers will be meeting tomorrow afternoon 20th September, to draft final instructions for M. Schuman. The Ambassador said that the Ministers were unanimous at yesterday's meeting that they could not (repeat not), accept in a communiqué to be issued in New York, any reference whatever to an agreement, even in principle, to German participation.[2] They believed that the effect upon opinion in France would be deplorable and that any such communiqué would be a provocation to the Russians at a time when neither the Germans themselves nor the Western allies were in a position to take effective measures if the Russians started trouble of any kind in Germany.

2. In this connexion the Ambassador told me that Field Marshal Montgomery had seen M. Pleven yesterday, and had told him that in his view any official acceptance of German rearmament at the present time would be most dangerous. The Field Marshal said that once German participation had been officially accepted, the Western powers would have an obligation to defend Western Germany. He emphasised that with the present resources at his disposal he would think it out of the question to contemplate a defence line east of the Rhine.[3]

---

[1] Minister of the Interior.

[2] Clarification on this point was sought by Mr. E. Davies, Parliamentary Under-Secretary of State for Foreign Affairs, at lunch with M. Massigli after the Ambassador's meeting with Mr. Younger: 'I said that we were not quite clear as to whether the decision taken at the meeting of French Ministers yesterday not to include a reference to German units in the communique was a decision on the principle of including German units in a European defence force or whether it referred merely to mentioning German units in the communique. 2. M. Massigli replied that there was no question of the latter: the Ministers had found it impossible to agree even to the principle of including German units. He added that M. Pleven had remarked that he could not possibly recommend the acceptance of the principle that German units should be included in a European defence force to the French Parliament. 3. I remarked that this appeared to be a very definite decision. M. Massigli replied that there was to be another meeting of French Ministers tomorrow but that he had represented the position as it now stands' (minute of 19 September by Mr. Davies on C 6002/27/18). The substance of this minute was telegraphed to New York that evening.

[3] These observations by Field-Marshal Lord Montgomery were included in his long memorandum entitled 'Western European Defence: some matters that give cause for alarm'

3. I thanked the Ambassador for his information. I told him that His Majesty's Government had not altered the attitude of which he already knew. So far as provocation of the Russians was concerned, however, I said that so much had already leaked out in America, that I doubted whether Russian reactions would be determined by the nature or the absence of an official communiqué. Even if nothing was officially announced they would be likely to calculate that agreement in principle had in effect been reached.

4. The Ambassador also said that M. Moch was very doubtful whether he ought to go to New York as proposed, since to do so might imply that French Government were half ready to give way on the question of German participation. I told the Ambassador that Mr. Shinwell is definitely leaving for New York tomorrow night.[4]

which he sent to Mr. Attlee on 19 September. In his covering note the Field-Marshal informed the Prime Minister that he 'had a long talk on the subject in Paris yesterday with M. Pleven and he was in general agreement with me'. M. Pleven evidently asked Field-Marshal Montgomery to tell British Ministers about their conversation. Commenting on this in a minute to Mr. Attlee of 12 October, Mr. Rickett observed: 'The implication was that there was a discrepancy between the views of the British Government and those of Field-Marshal Montgomery'. Mr. Rickett regretted the timing of Field-Marshal Montgomery's remarks in relation to discussions in New York, and in the context of recent concern by Mr. Bevin at Field-Marshal Montgomery's repeated direct approaches to Defence Ministers of Brussels Treaty countries. This matter was satisfactorily resolved at a meeting between Mr. Attlee and Field-Marshal Montgomery on 17 October: see correspondence on PREM 8/1154.

[4] Mr. Younger's account of his conversation with M. Massigli on 19 September was seen and noted by Mr. Attlee that day.

No. 37

U.K. Delegation (New York) to Ministry of Defence
(Received 21 September, 9.45 a.m.)

COJA 122A Telegraphic [WU 1198/419]

Emergency. Top secret   NEW YORK, *20 September 1950, 10.33 p.m.*

For Price from Elliot for Chiefs of Staff.

Following is brief which I will hand to Minister[1] on his arrival tomorrow. Grateful for any comments which you may wish to make on it to help him in his forthcoming discussions in New York and also those of Lord Tedder in Washington.

(*Begins*)

You may find it useful if I summarise the position that has now been reached with regard to the constitution of a unified force under a Supreme Commander for the defence of Western Europe and the related problem of German rearmament—those two related subjects being the

[1] Mr. Shinwell.

79

essence of the problem which has brought you here to join General Marshall and M. Moch and to help the three Foreign Ministers to resolve the deadlock which has arisen. The reason for this deadlock is that the Americans have made it clear that their proposals for an integrated European Defence Force and for the incorporation of German units in that Force must be treated as a whole. That part of the American memorandum[2] which relates to the integrated force and the provision of a command and staff for the force have been accepted in principle by most members of the North Atlantic Council but the French have refused so far to agree to an acceptance in principle of the incorporation of German units in the integrated force.

French attitude

2. The main French objections to the German rearmament proposal appear to be as follows—

(a) Public opinion in France and elsewhere in Western Europe is not yet sufficiently prepared. An immediate decision on German rearmament might it is suggested affect adversely the present defence efforts of the Western European countries because of the shock that it would cause to public opinion in those countries.

(b) Germany itself is still only convalescing from militarism and is not yet cured. There had already been a stiffening in the German attitude ever since the question of German rearmament had been broached. German policy would become still less tractable if we now agreed to a measure of rearmament particularly if we were put in the position of petitioners asking for German military assistance.

(c) The proposal might have serious reactions in Russia and the Soviet satellite countries. Russia might be provoked into taking immediate action in Germany before German rearmament could take place. Moreover Soviet propaganda would certainly seek to suggest—no doubt with some reason—that the German units in the integrated force were being manned by refugees from the East.

(d) Germany would not long accept the position of providing units for the integrated force without demanding full membership and rights of N.A.T.O. but it was not yet possible to allow Germany to resume her full status as an independent nation since European opinion was not ready for it and in any case the occupation must be maintained.

(e) It was not altogether clear that German opinion would accept the proposals. There was some reason to think that German opinion regarded her own rearmament as premature.

Attitude of the remaining N.A.T.O. powers

3. While there was some disposition, particularly among the Benelux powers to agree with the French attitude over German rearmament when

[2] No. 33.

the matter was first raised in the Council, there is now no doubt that the rest of the Council are prepared to accept German rearmament in principle. Some however may change their minds if the French continue to maintain their opposition. This would in effect render a collective defence of Europe virtually unattainable.

U.K. attitude

4. The Foreign Secretary made a statement[3] at the closing session of the Council about the U.K. attitude to the American memo. which may be summarised as follows—

(a) The U.K. accepts in principle the conception of an integrated force under a Supreme Commander with an international staff.
(b) It would not be appropriate for the Council to elaborate the way in which the force should be constituted or the command structure organised. These are details which must be worked out under the supervision of the Defence Committee.
(c) The U.K. accepts in principle German participation in Western defence. This is a matter however which will take time and implies a period of planning so that there is no question of immediately constituting German military units.
(d) The U.K. believes that if the American memo. is accepted in principle the next stage should be the examination of details by the Defence Committee and other appropriate N.A.T. bodies; the matter should be explored with the German Government, by the Occupation Powers, in order to find out what part Germany can be induced to play and to prepare German opinion: the three High Commissioners are to pursue this aspect of the matter on their return to Germany.

5. Subject to the advice that you received before you left London I suggest that the line that you should take when you see M. Moch and during the Tripartite meetings might be as follows—

(a) You recognise fully the French position and the very understandable fears which they have expressed about German rearmament but the overwhelming need at the present time is to provide sufficient forces to meet Russian aggression. France and the U.K. who, between them, can alone provide the major European contribution, know better than the other countries of N.A.T.O. not only how inadequate are our present forces to meet a Russian attack but also how very great will be the difficulties which will confront them and the other European members of N.A.T.O. in providing—if left to themselves—even the minimum target force of 56 divisions and 6,000 aircraft for the defence of the Rhine–Ijssel line. It is therefore of the utmost importance that the European countries should neglect no opportunity of supplementing such forces as they themselves can raise by whatever

[3] See No. 35.

81

reasonable means they can. The only major source of supply for these *additional* forces, outside Europe, is the U.S.A. Inside Europe it is Germany.

(*b*) Meanwhile serious doubts have been expressed, on political grounds, about the adequacy even of the Rhine–Ijssel line as a plan for the defence of Western Europe.[4] The argument runs that the ultimate success of an operation depends on the morale of the countries which are asked to be a party to it and that it will fail unless the people of those countries believe that the plan has some real chance of success. The plan based on the Rhine–Ijssel line condemns a large part of Europe to invasion and evacuation and consequently to the risk of defeat. Therefore if the countries concerned are to make the sacrifices demanded of them in producing the forces necessary for a successful defence of Europe, the plan for this must provide for a defence much further east of this line. This in all probability will demand *more* forces. In any event it carried with it the inescapable fact that the battle will be fought in Germany itself. It is therefore reasonable to take steps which will ensure that in such a contingency we shall have the active support and sympathy of the Germans themselves.

(*c*) It is important to emphasise that the American memo. stands or falls together. If Western Europe does not accept those parts of the memo. which call for German rearmament there is every danger of the U.S. refusing to carry out the remainder of her proposals which of course involve the provision of greatly increased American forces in Europe.

6. The main object of your participation in these Tripartite talks is as I have said to help to secure French agreement in principle to the American memo. but you should also I suggest make it clear in discussions with your American and French colleagues that the U.K. acceptance of the American memo. in principle will not of course prevent us from expressing strong views about the detailed implementation of the American proposals.

7. Whilst it is not necessary for you to mention them to the Americans and French it seems to me that the following are the kind of detailed matters to which we shall attach importance when the American memo. is under discussion in the Standing Group and elsewhere. These matters fall broadly under the two headings—

(*a*) The command organisation and (*b*) German participation in the integrated force.

(*a*) *The command organisation*

(i) What are to be the powers of the 'Chief of Staff' who is to be appointed immediately? In our view he should be more nearly akin to a Deputy Supreme Commander than a Chief of Staff.

(ii) While the Americans are not going to accept the location of the

[4] See No. 29.i.

Supreme Commander's H.Q. at Fontainebleau, we could no doubt persuade them to make use of some of the staff machinery which is now in existence there.

(iii) The functions of the Standing Group as a kind of 'Combined Chiefs of Staff' for the N.A.T.O. area will require much careful thought. In particular the smaller powers not represented on the Standing Group have expressed great anxiety lest their opinions shall not be adequately represented there. These misgivings are healthy and reasonable and steps should be taken to cure them. They are fully prepared to support an increase in the authority of the Standing Group—which we ourselves would welcome—involving a loss of sovereignty but legitimately argue that this must receive compensation by ensuring that their accredited representatives have adequate rights of consultation. Canada and Holland in particular have expressed strong views on this point. In the same context the French moreover have shown unmistakable signs of a strong determination to press for the extension of the authority of the Standing Group to global dimensions.

(iv) The exact powers of the Supreme Commander in peacetime over the forces allocated and earmarked to him will need to be carefully worked out. What responsibility will he for instance have for the periods and nature of training of the forces earmarked but not actually allocated to him in time of peace.

(b) *German participation in the integrated force*

(i) In the preparation of plans for the participation of German units in the force there must be very close consultation with the Occupying Powers who will be responsible for ensuring political acceptance and implementation of the plans in Germany in order to ensure that the plans are realistically related to German opinion and resources and will not cause dangerously adverse reactions upon German morale or the position of the Occupation Authorities.

(ii) Before however the political aspect of German participation in Western defence can be adequately considered the Standing Group as the expert military advisers will have to pronounce on a number of essentially technical points. The American proposals at this stage go no further than to suggest that 'the German unit contemplated is the balanced ground division'. This little German embryo is not even—and quite rightly—to be allowed the benefit of a German mother in the shape of a German General Staff. It is therefore all the more necessary that the Standing Group should quickly assume this role of foster mother to decide such questions as the exact meaning of 'a balanced ground division', its strength, its officering, the nature and extent of its supporting arms etc. There will moreover remain to be considered such incidental matters as the provision of German naval and air forces on which the American proposals remain startlingly silent.

8. You will no doubt have received advice in London about those parts of the American memo. which relate to production.[5] The view that was expressed here was that para. 8 of the memo. contravened the whole philosophy of N.A.T.O. which is that we are all partners in a common effort. Moreover para. 8 is drafted in such a way as to suggest that the proposed new bonsy [sic] charged with production and supply should be able to dictate to us in the production and financial field which in our view must remain within the responsibility of individual governments.

9. I would suggest in conclusion that it is most important that the meetings in New York should not be bogged down in a detailed examination of the American memo. The purpose of the meetings is to resolve the deadlock on German participation in Western defence; the detailed implementation of the American proposals must be worked out under the direction of the Defence Committee later.

(Ends.)[6]

[5] See No. 17, note 7 and No. 33, note 4.
[6] This telegram was considered by the Chiefs of Staff committee at their 153rd meeting on 22 September, and a reply sent to Air Marshal Elliot that day: 'Chiefs of Staff are in general agreement with your admirable brief for the Minister provided it is read in conjunction with the minute submitted to him after their meeting on Wednesday [cf. No. 33, note 6] . . . Reference your paragraph 7(iii), they think French pressure to extend at this stage authority of Standing Group to global dimensions should be firmly resisted . . . As regards the German problem, the Chiefs of Staff . . . feel that, in discussions with the French, more might perhaps be made of the argument that with the atomic bomb in Allied hands, Germany is not far enough away from the West to become a menace since her war making capacity, centred in the Ruhr, could be pulverised in a few days' (telegram JACO 140 on WU 1198/431).

No. 38

Minute from Mr. Shuckburgh to Sir R. Makins

[C 6066/27/18]

FOREIGN OFFICE, *21 September 1950*

When I met the French Ambassador at the Permanent Commission[1] this morning, he started at once telling me how disastrous he thought was the American insistence on re-arming the Germans. He said that this was a culmination of what had been the military view in the United States for the last two years, namely that the United States should place her reliance on the Germans for providing the land forces necessary to defend Europe. This decision to rely on the Germans would, he thought, inevitably lead to a 'preventive war' being launched by the Americans

[1] The Permanent Commission, appointed by the Consultative Council of the Brussels treaty powers (see No. 2, note 8), met at ambassadorial level in London once a month as a forum for inter-governmental consultation and collaboration in social, cultural and civil defence matters.

within the next two years. He supported this view by the argument that the Germans have only one interest and that is the unification of Germany; and that they can only achieve this end either by going Communist or through a preventive war; therefore as soon as the Americans have built up substantial German armed forces and begun to rely on them, they will be led by the Germans into a preventive war. He thought that in any case there was a grave danger that the Americans, elated by their successes in Korea and perhaps in other places in the future, would themselves incline more and more towards the idea of knocking out Russia.

2. I did what I could to counter this by pointing to the essential hatred of war of the American democracy and to the recent statements of the President and Mr. Acheson,[2] and I said I thought that the Americans were in a more dangerous frame of mind when they were suffering reverses than when they were being successful. But M. Massigli was quite unimpressed.

3. Incidentally, M. Massigli also pointed out that, as soon as German units were associated with the forces of the North Atlantic Treaty and Germany thereby became practically a member of the North Atlantic Treaty Organisation, an anomalous situation would arise in regard to the Brussels Treaty. In the Brussels Treaty Germany is named as the potential aggressor against which the Treaty is directed.[3] Since the military structure of the Brussels Treaty is now part of the North Atlantic Treaty structure, you would have the Germans participating in a machine which was theoretically directed against themselves.[4]

C.A.E. SHUCKBURGH

[2] Cf. No. 1, note 7, and Nos. 13, 17–18, 21.

[3] The preamble of the Brussels treaty stated, among other things, the resolve of the signatory powers: 'To take such steps as may be held to be necessary in the event of a renewal by Germany of a policy of aggression.' A similar statement was included in article 7.

[4] Sir R. Makins commented below: 'M. Massigli is hardly open to argument on this issue.'

No. 39

Letter from Mr. Barclay (New York) to Sir R. Makins

[*F.O. 800/517*]

Personal and Secret   NEW YORK, *22 September 1950*

I was most grateful for your prompt action in response to my personal telegram No. 1064 of the 16th September.[1] The Prime Minister's message gave great satisfaction, as did his subsequent expression of approval of the settlement reached on East–West trade.[2]

The explanation of my message was that the Secretary of State was in a

[1] Not printed: see No. 30, note 5.   [2] Not printed: see No. 26.ii.

slightly jumpy state last week and inclined to alternate between excessive optimism and unjustified pessimism. He was also, as the Ambassador put it, 'seeing ghosts everywhere', and the first telegram,[3] informing him that the Cabinet had not given him the green light to go ahead on the question of German participation in Western defence, caused somewhat exaggerated alarm and despondency. The feeling that he had not perhaps got full support from his colleagues at home, combined with a tendency to excessive suspicion of the intentions of some of the other Foreign Ministers here (not always excluding the Americans), was leading him to be so extremely cautious in his utterances at the conference table that there was a good deal of uncertainty as to what his position really was. Even when he had received full authority from the Cabinet to commit H.M.G.,[4] Bob[5] and I had the utmost difficulty in persuading him to make a clear and positive statement.

However, I am glad to say that the atmosphere is now very much easier and I think that any irritation there may have been on the American side at our initial hesitations and prevarications have now been completely removed. Thanks to the progress made in other directions, e.g. Chinese representation, Formosa, Korea, etc., the points of particular difficulty between us and the Americans have been very considerably reduced in scope, and the Secretary of State and Dean Acheson are now finding it possible to go along together on the great majority of questions that arise. To-day the tendency has been for them to combine in expressing their great indignation at the tiresomeness of the French about Germany. At the moment of writing the position is somewhat confused, but it looks as though the American defence people are prepared greatly to reduce their demands as to the nature and extent of French commitments, so that some sort of compromise formula will probably be worked out.

The first week after our arrival was exceptionally strenuous, and by Tuesday night [19 September] most of us were feeling pretty exhausted. But the last three days, which, for the Secretary of State and me at least, involved spending a certain amount of time listening to speeches at the United Nations, have not been nearly so bad. Actually the Secretary of State has stood up to a very severe programme surprisingly well, and, though he naturally feels a bit jaded by the end of the day, he has really been in better shape physically, and indeed mentally, than at any other conference during the last year or so. We have managed to avoid any excessive amount of social activities, and at the few functions he has been obliged to attend he has really been in extremely good form. Next week he is taking a party, including the Achesons, Jessups,[6] Spoffords and others, to the Sadler's Wells Ballet, the Metropolitan Opera having very kindly offered to put two boxes at our disposal.

What with the Ambassador and others from Washington, in addition to

[3] F.O. telegram to New York No. 1233, for which see No. 18, note 3.
[4] See No. 27, note 5.   [5] Sir P. Dixon.
[6] Dr. P.C. Jessup was a U.S. Ambassador at Large.

the various experts who came out from London, we really had a very high-powered team for the tripartite and Atlantic Council discussions, but I do not think we were in any way over-staffed, and indeed we could hardly have done with any less. I am afraid our reports have sometimes been excessively lengthy, but the subjects were mostly of considerable complexity and importance and frequently also of some degree of urgency. Paddy Noble[7] must [nev]ertheless[8] have been shocked by the length of some of our telegrams.

The next major operation before us is the Secretary of State's speech in the United Nations Assembly, which is likely to be on Monday afternoon [25 September]. Once that is over, and assuming always that we are able to conclude a satisfactory agreement with the Americans and French about Germany to-day, our most serious and immediate difficulties should be over, though I have no doubt that we shall be very fully engaged until we actually embark. There are still several Foreign Ministers clamouring to see the Secretary of State whom we have not yet been able to fit in.

I hope you have not had too strenuous a time since William's departure,[9] but I have no doubt there is a good deal going on at the moment.

I have dictated this in haste, and I am sorry that I have not had time to prepare anything more useful about the general atmosphere, but I thought you would at any rate like to know that the S. of S. is keeping fit and on the whole in very good form.[10]

R.E. BARCLAY

[7] Sir A. Noble, Assistant Under-Secretary of State, superintended *inter-alia* the Communications department of the Foreign Office.

[8] The text is here defective.

[9] Sir W. Strang was presumably on leave.

[10] In a letter to H.M. The King on 17 September, Mr. Bevin himself reviewed progress at New York which he considered satisfactory overall concluding: 'We have had a very strenuous time since we got here, but I am glad to say that I am standing up to it pretty well. I have been able to drive out into the country for a little sun and fresh air today, and feel all the better for it' (F.O. 800/511).

No. 40

Minute from Sir D. Gainer to Mr. Attlee

[*C 6050/2/18*]

Top secret   FOREIGN OFFICE, *22 September 1950*

Sir I. Kirkpatrick has telegraphed (see Flag A)[1] asking for authority to

[1] Wahnerheide telegram No. 1408 of 21 September (Flag A) was in fact from Mr. Steel, who was acting for Sir I. Kirkpatrick during the latter's absence in New York. In this telegram Mr. Steel reported discussion that day by the Deputy High Commissioners of the proposals from the Berlin Commandants summarized below. Mr. Steel requested instructions before a further meeting on 23 September.

accept immediately joint proposals by the three Commandants in Berlin for:

(*a*) the strengthening and arming with light weapons of the normal German police force in Berlin;

(*b*) the formation of a Garde Mobile of 5,000 men built up from the existing police but additional to them;

(*c*) consideration to be given to the formation of a supplementary force or Home Guard of 10,000.

2. I have felt unable to let Sir I. Kirkpatrick have any final decision on these questions without the advice of the Chiefs of Staff and Ministerial approval.

3. It has already been agreed in New York that a Garde Mobile should be set up in the area of the Federal Republic and also that German auxiliary forces should be formed in Berlin.[2] Recommendation (*b*) of the Commandants would appear consistent with these decisions.

4. Recommendation (*a*) for arming the ordinary police force, however, goes beyond anything agreed in New York and I feel that we should examine carefully the possible disadvantages of such a course. We are still awaiting a joint report from the three Western Commanders-in-Chief in Germany on the capability of the Western Occupying Powers to resist aggression by German forces against Berlin, and until we have seen this and also the detailed arguments on which the Commandants base their present recommendation, it is not easy to recommend a firm decision.

5. As regards (*c*) it seems preferable to defer a decision pending the result of the New York discussions on a possible German armed contribution to Western Defence.

6. I have therefore sent an interim reply to the High Commissioner, (see Flag B).[3] In the light of his further comments I will prepare a fuller submission to you. The Secretary of State has been informed.[4]

D. St. Clair Gainer

[2] See No. 26.ii.

[3] Foreign Office telegram to Wahnerheide No. 1543 of 22 September (Flag B) instructed Mr. Steel to hold the position without commitment while Ministers were consulted. Mr. Steel was informed of Sir D. Gainer's preliminary view that action in Berlin should be confined to organising a Garde Mobile.

[4] Wahnerheide telegram No. 1408 (note 1) and the interim reply (note 3) were repeated to New York for Mr. Bevin who replied on 23 September: 'Question of Berlin police was scarcely discussed by Ministers here but proposals described in Wahnerheide telegram No. 1408 seem to me to go a bit too far and too fast. We do not want to get out of step in Berlin with what we are doing in Western Germany. And it seems to me unwise at this moment to take ostentatious steps of this nature which might well provoke some Russian reaction before we have been able further to build up our strength.' (New York telegram No. 1173 on C 6110/2/18). Mr. Attlee minuted on the bottom of his copy of Sir D. Gainer's minute filed on PREM 8/1429: 'I find it difficult to understand the procedure in this matter. The whole question of police arms etc. is under discussion between the 3 Foreign Ministers in N.Y. How do these separate proposals come forward? On whose initiative? I will see Gainer on Monday. C.R.A. 24.9.50.' After his meeting with Mr. Attlee on 25 September Sir

i   *25 Sept. 1950   C.O.S. Report (C.O.S. (50) 378) on strength of Bereitschaften* and capabilities of Allied forces to withstand an attack. Present strength of Bereitschaften calculated at 53,000. Its organisation, equipment and readiness for war compared in detail with existing Allied forces in F.R.G. and Berlin. Bereitschaften not yet strong enough to attempt invasion but might be so by winter of 1950–1. Recommendations include strengthening of Allied garrison in Berlin, arming of proposed Berlin police force to infantry rifle level and preparation of military plans for an emergency. Minuting on report on 6 Oct. Mr. Gilchrist considers how best to reconcile the fact that the Allied political commitment to Berlin is inconsistent with sound military strategy. Berlin is not defensible and likely to remain so even after strengthening. Considers in what circumstances (e.g. Russian attack) Allies should abandon attempt to defend Berlin [C 6823/27/18].

D. Gainer informed Mr. A. Gilchrist, Assistant Head of F.O. German Political department, that 'the Prime Minister is satisfied that we must not get out of step in Berlin with Western Germany; he is afraid that the liaison on political matters between Berlin & Wahnerheide is not adequate. I said that nevertheless all telegrams were repeated where it seemed essential from one to the other. This was, I thought, the Commandants in Berlin making suggestions to Wahn. which had been discussed only by the Deputies and that we must await the reactions of the High Commission in the light of our telegram No. 1543 which had been endorsed by the Foreign Secretary. The Prime Minister agreed and asked me to keep him informed. I then said I should be making a further submission to him regarding the Garde Mobile and I briefly explained our point of view with regard to a Federal Force versus a Force based on the Länder. The P.M. said the French were being very difficult and contributing very little' (C 6050/2/18). The question of security measures in Berlin was discussed by the A.H.C. with the Berlin Commandants at a meeting on 28 September. The Commandants were invited to submit a further report with recommendations for strengthening the existing municipal police force in Berlin without turning it into a fully armed gendarmerie.

No. 41

Sir G. Jebb (New York) to Mr. Attlee[1]
(Received 23 September, 12.5 p.m.)

No. 1167 Telegraphic [C 6105/27/18]

Immediate. Top secret   NEW YORK, *23 September 1950, 2.5 a.m.*

Repeated to Wahnerheide, Paris, Washington.

Following from Secretary of State.
Tripartite talks. German participation in Western Defence.
First meeting of three Foreign Ministers and their Defence Ministers was held on morning of 22nd September.
2. Mr. Acheson after thanking Defence Ministers for coming to New York explained that United States consideration of this problem had been

----
[1] See No. 6, note 1.

prompted by French memo. submitted to the Deputies on 17th August[2] which the United States Government had found very stimulating in the manner in which it raised important fundamental issues. United States proposals which had been approved by President on eve of present meetings committed the United States to stationing strengthened forces in Europe as part of the effective scheme for the strengthening and integration, under a Central Staff and Supreme Command, of a combined North Atlantic forces in Europe. Units to provide nucleus of integrated force must be identified at once and additional units would have to be provided later. In general an increased production programme was being set in hand in the United States to meet the increased requirements and the United States was also ready to examine with its allies questions of finance and to join them in a joint action body to replace the Military Production and Supply Board.

3. It was an essential feature of the United States plan that defence in Europe must be as far east as possible and must include Western Germany if German resources were to be denied to the Russians and a lead given to German opinion. This could only be achieved if German units were embodied in the integrated force under appropriate safeguards. Discussion in North Atlantic Council had revealed difficulties about these proposals in certain quarters. The Norwegians, Danes and Portuguese[3] had genuine difficulties about the integrated force itself but these could be discussed and resolved. The French Government's main difficulty was on the question of German participation. Here it seemed important first to distinguish between the need for an immediate decision as to our common direction and objectives which seemed essential and the need for a public announcement which should not necessarily be made at once. In the second place some time would be required for discussions with the Germans so that we could ensure that we were in a position not of asking the Germans for help but of examining German proposals critically and with clear knowledge of our own objectives. Thirdly it must be made clear that there was no question of arming Germans at the expense of the North Atlantic Treaty countries. Fourth, German rearmament must be kept fully under control by ensuring that German units were fully incorporated as an integral part of a combined force.

4. These were the problems which the Defence Ministers could help in examining. He thought all were agreed as to the need to bridge the gap between present resources and the needs of the situation. The problem was how to do it.

5. M. Schuman said that the French Government fully appreciated the historic importance of the United States proposals; but their own views were clear and fully confirmed the attitude he himself had adopted in the discussions hitherto.

A minority in the Government would have liked to turn down the

[2] See No. 9, note 4.   [3] See No. 35.i.

proposals completely but the majority was ready to discuss them in a positive manner subject to two conditions. Firstly before the Germans could be allowed to participate in an integrated force that force must be created and made strong enough under a Supreme Commander to prevent the Germans from dominating it. Secondly it should be understood that the immediate need in the first phase say until the end of 1951 was not manpower but material and efforts should accordingly be concentrated during that period upon rearmament of our own forces.

6. In these circumstances the French Government considered that a decision now even of principle to admit German units to participation in the integrated force at a later stage would be premature and only make attainment of our common aims more difficult.

7. The French Government agreed that Germany must be induced to join forces with the West rather than the East and to this end France had supported Germany's economic integration with Western Europe. But now that German rearmament was being mentioned new hesitations were already becoming apparent on the German side in the discussions on the Schuman Plan.[4] It was evident that the Germans were already asking whether if they were in any event likely to achieve equality in the military field they need make any contribution at this stage in the economic sphere.

8. These considerations led him to the conclusion that while the question of German participation in defence could perhaps be discussed at the appropriate time any decision on the matter would be premature at present.

9. I then explained that while there had been much discussion in the United Kingdom of a German contribution to Western Defence public opinion was much more obsessed with the need to prevent a world war and with the question whether adequate forces could be built up to defeat the Russians. There was growing impatience at the slow progress since conclusion of the North Atlantic Treaty. I therefore agreed with Mr. Acheson that a decision must be taken now such as would enable the development of an integrated force to proceed. While I did not wish to draw exaggerated conclusions the tone of the Russian speeches in the United Nations Assembly indicated that we had the initiative. The moment had now come when Russian actions had opened the eyes of the whole free world to the real needs of the situation. The United States proposals put forward in response to French initiative provided the means of achieving what the situation demanded. We must not lose momentum and let slip the opportunity which they presented of making peace safe for 100 years.

10. We also agreed that the view put forward by the Americans and supported for their own reasons by the Dutch, that Europe must be held as far east as possible and that to this end we should agree in principle now

[4] See Volume I, No. 170.

that at the right moment German units must be used. We would accordingly propose first that the integrated force should be built up until it was strong enough to warrant the appointment of a Supreme Commander and Staff and second that it should be agreed now that at that moment German units should be organised.

11. We understood French doubts but considered that when we like the United States were committing ourselves to station forces permanently on the Continent we were entitled to be clear that all the decisions necessary to the creation of an effective force had been taken. Britain would resolutely follow the course we had embarked on whatever Government were in office. But we must not be obliged to argue the question of German participation again at a later stage after our joint enterprise was under way. The question must be settled now.

12. Mr. Acheson agreed that the North Atlantic Council must be enabled to take the necessary broad decisions which would enable the Defence Committee hereafter to work out the specific details. He thought there was agreement on the main issues except on the nature of the decision regarding German participation to be taken now.

13. M. Moch began by explaining that the French Government was unanimous in support of the position M. Schuman had outlined and considered that Parliament except the Communists would also support it. He feared that a decision that Germany would ultimately be rearmed would provide valuable ammunition for Soviet psychological warfare and agitation and also that by increasing the risk of war it would have dangers disproportionate to the immediate advantages to be gained.

14. The problem for the next 15 months was not one of manpower. The French Government's decision to seek Parliamentary authority for the extension of military service to 18 months had been taken not because it was necessary on manpower grounds but for purposes of psychological warfare and to help the United Kingdom. The immediate needs were first to speed up the medium term plan so that it could be completed by 1952 or even at the end of 1951 rather than in 1954 (so far France had received only 10 per cent of the supplies promised for the first stage of the Military Assistance Programme); second to make arrangements for the proper disposition of the increased Allied Forces in Germany in accordance with the strategic requirements; third to reach agreement on production programmes such as would enable military production to go ahead which in France was now held up: fourth to deal with the problem of finance; and fifth to make provision for the control of the price of raw materials by some form of combined board.

15. The problem therefore was to decide in this context what participation Germany could make until the end of 1951 to the collective security of Europe. A German contribution should be asked for and if necessary required, in the form of production, raw materials and labour. As regards production it would be wrong that Germany should be allowed to concentrate on building tractors or consumer goods while the allied

countries were devoting their resources to production of armaments. As regards labour, modern conditions required careful preparation of airfields, minefields, barbed wire entanglements and strong points and immediate consideration should be given to the question of how German labour could contribute to this work. In this way the necessity for creating armed German units would be avoided but it might be that if it were decided to establish immediately some German Labour Force on the lines of the Todt Organisation[5] that could later be transformed into armed units when the time came for a decision to create such units. But no decision of principle should be taken on this latter question now. The other immediate problems to which he had referred must have priority.

16. The meeting adjourned to enable the six Ministers to have lunch together with Mr. Acheson as host and decided to resume at 3 p.m.

Foreign Office please repeat immediate to Wahnerheide as my telegram No. 31 and Paris as my telegram No. 27.

[5] Semi-military labour battalions from territories occupied by Nazi Germany.

No. 42

Sir G. Jebb (New York) to Mr. Attlee
(Received 23 September, 12.12 p.m.)

No. 1168 Telegraphic [C 6106/27/18]

Immediate. Top secret   NEW YORK, *23 September 1950, 3.2 a.m.*

Repeated to Paris, Washington, Wahnerheide.

Following from Secretary of State.
My telegram No. 1167.[1]
Tripartite talks.
German contribution to Western defence.
Meeting of three Foreign Ministers and Defence Ministers was resumed on afternoon of 22nd September.

2. Mr. Shinwell stated that we must admit that the efforts we had made for twelve months and more to build up adequate forces in the West had so far failed. Now the United States had declared its intention of putting increased forces into Europe,[2] and we must grasp the offer with both hands.

3. We were confronted with forces vastly greater than anything we could hope to pit against them in the foreseeable future. All military advisers were agreed that we must try to fight east of the Rhine. It was also clear that the need for equipment was the crux of the present problem. There was no time to be lost. 1951 was the critical year, and he agreed with M. Moch that 1954 – the date of the medium term plan – was too remote a target.

[1] No. 41.   [2] See No. 1, note 7.

4. There would be chaos in Germany unless we could prepare some organisation capable of maintaining order in an emergency. Moreover the psychological effect upon opinion in Allied countries would be bad if no means could be found of enabling the Germans to participate in the defence of their own country.

5. After reciting the present proposals of the United Kingdom, France and Benelux countries for increases in their own forces,[3] Mr. Shinwell stated that it was clear that further help in the form of a United States contribution would be needed to produce an adequate defence force. On the question of German participation, the present issue was not how German units were to be formed, organised and integrated with the North Atlantic Pact defence forces, but the simple question whether, as and when these forces were built up, German units should be incorporated with them. Were we not agreed that while German military units should not be created now, they would be essential at some stage and would have to be provided, subject always to appropriate control and safeguards? If so, could agreement not be reached upon a formula that clearly indicated the intention of the three governments to use every possible means of defence, including the examination now of the possibility of using German units at some later stage. If no solution of this problem could be found now, the result would merely be to create an atmosphere of despair and defeatism in Europe.

6. General Marshall agreed with my remarks on the importance of maintaining the present momentum and with Mr. Shinwell's on the importance of the time factor. From his past experience he was well aware of the time needed to form and equip military units: he was satisfied that if a decision were taken now to create German units, by the time they were in being production in the United States would have increased to such a point that no problem would arise over their equipment. But if the necessary production plans were to be made, and in particular, if authority were to be secured from Congress for the appropriation of the necessary funds, there was no time to be lost. If a decision of principle were delayed until late in 1951 no practical results could be achieved until the end of 1952. He understood the French Government's difficulties with their public opinion in view of Communist clamour, but if they were not able to take the necessary decision of principle now, it was up to them to say what they thought could be done, in order to enable a start to be made.

7. M. Moch, after pointing out that the objection to the idea of German divisions was held unanimously by all sections of public opinion and by no means only by the Communists, asked if General Marshall could tell him:

(1) How many German divisions the United States Government had in mind;

(2) How many United States divisions they proposed to send to Europe, and

[3] See No. 1, note 3.

94

(3) When the United States divisions would be sent.

This information would be necessary if the French Government were to bring themselves and French public opinion to face the prospect of German divisions at some future date.

8. At my suggestion it was agreed that the replies to M. Moch's questions should be given to him at a private meeting of the three Defence Ministers.

9. M. Schuman asked what practical steps would follow if a decision of principle in favour of the participation of German units were taken. Mr. Acheson replied that such a decision was highly desirable in the United States to persuade Congress to vote further funds for European defence, and in Germany to enable a start to be made with discussions with the German Federal Government on ways and means of forming the units in due course.

10. Mr. Shinwell asked whether there was not agreement that ultimately German units would be needed. M. Schuman said that he could not agree to this at the present stage. For the moment, the French Government could agree to a German contribution only in the form of production and labour. They could not agree to discussing the question of German units for, say, another nine months.

11. In reply to my request for elucidation, M. Schuman explained that a delay of nine months would enable the French Government to see what progress had been made towards the strengthening, equipping, and integration of existing Allied forces, and would also allow for the necessary preparation of the ground with parliamentary and public opinion. If the French Government were to take a decision now, before Parliament reassembled on the 17th October, their position would be untenable. Moreover, if Parliament subsequently disapproved the decision, further progress might be delayed for an indefinite period.

12. Mr. Acheson recalled that a decision had already been taken to authorise the three High Commissioners to explore the question of German participation with the German Federal Chancellor.[4] M. Schuman agreed, but said that these discussions were to be purely exploratory, so that the three governments might be informed what Dr. Adenauer had in mind, and were not to be regarded as based upon any decision whatever by the three governments.

13. Mr. Acheson pointed out that there were many details related to the concept of German participation which called for further examination: for instance, the size of the units and how they were to be raised, organised, officered, etc. We must try to move near enough towards a meeting of minds to enable such examination to proceed. If the French Government could not take any decision of principle now, that must be accepted. But if on the other hand, the French attitude remained purely negative, no progress could be made. It was thereupon agreed that the

[4] See No. 26.ii.

meeting should adjourn while the three Ministers of Defence met alone without advisers to discuss the matter further.[5]

14. Upon resumption M. Moch announced that Mr. Marshall had outlined ten measures proposed by the United States Chiefs of Staff.[6] After consulting M. Schuman, he was able to say that the French Government could agree to them all.

15. Mr. Acheson said that while this marked a decided step forward, decisions on the creation of an integrated force in Europe and on German participation in such a force could not be put behind us entirely. A resolution on all these matters must be prepared for the North Atlantic Council.

16. I said that, while I understood from what Mr. Shinwell had told me that the ten points seemed generally acceptable, it would be necessary [to examine them to consider what points, if any, could be made public and][7] to set them all down in a document or documents which might be prepared by the Deputies. It would be necessary to proceed cautiously before deciding to make all our plans for Germany known to the North Atlantic Council. In principle, however, I should see no objection, if Mr. Acheson, as chairman, were privately to inform certain members of the Council, such as Messieurs Stikker, Van Zeeland, Bech and Lange,[8] of

[5] Commenting on discussions up to this adjournment on 22 September, Air Marshal Elliot added in COJA 128 that 'Tripartite Talks prior to the tea interval did not result in the gap between the American and French positions over German participation in Western Defence being in any way closed. Indeed, as was anticipated, the intervention of M. Moch served only to lay greater emphasis upon the French attitude which continued to be a refusal to admit now the principle of the participation of German armed units in the integrated force but laid emphasis on the harnessing of German labour, manpower and economic resources for defence purposes. M. Moch mentioned, in particular, German contributions to the production of raw materials and the provision of a labour force and he came forward again with the half baked proposal already made by M. Schuman [No. 35.i.] that a German labour force should be specifically employed for the building of airfields, minefields, barbed wire entanglements and other "Fortifications" in Germany' (C 6137/27/18).

[6] In COJA 128 Air Marshal Elliot reported that when the Defence Ministers met privately 'General Marshall quoted extracts from a document which had been hurriedly prepared the day before by the American Chiefs of Staff, themselves and which sought to enumerate the steps which, in the American view, could be taken immediately to secure German participation in Western defence.' Sir P. Dixon further explained in New York telegram No. 1169 that 'the proposals which Marshall put forward appear to be fundamentally different from the proposals which Acheson has been urging on us all hitherto. We are not yet entirely clear what these new proposals precisely amount to, but it seems that the Americans have substantially accepted the French view that no decision regarding the formation of German military units can be taken at present and are prepared to confine themselves to arming the police and building up and extending the functions of the German labour units. It is not yet clear whether their idea is that the Police should be formed into cadres which might form the basis of eventual military units. 3. The Americans in fact appear to have altered the ingredients of the "packet". This sudden change of front visibly took Acheson and other members of the American delegation aback' (C 6107/27/18).

[7] Text in square brackets is inserted from an amendment slip attached to this telegram.

[8] MM. J. Bech and H.M. Lange were respectively Luxembourg and Norwegian Ministers for Foreign Affairs.

what we had in mind.

17. It was agreed that the Deputies should meet in the evening to draw up appropriate documents for consideration by the six Ministers the following morning.[9]

Foreign Office please repeat to Paris and Immediate to Wahnerheide as my telegrams Nos. 28 and 32 respectively.

[9] At the meeting of officials on the evening of 22 September the Americans produced a paper summarizing the steps outlined by General Marshall to which the Defence Ministers had agreed. The text of this paper, as amended by the British and French delegations at the meeting, is printed at No. 43. Sir P. Dixon reported that at this meeting 'it emerged that a difference of opinion still exists between Americans and French on question whether a decision is to be taken *now* on eventual formation of German military units. 2. French maintained that they had not accepted this principle and that M. Moch had only agreed to the other steps (affecting police, labour units etc.) being taken on the understand[ing] that question of eventual formation of military units was left quite open for the time being. 3. Americans for their part said that their understanding was that M. Moch had agreed to the other steps being taken as a preliminary to the formation of German military units. 4. Question will no doubt be fully discussed by the six Ministers, at 10 a.m. on 23rd September' (New York telegram No. 1170 on C 6108/27/18).

No. 43

Sir G. Jebb (New York) to Mr. Attlee
(Received 23 September, 12.55 p.m.)

No. 1171 Telegraphic[1] [C 6109/27/18]

Immediate. Top secret   NEW YORK, 23 September 1950, 5.58 a.m.

Repeated to Wahnerheide, Paris, Washington.

My immediately preceding telegram.[2] Tripartite talks: German contribution to Western Defence.

Following is text of paper.

(*Begins*).

The three Foreign Ministers are agreed that certain minimum measures should be taken immediately in Germany [as steps toward the attainment of their eventual objective of the creation of German units to serve within the integrated force for the defence of Europe].[3]

These measures are as follows:

[1] Amended copy: see note 6 below.   [2] See No. 42, note 9.

[3] Passages in square brackets were reserved by French officials at the meeting on the evening of 22 September. In the final text, agreed by the Foreign and Defence Ministers in private session on 23 September (see note 9 and No. 44), this first sentence was replaced by: 'At a joint meeting of the three Foreign Ministers and Defence Ministers it was agreed that certain minimum measures should be taken immediately in Germany as steps towards a fuller participation of Germany in the build-up of the defence of Europe' (amendments transmitted in New York telegram No. 1181 of 23 September on C 6111/27/18).

A. The immediate strengthening of the West German Laender Police as agreed by the Foreign Ministers, to make them capable of preserving internal security against Soviet-inspired[4] disorders or sabotage. They should be equipped with automatic hand arms, light and heavy machine guns, hand grenades, and mortars. They should further have light armoured and engineer units with necessary equipment and should be fully motorised so as to ensure sufficient mobility. In addition, they would be used in the event of any East German para-military attack.

B. Increase the strength and improve the quality, morale, discipline and training of the 'Dienstgruppen' (labour service units). German personnel for these units should be selected with view to the formation of cadres for units up to a regiment. [The purpose of the cadres would be to form the nucleus of units to be contributed eventually by Germany to the European defence forces and to provide the skeleton of organisations to be filled in by volunteers in the event of emergency].[5]

C. Authorise the Allied High Commissioners and the Military Commanders to make additional use of German manpower as follows:

1. The establishment of sabotage security units for protection against fifth column activity and sabotage.

2. The establishment of a civil defence organisation which would provide for air defence and disaster plans and organisation.

3.[6] Authorise the organisation of appropriate German engineer units to include minelaying and fortification construction units.

In addition, plans should be completed now for the eventual utilisation for the benefit of the common defence programme of the West of the industrial potential of Western Germany in the production of finished light military equipment only, to include, subject to appropriate safeguards, such items as individual equipment [light weapons],[7] vehicles and transportation equipment, and optical equipment. However, West Germany should not be restricted from producing [subject to existing

[4] 'Soviet-inspired' was deleted in the final text (New York telegram 1181).

[5] This sentence was omitted in the final text (New York telegram 1181).

[6] In the original text of this telegram, not preserved in Foreign Office archives, this was numbered 4. Sub-para. 3 read: 'The establishment of a guerilla warfare organization and the initiation of procurement of supplies for guerilla warfare in Russian-held areas' (F.R.U.S. 1950, vol. iv, p. 724). On Mr. Bevin's instructions, issued from New York on 26 September, telegram 1171 was withdrawn from circulation, and sub-para. 3 deleted. Sub-para. 4 was renumbered 3 and the present amended text re-circulated. Similar treatment was given to the reference to guerilla warfare in Air Marshal Elliot's parallel telegram to the Chiefs of Staff (COJA 128, for which see No. 42, notes 5–6). On 26 September Mr. Bevin informed the Foreign Office that he had secured French and American agreement to this deletion on security grounds and that French and American texts were being similarly expurgated. He explained that old paragraph C3 now stood 'as a purely oral agreement between the three Governments' (New York telegram 1216 on C 6169/27/18).

[7] Square brackets in this and the next paragraph were deleted in the final text.

agreements as to the production of steel][7] raw materials for fabrication outside Germany into heavy military equipment for N.A.T.O. forces and German army units.[8]

It is further agreed that, as N.A.T.O. forces are equipped and deployed, the initial measures outlined above should be accelerated [in order to more quickly attain the eventual objective].[7]

(*Ends*).[9]

Please repeat to Wahnerheide (Immediate) and Paris as my telegrams Nos. 35 and 30 respectively.

[8] 'and German army units' was omitted in the final text.

[9] The amended wording of the paper above was agreed by the Foreign and Defence Ministers in a restricted meeting on the morning of 23 September. The final and unexpurgated text is printed in *F.R.U.S. 1950*, vol. iv, pp. 723–4. When Ministers returned to full session after two hours, Mr. Acheson announced their agreement and stated that he and General Marshall 'had made it clear that the entire scheme must be regarded as constituting a single whole and that the United States would have difficulty in carrying it out so long as the German problem remained unsettled' (New York telegram No. 1181).

No. 44

United Kingdom Delegation (New York) to Ministry of Defence
(Received 24 September, 7 a.m.)

COJA 129 Telegraphic [*WU 1198/430*]

Emergency. Top secret　　　　　　　　NEW YORK, *23 September 1950, 9.57 p.m.*

For Price from Elliot for Chiefs of Staff.
Further to my COJA 128.[1]

The six Ministers met this morning without officials in an attempt to narrow the gap which still exists between the American and French position over German participation in Western Defence. At this meeting the French continued to maintain the position which they have taken up since the beginning of the discussions in New York of refusing to accept the inclusion in any document – even if it is secret as between the Three Tripartite Ministers – of any form of words which implies their acceptance of the principle of a German rearmament. But the document referred to in paragraph 2 of my COJA 128 which was produced by the Americans in an attempt to meet the French point of view has had to be emasculated of all reference to the possible creation of German armed units. Its full and original text and subsequent amendments are set out in New York telegrams 1171 and 1181.[2] In its amended form the document has been turned into a formal Tripartite Agreement which is to be secret as between the three Powers. Its terms however will be explained orally by Mr. Acheson to the three Benelux Foreign Ministers and to Mr. Lange

[1] See No. 42, notes 5–6.　　　　　　　　[2] See No. 43 and notes 3–9.

(Norway) and Mr. Rasmussen (Denmark) all of whom have, understandably, shown a special interest in the question of German rearmament.

2. Meanwhile that part of the American 'packet' which relates to the integrated force and to a command and staff structure are being drafted in the form of a resolution to be placed before the meeting of the North Atlantic Council on Tuesday 26th September. The text of this resolution as originally drafted is set out in New York telegram No. 398 Saving of the 20th September.[3] That part of the resolution which relates to the embodiment of German units into the integrated force has had to be amended and the amended text is contained in New York telegram No. 1182.[3]

3. It has been agreed by Mr. Marshall, Mr. Shinwell and M. Moch that the North Atlantic Defence Committee fixed for 16th October be postponed until 28th October. This postponement is for two reasons

1. To see whether the French are able by then to accept the principle of German rearmament and
2. To give the Standing Group more time to carry out the detailed work necessary to enable the Defence Committee to reply to the requests contained in the resolution[3] referred to in paragraph 2 above.

4. As you see it has thus not been possible to obtain French agreement to accept the principle of German rearmament and therefore the whole content of the American 'packet' is in danger. Nevertheless the Americans have agreed that we should proceed on the assumption that the 'packet' will eventually be accepted in its entirety and for military staffs on that assumption to undertake immediately the elaboration of those parts of the 'packet' which are not concerned with German rearmament.

5. Since much of the success or otherwise of the meeting of the Defence Committee of 28th October will depend on work which will be done in the interval by the Standing Group I propose, with the Ministers concurrence, after seeing the resolution through the Council at its meeting on Tuesday to fly to Washington in order to put Lord Tedder in the picture. I saw him yesterday but only for half an hour in the middle of meetings. This will mean that I shall not leave New York for London until Friday or Saturday next at the earliest.[4]

[3] Neither the first draft of the N.A.C. draft resolution, referred to in No. 35, note 5 and transmitted in New York telegram No. 398 Saving (WU 1198/427), nor subsequent amendments transmitted in New York telegram No. 1182 on 23 September (C 6112/27/18) are printed: for final text, see No. 47.
[4] The American proposals and position reached, as reported in COJA 128–9, were discussed by the Chiefs of Staff on 25 September. The proposal to strengthen the Laender police rather than arm a Federal police as part of an integrated force was considered 'not militarily sound'. However, the Chiefs of Staff agreed that a start could be made with the raising and organizing of the forces. On 27 September the whole package was referred by the Chiefs of Staff to the Joint Planning Staff for further study: see No. 60, note 9.

No. 45

Sir I. Kirkpatrick (Wahnerheide) to Mr. Attlee
(Received 24 September, 1.45 a.m.)

No. *1418 Telegraphic* [C 6102/20/18]

Priority. *Confidential*   WAHNERHEIDE, *23 September 1950, 11.30 p.m.*

Repeated to Washington, Paris, New York.

My immediately preceding telegram.[1]

After Poncet had concluded his statement the Chancellor replied briefly. He began by expressing his warmest thanks for the statement which he said had increased the weight and importance of the Foreign Ministers' communiqué.[2] Though not all German wishes had been fulfilled to the extent to which they had been made they existed as [*sic*][3] expectations. (He said the same to Lord Henderson yesterday.) He was especially pleased at the full and water-tight character of the security guarantee which he said would combine [with] American successes in Korea greatly to reassure public opinion. He was also pleased at the reference to the unity of Germany. He understood the connexion between the existence of a state of war and the Occupation Statute. It was quite clear why the transition would have to be made step by step. As regards the police, he would have to talk to the Land Government(s) and hoped that a workable system would be arrived at but he was grateful for the offer of assistance in case of difficulty. In particular he agreed with McCloy, who had previously drawn attention to the need for purging the existing regular police.

2. As regards the further contents of the communiqué, he asked to be excused from commenting today, in particular on the question of the debts. These matters, he said, would need to be discussed in the Cabinet. At the same time he welcomed the proposal to set up Joint Committee(s) for the study of the various items in the Foreign Ministers' decision and agreed with McCloy's proposal that he should place a high-ranking member of the Government in charge of the conversations generally on the German side.

---

[1] This telegram, calendared at i below, contained the text of a statement made by M. François-Poncet, as Chairman of the A.H.C., at a meeting between the A.H.C. and Dr. Adenauer on 23 September in which Dr. Adenauer was informed of the New York decisions on Germany. Also present at this meeting were Herr H. Blankenhorn, Ministerial Director at the Federal Chancellery, and Dr. L. Erhard, Minister for Economic Affairs.

[2] See No. 26.ii.

[3] 'Existed as' appears to be a transmission error for 'exceeded his'. This was what Dr. Adenauer said to Lord Henderson at lunch on the previous day (see calendar ii). The corresponding passage of the verbatim minutes of this meeting reads 'it was true that it had not been possible to give immediate satisfaction to all the wishes of the Federal Government, but he [Dr. Adenauer] felt bound to state that the final decisions had gone beyond German expectations' (C 6454/4546/18).

3. At the close he said he regretted that he had one less agreeable matter to raise, this was Law 27.[4] He complained that in the drafting of the implementing regulations no German authority whatsoever had been consulted and that the Allies were proceeding to the liquidation of the various enterprises before having made any provision for a substitute organisation. Poncet, on our behalf, undertook that the Economic Advisers would go into the matter with Erhardt.

4. In the few words which I for my part appended to Poncet's main statement, I drew attention to the Secretary of State's conviction of the importance of the present stage in our relations and told the Chancellor how much Mr. Bevin hoped that the Federal Government and all concerned would devote themselves wholeheartedly to the success of the policy on which we were now embarking. The Chancellor replied that we could rely on him and the Federal Government to make a success of the present stage. In taking his leave, the Chancellor again thanked us very warmly for our personal efforts and the meeting closed on a most cordial note.

5. After the meeting I impressed on Blankenhorn the importance of getting a satisfactory assurance about Germany's financial obligations. He replied that the Chancellor had already resolved to meet us on this point, but he must carry his Cabinet. The Chancellor repeated to me that the Secretary of State could rely on him to play his part during the forthcoming stage.[5]

Foreign Office please pass to Washington, Paris and New York (U.K. Del.) as my telegrams Nos. 165, 202 and 22 respectively.

---

[4] Allied High Commission Law No. 27 set out the principles for the liquidation of the old German coal, iron and steel combines and the reorganisation of these combines into new companies (*D.G.O.*, pp. 335–43, 490–2). Negotiations were in progress between the A.H.C. and the Federal Government for the implementation of this Law promulgated on 16 May 1950 (see Volume I, No. 202 for the position in January 1951).

[5] On 26 September Sir I. Kirkpatrick reported that at lunch that day Dr. Adenauer had asked when would the Allied High Commission receive instructions 'to get to grips with him' on the question of a German contribution to defence. Dr. Adenauer warned that 'the longer a decision were delayed the more time there would be for the many opponents of German rearmament in any form to get to work and the more difficult it would be for him to get parliamentary support for German participation in an integrated force if this were the wish of the Western Powers ... I told him that as he would see from M. François-Poncet's statement we already had instructions to discuss the matter of the German contribution in a general way, but I did not know when we should be authorised to go further than this. I would, however, like to put a personal non-committal question to him. What would be his answer if we invited him to raise a German contingent for an integrated army. He replied that, provided this German contingent was admitted on exactly the same footing as any other contingent, he would personally agree without any further condition. Under cross-examination he said that Germany would not require a strategic air force but that she would ask that the German contingent would have the same weapons, the same staff arrangements and the same air support as any other contingent' (Wahnerheide telegram No. 1429 on C 6170/27/18).

i *23 Sept. 1950   A.H.C. statement of New York decisions on Germany* as given to Dr. Adenauer by A.H.C. chairman (Wahnerheide telegram No. 1417). Allied position explained on termination state of war; introduction of occupation regime on a contractual basis (Allies still against); external and internal security (question of German participation in Western defence to be discussed later with Chancellor); relaxations and revision of Occupation Statute; conduct of foreign affairs; economic relaxations; control of legislation [C 6101/20/18].

ii *7 Oct. 1950   Report by Lord Henderson of his visit to Bonn, North Rhine Westphalia and Berlin from 21 Sept.–2 Oct.*, records discussions with Dr. Adenauer, Dr. Schumacher and other leading German politicians and trade unionists. General reaction to New York favourable. Even Dr. Schumacher though 'cagey' appeared more satisfied than prepared to admit publicly. Henderson impressed by strength of S.P.D. feeling against any attempt to mould police force as embryo army: Mr. Bevin instructs 'See me Monday morning, I must refer to this at the Cabinet': cf. Nos. 58 and 60, note 17 [C 6464/2/18].

No. 46

Sir G. Jebb (New York) to Mr. Attlee
(Received 26 September, 11.15 a.m.)

No. 1204 Telegraphic [*WU 1198/467*]

Priority. Top secret   NEW YORK, *26 September 1950, 12.17 a.m.*

Repeated to Paris, Wahnerheide, and Saving to Washington.

Following from Secretary of State.
My telegram No. 1181.[1]
Tripartite talks. Defence of Western Europe.
It may be useful if I attempt to assess the position we have now reached and estimate what our future course of action should be.

2. The French finally agreed to a form of words in the Tripartite Top Secret Agreement which could be read as implying that the measures for the strengthening of the German Police, etc., are only minimum preliminary steps towards the participation of Germany in the defence of Europe by means of military units. M. Schuman and M. Moch made it clear in discussion, however, that the French Government are at present not in a position to consider, even in principle, the creation of German military units and that all they have agreed to are the measures regarding the police etc. They held out some hope that after the meeting of the French Chamber later this month[2] the French Government may find themselves freer to discuss the creation of German units and their participation in Western defence, and it was with this idea in mind that Mr. Acheson and General Marshall proposed that the meeting of the

---

[1] See No. 43, notes 3–9.   [2] See No. 25, note 2.

N.A.T.O. Defence Committee should be postponed to October 28th in order to give the French Government time to bring Parliamentary opinion round.

3. While I do not doubt that M. Moch's Parliamentary difficulties are genuine and that he would have a hard task to persuade the French Socialist Party to accept German rearmament, my impression is that these difficulties are a pretext and that the real trouble is that the present French Government or certainly M. Moch himself, is fundamentally opposed to the conception of rearming Germany. M. Moch revealed his mind very frankly on the subject at a dinner on September 23rd given for him and the Minister of Defence by the Americans, where he was 'grilled' by Findletter,[3] Spofford and Jessup. A note of the discussion is being sent to the Chiefs of Staff by Air Marshal Elliot who was present.[4]

4. To turn now to the American position; Acheson and Marshall finally deferred to the French contention that all they were in a position to accept now was the immediate institution of measures to strengthen the German Police etc., and they agreed to insert words in the documents to paper over the cracks. They made it plain, however, that taking M. Moch's Parliamentary difficulties at their face value, they expected the French to be more forthcoming about German rearmament at the meeting of the Defence Committee, their view being that in the interval M. Moch should have been able to bring his party into line. Meanwhile the Americans indicated that the whole defence plan was to be regarded as in suspense, and insisted on words to that effect being written into the draft resolution for the N.A. Council.[5]

[3] Mr. T.K. Finletter was U.S. Secretary of the Air Force.

[4] The account sent by Air Marshal Elliot in COJA 134A of this dinner-party conversation was largely concerned with a long explanation from M. Moch of the 'psychological factor' in French opposition to German rearmament: 'France within the last three generations had been invaded three times by Germany. On the last occasion she had been occupied. She had a common frontier with that enemy. A geographical fact which inevitably made Frenchmen feel and think differently from those who were separated from the Germans by a channel or an ocean. The case for rearming the Germans, however rational on purely military grounds, lost sight of the moral forces . . . The French feared the threat present in such a revival [of German militarism] more than they did the Russians. (This was a flaw in Monsieur Moch's argument. Tackled later by Mr. Shinwell he recanted, admitting an actual Russian menace to be greater than a hypothetical German bogey, but maintained that the former would not be serious for two years, by which time the latter might be still more serious). Once we decided to re-arm the Germans we would be starting a process over which we would very quickly lose control. For every German division which we created, we should need two of our own to supervise it. If and when war came, the Germans would betray us . . . With great emphasis Monsieur Moch said that the views which he had expressed were not personal. They were those of all his colleagues in the French Cabinet.' In private conversation with Air Marshal Elliot afterwards M. Moch 'went on to declare that if the Americans insisted on making German re-armament a condition of the acceptance of the help which they were offering, he would prefer to forego both, and content himself with five instead of ten French divisions, and place these on the French Frontier instead of in Germany' (WU 1198/481).

[5] See No. 47.

5. Thus we seem likely to drift into a highly unsatisfactory position where the French maintain their opposition to what the Americans regard as an essential feature of the whole defence plan, and the Americans in consequence are unwilling to start on other features of the plan. If the meeting of the Defence Committee were to result in the same impasse being reached, I should be very apprehensive of Americans' reactions. They might well lose heart.

6. The question then arises whether there is anything we can do to stop this ugly drift. The obvious course is for us to bring the maximum pressure on the French to state their agreement at the meeting of the Defence Committee to the principle of German rearmament. But I fear that for the reasons I have given we should be beating against a brick wall.

7. Should we not therefore represent to the Americans that in their present mood the French seem unlikely to agree to accept the principle of German rearmament, and try to persuade them to proceed vigorously with the rest of the plan? This would mean in effect that steps for establishing the integrated force would start as soon as the Defence Committee had worked out the details, and the Americans would proceed with their plans for the despatch of divisions to Europe. So far as a German contribution was concerned, we would make the most effective possible use of the agreed provisions regarding the build up of the police. Dientsgruppen, etc., leaving ourselves free to reopen the question of German rearmament with the French later on. If by next summer the French had some fully equipped divisions of their own, and if more foreign and above all more American divisions were by then stationed on the continent, the French would find it much more difficult to maintain their opposition to a start being made on rearming the Germans, since their argument has been that Germany must not be more strongly armed than France.

8. The Americans seem to have made their minds up that the job cannot be done unless they can fight on German soil with a Germany helping to defend it, and the question is whether they will take the risk of going in now without being sure that they can use the Germans if the battle starts. It is very much in the interests of all of us that they should forge ahead now while maintaining pressure on the French to agree to German rearmament. The Administration will certainly be under considerable political compulsion to go ahead. The President's declared intention to send more American divisions to Europe and the amount of information which has been given or leaked to the press about the intended defence of Europe will make it difficult for them to admit failure to reach agreement on a plan, and Acheson personally would be in a difficult position if he had to admit so near to the elections[6] that the bottom of the Administration's defence policy for Europe had fallen out.[7]

[6] Mid-term Congressional elections were held on 7 November.

[7] This telegram was the subject of extensive minuting within the Foreign Office (calendar i). Arguments deployed by Mr. Shuckburgh in favour of continuing to support the defence

Please repeat to Paris and Wahnerheide as my telegrams Nos. 34 and 40 respectively.

CALENDAR TO NO. 46

i *27 Sept.–4 Oct. 1950 F.O. minutes* (see note 7) on future tactics. Dangers of abandoning whole defence package for 'roundabout means' of securing German defence contribution through building up police and Dienstgruppen pointed out by Mr. Shuckburgh on 27 Sept. Furthermore this would go against Mr. Bevin's desire to keep internal German security separate from external defence. F.O. agree on desirability of applying pressure to French govt. Warning sounded by Mr. G.P. Young, Head of Western department, on 2 Oct. about weakness of present French govt: acceptance of German rearmament could lead to its fall. Advises delaying démarche for month or so to give M. Pleven time to consolidate his Parliamentary position and when 'there will be less likelihood of our finding ourselves landed with an even more unsatisfactory French Government' [WU 1198/467–8].

plan as a whole and making further attempts to win over the French, rather than press the Americans to proceed with only part of the plan were accepted by Mr. Davies, Sir D. Gainer and Sir R. Makins. Mr. Davies commented 'As regards the Americans it may well be that the Secretary of State's apprehension will not be justified. America is so far committed that I cannot see withdrawal and to put pressure on her now might have harmful results. After all it is the French and not the Americans who are holding back and it is they who need to be worked on.' It was agreed that the question of whether to press the French or not should await the return of Mr. Bevin from New York. Meanwhile action was set in train for obtaining the views of H.M. representatives at Wahnerheide and Paris.

No. 47

Sir G. Jebb (New York) to Mr. Attlee
(Received 27 September, 5.8 p.m.)

No. 1222 Telegraphic [*WU 1198/445*]

Secret   NEW YORK, *27 September 1950, 5.35 a.m.*

Repeated to Wahnerheide, and Saving to Paris, Washington.

Following from Secretary of State.
My immediately preceding telegram.[1]
Following is text of resolution on integrated force as finally approved by Council:

The North Atlantic Council:
Having fully discussed the measures taken and planned for the defence of Western Europe:

[1] This telegram, calendared at i below, gave an account of the N.A.C. meeting on the afternoon of 26 September when the resolution printed below was approved.

And

Noting the resolution of the Council Deputies concerning the adequacy of such measures and agreeing with the Deputies' conclusions that the aggregate of the efforts so far reported are still far short of the requirements for the defence of Western Europe;

Concludes:

That the defence of Western Europe will require:

(a) the establishment at the earliest possible date of an integrated force under centralised command and control composed of forces made available by Governments for the defence of Western Europe;

(b) the full utilisation of manpower and productive resources available from all sources;

Approves:

The concept of an integrated force adequate to deter aggression and ensure the defence of Western Europe, including Western Germany,

Agrees:

That such an integrated force shall be established at the earliest possible date, and that the composition, organisation and command of such force shall be based upon the following principles:

1. The force shall be organised under the North Atlantic Treaty Organisation and shall be subject to political and strategic guidance exercised by the appropriate agencies of the North Atlantic Treaty.

2. The force shall be under the command of a Supreme Commander. The geographic limits of his command in peace time shall be clearly defined. He will in peace time have sufficient delegated authority to ensure that the National units allocated to his command are organised and trained into an effective integrated force. He will exercise the full powers of a Supreme Commander in the event of war.

3. The Supreme Commander shall be appointed as soon as there is assurance that National forces will be made available for the integrated force adequate to enable the latter to be reasonably capable of fulfilling its responsibilities.

4. Pending the appointment of a Supreme Commander, there shall be appointed forthwith a Chief of Staff who shall be responsible, and be endowed with the necessary authority, for the organisation and training of forces made available by the National Governments.

5. The Supreme Commander, and pending his appointment the Chief of Staff, shall be provided with combined international staff drawn from the Nationals of all nations contributing to the force. The first task of the staff should be to plan and take the measures necessary to implement the organisation of the integrated force.

6. The integrated force should be composed of National units. Governments concerned should make firm commitments at the earliest

possible date as to the forces to be placed under the control of the Supreme Commander in peacetime, including the date upon which they will be placed under his control, and as to the additional forces which will initially be placed under his command in the event of war.

7. The Standing Group shall be responsible for higher strategic direction in areas in which combined North Atlantic Treaty forces are operating. As such it will be the superior military body to which the Supreme Commander, and pending his appointment the Chief of Staff, will be responsible. It will also determine the military requirements of the integrated force.

Requests:

That the Defence Committee consider and recommend to the Council as a matter of urgency:

A. The detailed steps necessary to establish the integrated force in accordance with the foregoing principles.

B. The powers to be exercised by the Supreme Commander in peacetime and the geographic limits within which he should exercise them.

C. The method and timing of contributions by Governments of National units in being to the integrated force.

D. The further authority, if any, which the Standing Group would require so as to ensure effective discharge of its responsibilities and also what adjustments in its organisation and its present relations with the accredited representatives may be required to assure and improve the necessary close working relationship between the Standing Group and the member governments not represented on it.

E. The consequent changes and simplifications required in the existing military structure of the North Atlantic Treaty Organisation and related military organisations.

F. The channel by which the higher direction of the integrated force as regards political considerations upon which strategic decisions should be based, can most effectively be conveyed by the Council to the military agencies of the North Atlantic Treaty Organisation.

Further states:

That it has considered the question of the nature, extent and timing of German participation in the build up of the defence of Western Europe, and has noted that this matter is now under discussion by the three Occupying Powers with the German Federal Government. Since in the view of many of the Ministers the proper and early solution of this problem is intimately connected with the successful implementation of the plan outlined above, that plan is not finalised at this time.

Accordingly requests:

The Defence Committee in the light of the information available at the time of its meeting, to make specific recommendations regarding the method by which, from the technical point of view, Germany could make its most useful contribution to the successful implementation of the plan, bearing in mind the unanimous conclusion of the Council that it would not serve the best interests of Europe or of Germany to bring into being a German National Army or a German General Staff.[2]

Please repeat to Wahnerheide as my telegram No. 43 and to Paris as my telegram No. 198 Saving.

CALENDARS TO NO. 47

i *26 Sept. 1950 N.A.C. Meeting* summarized in N.Y. tel. No. 1221: approval of resolution on integrated force. Statements from Denmark, Norway, Portugal of basic support for plan. Drafting contributions from U.K., France, Italy, Netherlands and Canada [WU 1198/437].

ii *29 Sept. 1950f. F.O. assessment of N.A.C. resolution:* F.O. minutes consider rôles of Defence Committee, Standing Group and Supreme Commander [WU 1198/445].

[2] The main points of this resolution, also printed in *F.R.U.S. 1950*, vol. iii, pp. 350–2, formed the substance of the communiqué issued by the N.A.C. after its meeting on 26 September and fully reported in *The Times* on the following day.

No. 48

Mr. Attlee to Sir I. Kirkpatrick (Wahnerheide)

No. 1575 Telegraphic [*WU 1198/467*]

Priority. Top secret FOREIGN OFFICE, *27 September 1950, 11.10 p.m.*

Repeated to New York.

United Kingdom Delegation New York telegram No. 1204.[1]

There now appear to be three possible ways in which the main German contribution (apart from such relatively minor matters as industrial assistance and auxiliary contingents in our service) can be made.

(*a*) A German contingent in an integrated force.
(*b*) A German gendarmerie armed up to the standard mentioned in New York telegram No. 1171,[2] organised on a Land basis.
(*c*) The same as (*b*) but organised on a Federal basis.

2. In considering which of these courses we accept or work for in further discussions with our Allies before October 28th the advantages of the respective courses from the purely German point of view cannot be decisive. But the German aspect will be of very great importance, and I shall therefore be grateful if you will let me have urgently an appreciation, prepared in consultation with the Commanders-in-Chief Committee,[3] on

[1] No. 46.   [2] No. 43.   [3] See No. 2, note 8.

the above question. You might cover the following points:

(a) which of the three courses mentioned above would be most acceptable to

    (i) Adenauer,

    (ii) Schumacher,

    (iii) German public opinion in general?[4]

(b) Which course presents the most serious constitutional obstacles and is this a factor to which we ought to attach serious importance?[5]

(c) Assuming the same numerical strength throughout, how do you rate for purposes of effective action in an emergency the three forces mentioned above?[6]

(d) On the same assumption, how long would it take to make each of these forces operationally efficient?[7]

(e) Which form of force would be likely to foster the least desirable political elements in Germany?

(f) Over which force would we be likely to be able to exert the most effective and long-lasting measure of control?[8]

3. Please state also whether in your opinion we are likely to be able to build up military effectives in the guise of auxiliaries to any appreciable extent on the lines mentioned in New York telegram No. 1171[2] without political trouble.[9]

[4] In his reply to these specific questions, transmitted in Wahnerheide telegram No. 1447 of 30 September, Sir I. Kirkpatrick stated that 'Adenauer would prefer the first course . . . Schumacher could probably be brought to accept the first course. But he would categorically reject the other two. He has already in public and private voiced his fear that the intention is to use the police force as cover for an army . . . If the German contingent were initially so small that conscription were not required, it would be easier to obtain public support. Courses two and three are acceptable to the broad masses. If however, the public were told that course one would bring political advantages whereas courses two and three would not, they might eventually prefer course one' (C 6262/27/18).

[5] Sir I. Kirkpatrick replied that Parliamentary approval for course one 'might cause difficulty but it presents no constitutional problem'. However, 'account should be taken of the S.P.D. opposition to courses two and three' (Wahnerheide telegram No. 1447).

[6] Sir I. Kirkpatrick considered course one as 'clearly the most effective'.

[7] Sir I. Kirkpatrick estimated 'about a year in each case'.

[8] As regards (e) and (f) Sir I. Kirkpatrick thought that a military force, under the control of an Allied Commander, would be the least dangerous and warned that 'a so-called police force would not in peace-time come under our control'.

[9] With regard to the measures outlined in New York telegram No. 1171 and COJA 128 (No. 42, notes 5–6), Sir I. Kirkpatrick commented (a) on strengthening Länder police: 'trouble with the S.P.D.' (b) on strengthening the Dientsgruppen: 'it is unrealistic to think of them as cadres for potential German infantry regiments' (c i) establishment of sabotage units: 'no objection' (c ii) establishment of civil defence organisation: 'this would be welcomed' (c iii) organization of engineer units: 'there is strong feeling in all parties against the conception of German mercenaries.' In a separate reply of 4 October on the question of what steps were being taken to implement the defence measures which had been agreed at New York, Sir I. Kirkpatrick reported the establishment of an Allied–German committee to work out the practical details (Wahnerheide telegram No. 1454 on C 6352/27/18: quoted in No. 60).

No. 49

Memorandum by Sir O. Franks (Washington)[1]

[UE 11914/106]

Secret   WASHINGTON, 27 September 1950

This short memorandum contains considerations and suggestions which have occurred to me about the situation created by the decisions of H.M.G. in recent months greatly to enlarge the Defence Programme and the American offer of assistance to us in carrying the resultant burden.

At the time of the North Korean aggression the British economy was doing better than could have been hoped at the inception of the European Recovery Programme three years earlier. The internal position was healthy. We had full employment but suffered from neither inflation nor deflation. There was a steady and rapid increase in production and productive efficiency. It had been possible to ease or abolish a number of restrictions on home consumption. The external position was equally satisfactory. On the three months, May, June and July taken together, there was no increase in the sterling balances.[2] In the same period there was a large increase in our reserves of gold and dollars, considerably greater than the amount of aid we received under the European Recovery Programme. We were earning therefore a sizeable surplus on our whole overseas balance of payments. In addition the effort put into the dollar drive was bearing fruit: our exports to North America were breaking records in value as well as volume.

In short, the resolute action of the British Government and people alike, building on aid received under the European Recovery Programme, had made us in mid year 1950 independent of extraordinary outside assistance. Given one assumption which seemed likely to be valid for some time ahead, that the American economy would continue at a high level of activity, there was good reason to believe we should continue to balance our overseas accounts, earn a surplus and consolidate our position. We had won our economic independence and seemed likely to be able to keep it.

The political effects of this achievement were already apparent. As the strength of sterling steadily increased, so did the power and influence of Britain. We no longer had to rest content with the knowledge that we were a great power. We could behave like one, for we were becoming able for

---

[1] Copies of this memorandum were addressed to Mr. Bevin, Mr. Attlee, Mr. Gaitskell and Sir R. Makins. The present copy is the text sent to Mr. Bevin at New York for perusal on his return voyage to England. In his short covering letter to Mr. Bevin, Sir O. Franks explained: 'Since returning from New York I have found myself thinking about American assistance to our Defence Programme and the form it should take. I believe the form of assistance is of great importance.'

[2] In spring 1950 the British war-time debt held in sterling balances amounted to £3,500 millions: for the detailed figures, see Volume II, No. 43.i.

the first time since the war to sustain our world-wide commitments. The visible growth of economic independence gave us weight in the counsels of the nations. Real friendship became easier with the Americans because they were ceasing to have to befriend us.

The aggression of the North Koreans has radically altered this picture. It disclosed a threat to the free world which caused the free nations, particularly those associated in the Atlantic Pact, to take progressively far-reaching steps to increase their defence programmes. H.M.G. has decided upon a three year programme of 3.6 billions sterling, an increase of some 400 millions a year on average above the level of expenditure before the aggression in Korea. This programme as it goes into effect will cause great difficulties to the British economy. Its main impact will be on the overseas balance of payments. When the consequences of the increased defence expenditure of other nations, particularly the vast expenditure decided upon by the United States, are also taken into account, our overseas indebtedness is likely to increase over the three year period by some hundreds of millions sterling. The main problem will not lie with our dollar balance: it will be reflected in the steady increase of sterling balances held by those countries which supply raw materials and to which our exports will be curtailed. This means that the strengthened position of sterling will again be weakened. Our general recovery at best will suffer a grave setback. The tendency on the part of holders of increasing sterling balances may well be to demand dollars from us as they find that we cannot export to them all they would like to buy. We risk re-entering the vicious circle from which we had just escaped.

It is in this context that the United States Government has offered financial assistance, recognising that continuance of economic recovery in the near future, although possibly at a less rapid rate than heretofore, will be essential. After some preliminary talks in London with members of the U.S. Embassy there are now two sets of discussions going on in Washington.[3] The first of these is general in character and is an attempt to elucidate the principles and methods which should be employed in our case and in those of our Western European allies to assess the burden of the new defence programmes on the national economies so that a determination of the amount of American assistance required can be made. These discussions have taken the form of informal exchanges of views preparatory to large scale exercises which would give the American Administration a good case on which to go to the Congress next year. They have considered our three year Defence Programme as a whole and it is evident that some months will elapse before any final results are reached. The second set of discussions is of a shorter term character. Here the exploration has been designed to discover, with reference in the first instance to the two 100 million sterling tranches of Defence Programme expenditure on which H.M.G. have already embarked, the types and extent of financial assistance the American Administration is able and

[3] See No. 11, note 7.

willing to give from the existing appropriations voted under the M.D.A.P. Act. It was decided as the result of a conversation earlier in the month between the Foreign Secretary and Mr. Acheson to push on with these conversations immediately as these two tranches of Defence Programme expenditure contained many of the high priority items urgent production of which was recommended by the Standing Group to the Atlantic Pact Deputies.

Both sets of discussions have made progress at least in the sense of getting the various American Departments and Agencies concerned to meet together and endeavour in conversation with us to formulate a common approach. But they have moved wholly within the orbit of the original offer of American assistance and the subsequent statement of H.M.G. that they were unable to undertake so full a diversion of resources as was required by the three year Defence Programme unless the United States was able to give substantial financial assistance. The original request of H.M.G. was for direct aid to the extent of 550 millions sterling over the three years of the full new Defence Programme. The present discussions with the Americans envisage the receipt of substantial direct aid by Britain over the next three years.

The proud achievement of mid-year 1950 is therefore being reversed. Instead of economic independence we envisage for a further period of years the economic dependence of Britain on the United States. And the new phase of economic dependence will differ from the old in several ways. In the first place it is likely to last longer. If the defence measures of the members of the Atlantic Pact are successful in averting war and ensuring peace, it is still most improbable that the heavy burden of armies and armaments will be suddenly lifted after three years or that defence expenditure will suddenly shrink to something like a pre-Korean level. On the contrary, the prospect is that the burden will remain very heavy for a longer time and therefore that the need for substantial American aid will also be prolonged. Secondly we cannot expect that the American administration of this new period of aid will be as considerate to the recipients as has been the Economic Cooperation Administration. The Americans are spending vast sums themselves on defence; they have already committed themselves to an expenditure of 25 or 30 billion dollars next year. They are planning to increase this to 50 or 60 billion dollars, say, 20% of the national income. They are putting themselves about: they will be the less hesitant to apply the same medicine to those to whom they give aid. Again, the emotions which lie behind present American policies and programmes are stronger than in the case of the European Recovery Programme. These feelings of generosity gave power to the enlightened self-interest of policy: now policy is spurred by fear. The Americans will be less patient of opinions not exactly coincident with their own. Thirdly the very fact that this will be a second period of direct aid will make it harder for giver and recipient alike to complete the transaction gracefully and without bad feeling.

These considerations alone would justify raising the question whether, given that we need American assistance to carry out the Defence Programme, we must necessarily take the assistance in the form of further substantial direct aid. But the political consequences of the position are far more important. It is here that the renewed loss of economic independence strikes hard. Once more we shall lose the position we were just attaining, the partner in world affairs of the United States. We shall be back again in the European Queue as in 1947, one of the countries helped by the United States.[4] This loss of influence and power will reflect itself in many ways. It will make it more difficult to hold the Commonwealth together. It will weaken our position in Europe. It will work to our disadvantage in many negotiations and arrangements to be made in the months ahead. For example we shall find—the tendency is already there—that the Americans are most interested to hear from us our proposals on stockpiling, but they are not willing to tell us what they are doing. Whether we are arguing about the number of divisions we should specify and commit to the defence of Western Europe to serve under the unified command, or about our needs and commitments as a world power outside Western Europe, or about our position in relation to the Americans and our other allies on such matters as a Combined Chiefs of Staff or Combined methods for dealing with defence production or the international supply and distribution of raw materials, we shall not be, or be treated as, partners though of unequal power. All in all, the preservation of good relations between Britain and America would become very difficult for, as all recent American observers have reported, Britain is the only Western European country which dislikes having to receive aid. It is therefore important to ask whether, given that American assistance is needed, it must take the form of direct aid.

The consideration of this question must take into account the fact that we shall be invited to increase further our Defence Programme for the three year period. It is almost certain that American expenditure on defence will far exceed 10% of their national income and they will look at us to match their effort. The root of most of the criticism that has been made here of the British defence effort is that the American Defence Programme that we were matching by our decisions had already been outstripped in American planning and to some extent in American action. But apart from this it was apparent in the Ministerial conversations in New York that the Americans were basing themselves in all phases of the discussion of the defence of Western Europe on the Medium Term Plan now being elaborated for the Atlantic Pact Defence Committee by the Standing Group. It was with reference to this Plan that the Americans were calculating the number of divisions which each member nation should be invited to create, train, specify and commit to the unified command. It was with reference to this Plan that the Americans were working out the contribution that each nation should make to a sufficient

[4] i.e. Marshall Aid: see No. 11, note 3.

defence production. The formula they had provisionally adopted was 170% of the pre-Korean rate of defence expenditure. It was clear that their ultimate decisions on assistance and aid would be made in the light of the performance of individual nations against targets so set up rather than by reference to what each nation had already decided it could do. The Americans followed this line of thought because they held that the Medium Term Plan offered the minimum provision for a satisfactory defence of Western Europe and it was not meaningful therefore to go ahead on any lesser basis. I should suppose that according to this thinking the British Defence Programme over the three years might be expected to rise to approximately 4 billions sterling or 1350 millions sterling a year on average. It cannot be assumed that we shall not be asked to increase our already heavy burden.

If we accepted the thesis that general war is inevitable we should now be putting the country on a war footing. Everything would be subordinated to preparation for war. In such circumstances it would not matter so much if American assistance took the form of substantial direct aid. Present policy would be preliminary to general war and, when this broke out, Britain would have no choice but to look to the United States for the financing of all or virtually all her overseas purchases. The stage of recovery now reached would be lost and overwhelmed in the general catastrophe and we should have to begin afresh when the war was over. While the war endured we should be utterly dependent on an immense volume of direct American aid, so that considerable dependence in the preliminary stages would not make much difference. But this is not the position. We are preparing for peace, not war. We believe that, if we and our allies prepare sufficiently quickly and thoroughly and are well organised and strong, war can be averted. It is from this point of view that it makes sense to the Americans as well as ourselves to insist that the continuance of the economic recovery of Britain is essential. It is this that makes the Americans ready to offer assistance to us in order that the heavy impact of the Defence Programmes should not dislocate and halt recovery. It is this that makes it so important that our independence for an indefinite period of the future should not be destroyed by American assistance taking the form of direct aid.

How can the Americans give us adequate assistance without direct aid? The main effect of the Defence Programme will be seen in our general balance of payments and the accumulation of further sterling balances, not offset by equivalent increases in our gold and dollar reserves. This adverse result could be neutralised if there were a way of diminishing our total overseas indebtedness to an extent which roughly corresponded to the new debts created by the operation of the Defence Programme. There is such a way. For example in the years 1951, 1952 and 1953 the first instalments of capital and interest fall due for repayment on the American and Canadian loans.[5] Together they involve dollar payments to the value

[5] The texts of the Anglo-American Financial Agreement of 6 December 1945 and the

of nearly 200 millions sterling. Then there are the loans under the European Recovery Programme amounting in all to some 120 millions sterling. These might be written off over the three years of the Defence Programme in proportion as we successfully accomplished our task. If this occurred our total overseas indebtedness over the three years would be diminished by nearly 310 millions sterling, an amount not too greatly out of accord with the latest estimate of the amount of assistance we might need; the figure was put at 350 millions sterling.

If this course of action were successfully pursued we should obtain sufficient assistance to our general balance of payments and total overseas indebtedness without the receipt of substantial direct aid. Our economic independence would be preserved. Neither the British nor the American public would see themselves as involved in a giver–receiver relationship. While the economic needs would be met, the political consequences of renewed loss of economic independence would not occur. We should be in a different position from all or most of our Continental neighbours. And, most important of all, we should by progressive action habituate the Americans to the idea that the whole British loan must eventually be written off as to both capital and interest.

This procedure could be used to meet the economic consequences of heavy defence expenditure beyond the period of the three years' programme. There are many annual instalments of capital and interest on the American loan which could be cancelled. If the burden of the Defence Programme for the next three years has to be increased, the additional deficit on our general balance of payments could be met by the cancellation of the payment of capital and interest for particular years beyond the three year period.

Since this procedure would not involve new money raised from the American taxpayer and transferred to foreign hands it would commend itself to American opinion on both points. The American taxpayer is going to be very heavily taxed for his own Defence Programme. It is much easier for him to assist the British in relation to moneys raised in the past. In the second place new dollars will not be placed in foreign hands which may be spent in the United States and so add to the already powerful inflationary tendencies. The American Treasury is very much alive to the danger of foreign assistance increasing domestic inflation, with the dangers of which they are increasingly preoccupied as the planned figure of Defence expenditure mounts beyond 50 billion dollars in the year.

In addition it would be easier to satisfy the American Administration and Congress with a fairly general assessment of the effects on our economy and balance of payments of the Defence Programme. This would in any case be sensible for there are far too many unknowns for any

Anglo-Canadian Financial Agreement of 6 March 1946 are printed in L.S. Pressnell, *External Economic Policy since the War*, vol. i (H.M.S.O., 1986), pp. 416–20 and 424–7. The negotiation of these loan agreements ($3.75 billion from America and $1.25 billion from Canada) is documented in Series I, Volume III: cf. also Volume IV, No. 41.

exact assessment to be possible. For example the recent exercises in the British Treasury and equally the present discussions in Washington have had to make certain assumptions about the course of raw material prices. What is the value of these assumptions when none of us know, when no American official in State Department, Treasury, or E.C.A. seems to know the projected range, extent, or price policy of American stockpiling? Again it offers escape from any detailed inquisition into the main uses of the British national resources, the level of home consumption, the expenditure on social services, or the size of the capital investment programme. Lastly it would mean that we should not have to justify our claim to dollar aid in respect of raw materials or machine tools by procedures as hampering to the conduct of our export trade as were those of the famous wartime White Paper.[6]

In sum, if this approach were adopted, we could continue to act as the partners of the United States. We should not rejoin the European queue. Once the main issue of principle had been settled, we should not annually be criticised at length and at a distance by a succession of Congressional Committees. Assistance in this form would not diminish our power and influence in the world.

Are the Americans likely to fall in with these thoughts? I cannot say. I can only report that two weeks ago I had a secret, informal and wholly personal conversation with Dean Acheson. I then tentatively advanced the idea that direct aid and the continuance of the giver–receiver relationship was a very bad thing for both our countries and asked him what he would think of the notion that we should carry the whole of the Defence Programme, the Americans in one grand gesture cancelling the American Loan and all E.R.P. loans. I suggested that the times were sufficiently abnormal for things to be politically possible with the Congress which otherwise would not be. To my surprise Acheson was interested, asked for time to think these ideas over and questioned me on my judgment about whether if these actions were taken Britain would be able to manage for the three years. Was I sure that we would not have to come back and ask for more? That he thought would be very difficult. After the lapse of several days Acheson reverted to these ideas. He had talked them over within the State Department and the general feeling was that they were interesting but too bold and too difficult. Later I was told in great confidence by Ambassador Douglas that he had had a conversation with George Perkins and Nitze of the State Department on these notions and they had tentatively thought that something might be done on a year by year basis. They were not prepared for immediate total cancellation of the American Loan.[7]

[6] In a memorandum to the U.S. Government of 10 September 1941 the British government undertook that Lend-Lease materials received from the U.S. would not be used to further British exports. This paper, withdrawn in 1944, was issued as Cmd. 6311 of 1941 and known as the 'Export White Paper': see further L.S. Pressnell, *op. cit.*, pp. 10–11.
[7] Sir O. Franks further discussed his ideas with Mr. Perkins, U.S. Secretary of State for

I would urge that consideration be given to these suggestions. They are clearly of a most tentative character. But they illustrate the principle to which I attach importance, the discovery of a form of American assistance which does not entail direct aid. I have given reasons for the importance I attach to this principle. I would further urge that if it is felt that these suggestions have merit they should be reflected on very thoroughly so that a completely firm and decided British position can be reached, advocated and defended. I believe the Americans to be sufficiently unclear and uncertain for a good case to have a real chance with them.

I would finally say that I believe this to be a time of decisions which will influence the pattern of events for many years ahead. This is demonstrably true of the political decisions taken or under consideration concerning Germany and Japan. It is also true of the individual and collective decisions of the members of the Atlantic Pact on rearmament and defence. I believe it to be not less true, so far as Britain is concerned, that the form American assistance takes in relation to our Defence Programme will decisively affect Anglo-American relationships and determine the judgment of the world on the economic independence or dependence of Britain with all the political consequences which attain to the one verdict and to the other.[8]

OLIVER FRANKS

CALENDAR TO NO. 49

i *2 Oct. 1950 Treasury criticisms of No. 49* contained in comments from (*a*) C.E.P.S.: figures do not balance out. Waiver of loan interest therefore insufficient: U.S. aid still required. (*b*) Sir H. Wilson Smith, Second Secretary at H.M. Treasury, doubts practicalities and wonders as to effect on European morale of U.K. making what amounts to a 'side deal'. Agreement at inter-dept. meeting with Sir O. Franks' analysis and with desirability of trying to find means to 'free ourselves from dependence on direct American aid'. However general consensus is that too many difficulties are in way of particular proposal advanced by Franks [UE 11914/106; T 273/289].

European Affairs, on 29 September. Mr. Perkins assured Sir O. Franks that the State Department was continuing to think about the question 'although we did not see at all clearly what, if anything, should be done' (*F.R.U.S. 1950*, vol. iii, p. 1683).

[8] Mr. Bevin initialled Sir O. Franks' covering letter (note 1) without comment. It was arranged that he would discuss the paper with Mr. Gaitskell and Mr. Attlee on his return to London. On 30 September Mr. Attlee thanked Sir O. Franks for his 'most valuable' paper and commented: 'I have read it with great interest and will take an early opportunity of discussing it with some of my colleagues' (UE 11914/106). In the Treasury, where consideration earlier in September of the future of U.S. aid to Europe had included the idea of a loan-waiver (see T 273/289 and T 232/128), Sir O. Franks' suggestions were discussed by an interdepartmental meeting held by Sir E. Bridges, at which the Foreign Office was represented by Sir R. Makins (record at calendar i).

No. 50

Sir G. Jebb (New York) to Mr. Attlee
(Received 29 September, 1 p.m.)

No. 1255 Telegraphic [WU 1198/451]

Priority. Top secret   NEW YORK, *29 September 1950, 2.21 a.m.*

Repeated Saving to Paris, Wahnerheide, Washington.

Following from Secretary of State.

I had a farewell talk with Mr. Acheson this evening [28 September] and took the opportunity to review with him the position reached in the Tripartite and Atlantic Council talks with regard to western defence. I said that I was not sure how we should try to handle the French particularly with regard to the German problem. I thought we must recognise that though there had perhaps been a slight improvement recently the morale of the French was none too good and it would be unwise to build too much on them. I said that His Majesty's Government did not at all like the idea of a European army or European Minister of Defence which had been ventilated at the Council of Europe.[1] They thought that the only solid basis on which to proceed was the Atlantic Pact.

2. Mr. Acheson replied that the United States Government had first considered whether the right course might be to work for German participation in the form of a concealed army like the Bereitschaften but had rejected this. It was also clear that there could be no question of a German national army. They had therefore decided that the only solution was to have German units in an integrated Atlantic Army. The United States Government quite realised that a purely European Army in which the Americans were not full members would not work and that they must come in on equal terms with the rest of us.

3. Mr. Acheson said he must emphasise that the United States Government were having to take on tremendous new responsibilities in providing troops, equipment and financial assistance on a vast scale. It was a revolutionary step in United States policy. It seemed to the United States Government that it was essential that we should plan to be in a position to defend Western Europe as far to the east as possible. A defence based on the Rhine would mean losing the Norwegians, the Danes and the Dutch and was obviously very unsatisfactory even from the point of view of the French. The inescapable conclusion seemed to be that the Germans must participate. The United States Government were determined to push ahead but before they took the final commitment and actually sent their additional troops to Europe they wanted to get a decision from the French in favour of German participation. If the French continued to stand out the United States might be obliged to modify their plans somewhat and

---

[1] See No. 20, note 3.

119

proceed on a slightly different basis. He himself believed that the French would come along and he had made it quite clear to M. Schuman that he relied on him to bring his Government round. Mr. Acheson suggested it might be possible for His Majesty's Government to help to bring the French Socialists to accept the necessity of German participation.[2]

4. I said that we were very anxious to keep in step with the United States Government and I undertook to keep in constant touch with the United States Embassy in London.

5. Mr. Acheson said he thought that the Defence Ministers would need a lot of political guidance at the forthcoming meeting of the Defence Committee. He would ensure that General Marshall had strong State Department support. I said that I fully agreed about the political importance of this meeting and I should be sending a Foreign Office representative with Mr. Shinwell. Mr. Acheson said he thought the deputies would have to do a good deal of preparatory work. They knew better than anyone what was required and could help to ensure that full weight was given to political considerations. He would like Sir D. Hoyer Millar and Mr. Spofford to work very closely together. He thought it would be necessary for Mr. Spofford to return for the meeting. He said he did not expect the Defence Ministers to make final plans but he hoped that matters would be carried a stage further. He said he assumed that I would be working closely with Mr. Shinwell in trying to establish what we hoped to get out of the meeting.

Please repeat to Paris and Wahnerheide as my telegrams Nos. 207 and 24 Saving.

---

[2] See No. 46, note 7. On 3 October M. Stikker suggested to H.M. Ambassador at The Hague, Sir P. Nichols, that the British Labour Party might bring pressure to bear on the French Socialists in the same way as the Dutch Socialists were doing. Mr. Davies discussed this suggestion with Mr. Denis Healey, Secretary of the international department of the Labour Party on 9 October. Mr. Healey said that he personally was opposed to German rearmament and that the Labour Party had taken no stand on the matter. He thought it likely that the question would come up at the meeting of the Committee of the International Socialist Conference (C.O.M.I.S.C.O.) in Paris on 20 October, which he was attending with Mr. Morgan Phillips, General Secretary of the British Labour Party and chairman of C.O.M.I.S.C.O. Mr. Healey mentioned difficulties between the French and Dutch Socialists and 'added that the British Labour Party was not altogether in a favourable position to influence the French because of the differences over European unity . . . All the same, Mr. Healey agreed to sound out the French attitude, and despite his personal feelings in the matter he would report our conversation to Mr. Morgan Phillips and do what he could to further British policy in the matter. He thought, however, that for the reasons stated, it would be a mistake for us to take the initiative' (minute by Mr. Davies on WU 1195/361).

No. 51

Sir I. Kirkpatrick (Wahnerheide) to Mr. Attlee
(Received 30 September, 11.30 p.m.)

No. 1448 Telegraphic [C 6263/27/18]

Priority. Top secret   WAHNERHEIDE, 30 September 1950, 9.20 p.m.

My immediately preceding telegram.[1]

1. You will see that looking at the problem through German eyes I have come down heavily in favour of course one.

2. The reason is that the Germans are realistic in military matters and know quite well that if they are to contribute to Western defence against external aggression, the only effective solution is for them to contribute a military contingent to an integrated army. For use against aggression a para-military police force is a makeshift. This was recognised in our paper[2] written before the New York Conference in which the thought was expressed that the participation of a German military contingent was essential to Western defence but that since it did not seem practicable at that stage to achieve it, we must for the moment be content with less.

3. This seems to me the position today. If the French will not agree to the participation of a German contingent there will be a fatal gap between what is required and what the Western Powers can provide. This gap cannot be filled by a police force armed as proposed in New York telegram No. 1171,[3] and we should not attempt to delude ourselves or the Germans that it can.

4. There are therefore two courses open to the Western Powers. Either to take effective steps now to assure Western defence and this means a German military contingent, or to recognise that for the moment it is not practicable and to take such admittedly inadequate interim measures as are practicable, in the hope that the French will before long . . .[4] brought to agree to the participation of a German military contingent.

5. In order to break the deadlock between the Americans and the French we should as proposed by the Secretary of State, seek to persuade the Americans to put the programme in train in the expectation not unjustified by past experience, that the French will shortly come along with us. If the United States Government remains adamant, we should have no alternative but to put the strongest pressure on the French by pointing out that we should be compelled to reveal that owing to their attitude, Western defence cannot be assured and that in consequence the Atlantic Powers, whilst ready to attempt to liberate France again, cannot make adequate plans to defend her.

6. There is another point to which I should call attention. In conversation with the C.I.G.S. yesterday, I learnt that the French may be

---

[1] See No. 48, notes 4–9.
[3] No. 43.
[2] i.e. D.O. (50) 66, for which see No. 3.i.
[4] The text is here uncertain.

toying with the idea of agreeing to German participation on condition that it is on battalion level and that German battalions are integrated in Allied brigades. You will be aware that such a proposal would be rejected on principle by the German Government and to [*sic*] the whole German people. There is no chance of securing its adoption. Moreover on purely practical grounds it seems to have little to recommend it. I calculate that if we raised a modest German army of 100,000 men on this basis, every single brigade or regiment in 33 Allied divisions would have to have one German battalion. The consequent administrative difficulties alone would scarcely compensate for the relatively small addition to Western trained manpower, moreover such an arrangement would not help us where we most need help in the specialised branches of the service where thorough training is more essential than in the infantry. Nor would it bridge the gap between the tactical air force required and what we are likely to be able to provide. These practical considerations would reinforce the fundamental opposition of the Germans to the participation of a German contingent, except on terms comparable to those applicable to the other participating nations.

7. If the French are afraid that the Germans might play too great a role in the integrated army, we might propose that the number of German divisions should not exceed 20 per cent or 25 per cent of the total number in the whole army. I put this thought to General Guillaume[5] yesterday and he replied that it seemed to him acceptable, but he is far in advance of his Government, because he both admits that we must have a German military contribution and is prepared to draw the logical conclusion.

[5] Commander-in-Chief of the French forces in Germany.

No. 52

Letter from Mr. Barclay (Queen Mary) to Sir D. Gainer

[*C 6457/27/18*]

Top secret and personal   QUEEN MARY, *3 October 1950*

Dear Gainer,

When the Secretary of State had his final talk with Dean Acheson on the evening of September 28th,[1] Acheson told us in strict confidence that the confusion caused by the apparent change of front on the part of the Americans on the subject of the German contribution to Western defence, on the afternoon of September 22nd (see our telegrams Nos. 1168, 1169 and 1170 from New York)[2] was entirely due to a mistake on the part of General Marshall. The U.S. Chiefs of Staff paper which General Marshall produced at the private meeting of the three Ministers of Defence had only been intended to show him what immediate steps might be taken if

[1] See No. 50.   [2] See No. 42 and notes 6 and 9 *ibid.*

agreement in principle could not at once be reached on the inclusion of German units in the proposed integrated Western force. Instead of keeping it to himself he showed it to M. Moch, who naturally seized upon it and said that it provided the basis for a settlement which he would be ready to accept. Marshall soon realised his mistake but the harm had already been done and it was very difficult for Acheson to retrieve the situation. There was in fact no change at all in the American attitude, nor was there any difference between the views of the U.S. Chiefs of Staff and the State Department.

As soon as it became clear at the meeting of officials on the night of September 22nd (see our telegram No. 1170) that the Marshall memorandum did not by any means represent the full U.S. requirements, we rather suspected that something like this must have occurred.

Acheson spoke very warmly about Marshall and excused his mistake by saying that he had had to hurry into the meeting without having any time for preparation.[3] He asked that we should keep this story to ourselves, but I thought you should know the true explanation of the apparent sudden change of front on the part of the Americans and its subsequent reversal.

I am sending copies of this letter to Kirkpatrick, Makins and Elliot.

Yours ever,
RODDIE BARCLAY

[3] See No. 31, note 3.

No. 53

Memorandum by Mr. Gaitskell (Treasury) for Mr. Attlee[1]

[*UE 11914/106*]

TREASURY, *3 October 1950*

1. I have carefully considered Sir Oliver Franks' memorandum of 27th September[1] in consultation with officials of the Treasury and the Foreign Office. We are in general agreement with the analysis, and especially the political analysis in the earlier part of the paper regarding the difficulties

[1] In a covering minute to the Prime Minister, Mr. Gaitskell explained that this memorandum on No. 49 'represents the views I have formed after full discussion with the officials concerned in the Treasury and the Foreign Office. I am sending a copy to the Foreign Secretary with whom I hope to discuss it tomorrow evening. No doubt you will also wish to discuss it with him at Margate, and I hope that it will be possible for you to let me know that you approve it so that I can use it as the basis for my discussions with Sir Oliver Franks in Washington next week.' Mr. Gaitskell was going to Washington and Ottawa from 8–14 October for informal economic talks with Ministers and officials. On arrival at Southampton on 4 October, Mr. Bevin travelled up to London for his appointment with Mr. Gaitskell later that evening and left London early the next morning to attend the Labour Party Conference in its closing stages at Margate. On 6 October Mr. Bevin returned to the Foreign Office.

associated with United States financial assistance to us in the form of further substantial direct aid.

2. When, however, the Ambassador goes on to suggest as a possible alternative approach that we might endeavour to secure the cancellation of interest and redemption payments falling due in 1951, 1952 and 1953, on our dollar loans, we feel that he overlooks certain fundamental difficulties.

(a) In the first place, in order to make his case, he extends his proposal not only to the payments due in respect of the 1945 American Line of Credit,[2] but also to the corresponding Canadian Credit and to the loans which we have received from the United States under E.R.P. The E.R.P. loans were granted quite widely to other European (and, incidentally, N.A.T.O.) countries and it does not appear to us to be feasible that there should be a special waiver of these loan obligations applying only to the United Kingdom. As regards obligations to Canada, it is no doubt correct that the United States would expect any American waiver of our obligations to be accompanied by a similar waiver of our Canadian obligations. From the Canadian point of view this is not likely to be an attractive suggestion (especially in view of the current and prospective dollar position of the sterling area and of its reserves) and extremely difficult negotiations would be required here.

(b) It is, in our view, very doubtful whether it would be any easier to secure a waiver of loan payments than to secure dollars under N.A.T.O. or O.E.E.C. procedures. The waiver would require special legislation by Congress. This would bring the Loan Agreement to the immediate attention of Congress and raise once more all the old controversies about the terms of the original Agreement on convertibility and non-discrimination. Congress might well insist on new terms under those heads being written into any fresh legislation.

(c) It is almost certain that waiver of loan payments, if feasible at all, would be granted on a year to year basis. We should, therefore, have no security at all regarding continuing benefit to our dollar accounts. We should have an open-ended liability on the total of our defence effort without any satisfactory arrangements for the sharing of the resulting burden between ourselves and other countries. This would be especially serious if, defence expenditure and the resulting impact upon our general economic position become considerably greater than contemplated under the existing plan for total expenditure of £3,600 million over the next three years.

(d) The Ambassador seems to assume,[3] under his suggestions, that we should pay for any United States finished equipment which we obtain as well as for the dollar content of any materials required for our own defence production. If this were the case we should be undertaking a

[2] See No. 49, note 5.
[3] Sir R. Makins commented in the margin here: 'I don't think he does assume this.'

far greater burden than we have ever contemplated.

(*e*) There might well be an adverse effect upon our credit and on the general position of sterling in the world from any abrogation of our contractual debt obligations, even if agreed with our creditors.

(*f*) From the political and defence points of view we must remain full members of N.A.T.O. We must also participate in and be affected by the results of any general exercises required to establish the sharing of the resulting manpower, production, and financial obligations.

3. It seems to me that our aim now should be to get these arrangements on a sound basis (relating to the equitable sharing of burdens and not to the charitable doling out of dollars) rather than to adopt the kind of alternative approach suggested by the Ambassador. The negotiations with the Americans on this are at present being carried on in Washington in two parts. First, there is a bipartite discussion with them on the assistance we might receive on account towards the two separate tranches of £100 million each of production expenditure which have already been sanctioned, and on such further production as may be sanctioned as the programme is worked out. These discussions are proceeding satisfactorily though no definite conclusions have yet been reached. They will presumably continue in Washington.[4]

4. Secondly, there is tripartite discussion on the longer term arrangements for sharing the burden of defence in which the French are joined with the United States and ourselves.[4] Both these discussions and those on immediate assistance have been confused by a French proposal for a common defence budget between all the North Atlantic countries which does not appeal either to us or to the Americans, but which it has not yet been possible to dispose of finally. The more practical line of approach is based on a memorandum[4] by Mr. Nitze of the State Department suggesting as a principle that there should be an equitable distribution of economic burdens in carrying out the medium defence plan, and that there should be studies of each country's military programme and an analysis made of its effect on her national accounts to reach what Mr. Nitze calls a critical evaluation of the data bearing on the equitable distribution of the economic burden. We have accepted this in principle. Further discussion is to take place under the N.A.T.O. deputies, in order to agree on the size of the programme and the exact meaning of fair shares. We cannot decide on the precise formula which we should like to put forward until we know in more detail the size of the American defence programme.

5. I believe that we have good grounds for hoping that if we play a positive and constructive part in these talks we can get agreed an

---

[4] See No. 11, note 7. When the bipartite official talks on interim aid resumed in Washington on 3 October, discussion focused on an American offer, made that day, of assistance with the first £200 million stage of the British defence programme without commitment towards any further aid in the full £3,600 million programme (text of U.S. aide-mémoire at No. 79.i).

arrangement for the sharing of the common defence burden which would go a long way to avoid the political difficulties envisaged by Sir Oliver Franks, and at the same time not saddle us with the difficulties set out in paragraph 2 above.[5]

CALENDAR TO NO. 53

i *10–11 Oct. 1950 Gaitskell meetings in Washington.* Discussion between Sir O. Franks and Mr. Gaitskell of Ambassador's ideas at Embassy meeting on 10 Oct. Mr. Gaitskell on the whole agrees that U.K. cannot make a case for special U.S. assistance to British economy—but it is awkward that Parliament has been told that U.K. will only go ahead with £3,600 m. defence programme if substantial U.S. aid available. In discussions with Americans Mr. Gaitskell pursues idea of getting away from concept of givers and receivers towards equitable sharing of burden. Raw materials and progress of Nitze exercise discussed—also question of U.S. aid for development in South East Asia—£1,000 m. required over 6 years [T 273/289; F.O. 115/4490].

[5] Mr. Attlee minuted below on his copy: 'I agree C.R.A. 4 x 50.'

No. 54

Memorandum from Sir R. Makins to Mr. Bevin

[*WU 1198/457*]

FOREIGN OFFICE, *4 October 1950*

1. Please see Sir Oliver Harvey's telegrams 396, 397 and 398 Saving,[1] (Flags A, B and C respectively) which give the latest position from Paris about the French attitude towards a German contribution to Western Defence.

2. Sir Oliver Harvey has been in London today and I have had a talk with him. His opinion is that the right course is to keep sustained but fairly gentle pressure on the French to accept the Anglo-American view. We all agree with this. Massigli has been round (probably not on instructions) to say that the French will never agree. He has asked us to call off the Americans.[1] Massigli is very prejudiced on this subject and is not a sound guide to French opinion. Sir O. Harvey thinks there is a fair prospect of bringing them round.

3. Sir O. Harvey subsequently discussed the matter with Sir William Elliot and as a result of these talks we have sent him a reply (telegram No. 2744 to Paris—Flag D).[2]

4. Sir O. Harvey will see M. Parodi[3] today, October 4th, prior to the meeting of the French Cabinet, and will give him all the arguments he can for use with the French Ministers. It is improbable, however, that the

[1] See calendar i.   [2] See calendar ii.
[3] M. A. Parodi was Secretary-General at the French Ministry of Foreign Affairs.

French Cabinet will take any firm decision this week and Sir O. Harvey thinks that it would be very useful if, on your return to the Foreign Office next week, you could send him some further instructions of a more personal character which would enable him to discuss the whole matter with M. Schuman, and if possible, M. Pleven.

5. The main burden of these instructions would be that after returning to England and consulting your colleagues, you had become more than ever convinced that the principle of a German contribution must be accepted however difficult it might be for Germany's ex-enemies in Europe; but that you sympathised with French difficulties and would certainly help them to ensure that there were proper guarantees against a revival of German militarism. This would give the French the feeling that we were not deserting them and leaving them to the mercy of an American–German alliance.

6. Sir William Elliot suggested that he himself might go to Paris to help Sir Oliver Harvey with his conversations with M. Parodi; but Sir Oliver Harvey—rightly in my opinion—discouraged this. First because it might look as if we were trying to influence the French Government behind the backs of their Ministers, and secondly because our own instructions had no Ministerial backing. Sir William Elliot then suggested that it might be valuable if Mr. Shinwell were to meet M. Moch in Paris before the latter leaves for New York on October 7th.[4] Sir Oliver Harvey was not sure whether this would be a good idea as he felt that more progress could probably be made through M. Schuman and M. Pleven than through M. Moch at this juncture. I agree.

ROGER MAKINS

CALENDARS TO NO. 54

i *29–30 Sept. 1950   French attitude to German rearmament*: French Cabinet endorse Schuman/Moch line at New York on 28 Sept. but defer discussion on future policy (Paris tel. No. 391 Saving). In conversation with Sir O. Harvey on 30 Sept. M. Parodi asks for British ideas on safeguards to be imposed on German units, which he could use for bringing French Ministers round before their next Cabinet discussion. Parodi refers to 'grave problem' of armament production: 'If the Germans were not allowed to make armaments and the French factories were turned over to rearmament, then the Germans would gain all the markets' (Paris tel. No. 397 Saving). Divisions within French Cabinet, political parties and general public assessed by Harvey who concludes that real difficulty lies within Cabinet (Paris tels. Nos. 396 and 398 Saving). Much harder line against German rearmament taken by M. Massigli with Mr. Davies on 29 Sept. [C 6256/27/18; WU 1198/455–457; F.O. 800/517].

ii *3 Oct. 1950   Proposed British safeguards on German rearmament* for M. Parodi, transmitted in F.O. tel. to Paris No. 2744 Saving: (1) neither German national

[4] M. Moch and M. M. Petsche, French Minister of Finance, went to Washington for Franco-American ministerial talks, from 13–19 October, on U.S. aid for French defence within N.A.T.O. and in Indochina: *F.R.U.S. 1950*, vol. iii, pp. 1396–1434.

army nor General Staff will be created; (2) no German air force; (3) no formation larger than a division; (4) only elementary training of those units under German control; (5) units to be scattered so as not to form a fighting unit by themselves; (6) restrictions on German military production. Parodi informed by Harvey of these safeguards on 4 Oct.: no immediate prospect of French acceptance [WU 1198/455, 461].

No. 55

Memorandum by the Secretary of State for Foreign Affairs[1]

C.P. (50) 222 [CAB 129/42]

Secret   FOREIGN OFFICE, 6 October 1950

New York Meetings

Tripartite Discussions on German Problems

The object of our discussions in New York on German problems was to lay the basis for a further development in the relations between the Occupation Powers and the German Federal Republic, such as would enable Germany to assume new responsibilities appropriate to her position in Europe while safeguarding the security of the Allies and the maintenance of the occupation. The necessity for steady progress in this direction had been foreseen at the tripartite meeting in London last May, when the Foreign Ministers of the three Occupation Powers set up a study group to undertake the necessary preparatory work to enable the existing Occupation Statute to be reviewed, as provided in the Statute itself, between the end of September, 1950, and the end of March, 1951, and to make recommendations for eliminating the major inconveniences arising from the state of war.[2] It was of course understood that the supreme authority of the Allies in Germany must be upheld pending the reunification of the country, and that any measures that might be regarded as constituting a separate peace with Western Germany must be avoided.

2. Since May new urgency had been lent to the study group's work by developments in the international situation. The Communist aggression in Korea came as a shock to German opinion, which was quick to perceive the parallel with Germany's case and demanded both reassurance as to the Allies' own plans for the defence of the Federal Republic and Berlin and guidance as to the role which the German authorities and the German

[1] The draft of this memorandum was prepared by Mr. Allen and approved by Mr. Bevin on the return voyage from New York. Three other Cabinet papers on discussions at New York were also prepared covering (i) general review (C.P. (50) 220: not printed); (ii) European defence (No. 56); (iii) Far East (C.P. (50) 221: see Volume IV).

[2] See No. 4, notes 3–4.

people should play. Communist propaganda from the Soviet zone played constantly upon German fears and hesitations and suggested that the elections to be held in Eastern Germany this October would mark a further stage in the consolidation of Communist power. Meanwhile German appetites had been whetted by the prospect of further advance towards equality of status held out by the Schuman Plan[3] and the Federal Republic's entry into the Council of Europe as an associate member.[4] Finally on the eve of our departure for New York Mr. Acheson informed M. Schuman and myself of the United States Government's intention to propose the establishment of an integrated defence force in Western Europe in which, not only American divisions, but also German units should participate.[5]

3. Against this general background the three Foreign Ministers had little difficulty in agreeing when we met in New York that early and decisive steps were called for if German morale were to be restored and the association of Germany with the free nations of the West made as firm and close as Allied interests clearly seemed to dictate. We were confirmed in this view by our three High Commissioners in Germany who came to New York to assist us in our discussions and who warned us in a report which they prepared for us there that, with German opinion in its present state of disillusionment, the ground would require careful preparation if the participation of Germany in Western defence were to receive the necessary degree of popular support.[6]

4. It was with these considerations in mind that we approached the recommendations made to us in the study group's report and reached the decisions outlined in our final communiqué on Germany (copy annexed)[7] and discussed in greater detail below.

5. In the political field we were able to agree that steps should be taken, as soon as constitutional procedures permitted, to put an end to the state of war in the domestic legislation of the Allied countries and of Germany. This is in itself a step of no great significance, since, in the international sense, the war between the Allies and Germany must be regarded as having ended with the unconditional surrender, but it is one which has psychological value for German opinion.[8]

6. We also reached agreement upon a formula defining the status of the German Federal Government, under which we recognise that Government as the 'only German Government legitimately constituted

[3] See Volume I, No. 170.   [4] On 13 July 1950.   [5] See No. 2.
[6] See No. 16, note 2.   [7] See No. 26.ii.
[8] It was explained in guidance for H.M. Representatives Overseas that the chief effect of the termination of the state of war would be to 'rectify the legal status of German citizens in Allied countries . . . It does not obviate the necessity which still exists for drawing up a peace treaty, which alone can settle such issues as Germany's frontiers and the termination of the Occupation. The termination of the state of war will become effective as soon as the United States, France and the United Kingdom are able to finalise the necessary changes in their domestic legislation and make a simultaneous announcement' (Intel 202 of 25 September on GC 11/95). This took place on 9 July 1951.

which can speak for Germany and represent the German people in international affairs' and as being in consequence the only Government entitled to assume the rights and obligations of the former German Reich pending a final settlement with a united Germany. On the basis of this formula we approved procedures for enabling the Federal Government to succeed to the treaty obligations of the Reich and for working out a provisional plan for the settlement, pending Germany's reunification and having due regard to the Federal Republic's capacity to pay, of all financial claims against Germany arising out of pre-war external public and private debts of all types and out of post-war economic assistance. In this latter connection I found it necessary to avail myself of the authority given to me by my colleagues (C.M. (50) 56th Conclusions, Minute 7)[9] to agree that claims relating to war damage to United Nations property in Germany should be excluded from the settlement plan and that the regulation of expenditure on external occupation costs should be deferred until a general peace settlement.

7. In addition we authorised the three High Commissioners to put into force, in consultation with the German authorities, agreed relaxations in the present occupation controls and to embody the changes in a document amending the present Occupation Statute. Before these changes come into effect the German Federal Government is to be required to give, firstly, a general undertaking of responsibility for the pre-war German external debt and in respect of post-war economic assistance to the Western Zones, and of co-operation in the working out and implementation of a settlement plan for claims and, secondly, an assurance that they will co-operate in the equitable apportionment of materials in short supply or needed for the common defence.

8. The foremost of the alleviations proposed is in the field of foreign affairs, where the Germans are to be allowed to establish a Foreign Ministry and to enter into diplomatic relations with foreign countries in all suitable cases. On the insistence of the French and United States Governments, which urged that such a step would be premature, they will not be permitted at the present stage to appoint Ambassadors to the capitals of the three Occupation Powers in view of the latter's special position in Germany. In internal affairs and particularly in economic matters the Allies's present powers of intervention and control will be substantially curtailed so that, in practice, they will be little used except insofar as may be necessary to carry out the essential needs and purposes of the occupation. The present procedure for prior review by the Allied High Commission of all German legislation before it can enter into force will be abolished and replaced by a simple right of repeal in grave and exceptional cases. In addition, relaxations will be made in a further series of controls, chiefly those relating to the accomplishment of specific Allied programmes in Germany (such as decartelisation, deconcentration, the care of displaced persons and the admission of refugees) as soon as the

[9] See No. 4.i.

German authorities have given specified assurances or enacted specified measures considered by the Occupation Powers to be necessary before they can relinquish their own responsibilities in these fields.

9. The three Foreign Ministers also gave instructions for the early review and revision of the Agreement on Prohibited and Limited Industries in order to remove restrictions which are found unduly burdensome in administration or no longer justified on security grounds or likely to impede the common defence effort.[10] Meanwhile it was decided as an interim measure to authorise the Allied High Commission forthwith, firstly, to permit German steel production to rise so that steel exported or otherwise devoted to the defence effort of the West will not reduce the amount available for German consumption and, secondly, to remove all restrictions on the size, speed, and number of commercial cargo ships built in Germany for export. The United States Secretary of State pressed strongly for these immediate concessions and, in the absence of French support and bearing in mind the Cabinet's discussion of these matters before my departure (C.M. (50) 56th Conclusions, Minute 6),[9] I thought it well in the circumstances to agree to them.

10. The discussions in New York on the crucial question of German participation in the common defence of Europe are described in a separate paper (C.P. (50) 223).[11] As there recorded, no final decision was reached on this matter. Meanwhile, however, certain decisions were taken which are of great importance to the security of Germany and an integral part of the new phase in relations with the Federal Republic which it was our aim to inaugurate. The three Ministers decided to announce in their final communiqué that they would treat any attack against the German Federal Republic or Berlin from any quarter as an attack upon themselves. This statement was of course designed both to restore confidence in Western Germany and Western Berlin and also to serve as a clear warning to the Russians and the East Germans against any ill-considered adventures, particularly the use of the East German military police for aggressive purposes. The Ministers also announced the intention of their Governments to strengthen their forces both in the Federal Republic and Berlin. Furthermore, they announced their resolve to help Berlin to maintain its freedom, by economic as well as military means. In an agreed document[7] which has not been published, they recorded their decision to take certain necessary measures to this end,

[10] These three principles gave rise to some difficulty when the Study Group met in London on 26 October to consider a review of the P.L.I. Agreement. The French delegation maintained that Ministers intended that priority should be given to the principle of eliminating restrictions which would impede the common defence programme. It was therefore argued that until the supply requirements of the Western Powers were determined by N.A.T.O., there could be no basis on which the P.L.I. review could usefully proceed. This interpretation was contested by the British and American delegations and eventually the French agreed to proceed with the review on the basis of all three principles: see further No. 140.

[11] No. 56.

including the building up of Berlin's stocks of fuel and non-perishable food to one year's supply and the preparation of plans for counter-measures against any renewed Soviet interference with Berlin transport. This unpublished document also recorded the decision of the three Powers to hold the Soviet Union responsible for any attack upon Berlin or Western Germany so long as the Russians remained in occupation of the Eastern Zone, and, in the event of an armed attack from whatever source, to defend Berlin by force, to bring the relevant provisions of the North Atlantic Treaty into effect and to present the issue to the United Nations.

11. As announced in the communiqué, agreement was also reached upon a plan for the formation of a German mobile police force for internal security purposes, with an initial strength of 30,000 men, equipped with light arms, organised on a Land basis but subject to a measure of central control and with a uniform system of recruitment, training and equipment. I should have preferred an outright Federal force, but the Americans and French were unwilling to agree and the final plan represented a necessary compromise with their concern for decen-tralisation. But it makes provision for full Federal control in an emergency, and will at least enable an immediate start to be made on remedying the present deficiencies in the field of internal security in Germany, pending, and without prejudice to, later decisions on German participation in the general defence effort. Moreover, as recorded in the separate memorandum on defence questions (C.P. (50) 223),[11] agreement was reached, with the assistance of the three Defence Ministers, upon certain further means of employing German manpower and resources for the benefit of the common defence effort, as steps towards a fuller participation of Germany in the build up of the defence of Europe.

12. All these decisions, taken together, cover the whole field of our relations with the German Federal Republic. They will be of great value in enabling the Western Allies to retain the initiative in the continuing struggle for Germany and to lay a firm foundation for the difficult negotiations that will have to be undertaken with the Germans when a decision has been reached among the Allies on German participation in the proposed integrated European defence force. But pending such a decision the present measures can only be regarded as provisional. Once the decision is taken a further review of the remaining Allied controls in Germany will have to be made. The three Foreign Ministers accordingly decided that the tripartite study group should remain in being and that, at a time to be determined, it should undertake this further review in the light of the circumstances and of the decisions made by the three Governments at the time. Meanwhile the study group is to address itself before the end of the year to certain immediate further tasks arising out of the decisions already taken. These are the agreed revision of the Prohibited and Limited Industries Agreement, the preparation of the agreed plan for the settlement of claims, further study of the questions of foreign interests in Germany and restitution preparatory to the relin-

quishment of the relevant reserved powers in these fields, and a review of the Tripartite Controls Agreement and the Charter of the Allied High Commission. At the same time the three High Commissioners, who returned to Germany from New York as soon as the three Ministers had reached agreement, will continue to work, in consultation with the German authorities, on the implementation of the decisions already reached.

E.B.

No. 56

Memorandum by the Secretary of State for Foreign Affairs

C.P. (50) 223 [CAB 129/42]

Secret   FOREIGN OFFICE, *6 October 1950*

New York Meetings

Defence of Europe and German Participation

Perhaps the most important subject discussed during the New York meetings was the United States plan for an integrated force for the defence of Europe and the participation therein of German units. The discussion of this plan took up most of the time of the tripartite meetings between Mr. Acheson, M. Schuman and myself, and also of the Atlantic Council. It was also discussed at a meeting, between the Minister of Defence and myself and our United States and French colleagues, specially convened in the hope of overcoming French objections to the participation of German units.

2. The Americans had already given some indication of what they had in mind before I left for New York; but it was not until I saw Mr. Acheson that the full implications of the American proposals were made clear.

3. The United States thesis as propounded by Mr. Acheson was roughly as follows. The essential aim is to defend Western Europe and not to liberate it. This can only be done by the full use of all available resources. For this purpose, as the President has announced, the Americans intend to send further substantial bodies of troops to Europe. The next step is the formation of these troops, and of the forces available in Europe of the other Treaty countries, into an integrated force under a Supreme Commander, with a unified international staff. But even this is not enough. The forces available are still insufficient for the defence of Europe. Moreover if Europe is to be defended and saved from occupation by an aggressor she must be defended in Germany. For these two reasons it is essential to make use of German resources. This can only be done with safety by the incorporation of German units in the integrated force. Only thus can the defence of Europe be assured without a revival of German militarism.

4. When Mr. Acheson first outlined the United States thesis to M. Schuman and myself, we both welcomed the American decision to send more troops to Europe and the proposed formation of an integrated force. We both expressed doubts, however, on the immediate necessity of including the Germans in this force. M. Schuman was particularly insistent that French public opinion would not tolerate even this measure of German rearmament at the present time, and argued strongly that the immediate need was not to rearm Germany but to arm and equip the forces of the Western Allies. He feared, moreover, the effect of such a decision on German opinion and also possible reactions in the Soviet Union and the satellite countries.

5. For my part, I said that we must proceed cautiously. We must not put the Germans in a position where they could bargain with us. The essential first steps, I thought, were to proceed with the organisation of the integrated force, and at the same time to build up the German Police. The question of German participation in the integrated force came second, and we should test out German opinion on this subject before taking any final decision.

6. It soon became clear that this practical approach to the problem would not satisfy the Americans. They felt strongly that their plan was a whole and must be accepted or rejected as a whole: and they left us in no doubt that their decision to contribute American troops to an integrated European force was conditional on a favourable decision regarding the participation of German units in that force.

7. At the same time, it was evident from the discussions in the North Atlantic Council that, although most of them were without definite instructions from their Governments, the majority of the Foreign Ministers were in favour of accepting the whole American plan. Some of them shared our own doubts about rearming the Germans, but were so conscious of the imminent danger and of the vital necessity of ensuring as quickly as possible an adequate defence of Western Europe that they were prepared to accept the lesser of two evils. The French alone, with some half-hearted support from the Belgians and Luxembourgers, stood out firmly against the American proposals.

8. In these circumstances I reached the conclusion that I must accept the principle of German participation in the integrated force and I sought and obtained the concurrence of the Cabinet in this line (C.M. (50) 59th Conclusions, Minute 1).[1] I made it clear, however, that the first step must be the organisation of the integrated force itself so that a position of strength was established on the Continent before the German units were brought in.

9. In spite of the virtually unanimous opinion ranged against them the French still refused to give in. It was therefore necessary to adjourn the Council for a week, firstly to enable the Ministers of some of the smaller countries to obtain final instructions from their Governments, and

[1] No. 27.

secondly in the hope that, in the interval the French might be brought round. With this second object in view, a meeting was arranged, at M. Schuman's suggestion, between Mr. Acheson, M. Schuman and myself and our three Defence colleagues. At this meeting the Minister of Defence and I on one side, and Mr. Acheson and General Marshall on the other, did our utmost to persuade M. Schuman and M. Moch to accept the principle of German participation in an integrated force. In this we failed utterly. M. Moch was adamant, and indeed very much tougher than M. Schuman had been. The three Defence Ministers were able to reach agreement on certain immediate measures such as strengthening the Police and Labour Service units, creating a Civil Defence Organisation and Engineer units, planning the production of light military equipment, etc.; but the French absolutely refused to agree that these measures were preliminary steps to the formation of German armed units.

10. The result of the French refusal to accept the principle of German rearmament was that the Americans, for their part, refused to give their final agreement to the formation of an integrated force. When the Atlantic Council reconvened, it was therefore obliged to pass a resolution which still left both these questions in some measure undecided. A copy of this resolution is annexed.[2] It will be seen that while it outlines the principles on which the integrated force shall be established and asks the Defence Committee and the North Atlantic Treaty Organisation to recommend detailed steps to that end, it specifically states (in the one but last paragraph) that the 'plan is not finalised at this time'. As regards Germany, the resolution leaves it to the Defence Committee of the North Atlantic Treaty Organisation 'to make specific recommendations regarding the method by which, from the technical point of view, Germany could make its most useful contribution to the successful implementation of the plan' (i.e. for the integrated force).

11. The present position is therefore as follows:–

(i) The Military Organisation of the North Atlantic Treaty is working out detailed plans for the formation of an integrated force for the defence of Europe.

(ii) These plans will not, however, be finally approved by the Americans until agreement has been reached on the principle of the participation of German units. In particular the United States Government will be most reluctant[3] to commit further American forces to Europe until agreement has been reached on this principle.

E.B.

[2] See No. 47.
[3] When submitting the draft of this paper (which here read 'U.S. Government are unlikely') to Mr. Bevin on 5 October, Mr. Barclay suggested that he might not wish to be so definite on this point. Mr. Bevin agreed that this phrase should be modified to the present text.

No. 57

Sir O. Harvey (Paris) to Mr. Bevin

No. 408 Saving Telegraphic [C 6424/27/18]

Priority. Top secret   PARIS, 7 October 1950

Repeated Saving to Wahnerheide, Washington, and New York.

German Rearmament.

M. Parodi told me this morning that the Council of Ministers yesterday had resulted in little more than a preliminary exchange of views between Ministers after hearing M. Schuman's report. The American Ambassador, who was returning to Washington on Sunday [8 October], had seen M. Schuman and M. Moch last night, when the difficulties of the French position had been fully explained to him.

2. M. Parodi said that he had really nothing more to add to what he had already told me.[1] The Ministers were acutely worried, and so far no way out of the difficulty had been found. Although French parliamentary opinion had evolved a great deal since last year as regards Germany the evolution was not by any means yet complete when it came to German rearmament. He could but deplore the way in which the Americans were insisting on a public acceptance of the principle now, when it might have been possible to reach a confidential agreement for action later whilst details and safeguards were being worked out. However, the public announcement was no doubt part of the bargain which the American administration wished to conclude with Congress. Once the principle was accepted he had little doubt that the Germans, who he understood, already had in their police archives all necessary mobilisation particulars, would in almost no time produce German formations. He was frankly alarmed, and so were the French Ministers, at what the combination of American and German efficiency would do in this respect. We had now got into the position which you had always so strongly deprecated of asking the Germans for favours.

3. I told M. Parodi that you had also been reflecting on the position since your return and that I would be receiving instructions to see M. Schuman on Tuesday on his return from his constituency. I could not foretell my instructions, but it must obviously be for our two Governments to ensure that German rearmament, once accepted was controlled and kept within safe and reasonable bounds.

4. The American Ambassador, whom I saw before he had seen M. Schuman, told me in confidence that he regretted the way in which the matter had come forward in New York, primarily through the military side and in such a form as to appear almost as an American ultimatum. He thought the French would have great difficulty in accepting by October 28th, and M. Pleven whom he had seen, had also said that he did not see

[1] See No. 54.i–ii.

136

any way at present of reconciling his Government to acceptance and of obtaining a favourable vote.

5. I had M. Bidault[2] to a quiet dinner last night to sound out his views. He said how embarrassing and difficult it was for France at this time and resented the hustling methods adopted by the United States and the way in which the German problem was being used for their internal electoral purposes. He recalled sadly how at Yalta the Americans had cried out for the dismemberment of Germany[3] and now, only a few years after, they wished to revive the German army. Where would it end? He, too, feared the influence of the Germans upon the Allies and did not doubt that they would soon insist on becoming members of the Atlantic Council itself. The position was extremely difficult from a parliamentary point of view here, and though I think resigned personally to the inevitable, he did not hold out much hope that agreement would be possible within the month.

[2] M. G. Bidault was President of the *Mouvement Républicaine Populaire* and a former Prime Minister.
[3] For discussions on German dismemberment at the Conference of Yalta, 4–11 February 1945, see Sir L. Woodward, *British Foreign Policy in the Second World War* (H.M.S.O., 1976), vol. v, pp. 272–5, 289–90.

No. 58

Extract from the Conclusions of a Meeting of the Cabinet held at 10 Downing Street on Monday, 9 October 1950, at 11 a.m.[1]

C.M. (50) 63rd Conclusions [CAB 128/18]

Secret

[Germany]

(Previous References: C.M. (50) 56th Conclusions, Minute 6 and 59th Conclusions, Minute 1).[2]

3. The Cabinet had before them two memoranda by the Foreign Secretary (C.P. (50) 222 and 223)[3] summarising the results of the recent discussions in New York on German problems generally and on the particular question of Germany's participation in the common defence of Europe.

The Foreign Secretary said that at the London meeting of the North Atlantic Council in May[4] it had been his primary object to convince the Americans that European defence could not be built up on the basis that in a future war the European Powers would again hold the front alone

[1] *Present* at this meeting were Mr. Attlee (*in the Chair*); Mr. Morrison; Mr. Bevin; Mr. Dalton; Viscount Addison; Viscount Alexander of Hillsborough; Viscount Jowitt, Lord Chancellor; Mr. Chuter Ede; Mr. Shinwell; Mr. Isaacs; Mr. Williams; Mr. Tomlinson; Mr. Wilson; Mr. Griffiths; Mr. Gordon Walker. *Also present* for item 3 were Sir H. Shawcross, Attorney-General, and Lord Henderson. *Secretariat*: Sir N. Brook and Mr. Johnston.
[2] No. 4.i. and No. 27.   [3] Nos. 55 and 56.   [4] See Volume II, No. 113.

until such time as American support was forthcoming: Europe must now be able to count on having effective support from the United States and Canada from the very outset of a future war. At the opening of the Council's meeting in New York in September it had at once become clear that the Governments of the United States and Canada had accepted the need for giving this assurance to Europe. The United States Secretary of State had put forward his plan for the creation of an integrated force for the defence of Western Europe, and his proposal that for this purpose substantial United States forces should be stationed in Europe in time of peace. The United States Government were in fact prepared to shoulder their full share of responsibility for the defence of Europe. This was a very significant development in American policy, and one of very great importance and value to the United Kingdom. It was, however, based on a careful and realistic appreciation of European strategy. The Americans recognised that the battle for the defence of Europe should be fought as far to the east as possible. This meant that it ought to be fought on German soil, and this in turn raised the question what rôle Germany should play in the defence of Europe. The Americans had reached the conclusion that the proper course was to invite Germany to contribute units to an integrated army for the common defence of Europe. The Foreign Secretary said that he himself accepted that conclusion; but, throughout the conversations in New York, the representatives of the French Government had declined to accept the principle of German participation in this European defence force. They preferred the alternative approach of raising in Germany an effective force of armed police which might be used for defence purposes in an emergency. This proposition would, however, give rise to conflict with the Social Democrats in Germany, who were likely to insist that a gendarmerie should be organised and used for the sole purpose of maintaining law and order within Germany and that any German contribution towards European defence should be made separately and openly by raising army units for purposes of external defence.

The Foreign Secretary said that the problem was largely one of timing. He sympathised with the French feeling that the pace and extent of German rearmament should be kept in step with the progress made by other Western European countries in raising and equipping forces for their common defence, and also with the arrival in Europe of forces from North America. At the same time he was most anxious lest the invaluable offer of North American assistance in the defence of Europe should be withdrawn by reason of French reluctance to accept the corollary of German rearmament. The offer had been made conditional upon this and, because of the attitude of the French Government, it was now in suspense. It would be a tragedy if this great opportunity were lost by reason of French reluctance to accept the lesser of the risks which Europe was now facing. He therefore proposed that further pressure should be brought to bear on the French Government, and he laid before the

Cabinet the draft of a message which he proposed to send to M. Schuman through His Majesty's Ambassador in Paris.[5]

The Minister of Defence said that French Ministers had from the outset taken the line that they could not agree to any rearmament of Germany until further progress had been made with the strengthening and re-equipping of their own forces. This, he thought, was still their position and it would be difficult to dislodge them from it. It was, as the Foreign Secretary had said, a question of timing. If the French could be brought to realise that effective steps would in fact be taken in the near future to strengthen the forces of the other European Powers, they might be persuaded to accept the principle that Germany should participate in the common defence of Europe. They would certainly be readier to accept this if the French Ministers of Defence and Finance received, in their forthcoming visit to Washington,[6] satisfactory assurances of American aid, in money and equipment, for the strengthening of the French forces. Meanwhile should we be wise to reject altogether the alternative of building up a strong police force in Western Germany? In the recent conversations which the three Defence Ministers had held in New York, the French had readily accepted the detailed proposals for the creation of such a force—and, indeed, all the other proposals for German contributions towards Europe's defence needs with the single exception of the creation of army units. With this in view he suggested that some adjustment should be made in the argument of the fourth paragraph in the draft telegram to Paris which had been circulated by the Foreign Secretary.

Finally, the Minister pointed out that everything that the Foreign Secretary had said emphasised the importance of the meeting of the Defence Committee of the North Atlantic Council which was to be held in New York on 25[28]th October. Hitherto there had been much discussion but, with the exception of the United Kingdom, none of the European Powers had made any practical contribution towards the common defence of Europe. At the next meeting each Government should state what contribution it was ready to make, and the Committee should show that effective practical steps would now be taken to build up forces capable of the tasks before them.

In further discussion the following points were made:

(*a*) The wording of paragraph 4 of the draft telegram to Paris should be reconsidered. As it stood, this paragraph might be thought to be inconsistent with the detailed proposals in paragraph 5.

(*b*) Paragraph 5 of the draft telegram proposed that there should be no German army units larger than a division. It might help to meet French susceptibilities if the largest permitted unit was a brigade. Alternatively,

[5] The draft of No. 59, prepared after an Office meeting with Mr. Bevin on 6 October, is not printed.
[6] See No. 54, note 4.

139

it might be preferable to make no reference to the maximum size of the units. The French were more likely to be impressed by the proposal that the German contribution to the integrated force should be limited to a fixed percentage of the total.

(*c*) Substantial concessions had been made in the relaxation of Allied control over Germany, described in C.P. (50) 222. It was reasonable that, in return for these, the Government of Western Germany should accept some obligation to contribute towards the common defence of Europe.

The Cabinet—

(1) Took note with approval of the relaxations in Allied control over Germany, outlined in C.P. (50) 222.

(2) Took note of the Foreign Secretary's report (C.P. (50) 223) on the conversations in New York regarding German participation in the common defence of Europe.

(3) Agreed that further pressure should be brought to bear on the French Government to accept in principle the incorporation of German army units in an integrated force for the defence of Europe; and invited the Foreign Secretary to instruct His Majesty's Ambassador in Paris accordingly, on the lines of the draft telegram which he had circulated, subject to further consideration of the wording of paragraph 4 of the draft.[7]

[7] Amendments to paragraphs 4 and 5 (iii) of the draft of No. 59 were subsequently agreed between Air Marshal Elliot and Sir P. Dixon.

No. 59

Mr. Bevin to Sir O. Harvey (Paris)

No. 1008 Telegraphic [*WU 1198/480*]

Immediate. Secret   FOREIGN OFFICE, *9 October 1950, 6.45 p.m.*

Repeated to Wahnerheide, Washington.

My telegram No. 2744 Saving[1] (of the 3rd October): German Participation in European Defence.

I shall be grateful if you will take an early opportunity of seeing M. Schuman and telling him that since my return from New York I have been able to discuss this question with my colleagues in the Cabinet and that I want him to know our views.

2. As M. Schuman knows, it was with no enthusiasm that I accepted in New York the principle of German participation in the integrated force for the defence of Europe. My attitude reflected that of the Cabinet. We do not like the idea of German re-armament any more than the French do. On the other hand, we are acutely conscious of the present

[1] No. 54.ii.

defencelessness of Western Europe. We are determined that the countries of Western Europe shall be defended next time and not liberated. It is clear that there is no chance whatsoever of the Western European Powers being able to achieve this unaided, and that very substantial help from the United States will be required. The Americans have accepted this position, and they also take the view (with which it is impossible to disagree) that the defence line must be in Germany, which means unavoidably that Germany must play a part. It is certain that we shall not get the contribution from the U.S. which is absolutely essential for the Defence of Europe unless we are prepared to accept that conclusion. The American offer of troops and an integrated force with a Supreme Commander is a unique opportunity at last to put European defences on a sure footing: and we should be playing with the safety of our peoples if we rejected it.

3. We understand and share the French Government's fear that the Germans will take advantage of our proposals to bargain and try to wring concessions from us. But we do not share the French view that this danger will be averted by waiting. On the contrary, we believe that German opinion will harden with the passage of time and that German demands will be stiffer and more difficult to handle in, say, six months' time than they are now. Whereas if we act now, we believe that there is every reason to expect that it will be possible to arrange for the participation of Germany in Western European defence on conditions which are acceptable to us. We must not lose this opportunity.

4. We are convinced that the only safe way for us to obtain German participation in European defence is through the integrated force composed of all Atlantic Treaty, including of course United States and Canadian, forces, because by that means alone can we be sure that Germany's defence effort is under allied control. The eight points proposed by General Marshall, and agreed in New York, (New York telegram No. 1171[2] (of 23rd September)) could not in our opinion be accepted as a satisfactory approach[3] to the wider problem of German rearmament, since they look to the strengthening or formation of specifically German units, which will come under German authorities and over which, if they were allowed to expand into armed units, it would be increasingly difficult to exercise adequate allied control.

5. It seems to us that the really important question is not whether military units should be formed, but the conditions under which they are formed. The idea of a German contribution is now public property. Sooner or later it is inevitable that Germany will have to be allowed to play some part in her own defence, if only because the Western European Powers are incapable of offering her security. Our problem is, therefore, to see that it takes place under conditions which we and not the Germans determine. Before accepting any practical proposals for the formation of

[2] No. 43.
[3] The draft circulated to the Cabinet (see No. 58, notes 5 and 7) here read 'an approach'.

141

German units, His Majesty's Government would certainly insist on safeguards with regard to timing, size and status. We have not yet been able to work out our ideas in detail, but the sort of safeguards we have in mind are the following:

(i) the formation of German units could be related in timing to (a) the despatch of further United States forces to Europe, (b) progress in the creation of the integrated force and the appointment of a Supreme Commander and (c) the build-up of sufficient forces of the European members of the North Atlantic Treaty, properly armed and equipped;

(ii) there should be no German strategic Air Force and no German Navy;

(iii) there should be agreement on the size of the German unit to be allowed;[4]

(iv) the German contribution to the integrated force might be limited to a fixed percentage of the total;

(v) the individual national units would be spread about the force, so that there would be no question of the Germans forming an army by themselves;

(vi) the equipment of German units with armour such as tanks etc. might be delayed until the requirements of the other allies had been met.

6. It seems to the Cabinet that with safeguards such as these the risks inherent in the formation of German military units will be reduced to a minimum and need not be seriously feared. I hope that M. Schuman will be able to persuade the French Government to take a like view. I believe that in this matter the interests of France and the United Kingdom are the same. We understand French hesitations and the French Government can rely on us to be at one with them in working out the details of this plan so as to minimise the German danger. At the same time, we both have a duty to ensure the immediate defence of Western Europe and we hope the French Government will be persuaded to agree with us that this cannot now be done without acceptance of the principle that German units should be incorporated in the integrated force. I am particularly anxious that we should all be agreed on this vital point in time to allow the N.A.T.O. Defence Ministers to carry further at their meeting at the end of this month the U.S. plan for an integrated force which was generally accepted in New York.[5]

[4] The draft (see note 3) here read 'there should be no German units larger than a division'.

[5] Sir O. Franks was instructed to inform the State Department of this approach to the French Government and to find out whether the U.S. government intended to make any similar approach. He replied on 11 October that the State Department 'are not at present making any approach to the French Government but are having discussions on this whole subject with the United States Ambassador in Paris who is here on a visit. They will let us know if they decide to approach the French' (Washington telegram No. 2737 on WU 1198/490).

No. 60

Memorandum from Sir D. Gainer to Mr. Bevin

[C 6624/27/18]

Top secret   FOREIGN OFFICE, 10 October 1950

With reference to the manuscript minute which I sent you on Saturday,[1] I now append a fuller report on recent developments in regard to Germany following upon the New York Conference.

2. First, the defence aspect. The only firm agreement reached in New York related to the *internal* security of the Federal Republic. Details of this agreement are contained in New York telegram No. 1171,[2] Flag A. Of the various items contained in this plan, only one, that relating to the expansion of the police, has been communicated to Adenauer, and that in somewhat general terms.[3] However, an Allied committee has been set up in Germany not only to advise the Federal Government on questions connected with the police but also to work out proposals for implementing the other items in the programme agreed in New York; to quote Sir I. Kirkpatrick,[4] 'We have agreed with the Chancellor that an Allied German Committee should consider the problems of equipment, terms of service, deployment and housing of the police. The terms of service of our and the American new G.C.L.O. (German Civil Labour Organisation) must be considered in relation to those of the mobile police. The competing claims of police and our troops for barracks must also be considered by a central body. The Committee should examine the problem of passive air defence, and finally consider whether in fact fortifications and mines are required, and if so how best Germans can be utilised for the purpose. I have nominated General Wansbrough-Jones[5] as British member. The Americans and French have respectively nominated General Hays and General Ganeval.[6] They are holding their first meeting today and hope shortly to meet the Germans.'[7]

3. As to the attitude which the U.K. representative will adopt in the discussions, it has become increasingly clear, as the result of an exchange of views we have had with Sir I. Kirkpatrick, that any attempt to use the interim New York programme (Flag A) as a covert means of achieving a

---

[1] In this minute of 7 October, Sir D. Gainer drew Mr. Bevin's attention to Wahnerheide telegrams Nos. 1447–8 (see No. 48, notes 4–9 and No. 51) in relation to the problems of internal and external security for Germany.

[2] No. 43.   [3] See No. 45.

[4] Wahnerheide telegram No. 1454, for which see No. 48, note 9.

[5] Chief of Staff to the U.K. High Commissioner in Germany.

[6] Respectively U.S. Deputy High Commissioner and French representative on the Military Security Board.

[7] In addition separate negotiations continued with regard to a Berlin police force (cf. No. 40). For the details of all negotiations, see F.O. 371/85324–7: C 3333/18 and 85901–4: CG 23/184 (Land/Federal); 84986–94: C 2/18 (Berlin) and further in this volume No. 113.

German military contribution would involve us in considerable political difficulties, and the line we propose to take in Germany is as follows:

(a) *The police is not an army in disguise.* As Sir I. Kirkpatrick points out,[8] 'the New York communiqué drew a sharp line between external and internal security. It thus gave the S.P.D. an implicit assurance that the proposed mobile police force would not be in any sense an army.' This renunciation of the possibility of organising a disguised army is complementary to our policy of bringing pressure to bear upon the French with a view to their acceptance in principle of the U.S. proposal for an open German military contribution.

(b) *We object on both military and political grounds to a multiplicity of small organisations not properly under the control of the integrated force.*

(c) *We cannot afford to allow Germany to be involved in heavy expenditure on non-essential items.* Germany's defence budget is limited and if we eventually want her to build her own divisions and/or pay for the maintenance of ours, it would be absurd to allow her resources to be committed to non-essentials.

(d) *We must therefore concentrate on implementing only certain realistic proposals such as the expansion of the police, the G.C.L.O., and the frontier police.*[9]

4. I hope you will agree that these are the right lines on which to proceed pending a clear decision on the main issue of a direct German contribution.

5. On this main issue, you will remember that the New York decision of the Atlantic Council provided for reconsideration of the subject on 28th October, and you have just secured Cabinet approval for further pressure on the French on this question.[10]

6. In Germany, Dr. Adenauer was on 23rd September told by the High Commission that he would be given an opportunity of discussing with them the question of German military participation in Western defence. Since then, in Sir I. Kirkpatrick's words,[4] 'as regards the participation of a German military contingent in Western defence, the High Commissioners have severally had conversations with the Chancellor. He has taken the

---

[8] In Wahnerheide telegram No. 1447 (see No. 48, notes 4–9).

[9] This line ran counter to the conclusions of the Joint Planning Staff in their study of the New York package (see No. 44, note 4) circulated as J.P. (50) 130 on 5 October (CAB 21/1897). In this paper the Joint Planners recommended, among other things, that the mobile police should be organised on a Federal basis and be so armed as to be able to counter an attack from the Bereitschaften. The J.P.S. represented the advantage of forming the police units in such a way as to facilitate their conversion to military units as soon as the French attitude became more forthcoming. In Wahnerheide telegram No. 1465 of 7 October Sir I. Kirkpatrick criticised these proposals not only on the grounds of the need to preserve the distinction between internal and external security but also as not taking sufficient account of the financial aspect. The U.K. High Commissioner warned that Germany could not produce unlimited funds for defence and that any deficit would have to be met by the Allies (C 6624/27/18).

[10] See No. 58.

line that if approached he will agree without imposing conditions on the understanding that Germany comes in on the same terms as the others. He is anxious for an early decision. At the moment we cannot profitably carry these exploratory discussions any further. The United States High Commissioner and I are, however, doing what we can in conversation with the S.P.D. and others to prepare the ground for German participation if this is eventually decided.' In a later telegram[11] Sir I. Kirkpatrick reports that after discussion among themselves the three High Commissioners had agreed that for the moment (i.e. until after 28th October) they could not usefully carry conversations with the Chancellor any further. I attach a copy of the telegram in question, since it records an important discussion on the question of how German agreement to direct participation in Western defence should be secured and announced; as you will see, the three High Commissioners agreed that 'it would be best if matters could be so arranged that the Germans appeared to be neither begged, coerced nor bought'.

7. Turning now to the development of our political relations with the Federal Republic, work is proceeding both here and in the High Commission as a result of the New York decisions on Germany. The present position is as follows:

(a) *Allied High Commission*:

(i) The High Commissioners have held general preliminary discussions with Dr. Adenauer, who has been informed of the relaxations in Allied control which are envisaged and of the counter-assurances expected.[12]

(ii) It has not yet been possible to transmit to the German Federal Government texts of the two undertakings which it was agreed they should be required to give before any relaxations entered into force. The text of the undertaking with regard to financial claims is now practically agreed between the three Occupying Powers. That relating to the equitable apportionment of the materials and

---

[11] In Wahnerheide telegram No. 1468 of 7 October Sir I. Kirkpatrick reported an informal meeting of the A.H.C. on 5 October when: 'We all agreed that any appearance of dictation or assumption that the Germans would do what was required would be undesirable. Our reasons for feeling this are, however, not the same as those which no doubt inspire Schumacher and particularly Adenauer. The latter no doubt hope that the Western Powers will decide to come to the Federal Government with a request that it should produce a military force which of course would establish their bargaining position. We felt however that both a brusque decision, appearing to impose a solution on Germany, and a request to Germany should be avoided. As McCloy put it, they should not receive a request, but be asked a question "are you ready to contribute". Poncet elaborated this by explaining that in his view the N.A.T. Governments should declare that the way is now open to all interested countries to contribute to a Western force. We should all do so and the Germans would then have to decide whether to do so or not, and could not claim that they were being pressed. We agreed that it would be best if matters could be so arranged that the Germans appeared to be neither begged, coerced nor bought' (C 6624/27/18).

[12] See No. 45 and No. 26.ii.

145

products in short supply or required for common defence will follow the wording agreed in New York and can, therefore, be transmitted as soon as the claims draft is agreed.[13]

(iii) A Sub-committee of the High Commission has drawn up a draft Instrument of Revision of the Occupation Statute which will shortly come before the High Commission itself.[14]

(b) *Inter-Governmental Study Group*:

The Study Group is due to resume its work in London on the 24th October.[15] It is due to complete all the work on its present agenda, except that on claims, by the 1st December. The working out of the claims settlement within the framework agreed at New York will require some months.

(c) *German Treaties and Termination of the State of War*:

Instructions have been sent out for a tripartite approach to each of the Governments still at war with Germany, informing them of the Ministers' decision and asking that they will endeavour to terminate the state of war according to their own constitutional practices at approximately the same time as the three Occupying Powers.[16] A further approach has been made to all 'non-iron-curtain' governments asking them to notify the High Commission of pre-war German Treaty obligations which they wish to see revived.[17]

D. St. Clair Gainer

[13] Separate letters from the A.H.C. to Dr. Adenauer requesting undertakings on external debts and raw materials were approved by the A.H.C. on 19 October (F.O. 1005/1114) and handed to the Chancellor on 23 October: texts printed in *D.G.O.*, pp. 528–32.

[14] When the A.H.C. considered this draft instrument of revision on 12 October (C 6536–7/20/18), reservations from Mr. McCloy as to the form of the document resulted in its referral to governments and a further round of drafting: see No. 147, note 2.

[15] The opening meeting was later postponed to 26 October: see No. 55, note 10.

[16] Cf. No. 55, note 8.

[17] Sir D. Gainer added below on 11 October: 'Seen by Secretary of State who approves the line being taken. He would like a letter to be drafted from him to the Minister of Defence drawing attention in the strongest terms to the impossibility of using the mobile Police force as a covert military force—to do so would imply almost a breach of faith with Schumacher and his party and lead to a political crisis of the first magnitude in Germany. He would like me to see Air Marshal Elliot myself to rub this in.' Mr. Bevin's views were conveyed to Mr. Shinwell in a minute of 13 October in which Mr. Bevin stated that he regarded 'this path as closed' (C 6624/27/18). When the Chiefs of Staff considered J.P. (50) 130 (note 9) on 11 October they agreed that the paper had been overtaken by events and should be withdrawn.

No. 61

Memorandum from Mr. Stevens[1] to Mr. Bevin

[CE 5240/45/181]

FOREIGN OFFICE, *10 October 1950*

German Contribution to Western Defence
Economic Aspects

You will recall that on the 27th September the NATO Council requested the Defence Committee 'at the earliest possible date to make recommendations as to the method by which Germany could most usefully make its contribution to building up the defence of Western Europe'.[2] There had been a previous agreement between the Foreign Ministers of the three Occupying Powers that 'plans should be completed now for the eventual utilisation for the benefit of the defence programme of the West of the industrial potential of Western Germany in the production of finished light military equipment only . . .'.[3]

The main emphasis in the Defence Ministers' discussions which are due to take place in Washington at the end of October will, no doubt, be on the German military contribution. There are, however, a number of questions on the economic side which may come up for discussion or which will call for consideration in some other context. You may wish to have the following brief report on the thought which has been given to these matters in London, and on the action which has been initiated.

The economic side of Germany's defence contribution can be viewed from two points of view:

1. *Financial and Budgetary*

It would seem desirable, if possible, that the cost of defence in its widest sense, chargeable to the German budget, should be roughly comparable to that borne by the NATO powers. On the other hand, it would clearly be undesirable that Germany should be required to carry so heavy a burden as to prejudice her economic stability. At the present time, the principle defence charge borne by the Federal Government is in the form of occupation costs. As a percentage of the National Income, this charge is low compared with the defence burden borne, e.g. by the United Kingdom (approximately 5 per cent as compared with nearly 10 per cent). With an increase in the Allied Forces of Occupation, however, and the prospect of an increase in German armed (including police) forces, these charges will rise. Unless care is taken, they may rise to a point which would impose an intolerable fiscal burden on Germany due in part to the division of budgetary responsibility between the Laender and the Federal

---

[1] Mr. R.B. Stevens was an Assistant Under Secretary of State in F.O. German Section.
[2] See No. 47.   [3] Punctuation as in filed copy: see No. 43.

Government. This points to the need for reducing occupation costs to the lowest possible *per capita* figure in order to leave the largest possible room for direct German contribution to her own defence. At the present time, the cost of the armed forces represents DM 3.7 milliard out of a total of DM 4.6 milliard occupation costs. As the armed forces of occupation increase, this figure will come under growing scrutiny and we are likely to find ourselves particularly vulnerable to criticism because, at the moment, the *per capita* cost of the British forces in Germany charged to the German budget is higher than that of either the United States or French armed forces. In order to anticipate such criticism and to avert the possibility that we may be called upon to make a Sterling contribution to the cost of our armed forces in Germany, we are suggesting to the War Office and other service departments that there should be instituted a joint enquiry to be undertaken by the Treasury into the possibilities of retrenchment in the present scope of expenditure. I believe that it may be possible for considerable economies to be effected if we go about this enquiry in the right way. Though it will be some time before any reductions take effect, this would enable the decks to be cleared for a larger real contribution to defence from the German budget than would be possible at the present time.

2. *Commercial and Industrial*

This is a very complex problem. As we see it, our broad objective should be eventually to ensure that German industry makes an adequate contribution to Western defence, whether by providing such items as she is permitted to manufacture to the armed forces of the NATO countries, or by supplying her own armed forces to the extent that she is allowed them with similar equipment. This is desirable both from the point of view of rapid progress with the defence programme and also from the commercial point of view. If, while the NATO powers are devoting an increasing proportion of their industries to defence production, the Germans are able to utilise increases in their steel production etc. largely for the manufacture of commercial goods which compete in export markets with our own, the long-term consequences to our own economy might be serious. It is felt, however, that this is not an immediate danger and that the first essential is to obtain what we can from Germany in the way of ancillary equipment for defence, machine tools, lorries etc., thereby relieving the burden on our own production. The Ministry of Supply is already proposing to place substantial orders for such equipment and the Americans are understood to be doing the same. We have asked the Ministry of Supply to let us have details of their purchasing programme, so as to enable us to see more clearly in what form the German industrial contribution to Western defence might best be made. It may be necessary in the light of this information to determine whether it is necessary, firstly, to coordinate purchases in Germany with other NATO powers so as to avoid competition and, secondly, whether any special steps need to be taken in Germany in order to ensure that the production of needed items is adequate. The information so obtained may also influence our attitude towards the revision of the Prohibited and Limited Industries Agreement which will be undertaken on a tripartite basis in November.[4]

To sum up, we are taking such steps as seem open to us, in the absence of any decisions about the future of Prohibitions and Limitations on German Industries or about the nature and scale of Germany's armed forces, to secure the following results:

(i) That Germany's ability to contribute financially to her own defence is not hampered by fiscal considerations and, particularly, by an unjustifiable burden of occupation costs.

(ii) That German industry is available to contribute within permitted limits to the defence programme of the NATO powers.

(iii) That German industry shall not obtain an unfair advantage in the commercial field as compared with the industries of other NATO powers.

(iv) That we are in possession of some factual information about the nature of the industrial contribution which Germany might most usefully make to the defence programme of the other NATO powers, for use in discussions within NATO either at the Defence Ministers' meeting at the end of the month or on some later occasion.

You may wish to indicate whether the lines along which we are working, as indicated above, have your general approval.[5]

R.B. STEVENS

APPENDIX TO No. 61

The Secretary of State spoke to Sir Donald Gainer and myself on 13th October about the problems discussed in the above minute.

2. As regards the financial and budgetary problems, he said that he considered that the question of Germany's contribution to defence would arise actively and urgently in the course of the next few months. He attached particular importance to getting the water out of Occupation costs and was much perturbed to learn that the *per capita* cost of the British forces in Germany charged to the German budget was higher than that of either the United States or French armed forces. He considered that something ought to be done about this right away and he doubted whether the procedure of writing to the War Office at the official level, as we were proposing, would produce sufficiently quick results. He instructed that a minute should be drafted for him to send to the Prime Minister drawing the latter's attention to the broad policy issues involved and suggesting to him that a directive should be used to the Departments concerned on the basis of which an enquiry

---

[4] See No. 55, note 10.
[5] Mr. Bevin minuted: 'I will see Gainer & Stevens.' Mr. Stevens' minute of this meeting is appended below, as on the filed copy.

should be undertaken by the Treasury in the manner suggested in the minute and without delay.[6]

3. As regards the commercial and industrial aspect of the German contribution to Western defence, the Secretary of State felt he ought soon to make a report on this subject to his colleagues, indicating the problems involved and the sort of solutions towards which we were working. He thought that Sir F. Hoyer-Millar ought to have in mind the possibility of a substantial German industrial contribution when discussing defence production problems with the Deputies. To this end he suggested that an Inter-Departmental Working Party ought to be established to get down, at once, to the problem of the German contribution with a view to securing objectives (ii) and (iii) in the penultimate paragraph of my minute with which he agreed. He considered it important that we should form as precise a view as possible of the items which Germany might make for the common defence and of what additional imports and financing would be required to make them. Unless we had our own ideas on these subjects, we should quickly find that the Germans were in the position of making heavy demands on limited stocks of raw materials etc., nominally for their defence production but, in fact, for commercial purposes as well. The Secretary of State expressed some concern lest German defence production were concentrated exclusively on items of a quasi commercial character, which would only serve to build up Germany's competitive position in the long run rather than develop production exclusively for defence purposes which could not be adapted to commercial ends. He recognised the relevance of the revision of the P. and L.I. Agreement in this connection.

4. I told the Secretary of State that we had asked the Ministry of Supply for details of their purchases from Germany and had also asked the British Element in Germany to supply us as soon as possible with the sort of information which the Secretary of State himself had in mind, with a view to briefing the U.K. Delegation to the Defence Ministers' meeting on the 28th October. The Secretary of State said that he thought that an effort ought to be made to coordinate this information in London as rapidly as possible through the Inter-Departmental Committee he had suggested.[7]

R.B.S.

13th October, 1950

[6] Mr. Bevin minuted accordingly to Mr. Attlee on 24 October whereupon the Prime Minister called a meeting of senior Ministers to discuss the matter. At this meeting on 1 November it was agreed that occupation costs should be reviewed by an expert appointed by the Chancellor of the Exchequer.

[7] Action was set in train accordingly and an interdepartmental committee was formed under the chairmanship of Mr. Stevens: see further No. 92, note 4.

No. 62

Letter from Mr. Penson (Washington) to Mr. Stevens

[CE 5041/45/181]

Secret. Personal   WASHINGTON, 10 October 1950

My dear Roger,

I am sorry I have not written you before since the end of the Tripartite

Meetings. You will, however, perhaps have seen my letter to Gainer of September 23rd[1] and have doubtless also discussed matters with Denis Allen. Since returning to Washington, I have endeavoured to take a few days leave, and this, for short periods only, has been welcome, but it has delayed my writing to you.

Our disappointment at the way things turned out in New York would be difficult to express adequately. I think most of our colleagues, in whatever field they were working, agreed that there was much confusion and frustration. This arose largely from the fact that the United States Government had not adequately prepared the ground for the initiative they intended to take in the field of defense. Their failure to get the French to agree with them on this point dominated the entire conference. Acheson made it clear at an early stage that his country's participation in additional European defense would be conditional upon French accept-ance of a plan for German participation in the defense programme. This, both in the substance and in the manner of it, was wholly distasteful to the French, who, not improperly, claimed that they had come insufficiently warned of the character of the problem which would be put to them.[2]

You may well ask how the difficulty in reaching a decision on this important matter should have had such an unfortunate effect in other fields where the ground had been thoroughly prepared. There is no real answer to this, except that whilst the French became more difficult on all points as a result of the pressure being put upon them in the defense field, the Americans made it clear that they would give way on everything else to win the French over on the main issue. Acheson had evidently given little consideration to the points arising from the Study Group's report. Had it been known in advance that this was the case and that he would treat the matter as light-heartedly as he did, our tactics would undoubtedly have been different. As it was, after a brief and rather flippant reference to the Study Group's work at the second meeting, and a rather cursory examination of one or two of the points of difference relating to foreign affairs, Acheson proposed that the whole matter be referred to the three High Commissioners.[3] I need not tell you that the result of this was most

[1] In this letter (not printed from C 6211/3780/18), Mr. Penson reviewed events at New York up to 23 September in the same vein as the more concise summary below.

[2] In the corresponding passage of his letter to Sir D. Gainer (note 1), Mr. Penson commented: 'The outstanding feature of the discussions generally was the omission on the part of the Americans of the necessary preparatory work to secure acceptance of their sudden change of views as to German rearmament. The integration of German units, up to a division, in a European army was put forward rather as a bright idea, so irrefutable from the American point of view as to merit immediate acceptance by the French as well as ourselves. We had only heard of this change twenty-four hours before the Secretary of State left London, and the same is more or less true of the French. The Americans are now paying for their clumsy approach and are finding it much more difficult to obtain acceptance of their proposals than would have been the case had they handled the matter more skillfully.'

[3] See No. 26.i.

unfortunate. For the moment it put Byroade and the State Department advisers in an even more embarrassing position than ourselves. Neither McCloy nor Kirkpatrick were very favourably disposed to the Study Group's report, and the main effect of the move was to not only jeopardise the comparatively few unagreed points, but the agreed parts also. A period of complete confusion resulted, which lasted for two or three days, the main question being whether any part of the Study Group's report could be saved at all.

In the end things did not prove quite as bad as this. But the Americans, avowedly with the view to saving the agreed portions of the report, proposed that we should compromise with the French by confining the relinquishment of the reserved powers on a temporary basis to those with which the French were in agreement. It became largely a series of 'majority' decisions, with the Americans siding with the French on two or three points where they had previously been with us. The French, for their part, showed no interest in retaining our wording on foreign trade and in general I fear that we came off very badly all round.

Even the temporary character of the present limited concessions disappeared in the last stages. The French were not prepared to agree to a resumption of the Study Group's work on the Occupation Statute by 1st December, as the Americans and ourselves had proposed, and this also we had to drop.

On the matter of claims, I insisted upon the post-war economic assistance being given the same priority as the pre-war debts. The Secretary of State was anxious to get this. On the other hand, Reinstein[4] insisted that if this were so he would not commit his Government to paying this in foreign exchange, but would leave it at foreign exchange or Deutschemarks. I think there is no doubt that there will be further arguments on this when the Study Group reassembles in London later this month. The French supported them on this and again made our position more difficult. I feel, however, that we had won a distinct point by getting the priority on the pre-war debts modified to this extent.

I will not attempt to adjudicate on the cause of our failure to secure a greater number of points. I believe that largely the matter was outside our hands and resulted from American anxiety, which of course our delegation largely shared, to secure agreement on the defense matter.[5]

[4] Mr. J.J. Reinstein was Director of the Office of German Economic Affairs in the State Department.
[5] In his letter to Sir D. Gainer (note 1), Mr. Penson pointed out that the substantial concessions made to the French on constitutional issues 'must be viewed, I think, in the light of the general problem of getting the French to agree to Germany cooperating in the defence of Western Europe. I understand that the Secretary of State felt that this was of such importance that we could agree to temporary postponement on some of the matters in the constitutional field, which we believe to be right, in order to get French cooperation generally. Looking at the matter from the viewpoint of the general purposes of the tripartite meetings, I would think that this view was fully justified.'

I have discussed both with Byroade and with Laukhuff[6] here in Washington the outlook for a further review of the Occupation Statute. They are both inclined to take a pessimistic view of the matter, though believing that the first step is to secure an agreement on German participation in defense measures. Once this has been done they believe the constitutional changes will follow. They agree that the work on the Occupation Statute is now left in an untidy state, and I think they deplore this as much as we do. But they do not feel that an immediate approach to the French to fix a date in present circumstances would lead to any useful result. They think that it is best to proceed with the Study Group matters, including claims, which the French are ready to go on with, leaving the constitutional questions for consideration after progress, at least in principle, has been made with defense.[7]

Yours sincerely,
J. HUBERT PENSON

[6] Mr. P. Laukhuff was Director of the Office of German Political Affairs in the State Department.

[7] Sir D. Gainer minuted on Mr. Penson's letter of 23 September (note 1): 'Once again the French have won! Both the Americans and ourselves have abandoned agreed positions in the hope that the French would play in regard to defence. The French accepted our surrender and stopped there! Let us hope we have now learnt our lesson and will be prepared to be tough in the next round.' The substance of this minute was incorporated into Sir D. Gainer's short letter of thanks to Mr. Penson on 28 September.

CHAPTER II

British reactions to the Pleven Plan and Soviet proposal for a Council of Foreign Ministers

11 October – 20 November 1950

No. 63

Sir O. Harvey (Paris) to Mr. Bevin
(Received 11 October, 3.48 p.m.)

No. 267 Telegraphic [WU 1198/487]

Immediate. Secret PARIS, *11 October 1950, 2.46 p.m.*

Repeated to Washington and Saving to Wahnerheide and New York.

German rearmament.

The Minister of Defence, Air Marshal Elliot and myself lunched with M. Moch yesterday.[1] He left for New York last night to help M. Petsche in his discussions with particular reference to equipment of the French forces.[2] He will return for the reopening of the French Assembly on October 17th. At the Cabinet meeting yesterday he had secured agreement on the bill for prolonging the military service to 18 months whose passage was now assured.

2. M. Moch at once brought up the question of German rearmament upon which I fear he appeared absolutely adamant. Although Mr. Shinwell put forward the views of His Majesty's Government both forcibly and persuasively, M. Moch made it clear that he personally would be opposed to the recreation of German military forces either now or even in the future. If, therefore, there were any question of acceptance in

---

[1] Mr. Shinwell was in Paris for a private lunch with M. Moch to discuss German rearmament. This engagement was arranged between the two Ministers in New York and gave rise to some concern in the Foreign Office (see No. 54). Mr. Barclay informed Mr. Bevin on 6 October that neither he nor Sir P. Dixon 'think that this is a very good plan. However ... it would, I think, be very difficult to get the visit cancelled'. Mr. Barclay's suggestion that 'we might ask that Sir O. Harvey should be included in the lunch party' was evidently taken up (WU 1198/500).

[2] See No. 54, note 4.

principle now he, M. Moch would resign and the government would fall, since the Socialist Party Executive had confirmed his attitude by 29 votes to one. The President of the Republic[3] also endorsed it. In spite of all our arguments as to safeguards and as to the priceless American counterpart, we failed to shift him. Indeed, he said at one moment that even if the Americans refused to help France any more, he could still alone rearm ten French Divisions promised for next July.

3. When pressed as to his objections, he declared that having fought in two wars to eradicate the German military spirit he would not now be himself a party to recreating it. Moreover, German troops would not be reliable troops, for each German unit would require two allied units beside it to ensure it did not go over to the east Germans. In other words, German units would not add to allied strength but would be a source of weakness. He thought the Germans should be used for police and for anti-fifth column activities but not as soldiers. We [sic] believed, moreover, that the line of the Elbe could be held without the Germans. He was not prepared to see a fresh war for the recovery of Koenigsberg.

4. M. Moch, although inflexible, was good humoured throughout, and most obviously concerned to avoid a deadlock in New York on October 28th. If the French Government, however, were then required to say 'yes' or 'no' to German rearmament, it was inevitable, he said, that the answer would be 'no' and a deadlock would result. It was necessary to save the face of the United States. Although His Majesty's Government no longer supported the French view, he hoped that it might be possible for them to help circumvent the deadlock.

5. Mr. Shinwell, making it quite clear that it was a purely personal suggestion, then enquired whether the French Government would be willing to agree in October to the study of the question of German rearmament and its military and political implications by a committee without commitment or even acceptance of the principle. Such a committee might report within nine months but meanwhile progress should be made on the other points (viz Federal Police etc.) upon which agreement had been reached at New York. M. Moch was rather attracted by the idea and seemed to think something like this might afford a way out of the immediate deadlock, but he maintained that as far as he himself was concerned, and he believed it would be true of the Socialist Party, he would never accept German rearmament. While in Washington this week he would decline to give any indication of the French Government's attitude, which would only be revealed at the end of the month.

CALENDAR TO NO. 63

i *9 Oct. 1950 M.O.D. Brief for Mr. Shinwell's talks with M. Moch* suggests Mr. Shinwell should tackle M. Moch on the military rather than political angle and 'talk it over with complete frankness as a matter between two friends' [DEFE 7/681].

[3] President V. Auriol.

No. 64

Sir O. Harvey (Paris) to Mr. Bevin
(Received 11 October, 6.36 p.m.)

No. 268 Telegraphic [WU 1198/488]

Immediate. Secret   PARIS, 11 October 1950, 4.20 p.m.

Repeated to Washington and Saving to Wahnerheide, New York.

Your telegram No. 1008.[1] German rearmament.

M. Schuman received me last night. He was as usual calm and reasonable. He reminded me cheerfully that only a few months ago it was we who were refusing to agree in principle subject to conditions to the Schuman Plan, now our rôles were reversed. We went through the views of His Majesty's Government and I left with him an aide memoire.

2. He said that these furnished him with useful particulars for the discussions which were taking place with his colleagues. The Cabinet would not take its final decision until October 18th after M. Moch's return when agreement would have to be reached on the line to be taken in the debate at the Assembly. He did not question any of the arguments used except paragraph 5(vi): (Delay in equipping German units with armour until after the requirements of the allies had been met). This, he thought, would be dangerous as implying that the German units should be maintained for some time in a position of marked inferiority. He agreed that this was a relatively minor matter subject to discussion.

3. What worried M. Schuman however, was the way in which we had got into the position of asking favours of the Germans. There was division in the German ranks on rearmament and Herr Heinemann had just resigned rather than accept,[2] whilst even in the Christian Democrat Party there were elements opposed to rearmament. In any case there was no German offer before us which we were asked to accept. It would be the Allies who would be making an offer to the Germans.

4. From the French point of view, whilst excluding the word 'never', M. Schuman said that the question had certainly been raised prematurely.[3]

---

[1] No. 59.

[2] On 9 October Dr. Heinemann resigned his post as Minister of the Interior after refusing to comply with a request from Dr. Adenauer that he dissociate himself from an open letter from his close associate Pastor Niemöller which stated the unequivocal opposition of the German Evangelical church to re-militarization. The public controversy surrounding Dr. Heinemann's resignation, for which Dr. Adenauer claimed he had the full support of his Cabinet, prompted the Chancellor to broadcast a public denial on 11 October that he had made any secret arrangements with the Western Occupying powers for re-militarizing Germany.

[3] In a public speech at Metz, reported by Sir O. Harvey on 9 October, M. Schuman said that while Germany must take its share in the burden of Western defence 'the idea that German military units should be immediately associated in this defence is premature since France is herself unprovided with arms and Germany must not be rearmed before France' (Paris telegram No. 411 Saving on C 6437/57/18).

Opinion in the Government was not yet ripe to take a favourable decision. I mentioned how stiff M. Moch's attitude was and M. Schuman said that it undoubtedly represented the attitude of the Socialist Party. Nonetheless, it had done M. Moch good to go to New York though I confess we did not notice it at our luncheon.[4] I spoke of the necessity of avoiding a deadlock at the end of October and M. Schuman showed that he was acutely alive to this. He was actually seeking a formula which would be somewhere between 'yes' and 'no', which would be sufficient to gain the approval of the French Assembly and yet would also be enough to persuade the Americans and their Congress to go ahead with the rest of the plans. It would then be for the French themselves to put this forward at New York on October 28th.

5. M. Schuman referred to a letter just received from General Marshall asking for the despatch of a special representative to Washington, from the contents of which he had concluded that the Americans were about to put forward definite proposals for German rearmament.[5] He was embarrassed by this request as he thought there were already sufficient military representatives in Washington and M. Moch himself would be there this week. I said that Mr. Shinwell had received a similar letter[6] and our reactions were, I thought, much the same. M. Schuman was anxious to know whether he had yet sent a reply and rather hoped, I think, that we would also decline to send a special representative. In any case the French Government would not have made up its mind about German rearmament until October 18th.

6. I asked M. Schuman to let me know if there were any further points upon which he would like the views of His Majesty's Government adding that I knew you were most anxious that the two Governments should be in agreement at the meeting on 28th October.

[4] See No. 63.

[5] The substance of the first American draft resolution for the N.A. Defence Committee on 28 October had been communicated informally to Mr. Penson by Colonel Byroade on 9 October: see No. 67, note 1.

[6] This letter (untraced) evidently followed up a proposal from Mr. Spofford to Sir F. Hoyer-Millar on 3 October that a meeting of personal representatives of the North Atlantic Defence Committee should be held to prepare the ground for the Defence Ministers' meeting on 28 October. On 11 October Mr. Shinwell replied to General Marshall, in a message transmitted in telegram DEF 17, that he doubted the necessity for a meeting of personal representatives and that the question was best confined to tripartite discussion at this stage. However he agreed that Marshal of the R.A.F. Sir J. Slessor and Air Marshal Sir W. Elliot could be available to attend a special meeting of personal representatives on 18 or 19 October if required.

Sir O. Harvey (Paris) to Mr. Bevin
(Received 11 October, 5 p.m.)

No. 269 Telegraphic [WU 1198/489]

Immediate. Secret   PARIS, 11 October 1950, 4.47 p.m.

Repeated to Washington and Saving to Wahnerheide, New York.

My two immediately preceding telegrams.[1]
German rearmament.

I am afraid it is now clear that there is no hope of getting the French Government to agree to the American proposals by the end of this month. Though M. Schuman was more reasonable than M. Moch, he did not differ on this point. All the politicians I have seen here lately have taken the same line on this, and it is clear that there would be no hope of getting the proposals through the French Parliament without a very strong line from the Government, which in view of M. Moch's attitude will clearly not be given. Though of course there is a good deal of dislike and fear of Germany here, I believe that French apprehensions are less of a German attack on France than of being drawn by the Germans into a war for Koenigsberg. The President of the Council made this point strongly to me in a conversation at the Elysee last night. There is also great dislike of having to ask the Germans to rearm as a favour to us, thus enabling them to make their own terms.

2. However I do not think we should take M. Moch's 'never' too seriously. In taking this very negative line I am sure he does not represent the attitude of the whole Government, or even of the whole Socialist Party; M. Lapie, the Socialist Minister of Education, was much less vehement on this topic when he lunched with me recently, though he made it clear that the party much disliked the idea. Moreover although the politicians have worked themselves up considerably about this the country as a whole is apathetic and would probably not react too strongly against a decision to rearm Germany, particularly if the alternative of a greatly increased military effort by France, as suggested by M. Moch, were put clearly before them. I have therefore very little doubt that given enough time we can bring the French round. But I should add that there is considerable resentment here of the Americans' bad timing in bringing this question up at this time, and a feeling that they do not understand the attitude of the average European towards Germany in the light of what they have suffered at German hands in recent years. M. Pleven said to me last night that he thought the Americans had incurred a grave responsibility in raising at this time a question which stirred men's consciences here.[2]

[1] Nos. 63–4.
[2] On his return from a visit to Paris, M. Massigli informed Sir R. Makins on 10 October of the 'great uneasiness' in France about German rearmament. 'In this atmosphere he did not

3. I think therefore that we should try to persuade the Americans to be patient with the French for a bit, and I hope that they will not press M. Moch too hard during his visit to Washington. I was impressed again at the lunch yesterday by the energy with which he is pursuing the task of recreating French armed strength, and I think it would be a great pity if he were forced to resign. I believe the American Embassy here agree with my view that he is the best possible French Minister of Defence, and I have no doubt that my United States colleague is urging patience in Washington. The best course therefore seems to be to work for some kind of compromise solution which could be discussed at the meeting of the Ministers of Defence at the end of this month. The Minister of Defence's proposal for a Committee to study the question, as recorded in paragraph 5 of my telegram No. 267, might well afford a way out. But on the whole I think it might be wiser at this stage to leave it to the French to put forward a compromise proposal. Mr. Shinwell's discussion with M. Moch and my interview with M. Schuman have given them plenty of material to work on, and I think they are conscious that it is now for them to suggest a way of avoiding a deadlock.[3]

see how a solution of the present impasse was to be found.' Also 'he had found some dissatisfaction at the state of Anglo-French relations with particular reference to this question. It was felt, rightly or wrongly, that we had ranged ourselves too quickly on the American side in this matter and that had we stood shoulder to shoulder with the French it would have been possible to move the Americans from their position' (minute by Sir R. Makins on WU 1198/491).

[3] This telegram and Nos. 64–5 were discussed at a Foreign Office meeting with Mr. Bevin on 12 October, when it was agreed to take no further initiative with the French and to 'leave the French and Americans to fight this out between them for a time' (F.O. telegram to Washington No. 4554 on WU 1198/499). When informing Sir O. Harvey of this decision, Mr. Bevin commented: 'I am disappointed at the negative attitude of the French. I am particularly worried that they seem to show so little realisation of the Russian danger and thus take no account of this most vital factor in the whole situation. 2. Nevertheless I do not wish to press the French further at present . . . you should take no further initiative. On the other hand, if the French have proposals to make on their own account, we shall of course be interested to see them' (F.O. telegram to Paris No. 2866 Saving of 13 October on WU 1198/499). Sir O. Franks and Sir I. Kirkpatrick were similarly instructed with particular regard to any developments on the American side. Sir I. Kirkpatrick was further informed by Sir D. Gainer on 13 October that 'Secretary of State is much disturbed at the number and variety of statements recently made in Germany with regard to remilitarisation and cognate questions . . . At this moment when difficult and delicate negotiations are going on between governments . . . he feels that all public references to these questions should now cease, as a continuation may lead to complications to the sole advantage of Russian propaganda. 3. Would you therefore see your colleagues urgently and try to induce them to hold their peace' (F.O. telegram to Wahnerheide No. 1630 on C 6543/57/18).

No. 66

B.J.S.M. (Washington) to Ministry of Defence
(Received 13 October, 4.34 a.m.)[1]

AWT 68 Telegraphic [CAB 21/1897]

Top secret. Immediate   WASHINGTON, 12 October 1950, 11.16 p.m.

For Air Marshal Elliot from Lord Tedder.
Your DEF 17.[2]

Please inform Minister that in Marshall's absence today I gave message to Mr. Lovett.[3] He explained that object of the proposed preliminary discussions was two-fold; to clarify minor questions so that Ministers could concentrate on major points and also to have preliminary N.A.T.O. and not merely Tripartite discussion on German question.

2. I explained that we hoped the Military Committee would largely meet the first object.[4] As regards the second object I think Marshall wants to get away from the position that the German rearmament is a unilateral U.S. proposal. Lovett said he had some reason to think that the French Cabinet might be preparing another 'Schuman' plan for 'Pooling' European manpower which could serve them as a political smoke-screen behind which a reasonable measure of rearmament could be accepted.[5]

3. The underlying object therefore of the preliminary talks is to 'keep the heat on' the French by all the other N.A.T.O. Nations so that the French will either accept our proposals or come up with an alternative. Lovett said he would welcome your being represented as you suggest.[6]

[1] Telegrams in this volume between the British Joint Services Mission and the Ministry of Defence (AWT, ZO, DEF), were transmitted and received according to Greenwich Mean Time. Where the time of despatch is not recorded, as in the present case, the time of origin is given.

[2] See No. 64, note 6.

[3] Mr. R. Lovett was U.S. Deputy Secretary of Defence.

[4] The Military Committee of N.A.T.O. was meeting on 24 October.

[5] French plans for a European Army were communicated to the U.S. Chargé d'Affaires, Mr. C. Bohlen, in Paris on 15 October (F.R.U.S. 1950, vol. iii, pp. 377–80). In reply to M. Schuman on 17 October Mr. Acheson stated: 'We are willing to consider some application of this [Schuman Plan] concept to the mil. field, although we envisage certain difficulties connected with its implementation . . . We wld. consider sympathetically and earnestly a specific French proposal on this matter . . . We do feel that any such initiative shld. be concretely expressed before or at the Oct. 28 mtg. of the Def. Mins.' (ibid., p. 385): see further No. 80.

[6] This telegram was discussed by Air Marshal Elliot and Sir P. Dixon on the morning of 13 October. Air Marshal Elliot evidently suggested that Sir O. Franks should attend the proposed meeting 'in view of the political issues which Lovett seems to expect the French to raise'. Sir P. Dixon advised against this as 'it is important that we should keep clear the distinction between the Council as the political body in the North Atlantic Treaty Organisation, and the Defence Committee with its military functions . . . Our view is that, if political issues are raised at this preliminary meeting, the right line for the Minister of Defence's Personal representative to take would be to recall that the Defence Committee were only asked by the Council to examine the question of German participation from a technical point of view' (letter from Dixon to Elliot on WU 1198/545).

No. 67

Letter from Mr. Gilchrist to Sir I. Kirkpatrick (Wahnerheide)

[WU 1198/520]

Secret   FOREIGN OFFICE, 13 October 1950

You will have seen Washington telegram No. 2730 of 10th October.[1] I now enclose a copy of a Ministry of Defence telegram[2] giving a fuller version of a draft memorandum which the U.S. side are proposing to put up to the Atlantic Council Defence Committee on 28th October. As you will see, this draft does not leave the French any loophole by way of offering to consider German participation *in vacuo*; i.e. without specific commitment on the main issue of principle; on the contrary, it compels acceptance of the main issue at the outset.

We had a meeting with the Secretary of State yesterday at which we considered the position arising out of Oliver Harvey's telegrams from Paris Nos. 267, 268 and 269.[3] After some discussion, the Secretary of State decided that we should do nothing at present in the way of bringing further pressure to bear upon the French, and that it would be better to allow the Americans to take up the running for the present; the outcome of the present visit to the United States of MM. Moch and Petsche[4] may help to clear the position for us. It was felt that any further pressure on the French might do more harm than good at present.

Thus, we are not yet in a position to define our attitude to the situation which will arise if the French maintain their present recalcitrant attitude on 28th October. The Chiefs of Staff, however, have prepared a draft brief for Mr. Shinwell for the Atlantic Council meeting, of which I enclose a copy herewith.[5] It is obvious that the point mentioned above will have to

---

[1] Sir O. Franks here gave the substance of a draft Defence Committee resolution, prepared by U.S. officials, recommending German contributions to defence of which Mr. Penson was informed by Colonel Byroade on 9 October (WU 1198/519). The full text of this paper, an early draft of No. 72.i, was transmitted from B.J.S.M. to London on 11 October in telegram ZO 324 (WU 1198/520). The summary sent in Washington telegram No. 2730 concentrated on the safeguards proposed by the Americans (1) no German unit larger than a division (2) German troops not to exceed one fifth of total force (3) no German General Staff (4) Allied control over officer personnel (5) no heavy weapons (6) continuing P.L.I. control. On 17 October Sir O. Franks reported a misunderstanding over heavy weapons. State Department proposed to allow tanks, if manufactured outside Germany (C 6623/27/18).

[2] ZO 324: see note 1.

[3] See Nos. 63–5 and No. 65, note 3.

[4] See No. 54, note 4.

[5] The draft brief (J.P. (50) 137 of 12 October) prepared by the J.P.S., in accordance with instructions (see No. 44, note 4), on the military case for German participation in the defence of Western Europe was amended by the Chiefs of Staff at their meeting on the morning of 13 October and circulated later that day as D.O. (50) 85. It is not clear which version was sent with this letter (see further No. 70, note 5). The brief was scheduled for discussion by the Defence Committee on 16 October: see further No. 68, note 9.

be covered by a supplementary brief at a later stage, but in the meantime we can perhaps make progress on the rest of the paper.

The first part of this brief is a somewhat academic recapitulation of the political arguments in favour of a German defence contribution; it may however serve as useful background for the Minister in case the French should trot out their old political objections to the proposal.

The main part of the paper, as we see it, is the section on safeguards. The Chiefs of Staff point out that they have only worked out the safeguards which seem to them desirable from the point of view of military security, and have not approached the problem from the political point of view. As you will see from the Ministry of Defence telegram[2] which I am enclosing, there are certain differences between our Chiefs of Staff's ideas and those of the Americans about the safeguards that will be necessary. I attach a short minute [i] which analyses those differences.

On this question of safeguards we have to strike a delicate balance between three factors:

(*a*) the need for achieving military efficiency;
(*b*) the need to provide safeguards sufficient to give the French confidence in accepting the plan and incidentally to protect ourselves against certain contingencies inherent in a revival of German military power;
(*c*) the need to provide the Germans with fair and honourable conditions of entry.

On these points our feeling is that we need not concern ourselves too seriously over (*a*), since once the main principle is accepted it should not be unduly difficult to secure an efficient working system. Our own Chiefs of Staff are thinking mainly in terms of the contribution which Germany could most usefully make to the Medium Term Plan.

The main danger is that by leaning too heavily on (*b*), we will land ourselves in serious political trouble over (*c*), and I am most anxious that we should not go forward in the N.A.T.O. Defence Committee at the end of this month on a basis which is destined to prove unacceptable to the Germans. It would obviously be best if the safeguards could be of a quantitative rather than a qualitative nature, i.e. that we should depend mainly on an accepted ratio between Allied and German troops in Germany. It is also desirable that the restrictions should be tacit and implicit rather than public limitations upon Germany which the Federal Republic would be expected to accept and endorse.

We shall be most grateful if you will look at this paper urgently in the light of the above considerations and telegraph your comments, particularly on the section on 'safeguards', so that we can have them by Monday morning [16 October].[6]

[6] This letter, together with a separate personal letter of even date from Sir D. Gainer (C 6425/27/18) apologising for asking Sir I. Kirkpatrick to work yet again over a week-end and

i *13 Oct. 1950 Enclosure*: comparison of U.S. and U.K. proposed limitations on German forces [WU 1198/520].

expressing appreciation for comments already sent (e.g. No. 60, note 9), crossed Wahnerheide telegram No. 1492 (received at 10.37 p.m. on 13 October). In this telegram Sir I. Kirkpatrick commented on the American draft resolution summarized in Washington telegram No. 2730 (note 1). He warned of the danger of drafting safeguards 'in such a form as to make them unacceptable to the Germans' and suggested that the A.H.C. might be able to secure the assent of the Federal government to conditions 'provided they were not officially published and made the subject of public debate' (WU 1198/553). Sir I. Kirkpatrick went on to criticize the proposed American safeguards in detail: see further No. 70.

No. 68

Memorandum by the Minister of Defence

D.O. (50) 80 [CAB 131/9]

Top secret   MINISTRY OF DEFENCE, *13 October 1950*

German Participation in the Defence of the West

Before I attend the meeting of the North Atlantic Defence Committee in Washington on 28th October, I wish to obtain the preliminary views of my colleagues on the question of German participation in the defence of the West. Discussion of this problem in the North Atlantic Defence Committee will be on the basis of the Resolution[1] approved by the North Atlantic Council at its meeting in New York on 26th September last, which requested the Defence Committee:

'In the light of the information available at the time of its meeting, to make specific recommendations regarding the method by which, from the technical point of view, Germany could make its most useful contribution to the successful implementation of the plan, bearing in mind the unanimous conclusion of the Council that it would not serve the best interests of Europe or of Germany to bring into being a German national army or a German general staff.'

2. My colleagues will recall that at its meeting on 1st September last,[2] the Defence Committee agreed that the United Kingdom should press for the creation of a German gendarmerie, 100,000 strong, under federal control as a step towards associating Germany with the defence of the West.

3. The United Kingdom proposal for the immediate creation of a federal gendarmerie 100,000 strong, was not accepted at the Tripartite

---

[1] No. 47.
[2] *Note in filed copy*: 'D.O. (50) 17th Meeting, item 3' (see No. 3.i).

Foreign Ministers' discussions in New York last month. Instead the Foreign Ministers agreed that a security police force with a total initial strength of 30,000 could be formed on a Land basis. Although this force is not to be a federal gendarmerie, it is to be provided with an Inspector-General and is to have a uniform system of recruitment, training and equipment prescribed by the Federal Government.

4. During the course of the tripartite discussions in New York, the United States Government came forward, as my colleagues will recall, with certain proposals for an integrated force for the defence of Western Europe and for the incorporation of German units in that force. These proposals envisaged certain safeguards to prevent the re-creation of a German general staff and a German national army. In consequence, the United Kingdom and France were invited to accept forthwith the principle of German participation in Western defence on the lines put forward by the United States Government subject to the safeguards proposed.

5. As the result of the United States proposal, the Cabinet[3] authorised the Foreign Secretary to signify the acceptance by His Majesty's Government of the principle of German participation in Western defence on the lines referred to in the previous paragraph; but the French Government indicated that it was not prepared to accept the United States proposals on Germany at that time.

6. In the course of the discussions, the United States Government put forward certain subsidiary proposals which were intended to be regarded as interim measures whereby Germany could gradually become associated more closely with the defence of Western Europe. These measures, which have come to be known as 'General Marshall's Eight Points,'[4] include proposals for the immediate strengthening of the West German Länder Police by providing them with automatic weapons, mortars and light armoured and engineer units; measures for the strengthening of the 'Dienstgruppen' or labour service units; proposals for the establishment of special sabotage security units and for the organisation of engineer units for minelaying and fortification construction. A Civil Defence Organisation was to be set up and plans were to be set on foot for making use of the industrial potential of Western Germany in the production of light military equipment and for using German raw materials for the production of heavy equipment outside Germany.

7. The results of the New York discussions may therefore be summarised as follows:

(a) The United States Government proposed that the three Occupying Powers should accept the principle of German participation in an integrated force for Western defence, subject to certain safeguards. The United Kingdom accepted the principle; France refused.

[3] *Note in filed copy*: 'C.M. (50) 59th Meeting, item 1' (see No. 27).
[4] See No. 43.

(*b*) The three Powers rejected the United Kingdom proposal for a federal gendarmerie, 100,000 strong, but accepted a modified scheme for a security police force of 30,000, organised on a Land basis but giving certain overriding authority to the Federal Government.

(*c*) The three Powers accepted General Marshall's so-called 'Eight Points' referred to in paragraph 6 above.

(*d*) The North Atlantic Council called upon the Defence Committee to make recommendations about Germany, as indicated in the draft Resolution in paragraph 1.

8. After the Tripartite discussions in New York had finished, my colleagues will recall that His Majesty's Ambassador in Paris was instructed to discuss the German problem with M. Schuman in order to try and see whether the French were willing to modify the views which they had expressed in New York about the American proposals.[5] At the same time, I discussed the matter with M. Moch in Paris on 10th October.[6] My talk with M. Moch left me with the feeling that there was little hope of the French Government modifying their present views on German rearmament, but recent telegrams[7] from His Majesty's Ambassador in Paris seem to give some ground for thinking that the views which M. Moch expressed to me are not shared by all his colleagues in the Government and are not reflected by French public opinion.

9. I may mention that when I was in Paris I suggested to M. Moch—making it clear that this was purely a personal idea of my own—that the French Government might agree to the study of the question of German rearmament and its military and political implications by a representative committee of the Occupying Powers. The committee could meet without being committed in any way. M. Moch was rather attracted by the idea and seemed to think that it might be one way of breaking the present deadlock.

10. Meanwhile, I would remind my colleagues that the German problem is to be discussed by North Atlantic Ministers of Defence, at the meeting of the Defence Committee on 28th October, and I therefore feel that it is not too soon that I should seek for their preliminary views on this crucial and controversial subject. We have just learnt that the United States Government have already prepared a memorandum[8] for consideration by the Defence Committee which makes it clear that they adhere firmly to the view that German participation both in man-power and industrial potential is essential to provide a force that can effectively ensure the defence of Western Europe, including the defence of Western Germany. The United States Government continue to recognise that certain safeguards are necessary to prevent the re-creation of a German

---

[5] See Nos. 59 and 64. [6] See No. 63.

[7] *Note in filed copy*: 'Paris telegrams to Foreign Office Nos. 267, 268 and 269 of 11th October' (Nos. 63–5).

[8] See No. 67, note 1.

general staff or a German national army but, subject to these safeguards, it is quite clear that they will continue to press strongly for German participation in Western defence on the lines that they have already proposed.

11. We can thus estimate fairly clearly what are likely to be the respective attitudes of the United States and French Government to this problem when the meeting of the Defence Committee takes place in Washington. It is for consideration whether there should not be at least a preliminary exchange of views between the three Occupying Powers in Washington before the meeting of the Defence Committee. In any case, however, I should like to have my colleagues advice on the problem in general and, in particular, on the questions—

(a) whether we should continue to do our best to persuade the French Government to accept the American proposals for Germany; and
(b) what line we should adopt if the French refuse to modify their present attitude and suggest that we should regard 'General Marshall's Eight Points' as a substitute for the American proposals.[9]

E.S.

[9] This paper was scheduled for discussion by the Cabinet Defence Committee on 16 October together with D.O. (50) 84 on the British contribution to an integrated force and D.O. (50) 85 on the military aspects of German participation (see No. 67, note 5). The Foreign Office brief for Mr. Bevin on D.O. (50) 80 recommended that he take the line (i) It was still too early to take a decision on general policy (ii) When in Washington the Chiefs of Staff should not bring special pressure on the French (iii) General Marshall's eight points were not an acceptable substitute for German participation in an integrated force. In order to allow more time for consideration of Sir I. Kirkpatrick's views (No. 70), discussion of D.O. (50) 80 and 85 was deferred (see further No. 70, note 7). In D.O. (50) 84 Mr. Shinwell proposed to offer at Washington one more division for Germany bringing the British peace-time total to just over four divisions. This proposal, made dependent on the materialising of French and American offers to increase their respective totals to 10 and 7½ divisions, was approved by the Defence Committee on 16 October (CAB 131/8 and 9).

No. 69

Minute from Sir R. Makins to Mr. Bevin

[UR 1027/16]

FOREIGN OFFICE, 14 October 1950

You may be interested to know that I had a brief conversation with Mr. Robert Hall who returned from Washington this morning.[1]

2. He said that in his opinion the visit of the Minister of State for Economic Affairs had been quite successful.

[1] Mr. Hall, Director of the Economic Section of the Cabinet Office, had accompanied Mr. Gaitskell on his visit to Washington (see No. 53, note 1).

3. As far as aid for rearmament was concerned, the Americans were not at present prepared to give up any forward assurance of a fixed sum covering a period of three years. They want to await the discussion which is to take place in N.A.T.O. on the equalisation of defence burdens.

4. Mr. Gaitskell's advisers are convinced that the proper course is for the United Kingdom to go ahead at once with the full £3,600 million programme, subject

(a) to the result of the N.A.T.O. discussions on the equalisation of the burden, and

(b) to a right to reconsider the United Kingdom position when the full impact of the programme has become apparent.

5. The Treasury hope that the Secretary of State will agree to a joint paper going forward to the Cabinet, put in by himself and the Minister of State for Economic Affairs, soon after the latter's return from Washington towards the end of next week.[2]

ROGER MAKINS

[2] Mr. Bevin minuted below: 'Subject to the Paper being agreed, I agree in principle to a joint paper E.B.' On 20 October Treasury officials returning to London with Mr. Gaitskell, who succeeded Sir S. Cripps as Chancellor of the Exchequer on 19 October, brought with them the first draft of No. 79 for discussion with the Foreign Office and Ministry of Defence.

No. 70

Sir I. Kirkpatrick (Wahnerheide) to Mr. Bevin
(Received 15 October, 4 p.m.)

No. 1499 Telegraphic [WU 1198/553]

Immediate. Top secret   WAHNERHEIDE, *15 October 1950, 2.10 p.m.*

Following for Gainer from High Commissioner.
Your letters of October 13th.[1]
We are clearly thinking very much on the same lines. The problem is to devise conditions of German participation which will alleviate French fears but will not prove unacceptable to Germany. I agree that any restrictions should so far as possible be tacit and not published. That is why I suggested in my telegram No. 1492[2] a public announcement of the principle and a confidential directive to the High Commissioners. You will remember that this procedure worked well before the Petersberg Agreement.

2. In general the conditions laid down in our draft brief for the Minister of Defence are obviously better thought out than those in the American paper.[3] But in my view we could go further than the joint

[1] See No. 67 and note 6 *ibid.*   [2] See No. 67, note 6.   [3] See No. 67, notes 5 and 1.

167

planners do in order to meet the French without colliding with the Germans. I believe that the Germans might be brought to agree to the following conditions. I prefer the phrase 'conditions of participation' to 'safeguards'.

(*a*) Germany would possess no national army.

(*b*) The German contingent like every other contingent would be integrated in Atlantic Force and would come under the operational control of the Supreme Commander and his staff.

(*c*) Germany would be suitably represented on the staff of Supreme Headquarters.

(*d*) Overall and higher operational command would be exercised in an integrated staff. Consequently since Germany would possess no national army, she would require no separate German operations or intelligence staff. But she could have the necessary administrative staff.

(*e*) In all the contingents the appointment of senior officers and of officers on the headquarters staff would be subject to the concurrence of the Supreme Commander.

(*f*) There would be joint higher training establishments. Direction and inspection of training would be under the supervision of the Supreme Commander.

(*g*) The highest German formation would be the division.

(*h*) The number of German Divisions will not exceed one fifth (or one quarter) of the total number in the Atlantic Force.

(*i*) The German contingent will have armour and a tactical air force in proportion to its strength. But tanks and aircraft will not be delivered except in small quantities for training until the Allied forces are equipped.

(*j*) German war production will be restricted to items specified by the Supply Board. All other equipment will be furnished by the Allies. The Military Security Board will be retained to ensure observance.

(*k*) In any event the Germans would possess no major war vessels, airborne forces, heavy and medium bombers, atomic, biological or chemical weapons, long range missiles.

(*l*) For the reasons stated in the Foreign Ministers London communiqué[4] the occupation regime will have to continue so long as the present international tension requires it.

3. I have not included in the above list of the conditions we might envisage the *arguments* adduced in the draft brief notably in paragraphs 29 and 31.[5]

[4] Of 13 May 1950: text in Volume II, No. 98.i.

[5] This appears to refer to J.P. (50) 137 rather than D.O. (50) 85 (see No. 67, note 5). Paragraph 31 of J.P. (50) 137 corresponds to paragraph 26 of No. 74 (D.O. (50) 89). Paragraph 29 (omitted from D.O. (50) 85 and 89) read '*Air Power*. There is the overriding insurance that the heart of Germany's war-making capacity lies within easy striking distance of British and American air power based on the United Kingdom' (CAB 21/1897). Paragraphs 29 and 31 of D.O. (50) 85 correspond to paragraphs 23 and 27 of No. 74.

4. You will see that I propose a fairly rigorous quantitative restriction of German Divisions. I do so because I believe that in no case would the French at this stage agree to 15 German Divisions. Secondly I doubt if the Germans themselves want to contribute a large contingent. I am not at all sure that 15 divisions could be raised by voluntary enlistment. If we had 5 or 6 German Divisions we could possibly recruit Germans for railway and other technical services for the whole force.

5. I doubt whether we need tell the French just now that we want the Germans to have local naval forces. The Germans show no particular desire to go to sea and I believe that we might attain our ends by quietly expanding our present German minesweeping force.[6]

6. The Minister of Defence knows all the arguments and it is therefore superfluous to brief him. But in my view the brief does not set forth sufficiently cogently or clearly what I conceive to be the main line of arguments: 'Nobody denies that the gap can only be filled by a German contribution. Unless the gap is filled the battle must be lost. Consequently the Americans cannot reasonably be expected to involve still more troops in an inevitable catastrophe. But if the Americans decline to commit more troops to Europe the gap will be still larger. In fact so large that the Western Powers will have to abandon any idea of effectively defending Western Europe.'[7]

[6] With reference to this paragraph Mr. Young warned of the risk to Anglo-French relations of going 'ahead on the sly like this'. Mr. Shuckburgh retorted: 'It is surely unnecessary to dot the "i"s of this by pointing out that it means they [the Germans] could have smaller, local vessels e.g. minesweepers. It will be clear to the French that this is implied, and I should not have thought they would object particularly, once the principle of defending Europe in *Germany* is adopted' (WU 1195/384).

[7] With regard to Sir I. Kirkpatrick's twelve points on conditions for German participation, Sir P. Dixon informed Mr. Bevin on 16 October that 'the first view of the Foreign Office is that they offer a better chance of being accepted by both the French and the Germans than either of the other two sets of proposals. On the other hand they clearly need looking into in detail' (WU 1198/553). It was agreed that the Chiefs of Staff and Foreign Office should concert to work out a further set of conditions of participation on the basis of Sir I. Kirkpatrick's twelve points. Action was then set in train for the revision of D.O. (50) 85 which included the recall of Sir I. Kirkpatrick and Sir O. Harvey to London for discussion on 20 October (see further Nos. 74 and 76). At the same time Sir O. Franks was instructed on 16 October to ask for postponement of the meeting of personal representatives from 19 October to the week beginning 23 October. He was also told to inform State Department that their proposals were being considered in London and to ask that no wider circulation be given to them until British views were available. Sir O. Franks replied on 17 October that State Department did not wish to postpone the meeting of personal representatives at which the American paper would be tabled. However State Department agreed to consider British views at a meeting with Embassy officials on 18 October. A Foreign Office redraft of the American paper, in line with Chiefs of Staff's views, was then telegraphed to Washington (F.O. telegrams to Washington Nos. 4620–2: not printed from WU 1198/514).

No. 71

Sir O. Harvey (Paris) to Mr. Bevin
(Received 19 October)

No. 433 Saving Telegraphic [C 6653/57/18]

Confidential   PARIS, *18 October 1950*

Repeated Saving to Washington, The Hague, Brussels, Luxembourg, Wahnerheide.

My telegram No. 430 Saving:[1] German rearmament.

His Majesty's Minister had a conversation on this subject on 17th October with M. de Margerie, Assistant Political Director at the Quai d'Orsay.

2. M. de Margerie complained of the bad timing of the Americans and our change of attitude at the New York meeting.[2] On the whole he thought that the results of this meeting had not been unsatisfactory. Though he had at first thought otherwise, he did not now believe that the Americans would make the despatch of their troops to Europe and their agreement to combined command dependent on French acceptance of German rearmament. He thought that the Americans were too deeply committed to both these measures to withdraw. What he did fear was that the Americans might get together with the Germans by themselves and

[1] In this telegram of 17 October Sir O. Harvey reported renewed public debate in France on the question of German rearmament: in particular an article by M. Aron in *Le Figaro* in which he argued the case for German rearmament and 'criticised M. Schuman's policy as tending to isolate France successively from all her friends, without any counterbalancing benefit to France' (WF 1022/48).

[2] In conversation with Sir W. Strang on 18 October M. Massigli returned (see No. 65, note 2) to this charge saying 'he did not think that the Secretary of State realised the extent to which M. Schuman and other French Ministers, particularly M. Pleven, had been pained by the rapidity with which we had changed our position on the question of German rearmament in New York and had come round to the United States view. If we had stood with the French rather longer than we did, we might have brought the Americans to change their attitude. It would have been more in keeping with the relationship of one Brussels Power to another, if we had not parted company with them quite so quickly' (minute by Sir W. Strang on C 6690/57/18). On 21 October the matter was raised further by the new French Minister in London, M. de Crouy-Chanel, who informed Sir P. Dixon in conversation that as a result of New York, 'relations between France and Great Britain could not be described as good at the moment'. Sir P. Dixon concluded that 'the object of the complaints which are now being made by the French is to bring pressure on us to be helpful to them at the forthcoming meeting of the N.A.T.O. Defence Committee. In fact what they are asking us to do is to go back, at least to some extent, on our declaration that we support in principle the idea of German rearmament. This of course we cannot do' (WU 1195/370). The memorandum at calendar ia was prepared as briefing for Sir P. Dixon when endeavouring to smooth the matter over with M. Massigli on 30 October. Sir P. Dixon then emphasised the efforts made by Mr. Bevin to consult M. Schuman at New York. M. Massigli 'admitted that it helped to clear up a misunderstanding. At the same time the fact remained that, although we had informed the French before we acted, we did not try to make a common front with them' (WU 1195/398).

create a German army in their own zone. He thought that Count Schwerin, who is apparently Dr. Adenauer's adviser on defence matters, was a sensible man, but he feared that General Guderian, under whose influence General Hays might well come, was a dangerous man with some very strange ideas.[3] M. de Margerie thought that German rearmament was now inevitable and agreed with the view expressed by M. Aron, quoted in my telegram under reference that now the matter had been raised the danger of provoking the Soviet Union already existed, and therefore the sooner action was taken the better.

3. Mr. Hayter asked whether the French Government intended to come forward with any proposals. M. de Margerie said that this point would be discussed at the Cabinet meeting on 18th October which is the only one before the debate on German rearmament in the National Assembly and before M. Moch leaves for the meeting of the Atlantic Treaty Defence Ministers in Washington. He was doubtful whether a real decision of substance could be reached at this meeting, since the Socialist Party, including the President of the Republic, was strongly opposed to agreeing with the American ideas.

4. M. de Margerie understood that M. Moch had not discussed German rearmament at all during his recent visit to the United States. American labour organisations had been persuaded to lobby him on the subject but M. Moch had replied that his Government had forbidden him to discuss the matter. M. Moch had received the impression that American views were very firm and unwavering. Good progress had been made, however, towards reaching agreement with the Americans on the French rearmament programme and agreement had been reached on the organisation of the French army and the number of divisions to be created. As regards French rearmament production, the Americans had maintained that they could produce heavy equipment more cheaply and quickly than the French. This no doubt was true, but the French were reluctant to make themselves entirely dependent on the Americans in the matter of arms. The Americans had been maintaining that it would be possible to retain control over the German army because the Germans would be unable to manufacture their own equipment, and this made an unattractive analogy when applied to the French army. This question was apparently not settled.[4]

[3] General Guderian, Chief of German Army General Staff 1944–5, issued a pamphlet in the autumn of 1950 entitled '*Kann Westeuropa verteidigt werden?*' in which he drew attention to the superior forces of the Soviet Union and the need for including German forces in a reinforced Western force as a counterweight.

[4] On 19 October Sir O. Harvey reported further that 'M. Parodi told me today that no final decision had been taken on German rearmament at yesterday's Council of Ministers but that a further meeting would be held on Monday [23 October]. He said that the French Government had become convinced now that the Americans were determined to go forward with German rearmament, and there was a tendency in the Government in favour of accepting the inevitable. But the opposition of the Socialists still remained' (WU 1198/518).

i *Oct. 1950 French complaint of rapidity of U.K. change of front at New York* is rebutted in F.O. memo. (see note 2) which traces events at New York with particular regard to stages of consultation with French delegation. Separate memo. for Mr. Bevin lists statements to French govt. on German rearmament since Nov. 1949. Shows some assurance that any change in policy must be a joint Allied decision, but no U.K. commitment to oppose German rearmament indefinitely [WU 1195/398; C 6594/57/18].

No. 72

Sir O. Franks (Washington) to Mr. Bevin
(Received 20 October, 7.10 a.m.)

No. 2825 Telegraphic [WU 1198/527]

Priority. Top secret   WASHINGTON, *19 October 1950, 9.58 p.m.*

Repeated to Wahnerheide and Paris.

My telegrams Nos. 2809 and 2810:[1] German participation in European defence.

After discussion with Lord Tedder it was agreed that I should attend the meeting of the personal representatives on October 19th at the Pentagon.

Lovett who was in the chair circulated the American paper, text of which is contained in my immediately following telegram.[2] The French

---

[1] Washington telegrams Nos. 2809–10 of 18 October reported discussion with American officials that day on the British redraft of the American draft resolution for the Defence Committee (see No. 67, note 1 and No. 70, note 7). The Americans explained that their own draft had now been expanded and already covered most of the British points. It was agreed that at the meeting of personal representatives 'we could not circulate any proposed amendments to the American paper as this would show that we had prior knowledge of it which would offend the French and others. But the Americans would have no objection if we introduced some of our points by means of questions designed to clarify the American paper' (Washington telegram 2809 on WU 1198/517). As regards the French attitude Mr. Perkins said that 'they did not expect that the French would be willing to discuss this paper or indeed any aspect of German participation in European defence before the Defence Committee meeting on October 28th. Their conversations with the French here had not thrown any clear light on the attitude the French would adopt at the meeting . . . the Americans had so far been basing their thoughts on the assumption that the French would somehow or other be able to accept the principle of German participation sufficiently to enable them to take part in the discussions. The American position had been that their proposals were a single-package offer. They had not begun to think what would happen if the French refused to accept the principle' (Washington telegram 2810 on WU 1198/516).

[2] This text, calendared at i below, was substantially the same as the paper of 26 October circulated by the American delegation to the Defence Committee as D.C. 29 and printed in *F.R.U.S. 1950*, vol. iii, pp. 406–9. British comments and suggestions for redrafting this text which was considered 'otherwise generally acceptable' were telegraphed to Washington on

Ambassador at once commented that he thought that no useful discussion of the paper could take place. He said there had been a misunderstanding if the Americans thought it had been agreed in New York that any discussion of the problem of German participation could take place before October 28th when the Ministers would assemble. Lovett urged the importance of giving the Governments opportunity to consider in good time the lines on which the United States Government for its part believed that this problem could be solved. Bonnet continued to object and asked that his views be recorded. Lovett maintained United States view.

2. The representatives were asked to communicate the paper to their Governments with a view to further consideration being given at the next meeting of the personal representatives on October 23rd. It was subsequently agreed that this date be changed to October 24th to avoid clashing with other meetings.[3]

3. In the circumstances I considered it would be unwise to attempt to introduce either by way of questions or otherwise the additional points contained in your telegrams[4] since it seemed likely that this would arouse further French objections possibly in an aggravated form, thus adding to the difficulties of the situation.

4. It will be seen that the Americans have incorporated in their revised paper the latter part of paragraph 2 of the text contained in your telegram No. 4621.[4] We had understood from the State Department that they were including certain other ideas from zone[5] redraft and would at least omit language prejudicial to the Germans providing their own tactical air support. They do not appear to have made this latter change though the draft has now been considerably expanded and strengthened in certain respects to which you drew attention.

Foreign Office please repeat to Wahnerheide and Paris as my telegrams Nos. 54 and 70 respectively.

CALENDAR TO NO. 72

i *19 Oct. 1950 U.S. Plan for German contribution to defence* as formulated in text transmitted in Washington telegram No. 2826 [WU 1198/528].

23 October and were evidently not taken up before its circulation to the Defence Committee as the basis for discussion on 28 October: see further No. 91.

[3] The British and American Chiefs of Staff were meeting on 23 October. At this meeting the British Chiefs of Staff followed instructions with regard to German rearmament (cf. No. 68, note 9). It was agreed that the question of pressure on the French government was a delicate one and that the matter should be pursued at a further meeting, this time with Political Representatives on 26 October: see No. 82, note 3 and *F.R.U.S. 1950*, vol. iii, pp. 1686–98. On 23 October the Americans deferred the next meeting of the Personal Representatives until 25 October: 'Reason given is absence of Lovett to attend funeral of Mr. Stimson. We believe they are also influenced by likelihood that few countries would be ready with comments on their paper' (Washington telegram No. 2854 on WU 1198/532: see further No. 80, note 4).

[4] See No. 70, note 7.   [5] This is evidently an error for 'our'.

173

No. 73

Memorandum by Air Marshal Sir W. Elliot

[CAB 21/1897]

Top secret   MINISTRY OF DEFENCE, *19 October 1950*

Some reflections on the present deadlock over the question of German rearmament

1. At the meeting of Foreign and Defence Ministers which was specially convened in New York at the end of September to consider the difficulties which the French had raised over the question of German rearmament, the Foreign Secretary made a very significant statement.[1]

2. Recalling how he, himself, had been the architect of the Brussels Treaty—and that from this had grown the Atlantic Pact—he confessed that the results hitherto had been a great disappointment to him. There had been much discussion and a great deal of planning, but little or no real progress had been made towards an effective defence of Europe which it had been the purpose of these two Treaties to create. In the American proposal for an 'integrated force', to which the Americans would contribute 'substantial forces', to be placed in Europe in peace under an American Supreme Commander, and in which they advocated the ultimate inclusion, under proper safeguards, of a limited quota of German military units, he saw, for the first time, some real hope of achieving that defence of Western Europe for which he had been striving so long.

3. The French do not, however, see the American proposal in this light. In their eyes, the recognition, even in principle, of a right, on the part of Germany, to rearm in any form, is denied on moral, psychological, and military grounds. The French case as it was put at New York by M. Schuman, the talk which Mr. Shinwell had with M. Moch in Paris on the 10th October, and the reports by Sir Oliver Harvey of his conversations with the French in Paris, all go to show that the French—or at least the present French Government—have no intention of giving way on this point.

4. We have thus reached a position where the Americans have made a proposal in which we all see great hope for the future of Europe. Part of this proposal includes the acceptance in principle of a measure of German rearmament. This has been accepted by us and rejected by the French. The question will come before the Atlantic Treaty Defence Ministers at their meeting in Washington on 28th October, when there is every probability that the Americans will force the issue in front of the other nine Nations of the Atlantic Treaty.

5. As in New York, so at Washington, much will depend on the attitude which we adopt. It is therefore of great importance that we should make up our minds on what our attitude is to be on this crucial matter. In order

[1] See No. 41.

to do so, it will, I feel, help us if we can find the answers to the three following questions:

(i) What is the true value of the American proposal?
(ii) How valid are the French objections to German rearmament?
(iii) Where do our interests lie?

The American Case

6. It is only necessary to contrast the American case today with that of a year ago to realise how profoundly the American outlook has changed. Almost to the day a year ago I was with Lord Tedder in Washington discussing round a table with the American Chiefs of Staff what they might be prepared to do for the land battle in Europe. The initial answer, given by General Bradley, was that they would do virtually nothing. A small American force would be sent to Casablanca whence it would survey the strategic scene and then decide where it would go next—perhaps northwards through Spain; perhaps, as in 1942, eastwards along the North coast of Africa to join hands with our own forces based on Egypt. Later, in discussion, we persuaded the Americans to modify this answer to the extent that they would at least give thought to the possibility of sending their forces to Europe, should the line there be holding. In practice this concession could not mean much, since the time which it would take the Americans to reach Europe, after the outbreak of war, would be such that their help would arrive, almost certainly, too late.

7. Thus, a year ago, American strategy was content to *liberate* Europe. Today it insists on *defending* Europe. Like ourselves, the Americans have reached the conclusion that an essential part of their protection lies in meeting and fighting the enemy on land in Europe. Like ourselves, they have come to this conclusion only after much profound heart-searching. Moreover, for them, it represents a departure from traditional thought even more radical than for us.

8. Though the decision to send American troops to Europe has been taken, and the announcement has been made by the President,[2] there is always the danger that the Americans may whittle down, or even withdraw, their offer. It has been made in the flush of the self-righteous enthusiasm—at times approaching spiritual elation—which the Americans are experiencing as the champions, as they see themselves, of freedom against aggression in the action which they have taken in Korea. This mood may, however, evaporate, and evaporate quite quickly. At the moment great pains are being taken by the Administration, in support of their own policy, to keep up the enthusiasm, but when the danger passes or appears to have passed, in Korea, and the full significance comes home to the Americans of what they are committing themselves to for the defence of Europe, this enthusiasm may wane; and nothing is more likely to make it wane than an apparent failure on the part of some of their

[2] See No. 1, note 7.

European partners to appreciate their offer at its true worth. They have already shown resentment at the way in which the French have looked their gift horse in the mouth.

9. What the Americans are offering us—substantial forces—present, ready, and fully armed in Europe before the outbreak of war—and an American Supreme Commander, is, in itself, of very solid military worth. Much more far-reaching, however, is the fact that implicit in the appointment of an American Supreme Commander is the unequivocal identification of the United States in the defence of Western Europe. We should, to put it no stronger, be very imprudent to do anything which might lose us the powerful military benefits which such an Ally can, and now appears willing to bring, to our need in Europe.

The French Case

10. The French welcome those parts of the American proposal which deal with the 'integrated force', and the Supreme Commander—as well they may since, understandably, it is they, first and foremost, who have always argued that the real danger lies in Europe, and that it is one which can only be averted by the creation of strong land forces. But they will have none of German rearmament. This, they insist, would be a mistake, both on psychological and on military grounds.

11. The arguments on the psychological side are familiar and easier to follow than are the military objections. Even so, the psychological arguments are not peculiar to France. No one will dispute the justice of the contention that the separation from the Germans by a Channel—and how much more so by an Ocean—induces a different mentality from that of those who share a common frontier with Germany. But France is not unique in sharing such a frontier. Nor is she alone in her experiences of invasion or of occupation by the Germans. Mr. Stikker put this point with moving clarity at New York.[3] He was prepared, on behalf of Holland, to accept 'eighty per cent of the American proposal', not because the Dutch were under any illusions about the nature of the Germans or about the risks which they would be running in agreeing to rearm them. The memories of German treachery and occupation remained all too vivid and painful. He had, himself, witnessed the shooting of over 100 innocent youths. The position which he had held in the Underground Movement enabled him to speak with authority about the hardships and privations which had been suffered under the occupation, by his countrymen— many of whom had died of starvation.

12. What is it therefore which makes it seem reasonable to the Dutch, the Belgians, the Norwegians, the Danes, and even to the Luxembourgers, to agree to a measure of German rearmament but impossible for the French to accept even the principle of such a step, when each is able to draw from its past experience arguments which apply more or less equally to the common problem which confronts them all today? The explana-

[3] See No. 32, note 3.

tion, I believe, is that the Dutch, without minimising the risks involved in rearming the Germans, assess the existing Russian threat at its true value and, confronted with the choice of two perils, they are in no two minds as to which is the greater. Clearly and dispassionately they see that, without German help, the battle for Holland—and, at least to that extent, for Europe—will be lost before it is begun.

13. The French, in their present mood, seem to be incapable of looking at the problem dispassionately, and therefore they cannot see it clearly. The whole of their outlook is poisoned by hatred, distrust, and fear of the Germans—a hypothetical fear of a possible future German menace so great that it has even eclipsed the fear of an actual and existing Russian menace. This unreasoning, if psychologically understandable, fear permeates and distorts all their thinking on this subject. They fear the Germans most—so much, indeed, that it will need two Allied Divisions to supervise every German Division. They fear not only the results which rearming the Germans will produce in Germany, but also in provoking the Russians. Thus, indirectly, they still fear the Russians. They fear the effect of German rearmament on the satellite countries. They fear their own public opinion. They fear their Communists. They fear—a fear to which one would have thought they might by now have become innured—the fall of their present Government. They are full of fear.

14. Worse than this, their fear leads them to the most wild and irrational arguments. It is they who, hitherto, have been loudest in their insistence that the safety of France demands that the battle shall be fought east of the Rhine. General de Lattre[4] was taken severely to task by M. Moch himself for lending himself to the very notion of a battle of withdrawal. Everyone recognises the elementary fact that the battle East of the Rhine will require more forces than one on or West of the Rhine—for which we already cannot find a sufficiency of forces—and that the gap cannot be filled other than by the Germans. The French, blinded by the fear of the Germans, ignore this. If German divisions, they say, are the price which we must pay for American divisions, and an American Commander (and all the consolidation of European defence which goes with this), then we would be happier to forego both.

'We will, if necessary'—said M. Moch to Mr. Shinwell, in Paris on 10th October—'form our ten divisions by next summer *without* American aid.'[5]

This, as a matter of military fact, we know to be impossible. But even if it were true it would get us very little way along the road to the defence of Europe east of the Rhine.

15. Equally irrational is the French attitude towards the Bereitschaften. Such are the martial qualities of the Germans that no safeguards will

[4] General Jean de Lattre de Tassigny was Commander-in-Chief of the Land Forces in Western Europe.
[5] See No. 63.

suffice to arrest the impetus of German rearmament once this is set in motion by ourselves in the western zone. Yet, begun as it has been by the Russians in the eastern zone, it constitutes no cause for alarm.

16. Finally, the French offer no solution to the very real problem—both a physical and a moral one—of how the Germans can be expected to accept the role of passive spectators in the battle for their Fatherland— other than the purely negative one of supposing that we can indefinitely continue to employ the same martial people as our hewers of wood and drawers of water.

17. The truth is that the French are refusing to face unpalatable facts. M. Moch, during his talk with Mr. Shinwell in Paris on the 10th October, said that not only he, but the whole French Cabinet, were unanimous in their refusal to consider now, or at any later date, the recreation of German military units in any form. We were mistaken, or had been misinformed, if we imagined that M. Schuman had spoken with another voice at Metz.[6]

Our own position

18. A profound change has recently overtaken our strategy in relation to the defence of the British Isles. We have accepted the view that our defence lies along a land line in Europe, as far east as we can make it.[7] A number of influences have worked to bring about this revolution in our military thought, politics, geography, strategy, the nature of the enemy and the threat which he presents to us, the trend of modern weapons, etc. etc. Another, and not least among these influences, has been the constant pressure which the French justifiably have brought to bear on us. We, in turn, have passed much of this pressure on to the Americans. They, in turn, have undergone an even more astonishing conversion.

19. The American proposal represents for us—and, one would have thought for the French—far more than we could have ever hoped for. The German clause should cause no surprise or alarm. As soon as thoughts about European defence began to take definite shape in Western Union, it became evident that sooner or later German participation would be inevitable. As Sir Ivone Kirkpatrick has clearly put it:

> 'Nobody denies that the gap can only be filled by a German contribution. Unless the gap is filled, the battle must be lost. Consequently the Americans cannot reasonably be expected to involve still more troops in an inevitable catastrophe. But if the Americans decline to commit more troops to Europe, the gap will be still larger. In fact, so large that the European Powers will have to abandon any idea of effectively defending Western Europe.'[8]

The present deadlock has been reached because the French *do* deny this. To fill the gap with Germans would, they contend, be the beginning of the

[6] See No. 64, note 3.   [7] See volume II, No. 43, note 2.
[8] See No. 70.

end of Europe. M. Moch made it perfectly clear when subscribing to Mr. Shinwell's suggestion in Paris that a commission should be appointed to study the question, that he did so only on the understanding that this would be a device 'to play for time and to save the face of the Americans'. Asked what he meant by time, he replied 'nine months, if you like'.

20. In these circumstances, where do our interests lie? We are committed to the defence of a land line in Europe. For us, the American offer—including German participation, of which we have declared acceptance by H.M.G.—is crucial. The offer is now in suspense because of French fears. The simple issue is—can we afford the loss of the substance of the American offer, with all that it means to us and Western Europe, for the shadow of French fears? From the military point of view, there can be only one answer. And this answer must, I feel, be given at Washington on 28th October. Time is *not* on our side. We cannot afford to delay. In a few months, if not weeks, American enthusiasm will wane; the Germans will become less tractable; the Russians will become more aggressive; the French will grow more cynical and apathetic; Benelux, Scandinavia and Italy will lose heart. If we pay too much attention to French susceptibilities at the forthcoming meeting of Defence Ministers at Washington, we shall take the heart out of the Atlantic Pact and be left to console ourselves, in Europe, with Portugal and Iceland.

21. Let us at least be sure of taking this 'current when it serves' and leaving it to others, if necessary, to be 'bound in shallows and in miseries'.[9]

WILLIAM ELLIOT

CALENDAR TO NO. 73

i *23 Oct. 1950 Letter from Mr. Shinwell to Mr. Bevin* enclosing notes by General Strong, Director of Joint Intelligence Bureau, of his conversations with German military experts, principally Count von Schwerin (defence adviser to Dr. Adenauer), during visit to Germany, 7–15 Oct. Germans consider that the danger of a Soviet attack in the West has now 'practically disappeared' as result of Western rearmament programme. Pace of Western rearmament should continue if Soviet threat is to remain abated. Bereitschaften are not considered a great menace but Soviet Union should not be underestimated. German conditions for rearmament include equality of status and treatment. Difficulties for von Schwerin include existence of 2,500 out-of-work and pensionless Generals in Germany. Germans doubt U.S. will remain in Europe long term. Importance attached therefore to France becoming an active and strong member of N.A.T.O. German military is fairly equally divided over N.A.T.O. membership: balance would swing towards joining once 'N.A.T.O. is a real live organisation' [C 6991/27/18].

[9] William Shakespeare, *Julius Caesar*, Act IV, Scene III. A copy of this paper was sent to Mr. Attlee, who instructed on 20 October that it be included in his week-end box for Chequers (PREM 8/1429).

No. 74

Extract from a Brief by the Chiefs of Staff[1]

[*CAB 131/9*]

Top secret   MINISTRY OF DEFENCE, *20 October 1950*

Part II
The urgent necessity for German military participation in the defence of Western Europe

9. The threat now confronting the Western world is the real threat from Russia, rather than a hypothetical threat from a rearmed Germany. If we do not make adequate arrangements for the defence of Western Germany she may well come to terms with the Russians. The greatest military threat that could confront the West would be for Western Germany to be aligned with the Russians.

Defence of Western Europe

10. Western Europe is the vital area—vital to the survival of both France and the United Kingdom. It must be defended—not liberated.

11. The present plan for the defence of Western Europe is inadequate even with expected United States aid, since it is based on the Rhine–Ijssel line, and would therefore:

(*a*) Abandon a part of Holland and leave Scandinavia open to direct attack.
(*b*) Lose Germany to communism and make the Tripartite Powers unable to implement their pledge to protect Germany.

12. The defence of Western Europe must therefore be planned to include Western Germany in order to:

[1] This brief was annexed to a covering memorandum by the Chiefs of Staff, D.O. (50) 89, entitled 'The military case for German participation in the defence of Western Europe'. The whole paper was circulated as a revision of D.O. (50) 85 (see No. 67, note 5 and No. 68, note 9) in the light of Sir I. Kirkpatrick's views recorded in Wahnerheide telegram Nos. 1492 and 1499 (see No. 67, note 6 and No. 70). In the covering memorandum, D.O. (50) 89, signed by the Deputy Chiefs of Staff, it was stated: 'It is not our province to say whether the time is now ripe to press the French to accept the principle of German rearmament. We can only point to the military necessity for it, marshal the military arguments in its favour and stress its urgency. This we have done in the form of a brief for the Minister of Defence, should it be decided that the United Kingdom should take this line when the question is discussed in Washington. 4. In the attached brief we have discussed the scale of a German contribution to Western defence in terms both of actual German strength and of the ratio of German strength to total Allied strength. We recognise, however, that the manner in which this aspect of the problem is handled is largely a matter of negotiating tactics. Since, therefore, it cannot be determined at this stage whether a ratio or a quantitative limitation is likely to prove more acceptable to the French, the United Kingdom Delegation must be free to decide which is most likely to serve our purpose, bearing in mind that our ultimate aim is the creation of 15 German divisions with appropriate air forces.' Part I of the brief, not here printed, recounted the background with particular reference to developments at New York.

(*a*) Have an adequate bulwark in front of France.
(*b*) Give proper protection to Holland and Denmark.
(*c*) Ensure the co-operation of Western Germany and firmly align her with the Allies;
(*d*) Ensure full American participation.

The defence of Western Europe, including Western Germany, will require greater forces than those required for the defence of the Rhine–Ijssel line.

13. The revised Medium Term Plan for the defence of Western Europe on the Rhine shows a requirement for 54 Divisions and 6,244 first-line aircraft by D+30 days.

Information given by Defence Ministers of their plans for the build-up of forces in Western Europe by 1954 indicates that there will be a gap of 20 Divisions and 3,700 aircraft in the forces required for resisting the initial attack alone.

We consider the most optimistic estimate of forces available, including an extra American contribution of five Divisions and 2,000 aircraft and greater planned European forces, would still leave a gap of the nature of ten to twelve Divisions and 1,700 aircraft.

14. The only method by which the necessary forces can be found to ensure Western Europe defence is by Western German participation. In addition, to incorporate German units in the integrated Western European Defence Force would also be an important 'Cold War' factor.

Unless adequate forces can be provided to close the gap between force requirements and present availabilities, there can be no prospect of a successful defence of Western Europe and there is even a danger that the Americans may refuse, with good reason, to increase their stake here. The result will be an even larger gap; in fact so large that the Western Allies would possibly have to abandon any idea of effectively defending Western Europe. Moreover, apart from the positive help which German Forces would give, there is the negative consideration that it would be militarily impossible to fight successfully East of the Rhine with Germany in a helpless state. There would be evacuation and policing problems of such magnitude that a large proportion of the Allied Forces would be required to solve them; and the confusion in the battle area would be such as to preclude effective military operations.

15. Britain and America, therefore, neither of whom likes the idea of German rearmament, have now accepted it as the only realistic means of ensuring the effective defence of Europe against the immediate Russian Communist military menace. On account of the defeat and occupation of Germany, any form of rearmament will take time. There is also the fact that indecision on the part of the Allies at the present time may eventually lead to a situation in which West Germany would be in a better position to bargain with us over the conditions we would wish to impose. It is therefore essential to accept the principle of German rearmament now so

that planning may start under conditions likely to be the most suitable to the Allies.

Why the United Kingdom has accepted the Need for German Participation

16. It is probable that the present inadequate build-up of forces is the maximum which can be achieved within the limits of the economies and world-wide responsibilities of the Western Powers, bearing in mind that they have all given first priority to Western Europe.

17. The United Kingdom considers that France should be the predominant military Power in Western Europe and appreciates her inevitable psychological reaction against German rearmament. However, her military security can only be ensured by a collective defence which would include Western German participation.

18. The recent United States offer is a unique opportunity which the Western Powers cannot afford to reject.

19. In view of the above conclusive military facts regarding the present indefensibility of Western Europe, the United Kingdom has weighed the risks and is convinced that subject to adequate safeguards such risks are acceptable. The safeguards are discussed below.

20. *The Risks of Militarily Strong Western Germany*—Like France, the United Kingdom recognises the dangers of a strong and independent Western Germany. It is considered, however, that these dangers can be avoided for the following reasons:

(*a*) German forces will be subject to limitations and integrated into an Allied Force (see Part III below) in such a way that they should not constitute a military menace to France.

(*b*) Perpetuation of unnecessary restrictions would cause German intransigence and might lead her to abuse her ultimate military strength, no matter how long it is delayed. Furthermore, compulsory restrictions on Germany can only be imposed by the maintenance on a permanent basis of the present occupation system. This is out of the question.

(*c*) Germany must, therefore, move towards equality of status with the rest of Europe, which means that she must voluntarily acquiesce in the measures of collective defence. Our political and military objectives can only be achieved if we lead her in this spirit with acceptable conditions.

Part III—Safeguards

21. It is essential to obtain German co-operation and this must be based on an identity of interest. Thus we can obtain the maximum safeguards for our own security against her future military resurgence. Whilst these are described as 'Safeguards' to satisfy French fears, some term such as 'conditions of participation' would be more appropriate in negotiations with the Germans.

22. The safeguards which we propose below are the most stringent which we consider are militarily acceptable, if the German contribution is

to be effective. Moreover, increased limitations over and above those proposed run the risk in our view of failing to gain German co-operation and incurring all the political difficulties without corresponding military results. We believe that the longer we delay approaching the German Government, the more likely they are to refuse to accept these conditions.

In general the safeguards would be that Western German forces would only be complementary to and integrated with Allied forces, numerically inferior to them and armed as far as possible with weapons of a defensive character.

The detailed safeguards envisaged are as follows:

General

23. *Occupation*—Allied occupation would continue until Western Germany's whole-hearted allegiance to Western ideas was assured. Thereafter Allied forces would continue to be located in Germany as long as the Russian threat existed, i.e., in the foreseeable future.

Integration of German Forces into N.A.T.O.

24. The German contribution to the integrated Allied Force under the Supreme Commander would not constitute an independent German National Force. The result of this would be that:

(*a*) Overall and higher operational command would be exercised by integrated international staff on which the Germans would be suitably represented.

(*b*) German formations could be disposed throughout the force as decided by the Supreme Commander.

(*c*) There would be no requirement for a German General Staff (Operations and Intelligence) above the Divisional level. There would, however, have to be a centralised national administrative agency with adequate representation at all necessary Headquarters in the field.

(*d*) There would be no German higher training establishments. Direction and inspection of training would be under the Supreme Commander.

25. It should be noted that the Americans propose[2] that the Allies should retain supervision of German officer recruitment.

We do not think that this is militarily necessary, and it would be very difficult to get the Germans to accept such a condition. We would prefer, as suggested by Sir I. Kirkpatrick,[3] to leave this problem to be worked with the Germans by the High Commission. There would be no objection, as he also suggests,[4] to the Supreme Commander having a voice in the appointments of senior officers.

Balanced Forces

26. The Germans would have to depend upon the Allies for certain major offensive forces and weapons. The type of forces, and the

[2] See No. 67, note 1.　　　　[3] See *ibid.*, note 6.　　　　[4] See No. 70.

arguments for them are set out in the previous Chiefs of Staff paper,[5] which can be summarised as follows:

(a) The Western Germans would not be permitted to possess the following types of forces and weapons:

(i) Major war vessels, including submarines.

(ii) Airborne forces.

(iii) Heavy and medium bombers, and long-range maritime aircraft.

(iv) Atomic, biological and chemical weapons, and long-range missiles.

(b) They would, however, be required to possess the following forces:

(i) Local naval forces, e.g., minesweepers, river craft and coast defence.

(ii) Conventional land forces. The highest formation would be the division.

(iii) Tactical and air defence air forces.

(c) The forces denied to Western Germany would make her incapable of aggression in a modern war against a well-armed adversary. *We suggest that detailed discussion of the military and air forces required be avoided.* Should this be necessary, it should be pointed out that from the military point of view:

(i) It would be unsound to deny Armoured forces to the Germans and they would not be likely to agree to their exclusion.

(ii) It would be equally unsound not to allow the Germans a divisional organisation and they would not co-operate if they were employed either individually or by units as mercenaries.

(iii) Tactical air forces and air defence forces must be permitted as there is a dangerous deficiency in the revised medium-term plan and the required balance could not be provided by the Allies.

It should be noted that the Americans do not mention naval or air forces, but it is not clear whether it is their intention to exclude these.

Size of Forces
(NOTE—Precise figures would be better unspecified at present)
27. *Ratio with Allied Forces*

(a) *Land Forces*—It is considered that if the Allied divisions which were either in Western Europe or could arrive there by D+30 days could outnumber the Germans by two to one the demands of Allied security would be more than satisfied. The Allies would have a greater actual superiority in view of their other forces stationed in France and Britain.

(b) *Air Forces*—It is considered that provided the Allied tactical air forces maintained a superiority of three to one, the Allies would be sufficiently secure.

[5] See No. 3.i for D.O. (50) 67.

28. At present the requirements of Western European defence, including the territorial defence of Western Germany, have not been calculated. It is probable that under the new proposals only the following forces, which are fewer than those which would be permitted by the above ratios, would be required:

(a) *Land Forces*—About fifteen divisions.

(b) *Air Forces*—Less than a thousand tactical aircraft, a thousand air defence aircraft and anti-aircraft artillery.

29. The above ratio is larger than that proposed either by the Americans[2] or the High Commissioner,[4] who, in addition, points out that the Germans may not be willing to raise forces of this size.

We do not, however, wish to limit ourselves to a ceiling which would mean that our military requirement could not be met. It could, of course, be pointed out to the French that this ceiling need only be reached if it was manifestly required and, in any case, would take a considerable time to achieve.

Equipment, Production and Research

30. *Equipment*—All warlike equipment would have to be manufactured to specifications agreed by the Allies. The rearmament programme and the issue of equipment would be subject to Allied control.

31. *Production*—German war production would be restricted to that required to fit in with integrated requirements as directed by the Military Production and Supply Board.

This appears to be a sufficient safeguard without the restriction to the manufacture of light equipment only as proposed by the Americans.[2]

32. *Research and Development*—Research and development would be limited according to requirements laid down by N.A.T.O. and controlled by the Military Security Board.

Time Factor

33. It would inevitably take some years to build-up and equip the required Forces. For instance, it would take one year before any divisions could be formed and at least two years for air force units, and before war production could be effective.

Summary

34. The building-up of the German contribution would take place in such a form and at such a limited pace that apart from her deficiencies of major modern weapons, Allied security under the conditions laid down would be ensured to the maximum extent. The time required, however, is of such a length that agreement to proceed with the necessary negotiations with the German Federal Government must be obtained now if the Communist threat is to be matched in sufficient time.

No. 75

Minute by Mr. Young

[WU 1195/384]

FOREIGN OFFICE, 20 October 1950

German Re-armament

At the risk of labouring this point,[1] I feel I should emphasise again that French inability to accept German Re-armament in principle now is not something that can be changed by the application of the necessary pressure, but is a fact deriving from the French political set-up, and must be faced as such. Were France governed by a dictator, he would doubtless be convinced by the remorseless logic of the Anglo-American case. But M. Pleven has to carry a vote in the Chamber, and if he fails on two votes of confidence the Chamber is dissolved,[2] which means, constitutionally, that a new Government has to be formed in which Ministers are represented in proportion to the number of seats held by the parties, i.e., there would be several Communist Ministers. Thus, pressure on the French may very well bring about a far worse state than exists now.[3]

2. This being so, it surely follows that, since we can't bring pressure to bear on the French, we should bring it to bear on the Americans, whom we need only ask for *time*, not concessions of substance. The alternative of us sitting it out altogether might well mean that the Americans will bring pressure to bear on the French on their own, and produce the same disastrous result.[4]

G.P. YOUNG

[1] See No. 46.i.

[2] Under Article 51 of the French constitution, two formal votes of no-confidence against the government during an eighteen month period could lead to the dissolution of the National Assembly. M. Bidault's government had been defeated on a formal vote of confidence in June, therefore only one more was sufficient to bring the dissolution procedure into operation.

[3] The constitutional position and alternatives to M. Pleven's government were examined in greater detail by Mr. Young in a memorandum of 19 October in which he concluded that although over the issue of German rearmament, 'the French Socialist Party may be more difficult to deal with than the other parties of the Third Force, there is at present no acceptable alternative to coming to terms with them' (WF 1019/62).

[4] In minutes below of 21 and 23 October Mr. Shuckburgh, Mr. Gilchrist, Sir P. Dixon and Sir W. Strang endorsed the principle of pressing the Americans rather than the French for concessions. Mr. Bevin minuted in reply: 'I decided, you will remember, not to press the French. I am ready to discuss next steps with the French after the vote. I was not aware of the constitutional issues.' On 21 October Mr. Hayter reported that M. Moch had succeeded in forcing the French government to agree to a full debate on German rearmament beginning on 24 October and commented 'It seems at present difficult to see how the Government can survive this debate intact other than by surrendering to M. Moch's views' (Paris telegram No. 442 Saving on WF 1019/60). Mr. Hayter's comments followed warnings from the Ambassador on 12 and 19 October (Paris telegram 418 Saving and Paris despatch 575 on WF 1019/53, 57) of the difficulties the French government were likely to face on

Indo-China, electoral reform and German rearmament once the National Assembly reassembled on 17 October. Despite M. Pleven's efforts at consolidation during the summer recess, Sir O. Harvey did not think his government would last long: see further No. 81.

No. 76

Note of an Informal Meeting held at No. 10 Downing Street on Friday, 20 October 1950 at 5 p.m.[1]

[CAB 21/1896]

Top secret

German Rearmament

The Secretary of State for Foreign Affairs said that there were four main subjects on which the Minister of Defence would require the advice of his colleagues before the meeting of the North Atlantic Treaty Defence Committee in Washington on 28th October:

(*a*) The re-organisation of the North Atlantic Treaty Organisation and the establishment of an effective command organisation to take control of an integrated force for the defence of Europe, irrespective of whether the Germans were included in this force or not.

(*b*) The financial and supply problem of equipping this integrated force effectively and in time.

(*c*) The problem of finding the necessary man-power and of deciding on the contribution which the United Kingdom might make to the integrated force.

(*d*) The question of rearming the Germans.

On the above four points, the first three were no longer controversial but it would be necessary for Ministers to approve formally a directive which the Minister of Defence might use in Washington. On the fourth point, however, there was still a great deal of controversy. The present position was that at the meetings of the Atlantic Council in New York the United Kingdom had accepted the principle of German rearmament. This had been thought the right decision in order that advantage might be taken of the American offer of substantial assistance to Europe. It had always been felt that it was necessary to defend Europe as far to the East as possible. The French themselves had insisted upon this point and the Dutch felt strongly that if the defence was to be conducted on the Rhine that would be catastrophic from their point of view, since they would have to surrender a large portion of their country without a blow. If the defence were to be conducted East of the Rhine, then it appeared essential to make

[1] *Present* at this meeting were Mr. Attlee (*in the Chair*), Mr. Bevin, Mr. Shinwell, Lord Henderson, Sir O. Harvey, Sir I. Kirkpatrick, Air Marshal Sir W. Elliot. *Secretary* Mr. G. Mallaby.

use of German production, German man-power and to integrate German divisions into the forces of the Atlantic Powers. There had never been any question of creating a separate German Army. The French, however, were unwilling to accept the principle of German rearmament and had still not made up their minds what position they would adopt at the forthcoming meetings in Washington. The French Government intended to decide a line of policy on 23rd October and to lay this before their Parliament on 24th October. It was probable, therefore, that by 25th October the decision of the French Parliament might become known. It was not possible to ask Ministers to decide a final line on German rearmament until this had taken place.

The following possible cases had to be considered:

(a) *French acceptance of the principle of including German forces in the Integrated Force.* In this case there was no problem and the way would be clear for detailed planning.

(b) *French Refusal.* In this case the United Kingdom should stand by the principle of German rearmament which it had already accepted and marshall every possible argument to convince the French to accept it also. The French were in a poor bargaining position. Although there had been some improvement in recent months and national service had been extended to 18 months and 10 divisions had been promised for next year, it remained unfortunately true that French morale was weak and that the French continued to depend upon the United States for equipment and aid. It was therefore difficult to see how the French could resist the pressure in the long run. Even if they could not be persuaded to accept the principle of German rearmament straight away, they might agree as a start that a scheme for German rearmament and integration in the defence forces should be prepared without commitment at this stage. It would be desirable that the Germans themselves should be included in this planning.

(c) *French refusal and unilateral United States decision to rearm the Germans.* This was a situation which might arise and which the French feared. It would probably drive the French into acceptance, but it would create an undesirable atmosphere. In any case the action to be taken in this eventuality could hardly be settled before it happened.

It was generally agreed by Ministers that, while there was every advantage in discussing these possibilities, no firm decision could be reached until after the meetings of the French Parliament in the following week. It would then be necessary to submit for the decision of Ministers a paper which would give the Minister of Defence a comprehensive brief for his meeting in Washington, in particular on the question of German rearmament. The line which he should follow could not be settled precisely until the decisions of the French Government were known, but in the meantime the Chiefs of Staff had already circulated a report on the safeguards which might be applied in the event of German rearmament (D.O. (50) 89).[2]

The Prime Minister emphasised the importance of reaching a decision one way or the other in the meeting at Washington. It was not acceptable that the present situation of doubt and hesitation should continue. The French should be pressed by every form of argument to come to some positive and helpful conclusion.

In the meantime, as Air Marshal Elliot had to take part in preliminary discussions in Washington during the following week, he should be authorised to say that in any event the United Kingdom stood by the principle which it had accepted at the Atlantic Council meetings in New York. He could also discuss, subject to final decisions by the Ministers of Defence, the various safeguards which the Chiefs of Staff were proposing against the dangers of a German military resurgence.

The Meeting:

(1) Invited the Foreign Secretary and the Minister of Defence to prepare a comprehensive brief which the latter might use at the forthcoming meeting of the North Atlantic Defence Committee in Washington.

(2) Authorised Air Marshal Elliot to follow the line agreed in discussion.[3]

---

[2] No. 74.

[3] In a note to Mr. Bevin after this meeting Sir P. Dixon put forward suggestions as to immediate procedure (i.e. to continue to leave the French alone) and the line Mr. Shinwell's brief for Washington should take. Sir P. Dixon suggested that 'the object should be to persuade the French to agree to a *discussion* at the N.A.T.O. Defence Committee of the conditions of German participation, even if they will not commit themselves to the principle of a German contribution'. Sir P. Dixon hoped discussion at Washington would enable the military experts to get ahead with working arrangements for an integrated force and that if possible the French should be persuaded to agree that the Germans themselves could be brought into such planning discussions 'on the basis of asking them what sort of contribution they had in mind to make when Dr. Adenauer made his offer. This could be done without necessarily implying acceptance of German rearmament . . . If the French can be brought along as far as this, the Americans should be induced to regard it for the time being as an adequate substitute for formal acceptance by the French of the principle of a German contribution. The above would give Mr. Shinwell and his representative something to go on, on the assumption that the French Government's decision is not entirely negative.' Sir P. Dixon doubted French response would be completely negative since 'I cannot help feeling that the French Government will do their utmost to avoid placing themselves in so extreme a position of isolation' (WU 1198/544).

No. 77

Mr. Bevin to Sir O. Harvey (Paris)

No. 3015 Saving Telegraphic [WU 1195/381]

Confidential   FOREIGN OFFICE, 23 October 1950, 3.5 p.m.

Repeated to Washington.

(German contribution to European defence.)
Please pass following personal message to M. Schuman.

(*Begins*)

I have been anxious not to burden you with any further expression of my views on the question of Germany's contribution to European defence on which you are now having to take difficult decisions in the French Cabinet. Unfortunately a statement attributed by the British press to Mr. Morgan Phillips at a meeting of COMISCO in Paris yesterday has given the impression that His Majesty's Government are still undecided on this subject which, as you know, is not the case.[1] I have therefore felt obliged to put out a statement, of which I am sending you the text. I have done my best to draft it in a form which will cause the least embarrassment to the French Government, while at the same time making clear our position.
(*Ends*)

2. My immediately following telegram contains text of statement.[2]

---

[1] See No. 50, note 2. On the morning of 23 October Mr. Morgan Phillips was reported in the *News Chronicle* as having said in a C.O.M.I.S.C.O. speech the previous evening that 'neither the British Government nor the Labour Party have yet made up their minds on the problem of German rearmament' (minute by Sir P. Dixon on WU 1195/381). In a letter to Mr. Bevin on 23 October Mr. Phillips confirmed an earlier telephone conversation with the Foreign Office in which he claimed to have been misrepresented: 'In fact I began my speech by saying "The British Labour Party as such has not adopted any clear policy on the question of German rearmament. I do not know whether the British Government has yet taken any final decision"' (WU 1195/397).

[2] In this statement, published in *The Times* on 24 October, it was made clear that the attitude of the British Government towards German and European defence remained the same as that stated to governments during the N.A.C. meeting in New York, namely that 'Germany should be enabled to make an appropriate contribution to the build-up of the defence of Western Europe' (F.O. telegram to Paris No. 3016 Saving on WU 1195/381). Sir O. Franks was instructed to inform Mr. Acheson in confidence of the action taken. When informing the Cabinet on the morning of 23 October of the 'alarm in official circles in Paris and in Washington' at the report of Mr. Phillips' speech, Mr. Bevin observed that 'the negotiations about Germany's part in the defence of Western Europe were now at a very delicate stage; and he hoped that Ministers would be careful to consult him before making any reference to this question in public speeches over the next few weeks' (CM (50) 67th Conclusions, minute 2 on CAB 128/18).

No. 78

Brief for Mr. Attlee[1]

[C 6737/386/18]

Confidential   FOREIGN OFFICE, 23 October 1950

The Prague Conference on Germany

Until a few days ago the Soviet and East German reaction to the decisions on Germany taken by the three Western Foreign Ministers at New York in September had been remarkably quiet. Some *riposte* was however to be expected, since the New York decisions had once again given the West the initiative in German policy.

2. The first Soviet step came on October 19th, when the Soviet Government replied to the Western Powers' notes of protest against the military character of the East German People's Police.[2] (These notes had lain unanswered since last May.) Both the tone of this belated Soviet reply, its instant publication, and the fact that it has not yet been received by His Majesty's Government, indicate that the Russians seized a moment of propaganda advantage. The note denied that the East German police was anything more than a normal police force and made counter-allegations that the Western Powers had abandoned the principle of German disarmament at the New York meeting and were going ahead with rebuilding the German Regular Army in the Federal Republic. The Soviet Government 'would not acquiesce' in these measures.

3. The next step was the Conference at Prague on October 20th and 21st, attended by M. Molotov[3] and the Foreign Ministers of Poland, Czechoslovakia, Roumania, Hungary, Bulgaria and Eastern Germany and by an Albanian representative. The Conference ended by issuing a long statement[4] containing four proposals:

(i) a declaration by the four occupying powers that they will not permit remilitarisation of Germany or its inclusion in any plans of aggression, and that they will carry out the Potsdam decisions[5] for creating a unified, peace-loving, democratic Germany;

[1] Mr. Attlee asked the Foreign Office for this brief in time for his weekly meeting with H.M. The King on 24 October. The brief, prepared in Northern department in conjunction with German (Political) department, was amended by Sir P. Dixon to include the views of the Russia Committee. This Committee of Foreign Office officials and representatives from the Chiefs of Staff, C.R.O., C.O. and B.B.C. met at fortnightly intervals to review the development of Soviet policy, propaganda and activities. For papers and meetings in 1950 of this Committee, see F.O. 371/86750–62.

[2] The Soviet note of 19 October is printed in *D.G.O.*, pp. 520–1: *ibid.*, pp. 493–5 for the Allied notes of 23 May and Volume II, No. 96, note 14. A text of the Soviet note, fully summarized in *The Times* on 21 October, was transmitted to the British Embassy in Moscow on 20 October and received by the Foreign Office on 23 October (C 6737/386/18).

[3] Deputy Chairman of the Soviet Council of Ministers.

[4] Printed in *D.G.O.*, pp. 522–527: F.O. text on C 7166/65/18.

[5] See No. 24, note 2.

(ii) removal of all restrictions on the development of German peace industry and prevention of the restoration of German war potential;

(iii) immediate conclusion of a peace treaty with restoration of German unity and a provision that all occupation forces shall be withdrawn within a year after concluding the treaty;

(iv) establishment of an all-German Constituent Council composed equally of representatives from East and West Germany to prepare for formation of an all-German Government and to be consulted in drawing up the peace treaty; in certain circumstances an immediate plebiscite of the German people can be held on this proposal.

The statement repeats the Soviet attacks on the New York decisions described above.

4. Like the Soviet notes, the purpose of this conference appears to have been largely propaganda. Both the conduct of the Conference and the resulting proposals bear a very close resemblance to those of the Warsaw Conference of June 1948,[6] which was held to counter the Western Powers' decision to set up a Federal Republic. The Prague programme is no more likely to be acceptable than the Warsaw one. Moreover the Conference has been held in a blaze of publicity; when the Soviet Government is really contemplating an agreement it usually makes the first approach in secret (as before raising the Berlin blockade).

5. In view of this the following seem the four motives most probably behind the Conference:

(a) The Soviet Union has suffered a damaging setback to its prestige in Korea and it has no doubt been casting about for an opportunity of diverting attention from the Far East and regaining the diplomatic initiative.

(b) Since the Communist defeat in Korea, there have been signs, as often after a Soviet setback, of a tactical pause in the Soviet offensive against the West. The Soviet delegation at the United Nations have been hinting at the possibility of a top-level Conference of the Great Powers to discuss outstanding questions, and the Prague proposals fall appropriately into such a phase of Soviet policy. The possibility cannot be excluded that the Russians may propose a meeting of the Council of Foreign Ministers, perhaps in the expectation that it would be refused. In that case Russia would hope to derive further propaganda advantage.

(c) The Soviet Government is genuinely concerned to prevent Western German rearmament, both for itself and as a contribution to the efficiency of Western rearmament as a whole. They can be sure of rallying Satellite opinion against it, though it may be doubted whether the German bogey is still as potent to frighten the Satellite countries

[6] For the statement on Germany issued on 24 June 1948 by the Foreign Ministers of the U.S.S.R., Albania, Bulgaria, Czechoslovakia, Yugoslavia, Poland, Roumania and Hungary after a conference in Warsaw, see *D.G.O.*, pp. 300–307.

after their experience of Soviet domination.

(*d*) They are equally aware that German rearmament is still a controversial subject for the West. The French Government and French opinion have been worried and divided over the whole question since the New York meeting. Next week the Defence Ministers of the Atlantic Powers have a meeting at which M. Moch will have to declare his Government's attitude to German participation in Western defence. By calling the Prague Conference now, the Soviet Government must hope further to divide and confuse French opinion, to make the French Government fear that any measure of German rearmament will be an undue provocation of the Soviet Union now that the chance of a settlement is again offered, and so to drive a wedge between the Western powers in the vital matter of defence.[7]

6. The meeting of Satellite Foreign Ministers may involve some action in respect of the network of agreements between the Soviet Union and its Satellites. Some of these agreements empower the Soviet Government to call for the help of the Satellites in the event of 'aggression by Germany or any Power directly or indirectly allied with Germany'; others, particularly the later agreements, refer to joint action to remove any threat of aggression. The possible courses open to the Russians seem to include:

(*a*) They can claim, as they seem to do in the Note that German rearmament has already taken place and can interpret this rearmament itself as an act of aggression.

(*b*) They can stage an attack by the East German Bereitschaften and describe it, as was done in Korea, as aggression by the Western Powers.

(*c*) In either of these cases it would be possible for the Soviet Union to call upon the Satellites to act with her or, if the Soviet Union did not wish to involve her own forces, one Satellite could no doubt be brought to call upon another.

---

[7] When discussing reasons behind the Prague statement in Cabinet on the morning of 23 October, Mr. Bevin thought that while it was probably aimed at influencing the French Government: 'At the same time it was probably true that the Russians were apprehensive about the consequences of rearming Germany . . . The *Foreign Secretary* also attached some importance to the failure of the political *coup* which the Russians had tried to stage in Austria. There seemed no doubt that the Soviet Government were nervous about the safety of their lines of communication in Eastern Europe and also of the position of Soviet citizens in the satellite countries. There were indications that they might shortly take further steps to consolidate their influence in those countries' (C.M. (50) 67th Conclusions, minute 2 on CAB 128/18). On 25 October H.M. Ambassador in Moscow, Sir D. Kelly, agreed that the Prague communiqué might increase the divisions in the French Government over German defence, but thought that the communiqué was primarily intended to reinforce the Soviet peace campaign and to give impetus to the National Front's campaign for the reunification of Germany. Sir D. Kelly warned of the difficulty of a Western refusal of Four-Power talks and wondered whether 'a non-committal but fairly conciliatory response, coupled with a suggestion that the Soviets should demonstrate their good faith by prompt settlement of the Austrian Treaty, would not be the best tactical line' (Moscow telegram No. 969 on C 7149/65/18: see further No. 86).

(*d*) They can streamline all the treaties so that they all take effect in the event of a threat of aggression only. If so, they could be made to refer to Western German rearmament much more easily than in the case of (*a*) above.

7. Although the general build-up of Russian propaganda makes it possible for the Russians to invoke the treaties if they wish to, it seems unlikely that they are contemplating any physical move, nor is there any evidence of such a move. References to the treaties are more likely to be intended to leave the Western Powers in doubt of the effect which their plans for European rearmament, including Germany, will have if pressed forward.[8]

[8] In a statement, issued on 25 October and printed in *D.G.O.*, pp. 533–5, Mr. Acheson dismissed the Prague communiqué as 'a return to old and unworkable proposals'. The immediate French response, as expressed by M. Massigli to Mr. Bevin on 23 October, was more cautious. M. Massigli observed the Prague proposals had in some ways made the position of the French Government over German rearmament more difficult: 'On the other hand, public opinion had been quick to note the implication that the determination of the Allied countries to defend themselves had brought about the Soviet proposals for a settlement in Germany. Speaking without instructions, M. Massigli said that he thought it most important that this proposal should not be ignored. The Western Powers should make some response. As the whole thing turned on the factual question whether or not the East German police were an armed force, he wondered whether it might not be possible to propose a Four-Power investigation to establish the facts. It would be difficult for the Russians to refuse this, and the situation might be turned to good account for the benefit of public opinion' (F.O. despatch to Paris No. 1054 on WU 1195/373).

No. 79

Memorandum by the Secretary of State for Foreign Affairs and the Chancellor of the Exchequer[1]

D.O. (*50*) *91* [*CAB 131/9*]

Top secret   LONDON, *23 October 1950*

The Finance of Defence

Our discussions with the Americans on the finance of rearmament have now reached the point where we can take stock of the position and consider what our future course should be. The decisions which we, in co-operation with the Americans and our other allies of the North Atlantic Treaty, must take in the next few months will be of far-reaching significance for the future not only in respect of our defence and economic policy but also for our foreign policy. This memorandum, after summarising the course of the recent discussions, sets out the considerations which we must take into account in making up our minds.

[1] For the origins of this paper, see No. 69, note 2.

2. By the middle of this year the British economy was doing better than could have been hoped at the beginning of the European Recovery Programme three years earlier. The internal position was healthy; we had full employment but suffered from neither inflation nor deflation. There was a steady and rapid increase in production and productivity. The external position was developing satisfactorily. The sterling area as a whole was earning a dollar surplus and the gold reserves were increasing rapidly. The United Kingdom was also in surplus on its current balance of payments, so much so that in May, June and July taken together there was no increase in the sterling balances and at the same time a large increase in our reserves of gold and dollars. In short, we were, provided the current trends continued, within sight of the objective which we had set ourselves at the beginning of the European Recovery Programme—independence of external assistance and a level of reserves at least equal to that which obtained when the European Recovery Programme started.

3. The aggression in Korea and the reaction to it of the United States Government was, in the short run, favourable to the continuance of this improvement for the sterling area as a whole, since it assured the maintenance for a further period of a high level of United States business activity. At the same time, however, from the longer-term point of view, the need for a substantial measure of rearmament on the part of all N.A.T.O. countries, accentuated as it has been by the worsening of the terms of trade for the United Kingdom, were new and unfavourable factors which radically altered the picture and threatened to impose a set-back to our recovery as well as that of the other free nations of the Western world.

4. This was the situation when towards the end of July the United States Government approached us and other N.A.T.O. countries with a request for 'information concerning the nature and extent of the increased effort both as regards increases in forces and increases in military production which His Majesty's Government and other North Atlantic Treaty Powers were willing and able to undertake as well as information concerning additional military production programmes which could be initiated with United States assistance.'[2] The United States memorandum added:

> 'The conviction of the United States Government that the achievement of security, economic well-being and cohesiveness in the Western World should be our continuing objective, remains unchanged. It is recognised that continuance of economic recovery in the near future, although possibly at a less rapid rate than heretofore, will be essential not only to the attainment of that broad objective but to the attainment of the immediate objective of greater military strength. While the United States recognises that rearmament will necessitate economic

[2] See No. 1, note 5.

sacrifices, including a reduced level of consumption, and retard the pace of recovery, it does not believe that the means which will be required to achieve increased military strength are inconsistent with the broader objective mentioned, but will, on the contrary, be essential to the eventual achievement of that objective.'

5. The United States Government requested an immediate reply in a form which could be published, and our reply,[3] which was delivered within ten days of the receipt of the United States request, stated that we were prepared to undertake over the next three years a programme, which it is now estimated would amount to £3,600 million, i.e., an average of £1,200 million a year, subject to the following qualification:

'His Majesty's Government does not, therefore, feel able to undertake consistently with the objectives indicated by the United States Government so full a diversion of productive resources to defence purposes unless the United States can offer financial assistance.'

Shortly afterwards a top secret memorandum was sent to the United States Government intimating that the assistance required was calculated at £550 million over the period.[3]

6. This exchange of memoranda was followed by discussions at the official level with the object of seeing whether the Americans would in fact be prepared to give assistance on the scale proposed.[3] These discussions made no progress and the Foreign Secretary was authorised to take the matter up with the United States Secretary of State in the discussions between the British, American and French Foreign Ministers in September at New York. As a result of this and in view of the urgent need to get the increased production programmes started, it was agreed to divide the problem into two parts:[4]

(a) American and British officials should discuss what immediate assistance the United States Government could give us on an interim basis towards the high-priority programme, totalling £200 million, which we had agreed to put in hand at once.
(b) American, British and French officials should discuss the longer-range problems of the implementation of the Medium-Term Defence Plan.

7. It is important to distinguish between the United Kingdom programme of £3,600 million and the United Kingdom share of the Medium-Term Defence Plan. The former represents our total defence effort over the next three years which we have offered to undertake with American assistance. It is based on the cost of forces and their equipment, and the figures are based on estimates of the most that our productive and other resources are capable of providing without mobilisation measures, such as restoring the direction of labour and the requisitioning of

[3] *Ibid.*, note 6.   [4] See No. 11, note 7 and No. 53, note 4.

factories. The Medium-Term Defence Plan is a statement of the military requirements in men and material for the defence of the North Atlantic area, i.e., it is prepared from the standpoint of what the military authorities consider to be needed, not from the standpoint of what can be provided. The cost of the Medium-Term Defence Plan is now being studied by the N.A.T.O. organisation and definite results are not yet available. But the stage has been reached in this study at which the countries are reporting the expenditure required to raise and equip their respective shares of the forces making up the Medium-Term Plan. The report for the United Kingdom shows that our total defence budget over the next three years, if it included the United Kingdom share of the Medium-Term Plan, would be of the order of £6,000 million. Any figures given at the present stage are, of course, provisional, and there are many uncertainties in the calculation. But it is clear at the outset that the United Kingdom defence budget over the next three years, on the basis of the Medium-Term Defence Plan, would far exceed £3,600 million.

8. The discussions on interim aid have now reached the stage at which the United States Government, in an aide-memoire dated 3rd October, 1950 (of which a copy is reproduced as Annex I to this memorandum),[5] made a definite offer to provide the dollar components of the £200 million programme (valued at $84 million) together with $28 million made available by the purchase by the United States Government of equipment produced in the United Kingdom. It was made clear that this offer, which was considerably less than we had hoped, was the best that the Americans could do in the light of our position and their existing legislative authority. It was also made clear that the United Kingdom equipment to be purchased by the United States Government would pass into their complete control and would not necessarily be transferred back to us.

9. Meanwhile, the tripartite talks on the long-term problem had resulted in the production of what has come to be known as the Nitze Memorandum, a copy of which is reproduced as Annex II to this memorandum.[5] (It is named after the author of the first draft, who is the Director of Policy and Planning in the State Department; but the revised form appended to this paper represents a proposal made officially by the United States Administration.) This document sets out a procedure for a multilateral approach to the fair division between the North Atlantic countries of the burden of implementing the Medium-Term Defence Plan, and represents the present view of the United States Government under which the long-term problem of the finance of defence is to be solved by allocating the measures required to carry out the Medium-Term Plan between the countries and distributing the cost.

II—*Political and Economic Considerations*

10. Before the implications of the Nitze Memorandum are examined, it

[5] See calendar i.

will be convenient to set out the main political and economic considerations which must be taken into account in determining our attitude towards it. The first point is that the objective of our whole endeavour is not to prepare for war but to seek to ensure peace. If we regarded war as inevitable, we should now be putting the country on a war footing and subordinating everything else to war preparation. The stage of recovery now reached would be overwhelmed in the general catastrophe and since we should, from the moment war broke out, be utterly dependent on an immense volume of direct American aid, considerable dependence in the preliminary stages would not make much difference. This, however, is not the position. We believe that, if we and our Allies prepare sufficiently quickly and thoroughly and are well organised and strong, war can be averted. It is this that leads the Americans as well as ourselves to insist that the continuance of our economic recovery is essential; it is this that makes them ready to offer us assistance so that recovery should not be dislocated and halted by the heavy impact of rearmament.

11. But the very state of affairs which makes the Americans ready to offer us assistance makes it desirable that the assistance should not take the form of direct aid on the lines of that given under the European Recovery Programme. The experience of the middle months of this year already referred to in paragraph 2 above showed what a difference to our position in the world was made by our rapid progress towards the attainment of economic independence. As the strength of sterling steadily increased so did the power and influence of Britain. We no longer had to rest content with the knowledge that we were a Great Power, but we were becoming able, for the first time since the war, to sustain our world-wide commitments. The visible growth of economic independence gave us weight in the counsels of the nations. If by accepting direct aid for military purposes we were to forfeit our economic independence we should lose the position we were just regaining as the principal partner in world affairs of the United States. We shall be back again in the European queue and our loss of power and influence will reflect itself in many ways. It will be more difficult to hold the Commonwealth together. Our position in Europe will be weakened. In the many negotiations and arrangements to be made in the months ahead we shall find that we are treated not as partners, though of unequal power, but as just another necessitous European nation. In general, the preservation of good relations between ourselves and the United States would become increasingly difficult.

12. An up-to-date assessment of the relevant economic considerations points in the same direction as the political arguments outlined above. Since the war we have lived under conditions of dollar shortage, with the reserves of the sterling area at or below danger point and with the ever-present need for dollar grants and loans to enable us to secure our essential dollar imports and to keep the sterling area together as a going concern. There has been no particular difficulty in proving our need, and since it was for dollars, it was natural that aid should be given by the

United States itself in this form. This is not the position to-day or for the immediate future. The sterling area is balancing and is likely to continue to balance its dollar accounts. The reserves, though still much too low for any striking change in our fundamental financial and economic policy, are certainly well above danger point and are still rising. We have indeed been told by United States representatives that it is their intention that we shall receive no more E.R.P. assistance after the allotment of $175 million for the current six months.[6] We cannot ignore this when we are considering the likelihood of our succeeding in any bilateral negotiations for further dollar assistance to us as the result of rearmament.

13. As has been said in paragraph 2, the British economy has shown a great deal of strength in the early part of this year, and the continued increase in production gave reasonable grounds for hoping for some easing of the burdens we had been carrying. As a result of the continued rise in the cost of our imports since Korea, however, the cost of living will certainly increase over the next six months. This increase is taking place as a consequence of general rearmament rather than of our own, but it is against this background that our new commitments must be considered. The addition of very substantial amounts to our defence expenditure will mean a direct burden on the Budget, and will involve either additional taxation or the reappearance of some inflation with all the adverse economic consequences that this entails. In the context of an inevitable rise in the cost of living, the political and social difficulties of increased taxation or renewed inflation are obvious.

14. Rearmament will compete with exports for our production, and at the same time the rapidly rising price of imported raw materials is causing a further deterioration in the terms of trade. It will therefore become increasingly difficult to avoid a deficit on the United Kingdom overall balance of payments, which will show itself in a rise in our overseas sterling liabilities. It will be still more difficult to attain that surplus which our external commitments require if we are not to run into debt.

15. These are serious issues. But they are issues which are facing all the North Atlantic Treaty countries, including in some respects the United States itself. They make inappropriate in the future the presentation of a

[6] On 19 October the E.C.A. informed British authorities that in view of the strengthening of central reserves of the sterling area, it was likely that E.R.P. allocations to the United Kingdom would cease at the end of the year (UR 2848/5). After bilateral discussions, Mr. Gaitskell announced in the House of Commons on 13 December an agreed formula whereby Marshall Aid to the United Kingdom was suspended as from 1 January 1951. British receipts of Marshall Aid then totalled $2,694.3 millions overall. In his statement Mr. Gaitskell expressed H.M.G.'s 'deepest gratitude to the Government and people of the United States for their unprecedented generosity in giving freely to Britain at a critical moment in history the means to regain her economic independence and power' (*Parl. Debs., 5th ser., H. of C.*, vol. 482, cols. 1162–1164). The next day Mr. Bevin sent the following personal message to General Marshall: 'I sat in House of Commons yesterday and heard Chancellor announce suspension of Marshall Aid and had you been there I should have wanted to go and say to you with a full heart "Thank you"' (F.O. 800/517).

special United Kingdom case calculated to convince the United States in bilateral discussion of our need for dollars. The arguments which we would now wish to put forward turn on a comparison between the worsening of our whole economic position as a result of rearmament both here and elsewhere, with the changes which will be taking place in the other countries concerned and particularly in the United States. Our arguments are entirely appropriate to a multilateral examination of what constitutes an equitable distribution of the new burdens. But they are not suitable to an examination of the position of the United Kingdom in isolation, and we would be unable in such an examination to provide adequate statistical justification for a direct plea for dollar assistance. Nor could we easily reconcile such a presentation with our basic determination to stand on our own feet at the earliest possible moment.

III—*The Division of the Burden*

16. The procedure envisaged in the Nitze Memorandum is—

(*a*) On the basis of the Medium-Term Defence Programme, there will be drawn up a statement of the military requirements in men and material.

(*b*) The requirements of material will be translated into broad production programmes for each of the N.A.T.O. countries, each being allotted the work it can best carry out from the technical point of view.

(*c*) The Governments will work out the cost to them of the tasks allotted to them.

(*d*) An assessment will then be made of the economic burden on each country—the assessment to take account of the total proposed defence expenditure of each country, including the expenditure required to carry out its share of the Medium-Term Defence Plan.

(*e*) On the basis of this economic analysis, decisions will be taken on the equitable distribution of the economic burden.

The method for reaching such decisions has still to be negotiated. But, in our view, there is one point, of first importance, for which the scheme must provide. It must not be confined to the fair distribution of a given total burden: it must also ensure that the total is not of such an order of magnitude that the division, however made, results in allocations which are intolerable for any of the countries concerned. In other words, the plan must be so framed that the assessment of the economic burden leads, not only to proposals for distributing the burden, but also to a review of the scale of the defence plan itself in the light of its economic consequences.

17. Given a tolerable total, the fair share for each country may be established by comparing the cost of each country's allotted task with a figure which is agreed to be the equitable share of the common burden for that country, having regard to its economic position in relation to that of the others. The principles by which this equitable share is to be

determined and the precise factors to be taken into consideration are not yet settled, but, roughly speaking, it may be assumed that the richer countries will be required to bear a proportionately greater share of the burden than the poorer and that the result will be to show that if the tasks allotted under paragraph (b) above were carried out, some countries would be bearing more than their share and others less.

18. The next stage would be a series of adjustments to secure that the object of the plan as a whole is achieved while, at the same time, each participating country bears its fair share of the burden and no more. These adjustments may take the form of some re-allotment of the tasks under the plan, or some revision of the scale of the plan itself, if required to ensure that the allotted tasks are tolerable. In addition, however, there will inevitably have to be arrangements whereby those countries whose effort in physical terms proves to be less than their fair share make up the balance financially, the money being made available to those countries whose effort in physical terms is greater than their fair share.

19. It is clearly of the utmost importance that the implications of this procedure should be clearly accepted by all concerned. From our point of view, they may be expressed as follows:

(a) Under the North Atlantic Treaty twelve countries are freely allied together to pursue a common end, each contributing to that end according to its ability.

(b) Under the procedure proposed in the Nitze memorandum the twelve countries sitting together will reach decisions on the magnitude of the tasks which each can reasonably undertake and on the fair and equitable contribution which each shall make to ensure that means are available for attaining the common end.

On the basis of these two concepts, any contribution made by any country, whether expressed in physical terms or financial, is a contribution to the attainment of the common end and this applies whether the contribution takes the form of supplying man-power, equipment or finance. The plan itself, with its allotment of production tasks to the countries technically best fitted to carry them out, envisages that some of the equipment produced in one country will be used in another; under the Nitze proposals, when the economic position of the various countries is brought into the account some countries will make financial transfers to others. In neither of these cases should the transfers be regarded as 'assistance' or 'aid'; they are merely the practical expression of the common agreement that will have been reached as to the best and most equitable way of achieving the common end.

20. One consequence of this is that each country will have the fullest rights to assure itself, through N.A.T.O., that any other country is carrying out its obligations. Indeed, without this, there could be no sound basis for continuing the alliance. Moreover, it must be recognised that the United States, as in all probability the largest contributor, will have a

particularly large interest in the procedures designed to ensure the due carrying out of obligations, but the relationship would be essentially different from that prevailing for Marshall Aid, when the United States alone, as the giver of aid, had rights of that character recognised under its bilateral agreements with the individual O.E.E.C. countries.

IV—*Conclusions*

21. The conclusions which we draw from the considerations set out above may be stated first with reference to the long-term problem and secondly in relation to the immediate situation.

22. *The long-term problem*—If it is accepted that it is neither desirable nor practicable that we should receive direct assistance from the United States, then we are irresistably drawn to the proposals of the Nitze memorandum.

23. It is important that we should not decide to embark on the Nitze plan without realising that it carries financial and economic risks as well as advantages. On the one hand, it is clear that the Nitze proposals offer virtually the only hope that the economic burden we shall have to bear will be tolerable in itself and equitable in relation to that borne by the others. On the other hand, the starting-point of the Nitze memorandum is the adoption of the Medium-Term Defence Plan as the basis for calculating the total burden to be distributed. We know that our share of the Medium-Term Plan involves a military effort for the United Kingdom far in excess of our £3,600 million programme and one which would not be practicable without departing from the basis on which our £3,600 million programme was based, that is (as stated in paragraph 5 of the published memorandum of 3rd August, 1950: 'It is the largest programme practicable within the period envisaged and without restoring the direction of labour, the requisitioning of factories or embarking on the slow process of building and equipping new industrial capacity which could not have rapid results.') It is therefore essential for us to establish that any plan for multilateral distribution provides that the shares allotted to each country are not only equitable but also tolerable, and that this may involve a revision of total defence requirements as well as their distribution.

24. We therefore conclude that it is right to proceed with the Nitze plan, provided always that the concepts which we see as the basis of the Nitze memorandum are understood and accepted by all concerned and, in particular, by the United States Government itself.[7] The tasks of securing the acceptance of these concepts and of carrying out the procedures will be of great technical complexity. We shall have to face United States insistence that they should have some close supervision both for Congressional reasons and to ensure that any transfers of dollars and equipment that they make are used for the purposes contemplated by

[7] A Treasury paper summarizing the British understanding of the Nitze concepts, as explained above, was sent to Mr. Nitze on 19 October (UR 1027/17).

N.A.T.O. We shall probably find other European countries more ready to accept this in return for the assistance which they feel they so desperately need. Nevertheless we feel that these difficulties must be faced and overcome if we are to secure not only the defence of the West but also the maintenance of our economic independence and political influence.

25. At this point it may be convenient to refer briefly to the outcome of the recent bilateral negotiations conducted between the Americans and the French. The French problem was particularly urgent because they must prepare their budget for their new financial year which starts on 1st January next. The assistance they have obtained, as published by the French on 18th October, may be summarised as follows:

	$ million	£ million
(1) Military equipment	1,600–2,200	786
(2) Equipment for Indo-China	275	98
(3) Dollar aid, described by the French as a first instalment of United States credits to go against French Budget deficit to 30th June, 1951 ... ... (Another $200 million expected from Congress in second half of 1951.)	200	71
	2,675	955

26. This treatment may appear generous, but these points should be remembered:

(a) It is greatly in our interest that there should be American troops stationed in Europe, and, as the condition precedent to this, a large and fully-equipped French force.

(b) The equipment and finance which the French are to receive must be regarded as an instalment, on account, of the arrangements which will be finally made under the proposals of the Nitze memorandum.

(c) The Americans have told us that, apart from finished equipment, the interim aid for the French will consist of dollar materials or off-shore purchases in France, and that the United States regard the interim settlement with France as on all fours with the interim offer they have made to us.

27. *The immediate situation*—We are here concerned with two main points: first, the reply to be made to the United States aide-mémoire referred to in paragraph 8 above, and, secondly, the status of the £3,600 million three-year production programme.

28. As regards the aide-mémoire it seems clear enough that we should accept the $84 million worth of dollar components in the £200 million high priority programme. This fits in with long-term concept under which end-items or components are produced by the countries technically best

fitted to do so and transferred to those who require them for the carrying out of their share in the common plan. On the other hand, the proposal that the United States Government should purchase $28 million worth of our equipment does not appear to fit in with basic concepts and a decision on it should therefore be deferred until the arrangements under the Nitze memorandum have been worked out in greater detail.

29. As regards the £3,600 million programme which we have announced we would undertake with United States assistance, it is clear that the basis upon which the United States request and our reply were made will be rendered obsolete if the proposals of the Nitze memorandum are accepted since we shall be considering our effort from an entirely different starting-point—the medium-term defence plan—and relying on multilateral agreement to secure that as a result the economic burden we undertake is equitable. This may well mean that our actual military effort over the three years may be greater than £3,600 million; but it also means that, to the extent that we secure a just multilateral settlement, the economic burden actually imposed on us will be no greater than we can fairly bear. Meanwhile, there remains the urgent need to get ahead with the placing of orders so that the production urgently required can be obtained in time. The authorities given under the £200 million programme will be used up by the end of this month and we must therefore give further authority so that production will not be delayed. This is a necessary interim measure and does not mean that we are committed either in practice, or in international discussion, to carrying out the whole of the £3,600 million programme; the worst that could happen, if in the event it proves that we are to undertake a smaller or different programme, is that we shall have involved ourselves in a certain amount of nugatory expenditure.

V—Recommendations

30. We therefore make the following recommendations:

(1) We should accept the United States offer of interim aid of $84 million for the dollar content of the £200 million instalment of the production programme to which we are already committed.

(2) We should reserve our position on the United States offer of interim cash aid of $28 million to be given by purchase of $28 million worth of our equipment, so as not to prejudice our position under the final arrangements for equitable distribution of the economic burden.

(3) We should proceed with the Nitze plan, that is, collaborate with the other N.A.T.O. countries in working out the procedure for determining on a multilateral basis the equitable division of the burden of North Atlantic defence between the partner countries. Our participation must be on the footing that the aim is to produce not only a fair distribution, but also results which are tolerable for our economy. The scheme must therefore provide, if necessary, for the review of the scale of the Medium-Term Defence Plan in the light of its economic consequences.

(4) Meantime a decision must be taken on the extent to which further commitments are undertaken on the £3,600 million programme before a final settlement is reached on the distribution of the defence burden between the N.A.T.O. countries. On the one hand, the stage has been reached at which further orders must be placed for many items over a considerable range of the complete programme if we are to avoid loss of time and the dissipation of capacity. On the other hand, the more we engage in commitments on our domestic programme, the more likely we are to suffer disadvantage in two ways. In the first place we prejudice our prospects of not being asked to carry more than a fair share of the burden under the Nitze procedure. Secondly, the programme itself may change as a result of the review of collective N.A.T.O. defence requirements and the capabilities of the partner countries, and we may find that time and money has been wasted by our embarking on the production of the wrong things.

In the light of these conflicting considerations, if our colleagues are satisfied that, notwithstanding the economic and financial consequences, we must proceed on the basis of the full £3,600 million programme, we recommend that authority should be given to place further orders, so far as these are needed to create or maintain productive capacity and avoid loss of time, within the £3,600 million programme and beyond the instalments of £200 million to which we are already committed. On the other hand, we should not be financially committed to the full programme of £3,600 million till progress has been made, with the determination of our share of the collective defence plan and the distribution of the economic burden between the North Atlantic countries.[8]

E.B.
H.G.

CALENDARS TO NO. 79

i *Annex I: Text of U.S. Aide-Mémoire of 3 October on Interim aid.*

Annex II: Nitze Plan suggests method for arriving at equitable distribution of economic burdens in carrying out Medium Term Plan [CAB 131/9].

ii *21 Oct. 1950 Practical difficulties of Nitze exercise* pointed out in letter from Mr. F.W. Marten (First Secretary, H.M. Embassy in Washington): in particular the gathering of facts and figures from each N.A.T. country likely to be long and difficult [WU 1114/1].

[8] The details of the £3,600 million defence programme were contained in a report by the Chiefs of Staff on the size and shape of the armed forces 1951–54 circulated by Mr. Shinwell to the Defence Committee with a covering paper, D.O. (50) 81, on 12 October. Mr. Shinwell estimated that the total cost of the programme was now in the region of £3,700 millions. Although the programme might require revision in detail, Mr. Shinwell asked the Defence Committee to accept it in broad outline: partly so that detailed planning could proceed and long-term contracts be placed and partly so that he would be in a position at the North Atlantic Defence Ministers meeting in Washington to give a forecast of the British contribution to the Medium Term Plan. On 24 October the Foreign Office was

informed that Mr. Shinwell did not feel that the conclusion of D.O. (50) 91 was sufficiently precise as to enable him to take a clear enough line in Washington. However, provided he could get a decision on his own paper, D.O. (50) 81, he would be satisfied. Both papers were therefore taken together by the Defence Committee at their meeting on 25 October with the emphasis on D.O. (50) 81. The conclusions of the Defence Committee included agreement to consider the American offer of interim aid and authorization for the Minister of Defence to put forward the proposals in D.O. (50) 81 as the British contribution 'it being understood that the commitment of the United Kingdom to the full programme of £3,600 millions was dependent upon several factors including in particular agreement on its share of the collective defence plan and the distribution of the economic burden between the North Atlantic Treaty countries'. Authority was also given for proceeding with detailed planning and the placing of orders (D.O. (50) 20th meeting on CAB 131/8). On Mr. Attlee's instructions, D.O. (50) 91 and 81 were then circulated to the Cabinet as C.P. (50) 247 and 248 respectively, together with a memorandum from the Prime Minister (C.P. (50) 246) in which he invited the Cabinet to endorse the conclusions of the Defence Committee on 25 October and to approve the recommendations in paragraph 30 of D.O. (50) 91 (now C.P. (50) 247).

No. 80

Sir O. Harvey (Paris) to Mr. Bevin
(Received 24 October, 1.10 p.m.)

No. 286 Telegraphic [WU 1195/366]

Emergency. Confidential   PARIS, *24 October 1950, 2.08 p.m.*

Repeated to Wahnerheide, Washington.

German rearmament.

The Quai d'Orsay have shown us advance text of statement to be made by M. Pleven this afternoon. This is still subject to alteration and must be regarded as confidential until he speaks. Summary in my immediately following telegram.[1]

2. Two points seem to require immediate consideration. In the first place there is the question of delay. It is clear that under the French plan no start can be made with raising German units until agreement has been reached on setting up a European Ministry of Defence and other political institutions, and further that negotiation for such an agreement cannot start until the Schuman Plan Treaty is signed.[2] I expect the French will ask

[1] Not printed: see calendar i for the final text of M. Pleven's statement to the National Assembly on 24 October in which he announced proposals for a European Army under a European Command and European Minister of Defence, communicated in outline to the American government on 15 October (see No. 66, note 5). When handing the final text to Sir O. Harvey shortly before M. Pleven began his speech on 24 October, 'M. Parodi said that the Government's declaration had only been agreed with greatest difficulty owing to the strong conscientious scruples held by various Ministers' (Paris telegram No. 289 on WU 1195/369).
[2] These conditions were expressly stated in M. Pleven's declaration, calendared at i below. For the progress of the Schuman Plan negotiations in October, see Volume I, No. 169. M. Parodi (see note 1) envisaged that 'by hurrying up the negotiations the Schuman pool

us to join them in pressing the Americans to accept this amount of delay.

3. Secondly there is the question of British participation. Nothing is said in the French plan about which countries are to be members, though the final version may include the United Kingdom among countries to be invited to negotiate,[3] meanwhile there is much speculation in the press here about possible British opposition to the plan on the grounds of our supposed dislike of European federation, allegedly on the principle of 'divide and rule'. No doubt the French Government would like us to come in, but I do not think they will make our participation a condition of proceeding with the plan. If, as I imagine, His Majesty's Government will not wish to come in themselves, I hope they will make it plain that they are nevertheless not opposing any wish of European Governments to federalise. We might make it plain that our attitude would be the same as towards the Schuman pool, i.e., benevolent support from the outside, and that our position in the military organisation would be the same as that of the United States, i.e. we would place our troops under the Supreme Commander in the unified force, (which would thus contain British, American, Canadian and European contingents).

4. I understand that it is intended that Germany should participate from the start in the negotiations for setting up a European Ministry of Defence, but that no German contingents should be raised until these negotiations are complete.[4]

CALENDAR TO No. 80

i *24 Oct. 1950 Text of Pleven Plan for European Army* as contained in address given by M. Pleven to National Assembly [WU 1195/383].

agreement might be signed by the end of November; the way would then be clear for negotiations for the European Army. The French proposals were definitely not intended to delay action. As the declaration indicated, the already existing national European forces would be at the disposal of the Atlantic Organisation from the outset.'

[3] In the final text it was stated that invitations to participate in negotiations for a European Army would be addressed to Great Britain and the free countries of Europe. In conversation with Sir O. Harvey (see note 1) 'M. Parodi implied that whilst the French Government naturally hoped that Great Britain would participate, they were prepared for adopting the same position as in the case of the Schuman pool, i.e. cooperation from outside.'

[4] According to M. Parodi (note 1) 'In the negotiations for the new European organisation, the Germans would take part on a footing of complete equality as in the Schuman pool negotiations'. Sir O. Harvey concluded that 'the French proposals must be regarded as the highest common denominator of what the French Parliament will accept and that were the proposals to be turned down flat in Washington, neither this nor any other French Government would be able to improve upon them substantially, and, if this government fell, a very difficult and unpredictable situation would arise here'. On receipt of Paris telegram No. 286, instructions were immediately telegraphed to Sir O. Franks for obtaining Mr. Acheson's reactions. It was explained in a following telegram that 'the Secretary of State does not wish to express any opinion on these proposals until he knows how they strike Mr. Acheson' (F.O. telegrams to Washington Nos. 4718–4719 on WU 1195/367). Sir O. Franks sent an interim reply on 25 October that Mr. Acheson had only just returned to Washington

from New York and was now working on the French plan. That day at the meeting of Personal Representatives (see No. 72, note 3) the French representative gave a short account of the plan. No comment was made by American or British representatives and a further meeting was scheduled for 27 October. Meanwhile Air Marshal Elliot was informed that in London: 'Plans for further discussion of German rearmament amongst Ministers have been upset by revolutionary proposals of French Government . . . Foreign Secretary is unwilling to reach firm conclusions until he knows something about American reactions. It is therefore difficult to give Minister of Defence a firm line before he leaves on Thursday [26 October]. Present proposal is however that he and Prime Minister and Foreign Secretary should have private discussion on this subject . . . just before he leaves' (DOTEL 378 of 25 October on CAB 21/1898).

No. 81

Sir O. Harvey (Paris) to Mr. Bevin
(Received 25 October, 10.9 p.m.)

No. 290 Telegraphic [WU 1195/374]

Priority. Confidential   PARIS, 25 October 1950, 9.56 p.m.

Repeated to Wahnerheide and Washington.

My telegram No. 289:[1] German rearmament.

The debate in the Assembly is still continuing and there are some important speakers still to come. But two points seem already clear. In the first place the House will probably approve the proposals by a fairly substantial majority. In the second place, anything going further in the direction of the constitution of German armed forces would have been rejected by the Assembly.

2. The conclusion to be drawn from this seems to be that if we wish the French to come along with us on this path we shall have to accept something on the lines of their proposals for a European army. I am not sure how important French assent is, but I assume that French divisions are not less important than German divisions in building up a unified force to resist Soviet attack. If this is so we must presumably make certain concessions to secure these divisions.

3. The French proposals seem to be open to objection on two grounds, that they are visionary or impracticable in themselves, and that they are liable to give rise to delay in proceeding with German rearmament.

4. As regards the first objection, the French Government agree, see paragraph 1 of my telegram No. 287,[2] that they are proceeding on untried lines, and they would undoubtedly have preferred to see whether the Schuman Plan would work before putting proposals of this kind. But the fact that nothing of this sort has been tried before does not necessarily mean that it is entirely unworkable, many though the difficulties will undoubtedly be. Though it was no doubt primarily Parliamentary

[1] See No. 80, notes 1–4.   [2] Ibid., note 1.

considerations which induced the French to put forward this plan, there is little doubt that the ideas contained in it correspond to a genuine feeling in France, and I believe in other European countries, that old fashioned nationalism is now out of date and that the only solution for Europe is some form of federalism. I hope therefore—as I said in paragraph 3 of my telegram No. 286[3]—that we shall not oppose this proposal purely because we think that the federalist ideas it contains are novel and untried.

5. The objections to the proposals on the score of delay are undoubtedly, in the present dangerous state of the world, more serious. The French are conscious of this and, as is apparent from M. Pleven's statement, are at pains to emphasise that negotiations for the constitution of a European army should not interfere in any way with the constitution of a unified Atlantic Force. They believe that the European nations, apart from Germany, could make their contribution to this force at once, without waiting for the prosecution of a European army, and that the negotiations for the creation of the latter could proceed simultaneously.

6. Nevertheless a factor of delay remains as regards the constitution of German units. The French comment on this is that Mr. Acheson said in New York that it would take two years to constitute German divisions; the French believe this estimate to be exaggerated and that German units could be created in not much more than a year, and that consequently Mr. Acheson's two year date line could be met while allowing a few months to elapse for the negotiations about a European army.

7. Whether this is so or not, it is clearly necessary to do everything possible to compress the delay imposed by such negotiations. It had occurred to me that it might be possible to begin discussions with the German Government about the constitution of German units, and possibly certain preliminary training, simultaneously with the proposed negotiations in Paris about a European army. But I fear that the French would be very strongly opposed to this, on the grounds that it would enable the Germans to play off the two sets of negotiations against each other and would make it more difficult for them to tie up the Germans in the European army. As a possible alternative we might consider laying down that the negotiations in Paris must be concluded by a certain date, say March 1st next. Meanwhile the Atlantic Powers, and in particular the Occupying Powers might be considering what contribution is required from the European army and the form and size of any German component in it. With a view to giving guidance to the French in their negotiations for constituting the European army, since clearly the other two Occupying Powers could not be expected to abdicate their responsibilities entirely in favour of the French in so important a matter.

8. Since the above was drafted United States Chargé d'Affaires here has told Minister that he is reporting in substantially similar terms about the French attitude. Mr. Bohlen believes that if we desire French

[3] No. 80.

cooperation it can only be got on the basis of something similar to present French proposals. In any case his advice is that the United States Government would be very ill-advised to reject them out of hand, though it might be found on examination that they would need very considerable modification. He has in any case warned the French (in particular MM. De Margerie and Alphand), that M. Moch, when he goes to Washington, will be subjected to very close cross examination by General Marshall on the precise significance of their plan, and that he will be expected to return detailed answers to questions about the relations between the European army and the Atlantic Force and about the exact meaning of the expression 'the level of the smallest possible unit' (see paragraph 3 of my telegram No. 287).[4]

9. M. Pleven is speaking at the end of the debate, but we shall not get the text of his speech until tomorrow morning. If he makes any important new points, I will telegraph them as soon as possible.[5]

[4] Paragraph 3 of this telegram (see No. 80, note 1) read 'The contingents to be supplied by high contracting parties would be incorporated in the European army at the level of the smallest possible unit' (WU 1195/367).

[5] On 26 October Sir O. Harvey reported that the National Assembly had approved M. Pleven's statement that morning by adopting a resolution in the following terms: 'the Assembly approves the Government's declaration, notably their determination not to permit the re-creation of a German Army or a German General Staff.' Sir O. Harvey observed that 'the terms of this resolution would appear to leave to the Government some latitude for negotiation' (Paris telegram No. 291 on WU 1195/376). French press reaction to the Pleven Plan was described by Sir O. Harvey as 'restrained approval' with some criticism that it showed 'more opportunism than realism . . . designed more to obtain parliamentary approval than to meet international needs in a realistic way' (Paris telegram No. 453 Saving on WF 1022/52). Immediate German reactions were more negative. Following on from his press statement on 24 October of the unequivocal opposition, in present circumstances, of the S.P.D. to German rearmament (Wahnerheide telegram No. 1534 on C 6791/57/18), Dr. Schumacher told Sir I. Kirkpatrick on 25 October that the Pleven Plan 'constituted a deliberate insult to the German nation and was wholly unacceptable' (Wahnerheide telegram No. 1538 on WU 1195/380). Dr. Adenauer 'deplored the publication of the French requirement that the Schuman Plan should be concluded before German participation could be considered. He said that such a condition might have been laid down privately without damage . . . He recognised, however, that the important question was not whether Germany should participate in Western Defence but whether or not agreement could be reached on some formula so as to enable the Americans to put in train the overall plan for a combined command and the constitution of a strong Atlantic Army in Europe. He hoped without conviction that this would still be possible. Otherwise there might be another fall in German morale and encouragement to the Russians and those elements in Western Germany who are ready to compound with them' (*ibid.*).

No. 82

Sir O. Franks (Washington) to Mr. Bevin
(Received 26 October, 4.55 a.m.)

No. 2883 Telegraphic [WU 1195/379]

Immediate. Secret   WASHINGTON, *25 October 1950, 10.22 p.m.*

Repeated to Paris and Wahnerheide.

Your telegrams 4718 and 4719:[1] German rearmament.

1. I saw Acheson this afternoon about the French proposals. They had just been formally handed to him by the French Ambassador.[2] Acheson told me that the views which follow were his own and those of the State Department. They had been talked over with General Marshall but the General had not yet been able to consult his own people so that these views are not yet officially accepted by the Defence Department or the American Administration generally. My impression was however that Acheson expected something very like these views to be generally accepted.

2. Acheson thought the Americans would approach the forthcoming meetings with the implicit assumption that the French by their new proposals had accepted German rearmament. The Americans would talk on this basis taking care to keep the assumption implicit and not explicit because the French would be likely to deny its truth if it was openly stated. He hoped in this way to get examination of the problems of German rearmament without having to face issues of principle at this stage with the French.

3. He felt there were two chief dangers to be avoided in the next few days. First, that things might so shape themselves that a flat turn down of the French proposals became inevitable. Secondly, that we might find ourselves unable to discuss any practical questions about Germany and German rearmament unless we had first accepted the principles implied in the new French proposals.

4. He thought the conference should make it clear early on that the French proposals contained political propositions of great range and difficulty and that these would have to be examined by other people later on. The Ministers of Defence and their advisers should put these political questions on one side and concentrate on what in the broadest sense could be called technical issues, that is, how to get on with the creation of a

---

[1] See No. 80, note 4.

[2] The American records of Mr. Acheson's meetings on 25 October with M. Bonnet, French Ambassador in Washington, and Sir O. Franks are printed in *F.R.U.S. 1950*, vol. iii, pp. 403–6. At his weekly press conference that day Mr. Acheson welcomed the French initiative. This prompted Mr. Shuckburgh to suggest on 25 October that a comparable British statement should be issued in order to avoid charges of insufficient sympathy. Mr. Bevin replied: 'I want to see U.S. reaction in response to instruction to Franks before a plunge into publicity' (WU 1195/382).

sufficient force in Europe and how the Germans came into this picture. In this way he hoped the French might be drawn into practical discussion of what over the next period of time could be agreed upon and done. This was a policy of little steps for little feet.

5. He felt it of great importance that the conference should produce some practical results. He doubted whether it could produce anything very major or striking. It might be that the French really did need more time, but it was necessary that the momentum of September should not be lost and that further real progress should be made.

6. Acheson did not really address himself to the merits or demerits of the French proposals in general. I should guess that his views are about what you would expect. He thinks that the French views are vague and in many ways unclear but that they have sprung from deliberate long-range considerations on the part of the French about the position in western Europe if over the next decade or more the Russian threat disappeared and American and British forces were withdrawn from the continent. He believes the French proposals are directed to such a hypothetical future situation and designed to ensure that if the integrated force at that time disintegrated there should not be a complete German army ready to the hand of the German Government as a result. He is not likely to accept or reject the proposals without a great deal of examination and before a good deal of time has elapsed.[3]

Foreign Office please pass to Paris and Wahnerheide as my telegrams 73 and 56.

[3] The preliminary reactions of the American military to the Pleven Plan were given at the meeting of British and American Chiefs of Staff with Political Representatives on 26 October (see No. 72, note 3). According to General Bradley the main objections to the Plan were (a) how the appointment of a supra-national Defence Minister could be reconciled within N.A.T.O. (b) difficulties of a common budget (c) delay caused by link to Schuman Plan and (d) doubt as to German participation. Dr. Jessup added that 'These far reaching French proposals went far beyond the scope of Defence Ministers and it would be for the Committee of Deputies and the Atlantic Council to pronounce upon many features of the Plan. It would clearly be unwise to reject these French proposals out of hand.' Sir O. Franks agreed and hoped that the proposals might prove to be a formula under which the French would discuss German rearmament. He emphasised the need to proceed quickly: a point endorsed by the British Chiefs of Staff who 'hoped that immediate effect could still be given to the proposal to appoint a Supreme Commander whose arrival in Europe might well have a profound effect on the development of the French plan' (British record of meeting, C.O.S. (50) 461).

No. 83

Record of a conversation between Mr. Bevin and M. van Zeeland at the Foreign Office on 25 October, 1950

[*WU 1195/385*]

Secret

The following were present:
Mr. Bevin, Sir W. Strang, Mr. R.E. Barclay, Mr. C.A.E. Shuckburgh.

Monsieur van Zeeland, Belgian Ambassador.[1]

After extending a warm welcome to Monsieur van Zeeland, Mr. Bevin asked him what particular subjects he wished to discuss. Monsieur van Zeeland replied that he was primarily concerned with North Atlantic Treaty and defence problems. He wished to discuss them both from the point of view of Belgium, and also in the light of his position as Chairman of the North Atlantic Treaty Council.

As far as Belgium was concerned, Monsieur van Zeeland said he thought there was almost universal support in the country irrespective of party for the policy represented by the Brussels Treaty and the North Atlantic Treaty. He had found a very satisfactory attitude in both Houses of Parliament on the question of the prolongation of the period of military service, and he thought that the necessary bill would go through in December or January. If there were large votes against the bill this would be purely for internal political reasons, and did not signify any basic opposition.

Belgian opinion, however, was seriously preoccupied by the question whether other countries were going to do their full share. He was frequently asked how the Dutch could be allowed to do so little in the field of defence and how the French could manage with only eighteen months' military service. People were concerned that there should be an equitable sharing of the burden, and they were also, of course, very anxious to be assured that there was no risk of their being left in the lurch if trouble arose.

In his capacity as Chairman of the North Atlantic Treaty Council, he was concerned with the problem of relations with O.E.E.C. He had had some preliminary discussion with Mr. Gaitskell in Paris, but he would be glad for more information about the position of H.M.G. He also wished to hear Mr. Bevin's views on the problem of German participation in Western defence. He would be seeing Monsieur Schuman in Paris, and would no doubt be discussing these matters with him.

Mr. Bevin said that one of the difficulties was that it was impossible to tell another Government what they ought to do in the field of defence, e.g. as regards the period of military service. As far as the French were

[1] Vicomte Obert de Thieusies.

213

concerned, he could only accept their word that they would carry out their undertakings and make their full contribution. What worried him, however, was that every time one French demand was met they came forward with another. At one point it had been represented to him that if only he could offer two more British divisions they would be satisfied. H.M.G. had agreed to this. Then they said that they must have an undertaking that American divisions would be available on the Continent. The discussions in the Atlantic Council meeting in London in May had apparently convinced the U.S. Government that they must try to satisfy the countries of Western Europe that they would be defended against aggression and not first overrun and then subsequently liberated. The offer which the U.S. Government had now made involving the stationing of considerable American forces in Europe in peace-time represented a tremendous advance in American policy. (Monsieur van Zeeland inter-jected that he fully agreed.) Mr. Bevin said he thought that the Russians had been duly impressed. His fear now was that the French were going to behave in such a way as to give the Russians a great deal of encourage-ment. He must admit that there was grave disquiet in Great Britain about the French attitude, and people did not understand all the party manoeuvring which went on when vital questions of defence were at stake.

As regards the question of German participation, Mr. Bevin recalled that the U.S. Government had not sought to make a bargain, but had presented a perfectly logical case, pointing out that it was of the utmost importance to the countries of Western Europe that if a Russian aggression took place it should be met as far east as possible. It was scarcely possible to contemplate fighting east of the Rhine if the Germans were not participating. One of the troubles seemed to him to be that, whereas the other North Atlantic Treaty countries were thinking in terms of building up powerful forces to act as a deterrent, the French were inclined to think more of what might happen if fighting began.

Mr. Bevin said that the new French proposals insofar as he could understand them did not appear very realistic, and he doubted whether the U.S. Government would find them satisfactory. He thought it would be of the greatest assistance if Monsieur van Zeeland could persuade the French Ministers to make some offer which would satisfy the U.S. and so make it possible to proceed with the plans for an integrated force. He believed that in this matter the French people were considerably ahead of their Government.[2] As far as the United Kingdom were concerned he had been happy to find that the proposals discussed in New York seemed to be in general accordance with the desires of the people. There had been very little criticism, and on the contrary he found general support for the idea of an integrated Atlantic force. If only the French Government could accept some formula which would be acceptable to the U.S. Government and enable them to satisfy the requirements of Congress, it should be

[2] See No. 54.i and Volume I, No. 177.

possible to work out a programme of priorities which would ensure that no German divisions were actually created until great strides had been made with the re-equipping of the forces of the Western European countries.

Monsieur van Zeeland said that he was one hundred per cent in agreement with what Mr. Bevin had said, and he firmly believed that it was possible for the Western Powers to make themselves strong, and in so doing to save peace. He was puzzled and worried by the new French proposals. He agreed that French public opinion was ahead of the French Government with regard to German rearmament. He himself had been surprised to find how Belgians who had suffered terribly from the German occupation were quite ready to accept the idea of enlisting German assistance in the defence of the West. Monsieur van Zeeland added that some of his recent talks with French Ministers had seemed to him more encouraging, and he thought they were genuinely looking for a way to get round their difficulties.

Monsieur van Zeeland then asked what Mr. Bevin thought of the French proposal for a common budget.[3] Mr. Bevin replied that to be frank he thought that this was a device to delay matters. He did not see how anything of the sort could be worked out without very lengthy and difficult negotiations. It was quite possible to rationalise the production of arms and equipment, but the problems of the different countries varied, and he thought that special arrangements would be necessary to cover the financial problem in each individual case. In the end there must be some rough equality of sacrifice, but this could only be worked out in the light of experience. This was how O.E.E.C. had developed. In the meanwhile he thought that the U.S. had been very generous to the French.

Monsieur van Zeeland said he did not think the French necessarily wished to hold things up, and he had been encouraged by a sentence in Monsieur Pleven's statement to the effect that, pending the conclusion of an agreement on the proposed European army, arrangements would proceed on the basis of the Atlantic integrated defence force.

Mr. Bevin then said that he was impressed by the urgency of the problem. He believed that if by the Spring of 1951 it was clear to the world that the building up of the Western defences was progressing rapidly and effectively, it would have a great effect on the Russians, and it might determine the policy they would pursue both in Europe and in the Far East. Monsieur van Zeeland said he fully agreed.

Mr. Bevin then said that he was concerned about the problem of Franco-German relations.[4] He had the impression in the spring that the Germans were really anxious to improve relations with France. This had been true both of the C.D.U. and the S.P.D. The success of United

[3] French proposals for a common defence budget (see No. 9, note 4) were included in the Pleven Plan (No. 80.i).
[4] For a report from Sir I. Kirkpatrick, received by Mr. Bevin on 24 October, of the deterioration of Franco-German relations, see Volume I, No. 173.

Nations action in Korea had also had a good effect on the Germans. He had the impression, however, that in the last few weeks there had been a slipping back on the French side. This might have been caused by their concern with the problem of German rearmament. The fact was, however, that the Western Powers were going to need the Germans and they must be very carefully handled.

Monsieur van Zeeland said that he fully agreed and he thought it was all the more important to reach a speedy conclusion on the question of German participation in Western defence.

Mr. Bevin said that if the French were not careful, they might cause the Americans in exasperation to look to Germany rather than to France as the mainstay of Western Europe. Monsieur van Zeeland replied that would be a catastrophe, but he quite agreed that the danger existed.[5]

Monsieur van Zeeland then said that he wished to talk for a moment about production. He thought that everything possible should be done to increase the production of arms and equipment in the West and he believed that Belgium could do more in this field. It was, however, necessary to offer some sort of inducement. It was not possible to persuade Belgian firms to turn over to arms production unless they were satisfied that they were going to receive payment from someone. He had been toying with the idea of some sort of clearing arrangement so that the countries who produced armaments beyond their own requirements could count on some settlement in due course. Perhaps this could be linked up with the question of United States financial assistance. Mr. Bevin said that he was only anxious to have the most efficient arrangements possible and to avoid duplication. He would be glad to go into the matter further.

Finally, Monsieur van Zeeland asked Mr. Bevin what he thought about the future relationship between the North Atlantic Treaty Organisation and the Brussels Treaty.

Mr. Bevin replied that he thought that much of the Brussels Treaty would inevitably be absorbed in the larger organisation, otherwise there would be duplication.

Monsieur van Zeeland said he agreed as regards the military aspect of the Brussels Treaty. He would, however, like to see the Brussels Pact continue in existence for political reasons. He thought it provided most useful contacts and that it would be a pity if these were lost.

[5] On Mr. Bevin's instructions this paragraph was deleted from the text of this record circulated in the Confidential Print Series.

No. 84

Notes by Mr. Shuckburgh for Mr. Bevin[1]

[*WU 1195/400*]

FOREIGN OFFICE, *26 October 1950*

The French Proposals

Objections to the Plan

1. The French plan is entirely out of line with the broad principles of the North Atlantic Treaty. It departs from the conception of the 'North Atlantic family of nations' for whose security, according to the Strategic Concept, the member nations were to provide for the 'combined employment of the military forces available . . .'[2] It seeks to divide the North Atlantic forces into American and Canadian forces on the one hand and 'European' forces on the other (with the possibility of British forces forming a third group if we do not join). The conception of a European Minister of Defence acting as an 'intermediary' between 'the European community' on the one hand and third countries or international organisations (e.g. N.A.T.O.) on the other cuts right across the Atlantic principle of an integrated collective force.

2. The plan also appears designed to postpone for a long time any possibility of a German contribution. First, the Schuman Plan must be signed; then a European political authority, with Council of Ministers and Special Assembly, must be set up; and then the Germans can only be incorporated 'at the level of the smallest possible unit'.

3. The plan also includes the well-known impractical French proposals for a common budget and 'a European programme of armaments and equipment'.

4. In short, the proposals represent, at their face value, a conscious move away from the Atlantic conception of defence, which we have always favoured, and towards a European federal solution, which is impossible for us and which we consider futile; or, at best, it is assumed that a European federal system must be an essential part of the wider Atlantic defence system. It is to some extent directed against American 'domination' of Europe, and is a bid for French leadership. Primarily, however, it reflects the French obsession with the German menace: it overlooks the present Soviet threat and concentrates on the remoter danger of a rearmed Germany in Europe relieved of the Russian menace and abandoned by the U.S.A.[3]

---

[1] These notes were prepared as a brief for Mr. Bevin's discussion with Mr. Attlee and Mr. Shinwell recorded in No. 85.

[2] For the Strategic Concept, here quoted, see No. 17, note 2.

[3] When discussing the Pleven Plan with the Portuguese Ambassador on the afternoon of 26 October, Sir W. Strang remarked that 'so far as the French plan was based on considerations of long-term policy, its intention might be to ensure that Germany should

Points in Favour

5. On the other hand, having regard to the extreme political difficulties with which the French Government are confronted, it may well be that large parts of the plan, including its most objectionable features, are designed mainly for internal parliamentary purposes and are not intended as immediate practical objectives. Many of these points are recognisable as the special favourites with French Socialist leaders such as M. Monnet, M. Guy Mollet,[4] etc., and may well have been inserted to secure their support in the current debate, to counterbalance the fanatical opposition of M. Moch to any German rearmament whatever.

6. The Government may have regarded this as a necessary smoke-screen to secure the passage through Parliament of the 18 months military service bill.

7. The plan implies acceptance by the French of the fact that *some* contribution by the Germans to Western defence must be allowed. This in itself is something to hold on to.

8. Now that the debate is over, and as the principle of a German contribution begins to be more fully accepted by French opinion, there may not be the same insistence on the other elements in the plan especially if, as seems probable (Wahnerheide tel. 1538)[5] the Germans do not like it. It may then be possible to get down to a discussion with the French, within N.A.T.O., of the safeguards and conditions of German participation, leaving the political aspects of their plan for longer-term examination.

Attitude of the United States Government

9. Mr. Acheson has given a public welcome to the initiative of the French Government 'in proposing a method for organising the armed forces in Europe, including those of Western Germany . . .' while admitting that it contains 'many far-reaching concepts which require careful study'.[6]

10. The attitude of Mr. Acheson and the State Department as revealed in Washington telegram No. 2883[7] is one of great caution. They are determined not to reject openly the French schemes, but intend to make the most of the implicit assumption that the French have accepted some form of German contribution. Their intention is to try on this basis to bring about a discussion in the Defence Committee of 'the technical issues, that is, how to get on with the creation of a sufficient force in Europe and how the Germans come into this picture' and to leave aside for discussion 'by other people later on' the longer-term political aspects of the French plan.

---

not become a party to the North Atlantic Treaty, and to ensure that, if at some future time the United States and British forces should be withdrawn from the continent, the French should not be left face to face with an independent German army' (WU 1195/406).

[4] M. Jean Monnet was Commissioner General of the Plan for the modernization and equipment of France. M. Mollet was Minister of State for the Council of Europe.

[5] See No. 81, note 5.   [6] See No. 82, note 2.   [7] No. 82.

Attitude to be adopted by His Majesty's Government

11. Our main objectives must be:

(*a*) to preserve the principles of the North Atlantic Treaty in the matter of defence and to oppose any separation between 'American' and 'European' defence responsibilities;

(*b*) to promote the quickest possible progress in the establishment of a Supreme Commander and the integrated North Atlantic force, the reorganisation of N.A.T.O. and the despatch of the promised American divisions to Europe.

12. The line of action indicated by Mr. Acheson appears exactly calculated to meet these two points to the best advantage in the circumstances. It would bring discussion of the strictly defence aspects of the proposals firmly back into the N.A.T.O. context and it suggests that the Americans may be coming round to the view that some delay over the German contribution may be inevitable, and that provided there is an *implicit* acceptance of the principle, progress can be made with the rest of the broad N.A.T.O. plan.

13. It is suggested therefore that we should support the line taken by Mr. Acheson as indicated in Washington telegram No. 2883.[7]

14. Assuming that the French are ready to fall in with this course of action and not to insist on any immediate acceptance of their own proposals, the time will nevertheless come, probably in December, when they will want to call together their conference in Paris. We ought to make it clear that we ourselves will not be prepared to join in any European combination of the kind indicated in the French plan; but we should time this in such a way as not to prejudice the French acceptance of the course of action outlined by Mr. Acheson. In other words, in order to help the French acquiesce in the continued discussion of 'the technical details' within N.A.T.O., it may be necessary for us to delay any too explicit rejection of the French proposals as a whole.

Conclusions

(1) Mr. Acheson's general approach offers the best way out of this impasse.

(2) His Majesty's Government should not openly reject the French proposals and should consider expressing some guarded appreciation of the French initiative on the lines of Mr. Acheson's public statement.[6]

(3) The Minister of Defence should support discussion in the Defence Committee on 'how to get on with the creation of a sufficient force in Europe and how the Germans come into this picture', leaving the broader political aspects of the French proposals for discussion elsewhere. If obliged to express an opinion on this, he should make it clear that His Majesty's Government could not, for their part, join in the creation of a European Army under a European Minister of Defence but would not oppose efforts of other countries to do so.

(4) The Secretary of State should send a message to Mr. Acheson expressing broad agreement with the latter's point of view.[8]

C.A.E. Shuckburgh

Calendar to No. 84

i 25–31 Oct. 1950 *Interpretation of Pleven Plan by French Embassy. M. Lebel*: Pleven plan intended to meet a Parliamentary emergency and 'to paper over a crack'. Plan not workable—idea of smallest possible unit a 'military and political nonsense' clearly unacceptable to Germans [C 6862/57/18]. *M. de Crouy Chanel*: Pleven plan a '*canard*' to deflect Americans from immediate rearmament of Germany. Hopes Britain will not insist too much on the obvious inherent difficulties of plan but will regard it as long term plan which might ultimately have useful features. Nothing sacrosanct about plan. French govt. might be glad of a way out of it e.g. by positive response to Soviet proposal for a C.F.M. [WU 1195/394]. *M. Massigli*: also implies Plan devised as delaying tactic. 'Heart of the matter was that the French believed that under the American plan the emergence of a German national army . . . was inevitable in a comparatively short time.' Suggests tripartite meeting after Defence Committee meeting to examine U.S., French and any British proposals [WU 1195/399].

[8] Mr. Bevin square-bracketed this paragraph and instructed in the margin 'delete' (see No. 82, note 2). In a minute below Sir P. Dixon endorsed Mr. Shuckburgh's conclusions as 'the only possible line for the present'. However, he warned that there was 'a real possibility that the French will not be prepared to agree that their own proposals should be divided up in this way. They may insist that no further planning for the defence of Europe is possible until their proposals, or something like them, have been accepted . . . We may reach an impasse in Washington. If that were to happen, a critical situation would arise with which the N.A.T.O. Defence Committee would not be capable of dealing' (WU 1195/400).

No. 85

Note of an Informal Meeting of Ministers held at No. 10 Downing Street on Thursday, 26 October, 1950[1]

[*CAB 21/1898*]

Top secret

The Prime Minister said that the object of the meeting was to advise the Minister of Defence on the line he should follow at the meeting of the North Atlantic Defence Committee in Washington on 28th October. It was particularly important that he should know what attitude to adopt towards the latest French proposals for the creation of a European Army under a European Minister of Defence. There were, in addition, two proposals which the Minister of Defence himself wanted authority to put

[1] *Present* at this meeting were Mr. Attlee (*in the Chair*), Mr. Bevin and Mr. Shinwell. *Secretary* Mr. Mallaby.

before his Atlantic Treaty colleagues. (Memorandum by the Minister of Defence attached to this record as Annex I.)

The essential point was that the Ministers of Defence of the Atlantic Treaty Powers should come to decisions on the Agenda which had been prepared for their meeting and should not be drawn aside into discussions of the latest French proposals, which had not yet been sufficiently explained and which were in any case full of political implications. Nothing should be allowed to disturb the concept of the Atlantic Treaty and the smooth working of the organisation which had been established under it.

On the question of the re-organisation of N.A.T.O. there was no objection to the Minister of Defence putting forward his own proposals:

(*a*) That if the Americans were willing to go no further than the appointment of a Chief of Staff, then Lord Montgomery should fulfil the functions of the Supreme Commander until the American Supreme Commander had been appointed.

(*b*) That any group of European Defence Ministers should have liberty to meet as they pleased, to ensure that the defence objectives of the North Atlantic Treaty were being actively pursued by European national authorities.

The Meeting:

Agreed that their conclusions should be summarised in a brief for the Minister of Defence, which should also be telegraphed to H.M. Ambassador in Washington (attached as Annex II to this record).

Annex I to No. 85

Memorandum by the Minister of Defence

Reorganisation of the North Atlantic Treaty Organisation in Europe

In adopting a resolution on the defence of Western Europe at their meeting on the 26th September, the North Atlantic Treaty Council approved the concept of an integrated force adequate to deter aggression and ensure the defence of Western Europe, including Western Germany. In order to implement this concept, the Council directed the Defence Committee to examine, and make recommendations on, a number of detailed problems on which further agreement would have to be reached.

2. Accordingly the Standing Group have prepared the necessary papers on these detailed problems for consideration by the Military Committee at their meeting on the 24th October, who will forward them for the consideration of the Defence Committee at their meeting on the 28th October.

European Command

3. This re-organisation, with the consequent dissolution of the existing

European Regional Planning Groups, gives rise to the question of the future relationship between the defence organisations under the Brussels Treaty and those under the North Atlantic Treaty. When the North Atlantic Treaty Organisation was set up, the Western Union Defence Organisation became, in fact, the Western European Regional Planning Group but still retained its structure from the Consultative Council and Western Union Defence Committee downwards. In the other Regional Planning Groups, however, no provision was made for Defence Ministers of those groups to meet as a Committee.

4. It is likely that the Military Committee will now recommend that the Defence Committee should suggest to the Western Union Defence Organisation that it review, as soon as possible, its status in the light of the establishment of an overall North Atlantic Treaty Command Organisation, making available those elements which could advantageously be merged and disbanding those no longer required. However, it is likely that the Defence Committee will acknowledge that the Defence Ministers and Chiefs of Staff of the Brussels Treaty Powers should continue to be able to meet when they so wish in order to consider matters of mutual interest, but that the new Headquarters proposed for Western Europe should be directly under S.H.A.P.E. and should not be responsible to the Western Union Defence Committee.

5. I consider that such an arrangement must in itself be accepted. I should, however, like to take this idea a little further and obtain the agreement of the North Atlantic Treaty Defence Committee to an arrangement by which any group of European Defence Ministers can meet as they please to ensure that the defence objectives of the North Atlantic Treaty are being actively pursued by European national authorities.[2]

6. I accordingly propose to put forward this suggestion at the forthcoming meeting of the North Atlantic Defence Committee. Before doing so, however, I would like to obtain the agreement of my colleagues.[3]

[2] When briefing Mr. Bevin on 25 October on an advance copy of Mr. Shinwell's memorandum Mr. Shuckburgh suggested that 'the Secretary of State will wish to support this point of view. He may care to mention that M. van Zeeland has stressed to him only this morning [No. 83] the importance of not abandoning the machinery for consultation between the five Brussels Powers' (WU 11915/58).

[3] Canadian proposals for a more far reaching reorganisation of N.A.T.O., suggested at the N.A.C. meeting in New York in September, were revived on 18 October when Mr. D. Wilgress, the Canadian Deputy, informed Sir P. Dixon that his government was considering raising the matter at the Defence Committee meeting in Washington on 28–31 October. The essence of the Canadian scheme was to amalgamate the N.A.C. with the Defence Committee and the Defence Finance and Economic Committee and to simplify the sub-structure e.g. abolish the Military Committee. Mr. Bevin thought it a mistake to rush reorganisation and that in any case it should be referred in the first instance to the N.A.C. rather than the Defence Committee: 'If they start discussing these matters at defence meeting or finance, they will get in the same mess as the Council of Europe' (WU 1198/551). On Mr. Bevin's instructions the Canadians were discouraged from making more than a passing reference to their proposals at the Defence Committee meeting, although an

Appointment of Supreme Allied Commander

7. It is the present American intention not to appoint a Supreme Allied Commander until such times as the Western European countries had made increased contributions to collective defence but that meanwhile they should appoint a Chief of Staff to carry out his duties. Although we have stressed to the Americans the disadvantages of such an arrangement and urged them to appoint a Supreme Allied Commander forthwith, it at present seems that they are unlikely to do so. In the event of a Chief of Staff being appointed, Field Marshal Montgomery, as Chairman of the Commanders-in-Chief Committee, would be placed in an invidious position. If therefore the Americans persist in their present determination to appoint a Chief of Staff as an interim measure, I would like my colleagues to agree that I should make the alternative proposal that Field Marshal Montgomery should be appointed as Supreme Allied Commander pending the appointment of an American to fill this post. It would, however, be necessary to place some time limit on his tenure of office.[4]

ANNEX II TO No. 85

Brief for Minister of Defence for Meeting of North Atlantic Treaty Defence Committee in Washington on 28 October, 1950

Prime Minister, Foreign Secretary and Minister of Defence met this afternoon to decide the line to be followed by Mr. Shinwell in the Atlantic Treaty Defence Committee meeting in Washington on 28th October. The summary of their conclusions which follows is based on the underlying principle that nothing must be allowed to disturb the concept of the Atlantic Treaty, i.e. the concept of equal partners in an Atlantic community.

2. The meeting in Washington is an Atlantic Treaty meeting. It has a definite Agenda, prepared by Atlantic Treaty official bodies. The Agenda must be dealt with and not pushed on one side in order to discuss new French proposals not yet fully explained and full of political implications.

3. The Medium Term Defence Plan is one of the central points of this Agenda. All countries should devote every effort towards reaching that

outline paper was circulated informally to the Deputies there. Discussion of this paper was referred to the Cabinet Atlantic (Official) Committee which began formulating a response: see further No. 145.ii. The A.O.C. was an inter-departmental committee of officials, established in June under the chairmanship of Sir N. Brook to assist with the preparation of instructions for the U.K. Deputy of the N.A.C. The Foreign Office was usually represented on the A.O.C. by Sir R. Makins and Sir P. Dixon.

[4] This last point was Mr. Bevin's own suggestion conveyed to the Ministry of Defence earlier in October by Sir P. Dixon when passing on Mr. Bevin's approval of these proposed interim arrangements (DEFE 7/743). In his briefing on 25 October (note 2), Mr. Shuckburgh referred to press reports that morning of a statement by General D. Eisenhower, President of Columbia University, which 'suggest that the Americans may be getting nearer to the point of nominating a Supreme Commander than we had expected'.

target, irrespective of German problem. Minister of Defence is in a strong position to state proposed United Kingdom contribution to this plan and other countries should be urged to do the same, and to concentrate their energies on raising and equipping the maximum number of forces in the shortest possible time.

4. Another urgent object of the meeting is to press on with the integrated forces proposals, to establish unified command, and to amalgamate and streamline existing defence organisations. On this subject Minister of Defence has authority to suggest:

(a) That if the Americans are willing to go no further than the appointment of a Chief of Staff, then Lord Montgomery should fulfil the functions of the Supreme Commander until the American Supreme Commander is appointed.

(b) That any group of European Defence Ministers should have liberty to meet as they please, to ensure that the defence objectives of the North Atlantic Treaty are being actively pursued by European national authorities.

5. The Minister of Defence will insist on the full discussion and completion of the above points. He will not allow time to be wasted and results retarded by consideration of French proposals which appear at first sight to be conceived in a European rather than an Atlantic context. At the same time he will, if time and opportunity allow, seek clarification of French proposals.[5]

[5] A copy of this brief, prepared by Mr. Mallaby, after the ministerial meeting, was taken to Mr. Shinwell at the airport before his departure for Washington. Paragraphs 2–5 were telegraphed later that evening to Sir O. Franks (F.O. tel. to Washington No. 4750) and Air Marshal Elliot (DOTEL 384). In a separate briefing telegram Mr. Mallaby informed Air Marshal Elliot: 'The general background of these instructions is the vigorous determination of the Foreign Secretary not to permit any weakening of the Atlantic community idea. If the French are trying to create a federated European force, including the British, as a sort of makeweight to the power of the new world on one side and the Soviet Union on the other, then he is utterly and irrevocably opposed to the proposals. If the French wish to go forward with the creation of a European force without the British, then that might be acceptable if it was considered as one contribution to the complete Atlantic force which would include also the British, the Americans and the Canadians. From the French point of view, however, this would seem to be a dangerous move as in a European force without the British, the Germans would soon assert their native superiority as warriors. It would be far safer to proceed on the basis of an integrated Atlantic force with safeguards against German military resurgence on the lines proposed by Chiefs of Staff' (DOTEL 383 on CAB 21/1898).

No. 86

Memorandum from Sir D. Gainer to Mr. Bevin

[C 7149/65/18]

FOREIGN OFFICE, 28 October 1950

I attach an interesting telegram from Moscow (No. 969 of 25th October)[1] in which Sir D. Kelly makes certain observations on the Prague communiqué.

You will see that in paragraph 5 the Ambassador suggests that we might consider 'a noncommittal but fairly conciliatory response coupled with a suggestion that the Soviets should demonstrate their good faith by a prompt settlement of the Austrian Treaty.'

Mr. Acheson has already denounced the communiqué as in effect a dishonest piece of eye-wash and he is undoubtedly right in this view.[2] The French, however, are busy deploring the attitude which Mr. Acheson has adopted.[3] Contacts we have had with the French Embassy here, taken together with some of the remarks made by French Ministers in the Assembly in Paris, make it clear that the French would very much like to regard the Prague communiqué as an olive branch from the Russians. French representatives here have already suggested that we should get on speaking terms with the Russians by proposing a joint enquiry into the question of the militarised police[2] and have hinted also at the possibility of an initiative on our part on Austria.

While it is clearly necessary to avoid giving the impression that we will, in no circumstances, discuss a settlement with Russia it remains our view that any such initiative on our part at this time is undesirable. The French attitude springs not only from their inborn and perhaps ineradicable distrust of Germany but also from a tendency towards appeasement which we had hoped they might have shed. They may disguise their motives under phraseology about diminishing tension in Europe but in point of fact there is *less* tension in Europe now, when we have shown our teeth in Korea and indicated our intention to provide ourselves with new ones in Germany, than when we stood hesitant and had not decided which line to adopt.

If we allow ourselves to follow the present weak French tendency we might find ourselves involved in a Council of Foreign Ministers on the basis of the Prague proposals. Sir D. Kelly rightly characterises such an outcome as 'fruitless 4-power discussions whose breakdown the Soviets will try to use to further discredit the Western Governments.'

This is true; the discussions would be fruitless and breakdown would be inevitable; we should have a much greater sort of tension after the breakdown than we have at the present moment.

Furthermore we must look at the disastrous effects which might be

---

[1] See No. 78, note 7. [2] *Ibid.*, note 8. [3] See No. 84.i.

brought about in Germany by a willingness on our part to sit down to negotiations with the Russians on a free-for-all basis, implying thereby that we did not exclude from discussion proposals put forward at Prague. There are two aspects here. First, morale in Germany would suffer a very serious setback. Dr. Adenauer has already indicated that delay in coming to effective defence arrangements for Europe might lead to 'another fall in German morale, and encouragement to the Russians and those elements in Western Germany who are ready to compound with them';[4] and this links up with Sir D. Kelly's opinion that the Prague decisions are directed largely to the workers in Western Germany. This means that to accept Prague as an olive branch is to play the Russian game. Second, assuming that we survive this crisis of morale and the drift to re-insurance with the Russians which it will carry with it, we should find when we tried to resume our German programme where we left it off, that the price of securing German participation in European defence had gone up out of all proportion and that it had become impossible to secure it except on terms which might involve the re-establishment of an independent Germany with a national army. Thus our last chance of getting Germany into the European system on a basis of something less than full national sovereignty would have gone.

For the above reasons therefore it is our view that the empty and dishonest proposals made at Prague deserve no reply other than that made by Mr. Acheson. If the Russians really want to trade with us, they must come with real goods in their hands. They can do so by showing readiness to settle the Austrian Treaty, by disarming their East Zone police, by withdrawing their sabotage and resistance instructions to their friends in Western Germany, or by agreeing to our proposals for all-German elections. Until we see concrete evidence of real willingness to contemplate concessions on such questions, we should remain firm in our positions and carry on with our current programme as if nothing had happened.[5]

D. St. Clair Gainer

[4] See No. 81, note 5.
[5] Mr. Bevin minuted below: 'I go rather wider than Gainer. I am thinking about it. Meantime my priority is Atlantic Defence then talks. The exact order of talks I will discuss. E.B.' On 3 November the Soviet Government addressed identical notes to the British, American and French governments in which it was proposed that a Four Power Meeting of the Council of Foreign Ministers should be convened without delay 'to examine the question of the fulfilment of the Potsdam agreement on the demilitarization of Germany' (British copy printed in *D.G.O.*, p. 535). Action was immediately set in train for concerting a reply with the American and French governments. Mr. Bevin's preliminary reactions, as transmitted in Foreign Office telegram to Washington No. 4881 and Paris No. 1119 of 4 November, were: 'In considering the Soviet proposal for a meeting of the Council of Foreign Ministers, we shall naturally look for any evidence of Soviet intentions such as might hold out hope that conference had some real prospect of success and that Soviet proposal was more than a propaganda move. From this point of view we do not find the Prague communiqué encouraging' (C 7051/65/18). From Moscow Sir D. Kelly warned against outright rejection of the offer since although 'immediate motive behind this

initiative is to bedevil Western Defence Programme by creating hesitations and delay and accentuating existing divergences of view between France and the other Western allies' rejection 'would without question provide first class ammunition for peace campaign both within and outside Soviet orbit' (Moscow telegram No. 1000 on C 7062/65/18).

No. 87

B.J.S.M. (Washington) to Ministry of Defence
(Received 28 October, 10.7 a.m.)

ZO 378 Telegraphic [*WU 1198/558*]

Immediate. Top secret   WASHINGTON, 28 October 1950, 2.52 a.m.

From Minister of Defence to Prime Minister and Secretary of State for Foreign Affairs.

1. On arrival at Washington at 2 o'clock this afternoon [27 October] my first appointment was with Mr. Marshall at 3.30. As this was within an hour and a half of my arrival I did not have an opportunity of (talking ?)[1] to the Chiefs of Staff though I was able to obtain on my drive to the Pentagon some idea of what their views were on the question of German rearmament—This being I anticipated the question which Marshall would wish first and foremost to discuss with me.

2. My anticipation was right. Briefly I outlined our own attitude on this subject laying emphasis on the fact that we did not intend to be diverted by the French from the four main subjects for which the present meeting in Washington had been convened namely:

   (i) A discussion of the Medium Term Plan.
   (ii) The creation of the 'Integrated Force'.
   (iii) The appointment of a Supreme Commander.
   (iv) and as a corollary to (ii) and (iii) above German rearmament.

On the last point I remarked that the only virtue which the French Plan seemed to possess was the fact that it apparently implied acceptance by the French of the principle of German rearmament. For the rest I expressed the view that the French conception of a 'European Army' did not seem to us to hold out any real or substantial hope for the Defence of Western Europe. On the contrary it seemed to be a political manoeuvre which was designed to give the French 'a way out' of their difficulties.

3. Marshall had listened with an attention which clearly showed that the subject which we were discussing was something very near the heart of the Americans. He confessed that he was anxious. He himself had been at a loss to understand not only what the French Plan represented but also what had been the motive which had prompted the French to make it at such a time. He had seen M. Moch during his recent visit[2] and the latter had made it clear that his consuming anxiety had been to play for time. He

---

[1] The text is here uncertain.   [2] See No. 54, note 4.

Moch had asked Marshall whether he could see any opening for delay. With disingenous optimism the Frenchman had asked whether the necessary preliminaries to the appointment of the proposed American Supreme Commander would provide the delay which the French felt to be so essential. To these and similar enquiries—all aimed at seeking some avenue for delay—Marshall had repeatedly answered that he could not postpone the American decision beyond the 20th November when he would have to present his proposals to Congress.

4. On the general conception of the French Plan insofar as it was known Marshall said that the initial inclination of the Americans had been to endeavour to discover and give credit to its merits. In this spirit of good intention a good deal of hard work had been spent on it by his staff. The conclusions which had been reached as a result of this work had however been both disappointing and disillusioning. The more the French Plan had been examined the more it presented itself as a 'Niasmic [Miasmic] Cloud'.

5. On that note we parted through a door opposite to that through which Moch was about to enter. The account of Moch's interview with Marshall is continued in my immediately following telegram.[3]

CALENDAR TO NO. 87

i *27 Oct. 1950   Moch–Marshall Meeting*, as reported in ZO 379, at which M. Moch elaborates Pleven Plan. Initial target for European Army would be 100,000 men of whom 50,000 would be French. German manpower equivalent to some 10 German divisions would eventually be incorporated in European Army at battalion level: but no German divisions as such and no American units. Experimental nature of Plan emphasised by Moch who 'made it clear that France was driving towards European Federation' [WU 1198/557].

[3] See calendar i.

No. 88

Sir I. Kirkpatrick (Wahnerheide) to Mr. Bevin (Received 28 October, 1.33 p.m.)

No. 1548 Telegraphic [WU 1195/386]

Immediate. Secret   WAHNERHEIDE, *28 October 1950, 1.15 p.m.*

Repeated Immediate to Washington and Paris.

The United States High Commissioner informed me today that he had spent some hours yesterday with M. Monnet at his country home near Paris. To Mr. McCloy's surprise M. Pleven and M. Schuman arrived and in the course of a four hours conversation sought to explain the attitude of the French Government in regard to the participation of Germany in

Western defence. They assured Mr. McCloy that France had in effect accepted the principle of German participation and had thus satisfied the condition laid down by Mr. Acheson in New York. The terms of the French resolution[1] were not in any way designed to cause delay, still less to evade the issue. They were only drawn up in this form so as to secure the necessary parliamentary majority and the course of the debate showed clearly that the Government could not have survived had the issue been presented to the French Parliament in any other way.

Mr. McCloy was impressed by the sincerity of Pleven and Schuman and was satisfied that they would do all they could to secure the earliest possible participation of Germany in Western defence. He has communicated this view direct to Mr. Lovett.

On matters of detail Mr. McCloy reports Schuman and Pleven as being rather hazy about the powers of the proposed European Minister of Defence but they said that they thought he should have the same relationship to the Supreme Commander as the American Minister of Defence. The purpose of the proposed appointment was to prevent the Germans having an independent Minister of Defence.

M. Pleven attached great importance to the participation of Britain but Schuman seemed resigned to the idea that Britain would not come in and that the proposed European army would have to be constituted without her.

The French Ministers did not exclude the possibility that the smallest possible national unit might in fact be the division, but they emphasised that in training and composition the force should be completely integrated.

Finally Mr. McCloy reports M. Schuman as being conscious that the terms of the French resolution would create a bad impression in Germany. He admitted that in its present form they seemed to discriminate against Germany but that was not the intention of the French Government and he asked Mr. McCloy to tell the Chancellor that he would be prepared to receive a German journalist of Dr. Adenauer's choice in order to put the French proposals in a more favourable light. Mr. McCloy told M. Schuman that opinion here had resented the French condition that the Schuman Plan must be concluded before the French proposals for a European army could be put in train.[2] M. Schuman replied that the Schuman Plan negotiations could easily be brought to a successful conclusion in three weeks time and that consequently there need be no delay in proceeding to the constitution of a European army. McCloy retorted that in these circumstances it was all the more regrettable that the condition should have been publicly laid down and Schuman implicitly recognised the force of this observation.[3] At the conclusion of the meeting Schuman repeated earnestly that he personally was convinced

[1] See No. 80.i and No. 81, note 5.
[2] See No. 80, note 2.
[3] The preceding three sentences are quoted in Volume I, No. 178, note 2.

that Western defence could not be assured without both French and German participation.[4]

Foreign Office pass Washington and Paris as my immediate telegrams Nos. 181 and 201 respectively.

[4] With reference to this conversation, M. Massigli informed Sir P. Dixon on 30 October that the French account of the conversation 'did not represent the two French Ministers as having gone quite so far'. A copy of the French telegram was subsequently shown to Sir P. Dixon who recorded that it 'certainly represented M. Pleven and M. Schuman as considerably less forthcoming than Mr. McCloy's account. In particular there was no mention of the possibility of the German national unit being as large as a division.' However, in view of a recent conversation that between M. Stikker and M. Schuman along the lines of the present conversation, Sir P. Dixon thought that 'there can be little doubt that Mr. McCloy's account, on the latter point at all events, was the more faithful'. Sir P. Dixon concluded: 'All this goes to show that the members of the French Cabinet are speaking with divided voices. But it is at least consoling that M. Schuman should personally be apparently in favour of a German unit of militarily manageable size, since I suspect that when the military experts get down to brass tacks, it will be found that the central difficulty revolves round precisely this question' (WU 1195/407).

No. 89

Mr. Bevin to Sir O. Franks (Washington)

No. 4786 Telegraphic [WU 1195/379]

Immediate. Secret   FOREIGN OFFICE, 28 October 1950, 1.20 p.m.

Repeated Saving to Paris and Wahnerheide.

My telegram No. 4750 and your telegram No. 2883:[1] German rearmament and the Pleven Plan.

It may be useful for you to have the following account of our thinking which should be regarded as supplementary background to the brief for the Minister of Defence contained in my telegram under reference.

2. The Pleven Plan is objectionable on two main grounds. It is important to distinguish between these and to appreciate that both raise difficulties:

(a) it delays the moment of German rearmament and the participation of Germany in the defence of Europe;
(b) quite apart from the above, it introduces delay and complication into the setting up of the integrated N.A.T.O. force, i.e. the force comprising the European countries (less Germany), Great Britain, the United States and Canada.

3. As regards the delay, it is true that the French apparently contemplate that, while the European army is being created, existing national armies will be available for the N.A.T.O. integrated force, and

[1] See No. 85, note 5 and No. 82.

have stressed that their plan will not lead to delay in creating the latter force. But quite apart from the question whether the United States would be prepared to go ahead with the plan for a N.A.T.O. force until they know whether there will be a German contribution such as will make that force a reality, it is obvious that, in practice, delay would ensue, if only because two complicated sets of negotiations would be running concurrently, one for the N.A.T.O. integrated force on the basis of national contributions, and the other for the setting up of a European Army eventually to be merged as a federal unit with the N.A.T.O. force. I say nothing of the difficulties which would arise in reconciling the common budget of the European Army with the NITZE[2] and other exercises which are proceeding in connexion with the financing of the N.A.T.O. integrated force.

4. As regards complications, it is impossible to visualise how, in practice, a satisfactory relationship could be worked out between the N.A.T.O. chain of command (Supreme Commander, Atlantic Council organs and individual Governments) on the one hand, and the federal European Army (European Minister of Defence, European Committee of Ministers and European Assembly) on the other.

5. The question then arises whether the Pleven Plan represents, in its federal aspects, a fundamental attitude on the part of the French Government, or whether it has been devised largely for electoral and tactical reasons. It is true that the federal conception underlying the Plan responds to a widespread feeling in France that some form of federalism is the best safeguard against a revival of German aggression but if the start of German rearmament were put off until the French were stronger themselves and provided it were surrounded with sufficient safeguards, they would probably not die in the last ditch for their specifically federal solution.

6. The key to the problem therefore seems to lie in convincing the French that the proposed N.A.T.O. system of a Combined Atlantic Force provides, or can be made to provide, sufficient guarantees both in the short and the long term against the German dangers which they fear. This may require a little time. We have to reckon with the French fear (which however unreasonable is genuinely and deeply felt) that under present N.A.T.O. plans a national German army with its Chief of Staff and Ministry of Defence is likely to emerge whatever safeguards may be devised; and that as soon as the Germans have acquired a substantial military strength they will abuse it. At the same time, the safeguards which we introduce must not be such as to invite a German refusal to make any contribution to Western Defence at all.

7. I am not, at this stage at any rate, prepared to urge on the Americans any modification of their views on the timing and form of a German contribution. For the present I think that we should all be guided by two considerations:

[2] See No. 79.i.

231

(*a*) We ought not to take the French plan for a European Army too seriously. We should allow it to be discussed as a long-term plan provided that this does not in any way interfere with progress on the immediate problems of N.A.T.O. defence planning. Mr. Acheson's mind appears to be moving on the same lines.

(*b*) Secondly, it is much to be hoped that we can assume tacitly that the French have agreed to the principle of a German contribution (though not on the manner in which it should be brought about), and that this being so, it is unnecessary to press them for the moment to commit themselves to it more openly.

No. 90

Mr. Bevin to Sir O. Franks (Washington)

No. 4801 Telegraphic [*WU 1195/385*]

Immediate. Secret   FOREIGN OFFICE, *29 October 1950, 3.40 a.m.*

Repeated to Paris, Wahnerheide and Brussels.

Belgian Ambassador left with me this evening a message from M. van Zeeland on the subject of the French proposals for a European army, of which following are significant extracts.[1]

(*Begins*)

M. van Zeeland had a long conversation with M. Schuman on Thursday 26th October. He told him of some of the impressions he had gathered on his visit to London the previous day.[2] In particular he emphasised the perplexity which a preliminary study of the French Declaration of the 24th October on the subject of a European Army had aroused in his mind and in those of some of the best friends of France. M. Schuman had replied with a good grace and as completely as possible to the questions which were put to him and gave M. van Zeeland a number of explanations.

At the end of the conversation M. Schuman stated that in his opinion it would be useful in the present circumstances to call a meeting of the North Atlantic Council of Foreign Ministers. In effect the political aspects of the problem and the final decisions to be taken were obviously matters not for the Committee of Defence Ministers, due to meet on the 28th October but for the Supreme Council of the Atlantic Pact.

M. Schuman thought that it would be useful if this meeting could take place as soon as possible after the meeting of the Committee of Defence Ministers. He thought the meeting of the Council should take place in Washington.

[1] The full text of the Belgian note summarized below, was transmitted to Washington on 30 October (WU 1195/385).
[2] See No. 83.

On the basis of this suggestion M. van Zeeland told M. Schuman that he would get in touch with the principal members of the Council without delay and in particular with Mr. Bevin and Mr. Acheson, as well as Mr. Spofford, to put this idea to them and to obtain their reactions.

If these reactions were favourable it might be possible to arrange a meeting of the Council in Washington immediately after the conclusion of the meeting of the Committee of Ministers of the Council of Europe at Rome,[3] that is to say at some date towards the middle of November to suit the convenience of members.

The Belgian Ambassador in Washington would be asked to make a similar communication to Mr. Acheson and Mr. Spofford.

M. van Zeeland then summarised the further details and explanations given to him by M. Schuman in the course of their conversation on the 26th October. This summary he gave in the strictest confidence.

In the first place it was worth emphasising two essential ideas: the French declaration definitely contained a declaration of principle favourable to the inclusion of German military units in the integrated Atlantic Pact force in Europe through the medium of a European Army.

According to M. Schuman it would be possible by this means to give effect to the American desire which appeared in connexion with the various ideas put forward about Western defence at the meeting of Atlantic Foreign Ministers in New York, for an agreement in principle on the utilisation of German contingents for Western defence.

France's aim remained more than ever clear and unchanging. She was anxious to associate herself fully with, and to further without delay the rearmament plans put forward at the Atlantic Council meeting held in New York at the end of September, 1950. M. Schuman was particularly clear and precise on this point. At the end of the conversation, he declared that if it became evident that the French suggestions would hinder or retard, were it only for one month, the plans in preparation, this would cause him to review the position, but he was convinced that there were no such difficulties.

(*Ends*)

2. Message goes on to summarise a series of further explanations furnished to M. van Zeeland by M. Schuman, which amount in effect to an elaboration of the French proposals as announced by M. Pleven.

3. M. van Zeeland concludes his message as follows.

(*Begins*)

The general impression which emerged from these remarks and elaborations may be summarised as follows:

(*a*) the methods to which the French have resorted are necessary in order that they can associate themselves without delay with the rearmament proposals put forward at New York, and in particular are

[3] The Committee of Ministers met in Rome on 3–4 November: see Volume I, No. 180.

indispensable if they are to give their agreement to the principle, regarded as essential by the Americans, of the incorporation of German military units.

(b) the scheme, despite the various amplifications reported above, still does not seem altogether clear, or relevant. Its implementation would certainly be fraught with numerous difficulties. Meanwhile, it appears that the Atlantic Pact countries could now, first at a meeting of Defence Ministers and later at an early meeting of Foreign Ministers, take appropriate decisions for the setting up of a Unified Atlantic force and could then pass on without delay to the implementation of these decisions.[4]

(Ends)

[4] In telegram No. 4802 to Washington, despatched shortly before the present telegram, Mr. Bevin informed Mr. Shinwell and Sir O. Franks that he did not favour the summoning of the N.A.C. and suggested that it would be wise to make no commitment to the idea. After discussion with Mr. Attlee later that morning, a further telegram (No. 4803) was sent in which Mr. Bevin stated: 'Our feeling is that it would be premature to consider this proposal until the Defence Committee has completed its present discussions . . . Even if no solution of the difficulty can be found in the Defence Committee, we have grave doubts whether it would be wise to summon an immediate meeting of the Atlantic Council . . . Another failure to agree would be extremely serious . . . For your own information I incline to the view that M. Schuman, possibly at M. Moch's suggestion, has made this proposal with the idea of putting off the decision and easing M. Moch's position during the present discussions. The French proposals have not had by any means a unanimous welcome in the French press and have not been well received in Germany. The French may estimate that their proposals will have a better chance of being accepted at a dramatically summoned meeting of the Atlantic Council at which all concerned would be anxious to avoid another breakdown' (WU 1195/385). Mr. Acheson agreed with Mr. Bevin and said that 'he felt that to summon Council to meet before one knew what it was to discuss would only make confusion worse confounded' (Washington telegram No. 2920). The Belgian Ambassador in Washington was informed on the evening of 29 October of Mr. Acheson's views. The following day Mr. Bevin sent a personal message in reply to M. van Zeeland in which he suggested that the N.A.C. might usefully be convened once the Deputies had made sufficient progress (F.O. telegram to Brussels No. 377 on WU 1195/385).

No. 91

B.J.S.M. (Washington) to Ministry of Defence
(Received 29 October, 8.51 a.m.)

ZO 384 Telegraphic [WU 1198/573]

Top secret. Immediate   WASHINGTON, 29 October 1950, 3.40 a.m.

For Prime Minister and Foreign Secretary from Minister of Defence.
When the Defence Committee reached item 6 of its agenda at this afternoons [28 October] meeting[1] Mr. Marshall recalled the questions

[1] The Fourth Meeting of the North Atlantic Defence Committee was opened on the morning of 28 October by the chairman, General Marshall, with a long general statement reported in The Times on 30 October. Discussion continued throughout the day on 28 October and was resumed at further sessions on 30–31 October, for which see calendar i.

relating to a German contribution to European Defence which had been remitted to the Committee by the meeting of the North Atlantic Council in New York.[2] He also recalled that the U.S. Government had circulated its proposals[3] and suggested that they form the basis of discussion of the Defence Committees reply to the council requests.

2. M. Moch then embarked upon an exposition and defence of the French proposals on familiar lines making the points mentioned in ZO 379 27th October.[4] He began by explaining that since he left Paris the French Government had instructed him by telegraph to make a statement on this subject. He was to say that in the opinion of the French Government and debates that had taken place in the French Cabinet and Parliament had made it clear that the French Government's proposal[5] offered the sole possible means of bringing about an effective German military contribution to the defence of Europe. The proposals provided the most effective method of establishing an efficient European Defence Force within the N.A.T.O. framework. The details would have to be worked out by the European countries with the cooperation of N.A.T.O.

3. M. Moch again cited the figure of 100,000 men as the initial strength of the European army including a predetermined proportion of Germans. He remarked that while a start should be made on a modest scale the creation of the European army should in no way delay and might indeed accelerate the development of the integrated N.A.T.O. force. He also claimed that the French proposal had the advantage over the U.S. proposal of avoiding any discrimination against the Germans. Under the U.S. proposal the Allies would be in the position of requesting the Germans to cooperate thus running the risk of their imposing many and unacceptable conditions. Under the French plan they would be invited once the Schuman Plan had been signed to send a Delegate to the Paris conference where they would have equality of rights. The conference would begin within a week of the signature of the Schuman Plan agreement on coal and steel without waiting for its ratification by Parliaments and it would be attended by U.S. and Canadian observers. The eventual recruitment of Germans would be under the control of the proposed European Minister of Defence but he would use the services of the German Ministries of Labour and the Interior.

4. M. Moch said that he was not asking for an immediate decision upon the French Plan but he must equally ask that he should not be pressed to accept the principle of the creation of German divisions and of a German Federal Administrative Agency which in the French Governments opinion would inevitably develop into a German army and German general staff. He asked however that the French proposal should be seriously considered preferably by a Joint Political/Military Body.

[2] See No. 47.
[3] See No. 72, note 2 and No. 72.i for the actual text.
[4] No. 87.i.   [5] No. 80.i.

5. The Danish Minister of Defence then stated that while the French proposals no doubt reflected a desirable future trend they were premature at present and raised constitutional problems of such difficulty that inevitable delay would be caused. The U.S. proposals though less far-reaching did not in his view give rise to this difficulty and the Danish Government supported by a large majority in Parliament had agreed to accept them as a basis for negotiation.

6. The Portuguese Delegate spoke next stating that his Government agreed that Germany should contribute to European defence but could not accept the French proposal even as a basis for discussion. Portugal had never supported the idea of a European Federation and for this reason had not joined the Council of Europe.

7. I then said that while I did not wish to enter into discussion at the present stage I would like to ask four questions designed purely to elucidate the French proposals.

(a) Did the French government now accept the principle of the participation of German units in the common defence? M. Moch replied that the French Government could only accept on condition that the Germans were not grouped in large formations but were integrated in European Divisions.

(b) Did the French Government consider that the German troops should be enlisted voluntarily or by compulsion? M. Moch replied that this was a matter to be decided by the experts. He himself was indifferent. The Germans also would doubtless have a say.

(c) Would not legislation be required in the Parliaments of the countries concerned to regulate the status of their troops serving in the European army. M. Moch replied that the answer would doubtless vary in different countries. In France the matter would be regulated automatically by the ratification of the agreement arising out of the Paris conference.

(d) Pending the application of the French Plan and while the French Governments proposals were being studied could we proceed without delay with the implementation of the U.S. proposals and with consultation with the German Federal Government regarding the formation of German units? M. Moch replied that the French Government could not associate itself with the U.S. proposal in any event and when pressed for a fuller reply merely reiterated this statement with emphasis.

8. Mr. Marshall thereupon proposed adjournment until 0930 a.m. Monday [30 October] to allow time for reflection.

CALENDAR TO No. 91

i *30–31 Oct. 1950 Remainder of Defence Committee Meeting.* On 30 Oct. Moch pressed to discuss U.S. proposals. French plan not viewed as practicable (e.g.

by Canadians) but all (including U.K.) prepared to study it (ZO 388). Afternoon discussion concerned with respective competences of Defence Committee and N.A.C. to settle dispute. Bevin in favour of leaving it to Defence Committee. Compromise reached whereby question of German contribution referred to Military Committee and Deputies for separate consideration of military and political aspects followed by joint report to the Defence Committee (ZO 389). On 31 Oct. Marshall proposes that question of integrated force and supreme command also be referred to Military Committee and Deputies. Objections from Bevin who, dismayed at prospect of failure, proposes adjournment. This agreed. Length of adjournment is left to discretion of chairman (ZO 397). Outstanding business dealt with at closing session on 31 Oct. Agreement reached for some reorganisation of N.A.T.O. (command organisation for N.A. Ocean Region and military standardisation); association of Greece and Turkey with defence planning in the Mediterranean; and the need to control East–West trade (ZO 395). Reference included in communiqué (ZO 396) to agreement of Military Committee recommendations on Medium Term Plan i.e. restatement of force requirements and recommendations for interim national contributions (Defence and Military Committee discussions on M.T.P. are not preserved in F.O. archives) [WU 1198/574–5, 577–8].

No. 92

Extract from the Conclusions of a Meeting of the Cabinet held at 10 Downing Street on Monday, 30 October 1950, at 11 a.m.[1]

C.M. (50) 69th Conclusions [CAB 128/18]

Secret

Germany

Rearmament

(Previous Reference: C.M. (50) 63rd Conclusions, Minute 3)[2]

1. *The Foreign Secretary* said that, since the Cabinet last discussed the question of Germany's participation in the common defence of Western Europe, the French Government had produced their proposal for the creation of a European army, under a European Minister of Defence, into which individual Germans might be recruited. This proposal had caused some embarrassment to the Governments of Belgium and the Netherlands; and it had been suggested that there should be an early meeting of Foreign Ministers to discuss it. He himself had thought it would be

---

[1] *Present* at this meeting were Mr. Attlee (*in the Chair*); Mr. Morrison; Mr. Bevin; Mr. Gaitskell; Mr. Dalton; Viscount Addison; Viscount Alexander of Hillsborough; Viscount Jowitt; Mr. Chuter Ede; Mr. Isaacs; Mr. Bevan; Mr. Williams; Mr. Tomlinson; Mr. Wilson; Mr. Griffiths; Mr. McNeil; Mr. Gordon-Walker. *Also present* for item 1 Mr. W. Whiteley, Parliamentary Secretary, Treasury. *Secretariat*: Sir N. Brook and Mr. Johnston.

[2] See No. 58.

preferable to await the results of the current meeting of Defence Ministers of the North Atlantic Powers, who were examining the technical aspects of the Medium-Term Defence Plan for Western Europe, and to take up later, in the light of those results, the political examination of the French proposal. The Minister of Defence had been advised to avoid being drawn into discussion of these political questions at the current meeting in Washington. The Foreign Secretary had conveyed his views to the Prime Minister of Belgium,[3] who was for the time being Chairman of the North Atlantic Treaty Council; and he had since heard that these views were shared by the United States Secretary of State.

The Prime Minister of France had now indicated that his Government, in putting forward their proposal for the creation of a European army, had not intended to delay progress with the United States plan for the formation of an integrated force for the defence of Western Europe, in which Germany would play some part. It was apparently their intention that the European army should be a relatively small force, of the order of 100,000 men, and should be subordinate to the main force. This seemed to confirm the view that the French proposal was, in the main, a manoeuvre in French domestic politics—though it might also have the subsidiary purpose of securing that the Deputy Commander-in-Chief of the integrated force would be a Frenchman.

It was the provisional view of the Cabinet that, if the French were able to persuade the other Continental Powers of Western Europe to join them in forming a European army on this basis, the United Kingdom Government need not raise objection to it though they would be unwilling to join in promoting it.

Production of Military Equipment

In further discussion, *the Foreign Secretary* said that he had arranged for officials of his Department to examine, in consultation with the other Departments concerned, the economic implications of Germany's participation in the manufacture of armaments for European defence.[4] There might be some disposition to argue that on security grounds Germany should not be allowed to undertake the manufacture of certain types of military equipment; but restrictions of this kind might well have the effect of giving Germany an advantage over other European countries in normal civilian trade. *The Chancellor of the Exchequer* agreed that from this

[3] This is an error for the Foreign Minister, M. van Zeeland: see No. 90, note 4.

[4] See No. 61, note 7. The first meeting of this committee, chaired by Mr. Stevens, took place on 24 October when, among other things, the committee took note of the references to a German industrial contribution contained in the American proposals for German participation in defence circulated to the N.A. Defence Committee. In a letter of 31 October Mr. Penson, to whom the inter-departmental committee papers were copied, promised to find out more from State Department of American views on 'the equally important question of the economic contribution' which he considered was being overshadowed by the question of a manpower contribution (CE 5453/45/181). Meanwhile Mr. Stevens' committee began preparing the report calendared at No. 112.i.

point of view it was desirable that Germany should bear some part of the economic burden of the re-equipment programme; and he welcomed the initiative which the Foreign Secretary had taken in having this problem examined interdepartmentally.

The Secretary of State for Commonwealth Relations drew attention to the importance of keeping other Commonwealth Governments informed of these developments—which illustrated the difficulties of planning for total war through an organisation limited to the North Atlantic Treaty Powers.

The Cabinet:

Took note of the Foreign Secretary's statement and of the points raised in the discussion.

No. 93

Letter from Sir O. Harvey (Paris) to Sir P. Dixon

[*WU 1195/403*]

Secret   PARIS, *31 October 1950*

My dear Bob,

I had a talk to-day with David Bruce who returned from Washington at the end of last week as I wanted to find out his views and those obtaining in Washington regarding the French plan.

He said that he did not think that the United States plan, as originally put forward in New York, could possibly be accepted by the French and that the French Government could not have got the Chamber to adopt anything less than the French plan. He added, speaking very confidentially, that the trouble was of course that the United States military people had got control of the negotiations and had launched the United States plan in New York before the State Department had had an opportunity of looking at it from the political angle. As he said, the Pentagon boys had quite forgotten by now that there had been a war with Germany. Now, however, with the aid of General Marshall and given time, the State Department would be recovering control. General Marshall himself had very definite views about the danger of giving too much to the Germans.[1]

What David Bruce hoped, and had preached in Washington, was that the French plan should somehow be accepted in principle just as the French had now implicitly accepted the principle of German rearmament itself, and that careful study should be given as to how the French plan could be adapted to fit into the requirements of NATO. What the Americans were chiefly concerned about was lest the French plan should weaken the effective operation of NATO and its chain of command and

[1] Mr. Mallet, to whom this letter was circulated, side-lined this sentence and noted 'Good' in the margin.

control etc. He did not believe (nor did I) that the French plan was designed in any way to weaken the overhead NATO control since all the Foreign Ministers of the signatory Powers of the Atlantic Pact, including those who contributed to the 'European Army', would attend the Council meetings. The only personage who would be in a very awkward position would be the 'European Minister of Defence' who would seem to be answerable both to a European Assembly and to the various Governments. However, all that was a matter of detail and organisation which required working out.

We agreed that the French plan was mainly the concoction of politicians designed to meet political difficulties (i.e. Schuman, Pleven, Moch, René Mayer[2] *plus* Monnet), and that the French soldiers themselves had not had a sight of it before it was published.[3] Bruce considered that the best method might be for the United Kingdom and the United States to sit in at the negotiations contemplated under the French plan for setting up the 'European Army', if necessary only as observers. Meanwhile it should be possible for some provisional planning for the eventual German contingent to begin.

Altogether David Bruce took a comparatively hopeful view but said that much depended on Moch and the degree to which he could be shifted. He did not believe that he was not sufficiently a realist to be convinced by arguments, especially if he were satisfied by the nature of the safeguards proposed in the German forces. He confirmed that Acheson was opposed to an early meeting of the Atlantic Council of Foreign Ministers.[4]

Yours ever,

OLIVER HARVEY

[2] French Minister of Justice.

[3] On 30 October the British military attaché in Paris reported: 'Unilion inform us that latest proposals concerning European army as put forward by French Government have been formulated without consulting French military chiefs. Blanc [Chief of the Army Staff] apparently first heard of proposals in press reports of Pleven's speech. Deduction therefore is that French proposals are purely political bargaining factor' (Paris telegram No. 295 on WU 1195/387).

[4] Sir P. Dixon minuted on this letter before circulating it to Mr. Mallet, Sir W. Strang and Western Organisations department: 'I am sure that it will be impossible to adopt the French plan as it stands and fit it into NATO plans. But some middle course should be possible. First reports from Washington suggest that this is what the Defence Committee decided to ask the Deputies and Military Committee to try to work out. P.D. 1/11'.

No. 94

Sir O. Franks (Washington) to Mr. Bevin
(Received 2 November, 5.25 a.m.)

No. 2963 Telegraphic [WU 1195/402]

Priority. Top secret   WASHINGTON, 1 November 1950, 9.59 p.m.

German Rearmament.

Public Affairs Department and policy planning staff of the State Department raised with Watson[1] on November 1st question of activities outside ordinary diplomatic channels which we might be prepared to undertake to shift French Government from their present stand in opposition to the eleven other members of the North Atlantic Treaty over defence arrangements. General Marshall had asked State Department to examine possible methods of this kind.

2. State Department explained that the United States Government wished not to make things difficult for the French in public but rather to apply pressure by oblique means. French Socialists seemed a profitable point of attack and State Department were now actively considering what pressure could be brought to bear on them. State Department will probably approach American Federation of Labour and Congress of Industrial Organisation. They did not want to take up this issue through United States representatives in the United Kingdom but wondered whether some prominent figure in the Labour Party hitherto not associated with these discussions could try to influence French Socialist leaders. Other channels might also occur to us. The Americans are also considering what could be done through the Belgians (who have shown themselves rather helpful to the French in the defence meetings). They may approach Victor Larock.[2] Could we help here? An attempt may also be made to induce the German Socialists to point out to French Socialists the need for making proposals acceptable to German opinion. (Although German Socialists might favour 'European' solution State Department feel they might be able to help.) State Department have little hope that Italians would be much use. They wonder whether we could somehow bring Canadian influence to bear. It is reported that M. Moch is visiting Canada on his way home.

3. State Department plans are not yet crystallised and this approach is to be regarded as strictly *confidential* and *informal*. They would be very glad of anything we can tell them urgently about our own plans or what we would be ready to do to help them which they could then take into account when preparing their action.[3]

---

[1] Mr. J.H.A. Watson was a First Secretary in H.M. Embassy, Washington.

[2] Socialist Deputy for Brussels and prominent journalist.

[3] Sir W. Strang commented on this telegram: 'A typical bright idea from the State Dept. They have muddled the whole operation and this would only make things worse. W. Strang

3/11.' A telegram was accordingly sent to Washington on 9 November in which most of the ideas put forward by State Department were dismissed as 'over-optimistic', though Belgian and Canadian influences were considered of possible use. Approaches from European organisations were not thought likely to be of help 'since the various Socialist parties concerned are either themselves lukewarm about re-arming the Germans or on indifferent terms with their French opposite numbers . . . Intervention by British Labour Party would be useless. We have already done all we can with M. Moch and M. Guy Mollet [see No. 99, note 2] without effect' (F.O. telegram to Washington No. 4935 on WU 1195/402). This telegram crossed a further telegram from Washington (No. 3021, received on 8 November) which reported measures taken by the American Policy Planning department: 'These include influence on French left press. Latest reports are that French opinion is coming around nicely, with both Socialist party and Cabinet ready to try to shift Moch' (WU 1195/436). A later request from the Americans for British pressure on Belgium and Dutch Socialists was not taken up and the matter was dropped after reports from Ottawa on 13 and 15 November of less intransigence from M. Moch were ascribed to Canadian influence.

No. 95

B.J.S.M. (Washington) to Ministry of Defence
(Received 2 November, 10.30 p.m.)[1]

ZO 410 Telegraphic [WU 1198/582]

Top secret. Immediate   WASHINGTON, 2 November 1950, 4.50 p.m.

Personal for Foreign Secretary from Minister of Defence.

1. I understand that Moch does not propose to return to France for a fortnight. There is risk to my mind that when he does get back to Paris he will, as a result of the searching criticism to which he was subjected in Washington, be even more difficult than before. This could easily lead to a French Cabinet crisis.

2. Although the French offered us nothing during their meeting here and in general behaved badly the fall of their present Government at this crucial stage of NATO developments—before they have had an opportunity of reconsidering their policy in the light of the Washington talks—would merely add to the confusion and land us all in a period of delay during which no progress would be made with the defence of Western Europe.

3. It occurs to me that in these conditions you might think it useful to make an early approach to Schuman with a view to persuading the French that their best course would be not to persist with their own plan which it was clear from the Washington talks found favour with no one but instead to seek amendment of the American plan in such manner as to meet their understandable anxieties on certain matters, e.g. the German General Staff. If Schuman can be made to agree to this he should then give instructions which would ensure that the French representatives on the Military Committee and in the Council of Deputies are given the necessary latitude.

4. If on the contrary the French persist in their present attitude there is

every reason to expect that they will find themselves isolated and by delaying all progress in the matter of Western European defence will create a very serious situation in NATO itself since they will be frustrating the wishes of all the other members of the treaty.

5. My guess is that the adjourned meeting of the Defence Committee will take place in London about the first week in December.

6. The account which I have this moment seen of Moch's statement to the press here yesterday[1] confirms me in my feeling that if we are to move the French from their present attitude there is no time to be lost.[2]

[1] According to *The Times*, M. Moch informed the press on 1 November in Washington that 'France would never agree to the creation of German army divisions in the proposed west European army. But France would agree to permitting the inclusion in such an army of German units of battalion strength—between 800 and 1,200 men' (*The Times*, 2 November 1950, p. 4).
[2] In a review of the situation on 2 November, Sir P. Dixon suggested that the Consultative Council of the Brussels Treaty Organisation, which was due to meet soon, might provide a good forum to tackle the French. However, a decision on this should await the return of Mr. Shinwell from Ottawa on 7 November.

No. 96

Letter from Sir O. Harvey (Paris) to Sir P. Dixon

[*WU 1195/423*]

Personal and secret   PARIS, *3 November 1950*

My dear Bob,

I asked Margerie to lunch alone with me to-day to hear his views on the impasse we have reached over German rearmament. He said that Schuman was away[1] and therefore all that he said only represented personal views.

He first of all told me that the time-table, viz that the Military Committee were now studying the American and French plans with a view to seeing what elements they had in common, that on November 10th the

[1] M. Schuman was attending the meeting of the Committee of Ministers of the Council of Europe held in Rome on 3–4 November. At the opening session on 3 November, 'M. Schuman enquired whether the Committee of Ministers would think it proper that he or another French Minister should give an oral explanation of the "Pleven proposal" to the Assembly if the latter should invite him to do so' (Rome telegram No. 724 on WU 1079/120). Mr. Davies, who was attending for Mr. Bevin, opposed this suggestion on the grounds that it could only encourage the Consultative Assembly to discuss defence questions outside the scope of the Council of Europe. 'Eventually M. Schuman gave way gracefully' (*ibid.*). The question was revived later that month when M. Schuman received an invitation to address the Assembly. After further consultation with the Committee of Ministers, M. Schuman accepted, on the understanding that he would speak on a personal basis as French Foreign Minister and not as a member of the Committee of Ministers: see *C. of E. Official Report 1950*, pp. 1686–92 for the text of his speech on 24 November and Volume I, Nos. 180 and 182.i for reviews of the Committee of Ministers and Consultative Assembly meetings.

Deputies would meet in London to examine their political aspects, and that finally General Marshall would summon a meeting of the Defence Ministers in London for November 20th to examine the reports of these two committees.

It therefore was vital, Margerie said, for these committees and the Governments to use this time to try to arrive at a plan embodying common views to both. One common factor was that both plans contemplated German rearmament; a difference was that whereas the Americans spoke of divisions, the French talked of regiments. Another common factor was that under neither plan were the Germans to have a War Ministry and a General Staff. Under the United States plan German staff officers would figure in the upper strata of the integrated staff; under the French plan they would be in the common European staff.

On the other hand, he recognised very frankly the difficulties of the political provisions of the French plan. He deplored that the French plan had been drawn up largely by Monnet and the economists to the confusion of the Quai d'Orsay, who had not had any say in it whatever. It would obviously take time to constitute the European Assembly and the position of the European Defence Minister, responsible both to that Assembly and to the individual Governments, would be an impossible one. He also recognised that the French were for all practical purposes in a minority of one as none of the other Powers, with the doubtful exception of the Belgians, were in favour of it; even the Italians were not in favour, their role being confined to finding the compromise on procedure, for which the French were very grateful, to avoid an immediate deadlock.

He thought that it might be possible to help the French by giving, as he said, a European label to the General Staff which would be concerned with the European aspect of the Atlantic Defence.[2] Such a label would make it easier for the French to swallow the Germans being present in the upper strata of the Combined Staff, as contemplated by the American plan. He believed that Moch, in spite of his words in Washington, had been impressed by the American views and, on his return, might adopt a less rigid attitude. None the less, some gesture would seem necessary if the harmonisation of the two plans was to be brought about.

Then again there were the Germans, who must also be brought into our calculations. Poncet's recent interview with Adenauer,[3] according to

[2] Marginal annotation in the Foreign Office: 'but the essence of the plan is U.S. participation'.

[3] Following on from his public statement of 28 October that German participation in Western defence depended on equal status, Dr. Adenauer went to see the French High Commissioner, M. François-Poncet, on 30 October to discuss the Pleven Plan. According to press reports of the meeting Dr. Adenauer criticized 'the linking of the Schuman Plan with any German participation in European defence and the time-consuming methods proposed for organising the European army. Dr. Adenauer is also said to have called attention to his own difficult position in the Bundestag . . . and to have emphasised that the Pleven plan in certain particulars expressed mistrust of the Federal Republic' (Wahnerheide telegram No. 1558 on C 6933/57/18). Later press reports that the Federal government intended to ask to

Margerie, had not gone too badly. Poncet had explained the French plan and the way in which it was sincerely designed to give the Germans equality. Adenauer had expressed his concern at the attitude of some of the German Generals with whom he had been in contact, and had apparently said something to the effect that it would probably only be safe to make use of officers of the rank of Colonel downwards in the German contingent.[4] Both from his interview with Adenauer and from other indications, Poncet had reported that he felt the Germans were beginning to take more interest in the French plan, although they had been hostile to start with. This was apparently due to Adenauer's difficulties in his own party who had compelled him to dismiss Schwerin, as well as with Schumacher, who were adopting a very anti-militarist line.[5] From this angle he might perhaps finds it easier to sell the idea of a German contingent in a *European* Army as provided in the French plan rather than in an Atlantic Army under the American plan.

He had also turned over in his mind how the Germans were to do without a Defence Minister since somebody must be responsible, and it occurred to him that the German member of the military Security Board who sat in with the representatives of the three High Commissioners might fulfil this function.

Margerie regretted that Schuman had been absent at this time in Rome, although he would be back at the beginning of next week. He was a much wiser bird than Moch and had deliberately sent Moch to experience American pressure with a view to sobering him. Schuman would never have committed himself so definitely as Moch had done. Pleven was also fairly rigid, but he thought he could be satisfied, provided that the basic ideas of his plan—no large German units, no German General Staff and some European label—could be secured.

One further point, he said that the French now favoured the military aspect of the Brussels Treaty being taken over by the Atlantic Council, whilst retaining the political, social and economic aspects of the Treaty, which were extremely useful.

Yours ever,
OLIVER HARVEY

P.S. I forgot to add that Margerie said that if the Schuman Plan could actually be signed as was hoped, within a month, it would greatly help with public and parliamentary opinion here.

take part in discussions concerning German participation in defence were denied on 4 November: see, however, No. 103.i.

[4] Cf. No. 73.i.

[5] Count von Schwerin resigned his post as defence adviser to Dr. Adenauer on 28 October following criticism of his outspoken support for German remilitarisation. Although critical of the Pleven Plan in a statement at Frankfurt reported on 30 October, 'Dr. Schumacher did not entirely exclude the possibility of a German participation . . . and repeated that Germany could only participate if the Western forces were strong enough to undertake a counter-offensive against any Soviet attack' (Wahnerheide telegram No. 1555 on C 6896/57/18).

No. 97

*Extract from Conclusions of a Meeting of the Cabinet held at
10 Downing Street on Monday, 6 November 1950, at 11 a.m.*[1]

C.M. (50) 71st Conclusions [CAB 128/18]

Secret

Germany

Soviet Proposal for Meeting of Council of Foreign Ministers

(Previous Reference: C.M. (50) 67th Conclusions, Minute 2)[2]

2. Following the Prague conference of Foreign Ministers of Russia's satellite States in Eastern Europe, the Soviet Government had now proposed an early meeting of the Council of Foreign Ministers to discuss the demilitarisation of Germany.[3]

The Foreign Secretary said that he was seeking agreement with the Governments of the United States and France regarding the reply to be sent to this invitation. After consulting the Prime Minister he had suggested to those Governments (in Foreign Office telegram No. 4899 of 5th November)[4] that an interim reply should at once be sent which, while making it clear that the demilitarisation of Germany was not the only outstanding issue between the Western Powers and the Soviet Union, would indicate willingness to join in Four Power discussions in the hope that these might remove the underlying causes of the present situation, so long as it was understood that an agenda for the meeting would be settled in advance and that the communiqué issued at the end of the Prague conference would not be taken as the sole basis for discussion. The Foreign Secretary contemplated that the Foreign Ministers of the United Kingdom, the United States and France should then arrange for their deputies to draw up an agenda for the meeting, which would cover all the points on which the Soviet Government had failed to fulfil their undertakings, or had acted arbitrarily since the end of the war. When the

[1] *Present* at this meeting were Mr. Attlee (*in the Chair*); Mr. Morrison; Mr. Bevin; Mr. Gaitskell; Mr. Dalton; Viscount Addison; Viscount Jowitt; Mr. Chuter Ede; Mr. Isaacs; Mr. Bevan; Mr. Williams; Mr. Tomlinson; Mr. Wilson; Mr. Griffiths; Mr. McNeil and Mr. Gordon-Walker. *Also present* for item 2 was Sir H. Shawcross, Attorney-General. *Secretariat:* Sir N. Brook and Mr. Johnston.

[2] See No. 78, note 7.   [3] See No. 86, note 5.

[4] In this telegram, the most recent in a series of exchanges between Washington, Paris and London (cf. No. 86, note 5), Mr. Bevin proposed the procedure summarized below and warned: 'As regards tactics I think it would be a mistake to allow ourselves to be rushed into a conference or to appear ready to come running at Stalin's bidding. We must consider matter carefully among ourselves before replying, and should not allow our actions to be dictated by chance considerations such as Bundestag debate on November 8th though if thought desirable we could give Adenauer privately a preliminary indication of our views. Moreover, if we are to enter into further four power discussions with the Russians we must ensure this time that ground is very carefully prepared beforehand and that we go into them not only with clear idea of what we are going to discuss but also with some prospect that progress towards a real settlement can be made' (C 7299/65/18).

deputies' recommendations were available, a further communication could be sent to the Soviet Government, proposing that a meeting of the deputies of the four Foreign Ministers should be held in the first instance to prepare the ground for an eventual meeting of the Council of Foreign Ministers.

The Foreign Secretary had just received the first reactions of the State Department towards his proposals for handling the Soviet invitation. These were not very favourable. The State Department were at present inclined to send an argumentative reply which would, by implication, reject the invitation—offering merely to enter into negotiations when the Soviet Government had demonstrated 'by its behaviour and the character of its proposals a sincere desire to reach genuine settlements.'[5] The views of the French Government were not yet available.[6]

In the Cabinet's discussion there was general support for the line which the Foreign Secretary wished to take in replying to the Soviet invitation.

The Cabinet:

Endorsed the views expressed in Foreign Office telegram to Washington No. 4899 of 5th November,[4] and invited the Foreign Secretary to continue his attempts to persuade the Governments of the United States and France to reply on these lines to the Soviet proposal for a meeting of the Council of Foreign Ministers.[7]

[5] This quotation is from a paraphrase of an uncleared draft reply prepared by State Department and transmitted to the Foreign Office in Washington telegram No. 3002 on the evening of 5 November. Sir O. Franks commented that State Department's thinking was 'still fairly flexible . . . Main difference . . . seems to be that State Department draft implies unwillingness to enter into four-power talks except on proof of good behaviour by Russians, whereas your only condition appears to be a satisfactory agenda' (Washington telegram No. 3001 on C 7066/65/18).

[6] On 5 November M. Parodi gave Sir O. Harvey his own personal reactions that 'we should fall into a trap if we simply said yes, or if we simply said no'. On 6 November M. Pleven informed Sir O. Harvey that his government was thinking on similar lines to Mr. Bevin (Paris telegrams Nos. 307 and 311 on C 7069, 7130/65/18).

[7] In the ensuing round of consultations with the American and French governments, it was agreed that an interim reply, along the lines of the British proposal, would be made by means of separate public statements rather than a written reply. Mr. Acheson spoke first at a press conference on 8 November where, in terms agreed with Mr. Bevin, he stated the need for careful consideration of the Soviet proposal. Later that day the French government issued a brief statement to the effect that they would enter into consultations with the American and British governments to examine the conditions under which a positive response might be given to the Soviet government (French and American statements reported in The Times on 9 November, p. 4). Finally Mr. Bevin made a statement in the House of Commons on 13 November, approved by the Cabinet earlier that morning, in which he listed aspects of Soviet policy which would have to be taken into account when considering whether a four power conference would be worthwhile (Parl. Debs., 5th ser., H. of C., vol. 480, cols. 1383–5). M. Schuman followed Mr. Bevin's line in a long statement to the National Assembly on 14 November (C 7418/65/18). Dr. Adenauer was given advance notice of both American and British statements. Sir I. Kirkpatrick reported on 8 November: 'I gather that our readiness to keep the Chancellor informed has had a good effect and that he is not unduly apprehensive about the possible effects of this latest Russian move' (Wahnerheide telegram No. 1584 on C 7209/65/18).

No. 98

Memorandum from the U.K. Deputy on the N.A.C. to Mr. Bevin[1]

No. 54 [WU 1198/587]

Top secret   LONDON, 6 November 1950

The meeting of the North Atlantic Defence Committee, if it achieved little else, did at all events clear the air and bring out the following points:

(*a*) The United States Government are not prepared to untie their package, or in other words are not prepared to appoint an American Supreme Commander or agree to the implementation of the plans for the creation of an integrated force, &c., until they are satisfied that this integrated force will be organised on sound lines from the military point of view.

(*b*) The United States Government are convinced that the integrated force can only be organised on sound military lines if arrangements for the inclusion in it of German units are made more or less on the lines outlined in the American plan—i.e., the German units must be of reasonable size.

(*c*) The French Government are at present not prepared to agree even to the principle of the incorporation of German units in the integrated force unless this is done on the lines of their own plan—e.g., with very small units and with a whole lot of accompanying political conditions.

(*d*) The French in their present mood are prepared to sacrifice all the advantages of the appointment of an American Supreme Commander and the early constitution of the integrated force rather than accept the American plan and agree in principle to the eventual constitution of German divisions. The French were prepared to push their attitude regardless of the wishes and interests of the other countries and in fact took the line that France, and France only, was the country which had an interest in German rearmament. The French too came very nearly to maintaining that they had a right of veto and that the question of German rearmament could not be considered at all by the North Atlantic Treaty Organisation except on terms laid down in advance by the French. M. Moch's attitude was in fact at times strongly reminiscent of that of Messrs. Vishinsky[2] and Molotov.

(*e*) The French were virtually in a minority of one. The Dutch and the Portuguese disliked the French plan in itself. The Norwegians and Danes resented the way in which Scandinavian interests were ignored and the Italian was greatly concerned at the delay in the appointment of a Supreme Commander caused by the French tactics. The Belgians and

---

[1] An earlier version of this memorandum was circulated by Sir F. Hoyer Millar to the Foreign Office on 1 November, before the issue of the present text in the numbered series of U.K. Deputy memoranda.

[2] Soviet Foreign Minister.

Luxembourgers on the other hand, though showing no great enthusiasm for the French plan, seemed to feel that given time some compromise between the French and the American theses could be found.

(*f*) The Americans were strangely silent during the actual meetings. Although both General Marshall and General Bradley made it clear to the British and other representatives in private that they regarded the French plan as making no sense from the military point of view and that they would continue to press vigorously for their own proposals, General Marshall in fact said very little during the actual meetings except to remark that the United States Government felt that any plan for the incorporation of German units must be a realistic one.[3] The Americans never stated clearly that they were in fact not prepared to go ahead with the appointment of an American Supreme Commander until the German issue was disposed of to their satisfaction. It was indeed only as a result of statements by other representatives, and more particularly by Mr. Shinwell, that the American position was elucidated. The explanation of the American attitude may have been that they were anxious not to be too tough with the French or to drive M. Moch too far into a corner. Their attitude was, however, to some extent disappointing in that they did not seize the opportunity of bringing home to the French and other representatives how essential it is to find a solution of the German problem on lines acceptable to the Americans if we are to get an American appointed as a Supreme Commander in the near future.

(*g*) No indication was given by the Defence Committee as to the kind of solution they hoped the Deputies would produce nor of the way in which the Defence Ministers thought the problem could be settled. It was clearly in the minds of some of the Ministers, however, that some compromise might be found between the American and French plans and the State Department themselves are talking about trying to find a way of introducing some of the French ideas into the American plan. It may perhaps be possible to do something on these lines, though at first sight the two plans seem to be virtually irreconcilable. However that may be, it seems clearly important that every possibility of reaching some kind of agreement should be explored by the Deputies and the Military Committee before the matter is referred back to the Council. The Council should only be summoned when it is possible to lay some generally acceptable concrete scheme before it or, alternatively, when it has become clear that no agreement can be reached.

2. It is against the foregoing background that the Military Committee

---

[3] General Marshall's reticence was evidently part of deliberate American tactics, as revealed in an American report of the Defence Committee meeting in which Mr. Acheson praised 'Gen. Marshall's superb and impartial handling of Chairmanship' (*F.R.U.S. 1950*, vol. iii, p. 427).

and the Deputies will have to discuss the question. The Military Committee are going ahead at once with their consideration of the military aspects of the problem, but the Deputies have agreed that they will not attempt to take up the political side of things until individual Governments have had adequate time to go into the whole question and examine the political implications of the French plan. The Deputies are not likely to begin their consideration of the problem until about 13th November. It is important that by that time I should be fully briefed as to His Majesty's Government's views on the political issues involved.

3. Apart from the obvious objections to the French plan already set out in recent Foreign Office telegrams, which are based mainly on the inevitable delay and confusion in setting up the integrated force which the adoption of the French proposals would involve, guidance on the following points would seem to be necessary:

(a) His Majesty's Government's attitude towards the political principles involved in the French plan—i.e., the idea of federation, the setting up of a European Defence Minister, the constitution of a European Assembly, &c. If, as seemed to be generally anticipated during the Defence Committee meetings, His Majesty's Government are not prepared to participate in the French plan or contribute to the 'European army', what would their views be if the French decided to go ahead and discuss their plans at a meeting in Paris with such of the other European countries as are prepared to go along with them, including presumably representatives of Western Germany? Would we be prepared to stand aside as we have done in connexion with the Schuman Plan and take no part in such discussions in Paris?

(b) What are the German reactions to the French plan and is there the least likelihood of them being prepared to accept it or anything resembling it? What will be the effect on the Germans if the present impasse continues for any length of time and if it becomes increasingly obvious to them that the appointment of a Supreme Commander, &c., is dependent on the solution of the problem of German participation?

4. Apart from the above points, guidance is particularly necessary on the extent to which His Majesty's Government are prepared to go in bringing pressure to bear on the French Government in this matter of German rearmament. The plain fact is that at the moment the French are holding up all progress in the matter of the appointment of an American Supreme Commander and the constitution of an integrated force and are thereby prejudicing what practically all the other N.A.T.O. countries consider in the best interests of the North Atlantic Treaty Organisation as a whole. If the French persist in this attitude they may not only delay the rearmament of the West indefinitely but wreck the whole N.A.T.O. organisation. On the other hand, the French maintain that their own public opinion will not permit them to make any concessions and that if they are pressed too far, the French Government will fall and, in

particular, M. Moch's own position will be jeopardized. No one at the Washington meetings was disposed to question the accuracy of this French view, even though suggestions were made that it was up to the French Government to take some steps to try to educate its own public opinion in the matter of Germany rather than as at present sheltering behind their public opinion. It must, however, be for consideration to what extent we can continue to allow the French more or less to blackmail the rest of the North Atlantic Treaty countries, bearing in mind that our main objective must be the speedy rearmament of Western Europe on terms acceptable to the Americans. We may at some time have to decide what effect the fall of the French Government would have on this objective.

5. As explained above, the Deputies are not likely to begin their consideration of this problem for ten days or so. It is, I think, for consideration whether in the meantime His Majesty's Government should not make some representations to the French Government through the diplomatic channel urging them to reconsider the whole matter on the grounds that if they continue in their present attitude they will become more and more isolated and by delaying the appointment of a Supreme Commander, &c., prejudice the interests of the North Atlantic Treaty Organisation as a whole—as well, of course, making it increasingly difficult ever to get the Germans in on anything like reasonable terms. While the French have admittedly behaved badly and do not deserve much sympathy, it should presumably be our policy to try to make things easier for them and to help them to find a way out of the present impasse. A French Ministerial crisis at this time would do no one any good. Our best line would, therefore, seem to be to do what we can to persuade the French not to persist with their present plan, which really stands no chance of acceptance, but, instead, to concentrate on trying to obtain from the Americans such modifications of the American plan that the French consider necessary to meet their own legitimate apprehension on points such as that of the German General Staff. As far as we know, the Americans, at all event in the State Department, are quite prepared to consider any sensible suggestions that the French may put forward on such lines, and it would seem to be to our advantage to get the French and the Americans together on this kind of exercise.

CALENDAR TO No. 98

i *6 Nov. 1950   American views on how to proceed*: Question of how to solve *impasse* discussed by Sir F. Hoyer Millar with (*a*) Mr. Spofford (*b*) Mr. Perkins and Mr. H. Freeman Matthews, U.S. Deputy Under-Secretary of State. Americans working towards amending their own plan so as to accommodate French. Suggest British pressure on French [WU 1198/583, 589].

No. 99

Mr. Bevin to Sir O. Franks (Washington)

No. 4911 Telegraphic [WU 1198/590]

Priority. Top secret   FOREIGN OFFICE, 7 November 1950, 12.5 a.m.

Repeated to Paris and Wahnerheide.

My telegram No. 4910 (of 6th November)[1] German participation in European defence.

The United States Ambassador said that he understood that Mr. Bruce had already seen M. Pleven and M. Schuman, and had got the impression from them that they did not altogether endorse the attitude adopted by M. Moch in Washington, and that they thought that he had been unduly rigid. The French Ministers had emphasised their need for guarantees against a resurgence of German nationalism, but had implied that they believed that some arrangement acceptable to both sides could be worked out.

2. Mr. Douglas said that, though the United States Government were convinced that the French proposals were not workable, they were quite prepared to make concessions to the French with a view to devising some acceptable but realistic scheme. M. Moch had been extremely difficult in Washington, had misinterpreted the decisions reached by the Atlantic Council in New York, and had refused to discuss anything but the French proposals.

3. Mr. Douglas said he did not know whether it was possible for His Majesty's Government to do anything to help to bring the French into line. It might, for example, be possible for His Majesty's Government to use their influence with the Dutch or Norwegian Socialists. He asked whether I had had any success with M. Mollet.[2] I replied that I would certainly consider whether there was anything we could do to help, but I was not optimistic, and I thought that the attitude of M. Mollet had been, if anything, even worse than that of M. Moch.[3]

---

[1] In this telegram of 6 November Mr. Bevin informed Sir O. Franks of the receipt from Mr. Douglas that day of the substance of the instructions to the American Ambassador in Paris for representation to the French Government on 4 November (F.R.U.S. 1950, vol. iii, pp. 428–31 and 433–4).

[2] Mr. Bevin saw M. Mollet in London on 31 October: see records of conversation in Volume I, Nos. 179 and 181. Mr. Barclay, who was present only at the end of the meeting, added in a separate record: 'The Secretary of State then said that if there was a third World War it would be caused by the indecision and lack of preparedness of the Western Powers. It looked very much to him at the moment as though France was going to be responsible for this indecision. The Secretary of State then asked Monsieur Mollet if he did not believe in the reality of the Soviet threat or that there was any danger of war. Monsieur Mollet said "No". The Secretary of State then said that he thought Monsieur Mollet and his friends were as bad as the Chamberlain Government' (F.O. 800/465).

[3] Sir O. Franks replied on 7 November that State Department confirmed Mr. Douglas' impression of M. Pleven's attitude: 'They said M. Pleven had indicated that in any plan

acceptable to the French there would have to be some prospect of a movement towards European federation and a Franco-German rapprochement but he did not give the impression that this need be of nearly so definite a character as M. Moch had insisted here. M. Pleven also indicated that the French might be more accommodating as regards the size of the German units . . . M. Pleven had also said that French representatives on the Military Committee would be free to discuss any proposal and would not necessarily limit themselves to discussing the French proposals' (Washington telegram No. 3019 on WU 1195/416). This last point had already been communicated to Sir W. Strang by M. Massigli on 6 November. The French Ambassador had then suggested that 'it was now for the United Kingdom representatives to see whether they could find a compromise' (WU 1198/591). Overall Sir O. Franks reported that 'State Department are not dissatisfied with Pleven's remarks, but are cautious of expressing optimism' (WU 1195/416).

No. 100

Mr. Bevin to Sir O. Franks (Washington)

No. 4505 Saving Telegraphic [UR 1027/38]

Secret   FOREIGN OFFICE, 8 November 1950

My telegram No. 4467 (of October 7th)[1] paragraph (e) (i): Interim aid for rearmament.

We have been giving further thought to the suggestion in the United States Aide Memoire that we should seek a contribution from the Commonwealth portion of the sterling area towards the maintenance of our defence effort. We should be glad of your advice whether this particular suggestion can be regarded as having lapsed in view of United States Government's decision to put forward formally the Nitze Memorandum.[2] We are quite certain that United States suggestion is a non-starter. If it has lapsed we can leave the matter where it is, but if not we must do our best at the appropriate time to persuade the Americans to drop it. Our arguments would be as set out in the following paragraphs and if you think United States authorities have not dropped this idea we should be glad to know how you think these arguments could best be employed in doing so. We do not wish you to take this matter up with the Americans until we have had an opportunity to consider your views and in any case not in advance of our reply on other outstanding points in their Aide Memoire.

2. Objections we see to United States suggestion are as follows:

(a) It is based upon a complete misunderstanding of the constitutional position. Certain Colonies make financial contributions of this kind but we are responsible for their defence. Each independent Commonwealth country is constitutionally responsible for its own defence. It would be a retrograde step for us to try to persuade independent

[1] This telegram, which gave initial reactions to the U.S. offer of interim aid, contained in their *aide-mémoire* of 3 October (No. 79.i), is not printed from UE 11914/104.
[2] See No. 79.i.

Governments of the Commonwealth to go back to the Colonial model and completely out of accord with whole pattern of Commonwealth relations today.

(*b*) Apart from the constitutional difficulties it would be contrary to our whole Commonwealth defence policy to ask Commonwealth countries to make a financial contribution towards our defence expenditure. Most of the other Commonwealth Governments are now engaged (with our full support) in building up larger and more effective defence forces of their own so that, in addition to meeting the needs of local defence, they may be in a position to send self-contained units wherever these are needed in time of war, and to meet as high a proportion as possible of these units' needs in arms, equipment, vehicles, etc. It would be wrong to ask other Commonwealth Governments to make contributions towards the cost of United Kingdom Defence if this meant, as it would, a corresponding reduction in the expenditure that they would otherwise be able to devote to building up their own defence forces and their own industrial defence potential. Once-for-all monetary payments to the United Kingdom from Commonwealth countries, or even a system of regular monetary contributions would be a very poor substitute for the capacity which other Commonwealth countries are in process of building up for making a really effective contribution from their own resources in manpower and equipment.

(*c*) Since 1945 most of the other Commonwealth countries have assumed a much greater responsibility than they had before for the defence of given areas in war. These areas are altogether outside the N.A.T.O. (North Atlantic Treaty Organisation) sphere, e.g. Australia and New Zealand have assumed responsibilities in the South Pacific and Middle East and South Africa has assumed them in the Middle East. These areas are of great strategic importance, and the United States and we have a common interest in seeing that they are effectively defended in war. To ask the non-NATO Commonwealth countries to start contributing to *NATO* defence at the expense of these non-NATO areas would be a very retrograde step indeed.

(*d*) Following argument would be for oral (repeat oral) use only at your discretion. We see in fact no prospect of any Commonwealth Government being willing to make a financial contribution. Defence expenditure (admittedly directed to wrong purposes while tension between the two countries persists) already forms too high a proportion of the budgets of India and Pakistan. Whatever part India may decide to play in a future war, the present policy and public statements of her Government make it quite out of the question for her to contribute openly towards the defence expenditure of one of the Western Powers. Somewhat similar political considerations apply in the case of Pakistan. We are engaged at this moment in the difficult process of persuading Ceylon to spend more on her own defence. Australia, New Zealand and South Africa are already showing an encouraging readiness to accept wider defence responsibilities and these Governments, and we ourselves, would find it extremely difficult and unprofitable to reverse our present policies.

(e) As suggested in my telegram under reference a request to India, Pakistan and Ceylon for financial assistance towards the cost of our defence would be extremely difficult to reconcile with assistance which we are to give them towards development in South and South East Asia.[3]

CALENDAR TO NO. 100

i *20–4 Oct. 1950 Commonwealth and Defence Planning.* With reference to the agenda for the U.K./U.S. Chiefs of Staff meetings in Washington, Mr. Gordon Walker reminds Mr. Shinwell that any discussions towards enabling the Standing Group to act as the higher military agency in a global war should be without prejudice to discussions within the Commonwealth. This is strongly endorsed by Mr. Bevin on 21 Oct. Mr. Bevin is himself extremely doubtful about extending functions of Standing Group beyond the N.A.T. sphere and 'no commitment whatever' on this 'very difficult political question' should be made to Americans before thorough consideration by Cabinet Defence Committee and discussion with Commonwealth Prime Ministers. Mr. Bevin speculates on more prominent role of Asiatic Powers in future war but is against translating possibilities into advance arrangements. Mr. Shinwell agrees and C.O.S. are instructed accordingly [DEFE 7/743; WU 1198/546].

[3] A copy of this telegram was sent to all U.K. High Commissioners in the Commonwealth for their information only, together with a telegram which summarized the developments recorded in No. 79 with particular regard to the U.S. offer of interim aid and Nitze plan. U.K. High Commissioners were instructed to inform Commonwealth governments of these developments. On 21 November Sir O. Franks replied that there was no indication that the Americans had dropped their suggestion for Commonwealth contributions to defence. However he recommended that 'we should firmly and decisively wait upon events, i.e. we should not take any steps to raise this matter and should wait for the Americans to do so'. This view was endorsed in the Foreign Office and on 28 November Sir O. Franks was instructed to let the matter rest.

No. 101

Extract from Minutes of a Meeting of the Defence Committee of the Cabinet held in the Prime Minister's Room at the House of Commons on Wednesday, 8 November 1950, at 5.45 p.m.[1]

D.O. (50) *21st Meeting* [CAB 131/8]

Top secret

4. *North Atlantic Treaty Defence Committee Meeting, October 1950*

The Minister of Defence said that he had circulated a memorandum (D.O.

[1] *Present* at this meeting were Mr. Attlee (*in the Chair*); Mr. Shinwell; Mr. Bevin; Mr.

(50) 95)[2] which showed that the positive results of the North Atlantic Treaty Defence Committee had been diminished or frustrated by the attitude of the French towards the inclusion of Germans in the Atlantic Treaty Forces for the Defence of Western Europe. It had, however, been possible to agree that the Medium Term Defence Plan was the target for which all Signatories were under obligation to work and to take active steps forthwith. It had been possible for him, thanks to the decisions of the Defence Committee (D.O. (50) 20th Meeting, Minute 5),[3] to set an example of activity to his colleagues. Apart from that, the achievements of the meeting had been disappointing. The Americans had refused to discuss the questions of integrated forces, the establishment of a Supreme Command and the re-organisation of the Military side of N.A.T.O., until agreement had been reached on the inclusion of Germans in Atlantic Treaty Forces; while the French had refused to discuss the inclusion of Germans, except on the basis of the so-called French Plan. This French Plan, which entailed the creation of a European Army under a European Minister of Defence, apparently answerable to the Council of Europe, was totally unacceptable to all the other Signatory Powers, with the exception of the Belgians and the Luxemburghers, who had manifested a somewhat lukewarm support. The result had been a complete deadlock and a reference back to the Military Committee and the Council Deputies, who were charged with the responsibility of recommending some solution to the Atlantic Treaty Defence Committee at an early date, so that the latter could discharge the duty laid upon them by the Atlantic Council. If the Deputies and the Military Committee failed to propound an acceptable solution, it would be necessary to consider whether proposals for the inclusion of Germans in the defence of Europe could be pursued with the Americans and the Germans, and without regard to the French. In the meantime, it might be desirable to leave it to the Americans to exert pressure on the French, which in fact they had begun to do in vigorous terms.

The Prime Minister said that the disappointing results recounted by the Minister of Defence were entirely due to French intransigence and lack of realism. Valuable time was being lost: chances of substantial American reinforcements in Europe were being thrown away; and there was little prospect of being able to build up adequate strength against the real dangers of aggression in Europe in 1951. This dangerous situation was the direct result of the French attachment to an unworkable and unsound plan. The French attitude left the whole western world in doubt and

Gaitskell; Mr. Isaacs; Viscount Hall, First Lord of the Admiralty; Mr. J. Strachey, Secretary of State for War; Mr. Henderson, Secretary of State for Air; Mr. G.R. Strauss, Minister of Supply. *Also present* for Item 4 were Mr. Gordon-Walker; Field-Marshal Sir W. Slim; Marshal of the Royal Air Force Sir J. Slessor; Vice-Admiral Sir G. Creasy; Sir F. Hoyer-Millar. *Secretariat*: Air Marshal Sir W. Elliot; Mr. Mallaby and Wing-Commander F.O.S. Dobell.

[2] See calendar i.   [3] See No. 79, note 8.

anxiety. Were the French in fact intending to fight, or had they already made up their minds to give in? Had not the time arrived when there would be advantage in the Foreign Secretary putting this question bluntly to the French Cabinet?

The Foreign Secretary said that, while he was reluctantly forced to admit that in present circumstances he saw little chance of the French putting up any sort of resistance in war, he doubted whether the moment had yet arrived for him to make this blunt approach. The Americans had left the French Government in no doubt of their displeasure and it might be as well to await the outcome of their approach.

The following points were made in discussion:

(*a*) It was difficult to interpret the intransigence shown by M. Moch in putting forward the French point of view. This might have been due to political and party intrigues, which were known to exist between members of the French Government. It might be due to a latent determination on the part of the French to play once again the part they had played in 1940. In either case, it seemed desirable to take a strong line in negotiating with a Government, which had very little to contribute towards the common defence of the Atlantic Treaty area, but whose attitude was alienating the practical sympathy of the United States, on whose assistance the defence of the whole of Europe, including the United Kingdom, ultimately depended.

(*b*) It would perhaps be premature for the United Kingdom to push matters to the extreme until the results of the work of the Military Committee and Deputies were known. In the meantime, the Americans had already adopted a firm and uncompromising attitude towards the French Government on these questions and the disputes between the members of the French Government must, by their own violence, find some decisive issue.

(*c*) *The Chiefs of Staff* pointed out that the Military Committee and the Deputies had been allowed discretion to examine and report on both the American and the French Plans for the inclusion of Germans and to propose any additional plan, if they thought fit. They themselves in general supported the American Plan, but they would put themselves in the position of being able to offer some positive solution, and not merely to make destructive criticisms of the two Plans that existed, and so widen the gap which perhaps only the United Kingdom could bridge. To this end, they would study the problem and search for effective safeguards against the resurgence of an aggressive German Army and German General Staff—a possibility which the German people themselves, who saw daily before them the results of strategic bombing, feared almost as much as the French.

(*d*) While the attitude of the French towards any proposals for the inclusion of Germans in the Atlantic Treaty Forces was of vital importance, the attitude of the Germans was perhaps no less vital.

Europe could not be defended without their co-operation and assistance. The intention of the Foreign Secretary to visit Germany for discussions with the Bonn Government on this and other questions before the end of the year was warmly approved.[4]

(e) The uncertainty over the solution of the German problem, and, in consequence, over the intentions of the United States, with regard to the defence of Europe, made it even more essential that the United Kingdom should press on with its own rearmament programme on the conditions already laid down (D.O. (50) 20th Meeting, Minute 5).[3] All sections of the community had accepted the need and urgency, and it was most important that orders should be placed to the maximum of available capacity and finance.

The Committee—

(1) Took note of D.O. (50) 95.

(2) Invited the Foreign Office and the Chiefs of Staff to pursue jointly their search for a solution to the problem of the inclusion of Germans in Atlantic Treaty Forces, which the United Kingdom representatives in the Military Committee and Council Deputies might propose.[5]

(3) Reaffirmed the decision taken on the placing of orders, as shown in D.O. (50) 20th Meeting, Minute 5, Conclusion (2).

CALENDAR TO NO. 101

i 7 Nov. 1950 D.O. (50) 95. Review of Defence Ministers' talks in Washington by Mr. Shinwell with suggestions for future action (a) with French (b) with Federal govt. (c) possibility of proceeding with American plan without the French [CAB 131/9].

[4] Mr. Bevin's visit to Bonn scheduled for December was later cancelled owing to the Korean crisis.

[5] The idea of working out an alternative plan was put forward by Sir P. Dixon in a brief to Mr. Bevin for this meeting (not printed from WU 1195/427). A Foreign Office plan for a German contribution on a Land rather than a Federal basis was suggested to the Chiefs of Staff and Sir I. Kirkpatrick on 9 November as a solution of both German constitutional and French difficulties. Sir I. Kirkpatrick replied on 10 November that though the idea was 'ingenious and attractive. Nevertheless we must recognise that it would give rise to great practical difficulties.' Sir I. Kirkpatrick went on to list these difficulties and after further consideration in the Foreign Office, the idea was dropped (see C 7268–9/27/18). Meanwhile the Joint Planning Staff was instructed by the Chiefs of Staff on 9 November to produce a plan in conjunction with the Foreign Office based on a modification of the American proposals: see further No. 106.i.

No. 102

*Extract from Conclusions of a Meeting of the Cabinet held at
10 Downing Street on Thursday, 9 November 1950, at 10 a.m.*[1]

C.M. (50) 72nd Conclusions [CAB 128/18]

Secret

Defence

Previous Reference: C.M. (50) 70th Conclusions, Minute 1[2]

7. The Cabinet had before them a memorandum by the Prime Minister (C.P. (50) 246) inviting the Cabinet to endorse the conclusions of the Defence Committee on 25th October, 1950, about the financing of defence and to approve recommendations put forward by the Foreign Secretary and the Chancellor of the Exchequer about the attitude to be adopted towards United States offers of assistance. The Cabinet had also before them copies of memoranda on the financing of defence and on the size and shape of the Armed Forces, 1951–54, which had been prepared for the Defence Committee (C.P. (50) 247 and 248).

The Minister of Defence said that the Defence Committee had agreed that, at the meeting of the North Atlantic Treaty Defence Committee in Washington which he had recently attended, proposals costing £3,600 million should be put forward as the planned defence effort of the United Kingdom over the three financial years 1951–52, 1952–53 and 1953–54. The commitment of the United Kingdom to the full programme of £3,600 million was dependent upon several factors, including agreement on the United Kingdom share of the collective defence plan and on the distribution of the economic burden between the North Atlantic Treaty countries. The Chiefs of Staff had put forward proposals on the size and shape of the Armed Forces which would have cost £3,800 million, but it was doubtful whether a programme of this size could in fact be carried out in the time available, and it had been agreed to adhere to the earlier figure of £3,600 million. There had been agreement that orders totalling £200 million should be placed, notwithstanding that the total programme was not yet finally settled; and of this amount orders to the value of £103 million had already been placed, and further orders for £50 million would be placed in the near future in respect of aircraft. The Admiralty would be wishing soon to place substantial orders in respect of mine-sweepers. It followed that orders of an amount in excess of £200 million would shortly be placed, and the Treasury had accepted this because of the need to

[1] *Present* at this meeting were Mr. Attlee (*in the Chair*); Mr. Morrison; Mr. Bevin; Mr. Gaitskell; Mr. Dalton; Viscount Addison; Viscount Jowitt; Mr. Chuter Ede; Mr. Shinwell; Mr. Isaacs; Mr. Bevan; Mr. Williams; Mr. Tomlinson; Mr. Wilson; Mr. Griffiths; Mr. McNeil; Mr. Gordon Walker. *Secretariat*: Mr. Johnston and Mr. O. Morland.

[2] At this meeting on 2 November consideration of C.P. (50) 246–8 (see No. 79, note 8) was deferred until the present meeting in order that both Mr. Bevin and Mr. Shinwell could be present.

make speedy progress with the re-equipment of the Services. The North Atlantic Treaty Defence Committee, at its meeting in Washington, had approved the Medium-Term Defence Programme, but this country had worked out in greater detail than others its component of this programme and the stages by which it would be achieved. The North Atlantic Treaty Defence Committee had accepted the thesis, advanced by this country and the United States, that man-power and equipment must be increased as speedily as possible. There were formidable difficulties in the way of the speedy implementation of the Medium-Term Defence Programme. Agreement had not yet been secured about the appointment of a United States Commander-in-Chief in Western Europe, nor about the integration of the Western Union and the North Atlantic Treaty Organisations, nor about the precise assistance which the United States would give in the form of additional divisions stationed in Europe and of equipment for the Western European armies. The French objection to the rearmament of Germany had proved to be the real obstacle to building up an effective defence for Western Europe. It was to be hoped that further examination of the problem in European defence by the Military Committee and the Council of Deputies would make it possible for some kind of compromise plan to be agreed upon. Meanwhile, it was essential, in the interests of this country, that the strengthening of the Armed Forces should proceed as speedily as possible.

The Prime Minister agreed that the difficult attitude adopted by the French had seriously delayed the preparation of plans for the defence of Western Europe. Meanwhile, the Government, for the defence of this country, must proceed on the basis that the Medium-Term Defence Programme would ultimately be approved, and that financial assistance would be forthcoming. Progress could be made with rearmament while leaving some element of flexibility to take account of modifications of the programme which might ultimately be agreed upon.

In subsequent discussion, attention was drawn to the fact that events had falsified some of the assumptions on which the defence programme was originally drawn up. It had been assumed that assistance to the amount of £550 million would be secured from the United States and that on this basis the defence programme could be implemented without serious risk of inflation or of drastic retrenchment in other items of Government expenditure.

The Cabinet—

Agreed to resume their discussion of C.P. (50) 246 at a later meeting of the Cabinet.

No. 103

Sir I. Kirkpatrick (Wahnerheide) to Mr. Bevin
(Received 12 November)

No. 623 Saving Telegraphic [C 7293/80/18]

Confidential   WAHNERHEIDE, *11 November 1950, 8 a.m.*

Repeated Saving to Berlin, Washington, Moscow, Paris.

My telegram No. 1590.[1]

It may be useful to you to have the following comments on the Bundestag debate on Foreign Affairs.

2. It was made clear by this debate that the gap between the Government and the Opposition on the main question of principle, i.e. whether or not Germany should make a contribution to Western defence, is by no means so wide as it has sometimes seemed. In fact, there was almost universal tacit acceptance of an affirmative answer to this question. The debate therefore was not on the question of whether Germany should contribute, but on the question of the conditions which should be satisfied before she contributes. Schumacher's position is in fact revealed as differing from Adenauer's only on tactical grounds.

3. I must however point out that the fact that the debate was conducted on this basis means that it failed to give any expression to a large and active body of opinion in Germany, probably most widespread among the younger generation, which is not engaged on considering how and when and under what conditions Germany should make her contribution but which simply does not want to make any contribution at all.[2] Subject to this failure to reflect a significant part of German opinion the debate seems to me to have served a useful purpose in clearing the air and revealing where the political parties stand. In turn, the parties will be less restive now that they have had this formal opportunity of speaking their mind in Parliament.

4. Adenauer deserves credit for courage in making his positive declaration, on behalf of the Federal Government, of its readiness to make an appropriate contribution to the construction of a defensive front. This action exposed him once again to attacks from the Opposition for out-running events and weakening the Government's bargaining position. I think he deserves equal credit, though his action may prove embarrassing later and not only to him, for his acceptance of the Pleven plan as a

---

[1] See calendar i.

[2] In a brief to Mr. Bevin of 6 November, Sir D. Gainer ascribed lack of enthusiasm for German rearmament among the German people to: (a) war weariness (b) dislike of militarism, fostered by Occupying Powers and now taken up by some leading Protestants (c) appeal of neutrality (d) the element of *Schadenfreude* (e) reluctance to fight against fellow Germans in Bereitschaften (f) financial cost. These points together with the substance of the present telegram formed the basis of Intel No. 239 of 16 November to H.M. Representatives Overseas.

basis of discussion, although by claiming equal rights he really rejected it. He is about the only German who has accepted it; and he probably did so because of the need for good relations with France. Perhaps he calculates that the best way to kill the plan is by kindness to France; but we should not overlook the fact that its European federal character gives it attractions in Germany which it lacks for us.

5. Other noteworthy features of the debate were, first, the determination expressed by all parties, and perhaps most strongly by the CDU and FDP from the Government benches, that if Germany had to produce a military contingent there should be no restoration of the former trappings, manners and personalities of the former German army, but an entirely new force must be constructed in an entirely new spirit; and second, the hostility expressed by several speakers (notably Schumacher and Schaefer for the FDP) towards the German Labour Services employed by the British and American forces in Germany and the recent measures taken to reorganise them. We may run into more trouble on this front before long.

6. But undoubtedly the main feature of the debate was the discussion of the conditions on which Germany should insist before she makes her contribution to Western defence. Here the Chancellor set the example with his insistence on complete equality of rights with other participating powers; and other speakers were not slow to draw their various deductions from this principle. Equality of rights in defence was widely interpreted, and most forcefully by Schumacher, as implying equality of political status too. The Allies must not force the pace on the defence issue and expect at the same time that the Germans should refrain from forcing it in the political field. Many speakers demanded the termination of the state of war and the abolition of the Occupation Statute. One suggested that it should be replaced by a treaty. There were the usual demands for the release of war criminals; and Dr. Seelos for the Bavarian Party demanded that Germany should take her place as a full member in the Council of Europe, the Atlantic Council and the United Nations. One speaker observed pointedly that those who were called on to sacrifice freedom and rights in a common struggle must first possess them.

7. The concept of equal rights was approached more gingerly in connection with occupation costs, which figured largely in the debate. Some speakers observed that they must be reduced in order that Germany's contribution to defence should be no greater than that of other countries. More prudent orators stated simply that they must be reduced. In general the same concept prevailed namely that Germany might have to pay a proportionate share of the cost of defence, but should certainly not pay more. Many members of the Bundestag are probably under the impression that the occupation costs they pay represent a larger proportion of national expenditure than defence costs in other Western countries.

i *8 Nov. 1950 Bundestag debate on rearmament,* as reported in Wahnerheide tel. No. 1590 of 9 Nov. Major statement by Adenauer: (*a*) dismisses Soviet proposal for C.F.M. as an attempt to prevent or delay Western rearmament. Hopes that Western Govts. will consult Federal govt. before reply. (*b*) Welcomes Pleven Plan. Hopes for British and German participation. (*c*) F.R.G. has not yet made any offer of contribution to Western defence but is ready to be asked. Preconditions for German contribution include 'complete equality' with other participating powers. In reply Schumacher agrees that Prague resolution is 'completely unacceptable' and 'genuine equality' is a precondition for German contribution to defence. But criticises Pleven plan and says 'no' to German remilitarization [C 7217/80/18].

ii *16 Nov. 1950 A.H.C. meeting with Dr. Adenauer* reported in Wahnerheide telegrams Nos. 1648, 642–5 Saving. Long statement by Adenauer in effect asking for sweeteners e.g. on occupation statute and costs in return for German contribution to defence. Details contained in document of informal status left with A.H.C. This new catalogue of requests regarded by Kirkpatrick as 'unfortunate' though he later gathers from Chancellor that 'he does not really expect full satisfaction, but intended to make a list of all the items on which concessions would be helpful to him in the coming struggle'. F.O. reactions include memo. by Sir D. Gainer of 20 Nov. warning that issue of almost full sovereignty for F.R.G. will have to be faced soon: 'we may be forced to concede the maximum of political equality in order to bring about even the minimum of military equality' [C 7440, 7467–7470, 7607/27/18].

No. 104

Extract from Conclusions of a Meeting of the Cabinet held at 10 Downing Street on Thursday, 16 November 1950, at 10 a.m.[1]

C.M. (50) 74th Conclusions [CAB 128/18]

Secret

Defence

(Previous Reference: C.M. (50) 72nd Conclusions, Minute 7)[2]

4. The Cabinet resumed their discussion of a memorandum by the Prime Minister (C.P. (50) 246)[3] inviting the Cabinet to endorse the conclusions of the Defence Committee on 25th October, 1950,[3] about the financing of defence and to approve recommendations put forward by the Foreign Secretary and the Chancellor of the Exchequer about the attitude to be adopted towards United States offers of assistance. The Cabinet had

[1] *Present* at this meeting were Mr. Attlee (*in the Chair*); Mr. Morrison; Mr. Bevin; Mr. Gaitskell; Viscount Addison; Viscount Jowitt; Mr. Chuter Ede; Mr. Shinwell; Mr. Isaacs; Mr. Bevan; Mr. Williams; Mr. Tomlinson; Mr. Wilson; Mr. Griffiths; Mr. McNeil; Mr. Gordon Walker. *Secretariat*: Sir N. Brook, Mr. Johnston and Mr. Morland.
[2] No. 102. [3] See No. 79, note 8.

also before them copies of memoranda on the financing of defence and on the size and shape of the Armed Forces, 1951–54, which had been prepared for the Defence Committee (C.P. (50) 247 and 248).[3]

The Chancellor of the Exchequer said that he advised the Cabinet to accept the United States offer of interim aid of $84 million for the dollar content of the £200 million instalment of the production programme to which the Government were already committed, but to reserve their position on the United States proposal to purchase $28 million worth of British equipment. If the latter proposal were accepted it might prejudice the position of this country under the final arrangements for the equitable distribution of the economic burden of rearmament, and it was not clear that equipment which the United States purchased from this country would, in fact, be left here. He supported the working out of a procedure for determining, on a multilateral basis, the equitable distribution between the partner countries of the burden of North Atlantic defence; but at present the position was complicated by the fact that, not only had a basis to be found for the equitable distribution of the burden, but agreement had not yet been reached on the size of the military preparations which had to be made. The United States Government had made it clear that they were not committed about the size of their military contribution, pending a settlement of the difficulties raised by France to the proposals for German rearmament. He saw no alternative but to proceed with preparations on the basis of the £3,600 million programme, on the understanding that this programme would have to be reviewed in the light of later developments.

The Minister of Defence said that, as he had made clear at the Cabinet's meeting on 9th November,[2] he was anxious to make further progress on the basis of the £3,600 million programme. He did not ask for more than general acceptance of the programme, so that forces could be built up and production orders placed in an orderly and balanced way. He wished, however, to make it clear that, if present economic tendencies continued, there would be a sharp rise in the cost of defence in the fourth year because of the steep rise in prices. The position would have to be reviewed in the light of developments in the next three or four months. If the difficulties which had arisen in connection with German rearmament were resolved and a United States Supreme Commander were appointed, it might then be easier to anticipate the extent of the contribution which the United States were prepared to make to North Atlantic defence.

In further discussion the following points were made:

(a) This country should continue to make it clear that it could not devote more of its national resources to defence than what it had proposed in connection with the Medium-Term Defence Plan. This should be kept in mind in the working out of global defence needs by the military experts of the North Atlantic countries. While it was true that the United Kingdom Government could not be committed to a larger programme than the Government considered that they could afford on economic and financial grounds, there was a risk that undesirable pressure would be brought to bear on this country if, on military grounds, the military experts put forward a very large programme for consideration by the Governments of the countries concerned. Every endeavour should be made to ensure that what was economically practicable was kept in mind in the drawing up of military appreciations.

(*b*) This country should not undertake to implement a defence programme beyond its resources on the basis that substantial financial assistance would be forthcoming from the United States, since that assistance might be the means by which undesirable economic or other pressure would be brought to bear on the United Kingdom Government. From this angle it was satisfactory that the United States had shown a willingness to station substantial land forces on the Continent of Europe. It was preferable that the United States contribution to North Atlantic defence should take the form of troops and equipment rather than financial aid.

(*c*) In working out, under the Nitze Plan, the contribution which this country should make to North Atlantic defence, full regard should be had to this country's defence commitments in other parts of the world.

(*d*) The United States Government, in their aide-mémoire of 3rd October, 1950,[4] on interim aid, had suggested that other parts of the sterling area should contribute to the defence effort of the United Kingdom. They had been led to make this suggestion by reason of the substantial income which some countries in the sterling area were earning from the present high prices of raw materials. It would, however, be difficult to ask sterling area countries which were outside the North Atlantic Treaty Organisation to make financial contributions to North Atlantic defence while they were not part of that organisation and did not benefit by it. The United States proposal would have to be taken up at a later stage when, in connection with the defence of the Middle East and other areas, the question arose of enlarging the scope of the North Atlantic Treaty Organisation.

The Cabinet—

(1) Endorsed the conclusions of the Defence Committee about defence expenditure, as set out in paragraph 3 of C.P. (50) 246.

(2) Approved the recommendations of the Foreign Secretary and the Chancellor of the Exchequer about United States interim aid and the equitable distribution of the burden of North Atlantic defence, as set out in paragraph 30 of the memorandum annexed to C.P. (50) 247.[5]

[4] See No. 79.i.
[5] Instructions were sent accordingly to Sir O. Franks on 28 November for accepting the American offer of $84m. towards the first two instalments (£200m.) of the U.K. defence programme but deferring the question of U.S. purchase of $28 million worth of British

i *28 Nov. 1950   U.K. reply to U.S. offer of interim aid*: transmitted in F.O. tels. to Washington Nos. 5291 and 5332 [UR 1027/84].

equipment. It was pointed out to Sir O. Franks that reference to the figure of £3,600m. for the overall U.K. defence programme was deliberately omitted in the reply (calendared at i) since 'this figure may vary slightly according to whatever definitions of defence expenditure are adopted for the purpose of the Nitze Exercise, and, secondly, since it does not include expenditure in stockpiling which we may now wish to claim as relevant' (F.O. telegram to Washington No. 5290 on UR 1027/84). Sir O. Franks reported that the British reply was handed on 1 December to Mr. H. Labouisse of the State Department who 'made no special comment' (UR 1027/89).

No. 105

Memorandum by Mr. Mallet

[C 7523/27/18]

FOREIGN OFFICE, *16 November 1950*

Some consequences of German rearmament on relations between the Western Allies and the Federal Republic

The decision that Western Germany must be rearmed as part of Western defence against the Soviet Union will bring about consequences which we and our two Allies must be ready to face.

The chief consequence, the effects of which will be met in all spheres, is that Federal Germany will have to be treated as a partner and an equal. In the military sphere this means that, as Germany is to share the burden and dangers of the common defence, she must be given membership of the bodies which control that defence. She must in the long run be accorded the same degree of military sovereignty as is enjoyed by her partners. The Federal Republic is today probably still prepared to accept military restrictions which will save her from the risk of being dominated by the army and of being plunged into another war. But she will not indefinitely consent that such limitations be imposed upon her by others unless those others are prepared to impose corresponding limitations on themselves. We must not delude ourselves into thinking we can in the long run prevent Germany from having an independent general staff, a bomber and submarine force and a full armaments industry unless other Atlantic Powers are prepared to place at least their European forces under an international staff and command, and to agree to something less than self-sufficiency in regard to certain arms of the Services and to equipment and supplies.

If rearmament will involve military equality, military equality will involve political equality. Germany will have to be an equal member of such bodies as the Council of Europe. It will not be pleasing or easy to treat Germany as a partner and equal, but we cannot have it both ways. If we need Germany's help and want Germany to form part of our Western bloc, we must make her a full member of the club and reconcile ourselves to seeing her smoking a large cigar in a big chair in front of the fire in the smoking room. Otherwise, Germany will not pay the subscription we are asking; she may even join another club where she will be better treated. We have not only to give the Republic the social prestige of being an equal member of the Western confederation, but we have also to see to it that it is in her economic interest to belong to that confederation. We have not only to cease treating her as though we distrusted her or were frightened of her but must also give her political equality. This means that we must recognise that the occupation régime will have to come to an end much sooner than we anticipated and that Germany will recover complete sovereignty subject only to such military arrangements as may be made within the Atlantic Pact for stationing Allied troops on German soil. We must expect shortly to see Adenauer sitting at the conference table with the Americans, the French and ourselves.

These consequences will be extremely unpalatable to the French. The whole French policy in regard to concessions to Germany is to go gradually, waiting for Germany to justify each further step by giving 'guarantees' of good behaviour or by showing that she is well behaved. This attitude, though comprehensible, is unrealistic, since it shows that France still thinks that Germany may in the long run be a greater menace than the Soviet Union is today and still imagines that Germany can join the Western club as a second-class member.

Already the French are demanding safeguards, which we cannot accept, before they will agree to the limited degree of German rearmament now proposed. The recent paper by the Joint Planning Staff[1] indicates clearly that it is only in the political sphere that we are likely to be able to evolve alternative safeguards which the French would regard as anything like adequate. The Joint Planners are sceptical even about the political safeguards which they can suggest, and point out, quite rightly, that the really important thing is 'the speedy implementation of a policy so closely integrating the Federal Republic into the Western world, both politically and militarily, that the danger of independent German action is reduced to a minimum'.

If, in fact, as seems to be the case, the first steps in Germany's rearmament will lead before long to the complete equality and independence of the Federal Republic, it becomes all the more essential to prepare ourselves for the 'close integration' of the Federal Republic into the Western world. For military reasons we are unable, at least for the present, to envisage this 'integration' on a European basis. We must therefore face the fact that some form of Atlantic integration will be essential if the French are to be got to come along with us in our defence policy and in our German policy as a whole, and if it is to be made difficult for Germany to become an independent Power which could threaten our

[1] See No. 106, note 1.

position either by leading us into adventures in the East or by making an agreement with Russia.

This Atlantic integration will have, on the military side, to take the form of an Atlantic pool to which each North Atlantic Treaty member contributes a definite number of forces under an international command. On the political side it will involve some form of Atlantic federation which will be sufficiently close-knit to give every member—and not only the French—grounds for hoping that no one member will be able to act independently of the will of the majority.

I. MALLET[2]

[2] Mr. Mallet's views were fully endorsed by Sir D. Gainer (cf. also No. 103.ii). However Lord Henderson took issue with the notion of political equality for Germany: 'My view is that within the context of pooled defence resources, Germany should have equal rights, but that it is far too soon to think of equal rights politically in the wider context. I consider that the Occupation regime will have to come to an end much sooner than was perhaps expected, but even so I do not consider that its early ending should leave Germany free to set up a German army in the accepted sense and recreate the German General Staff. So long as that continues to be Western Allied policy it must involve a limitation on German sovereignty indefinitely'. Mr. Mallet agreed that it was desirable to avoid the creation of an independent German Army and German General staff. However, while he considered that 'given certain conditions, full German equality in the military sphere can be avoided, German equality in the political sphere will have to be granted very quickly. I think it is most important that we should recognise this consequence of our decision to rearm Germany'. Lord Henderson countered on 20 November that: 'We are not prepared to allow Germany to have a national army in the recognised sense nor a General Staff in the same sense . . . The Western Allies have committed themselves to the prohibition of these two organisations, and that is to me a denial of some measure of political equality or sovereign rights. I do not think this can be regarded as merely academic' (C 7523/27/18).

No. 106

Ministry of Defence to B.J.S.M. (Washington)

COS (W) 900 Telegraphic [WU 1198/641]

Immediate. Top secret   MINISTRY OF DEFENCE, 17 November 1950, 5.3 p.m.

For Lord Tedder from Chiefs of Staff.
German Re-armament.

1. We have examined, in conjunction with Foreign Office, the American plan for German re-armament to see whether this plan can be suitably modified to make it acceptable both to the French and to the Germans.[1] The results of this examination which have been approved by

[1] On 15 November the Chiefs of Staff Committee considered proposals produced by the J.P.S. as instructed (see No. 101, note 5) for modifying the American plan. This paper (J.P. (50) 161 Final) was agreed subject to certain amendments incorporated in the final text circulated as C.O.S. (50) 474 (calendar i below) on 17 November to Mr. Shinwell and Mr. Bevin. In discussion at the C.O.S. meeting on 15 November, 'Sir Pierson Dixon said that at the Defence Committee meeting the Foreign Secretary had originally asked that a new set of proposals for German re-armament should be prepared. Since that meeting it had,

Minister of Defence are summarised below for your use at to-morrow's meeting of the Standing Group with Accredited Representatives.

2. We believe that the fundamental difficulty with which we are faced is that the French still fear that if and when U.S. and U.K. forces are no longer stationed in Germany, a re-armed Germany will present a greater menace than does the Soviet Union to-day or in the immediate future. The French fear, not only an invasion of France by Germany, but also that she may be involved in a war provoked by Germany with the object of regaining her Eastern provinces. Our aim must therefore be to convince France that in the period for which it is possible to plan Russia presents a far greater danger than does Germany.

3. If our military requirements are to be met they must involve creation of German formations and this carries with it the ultimate danger of a German army with a German general staff on the old model. There is therefore a danger that our military requirements will eventually lead to something on the lines of what the French fear and although we may provide certain short term military safeguards long term safeguards must be largely political and come within the sphere of the deputies.

4. Existing safeguards for use in arguments with the French are considerable and are as follows:

(a) Atlantic forces must be under the Allied Supreme Commander and the French through the Standing Group will have a deciding voice in its control.
(b) U.K. obligation to France in Brussels Treaty will continue even after military organisation of Brussels Treaty has been dissolved.
(c) Whole of Germany is within easy range of escorted atomic bombers and with key industries concentrated in the Ruhr she is peculiarly vulnerable to atomic bomb attack. This fact must inevitably be a strong deterrent to any idea that she can gain anything by aggression.

5. We consider there are four main military modifications possible to the American plan. They concern:

(a) Basic Military formations.
(b) Appointment of political advisers to the Supreme Commander.
(c) Research and development.
(d) Limitation of German Armament Industry.

6. We consider that a Brigade Group or Regimental Combat Team would be acceptable as the basic military formation instead of the balanced

however, become clear that the French were not holding rigidly to their original proposals and he (Sir Pierson Dixon) therefore now agreed that, rather than prepare a further set of proposals, it was preferable that the problem should be negotiated within the North Atlantic Treaty Organisation, and that we should consider how best to make the American proposals acceptable both to the French and to the Germans. This had, in fact, been the method of approach in the paper before them and he would explain the reason for adopting this approach to the problem to the Foreign Secretary' (CAB 21/1898).

ground division *if agreement can be reached on no other basis.*

7. We consider that in exercising his function of political administration, Supreme Commander will have to be advised by a panel of political advisers appointed, subject to his approval, by the Council of Deputies to whom they would be responsible.

8. We consider that research and development should be limited to requirements laid down by N.A.T.O. and controlled by the M.P.S.B.

9. We consider that the manufacture of atomic, biological and chemical weapons and long range missiles should not (repeat not) be permitted in Germany.

10. We have examined and rejected the following proposals:

(*a*) Decentralisation of military administrative responsibilities to Laender Governments.
(*b*) Allied supervision of promotion and appointment of Officers in the German Forces.[2]

CALENDAR TO NO. 106

i *17 Nov. 1950   C.O.S. (50) 474:* Report by Chiefs of Staff on how U.S. plan can be modified. New safeguards to attract the French are an Anglo-American security guarantee and the reaffirmation of British obligations to France under Brussels Treaty and the tripartite declaration on Germany of 13 May (Volume II, No. 98.i). Development of European Army in parallel with U.S. plan is regarded as inefficient and should only be pursued 'as a last resort'. Report sent to Tedder with instructions as to its confidentiality [CAB 21/1898].

[2] At their meeting on 18 November the Standing Group approved a report on the military aspects of German participation in the defence of Western Europe for circulation to the Military Committee as M.C.30. This report is not preserved in Foreign Office archives. For summaries see Nos. 115–6: cf. also *F.R.U.S. 1950*, vol. iii, p. 488, note 1.

No. 107

Memorandum from Sir P. Dixon to Mr. Bevin

[*WU 1195/447*]

FOREIGN OFFICE, 17 November 1950

German Contribution to Defence of Europe

Since you last discussed this question there have been two developments:

(i) M. Alphand has made a statement in the Atlantic Deputies Council elaborating the French Plan. This statement adheres to the plan for a European army and a European Ministry of Defence, which is fundamentally objectionable, but it also makes certain concessions,[1] At least, therefore, the French now seem prepared to talk, though it is too early to say whether they are willing to negotiate a compromise.

(ii) The Chiefs of Staff have, on the instructions of the Defence Committee and in consultation with the Foreign Office, examined the possibility of producing a 'British plan'. Their general conclusions are that certain minor modifications can be made to the American plan to render it more acceptable to the French; that if military requirements are to be met, however, they must involve the creation of German formations and thus the danger that ultimately there may be a German national army with its own staff; that purely military safeguards cannot, therefore, give the French the security they seek; and that this can only be done by political means.

From these two developments I think we may draw the following conclusions:

(1) That there is now some hope of the discussions in the Deputies and the Standing Group making progress, and that we should therefore let the negotiations continue in those channels for the present;

(2) that any 'British plan' can, in the nature of things, only be a political plan.

We have therefore been thinking over what political proposals we might, at some stage or other, put forward in the Deputies. I have now embodied our thoughts in the attached draft of a paper for the Defence Committee.[2]

P. DIXON

CALENDAR TO NO. 107

i *18 Nov. 1950 Draft British Plan*: Alternatives for negotiating a compromise are (*a*) to seek agreement on immediate formation of an integrated force without German participation—dismissed as impractical (*b*) to persuade French to accept a modified U.S. plan in return for certain U.K./U.S. political assurances as proposed by C.O.S. (No. 106.i)—attractive but substantial objections (*c*) to persuade French to agree to implement a modified U.S. plan

[1] In his statement to the Deputies on 13 November, M. Alphand offered three concessions (i) national units in a European army should be Brigade Groups, three of which would constitute a Division (ii) French agree to establishment of a German Federal Agency, though not a Ministry of Defence, to administer German troops (iii) no objection to interim measures for recruitment and barrack-construction in Germany provided no forces raised at this stage. When elaborating the Pleven Plan, M. Alphand explained that the proposed European Minister of Defence would be responsible to the Parliamentary Assembly proposed for the Schuman Plan.

[2] This first draft of No. 115 is calendared at i. Sir P. Dixon's submission covering the draft was countersigned by Sir W. Strang on 18 November and discussed with Mr. Bevin at an Office meeting on 21 November when instructions were evidently given for the revision at No. 115.

in parallel with negotiations for a European Army—'politically unwise' (*d*) to persuade French to agree to implement U.S. plan and to agree to pursue idea of developing integrated force into an Atlantic federal force—'grave practical difficulties' but recommended as the line to pursue. At A.O.C. meeting on 22 November, Bevin's objections to European Army are represented by Dixon. Military view, given by Elliot, is that French plan is so unlikely to succeed that no harm in its being pursued [WU 1195/447; CAB 21/1898].

No. 108

Mr. Bevin to Sir O. Franks (Washington)

No. 5167 Telegraphic [*UR 1027/60*]

Immediate. Confidential   FOREIGN OFFICE, *20 November 1950, 8.10 p.m.*

Your telegram No. 3134 (of 19th November):[1] American Press articles about British rearmament expenditure.

The United States Minister called on officials of the Foreign Office and Treasury on 18th November to inform them of the story which American correspondents had got hold of, and emphasised that the correspondents had received the impression that His Majesty's Government had already decided to refuse American offers of dollar assistance for rearmament. He was informed that there was no foundation for the suggestion that His Majesty's Government had taken such a decision and was authorised to say so to the correspondents but he was told that His Majesty's Government attached great importance to the partnership concept and had always held the view that military preparation should be related to economic strength.

2. Mr. Holmes said that when the correspondents realised that no decision had in fact been taken in the sense which they had understood, they would probably refrain from making any use of the story. In this he was clearly wrong.

3. Text of Statement (as from a Government spokesman) issued this evening is given in my immediately following telegram.[2]

[1] This telegram gave details of American press reports on 19 November of 'alleged pressure by a section of the Cabinet for independence of American military aid and a reduction in British rearmament expenditure . . . We have been informed by Washington bureau of *Newsweek* that, according to their London correspondent, the background of these articles is as follows. The Minister of Health allegedly summoned the London correspondents of the *New York Times*, *New York Herald-Tribune* and *Newsweek* and gave them the substance of these articles without any restriction on its use. Further, it is alleged some repudiation of these views was conveyed yesterday to the American Embassy by the Foreign Office. 3. We believe that *Newsweek*, which appears on Thursday and goes to press on Monday night, is preparing an article giving what is said to be the inside story on differences in the Cabinet and Party revealed by this incident' (UR 1027/60).

[2] This statement, reported in *The Times* on 21 November, read: 'Articles have appeared today in two important United States papers alleging that three members of His Majesty's Government (the Minister of Health, the Minister of War and the Minister of Supply) are urging a cut in the British rearmament programme and the abandonment of any

4. We are not proposing to intervene with Newsweek.

5. If we receive enquiries we shall stress the following points, and we suggest that you do the same:

(a) His Majesty's Government have made clear their intention to play a full part in the collective defence programme.

(b) It has always been the view of His Majesty's Government that the burden of defence should be distributed equitably on a basis to be multilaterally agreed by the countries concerned.

(c) Such distribution of the burden would probably involve transfers of resources from one country to another which might loosely be described as 'Mutual Aid'.

(d) There has never been any question of His Majesty's Government deciding to refuse Aid of this character from the United States.

6. Record of the conversation with Mr. Holmes follows by bag.[3]

prospective American aid for that programme. A Government spokesman today officially denied that there is any truth in this suggestion. He was further authorised by the three Ministers concerned to deny the stories on their behalf' (UR 1027/60).

[3] Not printed from UR 1027/68.

Breaking the deadlock: the Spofford Plan, Mr. Attlee's visit to Washington and the Brussels Conference

20 November – 22 December 1950

No. 109

Memorandum from the U.K. Deputy on the N.A.C. to Mr. Bevin

No. 66 [*WU 1195/452*]

Secret   LONDON, *20 November 1950*

Mr. Spofford telephoned to me this morning to give me an account of his visit to Brussels. He said that he thought that he had persuaded M. Van Zeeland that it would be a mistake for him to intervene personally in the German problem at the present stage, and that it would be better to let the discussions in the Deputies and the Military Committee carry on uninterruptedly. In particular, it would be a mistake to summon any meeting of the Council itself until the situation in respect of the German question was a great deal clearer. M. Van Zeeland had agreed.

2. Mr. Spofford then went on to say that he had now received instructions from the State Department as to the line he was to take in the Deputies in the matter of the German contribution to the defence of Western Europe.[1] At his suggestion, his Assistant, Mr. Achilles, came to see me later in the morning to give me an account of the American position.

3. Mr. Achilles explained that, as a result of the deliberations here early last week between the United States Ambassadors in London and Paris, the United States High Commissioner in Germany and Mr. Spofford, a telegram[2] had been sent to the State Department expressing the view that while the French plan was clearly unacceptable from the military point of view as a solution to the short-term problem, yet if the French

[1] These instructions are printed in *F.R.U.S. 1950*, vol. iii, pp. 471–2.
[2] *Ibid.*, pp. 457–460.

Government were not to fall (an eventuality which it was assumed the American Government would wish to avoid), some sop would have to be given to the French in the matter of their plans for European federation. In these circumstances, the telegram recommended that an attempt be made to separate the military aspects of the German problem from the political conditions laid down in the French plan. The French should be pressed to agree to the immediate putting into force of the American plan (with perhaps some modifications, such as the substitution of Brigade Groups for Divisions) as a provisional solution of the problem. In the meantime, the French should be allowed, or encouraged, to summon their proposed meeting in Paris to consider whether, and if so how, their plan for a European Defence Minister, &c., could be put into operation. If agreement could be reached at this Paris meeting and a workable scheme could eventually be drawn up, then the provisional arrangements for dealing with the German contribution (i.e. the American plan) could be brought within the orbit of the French scheme.

4. Mr. Achilles went on to explain that Mr. Spofford had now received a telegram[1] from the State Department authorising him to go ahead on the preceding lines, and that he therefore contemplated speaking in this sense at this afternoon's meeting. In the meantime, he had had some preliminary discussion with M. Alphand yesterday afternoon and had found that the French delegation had also apparently been thinking along the lines of trying to separate the immediate military problems from the longer-term political considerations. In consequence, Mr. Spofford had got the impression that the French might be prepared to go along with the American proposals.

5. I told Mr. Achilles that while we, here, had also come to the conclusion some time ago that the French plans were quite unacceptable from the immediate military point of view, we too had been wondering whether some means could not be found of putting the American plan, with perhaps some additional safeguards to help the French, into immediate operation, while reserving the longer-term political problems for further consideration. We had not, however, yet reached any conclusions on the point. One particular point which was giving us concern was the extent to which we could accept the French insistence that the examination of the long-term political considerations must take place within their own French framework—i.e. the conception of European federation. There were obvious difficulties in this from our point of view, and we might feel that it would be better if the matter were looked at from the N.A.T.O. point of view rather than the purely European one. In any case, we would probably be reluctant to commit ourselves in advance to anything which suggested the acceptance in principle of the idea of a European army, &c., before we had any idea how it would work out in practice.

6. I was careful, however, to emphasise to Mr. Achilles that no decision had yet been reached on the British side, and that consideration of the

problem had not yet gone beyond the official level. I should not, therefore, I told him, be able to say anything definite about the British attitude at the Deputies' meeting this afternoon. However, I would probably want to ask some questions, both of M. Alphand and of Mr. Spofford, to clarify the situation. For example, I would want to know exactly what additional safeguards the French would wish to see inserted in the American plan to make it acceptable to them; and I should want to be sure that the French really agreed that this plan could then be put into effect and the necessary approach be made to the Germans forthwith. I should want to ask Mr. Spofford whether, if the French did accept the immediate application of the American plan, the United States for their part would be willing to proceed at once with the plans for the integrated force and the appointment of a Supreme Commander. And I might also want to suggest that rather a difficult situation might arise *vis-à-vis* the Germans, who would, on the one hand, be approached by the three Occupying Powers to come into the integrated force on the American plan and, on the other, would be being lobbied by the French to support the idea of a European force.

7. Mr. Achilles seemed to think that my questions were quite reasonable. He asked whether I thought that, in the event of the French holding their projected meeting in Paris to discuss the matter of a European force, His Majesty's Government and the United States Government ought to be represented. I told him that this was a matter which would clearly require careful consideration here, though I felt it might be difficult for His Majesty's Government to stand aside as they have done in the negotiations about the Schuman Plan. In this connection, Mr. Achilles reminded me that an important section of the State Department were in favour of the idea of a closer European federation, and spoke as if Mr. David Bruce and, to a lesser degree, Mr. McCloy were also supporters of it.

8. In the event, the discussions on other aspects of the German problem at the meeting of the Deputies this afternoon took so long that it was not until quite late in the meeting that Mr. Spofford had an opportunity of speaking on the lines foreshadowed by Mr. Achilles. When Mr. Spofford did make his statement, he spoke very vaguely and hesitantly, and though the other Deputies no doubt gathered the general trend of his thoughts they must have been left in considerable doubt as to his precise intentions. Mr. Spofford did, however, promise to circulate a paper setting out his ideas in writing.[3]

9. Not unnaturally, however, in view of their earlier conversation, M. Alphand knew quite well what was at the back of Mr. Spofford's remarks and at once said that he much appreciated this attempt of the United States delegation to find a compromise, and that he thought that the French Government for their part would be willing to agree to some arrangements on the lines suggested by the Chairman.

10. It was agreed that, in view of the new situation created by Mr.

[3] See calendar i.

Spofford's remarks, the Deputies would need a few days in which to consult their Governments. It was decided that at their next meeting on the morning of Thursday, 23rd November, they would take up some of the other outstanding questions and leave the German problem over for a day or two longer. In the circumstances, I did not put any questions referred to above, either to Mr. Spofford or M. Alphand. I should, however, be grateful for an early indication of the line which you would wish me to take when the Deputies resume their discussion of this matter at the end of this week or the beginning of next.[4]

CALENDAR TO NO. 109

i *23 Nov. 1950   Text of Spofford Plan* (U.K. Deputy Memo. No. 69). Details of provisional arrangements for a German contribution to defence to be put in hand at once. Concurrently European Powers with German representatives should meet to formulate proposals for a European Army [WU 1195/460].

[4] British and Dutch doubts about the compromise plan put forward by Mr. Spofford to the Deputies on 20 November were aired informally at a lunch the next day given by M. Alphand and attended by Mr. Spofford, Sir P. Dixon, M. Massigli and Dr. Starkenborgh (Netherlands Deputy). M. Alphand listed three stages of a German contribution (i) listing man-power (ii) recruitment (iii) formation. He conceded that stage (i) could start at once and stage (ii) could start under N.A.T.O. planning if the French plan for a European Army was not ready by the time recruitment was due to begin. After the lunch Sir P. Dixon explained to Mr. Spofford British objections to the French Plan and informed him on a personal basis of the four alternative solutions under consideration in the Foreign Office (see No. 107.i). Mr. Spofford said he was attracted by the idea of a N.A.T.O. Confederation and 'would see no objection if we were to launch the idea in the Council of Deputies, or indeed propose that the idea of a N.A.T.O. Confederation and the idea of a European army should *both* be examined as long-term projects' (WU 1195/457).

No. 110

Mr. Bevin to Sir O. Harvey (Paris)

No. 1242 Telegraphic [C 7202/65/18]

Immediate. Confidential   FOREIGN OFFICE, *22 November 1950, 9.30 p.m.*

Repeated to Washington, Wahnerheide, Moscow.

My telegram No. 3332 Saving[1] (of 16th November) Soviet Proposal for Council of Foreign Ministers.

[1] In this telegram Mr. Bevin informed Sir O. Harvey that he had floated to M. Massigli the idea of tripartite talks 'on the whole question of relations with Russia and of post-war tension' as the next move in concerting a reply to the Soviet note of 3 November following the issue of the interim statements (see No. 97, note 7). Sir O. Harvey was instructed to seek French views on the substance of an agenda. Similar instructions were sent to Sir O. Franks who was asked to discuss Mr. Bevin's ideas with the State Department (F.O. telegram to Washington No. 5096).

French Ambassador told me on 20th November that M. Schuman had considered my suggestion for a possible three power meeting at Ambassadorial level in Washington but wished to propose that these consultations should be held in London instead on the ground that there was too much risk of leakage and public pressure in the United States. In view of indications of State Department's thinking in Washington telegram No. 3112[2] I told him that provided the United States Government agreed I should see no objection to holding the meetings here.

2. I then told M. Massigli that in my opinion it was of crucial importance that our three Governments should reach agreement in principle on the arming of Europe before entering into any discussions with Soviet Government. The negotiations on a German contribution to Western Defence must not be held up for the tripartite consultations on the Soviet proposal and a real effort must be made to reach agreement. I asked M. Massigli to convey my views on this point to M. Schuman, making it clear that I was in no way seeking to interfere with the negotiations on the substance of the question which were proceeding through other channels.

3. M. Massigli said that he thought things were now moving on the defence front and that the beginnings of a solution were in sight. He was sure that M. Schuman would agree on the importance of agreement on this matter before any meeting with the Russians.

4. I then took the opportunity to suggest to M. Massigli that the continuous criticism of Britain's attitude towards Europe that was being voiced on the continent, particularly at Strasbourg, was not only unjustified but most unhelpful in present circumstances. Britain not only had her commitments as the centre of the Commonwealth, but was linked with the United States and Canada. It was in the interests of Europe itself that this link should be maintained and strengthened. We must also take account of developments in the Far East and Middle East, as well as the trend of American opinion, and should not allow ourselves to be lured into focussing all our attention on Europe. These considerations must also be present in the minds of officials when they came to examine the Soviet

[2] This telegram of 17 November reported that the State Department had no strong preference as to venue although they had been thinking of Paris. State Department was against sending a simple negative to the Soviet proposals and suggested that a reply should be in general terms rather than deal specifically with Germany. State Department indicated the possibility of testing Soviet intentions through quadripartite talks in New York as implementation of the Iraqi-Syrian resolution adopted by the U.N. on 3 November. This resolution (*U.N. Resolutions 1950*, No. 377) called upon the permanent members of the Security Council to meet and discuss, collectively or otherwise, all problems likely to threaten international peace. This idea was pursued by State Department in further inconclusive discussion with British Embassy officials on 24 November. In his report of these discussions, Sir O. Franks commented: 'they do not anticipate any encouraging reaction from the Soviets and their programme has been simply to find a decent burial procedure' (Washington telegram No. 3168 on C 7593/65/18).

proposal. The proposal must be studied in the light of the Soviet Government's behaviour and attitude throughout the world. This should be dealt with urgently.[3]

CALENDAR TO NO. 110

i *16–28 Nov. 1950   Tripartite views on agenda for proposed C.F.M.*

(*a*) *U.K.*: should seek wide agenda. Optimum terms for global settlement with U.S.S.R., listed in brief by Dixon of 16 Nov., include: 'Hands off Greece'; lifting of iron curtain; German unity; settlement in Far East; moves towards disarmament. In return West could offer to halt pace of rearmament. But no discussions until a watertight plan for German rearmament has been reached with France. On 23 Nov. Dixon wonders whether Polish reports received by French of Soviet war preparations were planted 'in order to make French flesh creep' [C 7601/65/18; NS 1023/47].

(*b*) *France*. Ideas thrown out by MM. Massigli and de Crouy-Chanel include possibility of a non-aggression pact. Enthusiasm in France for talks with Soviet Union analysed by Harvey in letter to Bevin of 21 Nov. Positive response from Atlantic Powers will help to win French people over to N.A.T.O. and to allay their fears and mistrust of the United States [C 7559, 7651/65/18].

(*c*) *United States*: broad lines for talks with Soviet Union suggested in draft reply of 27 Nov. (viewed by French govt. as 'on the negative side'). Agenda to include Germany, Austria and Soviet-satellite states. U.S. propose exploratory talks with Soviet representatives at the U.N. [C 7677/65/18].

[3] Sir O. Franks was instructed on 22 November to inform State Department of the substance of the present telegram and to seek their agreement to a meeting in London about the middle of December. On 25 November Mr. Bevin pressed the U.S. Chargé d'Affaires in London for agreement on a tripartite meeting which he conceded could be held in Paris. As regards a reply to the Soviet government: 'I explained to Mr. Holmes that there was a considerable and growing feeling in Parliament and in the country as a whole that it would be wrong to return a completely negative reply to the Russian note. There was a widespread feeling that it was wrong to leave the Russians, so to speak, under the impression that they were denied all opportunity of discussion with the Western Powers. This would only drive the Russians into a position of desperation and increase the danger of war. It was, moreover, the opinion of His Majesty's Ambassador at Paris that the state of French morale would be strengthened if we could return a positive reply to the Russian proposal. I thought furthermore that the effect of a positive reply to the Russians would be beneficial on the Chinese and might further the aim, on which the United States and ourselves were at one, of not driving the Chinese into the arms of Russia' (F.O. despatch to Washington No. 1518 on C 7633/65/18). On 26 November the Foreign Office received summary reports of an American draft reply to the Soviet government: full text, handed to Mr. Bevin by Mr. Holmes on 27 November, is calendared at i.*c* below. Agreement was reached the next day for a tripartite meeting of officials in Paris in early December. This was announced by Mr. Bevin, in a statement agreed by both Mr. Acheson and M. Schuman, in the House of Commons debate on foreign affairs on 29 November: *Parl. Debs., 5th ser., H. of C.*, vol. 481, cols. 1170–1171.

No. 111

Minute from Mr. Mallet to Sir P. Dixon

[*WU 1195/516*]

FOREIGN OFFICE, *22 November 1950*

Germany and Western Defence

The Secretary of State holds the view that before entering into any meeting with the Russians the three Western Powers must reach agreement among themselves on the organisation of Western defence, including the participation of Germany. Otherwise, we should be in a weak negotiating position.

Hitherto, attention has turned chiefly on the need for securing French acceptance not merely of the principle but of actual arrangements for German participation. It is, however, important not to overlook the necessity for securing German concurrence in the scheme for Western defence. Until we have secured such German concurrence, our arrangements will not be complete and we shall not be in a strong negotiating position vis-à-vis the Russians. If we go ahead without having tied the Germans in, we shall give Adenauer and Schumacher great scope for bargaining.

It is therefore necessary to examine what sort of agreement is likely to be acceptable to the Federal Republic. The Chancellor stated in the Bundestag Debate on 8th November,[1] on behalf of his Government, that the Federal Republic, if called upon by the Western Powers, must be ready to make an appropriate contribution to the defensive Western front. He has since stated that, in his opinion, in spite of the attitude of the Socialist Party, the majority of the Bundestag would agree if the Federal Republic were asked to contribute. Dr. Adenauer, however, has formally stated that a pre-condition for such a contribution is the complete equality of Germany in the defensive front with other participating powers, and that the defensive front should be of sufficient strength to make any Russian aggression impossible.

Since the Bundestag Debate, the Federal Chancellor has made an important communication to the High Commission in which in effect he states that, unless the Western Powers make certain concessions in regard to the occupation, it will be difficult for him to shake the German public out of their present attitude of hostility or indifference to the problem of rearmament.[2]

The Federal Government's demand for complete equality in the defensive front implies, I think, two things. It does not, I think, necessarily mean that the Federal Government will insist on complete freedom and sovereignty in the military sphere at present. There are strong psychological and financial reasons against the re-creation of an independent

[1] See No. 103.i.

[2] See No. 103.ii.

German army. But it does mean that if Germany is to accept limitations on her military sovereignty she will expect other partners in Western defence to accept comparable limitations. In other words, Germany will put her troops into a common pool under a common command if other European or Atlantic partners do the same and if the Federal Republic is represented on the Atlantic Council. Secondly, it does mean that in the political sphere Germany must be treated as an equal. That is to say, that if Germany is a partner and ally in Western defence she can no longer be treated as an occupied country. That means not merely that the occupation forces will have to be transmuted into N.A.T. garrisons but also that the present occupation régime will have to disappear.

I do not suggest that we shall have immediately to abolish the Occupation Statute as a pre-condition to Germany's consent to participate in Western defence. But we must recognise that we shall ourselves have to accept limitations on our military sovereignty and to begin to move towards the restoration of German political sovereignty if Germany is going to participate willingly in Western defence.

The upshot of this therefore is that before we can have a united Western front, which is a necessary pre-condition of negotiations with the Russians, we ought to decide among ourselves, and make it clear to the Germans, that we are prepared to give them at least a measure of equality in the military sphere, and to advance rapidly towards at least a delegation of full sovereignty in the internal political sphere.

To meet Adenauer's second condition we must also satisfy Germany that there will be at least the possibility of effective defence in the West.[3]

I. Mallet

---

[3] Sir P. Dixon minuted his agreement below and commented that as regards the question of equality, the French plan for a European Army was less well suited to the Germans than either the original American plan or the new British alternative of a N.A.T.O. Confederation (see No. 115). Sir W. Strang minuted on 26 November: 'The precipitate launching by the Americans in New York of the proposal for German rearmament has thrown Europe into confusion. It has thoroughly frightened the French, who are now more anxious than ever to cower down in a European environment which is more comfortable for them than the North Atlantic scene, the rigours of which they are unwilling to face. (M. Schuman said the other day at Strasbourg that the Atlantic Pact was temporary while Europe was permanent [see No. 117, note 3]). It has also polarized two tendencies in Germany which it will be hard to reconcile. It was obvious that the U.S. proposal would stimulate the German claim for equality of rights. I agree with Mr. Mallet that if the U.S. proposal is adopted there is no alternative but to move towards such equality, especially in the political sphere. But it is precisely this, among other things, that the French fear and will do their best to avoid or delay. This is part of the *raison d'être* of their plan. They will give the Germans equality within the limits of the Schuman plan and within the limits of the European army: but beyond that they will be loath to make any concession. To the German mind this will not be equality at all. I do not see how we are to reconcile this difference. The best solution, as some of us have said before, would be an act of faith by the Americans. Once the U.S. divisions were in Europe and the Supreme Commander was appointed, both French and Germans might see the situation in a new light and help to find an agreed way to bring the Germans in.' Mr. Bevin minuted: 'I will talk this over with Strang & Dixon.'

i *23–24 Nov. 1950 Legal aspects of ending Occupation.* F.O. consider with Legal Adviser the effect of Allied renunciation of Supreme Authority in Germany on the position in Berlin, status of F.R.G. and retention of Allied troops on German soil. Conclusion reached is that there are apparently 'no insurmountable legal obstacles in the way of doing whatever political expediency requires' [C 7685/48/18].

No. 112

Extract from the Minutes of the Economic Steering Committee[1] held in the Cabinet Office on Thursday, 23 November 1950, at 4.30 p.m.

E.S. (50) 6th Meeting [CAB 134/263]

Secret

3. *Germany's Industrial Contribution to Western European Defence*

The Committee considered a note by the Foreign Office (E.S. (50) 12) on Germany's industrial contribution to Western European defence.[2]

Sir Roger Makins said that Ministers had decided that maximum use should be made of permitted German industrial capacity to meet some of the United Kingdom's additional defence production needs.[3] To implement this decision fully it would be necessary for further consideration to be given to our requirements from Germany, and also to what Germany could provide having regard, among other things, to any conclusions reached by the Tripartite Study Group on the Agreement on Prohibited and Limited Industries.[4] In order to ensure that the maximum number of orders were placed in Germany, some further inter-Departmental machinery might be necessary. The paper attached to E.S. (50) 12 had been prepared for the information of the Foreign Secretary and it was intended that it should be submitted to him, amended to take account of any points raised by the Committee.

[1] The Economic Steering Committee of officials was convened in October 1950 to advise Ministers on the economic implications of defence policy and requirements. It reported to the ministerial Economic Policy Committee, chaired by Mr. Attlee (for terms of reference, see Volume I, No. 26, note 1). Members of the E.S.C. present at this meeting were Sir E. Bridges (*in the Chair*); Sir E. Plowden, Central Economic Planning Staff, Treasury; Sir H. Parker, Ministry of Defence; Sir G. Ince, Ministry of Labour and National Service; Sir J. Woods, Board of Trade; Sir D. Fergusson, Ministry of Fuel and Power; Sir A. Rowlands, Ministry of Supply; Sir R. Makins, Foreign Office; Sir N. Brook, Cabinet Office and Mr. R.L. Hall, Economic Section, Cabinet Office. *Also present* were Sir J. Lang, Admiralty; Sir H. Wilson-Smith, Mr. E.A. Hitchman, Mr. E.G. Compton, Treasury; Sir G. Clauson, Colonial Office and Mr. H. Campion, Central Statistical Office.

[2] This paper, calendared below, was prepared by Mr. Stevens' inter-departmental committee (see No. 92, note 4).

[3] See No. 11.i. [4] See No. 55, note 10.

In discussion the following points were made:

(*a*) It now seemed likely that the effect of the defence programme on the United Kingdom economy would be more serious than earlier estimates indicated.[3] It was therefore disturbing that the paper under discussion (paragraph 16(iii)) should suggest that Germany's most effective contribution to the European defence programme for some time to come might well lie in the export of coal and scrap. Should not more use be made of Germany's unused industrial capacity and of her unemployed man-power? In general, the paper might be recast to put greater emphasis on the necessity for every effort being made to overcome the difficulties which would be encountered in getting from Germany the industrial contribution we required.

(*b*) Germany was at present heavily in deficit with the European Payments Union.[5] Though this appeared to provide an added argument for increasing our purchases from Germany, it had been suggested by some experts that the deficit was due mainly to short-term causes, and that a decision to make increased purchases from Germany might take effect at a time when her present deficit had already been wiped out. *Sir Henry Wilson-Smith* said, however, that the experience of the last few weeks provided little evidence that Germany's financial difficulties were essentially short-term, and that he himself had formed the view that they might well persist for a long time.

(*c*) Indiscriminate use of Germany's industrial capacity would increase our difficulties in procuring adequate supplies of raw materials. But this should not preclude us from employing that capacity in cases where United Kingdom production was limited by factors other than raw material shortage.

(*d*) *Sir Archibald Rowlands* said that our most urgent requirement from Germany was steel scrap. It seemed most unlikely that we would obtain the amount we required for our steel industry to work to capacity in 1951. We also needed machine tools from Germany, both for their value to our own industry and to prevent the Germans from capturing United Kingdom export markets. The German textile industry was already of assistance to us in the supply of army clothing and this should continue. In addition, we required urgently certain types of electronics, which might be procured in Germany. As regards finished munitions, new factories would be necessary to produce these, and even if the factories were built, their output would probably be needed to arm any German forces authorised.

(*e*) *Sir Donald Fergusson* said that, as indicated in paragraph 13 of the paper, the coal and electricity available were likely to prove a limiting factor in any increase of German production. It was very doubtful

[5] The agreement of 19 September 1950 for the establishment of a European Payments Union, including tables of initial credit and debit balances, is printed in *B.F.S.P.*, vol. 156, pp. 883–915.

whether German industrial production could be matched by increase in the supply of German coal. Such increased production would, therefore, limit the amount of German coal available for export to Europe.

(*f*) *Sir Gerald Clauson* said that it was most undesirable that German production of synthetic rubber should be resumed. Such rubber was of inferior quality and high price. If its production were now authorised it was probable that the rubber would come on the market when the expected severe fall in the price of natural rubber had already begun. It was also relevant that German synthetic rubber was produced from coal. The limited amount of coal available could be put to better uses.

(*g*) *Sir Harold Parker* said that if it were decided to decrease the part of the £3,600 million defence programme to be spent in the United Kingdom, it might well be considered that increased purchases could better be made in other European countries than Germany. France, Belgium and Italy were known to have unused industrial capacity in plants already in production, and orders placed in those countries might come to fruition more quickly than orders placed in Germany.

(*h*) *Sir Archibald Rowlands* said that in order for progress to be made in procurement from Germany, we would require more detailed information about the supplies likely to become available. He suggested that economic experts from the United Kingdom High Commissioner's staff should be invited to visit this country for discussion with representatives of the Supply Departments.[6] The conversations need not be limited to defence requirements in the narrower sense. It was appreciated that the meeting of certain civilian requirements (e.g. boilers) was vital to defence production.

(i) The United Kingdom representative on the proposed N.A.T.O. Defence Production Board should be made fully aware of Ministers' views on the use to be made of German industrial capacity.[7]

The Committee—

(1) Invited the Foreign Office to make arrangements for the conversations proposed at 'X' above.[8]

(2) Took note that the Foreign Office would submit to the Foreign Secretary the memorandum attached to E.S. (50) 12, revised in the light

[6] This sentence was sidelined 'X'.   [7] This sentence was sidelined 'Y'.

[8] These discussions between economic experts of the Ministry of Supply and Control Commission took place in London on 7–11 December. The policy statement, calendared at ii below, was prepared as background for these meetings. On 23 December the Foreign Office was informed by the Ministry of Supply that the 'broad conclusion from these meetings is that there is a wide range of non-warlike equipment we can buy from Germany if the Germans are able to make it. German capacity is rapidly being booked up and delivery dates have lengthened, but the chief limitation is likely to be shortages of raw materials.' Principal items wanted from Germany included machine tools, galvanised sheet, cutlery, water bottles, cement, clothing and textiles, bomb components, packing materials (e.g. cartons), paint, forgings, boilers, piping, valves and chemicals (CE 6385/45/181).

of the points made in discussion.[9]

(3) Invited the Foreign Office to arrange for the Committee to have a further report on the use of German industrial capacity for defence purposes, when the conversations as in (1) above were concluded.[10]

(4) Invited the Ministry of Defence to arrange for the briefing of the United Kingdom representative on the proposed N.A.T.O. Defence Production Board, as at 'Y' above.

CALENDARS TO NO. 112

i *20 Nov. 1950 E.S.(50)12.* Report detailing the possibilities of a German industrial contribution to Western European defence [CE 6019/45/181].

ii *6 Dec. 1950 Policy Statement* on German contribution to U.K. defence programme compiled by Ministry of Supply. Primary object in placing maximum defence contracts in Germany is protection of British engineering industry. Willing to take 'some risks in reviving production in Germany which might be used against us'. However some safeguards outlined. No diversion of raw materials to Germany [CE 6128/45/181].

iii *17 Nov.–21 Dec. 1950 American ideas on size of German industrial contribution* reported by Mr. Penson in lengthy facts and figures correspondence with F.O. (cf. No. 92, note 4). U.S. thoughts of 10% of gross national product not in line with U.K. calculations and cause 'storm of protest' in Germany [CE 5742, 5836, 5978–9, 6022, 6260/45/181].

iv *11 Dec. 1950 Economic Recovery of F.R.G.* assessed in Wahn. despatch No. 131. Economic trend so upward that 'no economic reason why Western Germany should not be able to play an important part in Western defence' [CE 6181/45/181].

[9] The text at i below was submitted to Mr. Bevin on 24 November under cover of an explanatory minute from Mr. Stevens. Mr. Bevin noted on the minute that he had not read the actual report.

[10] No further report specifically on German capacity appears to have been prepared. Instead a paper on the placing of defence orders in the rest of Europe (E.S. (50) 26) was presented to the E.S.C. on 14 December with a view to obtaining a decision on priorities between purchases from Germany and the rest of Europe. 'The general view of the Committee was that it would be unnecessary to assign priority between the various European countries for this purpose, but that as much defence material as possible should be obtained from each of them' (E.S. (50) 9th Meeting on CAB 134/263).

No. 113

Letter from Sir D. Gainer to Sir I. Kirkpatrick (Wahnerheide)

[*C 7312/2/18*]

FOREIGN OFFICE, *23 November 1950*

Your telegram No. 1614[1] of the 12th November about the Berlin Mobile Police.

I fear we have frequently been in some danger of confusion over these police questions because of differing views as to their functions. This has particularly been the case over the proposed mobile police, whether in the Federal Republic or in Berlin. Here the confusion has resulted from lack of clarity at various times over the question whether the mobile police were intended to deal solely with threats to internal security or whether, on the other hand, they were meant to meet an actual attack from across the border, for instance by the Bereitschaften and possibly to constitute a first step towards the creation of a German army.

The Foreign Ministers' agreement in New York on the mobile police of the 19th September[2] was based on the first conception. The later agreement reached by the Defence Ministers and endorsed by the Foreign Ministers on the 23rd September (appendix to annex to J.P. 130)[3] to some extent reflected the latter. The second agreement has I think never been fully carried out and it is the Secretary of State's view that it must be regarded as being to some extent in abeyance pending final agreement on the whole question of Germany's contribution to Western Defence. (The United States and French representatives in the Study Group have recently taken a similar line in discussions on the Prohibited and Limited Industries Agreement.)[4] I do not think therefore that we should regard the agreement of the 23rd September as necessarily overriding the first, as you suggest, so far as the mobile police are concerned. The second agreement was the result of an attempt by the United States Joint Chiefs of Staff to set down measures that might be put in hand in Germany and

---

[1] In this telegram Sir I. Kirkpatrick reported discussion on the arming of police forces in Berlin between the Allied High Commission and the Berlin Commandants on 9 November (see No. 60, note 7). Sir I. Kirkpatrick explained why he had exceeded his instructions and had agreed to join with his A.H.C. colleagues in recommending to their respective governments that the proposed Berlin mobile police force should be armed up to normal infantry standard rather than with light weapons only. Also under discussion on 9 November was a proposal for a unified command in Berlin under a single commander. Sir I. Kirkpatrick resisted pressure from Mr. McCloy to support the idea of an immediate appointment. It was agreed that the question should be referred to governments and that meanwhile a tripartite military staff should be set up in Berlin for defence planning. This line was approved by Mr. Bevin: see note 5.

[2] As contained in the Foreign Ministers' communiqué calendared in No. 26.ii.

[3] This was the text transmitted in No. 43 as amended by New York telegram No. 1181 (*ibid.*, notes 3–9). For J.P. (50) 130 see No. 60, notes 9 and 17.

[4] See No. 140, note 1.

thus avoid the appearance of complete deadlock in New York over the question of Germany's contribution to Western Defence. Insofar as it referred to the armament and rôle of the mobile police it did so primarily by way of illustration and not in the deliberate intention of amending the Foreign Ministers agreement of the 19th September, which must remain the basic document on the constitution of the mobile police.

As you know our own view of the mobile police, whether in Berlin or in the Federal Republic, is that they are there for the purpose of maintaining law and order in the face of attempts at sabotage or disturbances, political or economic or both in origin. They are a gendarmerie and not a camouflaged army or even a para-military force. Even should the East German police invade Berlin or the Federal Republic, their first rôle would be the preservation of order among the civil population, dealing with refugees, saboteurs, etc. and their second rôle that of auxiliaries to the Allied troops who, in accordance with the Foreign Ministers decisions, will resist any invasion by East German police from the first.

It is in this light that we should interpret the words in the agreement of the 23rd September stating that the mobile police 'would be used in the event of any East German para-military attack', i.e. they would be used not as combat forces but rather as security and supporting forces.

It is presumably in the light of such considerations also that the Allied High Commission, which was deliberately left discretion by the Foreign Ministers to decide what was meant by 'light arms only' in the agreement of 19th September, decided that for the present the mobile police in the Federal Republic should be armed only with pistols, automatic rifles and light machine guns. They so decided despite the reference in the agreement of the 23rd September to heavy machine guns, mortars, light armoured cars and engineer units. In other words, they agreed that, for the time being, the mobile police in the Federal Republic should be armed up to a standard considerably short of anything that could be regarded as normal infantry standard. For this there is the very good justification that the mobile police are not intended for normal infantry duties but, in the words of the agreement of the 19th September, 'solely for the preservation of public order'.

Now it is the Secretary of State's view that, although the situation in Berlin may not in all respects be comparable to that in the Federal Republic, the same principles must be applied in deciding the rôle and armament of the mobile units to be formed in Berlin as in dealing with the West German mobile police. He approved the formation of the mobile units on the understanding that they, like the West German mobile police, would be used for internal security purposes only and that in consequence they should be armed on the same scale as the West German mobile police, no less and no more.

Since the Berlin mobile units, like the Federal mobile police, do not have a normal infantry rôle, the Secretary of State is therefore not willing to agree at present that they should be armed, as you have recommended in your telegram No. 1614, up to normal infantry standard. The Secretary of State attaches particular importance to our not taking in Berlin, where we are so vulnerable, more far-reaching and provocative measures than we are taking elsewhere and he is anxious that the measures taken in Berlin should not get out of step with those taken in the Federal Republic generally.[5] This is particularly important at the present time when (1) we are still increasing our own Allied garrisons in Berlin,[6] (2) we are considering the Soviet proposal for a Council of Foreign Ministers, and (3) we have not yet got a decision on the creation of German formations within an integrated Western Defence force.

In the circumstances, therefore, we are not prepared at the present time to press the Secretary of State to give a favourable decision on your recommendation that the Berlin mobile units should be armed up to normal infantry standard and I must ask that the matter be allowed to rest where it is for the present, subject of course to reconsideration later in the light of any new circumstances that may arise. I would hope that no great harm would be done by thus postponing a final decision since, as you state in your telegram, it is necessary to discuss with the Chancellor and the Magistrat the whole financial aspect of the Berlin mobile units and reach a decision on financial responsibility before even any recruitment can begin.

As regard the question which you raised in paragraph 4 of your telegram, we agree that the projected voluntary police reserve may be armed with pistols which would be kept in allied depots and issued only for training or for duty when the reserve is embodied.

D. St. Clair Gainer

Calendar to No. 113

i *24 Nov. 1950 Berlin Security*. F.O. objections to U.S. proposal at New York (see No. 26.ii) to hold Soviet Union responsible for any attack from G.D.R. on Berlin or F.R.G. are explained in memo. for Cabinet Defence Committee D.O. (50) 99 [CAB 131/9].

[5] For this reason, Mr. Bevin informed Sir I. Kirkpatrick on 25 November that he agreed that no arrangements should be made for a single command in Berlin 'until a Supreme Commander has been appointed in Europe by whom the necessary dispositions could be worked out in concert with the Occupying Powers' (F.O. telegram to Wahnerheide No. 1136 Saving on C 7374/2/18). On 9 December Sir I. Kirkpatrick reported that Mr. McCloy was pressing for an early decision on a unified command for Berlin. Action was subsequently deferred in the hope that a Supreme Commander would be appointed soon (C 7594/2/18).

[6] As agreed at New York (see No. 26.ii), Allied garrisons were being strengthened. The British garrison of 3 battalions was being increased in strength by 33%.

No. 114

Mr. Bevin to Sir P. Nichols (The Hague)

No. 386 [WU 1195/461]

Secret   FOREIGN OFFICE, 23 November 1950

North Atlantic Defence Problems

Sir,

The Netherlands Foreign Minister, who was in London in attendance on Queen Juliana,[1] came to see me to-day.

2. Dr. Stikker said he wished first to talk about the present position in the North Atlantic Treaty Organisation. He was very worried about the question of a German contribution to the defence of Europe. The French were still pressing their plan for a European Army under a Council of Ministers and a European Assembly. This army would not include all the North Atlantic Treaty countries but, apparently, only the six countries taking part in the Schuman Plan. This extension of the Schuman Plan into the military field was tantamount to European federation, since a European Army was impossible without common finance, &c. He would be quite frank. The Netherlands would never agree to take part in the French plan in this form. It would be another matter if the United Kingdom were to come in. As far as the Netherlands were concerned, such a European Army might embrace five nations (i.e., without the Netherlands) or seven (i.e., with the Netherlands and the United Kingdom), but never six (i.e., with the Netherlands alone). The United States might well press the Netherlands to join such a scheme, but the Netherlands would not give in.[2]

3. Dr. Stikker continued that he hoped that by discussion among the Atlantic Powers, and particularly with the French, it would still be possible

---

[1] Queen Juliana of the Netherlands paid a state visit to Britain from 21–24 November.

[2] In conversation with Sir F. Hoyer Millar the previous evening the Dutch Deputy, Dr. Starkenborgh, pointed out that Mr. Spofford's suggestion for a conference in Paris to study the French Plan for a European army was directed at all European members of N.A.T.O. including the United Kingdom. 'He feels that the attitude of the smaller countries towards the whole matter and, in particular, towards the question of acceptance of this invitation to attend the Paris meeting, will be greatly influenced by H.M.G.'s decision. He hopes, therefore, that we will be able to say very shortly whether H.M.G. are prepared to go to the Paris meeting or not. He feels that until the U.K. can give a clear indication of its views, the smaller countries will continue to hesitate (or perhaps, even worse, begin to succumb to French and American pressure), and that the Deputies will continue to achieve little or nothing.' Dr. Starkenborgh himself disliked the idea of being asked to pursue the French plan as 'being tantamount to saying that the European powers would have to accept in principle the French ideas about a European force, a European Minister of Defence, etc., and in fact agree to the European as opposed to the N.A.T.O. concept.' These remarks were recorded in a letter of 23 November from Sir F. Hoyer Millar to Sir P. Dixon which was shown to Mr. Bevin shortly before his meeting with Dr. Stikker that afternoon (WU 1198/644).

to find a compromise solution. In an attempt to do so, he had instructed the Netherlands Deputy to put forward a proposal for the appointment of a N.A.T.O. High Commissioner with powers not only over German units in the integrated force, but over all Allied forces stationed in Germany. This High Commissioner would be under instructions from a committee of N.A.T.O. Ministers but not from an Assembly. He had informed both the French and the United States of his proposal but was not at present sure of their reactions.

4. I said that we had come to the conclusion that France wished to keep Germany from any real participation in the Atlantic organism. Every move she made seemed to be directed towards that end, and that was, I thought, at the root of the proposal for a European Army. The United Kingdom, with its Commonwealth ties, could not afford to join or even to encourage an organisation in which the United States and Canada had no part. We were therefore thinking in terms of a comprehensive Atlantic Confederation which would include *all* Atlantic countries and also Germany. In this framework the Germans could do no harm. This Atlantic Confederation would have close links with the British Commonwealth, particularly in the economic and financial fields. The problem of raw materials, for instance, could never be solved, even on an Atlantic basis. I emphasised that I was speaking personally and that His Majesty's Government had not yet formally approved my idea of an Atlantic Confederation on these lines.

5. I thought we must face the French quite frankly with the question whether it was to be Europe or the Atlantic. On which basis were we going to build? In our opinion, the answer was the Atlantic, and I thought that in giving this answer I was speaking not only for my own party but also for the Opposition. I had reached this conclusion not because I was anti-European, but because I did not believe Europe alone could ever be strong enough to defend itself. It was a practical not a sentimental question. It seemed to me, and Dr. Stikker agreed, that the French did not want the Americans in their plan nor the United Kingdom. On the other hand, it was clear from what Dr. Stikker had said that the Netherlands would not go along with the French. Nor would Scandinavia; nor even, I thought, Italy. The Belgians alone might follow their lead. We had to try and convince the French that European unity was not possible on a purely European basis, but that it was possible on an Atlantic basis and only on an Atlantic basis. If it would please the French, I had no objection to recognising the special ties which bound the European countries together; but the organisation itself must, I was convinced, be Atlantic.

6. Dr. Stikker and I then discussed what could be done to persuade the French to accept the Atlantic idea instead of their own European idea. Dr. Stikker said he would be seeing M. Schuman in Paris next week and would do his best to bring him round. I said that I should have to be in London for the Foreign Affairs Debate in the House of Commons on 29th and 30th November, but that when that was over I would try to go to Paris to

see M. Schuman, perhaps on my way back from Germany. Meanwhile, I would see whether special instructions could not be sent to Sir O. Harvey to see M. Schuman personally.

7. Dr. Stikker and I also agreed that our representatives should exchange notes on the Netherlands proposal for a N.A.T.O. High Commissioner and also on our own scheme for an Atlantic Confederation. I would also let Mr. Acheson know the line our thought was taking.[3]

I am, &c.,

ERNEST BEVIN

CALENDAR TO NO. 114

i *24 Nov.–1 Dec. 1950 U.K. reactions to Dutch proposal for N.A.T.O. High Commissioner*: F.O. strong criticism of 24 Nov. endorsed by J.P.S. on 1 Dec. Among other things Dutch plan would present an unacceptable position of inequality to the Germans. Both agree on desirability of disposing of plan: revised Dutch proposal at No. 130.i [WU 10741/3; CAB 21/1899].

[3] When the Dutch proposals (circulated as D.D.191 and not preserved in F.O. archives) were discussed by the Deputies on 24 November, M. Alphand dismissed them as 'an entirely inadequate substitute for the French plan . . . The American attitude seemed to be that the control over the projected German Federal Agency had better be left in the hands of the three Occupying Powers . . . I [Sir F. Hoyer Millar] said that we had not yet had time properly to consider the Netherlands paper' (U.K. Deputy telegram No. 1 Saving on WU 1195/468).

No. 115

Memorandum by Mr. Bevin[1]

D.O. (50) 100 [CAB 21/1898]

Secret   FOREIGN OFFICE, *24 November 1950*

German Contribution to the Defence of Europe

Since this question was last discussed by the Defence Committee (D.O. (50) 21st Meeting)[2] there have been three developments:

(i) The Chiefs of Staff, in consultation with the Foreign Office, have examined the possibility of producing a British plan for a German contribution to the defence of Europe.[3] Their general conclusion is that the French are more afraid of the potential danger from a re-armed Germany than of the immediate menace from the Soviet Union; that, although it is possible to provide certain short term safeguards against this danger, there is no practical military safeguard which can give the

[1] For the origins of this paper, see No. 107, and note 2 *ibid.*
[2] No. 101.   [3] See No. 106.i.

291

French a genuine guarantee in the long term; and that long term safeguards can therefore only be of a political nature.

(ii) The Standing Group of the North Atlantic Treaty Organisation (N.A.T.O.), in consultation with the accredited military representatives of the other Atlantic Powers in Washington, have examined the French and American proposals for a German contribution to the defence of Western Europe, and have submitted a report on the military aspects of the question to the Military Committee,[4] which is due to meet in London at the beginning of December. The conclusions of this report are, briefly:

(a) that the defence of Europe requires a German contribution;

(b) that a European Army on the lines suggested by the French is militarily acceptable, but its achievement should in no circumstances delay the German contribution;

(c) that the only militarily practicable short term German contribution would be in the form of complete German units, preferably divisions, but failing that combat groups.

(iii) The Americans have made a compromise proposal in the Deputies.[5] Their proposal is that there should be a transitional period during which German units would be raised and incorporated in the integrated force on the lines of the American plan (perhaps modified to limit the German units to Brigade Groups): and that at the same time the French should proceed with their own plan for a European Army, a European Minister of Defence etc., and call a conference to that end in Paris. It would be understood that once the French had been successful in working out a scheme for a European Army and establishing the necessary political superstructure, a place would be found for the new European Army within the integrated N.A.T.O. force and the German units would be incorporated in it. By this means the Americans would hope to secure French agreement to the immediate raising of German units and at the same time to give them some satisfaction on the European federal issue. The French Deputy has already indicated that a compromise on these lines might be acceptable to his Government: but it is not yet certain that the French are prepared to consent to the actual raising of German units outside the European Army.

The Deputies are now discussing this question on the basis of the Standing Group's report and the United States compromise proposal which the American Deputy has undertaken to reduce to writing.[5] So that the United Kingdom Deputy can play his proper part in these discussions, it is important to decide at once what attitude His Majesty's Government should take towards the American proposal.

I think my colleagues will agree that, to be acceptable, any compromise proposal must be such as to permit the immediate establishment of the integrated force and the appointment of a Supreme Commander and,

[4] See No. 106, note 2.

[5] See No. 109.i.

since the Americans will not agree to this on any other terms, also an immediate start on the process of raising German units. From this point of view, the first part of the American compromise proposal is satisfactory.

It is only with regard to the second part of the American proposal (that concurrently with the establishment of the integrated force, the French should be allowed to proceed with their own plan for a European Army, a European Minister of Defence etc.) that I have doubts.

In making this proposal the Americans are probably influenced by two considerations. First, there has always been a strong body of opinion within the State Department and elsewhere in the United States Administration, which favours European federation. Secondly, the Americans anticipate no doubt that if they are allowed to go ahead with their scheme, the French will not in practice get very far with it and will run up against so many practical difficulties and receive so little support from other European countries that it will in the end die a natural death. But although things might well turn out this way, we cannot count on it. If we accept the American proposal, we must reckon with the possibility of the French having some measure of success with their scheme, and the consequent formation of a European Army with its connected political superstructure.

It seems to me that such a development presents serious dangers.

In the first place, the co-existence of two alternative and competing plans for the rearmament of Germany would be liable hopelessly to confuse the arrangements for the raising of German units and would place the Germans in a position to play off the French against the Americans and ourselves.

In the second place, agreement in principle to the formation of a European Army to be controlled by a European Minister of Defence and a European Assembly would be out of harmony with our general policy of building up the Atlantic Community as the major grouping for the future. One of the ideas underlying the French plan is, undoubtedly, that of a Continental bloc, under French leadership, which while linked with the Atlantic Community, would constitute in world politics a force with some measure of independence. Such a continental bloc, built out of a group of some but almost certainly not all Western European States united economically in the Schuman Plan, politically in the Council of Europe and militarily in the European Army might not only present certain dangers to ourselves if it were to adopt a policy of neutrality; it would also be in conflict with the basic principle of the Atlantic Treaty as a free association of 12 equal independent states. Such a *bloc* would be too feeble to defend itself and yet strong enough to assert itself in world politics. It would thus be a sort of cancer in the Atlantic body which would, I am afraid, constitute a serious disruptive element and might in the end endanger the Treaty itself: all the more so since it would be calculated to discourage instead of encouraging continuing American concern with the security of Europe.

Present French policy is, I believe, at bottom antipathetic towards N.A.T.O. and to the Americans. The proposal for a European Army is only one of many aspects of this covert antipathy. There have recently been other signs of it in the economic field. If we are ever to break down this antipathy and to make the French good members of N.A.T.O., we cannot afford to allow the European federal concept to gain a foothold within N.A.T.O. and thus weaken instead of strengthening the ties between the countries on the two sides of the Atlantic. We must nip it in the bud.

We can hardly hope to kill the French plan, however, unless we have some positive alternative to put in its place. I believe that we have such an alternative in the North Atlantic Treaty itself. The French propose to create a European Federal Army within an Atlantic integrated force. Why should not we propose that the ultimate goal should be to develop the whole integrated force into an Atlantic Federal or Confederate Force?

The ultimate goal would be the establishment of a self-contained and fully integrated Atlantic Army as distinct from an integrated force composed of separate national units. This Atlantic Army would not only be integrated operationally under the Supreme Commander; it would also be integrated administratively under a special N.A.T.O. body, under the direction of the Atlantic Council. Such a scheme would, of course, require time to work out and could not be fully implemented for several years to come. Once the principle was agreed and the goal set, however, it should be possible to proceed by stages and to take certain initial steps in the near future. It might, for instance, be agreed that, as a first step, the Supreme Commander, with the advice of a civilian officer, perhaps a High Commissioner, responsible to the Deputies, should exercise certain administrative functions (such as the appointment of all officers above a certain rank, the holding of courts martial, the supervision of training and the establishment of training schools, etc.) over all the forces under his command.

From the political point of view this line of approach has considerable attractions:

(a) It eliminates the European federal concept from N.A.T.O. defence and replaces it by an Atlantic federal concept, which is in line with our own general political thinking.

(b) It caps the French proposal with a broader and grander conception, which, because it involves the Canadians and the Americans, is more likely to appeal to some of the smaller European powers, such as Holland, Norway, Denmark and Italy. The Dutch have already proposed the appointment of a N.A.T.O. High Commissioner[6] to exercise certain administrative controls over the new German units and, to a lesser extent, over the units contributed by the other N.A.T.O. countries; and it seems likely that they would support a plan for a more

[6] See No. 114.

closely integrated N.A.T.O. army. The Americans for their part have already indicated that they would have no objection if we were to launch this idea in the Deputies.

(c) In the long run, it offers the French a much greater measure of security than their own plan. It brings in the Americans to counterbalance the Germans. It binds the Americans more closely to Europe, and all Treaty members, including the Americans, more closely into one whole. An Atlantic Army, in which both the Americans and ourselves participate, gives the best possible guarantee against a revival of German aggression.

(d) It is the most effective and least dangerous way of integrating Germany into the Western World and of giving her that equality which all Germans are united in claiming. An eventual consequence would inevitably be German association with, or membership of, N.A.T.O. and the transformation of the Allied occupation forces into Atlantic garrisons. On the political, as distinct from the military, side this would also involve the further modification of the occupation regime in such a way as to restore to the Federal Government full liberty of action, subject only to such ultimate authority as the three Allies may decide to retain with the object of concluding a final settlement with a united Germany.

On the other hand an 'Atlantic Confederation' is unlikely to have much appeal for the French, who greatly prefer the idea of a European Federation without the Americans. Dislike and fear of the Americans bossing Europe is, indeed, a fundamental element in the French approach to the present problem.

It must also be admitted that a proposal on these lines presents grave practical difficulties, more particularly for the Americans and ourselves. For both it would involve a greater sacrifice of the right of independent action than we have hitherto been prepared to contemplate. Ultimately we should have to be prepared to divide off a part of our armed forces for Atlantic use and to subject them to international administrative control. We should in fact have to have two different armies (our ordinary army and our share in the Atlantic Army) with different tasks and different administrations.[7] The political implications of such an arrangement would

[7] When the Chiefs of Staff considered the advance text of this paper on the afternoon of 24 November they regarded the idea of two armies as 'militarily unsound. The proposals, in addition, presented many other difficulties and had in fact, from a military point of view, most of the disadvantages of the French proposals for a European Defence Force with the added disadvantage that the United Kingdom and U.S.A. would now be involved. The Committee reached the conclusion that, from a military point of view, it would be most unwise to put these proposals forward as they stood'. The Committee went on to consider the Standing Group report M.C.30. The Chiefs of Staff were in general agreement with the report and did not agree with representations from Sir P. Dixon that the idea of allowing the French to try to develop the European Army in parallel with the creation of an integrated N.A.T.O. force was 'politically unacceptable' (Confidential Annex to C.O.S. (50) 186th Meeting on CAB 21/1898).

be very far-reaching. Against this, however, we must set the fact that some sacrifice is anyhow inevitable if we are to develop the unity of the Western World and that such sacrifice can more safely be made in an Atlantic than in a European framework.

Recommendations

I therefore recommend:

(1) That we should support the first part of the American proposal for the immediate implementation, as an interim arrangement, of the American plan for the raising of German units and their incorporation in the integrated force.

(2) That at the same time we should propose in the Council of Deputies the ultimate formation of an Atlantic Confederate Force.

(3) That, if no agreement can be reached on this proposal, we should only agree to study the French plan for a European Army on condition that our own plan for a N.A.T.O. Confederate Force is examined at the same time.

(4) That, in any event, we should make quite clear that the United Kingdom would in no circumstances take part in the formation of a European Army and could not, therefore, agree to participate except perhaps as an observer, in a conference called solely for that purpose.

E.B.

No. 116

Brief by Air Marshal Sir W. Elliot for Mr. Attlee[1]

[PREM 8/1429]

Top secret   MINISTRY OF DEFENCE, *25 November 1950*

German Contribution to the Defence of Europe
D.O. (50) 100[2]

You will remember that when the Defence Committee of the North Atlantic Treaty met in Washington in October, there was a disagreement on the question of the German contribution to the defence of Europe. The Americans put forward proposals for including German units in an integrated North Atlantic Treaty Defence Force under a supreme command in Europe. The French, on the other hand, insisted upon a

---

[1] This brief was prepared for the Defence Committee meeting on 27 November (No. 118). In accordance with instructions from the Chiefs of Staff at their meeting on 24 November (see No. 115, note 7), Air Marshal Elliot also produced a separate brief for the Minister of Defence. This brief (not printed from CAB 21/1898) followed the same lines as the present brief for Mr. Attlee but gave a fuller summary of the Standing Group Report, M.C.30 (see No. 106, note 2).

[2] No. 115.

European Defence Force under a European Minister of Defence. As nothing would move the French from this conception, the problem remained unresolved and instructions were given, on the one hand to the Military Committee of the North Atlantic Treaty, and on the other hand to the Council Deputies, to seek for an agreed solution and to submit proposals to the North Atlantic Treaty Defence Committee at an early date. In the discussions in Washington we supported the American plan.

The Standing Group of the North Atlantic Treaty Military Committee has now produced a paper, a copy of which you have seen (M.C.30).[3] This paper is to be considered at a meeting of the Military Committee, probably on the 5th December and subsequently at a joint meeting of the Military Committee and Council Deputies on the 7th or 8th December. If these bodies can reach an agreed solution, the solution will be submitted to the Defence Committee at a meeting about 12th December. It is important that the United Kingdom representatives in the Military Committee and Council Deputies should now be given firm instructions on the line they should pursue at these meetings.

The paper by the Standing Group, the conclusions of which you will see in paragraph 36, accepts the proposition that the only militarily practicable short term contribution by Germany would be the incorporation of complete German formations, no lower than brigade groups, into the integrated N.A.T.O. Defence Force. The paper, however, admits that if an effective European Defence Force can be created, it would be militarily acceptable, but that arguments about this European Defence Force should not be allowed to delay the contribution of Germany to the defence of Europe. The Chiefs of Staff recommend that on military grounds the conclusions of the paper by the Standing Group should be accepted.

Mr. Spofford, the Chairman of the Council Deputies, in an effort to make these proposals politically acceptable to the French, has now proposed that the organization of German units, as recommended by the Standing Group, should proceed immediately but that simultaneously 'the European Powers (including German representatives) should be convened to formulate proposals for institutions adequate to meet the objectives of the French proposals (i.e. the European Defence Force). To the extent such institutions were agreed upon by the European Powers

[3] Mr. Attlee had not in fact yet seen M.C.30. A copy of it was submitted to him on 26 November by Mr. Rickett who explained: 'You have not seen it yet because as you will see when it came down last night it was accompanied by a message saying that the paper had been withdrawn. I have since spoken to Air Marshal Elliot about this who was at a loss to understand why the paper should have been withdrawn and thought that you would in any case wish to see it. He also asked me to draw your attention in particular to paragraph 25 of the paper which makes the point that it is undesirable that the administration and the logistic control of any German forces should be in the hands of SHAPE. This however would inevitably be the case under the Foreign Secretary's proposal for an integrated North Atlantic Force and this paragraph therefore provides an additional argument against this proposal' (PREM 8/1429).

and were developed to the point where they should create and support effectively military forces of a European rather than National character suitable for integration into N.A.T.O. the arrangements for the creation of such forces would be implemented'.[4] In other words, the French should start discussions on a European Defence Force and, if these succeeded, well and good.

When Mr. Spofford's proposal became known to the Foreign Secretary he felt grave misgivings and it was for that reason that he has now circulated his own memorandum (D.O. (50) 100).[2] You will see on page 3 of this memorandum the forceful objections which the Foreign Secretary feels towards taking any risk whatever that the French might succeed in creating this European Defence Force. He feels that it would be a weakening of the Atlantic community as a whole and might well result, in the long run, in the emergence of a neutral third force in Europe. He, therefore, makes an alternative proposal and suggests that the British should now propose that the ultimate goal should be to develop the whole integrated force into 'an Atlantic Federal or Confederate Force'.

The Chiefs of Staff have discussed this memorandum amongst themselves and will be in a position to state their views. They feel in the first place that there is no alternative military plan. The only real plan is that originally proposed by the Americans, i.e. to incorporate German units into an integrated N.A.T.O. Force. They do not believe that a European Defence Force is a practicable possibility.[5] It is not only the British but the Scandinavians and the Dutch who are opposed to it and the Chiefs of Staff feel that there is no chance of the French succeeding in creating this European Force. It is for that reason that they would be prepared to accept both the paper by the Standing Group and the compromise suggested by Mr. Spofford. In other words, while the Foreign Secretary wants to kill the French idea by substituting a different idea, the Chiefs of Staff feel that the French idea is bound in any case to die.

There are, moreover, two objections to allowing the United Kingdom representatives to put forward an entirely fresh proposal for the creation of a N.A.T.O. Federal Force:

(a) The idea has no sound military basis. It was conceived as a method of killing a bad French idea but is itself open on military grounds to

[4] See No. 109.i.

[5] At the Chiefs of Staff meeting on 24 November, *Lord Fraser* 'doubted whether the European Defence force was militarily practicable. *Sir William Slim* said that although far from ideal, a European Defence Force might be a practicable possibility. He supported the Standing Group proposals, and considered the integration of German Brigade Groups in the divisions of the various N.A.T.O. nations was perfectly feasible, and was in fact very similar to what was happening in Korea on a small scale. He suggested that if the Standing Group's report, having been agreed by the Military Committee, was not accepted by the Deputies, we should raise no objection to the French holding a conference in Paris to work out detailed plans for the formation of a European Defence Force with those nations who were to take part' (CAB 21/1898).

very much the same objections as the French idea. Moreover, it has not been thoroughly considered and worked out from the military point of view. If, therefore, United Kingdom representatives put forward this proposal they would be doing precisely what we objected to, when the French put forward their half-baked proposals at Washington and succeeded in blocking all progress.

(*b*) Unless the Americans are prepared to accept the concept of an Atlantic Federal Force—which seems extremely unlikely—we should be in danger once again of losing the offer of additional American divisions in Europe and the establishment of a supreme command with an American supreme commander. That is a vital advantage which we must seize now or may lose forever.

My earnest recommendation therefore is that the Defence Committee should be persuaded to instruct the United Kingdom representatives in the Military Committee and the Council Deputies to accept the Standing Group report, and Mr. Spofford's compromise proposals if that is the only way of getting an agreed solution, in the knowledge that the chances of the French succeeding in the creation of a European Defence Force are practically negligible.

WILLIAM ELLIOT

No. 117

Brief by Sir P. Dixon for Mr. Bevin

[WU 1195/470]

FOREIGN OFFICE, 25 November 1950

German Contribution to the Defence of Europe
(D.O. (50) 100)[1]

This paper contains the Secretary of State's proposal for resolving the present deadlock on the question of a German contribution to the defence of Europe. The proposal is briefly that we should proceed at once with the formation of an integrated force and with the raising of German units: and that as a long-term objective, we should aim as the ultimate goal at developing the integrated force into an Atlantic Federal Army under the operational control of a Supreme Commander and the administrative control of a N.A.T.O. High Commissioner. Only thus do we stand any chance of defeating the French proposal for a European Army, which we believe to be fundamentally unsound and politically dangerous.

This proposal has already been discussed in a preliminary way by the Chiefs of Staff, whose first reaction was not very favourable.[2] Their point of view is roughly as follows: Though not enamoured of the French idea

---

[1] No. 115.

[2] See No. 115, note 7 and No. 116, note 5.

of a European Army, they are prepared to accept it as there appears to be no other way of persuading the French to agree to German rearmament.

The Chiefs of Staff feel in any case that the French idea can safely be accepted, since they doubt if it will come to anything. The proposal for an Atlantic Army is, in the view of the Chiefs of Staff, open to the same objections as that for a European Army from the point of view of military efficiency: but they like it less because it will include both American and British forces as well as those of the Continental countries. In short although they do not mind placing British forces under an international operational command, they are opposed to submitting them to any form of international administrative control.

The attitude of the Chiefs of Staff is not surprising. It is clear, as the Secretary of State's paper says, that the proposal for an Atlantic Federal Army presents grave practical difficulties in the field of military administration, and involves a greater surrender of our right of independent action than we have hitherto been prepared to contemplate. The question is not, however, whether those practical difficulties and surrender of independence are desirable in themselves: but whether they are a fair price to pay for the defeat of the French plan and the growth of a close Atlantic union on a scale hitherto unthought of. We believe that the French plan is dangerous, that in its emphasis on the European idea, its determination to exclude Germany from N.A.T.O. and its covert hostility to U.S. participation in European affairs it strikes at the very root of the Atlantic ideal and threatens to undermine the whole Treaty, and the whole system of North American–European cooperation which is being slowly built up on it. That French policy is, in fact, directed against the North Atlantic Treaty organisation is borne out by what M. Schuman is reported to have said in his speech to the Assembly of the Council of Europe at Strasbourg on the 24th November.[3] According to *The Times* he said:

'Finally, the Atlantic Pact has a *temporary* aim. The European Army in our view is a *permanent* solution and must ensure peace against all threats, internal and external, now and in the future.'

The question is therefore: are we prepared to sacrifice some measure of military sovereignty in order to safeguard the Atlantic concept on which our whole foreign policy is based and on which the security of the Western World at present largely depends. It is a choice of two evils. Which is the lesser?

In addition to the arguments in favour of the proposal for an Atlantic Federal Army, which are given in the paper, the Secretary of State may also like to mention his conversation on the 23rd November with Dr.

[3] See No. 96, note 1. On the same day the Consultative Assembly adopted a recommendation (No. 53) for the urgent creation of a European Army (*C. of E. Recommendations and Resolutions*, November 1950, p. 4).

Stikker[4] and the latter's support for the Atlantic idea. All the smaller European members of N.A.T.O., with the possible exceptions of Belgium and Luxembourg, are opposed to the French plan. All of them have pinned their hopes on the Atlantic Treaty. But all of them are waiting for a lead. That lead can only come from the U.K. Recently the French have been too fertile in ideas. It is now time for us to give the lead which the smaller countries expect from us: and to show the world, and not least America, that whatever our hesitations about European federation, the Schuman Plan and the Council of Europe, we are whole heartedly pledged to N.A.T.O. and ready to make real sacrifices in the cause of Atlantic unity.[5]

P. Dixon

[4] See No. 114.
[5] A copy of this brief was sent on 25 November to Mr. Rickett for the Prime Minister as 'the opposite point of view' to No. 116 (PREM 8/1429).

No. 118

Minutes of a Meeting of the Defence Committee of the Cabinet, held at 10 Downing Street on Monday, 27 November 1950, at 10 a.m.[1]

D.O. (50) 22nd Meeting [CAB 131/8]

Top secret

German Contribution to the Defence of Europe

The Secretary of State for Foreign Affairs said that he was most anxious to obtain unanimity of view with the French and the Americans on the question of German rearmament and the defence of Europe before there was a meeting, if a meeting in fact did take place, between those three countries and the Russians. It was for this reason that he had circulated his memorandum (D.O. (50) 100),[2] which contained proposals for a North Atlantic Federal or Confederate Force in place of the European Force favoured by the French. He feared that if the French succeeded in creating a European Federated Force, the result would be a mere façade and the Force would be no more capable of sustained resistance than were the French themselves in 1940. He was not intending to suggest in his proposals that we should surrender sovereignty in any greater measure than the United States were willing to do: that should be our standard in this matter.

[1] *Present* at this meeting were Mr. Attlee (*in the Chair*); Mr. Shinwell; Mr. Morrison; Mr. Bevin; Mr. Gaitskell; Mr. Isaacs; Viscount Hall; Mr. Strachey; Mr. Henderson; Mr. Strauss. *Also present* were Mr. Gordon Walker; Admiral of the Fleet Lord Fraser; Field-Marshal Sir W. Slim; Marshal of the Royal Air Force Sir J. Slessor; Sir F. Hoyer Millar; Sir P. Dixon. *Secretariat:* Air Marshal Sir W. Elliot, Mr. Mallaby, Brigadier Price, Wing Commander Dobell.
[2] No. 115.

The Prime Minister said that the most urgent need was to get a Supreme Commander appointed and German units incorporated into the Forces for the defence of Europe. This unified Force must be created within the N.A.T.O. framework but, as he saw it, if the French succeeded in creating a European Force, then the N.A.T.O. Force might be composed of the United States, Great Britain with Commonwealth support, and the Federated European Force. These three parts would make one whole under a North Atlantic Supreme Commander. This would not involve the entry of Great Britain into a European Force—a project to which he was totally opposed considering the commitments of Great Britain to the other Commonwealth countries and in overseas territories. It was quite likely that the French would fail to create this European Federated Force, but he could not see why they should not make the attempt. It should not be for us to veto their attempt, although we should stand out of any active participation. Meanwhile, the Supreme Commander should be appointed and a beginning made with the recruitment and training of Germans. He feared that the effect of putting forward a counter-proposition in the form of a N.A.T.O. Federated Force would only delay the achievement of the immediate objective of getting the Supreme Command set up and additional American divisions sent to Europe.

The Minister of Defence recalled the history of the negotiations on this subject up to date and suggested that the French had modified their original intransigent attitude and might now be prepared to accept the recruitment of Germans on the basis of units of brigade strength, provided that at the same time they were free to start their discussions on their own idea of a European Federated Force. His main concern was to ensure that an increase of strength on the ground was achieved by 1951. Nothing should be done which might delay that. Once additional American divisions had begun to arrive in France, he thought that the French attitude might well change and that they might feel it less necessary to insist upon their own idea. If a different proposition were now advanced, all this might be delayed and, moreover, he saw in the proposal to form an Atlantic Federated Force a great danger that we might be obliged to surrender political control of a part at least of our own Forces. It was one thing to surrender operational control to a Supreme Commander, but to surrender political control was a serious risk.

The Chiefs of Staff said that they were in general agreement with the views stated by the Prime Minister and the Minister of Defence. Although it was very unlikely that the French would succeed in creating an effective European Federated Force, nevertheless, if they did succeed, that Force could become one part of the integrated N.A.T.O. Force in the manner suggested by the Prime Minister. There might then be a risk of creating a defeatist Third Force in Europe, but that risk had to be weighed against the risk of doing nothing at all. We should certainly stay out of the European Federated Force and, indeed, of any Federated Force. There was, therefore, great danger in the alternative proposal for a N.A.T.O.

Federal Force, put forward by the Foreign Secretary. Moreover, if the Americans decided not to take part in such a scheme, then we should find it very difficult to stay out of a European Federated Force.

The following points were made in discussion:

(a) While the Atlantic Federal Force proposed by the Foreign Secretary was more in line with the general concept of an Atlantic community than the French proposals, it appeared at first sight to be open to both political and military objections. It was unacceptable that we should provide two Forces, one in the Atlantic Treaty Force and one outside it. It was unacceptable that we should surrender political and administrative control over any part of our Forces. Nevertheless, the proposal ought to be studied in greater detail in case at a later date in the negotiations it were found useful to put forward an alternative proposition. The Minister of Defence might therefore arrange for a more detailed study to be made, in consultation with the Departments concerned, of the proposals in D.O. (50) 100.

(b) The proposals put forward by Mr. Spofford, the Chairman of the Council Deputies—that the recruitment and training of Germans up to brigade groups for integration into N.A.T.O. Forces should begin and that, concurrently, the French proposals for a Federated European Force should be studied—seemed to offer the best hope of immediate progress. It was possible, however, that the French would seek to delay the training of Germans until their own proposals had been discussed and agreed. Moreover, the Germans themselves might refuse to take part until the outcome of the discussions on the French plan was known. That would mean that unless the Americans changed their attitude, there would be no Supreme Commander and no additional American divisions in Europe, since they had so far made these conditional upon the inclusion of German units being accepted by the Germans.

(c) While no doubt the French plan entailed some long-term dangers, it must not be forgotten that it was admitted, even by the French, to be an experiment. At the outset, they would detach a part of their army for inclusion in the European Force. During that period the French contribution to the N.A.T.O. Force would be partly French and partly the European Force. The intention was that if this was successful, which appeared extremely unlikely, then the whole of the French and other European Forces, except those required for overseas commitments, would be included in the European Force. The success of such a proposal was, to say the least of it, doubtful, especially as the Norwegians, Dutch and Danes were opposed to the conception and the Italians and Belgians hardly even lukewarm.

(d) Apart from the organisational problem, there remained the question of the United Kingdom being able to find the necessary manpower to fulfil all its commitments. This would apply, in particular, to the requirements of the Royal Air Force. The question was under continuous study.

(*e*) Whatever the ultimate form of the N.A.T.O. Force, there was a problem which remained unresolved, i.e., the link between N.A.T.O. and the Commonwealth. N.A.T.O. was not a world-wide organisation and before it found itself obliged to take up world-wide responsibility it was essential that its relationship with the Commonwealth should be carefully studied and devised. Work was being done on this subject in connection with the forthcoming meeting of Commonwealth Prime Ministers.

The Prime Minister said that it was necessary to indicate the line which should be taken by Ministers in the forthcoming debate on Foreign Affairs,[3] and by United Kingdom representatives in the Council Deputies and Military Committee. He summed up the sense of the meeting as follows:

(i) Our obligations for the defence of the West were in accordance with the North Atlantic Treaty. We should do nothing to weaken that Treaty, or destroy the concept of the Atlantic community. For that reason alone and because of our commitments to the Commonwealth and to our overseas territories, we could not ourselves take part in a European Federated Force.

(ii) If, nevertheless, European countries wished to follow the French initiative and discuss the formation of a European Force, we should raise no objection, provided that it was understood that that Force should be considered as a part of the N.A.T.O. integrated Force. In other words, European countries should be free to make their contributions to the N.A.T.O. Force either by way of national contributions or of a Federated European Force.

(iii) We should favour the immediate recruitment and training of Germans into units not lower than brigade groups, for integration into the N.A.T.O. Force, in accordance with (ii) above.

In addition, it was desirable to persuade the Americans to agree to the immediate appointment of a Supreme Commander, and the reinforcement of their divisions in Europe, since that alone could meet the vital needs of 1951, and since it would also go a long way towards dissipating the fears and hesitations of the French.

The Committee:

(1) Invited the Foreign Secretary and the United Kingdom representatives on the Council Deputies and Military Committee to follow, in the forthcoming debates and negotiations, the line indicated by the Prime Minister at 'X' above.[4]

(2) Invited the Minister of Defence to arrange for a more detailed study to be made of D.O. (50) 100 by the Chiefs of Staff, in consultation with the Foreign Office.

[3] See No. 110, note 3.   [4] i.e. points (i)–(iii) above.

No. 119

Mr. Bevin to Sir O. Franks (Washington)

No. 5318 Telegraphic [WU 1195/481]

Priority. Secret   FOREIGN OFFICE, 29 November 1950, 9.35 p.m.

Repeated to Paris and Wahnerheide.

German contribution to defence of Europe.

As you know, the Americans have proposed a compromise in the Deputies.[1] Their proposal is that there should be transitional period during which (a) the process of forming German units would be started (perhaps on a brigade group basis), and (b) at the same time the French would invite European Governments to Paris to discuss their plan for a European army, a European Minister of Defence etc.

2. I have given much thought to this proposal and have discussed it with my colleagues in the Cabinet.[2] Our conclusion is that we should accept it and Sir F. Hoyer Millar will today make a statement to that effect in the Deputies.[3]

3. We have reached this conclusion with great reluctance and only because we believe it offers the one hope of getting the integrated force established without further delay. The first part of the American proposal (i.e. to go ahead with the integrated force) is of course entirely acceptable to us. It is the second part (to allow the French to try out their scheme for a European army) which we think dangerous. We have two principal objections.

4. First, we fear that the co-existence of two alternative and competing plans for the rearmament of Germany is liable to confuse the arrangements for the raising of German units. It may place the Germans in a

---

[1] See No. 109.i.   [2] See No. 118.

[3] See calendar i for Sir F. Hoyer Millar's statement of 28 November. On 29 November Mr. Bevin made a similar announcement in the House of Commons debate on foreign affairs. Mr. Bevin reaffirmed British support for the American proposal for an integrated force with German units and explained why the British government could not accept the French proposal for a European Army. 'Nevertheless, if it is the wish of the French Government and of other Governments in Europe to proceed to examine the possibilities of forming a European Army as part of the integrated force for the defence of Europe, His Majesty's Government would not stand in their way' (Parl. Debs., 5th ser., H. of C., vol. 481, cols. 1172–1174). Advance notice of the line taken by Mr. Bevin in the House of Commons was sent to M. Stikker in a personal message from Mr. Bevin of 28 November. The considerations behind the Cabinet's decision to accept the compromise were explained along the lines of the present telegram to Washington. Mr. Bevin concluded by voicing doubts about the Dutch proposal for a N.A.T.O. High Commissioner which he suggested should be held in reserve (F.O. telegram to The Hague No. 626 on WU 1195/474). M. Stikker replied on 29 November that as regards (a) participation in a European Army: 'the Netherlands Government will conform their attitude to that of His Majesty's Government'; (b) N.A.T.O. High Commissioner: 'Mr. Stikker agrees with both your comments . . . this proposal had not he said, been acceptable in its present form to the United States Government' (The Hague telegram No. 246 on WU 1195/478).

position to play off the French against the Americans and ourselves. It may even give the Germans a justifiable excuse for postponing a decision on the whole question of rearmament until the negotiations for the French plan have been completed.

5. In the second place, we believe that one of the ideas underlying the French plan is that of a Continental bloc, which they no doubt hope will be under French leadership and which, while linked with the Atlantic community, would constitute in world politics a force with some measure of independence. Such a bloc would be in conflict with the basic principles of the Atlantic Treaty as a free association of twelve equal independent States. It would be a sort of cancer in the Atlantic body which would, I am afraid, constitute a serious disruptive element and might in the end even endanger the Treaty itself. In allowing this European federal concept to gain a foot-hold within the North Atlantic Treaty Organisation, we are therefore taking a grave risk.

6. Nevertheless, in spite of these objections, we are prepared to accept the American proposal because we can see no other way of getting ahead with the immediate and urgent task of establishing the integrated force. We know that the Americans attach as much importance to this as we do. We greatly hope therefore that if the American proposal is generally approved, the United States Government will, for their part, accept it as sufficient evidence of general agreement and will proceed with the appointment of the Supreme Commander and the first steps in the formation of the integrated force. As we see it, a stage has at last been reached in these negotiations when there is some prospect of ultimate agreement. There have been concessions on all sides.

The French have come down from their original stand. We are ready to acquiesce in an attempt to form a European army. It does not seem unfair therefore to ask if the Americans too cannot take a step forward by appointing the Supreme Commander as soon as agreement in principle has been reached between the Atlantic Powers.

7. I feel convinced that the appointment of a Supreme Commander will of itself have an incalculable effect in putting vigour into the North Atlantic defence system and in speeding up the arrangements for an integrated force. Even if the Supreme Commander was not able to take up his duties in Europe immediately, his mere existence would be an encouragement to us all.

8. I shall be grateful if you will see Mr. Acheson, explain our views to him on the above lines and urge him strongly to meet us with regard to the appointment of a Supreme Commander.[4]

---

[4] On 30 November, Sir I. Kirkpatrick strongly endorsed paragraphs 6 and 7 above. 'From the purely German angle it is now essential for the following reasons to proceed at once with the appointment of the Supreme Commander and the constitution of an integrated force. Ever since September the situation has been slowly deteriorating, the propaganda of Schumacher and S.P.D. has begun to take effect and time has been given for all the diverse elements who are opposed to rearmament on the American terms to get together in

i *28 Nov. 1950 Statements by N.A.C. Deputies on Spofford compromise* as reported by Sir F. Hoyer Millar in telegrams 5–6 Saving. All favour implementing U.S. plan for integrated force while pursuing French plan for European Army. *Canada* suggests N.A.T.O. structure should be strengthened. *U.K. and Netherlands* will not participate in European Army. *Norway and Denmark* doubtful about participation. *Portugal* fears German preponderance in a European Army—attracted by Dutch idea of N.A.T.O. High Commissioner. *Belgium, Luxembourg, Italy* and *Iceland* generally cooperative, but Luxembourg likely to be influenced by Anglo-Dutch attitude. *France* 'neither surprise nor disappointment at H.M.G.'s attitude' [WU 1195/473; WU 1198/653].

opposition to the Chancellor. The result of the recent elections have further weakened his position ... Every effort should be made to bring the Americans to understand that German opinion has gone quite sour and that we shall not carry Germany along unless they proceed on the lines you advocate' (Wahnerheide telegram No. 1695 on WU 1195/477). Sir I. Kirkpatrick spoke on these lines to Mr. McCloy, who recognised the force of these considerations, and General Hays, who 'was less encouraging. He maintained that it was necessary not only to have regard to German opinion but to American opinion also. It would be difficult for General Marshall to persuade Congress that it was right to go ahead before all difficulties with France and Germany had been ironed out' (Wahnerheide telegram No. 1699 on WU 1195/479). On 30 November Sir O. Franks replied that 'In view of Mr. Acheson's preoccupations with Korea today, Minister [Mr. C.E. Steel] spoke to Matthews as instructed' and used the arguments advanced by Sir I. Kirkpatrick. 'Matthews said that their latest information was hopeful as regards French acceptance of the Spofford plan. They were also already seriously thinking of the matter of the Supreme Commander and he undertook to put your views to Mr. Acheson at the earliest opportunity' (Washington telegram No. 3230 on WU 1195/480).

No. 120

Mr. Bevin to Sir O. Franks (Washington)

No. 5377 Telegraphic [*WU 1195/483*]

Immediate. Secret   FOREIGN OFFICE, *1 December 1950, 10.15 p.m.*

Repeated Saving to Paris, Wahnerheide, U.K. Deputy on N.A.C.

Sir F. Hoyer-Millar's telegram No. 11 Saving (of 30th November)[1] German Contribution to Western Defence.

[1] This telegram contained the text of a personal message from Mr. Acheson to M. Schuman, printed in *F.R.U.S. 1950*, vol. iii, pp. 496–8. In this message, delivered on the morning of 30 November, Mr. Acheson asked the French government to agree without further delay to the Spofford proposals. Mr. Acheson stated that the matter was now urgent in view of the deteriorating situation in Germany and 'the shocking turn of events in Korea in these last days', caused by the successful launch of a Chinese counter-offensive on 25–26 November. Mr. Acheson emphasised the importance of the Spofford proposals for European integration: 'I consider adoption of these proposals to be only a starting point. I do not need to remind you of the attitude which the Government of the United States has displayed on innumerable occasions and in many forms, towards European integration. We

I assume that Mr. Acheson's message to M. Schuman was sent off before you had spoken to him on the lines of my telegram No. 5318 (of 29th November).[2] Nevertheless I am disturbed by the emphasis placed in Mr. Acheson's message on support for European integration, about which, as you will have seen from paragraph 5 of my telegram No. 5318, I have grave doubts. I shall accordingly be grateful if you will let Mr. Acheson know my views as soon as possible on the following general lines.

2. I am grateful for the action which Mr. Acheson has taken with M. Schuman and hope that it will be effective in achieving the object we all have in view, namely, an early settlement of the Western Defence problem on the lines proposed by the United States Deputy. I fully share Mr. Acheson's views about the danger of further delay, particularly in view of the trend of German opinion and of the turn of events in the Far East, and I notice with appreciation Mr. Acheson's statement that the Supreme Commander should be appointed in order to give form and impetus to our military effort, and have also read what the President said about the need to establish the integrated force under the supreme command without delay.[3] As Mr. Acheson will have noticed from the message in my telegram No. 5318,[2] I attach the highest importance to such an appointment being made immediately.

3. At the same time I am concerned about the emphasis placed in Mr. Acheson's message upon the idea of European integration and the manner in which this question is related to the German problem. As Mr. Acheson will be aware, we have grave doubts about the feasibility or wisdom of any purely European solution. I recognise that the American approach to this matter may be somewhat different from our own, and that Mr. Acheson's references to it may have been designed primarily to help the French to agree to the American plan. Nevertheless, apart from the effect of such a European development upon N.A.T.O., I am

favor it. I favor it . . . if your government in close consultation with the German and other European Govts. could evolve the main outlines of a plan for binding the free nations of Europe more closely together in the spirit so well represented by the Schuman Plan, we could reasonably hope for long-term solution of our many problems, be they political, military, or economic . . . The U.S. has given every evidence in statements, actions, and treaties, of the depth and permanence of its interest in Europe, its support for closer European association, its willingness to cooperate with Europe. That this will continue and increase, is, I am convinced, the will of the American people.' When handing a text of this message to Sir F. Hoyer Millar, Mr. Spofford said that it had been made clear to M. Schuman that 'it represented the final views of the United States Government, and that the latter were not prepared to make any further concessions to the French. M. Schuman had apparently taken this communication quite well and had been particularly gratified by Mr. Acheson's references to the question of "European integration".' Mr. Spofford agreed with Sir F. Hoyer Millar 'when I said that I thought Mr. Acheson had gone rather far in what he had said about "European integration"' (WU 1195/482).

[2] No. 119.

[3] With regard to the situation in Korea (note 1), President Truman said, at a press conference on 30 November, that integrated forces in Europe under a supreme command should be established 'at once' (see *The Times* of 1 December and No. 121, note 1).

concerned lest the last three paragraphs of Mr. Acheson's message may not encourage the French to take the line that further relaxation of our Occupation controls over Germany can only be effected when progress has been made with European integration on the lines of the Pleven Plan. I consider that it would be highly dangerous if we were to get ourselves into such a position. I fully agree with Mr. Acheson that a continuation of the Occupation régime in its present form is rapidly becoming incompatible with many of our broader objectives and certainly with any Defence Programme for Germany. But the changes in the occupation régime, which will undoubtedly be necessary if a full and willing German cooperation in defence is to be secured, may well be rendered impossible of achievement if they are made too closely dependent on the specific French proposal for a European Army. Apart from the general difficulty, there would seem some danger in allowing a situation to arise in which the whole future of Allied controls in Germany were made dependent upon the results of a conference summoned by the French Government at which neither the United States nor the United Kingdom Governments are represented, except possibly as observers.

4. I do not, of course, suggest that Mr. Acheson can now modify his message to M. Schuman, but I should like to feel sure that he appreciates the risks set out above, and I hope he may find an occasion to make his position clear.[4]

CALENDAR TO NO. 120

i *1–4 Dec. German attitude on controls and defence* Hardening of German line evident at meeting of A.H.C. with Dr. Adenauer on 1 Dec. (Wahn. tel. 1706). Adenauer, 'rattled' by political difficulties and events in Far East, bids for contractual agreement and promise of ultimate equality as price of German contribution to defence. Kirkpatrick confirms on 2 Dec. that situation in

---

[4] Sir O. Franks spoke as instructed to Mr. Acheson on 2 December. Mr. Acheson 'said he realised fully the danger of getting into a position with the French which meant that we could not do what was necessary in relation to the Germans. His own thoughts were that two currents of thoughts could be discerned in Germany. One was a current in favour of an integrated European defence force . . . The second current was the demand of Germany for greater equality which meant that we should have to modify the occupation controls. He hoped that if elements in French and German thought could be brought together and harmonised in the creation of a European force it might be possible to evade the very real dangers you mention. His thinking on this subject was far from finalised . . . things would move very quickly in the next week or two and it would be necessary for all of us to think very hard if right solutions were to be found' (WU 1195/484). When following up Sir O. Franks' representations with State Department on 4 December, British Embassy officials were told that 'Mr. Acheson's message to M. Schuman had not (repeat not) been intended to give impression that a European army or European integration on the lines of the Pleven Plan was a necessary preliminary to further relaxation of occupation controls. Laukhuff confirmed that the purpose of the message was to get the French to agree to Spofford's proposal . . . Laukhuff further said that State Department was thinking most seriously of the steps necessary to secure further relaxation of occupation controls. State Department much regretted failure at New York in September to overcome French objections on this subject' (Washington telegram No. 3277 on WU 1195/488).

Germany has deteriorated and that concessions on controls will have to be made to secure German cooperation on defence (Wahn. tel. 1712). Mr. C. O'Neill, Political Director at Wahnerheide, considers on 4 Dec. that Germans would prefer a European Army to an Atlantic one [C 7774–5/20/18; C 7834/27/18].

No. 121

Record of a meeting of the Prime Minister and Foreign Secretary with the French Prime Minister and Minister of Foreign Affairs at 10 Downing Street on 2 December 1950[1]

[WU 1198/659]

Top secret

PART II[2]

Western Defence

Mr. *Attlee* suggested that it would now be desirable to consider the general strategic situation. He thought that there was a danger that the Western Powers might find themselves getting heavily committed in the Far East. He believed that responsible American opinion appreciated that Europe was the crucial area. It was possible that the Western Powers might at any time find a new threat developing in the West and they must therefore seek to make themselves as strong as possible there. It was of course in the interests of the Russians to get the Western Powers heavily committed in Asia. They would moreover take every opportunity to foster disagreements between Europe and the United States and indeed between different Western European countries. It was essential to prevent them from achieving this and the position in the West must be consolidated. It was very important that the United States should be satisfied that the countries of Western Europe were exerting themselves to the utmost and also that there were no serious disagreements among them. He believed that the appointment of a Supreme Commander-in-Chief in the West would have a very good effect.

M. *Pleven* said that the French Government much regretted that the

[1] M. Pleven and M. Schuman came to London on 2 December for talks with Mr. Attlee before his visit to Washington from 4–8 December. This visit was precipitated on 30 November by reports of remarks by President Truman that morning at a press conference (see No. 120, note 3), in response to questions about the use of the atomic bomb in the Far East. The circumstances and course of Mr. Attlee's visit to Washington in relation to the Far East will be documented in Volume IV. For coverage in the present volume, see No. 127, note 1.

[2] Part 1 was a separate record (F 1027/6) of the first Anglo-French ministerial meeting held that morning when the situation in the Far East was discussed. This second meeting took place in the afternoon. *Present* were *U.K.* Mr. Attlee, Mr. Bevin, Sir W. Strang, Sir R. Makins, Sir P. Dixon, Mr. Mallet, Mr. Barclay, Mr. Shuckburgh; *France* M. Pleven, M. Schuman, M. Massigli, M. Parodi, M. Le Roy, M. Lebel, M. André.

appointment of a Supreme Commander had been postponed because of the failure to reach agreement on Germany. In their view there was no real connection between the two. For their part, they would do their best to encourage the early appointment of a Supreme Commander and he recalled that the French Government had taken the initiative in proposing this in their memorandum of 17th August.[3]

Mr. Attlee pointed out that the Americans took the view that a Supreme Commander should not be appointed until there were respectable forces for him to command. He went on to say that in his view it was necessary to have a proper mobilisation of the economic strength of the West as well as co-ordination in the field of defence. In the long run defence was dependent on the economic strength of the countries concerned.

M. Pleven said that he was in full agreement on this point.

Mr. Bevin said that as he had said in the House of Commons,[4] he was always worried about the possibility of the U.S.S.R. striking in the West as well as in the East, and he quite agreed that it was essential to avoid getting too heavily committed in the East.

Mr. Bevin said that a deadlock seemed to have been reached on the question of an integrated Atlantic force or European Army. At the meetings in London in May he had stressed the importance of the idea of partnership between the North American countries and Europe as opposed to the idea of aid from the former to the latter.[5] When he went to New York in September he thought that the President's statement about the stationing of United States troops in Europe[6] and the composite proposals put forward by Mr. Acheson[7] offered just what he wanted and he felt that the opportunity was too good to miss.

Mr. Bevin said that he believed that if the West acted wisely in building up its defences, it would be possible to prevent aggression taking place. His Majesty's Government, like the French Government, must carry their public opinion with them. They had to take into account the requirements of the Commonwealth and of the present Far Eastern situation as well as of Europe, in considering how much they could put into Europe. As he had told the House of Commons, Europe in his opinion was no longer strong enough to stand alone.[4] That was why His Majesty's Government had turned to the Atlantic conception, and when the United States signed the North Atlantic Treaty he had felt that one of his great objectives had been realised. The United States had come a step forward at the meetings in London in May, and in New York in September, they had been ready to commit themselves even further. He had not been expecting them to raise the question of a German contribution to Western Defence in the way they did, but the United States Government had reached the conclusion that German man-power was necessary to any effective defence of the West, and he saw their point of view. He had told the House of Commons that

[3] See No. 9, note 4.   [4] See No. 119, note 3.
[5] See Volume II, e.g. Nos. 52, 74, 74.i., 78–9.
[6] See No. 1, note 7.   [7] See No. 2.

His Majesty's Government pinned their faith in the Atlantic conception. If the continental countries felt that they could do better by building up combined force than they could if they each made their own contribution, His Majesty's Government would not seek to prevent them. They had accordingly been prepared to accept the Spofford compromise proposals. He believed that the appointment of a Supreme Commander would be a most important step, since it would be possible to build round him. It was, in his view, essential to agree that the Germans should play their part in the defensive system, but he believed that the details of how they should do so could be worked out as they went along. As he had frequently told M. Schuman, he was opposed to written constitutions. In the meanwhile, in his opinion, there was no time to be lost. If it was possible to make rapid progress in the West it should be possible to save the East. It was, however, essential to get out of the present vicious circle. The Americans who in New York had only asked for agreement in principle on German participation in the defence of the West, now said that they wished to see German units being formed. They had made this a condition of further progress on their part. The French, on the other hand, said that the first step must be to create a European army, and so long as the two maintained these positions, no progress seemed possible.

Mr. Bevin invited Sir P. Dixon to explain the position now reached in the Deputies.

Sir P. Dixon explained that the 'Spofford compromise' contained two elements—

(1) that we should start the process of raising German units, perhaps on the basis of brigade groups;
(2) that the French Government would invite European Governments to Paris to discuss the European Army.

The question was how far could the progress under (1) go before the discussions under (2) had been completed. The American attitude was that they would not appoint a Supreme Commander or send American divisions to Europe until they could see a prospect of German units being formed, and since it must be uncertain how long the process of discussion on the European Army would take and what its results would be, this created uncertainty about the whole programme. M. Alphand, he understood, had returned from Paris the previous day and put a number of questions to the Deputies relating to relaxations of controls in Germany. One of these questions was whether, during the transitional period, the German combat teams should be attached to existing Allied divisions. Another was whether it would be agreed that controls on Germany would not be relaxed until a definitive military or political system had been established. The position thus was that it was still uncertain how far progress could be made on the first part of the Spofford compromise while the second process was going forward.

M. Schuman said that all were agreed that we must advance quickly. The question was how could we do so most surely. The Governments were agreed on the objective, but differed on certain points of application. The French Government accepted the idea of an integrated Atlantic Force; in fact, they suggested it in their note of 17th August.[3] They regretted that no progress had been made, especially as regards the appointment of the Commander-in-Chief. They had not considered that this question was linked with the question of German participation, but the Americans had preferred to seek agreement on a German contribution in advance and had thus put the French Government in a difficult position. Nevertheless, they were willing to look at it. They did not object to the principle of German participation. It was logical; we could not conceive of defending Germany on the Elbe without sacrifice and effort from the Germans. The difficulties began when you considered how to bring about this German participation. The French view was that, if the Germans were integrated *direct* into the Atlantic force, it would mean that Germany was being offered participation in North Atlantic Treaty arrangements just as if she were a member of the Atlantic Community and a signatory to the Treaty. But she was not a signatory, and when the Treaty had been ratified by the European Powers it had been expressly stated that Germany was not and would not be a member. There was no hope of the French Parliament ever voting for a proposal to admit Germany as a member of the North Atlantic Treaty and giving her equality of rights in that forum. He begged the British Ministers to take account of this just as the French were asked to take account of the American view.

The second difficulty arose from the German attitude. It had been agreed in New York that we must not go to the Germans as supplicants for their assistance. Unfortunately, this was what had happened, and the two parties in Germany were now competing with each other in setting higher terms for German participation. A German contribution in man-power could not be imposed on the Germans; they must accept it, and the fact was that all Germans were now united in demanding equality of rights as their condition for participation. In the Atlantic Treaty framework this could only mean their representation on the Atlantic Council and in the other committees and their admission to the Treaty.

The Prime Minister said he did not see how the position would be different in a European Army. Presumably the Germans would not join a European Army either except on a basis of equality.

M. Schuman said that the European Army would be organised, recruited, equipped and maintained entirely on a European basis through special European organs, in which the Germans would have precisely the same position as the other parties. In the Atlantic Pact, on the other hand, the only central control was in the matter of Command through the Supreme Commander.

The Prime Minister thought it was largely a juridical distinction, but *M. Schuman* did not agree.

M. Schuman said the third difficulty related to the reaction upon Russia

313

and the Eastern satellites. Korea showed what use the Soviets could make of satellites. The example might be followed in Germany. The three Allied Governments were meeting next week to consider how to answer the Soviet invitation to a Four-Power discussion on Germany.[8] It seemed to the French Government illogical that, in the very same week, irrevocable decisions should be taken about the rearmament of Germany. Such decisions would be taken by the Russians as a pretext for declaring the Four-Power discussions useless. The French Government could and must agree to the question of principle, but since a long period of preparation would be necessary, they thought it undesirable to decide upon the modalities. They were not far from agreement with the Spofford plan. They could agree to the preparatory measures preceding formation of German units either for a European or for an Atlantic force as the case might be. They could agree to discussions being undertaken with the Germans to prepare the necessary legal and administrative measures, but they must object seriously to the actual raising and training of German troops as provided in the Spofford plan. A decision to do this, if made public, would give the impression to public opinion that we had no intention of taking the Russian approach seriously. After all, it had been said in New York that it would take eighteen months to two years before German units could be equipped. The Korean developments might make the period longer. Why, then, was there such a hurry to decide now how the German units should be integrated in a broader force. In short, he thought the French Government could accept the Spofford plan, but with the reservation that measures of implementation (i.e., actual enrolment of German troops) would be delayed so long as there is any possibility of conversations with Russia.

The Prime Minister asked why the creation of a European Army, supposing everybody had agreed to that, would not equally give a pretext to the Russians to abandon the proposed talks. He did not think appeasement had ever had any effect with the Russians, who were much more impressed by determination.

M. Pleven said he did not think appeasement was the right word to describe what M. Schuman had in mind any more than our common desire to avoid a war with China was appeasement. Certain agreements had been signed with Russia explicitly prohibiting German rearmament.[9] The French reluctance openly to break those agreements was simply the desire not to give a pretext to the Russians at a moment when we were not ready to resist the consequences. True determination consisted in the utmost effort on the part of the United States, United Kingdom and France themselves. The trouble was, he thought, that in this matter of German rearmament military opinion had been allowed to outrun political thought.

M. Pleven, nevertheless, thought that considerable advance had been

<hr>

[8] See No. 110, note 3. [9] See No. 24, note 2.

made in the French position in the last few weeks, and he set it out as follows:

(1) The French Government agrees on the participation of German contingents in Western Defence.
(2) The French Government could probably very easily agree as to the percentage of German forces to Allied forces.
(3) They would agree to the establishment of a system of recruitment and to all necessary preparatory measures up to medical examination of personnel, provisional selection, census, &c., but *not* to the actual incorporation of personnel in armed units.
(4) They could agree to measures for the output of equipment as necessary for the speedy incorporation of the units.
(5) They agreed to the principle of the combat team as the basis for the German contribution.

This was as far as they could go for the moment, except through the European Army system which in their opinion would not give the Russians the pretext he had referred to.

The Prime Minister again asked why the position would be different with a European Army.

M. Pleven replied that there was no agreement prohibiting the creation of Europe or of a European Army. The German units in such an army would not be under German political authority, but under European authority and could, therefore, not be used for offensive purposes by the Germans.

The Prime Minister said that the Russians were after all realists, and he did not think they would take much account of this juridical distinction.

M. Pleven said it was not only a question of the Russians. Account must be taken of public opinion in our own countries and in the satellite countries. It was necessary to show that we had not broken engagements formally entered into.

Mr. Bevin said that the matter must somehow be brought to a head. He wondered whether the appointment of a Supreme Commander would not give the Russians as much of a pretext as the integration of German units.

M. Pleven said that there was no agreement prohibiting such an appointment and *M. Schuman* added that there was no distinction of principle between the appointment of a Supreme Commander and the signature of the North Atlantic Treaty itself, to which the Russians had not reacted. The recruitment of Germans under a German authority, however, would be quite a different matter. After all, until August last the Potsdam principle of German disarmament had never been questioned.

M. Pleven said it should be remembered that the United States, United Kingdom and France had never attacked Russia whereas Germany had, and a German army was quite a different matter. As for the risks, it would be less serious if we already had a strong Allied force in Europe.

The Prime Minister said he had always thought the two things could

315

proceed *pari passu*. It would in any case take time to get forces out of Germany, and in the meantime the Allied forces would get stronger. If, however, we delayed in our plans, we should make no progress.

M. Pleven said he thought we were making progress in the building up of our own forces.

The Prime Minister doubted this. It was a question where Europe was to be defended. If we could not make effective strategic plans to defend the Elbe line (which we could not do without a German contribution), we were in effect handing the whole of Germany over to Russia. So long as this question was left in doubt, no strategic plans could be made.

Mr. Bevin then said that, so far as the discussion went, it seemed to him that we must now ask the Americans whether they would be prepared to appoint the Supreme Commander and put in force the Spofford plan on the basis of the five points mentioned by M. Pleven. He asked whether M. Pleven insisted that it must all be dependent on the formation of a European Army.

M. Pleven said his reply was the same as before. He did not think it a good idea, from the point of view of reaching a solution, that the appointment of the Supreme Commander should be delayed. At the present moment the French Government (though they had tried to avoid it) were strictly limited by the decision of their Parliament. Apart from words and formulae, the essential principle to which the French Parliament was so attached was that no German armed force should be allowed to exist under the sole control of a purely German political authority. Any such force would constitute an element within the integrated army which might tend towards a policy of revenge and give an offensive spirit to the whole Atlantic force. If, however, there were an Allied Supreme Commander actually in existence, this would constitute a new factor which might enable the French Government to go back to Parliament and see whether further progress could be made. He did not want his words misunderstood. He had no new formula in mind, but in an attempt to reconcile divergence, he thought there might be a possibility there.

M. Schuman repeated that the French Government were bound by a formal Parliamentary text. Nevertheless, the French Parliament was realistic and took account of facts. If there were a new factor which met the broad line on which Parliament was thinking, it would give the possibility of a change of position. The French Government would reply in a day or two to Mr. Spofford's proposals in the Deputies. M. Schuman had had a message from Mr. Acheson, to which he must also reply. Their attitude would, therefore, be fixed in the near future.

M. Pleven said that he did not want Mr. Attlee to think from what he had said that the French Government had any illusions about Soviet aims. They did not know whether the Soviet offer to discuss Germany was sincere, but it was necessary to carry the moral support of public opinion and to show that the Governments had never neglected any possibility of meeting a sincere attempt to find a settlement.

Mr. Bevin said the question boiled down to what risks the Americans and the French were prepared to take. Would the Americans risk appointing a Supreme Commander in the belief that, if an organisation were built up around him, based on the acceptance of the five points of M. Pleven, there would be a chance of the French Government modifying their views.

M. Pleven agreed. There was a possibility of some solution here, but he hoped that he would not be pressed to say more.

M. Schuman said that if the French Government had had nothing but the original American proposal to put before their Parliament there would have been ten votes in favour.

M. Pleven said that the passage of time in this matter was not necessarily a loss. Public opinion needed time to reflect and to revise its judgement.

Concluding this part of the discussion, *M. Schuman* said the essential, from the point of view of any discussion with the Russians, was that though we should have agreed on the principles of German participation, we should not have taken a definite decision on the modalities or begun the actual enrolment. It would be a similar situation as had existed last year in Paris, when the principles of the new Bonn Constitution had been agreed but we had been able to discuss the details because they had been left open. The Russians had tried to stop the Constitution being put into force, but we had resisted this, without however giving the appearance of refusing to discuss the matter. If we now announced a final decision about German rearmament, we would either be wrecking the prospects of Four-Power discussions or we might find ourselves obliged to withdraw our plans, which would be bad for our prestige.

Four-Power Talks

Mr. Bevin said that the British Cabinet had not yet reached final conclusions on this subject. They would be considering the matter on Tuesday [5 December] preparatory to the meeting of officials of the Three Powers in Paris next week. His Majesty's Government thought the agenda proposed by the Russians too narrow. There were many other fundamental questions such as the cold war, the general attitude of Russia, the Austrian Treaty, the question of respect for international law, &c., which would have to be dealt with if there were to be any possibility of a settlement which would be more than an illusion. The British Government's policy was therefore to try out the possibilities of a meeting with the Russians with the object of ascertaining whether they have really any genuine desire for peace.

M. Schuman asked whether we thought about including the question of the Far East in the agenda.

Mr. Bevin said it was difficult to answer this. We must bear in mind the fact that the United Nations was dealing with these questions. There were such problems as interference with our institutions, promotion of civil wars, &c., of which the events in the Far East were merely examples. Even if we reached a settlement on Germany and Austria, we should be living in a fool's paradise if the cold war went on. It was, however, difficult to express these thoughts in terms of an agenda. We thought, in any case, that Austria should be high on the list for discussion, as it was regarded in Great Britain as a test of Russian sincerity. The Austrian Vice-Chancellor had told him that the Russians were beginning to organise a puppet State in East Austria and there was much alarm.[10] They must be faced with this amongst the other issues in any conversations.

M. *Schuman* said that the French Government agreed with this approach, especially as regards widening the agenda. He reminded Mr. Bevin that the United Nations had invited the Four Powers to hold such discussions, but he agreed that it would be wrong to deal in detail with the questions actually under consideration in the Security Council. The right thing to do would be to discuss the general prospects of peace and to deal with all the specific difficulties as illustrations of the main theme.

Visit of the Prime Minister to Washington

Mr. *Bevin* said that the British Government would keep the French Government informed of the progress of Mr. Attlee's talks in Washington. Mr. Attlee would naturally not speak for the French Government, but it would be very useful if we could make sure from time to time during the talks that we were keeping in step.[11]

The Prime Minister thanked the French Ministers for their visit and a short communiqué was adopted. It was agreed that there would be no press statements.

[10] Mr. Bevin entertained the Austrian Vice-Chancellor, Dr. A. Schaerf, to lunch in London on 1 December. No other record of these remarks has been traced in Foreign Office archives: cf. C 7874/942/3.

[11] The visit of MM. Pleven and Schuman to London gave rise to complaints from General de Gaulle, President of the *Rassemblement du Peuple Français*, that Mr. Attlee was being authorized to speak for France in Washington. This was denied by M. Pleven at a Foreign Press Association dinner on 5 December 'though he also expressed his satisfaction that his talks in London had revealed French and British ideas to be "orientated in the same way"' (Paris telegram No. 527 Saving on WF 1023/28). Arrangements were made in Washington for keeping the French Embassy there informed of the progress of the Attlee-Truman talks. On Mr. Bevin's instructions Sir R. Makins, who accompanied Mr. Attlee to Washington and to Ottawa (9–11 December), went to Paris on 13 December in order to inform MM. Pleven and Schuman personally of the course of the conversations.

No. 122

Memorandum by the Secretary of State for Foreign Affairs

C.P. (50) 294 [CAB 129/43]

Secret   FOREIGN OFFICE, *2 December 1950*

Soviet Proposal for a Meeting of the Council of Foreign Ministers

My colleagues will remember that in a note of the 3rd November[1] the Soviet Government proposed that the Council of Foreign Ministers of France, the United Kingdom, the United States of America and the Union of Soviet Socialist Republics should meet to examine the question of carrying out the Potsdam Agreement on the demilitarisation of Germany.

2. The United Nations General Assembly also passed on the 3rd November a Resolution[2] calling upon the permanent members of the Security Council to meet and discuss, collectively or otherwise, and if necessary with other States concerned, the problems threatening world peace and hampering the work of the United Nations.

3. In the House of Commons on the 13th November I made a statement,[3] of which my colleagues will be aware, setting out the view of His Majesty's Government on the Soviet Note. I also referred to the United Nations Resolution. My statement followed the lines of the draft circulated as Annex B to C.P. (50) 266,[4] as amended in the light of the Cabinet's discussion on 13th November (C.M. (50) 73rd Conclusions, Minute 3).[4] Since my statement it has become clear that there is considerable feeling in Parliament and in the country as a whole that the Western Powers should not return a completely negative reply to the Russian note but should demonstrate that they have given constructive thought to the possibilities of relieving the present international tension. This state of feeling assumes, of course, that the Russian note which, on the face of it, was designed to weaken the resolve of the West to defend itself and was carefully timed to prelude the World Peace Congress,[5] contains the elements of a desire on the part of the Soviet Union to meet with the Western Powers. This, however, is by no means certain.

4. It has now been agreed with the French and United States Governments that officials of our three Governments should meet in Paris during the week beginning 4th December to consider on what basis we could enter into an exchange of views with the Russians.[6]

---

[1] See No. 86, note 5.   [2] See No. 110, note 2.
[3] See No. 97, note 7.   [4] Not printed.
[5] A World Peace Congress was held in Warsaw from 16–22 November. Delegates from eighty countries, including the Soviet Union, the United Kingdom, United States and France, voted, among other things, for the establishment of a World Peace Council.
[6] See No. 110, note 3.

5. *Soviet objectives*

I think it is important first of all to be clear on the Russians' reasons for putting forward once again a proposal for such a meeting at this time and for linking it with the proposals in the Prague communiqué. As on previous occasions, when they have resorted to similar diplomatic manoeuvres, they are trying to stop a development in Western policy unwelcome to themselves. Their main purpose now is undoubtedly to delay the progress of plans to strengthen the defence of the West. They realise that these plans will have made a good step forward if agreement is reached on an integrated Atlantic force for Western European defence and on a contribution to that force from the great resources of Germany. They hope therefore to confuse Western counsels while this agreement is being sought and in particular to take advantage of the difference of opinion which is known to exist between the French and their partners in the North Atlantic Treaty on this issue.

6. Before we commit ourselves to inviting the Russians to a discussion with the three Western Powers we must be clear whether there is any basis for fruitful discussion. As I made clear in my statement in the House of Commons, we should not be prepared to enter into discussion on the basis of the Prague communiqué on Germany[7] alone. The United States and French Governments are also agreed on this point.

7. It seems to me that the possible lines of approach to this problem might be briefly described as follows:

Course A   We might try to confine any talks with the Russians to the problems of a particular region (such as Germany and/or alternatively, the Far East), on which there might be some hope of achieving a partial settlement and a partial relaxation of tension.

Course B   We might, in the same hope, invite the Russians to discuss only the major points of friction throughout the world with a view at least to eliminating them.

Course C   We might present the Russians with a full statement of our terms for a global settlement of all our differences with them in order to try to establish an enduring basis for better relations in future.

Course D   We might make the Russians some proposal, their agreement to which would be a test of the sincerity of their intentions and on which agreement would therefore be required before proceeding to any wider talks.

Course E   We might propose preliminary informal talks at the official level and should set out a selected list of subjects, on which we should require satisfaction from the Russians as a result of any subsequent formal Ministerial talks.

Course F   We might say that the existing Russian proposals based on the

[7] See No. 78, note 4.

Prague communiqué did not hold out adequate hope of successful talks and we might therefore call upon the Russians to put forward more attractive proposals if they really desire talks leading to a relaxation of tension.

Courses A, B and C

8. The first three courses outlined above would in fact represent an attempt to enter without further delay into talks designed to reach a settlement over a specified field. I have examined these three possibilities and have reluctantly come to the conclusion that none of them offers any hopeful prospect of coming to a genuine agreement which would increase our security or hopes of permanent peace. The arguments on which this conclusion is based are fully set out in Annex A[i] to this paper. Briefly I am convinced that any attempt to reach a settlement either in a single region or on major points of friction would at the present time be too dangerous for us to embark upon it.

9. With regard to a global settlement—Course C above—I have explained in Annex A why I do not think it would be possible for the Soviet Government to accept our terms and why no concessions that we could contemplate would persuade the Soviet Government to consider them. Moreover, if we published our terms for a global settlement in our reply to the Soviet note, the conclusion would probably be drawn that we were deliberately putting the price too high and were not serious in our attempt to find a basis for discussion. In order to meet such criticism it might be possible to set out in the form of an agenda for the meeting the subjects which we should wish to discuss in trying to reach a global settlement, without necessarily indicating what we should wish to obtain under each subject. I attach at Annex B[i] the terms of such a possible agenda, but, as I have indicated already, the presentation of this agenda would merely be a move calculated to appeal to public opinion and would not in my view increase the chances of a settlement.

Course D

10. The fourth possibility is to demand from the Russians some prior test of their sincerity before entering into wider talks. The sort of tests which I have in mind would be to conclude some sort of non-aggression pact between the four Powers and to reach agreement on a satisfactory plan for the international control of atomic energy and for the reduction of conventional armaments. It seems to me that this approach is open to three objections. First, it allows Russia to point to her existing disarmament proposals which are designed for propaganda purposes only and are in fact unacceptable. Secondly, it could be objected that, by putting an agreement on atomic energy as one of our essential pre-conditions for a wider agreement, we were insisting on settling one of the most difficult problems first and therefore trying to obstruct fruitful discussions. Thirdly, it would in my view be dangerous to embark on any general

scheme of disarmament until we had received some sign that the dangers against which we are now rearming had abated.

Course E

11. The fifth possible line of approach—to hold preliminary talks with a view to defining an agenda for a meeting of Foreign Ministers—is in essentials similar to the approach suggested in a draft reply to the Soviet note which the United States Government have sent to us with a request for our views. I attach the text of this draft reply at Annex C[i] to this paper. If we adopted this course I do not suggest that we should agree with the exact wording of the United States draft. In particular we should wish to define more clearly the subjects which we wished to discuss. It would have to be made clear that these subjects were not necessarily the main existing points of friction but were matters on which the Western Powers required satisfaction from Russia. In addition to such questions as the Austrian Treaty, the violation of the Balkan Peace Treaties, compliance with the United Nations Charter and the cessation of Communist propaganda under Soviet direction (subjects which the United States draft lists), they would, I suggest, have to include an agreement on the use of the veto and better treatment in the Soviet Union and other Communist-controlled states of Western nationals. I do not think that it would be appropriate to bring up Far Eastern questions in any such list of subjects. As I have made clear in Annex A these questions affect particularly the policies of the United States and Chinese Governments. The disadvantage of this line of approach is that it leaves it open to the Russians to raise a list of points of their own and to demand satisfaction on them from us. Nevertheless this line of approach shows a willingness to hold four-Power talks and widens their scope beyond the narrow basis proposed by the Russians.

The United States draft suggests that the proposed preliminary talks should be held between representatives of the three Western Powers and the Soviet Union at the seat of the United Nations in New York. I am in favour of this suggestion, since it would be difficult to persuade the Soviet Government to hold such a meeting in one of the three Western capitals, and there are obvious objections to the three Western Powers agreeing, so to speak, to be summoned to Moscow for the meeting.

Course F

12. The final course mentioned in paragraph 7 above is to ask the Russians to put forward fresh and more constructive proposals. The United States Government, who were at first attracted by this possible line, appear no longer to advocate it strongly. It has the disadvantage of handing the initiative back to the Russians and leaving the way open for them to make a new and specious 'peace' offer. On the other hand this course has considerable attractions. As I have already remarked, it is by no means certain that the original Russian proposal for a meeting of the

Council of Foreign Ministers to examine the question of Germany on the basis of the Prague communiqué was put forward with a genuine desire for discussion. Having rejected this basis for discussion, it would be logical for the Western Powers to ask the Soviet Government whether they can suggest any other basis. This would be a test of their sincerity. Moreover this course avoids most of the disadvantages which are inherent in the other possible courses of action. On the other hand I recognise that public opinion might not consider that we were making a sufficiently constructive approach to the Russians if we merely threw the ball back into their court.

13. I have set out these alternatives somewhat fully for the consideration of my colleagues. I consider that in reaching a decision we should take account of two main factors. First, although we should be prepared to enter into talks and to take any opportunity which offers of reducing tension even in a limited sphere, there is very little likelihood that talks will lead to any real settlement of differences. Secondly, we should so present our reply to the Soviet note as to make clear our genuine conciliatory approach to the possibility of talks without risking damage to any of our own interests.

14. It seems to me that in the light of these two factors the choice will really lie between a modification of Course C in paragraph 7 above, i.e. presenting the agenda on which a meeting might be held; Course E, in which exploratory four-Power official talks would first be held; and Course F, in which we should invite the Russians to put forward fresh and constructive proposals.

15. The choice is very difficult. I do not find myself prepared to recommend strongly any of the three courses suggested in the preceding paragraph, since I am conscious of the dangers attaching to all of them. Before I make up my mind I should like a thorough discussion with my colleagues.[8]

E.B.

[8] When the Cabinet considered this paper at their meeting on 5 December 'the Cabinet felt reluctant to discuss in detail the merits of the various alternative courses . . . since many of the main issues were under discussion in Washington and the outcome of these talks would greatly influence the course which the Cabinet eventually decided to take. Moreover, some of the alternative courses raised very important questions of policy, and the course of the talks in Washington might be prejudiced if some of these questions were raised in the Paris discussions'. However the Cabinet agreed that in any event Course F would be rejected and considered that Course E was 'less open to objection than some of the other courses proposed'. It was agreed that U.K. representatives at the Paris talks (Sir O. Harvey and Mr. Mallet) should be instructed, among other things, to concentrate on drafting a reply to the Soviet government 'on lines which would seek to broaden the agenda of any meeting of the Council of Foreign Ministers so as to cover, not only German problems, but all the main points of tension' and to try to avoid concluding the Paris discussions until the results of the Washington talks were known (C.M. (50) 82nd Conclusions on CAB 128/18). Sir O. Harvey was instructed accordingly. On 7 December he reported that at the first meeting with French and American representatives held in Paris that day it was agreed that 'we should confine ourselves to drafting a reply to the Soviet Note. We established broad identity of

i *Annex A* examines in detail British terms for (*a*) global settlement including 'lifting of the Iron Curtain' (*b*) partial settlement e.g. in Germany and Austria or in Far East (*c*) eliminating major friction only: would lead to bargaining and 'any advantages gained would be more apparent than real'.
Annex B agenda for 4-Power talks for a global settlement.
Annex C draft reply to Soviet govt. [CAB 129/43].

ii *1–3 Dec. 1950 Spheres of interest* With reference to draft of No. 122, F.O. consider at Mr. Bevin's request possibility of settlement with Russia by delimitation of 'spheres of influence' as in percentage agreement over Balkans in 1944 (see Series I, Volume I, No. 185, note 4). Difficulties explained in minutes by Mr. Mallet and Mr. G.W. Harrison, Head of Northern Dept. These endorsed by Sir W. Strang, who considers an indefinite continuance of the cold war is 'the best we can hope for' [NS 1023/48].

view on the form which the Note should take (i.e. on the lines of the American draft) and are meeting again on December 8th to try to reach agreement on an identic text' (Paris telegram No. 530 Saving on C 7925/65/18).

No. 123

Record by Sir W. Strang of a conversation with the French Ambassador

[*WU 1195/492*]

FOREIGN OFFICE, *3 December 1950*

The French Ambassador came to see me this morning to say that, after their meeting with the Prime Minister and Foreign Secretary yesterday,[1] M. Pleven and M. Schuman had given further thought to the problem of Western defence in the hope of finding a compromise solution of the question of the German contribution. They had had another look at the proposal put forward by the Netherlands Deputy, on the instructions of Mr. Stikker, for the appointment of a North Atlantic High Commissioner who would have special duties in Germany in respect of the German forces.[2] Pleven thought that this proposal offered a possible way out and was prepared to consider it further. When he reported to his colleagues on Tuesday, the 5th December he would put to them as possible alternative solutions

(1) the suggestion outlined at the close of the meeting yesterday, namely that if a Supreme Commander could be appointed immediately, this might enable the French to move beyond M. Pleven's four points in the direction of the incorporation of the German forces;
(2) the Dutch plan.

[1] See No. 121.   [2] See No. 114, note 3.

M. Massigli explained that from the French point of view the advantage of the Dutch plan was that it would place the German forces under a North Atlantic political authority and not directly under a German political authority. The Dutch plan was of course an alternative to the French plan for a European Army, and if it were adopted the whole scheme for a North Atlantic Commander-in-Chief and a German contribution could go forward.

M. Massigli said that M. Pleven wished the Prime Minister and the Foreign Secretary to know his latest intentions before Mr. Attlee left for Washington. He hoped that H.M.G. would, for their part, do their best to promote a solution along one or the other of the two lines suggested.

M. Massigli added that M. Pleven had seen Mr. Spofford before leaving for Paris yesterday evening and had explained to him the two suggestions which he proposed to put to his colleagues in Paris next week. Mr. Spofford had been much interested and thought that something could be made of this.

I promised to inform the Prime Minister and the Foreign Secretary as soon as possible.[3]

W.S.

[3] A copy of this record was sent over to 10 Downing Street in time for the Prime Minister's meeting recorded in No. 124. On 4 December Sir P. Dixon gave Mr. Holmes an outline of the discussions recorded in Nos. 121 and 123. Sir P. Dixon observed that while the suggestion that the appointment of a N.A.T.O. High Commissioner might provide a solution 'French thought was developing in favour of the N A.T.O. conception and away from the European conception. We, of course, favoured this development. Mr. Holmes none the less thought that the French attitude was bad owing to their evident fear of provoking the Russians' (WU 1198/691).

No. 124

Note by the Secretary of the Cabinet

GEN 347/2 [F.O. 800/517]

Top secret   CABINET OFFICE, *4 December 1950*

At a meeting at No. 10 Downing Street on Sunday, 3rd December, the Prime Minister left instructions that the following points should be further considered after his departure to Washington, and the views on them telegraphed to him as soon as possible:

(*a*) *Rearmament of Germany*. The Foreign Secretary said that as a result of the conversations with the French Prime Minister and the French Foreign Minister,[1] he desired more time to consider the attitude which the United Kingdom should adopt towards the problem of the German

[1] See No. 121.

contribution to Western defence. He undertook to send his considered views to the Prime Minister in Washington.

(*b*) *United Kingdom Rearmament.* The Chancellor of the Exchequer said that it would perhaps be desirable, and even necessary, for the Prime Minister to be able to state to the President that the United Kingdom was willing to go through with its defence programme of £3.6 billions over the next three years and to rely upon the results of the Nitze exercise[2] giving the United Kingdom the amount and type of assistance which was shown to be appropriate. He would, however, like to consider whether a formal decision on this point should be sought from the Cabinet. A telegram could be sent to the Prime Minister.

(*c*) *Higher Direction of the Cold War.* The Foreign Secretary said that there was need of some procedure to enable the nations which had contributed to the United Nations forces in Korea to share in the control of the operations. Apart from that question, to which the Chiefs of Staff had already addressed their minds, there was the problem of achieving a properly co-ordinated, firm and rapid control in all areas of the world where trouble was likely, and over all material factors which were essential to the effective prosecution of the cold war. Recent events had shown how dangerous it was for one country to stockpile raw materials to the detriment of the defensive effort of its Allies. Some continuing Allied organisation for political, economic and strategic control was increasingly needed. The Foreign Secretary undertook, in consultation with the Chancellor of the Exchequer, to telegraph proposals to the Prime Minister on the political and economic organisations required.

(*d*) *Shortage of Raw Materials.* The Chancellor of the Exchequer said that some public announcement would have to be made within the next few days on the shortage of raw materials and the need to re-introduce control over some of them. The announcement would emphasise that the object of control would be to limit the use of scarce materials for less essential civil purposes and it would avoid giving the impression that there would be any weakening of the rearmament effort, or that there was any lack of co-ordination between the defence efforts of the United States and the United Kingdom. The nature of the announcement would be considered by the Economic Policy Committee on 5th December.[3]

NORMAN BROOK

[2] See No. 79.i–ii.

[3] At their meeting on 5 December (not printed from CAB 134/224) the Economic Policy Committee of the Cabinet (see No. 112, note 1) took note of the statement on the distribution of scarce metals, to be made by Mr. Strauss in the House of Commons on 7 December (*Parl. Debs., 5th ser., H. of C.*, vol. 482, cols. *83–5*). After the meeting Mr. Attlee was informed by Mr. Morrison that 'Ministers felt strongly that your discussion of this problem with President Truman afforded only hope of quick improvement in our position. Our difficulties in respect of each raw material are primarily due to United States action, and our lack of success so far in getting their co-operation has been result of absence of

i *6 Dec. 1950 Briefing for Mr. Attlee on (a) U.K. Defence Programme* dependent on expanding economy which is threatened by shortage of raw materials, as explained in Washington brief. H.M.G. does not claim 'any special position' compared with other members of N.A.T.O. and 'fully accepts' a defence strategy as far east as possible. Nevertheless reasons for special treatment put forward. Economic problems of defence, in particular shortage of raw materials, further explained in F.O. tel. to Washington No. 5478. Allocation scheme only effective if associated with combined boards and coordinated purchases. Represents need for prior Anglo-American agreement on guide lines. Commonwealth angle developed in F.O. tel. to Washington No. 5491 [PREM 8/1200; UE 11915/92; UR 1030/13]. (*b*) *Liaison* (*Higher direction of Cold War*) F.O. tel. to Washington No. 5477 explains need for closer global planning and war preparation with U.S. and Commonwealth since N.A.T.O. is directed mainly to European defence [UE 11915/91].

co-ordination between branches of United States administration. We feel therefore that you will wish to seek some solution of our difficulties through thorough discussion with the President, even at the cost, if necessary, of prolonging your stay in Washington by an additional day or two. Your colleagues would not wish you to feel rushed if useful discussion remains to be completed' (F.O. telegram to Washington No. 5463 on UR 1030/14).

No. 125

Mr. Bevin to Sir O. Franks (Washington)

No. 5438 Telegraphic [*WU 1195/487*]

Emergency. Top secret   FOREIGN OFFICE, *4 December 1950, 7.50 p.m.*

Following for Sir R. Makins from Sir P. Dixon.

You will remember that at the briefing meeting on Sunday evening[1] the Secretary of State expressed his doubts as to whether we should proceed with the plan for a German contribution to Western Defence and promised to send the Prime Minister his considered views after further thought.

2. The Secretary of State still feels that it would be wrong to take this step at the present time and has been fortified in this opinion by Sir D. Kelly.[2] A telegram was prepared in this sense, but the Lord President of

[1] No. 124.

[2] Sir D. Kelly, who was on recall to London for talks with the Foreign Office had a meeting with Mr. Bevin at 10 a.m. on 4 December. No record of this meeting has been traced. Under discussion was presumably the report from Sir D. Kelly (also untraced) to which Mr. Shinwell referred in discussion with the Chiefs of Staff that afternoon. Commenting on the draft of No. 128, Mr. Shinwell said that it 'appeared to have been based very largely on His Majesty's Ambassador to Moscow's report to the Foreign Secretary in which he had expressed very strongly the opinion that a decision by the N.A.T.O. Powers to

the Council and the Minister of Defence have expressed doubts about it, and the Chiefs of Staff are far from satisfied that it is the right line. A meeting is being arranged for 3.45 p.m. our time tomorrow, December 5th, after which a telegram will be sent to you urgently.[3]

3. We hope, therefore, that the Prime Minister may be able to avoid committing himself on this point with Mr. Truman for the moment. In the meantime, the position is being held in Deputies, though it will be difficult to continue this beyond Wednesday [6 December].

rearm the Germans would be provocative to the Russians and might tip the balance in favour of counter-preparations for a European war'. Nevertheless Mr. Shinwell and the Chiefs of Staff were agreed that the dangers of delaying German rearmament outweighed the dangers of proceeding. It was agreed that Mr. Shinwell would represent this view to Mr. Bevin at an early opportunity (C.O.S. (50) 194th meeting, Confidential Annex, minute 1, on DEFE 4/38).
[3] When arrangements for this meeting fell through, Mr. Morrison suggested that the Chiefs of Staff might be invited to the Cabinet meeting that afternoon (see No. 122, note 8) to discuss the question. This was evidently declined by Mr. Bevin in favour of the separate meeting with the Chiefs of Staff recorded at No. 126. A message was accordingly sent to Washington that it would not be possible to despatch a further telegram before noon on 6 December.

No. 126

Confidential Annex to the Minutes of a Staff Conference held in the Foreign Secretary's Room at the House of Commons on Tuesday, 5 December 1950, at 4 p.m.[1]

C.O.S. (50) 197th Meeting [*WU 1195/519*]

Top secret

Rearmament of Germany

(Previous Reference: C.O.S. (50) 194th Meeting, Min. 1)[2]

The Committee had before them a draft telegram[3] which it was proposed should be sent to the Prime Minister suggesting the line to be taken with the President of the United States on German Re-armament. Preliminary consideration had been given to this draft by the Minister of Defence and the Chiefs of Staff at the Staff Conference the previous evening,[2] as a result of which the Minister of Defence informed the Foreign Secretary of their views.

The Secretary of State for Foreign Affairs said that he had no intention

[1] *Present* at this meeting were Mr. Bevin (*in the Chair*); Mr. Shinwell; Admiral of the Fleet Lord Fraser; Marshal of the Royal Air Force Sir J. Slessor; Lieut-General N.C.D. Brownjohn representing the C.I.G.S.; Air Marshal Sir W. Elliot; Sir W. Strang; Sir D. Kelly; Sir P. Dixon; Sir F. Hoyer Millar; Mr. Mallet; Mr. Shuckburgh. *Secretary* Captain M.E. Butler-Bowdon.
[2] See No. 125, note 2.
[3] The early drafts of No. 128 are not preserved in Foreign Office archives.

whatever of going back on our previous agreement to the principle of German re-armament. He was, however, worried about the effect which the present situation in Korea would have on the ability of the United States to organise and make available American contributions to the defence of Western Europe. This had caused him to calculate what the Russians could do if they were to regard the re-arming of Germany as a provocative act. Though he did not necessarily fear such an eventuality, he considered it was most important to take account of the resulting situation with which we might be faced. The result of the first day's discussion between the Prime Minister and the President of the United States was not encouraging and it confirmed his attitude because there was clearly a danger of impetuous action being taken by the Americans which might expose us to a serious situation before we had time to do anything about it. In the face of this and the fact that there was as yet no evidence of American preparations to move reinforcements into Western Europe we could clearly not afford to gamble on the result of any decision which might provoke the Russians into action.

The Minister of Defence said that the problems at issue were – first, the timing of any announcement to re-arm the Germans, and secondly, the subsequent implementation of this decision. There was no doubt that there would be an appreciable interval of time between taking the decision and it being implemented in adequate measure. The salient point in the draft telegram to the Prime Minister was the effect on the Russians of an announcement that the N.A.T.O. powers had agreed to re-arm the Germans. The telegram also went on to say that the appointment of a Supreme Commander should be the first step and the build-up of Allied forces in Germany the second. Since a Supreme Commander must obviously concern himself at some stage with the question of German re-armament, surely his appointment would have no less effect on the Russians than an announcement of our intention to re-arm Germany. A very real situation which must be faced was that if, after having given our agreement in Washington to the principle of German re-armament and having struggled to get the French to come into line, we were now to say that we did not wish to proceed with the re-armament of Germany, it would have a most adverse effect not only in America but in Europe as well. However, as stated in paragraph 2 of the draft telegram, our agreement to this principle was based on the expectation that before any German re-armament actually took place there would be substantial Allied forces (including new American divisions) on the ground in Europe. We must now face the fact, however, that unless America and ourselves were to go on to a war footing there was no reasonable hope of providing the necessary formations to stem a Russian attack in the near future. Even if United States divisions were to be available in Western Europe next year we should still not have built up an adequate strength before 1953/54. It might well be that before we had built up the necessary strength the Russians might decide to attack; in view of this possibility it might therefore be better for us to take the risk of going ahead as soon as possible with our plans for the re-armament of Germany. It would anyway be difficult to convince the Americans of the validity of our fears that to proceed now with the re-armament of Germany might provoke the Russians. Accordingly it would be far better for us to go ahead quietly and steadily with our plan to build up the German forces and, if this view was accepted, there would be no need to send this telegram to the Prime Minister. In any case before making known to the Americans any misapprehensions we may have concerning the re-armament of Germany, it would certainly be wise for one of our representatives in America to take some soundings of United States views.

The First Sea Lord said that there had been no great fundamental change in the situation in the last three or four months and that having gone as far as we had with the case for re-arming Germany it would be extremely difficult for us to go back on it. The Military Committee and Defence Committee were due to meet very shortly and some statement would have to be made afterwards. If no statement were made the general interpretation could only be that negotiations had broken down. However, in the implementation of our policy it should be possible if necessary to soft pedal a bit. There was no doubt that any reversal of our policy would have a very adverse effect in America.

Sir John Slessor said that any going back on our policy would probably result in the Americans dissociating themselves from us and Western Europe and there would be no question of them appointing a Supreme Commander. On the question of the degree of provocation which the re-armament of Germany might have on the Russians, the two main features which had so far prevented them from advancing in Europe to the Channel coast were – first, the possession by the Western powers of the atomic bomb and secondly, that it was not part of the Russian plan to carry out such an attack so long as they were getting what they wanted without resort to such a course. If however anything were to cause the Russians to revise their plan and to attack Western Europe it was clearly not in our best interests to have a break in our relations with the United States.

Sir Pierson Dixon said that as he saw it the moment at which the Russians might be provoked on this question of re-arming Germany was when we started talking to the Germans on the subject. We might therefore be better advised to defer making any announcement of our intention or approach the Germans until the Foreign Secretary had considered what could be achieved in the Four-Power talks.

Sir David Kelly said that, as he appreciated the Russian attitude, they made a definite distinction between the Western Powers building up their forces and the question of Germany being re-armed. They accepted that it was natural, that we should be building up our forces and this was discounted in their plans. He considered, however, that their planning made no allowance for Germany being re-armed and that when they saw this happening they might revise their basic policy which had hitherto been to leave Western Europe alone. Whatever was our intention they would see in the outcome a steady growth in the military capabilities of Germany, and historically they had very good cause to fear this. The dangerous time was undoubtedly between the moment when we committed ourselves irrevocably to re-arm the Germans and the time when there was even a small German army in being. The Russians had asked for a conference on the demilitarisation of Germany and he considered that we should go to this conference without having committed ourselves to such a step beforehand. He did not however think that the Russians would have any objection to an armed Gendarmerie in Germany.

Sir William Strang said that in the Russian Note dated 20th October[4] they had used the phrase:

'The Soviet Government declares that it will not reconcile itself to such measures by the governments of Great Britain, the United States and France directed towards a restoration in Western Germany of a German regular army.'

An analogous statement was made on 3rd October by the Chinese Peoples Government declaring that if the United Nations forces went near the Manchurian border they would not stand idly by. We had taken no heed of this at the time; had we not better be very careful before we ignored the Russian's warning.[5]

In discussion on the dates of the forthcoming meetings of the Defence Committee and the Atlantic Council there was general agreement that it would be dangerous if it was known that Ministers were discussing the re-armament of Germany. It would be better if, on the pretext of the present situation in Korea, arrangements could be made to defer the North Atlantic Treaty meetings of Ministers for the time being.

Sir Pierson Dixon circulated a re-draft[3] of the Foreign Office telegram

---

[4] See No. 78, note 2.

[5] Cf. Volume IV. Sir W. Strang was here repeating the arguments he had advanced in a minute to Mr. Bevin of 5 December in which he reiterated his 'grave doubts' as to whether Germany should be rearmed at all (see No. 24). 'Nevertheless, if it is to be done, it should not be done until the Atlantic Powers have built up their defences in Western Europe and the Americans are substantially committed by the presence of further divisions.' With regard to Soviet objections to a German army he observed: 'They are not likely to draw nice distinctions as to its being integrated in a European or North Atlantic setting: if we arm Germans, we arm them . . . there may be worse things than risking the displeasure of the Americans by speaking our minds and asserting our own judgment. I am not here arguing for appeasement of the Russians, but for a measure of realistic caution.' Sir D. Gainer agreed in a separate minute of 6 December to Sir P. Dixon and considered that the Soviet attitude should be 'disregarded at our peril. Granted that the object of the Soviet Union was and is to prevent German rearmament in which object she could count on the earnest support of her Satellites, especially Poland, for us to back down now might appear to be a major political victory for Russia . . . but such a victory would be a small forfeit for us to pay at this moment or indeed for some time to come in order to prevent or delay a general war for which we and our friends are utterly unprepared' (C 8028/27/18: see further note 6).

which he suggested might meet the various points made in discussion.

Lieut-General Brownjohn said that paragraph 4 of the re-draft made no mention of the effect which any back-pedalling on our part might have on the Germans. It was important to take account of the fact that no success would be achieved in obtaining the German contribution to the defence of Western Europe unless the Germans were wholeheartedly behind us. If they were to feel that we had gone back on our policy it would make it very difficult for Dr. Adenauer to sustain the morale of Germany.[6]

> (Owing to a Cabinet meeting the Secretary of State for Foreign Affairs, the Minister of Defence, Sir William Strang and Mr. Mallet left the Conference at this point.)

Sir Pierson Dixon in resuming the discussion, said that the Foreign Secretary was seriously alarmed that any irrevocable step, such as making a direct approach to the Germans, might be taken which would have the result of setting the Russians on a course towards the early staging of a European war. He was further concerned that present events in Korea might result in no U.S. forces being made available for Europe and that, by taking such a step, we might be committed to having a German Army on paper and no support by U.S. forces. The Foreign Secretary would, therefore, prefer to defer taking any irrevocable step both until he could be assured that the Americans were definitely sending armed forces to Europe and until discussions between representatives of the three Governments on the possibility of talks with the Russians had indicated what we could expect to get out of such talks. The French seemed to be dropping their concept of a European Army, and the United States attitude towards it was uncertain. The great thing was to get them to appoint a Supreme Commander in Europe.

Sir David Kelly said that his feeling was that if we were to take any irrevocable steps towards re-arming Germany, there could be no certainty what the Russian reaction might be. At present, he thought that the Russians felt that they could get what they wanted by waiting, but if we were to re-arm the Germans it might just tip the balance into provoking them into an attack on Western Europe. There was no doubt that they respected German military arms more than those of the Americans. He

---

[6] In his minute of 6 December (see note 5), Sir D. Gainer thought that it was by no means certain that a cautious line on rearmament would further demoralize Germany: 'It may be we should find there a measure of relief in all political camps that this issue has been postponed and we might utilize this breathing space to pursue our work of bringing Germany into closer political relations with Western Europe, work which at this moment is being gravely complicated by the question of German rearmament which tends seriously to confuse the issue.' Sir P. Dixon minuted below that the whole of Sir D. Gainer's minute 'accords very closely with the views of the Secretary of State. The view expressed by Sir D. Gainer in the last para. of his minute really clinches the argument in favour of caution: our one reservation had been on the score of the possible demoralisation which might ensue in Germany as a result of a go-slow policy over German rearmament.' These minutes were seen by Sir W. Strang on 7 December and later by Mr. Bevin and Mr. Mallet.

was pretty sure that they would raise no objection to the arming of a German gendarmerie; furthermore, they would have less objection to the participation of German units in a European Army than to the setting up of an actual German Army.

Sir John Slessor said that, after the pressure which the United States and ourselves had imposed on the French last September, there was no doubt that if we were to go back on our agreed principle to re-arm the Germans, we would disintegrate any hope both of getting American assistance for Europe and of eventually raising a German Army. Dr. Adenauer had, furthermore, recently pointed out that German morale was deteriorating and that there might come a stage when they would turn their allegiance towards the East.

The First Sea Lord said that it was most important that we should make it quite clear to the President of the United States that we remained firm in our agreement to the principle of German re-armament but that the only change we were making was a proposal to defer its announcement.

Sir William Elliot said that we recognised that the French plan was militarily impracticable. It was quite clear from what Mr. Marshall had said that he would not be prepared to appoint a high-ranking officer to the post of Supreme Commander if the European plan was an impracticable one. At the New York meeting in September, Mr. Acheson had made it clear that the sending of American forces to Europe depended on the situation in Korea.

Lieut-General Brownjohn said that we must remember that even if all had gone well in Korea, it would not have been physically possible for the United States to have provided forces in Europe as yet. However, if we were half-hearted in our attitude towards German re-armament it may well have the effect of causing the United States to drop any idea of sending their forces.

Sir John Slessor said that, in informing the President of the United States of our views, he suggested that the Prime Minister should take the line that, in view of the present situation in Korea and the possibility of war with China, we fully realised that the Americans were not in a position at the moment to send reinforcements to Europe and that, accordingly, whilst we still fully agreed with the principle of re-arming the Germans, we should defer any decision to do so at the moment.

Sir Derek Hoyer-Miller said that if we were to go back on the policy of re-arming the Germans, we should certainly set the smaller nations against us. However, we could say to them that surely it was better for them to continue in some uncertainty for a further six months rather than that action should be taken which might plunge them into danger now.

In discussion there was general agreement that, in the light of the above views the Foreign Office should prepare a redraft of the telegram to the Prime Minister with the object of getting agreement to it in time for despatch by noon to-morrow, Wednesday, 6th December.

The Committee:

Took note that the Foreign Office would as a matter of urgency, prepare a redraft of the telegram to the Prime Minister.[7]

[7] When this further redraft (text on CAB 21/1899) was discussed by the Chiefs of Staff on the morning of 6 December, Sir W. Elliot reported that the Minister of Defence 'still did not like the telegram . . . If a telegram was to be sent at all it should be sent from the Foreign Secretary giving only his views which seemed to be based very much on those of Sir David Kelly. The Minister of Defence was not equally impressed with Sir David Kelly's arguments . . . In discussion there was general agreement that although the Chiefs of Staff did not agree with the advice being given to the Prime Minister, they should not dissociate themselves from the telegram but should press for their views to be included in it. In the Foreign Secretary's opinion, to proceed at the present time with the announcement of a decision to re-arm Germany might be taking an undue risk of leading us into war, and the reason for postponing the matter was mainly political' (Confidential Annex to C.O.S. (50) 198th Meeting on DEFE 4/38).

No. 127

Sir O. Franks (Washington) to Mr. Bevin
(Received 6 December, 3.40 a.m.)

No. 3289 Telegraphic [WU 1198/661]

Emergency. Secret   WASHINGTON, 5 December 1950, 9.47 p.m.

Repeated to Paris and Wahnerheide.

At the end of the talk between the Prime Minister and President this afternoon, Acheson said that an urgent matter had arisen in connexion with the Spofford Plan now before the Atlantic Council Deputies and proposed that this should be followed up immediately between officials.[1] Acheson had mentioned this casually earlier in the day and remarked that some further thought would have to be given to the relationship of the United States, Canada and the United Kingdom to the European members of the N.A.T.O.

2. Accordingly Makins and Steel saw Perkins and other State Department officials this evening.

3. The position is that the French have proposed to the Americans that, in order to facilitate a favourable French attitude to the plan now before the Deputies, and (sic) United States Government should formally address to the French Government a statement on the lines of Mr. Acheson's

[1] Mr. Acheson was speaking at the second formal meeting between Mr. Attlee and President Truman on the afternoon of 5 December. The talks between Mr. Attlee and President Truman opened on 4 December and concluded on 8 December. Their discussions in relation to the Far East and use of the atomic bomb (1st, 2nd, 5th and 6th meetings) will be covered in Volume IV. The British records of the six formal meetings and related papers are filed on F.O. 371/124949: ZP 3 of 1951. The American records are printed in F.R.U.S. 1950, vol. iii, pp. 1706–1782: ibid., pp. 1783–7 and Cmd. 8110 for the communiqué issued on 8 December.

message to M. Schuman of 29th November (see telegram No. 11 Saving from United Kingdom representative on Atlantic Council to Foreign Office).[2]

4. The French prepared a text of this letter which has been redrafted by the Americans. The text of this draft which is not necessarily final is contained in my immediately following telegram.[3] The Americans have been informed that the French Cabinet will take a final decision on their attitude to the Spofford Plan and their instructions to Alphand at their meeting tomorrow morning December 6th and they wish to communicate this letter to the French Government before this meeting. The French Government would publish it at the moment when agreement in the Deputies was approved and announced. The United States Embassy in Paris had advised that the document was necessary if a favourable reply was to be obtained from the French and that it must be handed in tomorrow morning. The State Department admitted that they did not know precisely what decisions the French were prepared to take in return for the statement.

5. We first asked Perkins whether the prospective agreement in the Deputies would enable the United States Government to proceed with the appointment of a Supreme Commander. Perkins said that no decision had been taken on this but he thought that it was very probable.

6. We then asked what was meant by the expression 'a plan for bringing the free nations of Europe more closely together', in the third paragraph and the phrase 'European integration' in the fourth paragraph.[4] Perkins replied that they were not quite sure but that it meant something more than the European army. Subsequent conversation showed that they had in fact no clear idea what was meant but were thinking vaguely of Federal institutions.

7. We then said that a formal statement of this kind from government to government was a highly important matter. We drew attention to your speech in the House of Commons last Monday[5] and stressed the

[2] See No. 120, note 1.

[3] For the text of this redraft, in which Mr. Acheson welcomed the French initiative for a Paris conference to formulate proposals for a European Army and offered to send an observer to it, see *F.R.U.S. 1950*, vol. iii, pp. 523–4 and note 4 below for the text of paragraphs 3–4, as transmitted in Washington telegram No. 3290.

[4] Paragraphs 3–4 read: 'If your Government in close consultation with the German and other European Governments who wish to participate can evolve the main outlines of a plan for bringing the free nations of Europe more closely together in the spirit so well represented by the Schuman Plan, we can reasonably hope for long term solutions of many of our problems, be they political, military or economic. 4. I do not need to remind you of the attitude which the Government of the United States has displayed on innumerable occasions, and in many forms, toward European integration. My Government strongly favours it. If the European countries can work it out in a practical manner, a sound basis would be laid upon which military and economic strength can be built. A rallying point will be created around which a free and civilised Europe can muster its energies for a successful defense of its beliefs and the traditions of its history' (WU 1198/662).

[5] This is an error for Wednesday, 29 November: see No. 119, note 3.

335

difference of approach and emphasis between the two statements.[6] The Americans admitted this but said that in their view their draft was little more than a repetition of a number of declarations which they had made in the past.

8. We repeated that we thought that the effect of the document would be far-reaching and would be replied [*sic*] upon by the French Government in negotiations for a long time to come. We suggested that its precise implications should be fully thought out. In particular we said that it was essential that you should have an opportunity of considering the position which would be created by the delivery of such a communication and the line which His Majesty's Government might wish to adopt before action was taken in Paris. We were not impressed by the urgency of acting tomorrow. We therefore formally asked the State Department not to proceed until you had had an opportunity of seeing it.

9. Perkins subsequently telephoned to say that Acheson would hold up action until the matter could be considered tomorrow. It will come up at meeting between Prime Minister and President fixed for 4.00 p.m. tomorrow. I should be grateful for your views before then.[7]

Foreign Office please repeat Emergency to Paris as my telegram No. 96 and to Wahnerheide as my telegram No. 69.

[6] When making this point at the second Attlee-Truman meeting (note 1) Sir R. Makins added: 'The French position had changed in the last few days. On Saturday [2 December] they had favoured a proposal for a High Commissioner as an alternative to a European Defense Minister but now they had swung back to the latter alternative and were asking U.S. blessing on that. *Secretary Acheson* said that any solution to move forward was better than doing nothing. *The President* said he thought that something could be done' (American record: *F.R.U.S. 1950*, vol. iii, pp. 1738–9).

[7] This telegram and telegram No. 3290 (note 3) were considered by the Chiefs of Staff Committee on 6 December. Mr. Shuckburgh informed the Committee that 'the Foreign Secretary had only just seen these telegrams and was opposed generally to the text of the communication to be sent to the French Government. It in effect amounted to approval of the French Plan and indicated American support for European integration and a European Army. The policy in paragraph 4 would inevitably expose us to pressure to participate to some extent in any federation in Europe. He was not, however, opposed to the suggestion for holding a Conference. In discussion there was general agreement that this was largely a political matter. We were committed under the Spofford Plan to give further examination to this matter and, unless a matter of principle was at stake, we would not be justified in opposing the U.S. proposal to send this communication to the French Government' (C.O.S. (50) 198th Meeting, Confidential Annex, on WU 1195/511).

No. 128

Mr. Bevin to Sir O. Franks (Washington)

No. 5485 Telegraphic [WU 1198/683]

Emergency. Top secret   FOREIGN OFFICE, 6 December 1950, 5.10 p.m.

My telegram No. 5438[1] (of 4th December; Atlantic Defence).
Following for Prime Minister.

I have been giving further thought to the question of a German contribution to Western Defence, and have discussed the matter fully with the Lord President of the Council, Minister of Defence and Chiefs of Staff.[2] The following represents our views on the subject.

2. The position is that until the developments reported in your telegram No. 3289[3] the Deputies had thought they were on the point of reaching agreement on a plan, based on the 'Spofford compromise' perhaps modified to provide for some kind of N.A.T.O. (North Atlantic Treaty Organisation) Commissioner or Political Representative, under which a German contribution could be raised. The French were known to be seeking to preserve the chances of a European Army solution, but it was hoped that it might be possible to overcome this difficulty. Once agreement is reached in the Deputies the idea under present plans would be that it should be referred to the Military Committee later this week and then to the Defence Committee and the Council, and if nothing occurs to delay matters, the approach to the German Government might take place before Christmas. At any point from agreement in the Deputies to the actual approach to the Germans the world is likely to become aware that a definite and irrevocable decision has been reached to create regular German army units.

3. We are very much concerned as to the effect which this is likely to have on the general situation at the present time, having regard to the position of extreme weakness in which the Western Powers now find themselves and the grave doubts which we must feel as to whether any American reinforcement of Europe is possible in the near future. We think that you should discuss the position frankly with President Truman and see whether he does not share our doubts and whether he does not

---

[1] No. 125.

[2] See No. 126 and note 7 *ibid*. When Mr. Morrison saw the draft of this telegram, he minuted: 'It is difficult for me to accept this at such short notice. I have no objection to the Secretary of State sending it as his personal opinion with a warning that there may be other views in the Cabinet, including me. The Minister of Defence has a reserve on paragraph 5 which I share ... I am disposed to agree with the Chiefs of Staff's apprehensions (see paragraph 6 of telegram). I see the Foreign Secretary's case and am by no means indifferent to it. If we appear to be jittery and the Soviet see us on the run we may add to our troubles. This is high policy and should be decided by the Cabinet. H.M.' (WU 1198/683): see further note 8. Paragraph 5 was amended as requested and an emergency telegram sent after despatch with instructions for deleting the reference to Mr. Morrison in paragraph 1.

[3] No. 127.

consider some caution is required. We recognise of course that the matter is extremely delicate, as we must not give the Americans the impression that we are retreating from our agreement to the principle of a German contribution; but the issues are so serious for Europe that we think the timing of any announcement and approach to the Germans must be most carefully considered in relation to all the other factors in the world situation.

4. The first major factor which influences our thought is that the circumstances in which we would be initiating this action are entirely different from those which obtained when we first agreed with the Americans that it was safe to embark on German rearmament. It will be recalled that the American proposal for the rearmament of Germany was part of a 'packet' which included not only the appointment of a Supreme Commander but also the offer of the United States to send substantial reinforcements to Europe at an early date. It was of course always quite clear to us that the speed with which these reinforcements could be sent was conditional upon the satisfactory clearing up of the Korean situation, and this was expressly stated by Mr. Acheson at the New York meetings in September. At the same series of meetings, General Marshall gave a verbal assurance to M. Moch and Mr. Shinwell (at a private meeting of which no record was made)[4] that it was planned to send 5½ divisions to Europe during 1951. The situation until ten days ago gave good reason to hope that these expectations would be fulfilled, and that there would not be a very long gap between any invitation to the Germans to begin raising forces and the arrival of substantial Allied reinforcements in Europe. This no longer holds. Moreover we cannot even be sure, until the consequences of the present Korean developments are more clear, that we are not going to be faced with a situation in the Far East in which a large proportion of Allied military resources would be tied up for a long time to come. At the same time we are uncertain, until we know the results of your discussions with President Truman, whether American policy in regard to raw materials etc. is going to be such as will enable us to carry out our own rearmament programme, far less contribute to rearmament of Germany. A definitive and public decision to rearm Germany at a moment of such weakness and uncertainty is a very much more dubious proposition than we had previously envisaged.

5. We want to be sure that the President has fully considered the effects of the completely changed situation and the possible risks of the action proposed at this moment. We are assured by Sir D. Kelly[5] that the recreation of regular German armed forces is something which the Russians would regard as altogether different in character from, and more provocative than, any measures taken by the Western Powers themselves to increase their armed strength. They have a deep and

---

[4] See No. 42 and note 6 *ibid*.
[5] The phrase 'and we are impressed by his arguments' was deleted here before despatch (see note 2).

genuine fear of German armed forces, by which they were so nearly destroyed, and the reappearance of such forces, in numbers which they would not believe we had any intention of limiting, would be something which might lead them to re-cast the policy in regard to Europe. At present they are hoping that Europe will fall to them through its own weaknesses and under the weight of rearmament. The raising of German forces might tip the scale with them in favour of a policy leading to a European war. We think it should not be forgotten, moreover, that in their Note of 20th October[6] to the three Powers they used the phrase: 'The Soviet Government declares that it will not reconcile itself to such measures by the Governments of Great Britain, the United States and France directed towards a restoration in Western Germany of a German regular army.' It might be no less dangerous to ignore this warning in our present condition of weakness than it was to ignore the warning of the Chinese in regard to an approach to the Manchurian border by United Nations forces.

6. I feel you must have all points of view and the following is the Chiefs of Staffs' opinion. They feel that we must recognise the very serious result, after all the publicity that has been given to Allied policy on German rearmament, of any back-pedalling at the eleventh hour; that it would inevitably be taken by the Communist powers as a sign of weakness; that in Germany, its possible effects are clear from Adenauer's attitude as disclosed in Sir I. Kirkpatrick's telegram No. 1706 (of 1st December);[7] and that it would inevitably cause confusion and increase the tendency to defeatism in France. The Chiefs of Staff are extremely anxious about these factors and in addition they feel there are the gravest dangers in anything that might cause a serious disagreement between the United Kingdom and the United States at this time. They feel that unless United States themselves are thinking on these lines, the effect of this approach may be to eliminate all hope of getting a United States Supreme Commander or the despatch of additional American forces to Europe before the outbreak of war.

7. I understand these grave doubts on the part of the Chiefs of Staff. It seems to me that the question turns largely on how it is handled with the Americans, since, in their present excitable frame of mind, there might certainly be a dangerous reaction. Would it not therefore be wise for you to have a private talk with the President, Mr. Acheson and General Marshall, without advisers present, and make our position clear to them. You could then make it absolutely clear to them that there is no running away on our part; that we are speaking as friends, who are thinking of them in their present grave anxieties and responsibilities and who, for our part, have to remember our own exposed position in Europe. We are asking them to take into account our views before we take a final plunge which might bring a reaction before we are ready to meet it. There is no

[6] See No. 78, note 2.   [7] See No. 120.i.

question of our going back on our agreement to the principle of German rearmament which is essential for the defence of Western Europe. We think, however, that we should consider most carefully in the light of the Far Eastern situation the *timing* of any announcement of our intention actually to initiate the first steps in German rearmament. There are two main factors:

(*a*) Outcome of your discussions with the President on the overall strategic policy as between Far East and Europe, and on raw materials;
(*b*) Outcome of discussions between representatives of the three Governments on the possibility of talks with the Russians. We should perhaps wait to see whether definitive action in regard to German rearmament would not be of value as a bargaining counter in this connexion.

8. On balance I consider that, on the assumption that agreement is reached this week in the Deputies,

(*a*) no public announcement of that fact should be made for the present;
(*b*) further action would be considered in the light of the outcome of the discussions referred to in (*a*) and (*b*) of paragraph 7 above.
(*c*) the effect of this on the timing for the meetings of the Military Committee and the Defence Committee would have to be considered further.

9. As regards your telegram No. 3289,[3] please see my immediately following telegram.[8]

[8] No. 129. As this telegram was being prepared for despatch, Mr. Bevin was informed by his Assistant Private Secretary, Mr. K.M. Wilford, of Mr. Morrison's minute (note 2). Mr. Wilford added that 'The Lord President therefore wishes either: (1) that you should send the gist of this minute to the Prime Minister, or (2) that there should be a Cabinet meeting this evening to thrash out these points.' Mr. Wilford noted below that 'The Secretary of State decided to adopt course (1)'. At 6.22 p.m. that evening an emergency telegram was despatched to Washington (see note 2) which instructed that action be suspended pending receipt of a further telegram. This telegram No. 5498 despatched at 7 p.m. contained the substance of Mr. Morrison's minute and a message from Mr. Bevin to Mr. Attlee that 'Lord President and I feel that we can only leave it to you to decide whether to open this question with the President on the lines of my telegram. Should you decide to do so you will, I know, do it in an intimate and confidential way. 3. You will appreciate that with the rush of events I have not been able to send considered views of Cabinet' (WU 1198/685).

No. 129

Mr. Bevin to Sir O. Franks (Washington)

No. 5486 Telegraphic [WU 1198/661]

Emergency. Secret   FOREIGN OFFICE, 6 December 1950, 3 p.m.

Repeated to Wahnerheide, Paris and Moscow.

Your telegrams Nos. 3289 and 3290[1] (of 5th December): German contribution to defence of Europe.

This is of course intimately affected by the considerations in my immediately preceding telegram.

As we understand it, this proposal is in effect a new Franco-American package. The French will agree to the 'Spofford compromise' (see my immediately following telegram). In return for that agreement, and as part of it, the Americans will come out publicly in favour of 'European integration' and a European Army

2. Such a declaration on a fundamental issue on which, as the Americans well know, we and the French hold radically different views, would have far-reaching and lasting effects on our whole policy. We could not, therefore, possibly agree to approve at a few hours notice and in the midst of a crisis of first magnitude any package of which such a declaration was an essential part.

3. We must not be rushed into decisions of this importance. We cannot allow our whole future policy towards Europe to be settled merely on the ba[s]is of temporary expedients. We cannot even be sure that these expedients are necessary. The French Government have already changed their minds three or four times within the last week. Our last official indication of their views was that they were prepared to drop the European Army idea for the present, and to develop the Dutch proposal for a N.A.T.O. (North Atlantic Treaty Organisation) High Commissioner. Even the United States Government do not seem to be quite sure what they are about. In your telegram No. 3277[2] (of 4th December) the State Department say that Mr. Acheson's message to M. Schuman 'did not commit the United States in any way to a favourable view of a European Army'. In the midst of such uncertainty we cannot reasonably be expected to approve a proposal of such far-reaching and fundamental character as the new Franco-American package.

4. In any event, as you will see from my immediately preceding telegram, we do not think irrevocable decisions regarding a German contribution to Western defence can be taken at this moment. In our view, the Deputies and the military authorities should reach agreement on the plan, but nothing should be published for the present and there should be no meeting of Ministers. In these circumstances, we should see grave

---

[1] See No. 127 and note 3 ibid.   [2] See No. 120, note 4.

objection to the United States publishing their present views on European integration in this formal manner at this time.

5. In short, our position is:

(*a*) that, if an American declaration on European integration is the price of French agreement to the 'Spofford compromise' we for our part, shall have to reconsider our attitude to that compromise; and
(*b*) that there is no immediate urgency to reach a decision on this wider question, which requires much further thought.

6. We shall be seeing the Americans and the French today and will explain our views to them on the above lines.[3]

[3] At a Foreign Office meeting with Mr. Holmes and Mr. Spofford later that day Sir P. Dixon stated the British position and protested strongly about the proposed American letter to the French government. Mr. Spofford maintained that the only new element was the American offer to send observers to a conference on a European Army. Sir P. Dixon pointed out that under the new formula, 'the United States now proposed to take an active interest, as observers at the Paris conference, not only in the European Army idea but also in a wider confederation.' Mr. Holmes emphasised that undue delay in reaching agreement in the Deputies 'would be dangerous'. It was finally agreed to wait until more was known of the French position (record of meeting in WU 1198/693). When Sir P. Dixon and Sir F. Hoyer Millar saw M. Massigli immediately afterwards, they spoke on similar lines and repeated Foreign Office concern at the prospect of immediate publication of the letter. M. Massigli gave reassurances that he did not think this likely since 'from latest reports it appeared that the French Cabinet were not agreed on the subject of German rearmament. He thought, however, that the American proposal was probably needed by M. Pleven in order to carry the Socialists . . . M. Massigli later told me that, according to M. Alphand, there was no question of publishing the letter to M. Schuman until the Atlantic Council had met and approved the defence plan' (minute by Dixon on WU 1195/507).

No. 130

Mr. Bevin to Sir O. Franks (Washington)

No. 5487 Telegraphic [*WU 1198/663*]

Immediate. Secret   FOREIGN OFFICE, *6 December 1950, 4.45 p.m.*

Repeated to Paris, Wahnerheide, Moscow.

Your telegram No. 3292[1] (of 5th December) German contribution to Western Defence.

The position in the Deputies is as follows:

By the end of last week agreement had been reached on practically the whole of the draft report (document D.D. 196 revised),[2] the effect of

[1] With reference to No. 127, this telegram (WU 1198/663) asked for clarification of the basis on which the Deputies were nearing agreement and added 'It looks as if the United States Embassy in Paris may already be committed in principle to giving the French a document on the general lines of the draft in my telegram No. 3290' (No. 127, note 3).

[2] Not printed: see No. 133, note 3.

which was to recommend to the Defence Committee and the Council that the 'Spofford Plan' be adopted. Or in other words that an immediate approach to the Germans be made by the three Occupying Powers with a view to securing a German military contribution on the lines recommended by the Military Committee in their report (MC 30).[3] Simultaneously the French would summon those European Powers which wished to attend to meet in Paris to consider the French plan for a European army, etc.

2. The only passages in the report still in dispute concerned

(a) Whether or not it should ever be possible before the formation of a European army to turn the German brigade groups into larger units.
(b) Whether Germany should be allowed a tactical air force.
(c) Whether the Deputies should simply 'take note' of the French intention to hold their conference about the European Army or whether they should give the French proposals some kind of blessing.

The French reserved their attitude on (a) and (b) and were pressing for some wording in (c) more favourable to the French ideas, than the other Deputies, (barring perhaps the United States and Belgium) were prepared to agree to.[4]

3. Over the weekend the French let it be known that they would find it much easier to accept the 'Spofford Plan' and the Deputies' report if something could be inserted into the latter on the lines of the Dutch proposal for the appointment of a N.A.T.O. (North Atlantic Treaty Organisation) High Commissioner, one of whose tasks would be to assist the Allied High Commissioners in their supervision of German rearmament.[5] If and when the Allied High Commissioners were withdrawn, then the powers of supervision might be taken over by the N.A.T.O. High Commissioner. In consequence the Deputies spent Monday, December 4th in discussing this idea of a N.A.T.O. High Commissioner and we put forward a modified proposal (see my telegram to Wahnerheide No. 1945[5]). Subsequently we and the Dutch undertook to see whether we could produce a compromise proposal between us and after consultation with Sir I. Kirkpatrick and the Chiefs-of-Staff, we have now produced, in agreement with the Dutch and Americans, another formula. The effect of this would merely be to say that the Deputies had considered the idea of a N.A.T.O. High Commissioner, thought that it had a good deal to commend it, and recommended that further study be

[3] See No. 106, note 2.
[4] Discussion by the Deputies on the precise wording of the report is not followed through in detail in this volume. See, however, No. 136, note 10 for the eventual resolution of point (a), and para. 5(ix) of Annex A to No. 136 for agreement on (b). The wording as regards (c) was not significantly changed, the point being covered by a separate arrangement between the American and French governments: see note 7 below and para. 3 of Annex A to No. 136.
[5] See calendar i.

given to the matter and to the powers which might be given to the High Commissioner.

4. The French did give the impression to us and to several of the other Deputies that if we could meet them in this way by bringing in some reference to a N.A.T.O. High Commissioner they would no longer press for the Deputies to give a blessing to their own plan, and would in fact probably let the matter slip into the background for the time being at all events.

5. It had, however, been hoped that final agreement on the Deputies report might have been reached at the Deputies meeting this afternoon, especially since the Americans were apparently prepared to agree to a form of wording on brigade groups which was acceptable to the French. We heard yesterday afternoon, however, that the French had gone into reverse, had more or less lost interest in the N.A.T.O. High Commissioner and were once again pressing for a blessing, if not from the Deputies, then at all events from the United States Government for their own ideas.[6]

6. This reversal may well be due to the intervention of the United States Embassy in Paris which we know has been in close touch with the French during the last few days.[7]

[6] In a minute to Mr. Bevin of 5 December on this development, Sir F. Hoyer Millar suggested that 'what may have happened is that M. Pleven on his return to Paris has been encouraged by the American Ambassador there to pursue the French ideas. We know that Mr. McCloy has been arguing strongly in favour of the European idea and we know too that those elements in the State Department who favour the idea of an integrated Europe have been much disappointed by the apparent French abandonment of the idea.' Sir P. Dixon commented: 'This further change of front on the part of the French is irritating but perhaps not disastrous. Adoption of the French plan would involve delay in the formation of German units. The Secretary of State's view is that in present circumstances delay would be desirable in order to keep the door open with the Russians and prevent them from committing themselves to preparations for a European war. It remains to be seen whether the United States are prepared to announce that the plan for a European army is approved by them. If they are prepared to do this and to agree that a settlement of this question in principle will enable them to appoint the Supreme Commander and start the build-up of the integrated force, I think it might suit us to accept the new French proposal. Sir D. Kelly does not think that the calling of a conference in Paris to discuss the German contribution would be particularly provocative to the Russians' (WU 1195/506).

[7] Mr. Bevin, who had asked that morning for information on the Deputies, minuted on the draft of this telegram: 'This is all very puzzling. I will go into it again in the morning E.B. [see No. 133, note 2]. What do we do if Berlin is occupied by a large force immediately we announce E.B.' When the Deputies met on the afternoon of 6 December they agreed to defer finalising their Report until the following day when it was hoped the French representative would have his instructions. M. Alphand 'had every confidence that it would be favourable. He added that if his Government decided to accept the Spofford Plan, they would make a communication to all the other 11 member countries in which they would explain clearly to their partners the spirit which animated them in giving their approval to the plan by which he presumably meant that the French Government would reiterate their attachment to the idea of closer cooperation in Europe' (U.K. Deputy tel. No. 19 Saving on WU 1195/501). Sir O. Franks was informed that 'From what the Americans told us after the meeting it was clear that the French Government's acceptance of the Report tomorrow will be conditional on their receiving an assurance from the Americans that the latter will send them a letter on the lines indicated in your telegram No. 3290' (F.O. tel. to Washington No.

i *4 Dec. 1950 Revised Dutch proposal for N.A.T.O. High Commissioner.* F.O. tel. to Wahnerheide No. 1943 reports that proposal, originally dismissed by French (see No. 114, note 3), is being revived by them now that European Army is 'non-starter' so as to provide more permanent agency than A.H.C. for exercising controls over German rearmament. British objections to new text, transmitted in tel. 1944, are explained with alternative British text in tel. 1945, approved at C.O.S. meeting on 4 Dec. Strong criticisms from Sir I. Kirkpatrick in reply on 5 Dec. (Wahn. tels. 1733–4) include fact that 'Dutch proposal shows clearly that its authors have no conception whatever of the present situation in Germany.' Proposed appointment would undermine supreme authority of A.H.C. quite apart from 'insuperable political difficulties' of getting Germans to accept transfer of controls to a new agency. Publicity already given to proposal by *Die Welt* could be damaging. Issue settled by inclusion of a 'non-committal' paragraph (text in Wahn. tel. 1201 Saving) in the Deputies' Report [WU 1195/489, 494; WU 10741/4; C 7858/27/18].

5509 on WU 1198/680). On 7 December Sir O. Franks reported that 'active negotiation is evidently going on in Paris and the French are pressing for a reversion to something nearer to their own original text . . . State Department were informed flatly that their own text was bad enough from our point of view and that reversion to earlier drafts would make it worse. They promised to send instructions to Paris accordingly but I have little faith that they will hold fast. They had evidently already fully committed themselves in the matter' (Washington telegram No. 3313 on WU 1198/682). Sir O. Franks was instructed on 9 December to find out more about the proposed French statement and about the negotiations between the Quai d'Orsay and the American Embassy in Paris since 'French Embassy here claim to know very little about them' (WU 1198/682).

No. 131

Sir O. Franks (Washington) to Mr. Bevin
(Received 7 December, 4.47 a.m.)

No. 3309 Telegraphic [WU 1198/681]

Emergency. Secret   WASHINGTON, *6 December 1950, 8.59 p.m.*

Your telegrams Nos. 5485 and 5498.[1]
Following for Foreign Secretary from Prime Minister.
I gave a great deal of thought to your telegrams before I went into the meeting with the President, Mr. Acheson and Mr. Marshall this afternoon.[2]

2. I did so against the background of the talks in the last two days.

3. The talks on the Far East have been difficult owing to the reconciliation which has to be made between the American and British points of view but it is possible that this will be achieved before I leave.

[1] No. 128 and note 8 *ibid.*
[2] See No. 132 for the full telegraphic report of this fourth meeting between Mr. Attlee and President Truman of which part is summarized below.

4. On raw materials this morning [i] the attitude of the President and his advisers was markedly encouraging. The President has given directive to the heads of all the agencies that action must be taken on this problem before I leave and it was openly recognised on the American side that this raw material problem was one which had to be considered in the first instance by United States and United Kingdom although there will surely be the usual difficulties in reaching agreement on individual matters down the line the approach at the top level was all that could be desired.[3] At the same time Field Marshal Slim has had encouraging talks with General Bradley about Anglo-American military cooperation and organisation.[4]

5. At this afternoon's meeting I opened by endeavouring to ascertain the present American thinking on how to proceed with Western European defence.

6. The President began by saying that in spite of the Far Eastern situation Europe was their primary concern. They felt it essential to proceed to further action. They had heard that it was now possible to reach agreement with the French on the Spofford Plan in terms satisfactory to the United States military authorities and it could be recommended to Congress.[5] As soon as agreement was reached in the Military Committee and the Deputies (and they thought that the meeting of Defence Ministers might be dispensed with) they would proceed to nominate General Eisenhower as Supreme Commander.[6] They hoped

[3] The discussions at Washington on raw materials are calendared at i below. The agreement reached for 'best efforts both to increase production and to assure the most effective use of the limited supplies available' through the establishment of a network of commodity groups overseen by a small central group was pursued by negotiation at official level throughout December: correspondence on F.O. 371/82879–82 (UE 11915) and F.O. 371/86987 (UR 1030).

[4] Further to these talks (not here documented) Mr. Attlee handed a memorandum suggesting arrangements for greater liaison in the military and economic spheres to President Truman at their fifth meeting on 7 December. This memorandum, based on the telegram at No. 124.i(*b*), is printed in *F.R.U.S. 1950*, vol. iii, pp. 1782–3. That evening in conversation with President Truman after dinner at the British Embassy, Field-Marshal Slim and Lord Tedder 'urged very strongly both the feasibility and the desirability of some regular and closer contacts between the Chiefs of Staff on both sides and stated their view that this could be arranged without formally reconstituting the Combined Chiefs of Staff ... *The President* was sympathetic to these representations and without committing himself to any specific arrangements finally remarked that the United Kingdom and United States were the only people who could be relied upon to fight and he felt sure that good arrangements could be worked out' (F.O. 371/124949; ZP 3/1). At the sixth and last meeting on 8 December (see calendar i) President Truman repeated that the suggestion was a good one but that he would have to discuss further with his military advisers. On 16 February 1951 Mr. Attlee was informed by Mr. Younger of Anglo-American arrangements for regular but informal exchanges of views at Ambassadorial level on policy in the military and politico-military fields at the formative stage (F.O. 800/517).

[5] At a meeting on the evening of 6 December the French Cabinet agreed to instruct M. Alphand to accede to the Deputies Report: see further No. 133, note 3.

[6] At the Embassy dinner on 7 December (note 4) 'General Marshall made it clear that the Americans were anxious not to create a precedent in the matter of a Supreme Commander in Europe. He raised the question of the relationship which the Supreme Commander

that this might be done next week. They were also prepared to send reinforcements to Europe, though they would now be composed of national guard units. They believed this would encourage Europe and would also be encouraging to the American people. They were sure of us and now that the French had come into line they felt confident enough to go ahead.

7. In the face of these declarations which gave us the satisfaction on the broad issues which we have been seeking for many months it appeared to me to be unthinkable that we should say on our side that we now wished to pause and draw back. To have done so would, in the opinion of everyone here, have killed the present talks and dealt a body blow at the renewed Anglo-American partnership which seems to be developing.

8. It is evident that the Americans are in a mood to proceed to decisions and action and I feel it would be wrong not to take advantage of this.

9. I fully recognise your apprehensions but I feel that there is nothing unknown or new about the Spofford Plan. It has been discussed and debated for weeks and is known to be near acceptance. Moreover under the present American programme they will proceed to the appointment of a Supreme Commander before any discussion takes place with the Germans and before any steps can be taken to proceed to the formation of German units. If the Soviet Government were to take the adoption of this plan as the pretext for a move I suggest that they would have moved in any case. On the other hand to draw back from the adoption of the plan might well create a new situation and display dangerous weakness. There are risks in every course but my feeling is that the biggest risk at the moment is to stop the momentum which has gathered here.

10. There remains the question of European integration. It is very tiresome and unnecessary of the Americans to have fallen into the French trap here but they have done so and the integration letter has become a part of the general settlement. I recognise the inconvenience and embarrassment which this is likely to cause us and probably the Americans as well but in relation to our major objectives I feel that it is a secondary question. My general view on this point is that the French proposals will almost certainly fail and that we should not worry too much about them.

11. I have made our views clear on this to the Americans but I do not feel that we can make it a reason for rejecting the settlement.

CALENDAR TO No. 131

i *6–8 Dec. Economic Policy and Raw Materials discussions at Washington (a) Attlee-Truman 3rd meeting* on 6 Dec. U.K. defence programme of £3.6 billion dependent on adequate supply of raw materials. Position stated in (*b*) Memo.

would have to the governments participating in the integrated force. The Americans did not seem to have any particular ideas on this subject but the Prime Minister and President agreed that it was a matter which should be studied without delay so that a common viewpoint could be established' (ZP 3/1).

handed to Truman (*F.R.U.S. 1950*, vol. iii, pp. 1743–46). Suggestions for establishment of raw materials organisation pursued at (*c*) 3 working party meetings, 6–7 Dec., which produce (*d*) report (quoted in note 3 and printed *F.R.U.S. 1950*, vol. iii, pp. 1787–8), not formally taken at (*e*) *Attlee-Truman 6th meeting* on 8 Dec. Attlee then welcomes agreement reached; emphasises importance for U.K. defence effort of U.S. contribution of raw materials and hopes that central body of proposed organisation be restricted to tripartite basis. Control of strategic exports (East/West trade) also discussed at 6th meeting. Suggestion from Harriman that reference in communiqué to the need to prevent export of strategic materials getting 'into the hands of those who might use them against the free world' be further strengthened is rejected by Truman and Attlee. On 16 Dec. Sir R. Makins reviews Washington talks on East-West trade at (*f*) and warns that 'there is no doubt that we shall hear more of this question' [ZP 3/3; UR 3426/254].

No. 132

Sir O. Franks (Washington) to Mr. Bevin
(Received 7 December, 8.1 a.m.)

No. 3311 Telegraphic [WU 1198/675]

Immediate. Top secret   WASHINGTON, 7 December 1950, 1.41 a.m.

Repeated Saving to New York.

Fourth meeting took place this afternoon [6 December] at White House.[1]

2. President opened by reaffirming United States wish to pursue successful policies in Europe and Far East simultaneously while regarding Europe as of first priority. He hoped for agreement on the European situation during the present meetings so that Supreme Commander could be appointed and progress made with Defence Organisation.

3. Prime Minister said that in building up the North Atlantic Treaty Organisation main obstacle was the French attitude. This attitude was understandable but the delay was exasperating. The Spofford Plan now seemed to offer a chance of going ahead; although we were not attracted by the idea of a European army we agreed that the French must be allowed to try it within the Atlantic framework. The main Atlantic plan could only be agreed if the deadlock was broken whereby the appointment of a Supreme Commander waited on the building up of forces and the forces waited on the Supreme Commander. In our view the greatest impetus would be given if agreement on the Spofford Plan was followed by the appointment of a Supreme Commander. Although we agreed in principle with the United States on the need for a German contribution it would be impossible to obtain a contribution without German consent.

[1] See No. 131.

348

The French were trying to hang the German question on other arrangements. We must be careful not to let the essence of defence measures be hung up by waiting for chimerical ideas. We therefore need to examine what kind of strength we could build up and when we could build it, having regard to the deterioration in the position after the Korean retreats.

4. President and Marshall explained American ideas on build up of forces in Europe. They had intended moving in two divisions from the Far East and one from United States to Germany by early summer 1951. The changed position in the Far East made this impossible. They were therefore now considering mobilisation of some divisions from the National Guard since they regarded increase of American forces in Europe as an essential preliminary to securing French cooperation and to raising German forces.

5. President emphasised American desire to reach agreement during present conversations on means of breaking deadlock. Acheson then said that French Cabinet today had approved Spofford Plan provided United States Government's letter (see my telegram No. 3289)[2] was sent. If French notified agreement at meeting of Deputies tomorrow Military Committee could agree proposal next Tuesday [12 December]. It would then be necessary to secure formal approval of Defence Committee and Council but this might perhaps be obtained without formal meetings. The Americans said that in their view these steps must be taken before an approach could be made to the Germans but if they were taken the problem could be transferred to the Germans without making a condition of establishing complicated organisations. Acheson emphasised that McCloy thought that the European side of the proposal must be stressed if the Germans were to accept it. He stated that if French agreed and approval of Deputies and Military Committee was obtained Department of State and Defence and Joint Chiefs of Staff would recommend to President immediate appointment of Eisenhower as Supreme Commander.

6. Makins then asked whether the despatch of the integrated letter which blessed and encouraged not only the European army but also the political institutions that might go with it was now an essential element in putting the Spofford Plan into operation. Using some of the arguments in your telegram No. 5486[3] he pointed out that the emphasis in the letter was very different from the attitude so far adopted by His Majesty's Government and would be a source of serious embarrassment in the future.

7. Acheson confirmed that the letter was part of proposed arrangement. He agreed that there was a difference of emphasis. In his view the whole basis of the Spofford Plan was to separate the French proposal for a European army from the American plans for European defence. He

[2] No. 127.

[3] No. 129.

therefore thought it important for the United States Government to support the French part of the plan with real warmth; if it failed it would then not be the fault of the Americans. He thought the terms of the letter were secondary to the main object of achieving agreement on the Spofford proposals but argued strongly for its despatch tonight if the opportunity was not to be lost.

8. Prime Minister agreed that while he would like to think over the proposals as a whole he could not object to despatch of letter.[4]

9. Acheson then raised question of size of British defence effort over next two to three years emphasising that Britain was the United States' main ally and as the two countries might be left alone in the event of early trouble they must consider together what effort they could make. President and Marshall emphasised importance of convincing Congress that there would be real hope of defending Europe effectively. President outlined size of supplementary defence budget already proposed to Congress and said that there would be consequential increases in proposals for fiscal year 1952 with the object of having three million men under arms and equipped by the end of 1952. The Americans wanted assurances that the United Kingdom would go along with this effort.

10. Prime Minister replied that we had already started up as large a programme as seemed immediately possible. We would consider what more could be done but the effort now planned would already mean cutting back elsewhere and imposing new controls.

11. C.I.G.S. explained object of pounds sterling 3600 million programme and problems likely to arise on both equipment and manpower. He emphasised the beneficial effect which the appointment of a Supreme Commander would have on the confidence of the European allies. He also thought that the arrival of American reinforcements in Europe as originally planned even if they were National Guard divisions and not fully trained would have a great moral effect.

12. Acheson repeated that the Americans were now accepting a new basis for their defence effort in the form of partial mobilisation that the United Kingdom was the only real ally on whom they could rely and that they attached great importance to our efforts. Marshall who was concerned that a really effective agreement should be reached on the powers of the Supreme Commander also said that the chance of successful agreement depended on the character and spirit of the Anglo-American

[4] On 7 December the American Ambassador in Paris gave M. Schuman an amended and unsigned text of the letter printed in *F.R.U.S. 1950*, vol. iii, pp. 523–4 (see No. 127, note 3 and No. 130, note 7). M. Schuman was 'deeply gratified' and 'will immediately notify Alphand [in] London to go ahead but will not give Alphand text. He says he is very concerned about security of this paper and will keep it in his personal possession until time comes for it to be published, which time will be set by agreement between Secretary and himself or between Spofford and Alphand. He understands perfectly that letter can only be used in event complete agreement reached in London' (*F.R.U.S. 1950*, vol. iii, pp. 527–8): see further No. 133, note 3.

relationship as the backbone of the agreement. Prime Minister welcomed these observations.

No. 133

Mr. Bevin to Sir O. Franks (Washington)

No. 5524 Telegraphic [WU 1198/690]

Emergency. Secret FOREIGN OFFICE, *7 December 1950, 5.40 p.m.*

Your telegram No. 3309 (of 6th December).[1]

Following personal for Prime Minister.

I naturally accept your judgment and have authorised Sir F. Hoyer-Millar to agree to the Spofford plan in the Deputies this afternoon. I have, however, instructed him to make two reservations, namely

(*a*) that the approval of the plan by the Deputies does not commit the Governments as to the precise timing of the approach to the Federal German Government;

and

(*b*) that the Deputies should not attempt to decide at this moment whether the formal approval of the Defence Committee and the Council should be secured through formal meetings or not.[2]

2. My reason for reserving these two points is that I consider it essential that we should preserve some degree of control over the strategy to be pursued in this vital matter during the next few weeks. We cannot foresee how the situation will develop or what will be the reaction of the Russians to the various stages in the acceptance of the plan for German rearmament, and I think it would be wrong for me to commit His Majesty's Government, by a decision in the Deputies today (before there has been any discussion in the Cabinet or with you), to the timing of an automatic programme of action in the matter of this magnitude.

3. This reflects my natural anxiety about arming the Germans when we and our American friends are still so weak in Europe.

4. Since above was drafted the Deputies have accepted the point of view

---

[1] No. 131.

[2] Mr. Attlee gave President Truman British agreement to the Spofford Plan, subject to the above two reservations, at their fifth meeting in Washington on the afternoon of 7 December. 'The President and Mr. Acheson welcomed this statement' (British record on ZP 3/3). The reservations emerged from a Foreign Office meeting with Mr. Bevin on the morning of 7 December. Instructions were then given for the drafting of this telegram by Mr. Shuckburgh who had minuted that day on the need to hold the position (see calendar i). Mr. Shuckburgh's draft was amended by Sir P. Dixon 'so as to make it clear that what the Secretary of State is holding out for is control over the *timing*' rather than revising the commitment to re-arm Germany (WU 1198/690).

expressed in paragraph 1 (*a*) above, and Sir F. Hoyer-Millar has put point (*b*) to Mr. Spofford who agreed that the point could not be decided by the Deputies.³

CALENDARS TO NO. 133

i *7 Dec. 1950   Anglo-French hesitations on German rearmament.* Position reached is assessed by Mr. Shuckburgh in brief for F.O. meeting. Approval of Spofford Plan will lead to approach to Federal govt. (*a*) by A.H.C. for German participation in integrated force (*b*) by French govt. concerning European Army. In separate minute of 7 Dec. Mr. Shuckburgh considers the case for holding back. Arguments for and against marshalled by Sir P. Dixon on 9 Dec. in favour of proceeding. Sir W. Strang points out that decision to rearm F.R.G. has already been taken and 'whatever we may think of that decision, it is not now politically possible to try to go back on it.' Represents need to get on with approach to Federal govt. Mr. Bevin complains on 10 Dec. of too much haste: 'All war can be avoided if we time it right & present our case correctly. I still believe we are rushing headlong into it. Everyone seems in such a hurry.' Reports from France on 8 Dec. of French reluctance to proceed with German rearmament until question of 4-Power meeting is settled [WU 1195/508; WU 1198/711; C 7961, 8057/27/18].

ii *13 Nov.–15 Dec. 1950   Fourth Session of N.A.C. Deputies* reviewed by Sir F. Hoyer Millar on 30 Dec. [WU 10727/2].

³ At their meeting on the afternoon of 7 December, the Deputies approved their Report (*F.R.U.S. 1950*, vol. iii, pp. 531–8), subject to a French reservation on wording which was settled the next day (see No. 136, note 10). No mention was made by M. Alphand of the proposed French statement or the American letter (see Nos. 130, note 7 and 132, note 4). In reply to Foreign Office enquiries about these on 9 December, Sir O. Harvey reported that a statement had been drafted 'to the effect that France had agreed to the plan only in the interests of Atlantic solidarity and against her better judgement, since she believed the action proposed was both dangerous and unnecessary.' This statement had been prepared in order to pacify M. Mollet, who had threatened resignation. It was later thought that the idea of communicating the statement to other governments had been shelved. However, on 16 December it was sent as a formal note to all N.A.T.O. powers with accompanying assurances that it was chiefly for internal purposes. This was the view taken by Mr. Bevin who reassured Mr. Acheson at Brussels on this point. The position as regards the American letter remained less clear. The Foreign Office was unable to establish whether it had been sent or not, until informed by the State Department on 15 December that M. Schuman was in possession of two alternative drafts which were not yet validated. At the Deputies meeting on 7 December, the question of whether the Report would be taken by the Defence Committee or the N.A.C. itself was deliberately left open. On 9 December the Foreign Office were informed by the Belgian Embassy that Mr. Acheson had asked the N.A.C. Chairman, M. van Zeeland, to convene an N.A.C. meeting in Brussels on 18–19 December. This was confirmed by the American Embassy which added that Mr. Acheson also hoped for a tripartite meeting to discuss German questions. Mr. Bevin resisted pressure to agree immediately and telegraphed to Mr. Attlee in Ottawa for instructions. Mr. Attlee agreed that the proposal for a meeting should be accepted and arrangements were accordingly set in train. Meanwhile concern about the timing of proceeding with German rearmament, especially in relation to the German government and the Soviet proposal for Four-Power talks continued to be a subject of minuting in the Foreign Office, for which see calendar i.

No. 134

Record of a conversation held at Mr. Harriman's house in Washington on 7 December 1950

[*ZP 11/1*]

United Kingdom Rearmament Programme

Present: Prime Minister, Sir Oliver Franks, Sir E. Plowden, Mr. Acheson, Mr. Harriman.

Mr. Harriman began by saying that he wished to talk very frankly. He said that while he felt that the current discussion had gone very well and would be fruitful, he was concerned about the future.

2. The American people were firm supporters of the N.A.T.O. and the ideas of joint defence and equality of sacrifice. They were convinced since the aggression in Korea that a greatly increased defence effort was necessary. It was the intention of the Administration to increase their defence budget to some $45 to $50 billion.

3. While in July an effort of £3,600 million including American help was perhaps a reasonable contribution by the United Kingdom, he felt sure that it would be considered inadequate in the present situation. This he thought might make the American people – already somewhat disillusioned as to the prospects of N.A.T.O., in view of the difficulties with the French over Germany – be inclined to withdraw. He wished therefore to put forward a strong plea for a substantially increased defence programme in the United Kingdom.

4. *Mr. Acheson* confirmed that there was likely to be a demand by the American people for an increased defence effort by the United Kingdom.

5. *The Prime Minister* pointed out that the British people had been under continuous strain for ten years and were only just emerging from serious economic difficulties and that their present programme would be a very heavy burden particularly as the help that was likely to be received under the Nitze formula[1] was likely to be far less than had been expected when the proposal was first put to us by the Americans at the end of July.

6. In the course of discussion *Sir Oliver Franks* said that many people even in the United Kingdom did not appreciate what progress had been made in the economic field in the last twelve or fourteen months and that the United Kingdom economy was much sounder than it had been for many years.

7. After some general discussion about the state of the United Kingdom economy and the likely attitude of the American people to the armament effort of the United Kingdom, *Mr. Harriman* renewed forcibly his plea for an increased United Kingdom defence effort over the £3,600 million.

---

[1] See No. 79.

8. While Mr. Acheson did not speak much he appeared to agree with Mr. Harriman's analysis.[2]

[2] Mr. Bevin minuted on this record, prepared by Sir R. Makins on 8 December, 'We cannot stand more for the time being E.B.' When giving MM. Pleven and Schuman an account of the Washington talks in Paris on 13 December (see No. 121, note 11), Sir R. Makins warned that 'His Majesty's Government and other European Governments would be under some pressure from the United States Government to increase the scale and tempo of their rearmament effort. M. Pleven said he did not think that the French Government could do any more' (WF 1023/34).

No. 135

Sir I. Kirkpatrick (Wahnerheide) to Mr. Bevin
(Received 12 December, 12.20 p.m.)

No. 1759 Telegraphic [C 7996/27/18]

Priority   WAHNERHEIDE, 12 December 1950, 11.30 a.m.

Repeated Saving to Washington, Paris.

German defence contribution.

The Chancellor yesterday gave an interview to Kingsbury Smith (International News Service) in which he said that he wished in no way to impede the negotiations of the Atlantic Pact States. However, he wished to prevent the present plan from being put to him formally, since if this occurred he would be in the unhappy position of having to reject it.[1]

2. He did not wish to adopt an entirely negative attitude, and the Federal Republic would not insist on equality of numbers in the Atlantic Army. Numbers were a matter of secondary importance. 'But we must have full equality of rights with the others as regards armament and the structure of command', he said. This he considered necessary to avoid German soldiers being used as cannon fodder. Without heavy equipment, they would have no hope of defending themselves and would regard themselves as cannon fodder. Without their own leaders, they would have the impression of being regarded as second-class troops.

3. The Chancellor stated that he had last week made it clear to 'the spokesman of the French Government' that a plan such as the present one would be unanimously rejected by the German public, the Federal Government and Parliament.

[1] Prior to this statement from Dr. Adenauer, consideration had been given by F.O. German Political department to the question of an approach to the Chancellor on the Spofford Plan by the Allied High Commission (e.g. minute by Mr. Gilchrist of 8 December on C 8126/27/18). Following reports from Wahnerheide on 9 December that German opinion against rearmament was hardening, Mr. Mallet suggested on 12 December (WU 1071/238) that if the A.H.C. were to obtain a negative response from Dr. Adenauer on the Spofford Plan before the N.A.C. meeting in Brussels, the Plan might be referred back to the Deputies. This would gain time for holding the position: a course still under consideration in the Foreign Office (see No. 133.i).

4. He pointed out the dangers, on the other hand, of a neutralised Germany. With a strong Soviet Union on the one side and a weak Europe on the other, there would be a great danger that the stronger of these two magnets would draw Germany into its field.

5. He regarded the present situation as extremely serious not only for Germany but also for Europe and the United States. If the French Government, and above all Moch, had not opposed equality of rights for Germany, agreement could have been reached in September and the setting up of a European Army could have commenced. This would have strengthened the Western Powers if the proposed Four-Power conference with the Soviet Union took place.

6. In his view, a start could be made with the creation of a Franco/German army by means of a common military academy in which young Frenchman and Germans could be trained together and under certain circumstances incorporated as homogeneous units in a European army.

7. The Western Allies should not delay the appointment of an Atlantic Supreme Commander until an Atlantic Army was formed. He was in favour of a Supreme Commander being American.

8. Finally he believed that agreement on a German contribution could quickly be reached if the three High Commissioners were empowered to negotiate direct with the Federal Government.[2]

Foreign Office please pass to Washington and Paris as my telegrams Nos. 536 and 536 Saving.

CALENDAR TO NO. 135

i *Dec. 1950 Reunification of Germany:* Adenauer warns A.H.C. on 14 Dec. that Grotewohl proposals should be taken seriously (Wahn. tel. 1785). F.O. consider on 30 Dec. (letter to Wahnerheide) that Adenauer's own attitude seems sound but he may be pressed into talks by the growing tide of German opinion which thinks 'Germany is divided into two more or less equal halves, that there are two governments in being and that really there is nothing much to choose between them'. Significance of use of word 'Wiedervereinigung' (reunification) for German unity is discussed [C 8095, 8284/65/18].

[2] On 13 December Sir I. Kirkpatrick reported that the Chancellor's interview had been followed up by an interview between Dr. Schumacher and Mr. Kingsbury-Smith in which Dr. Schumacher condemned the Spofford Plan. In private A.H.C. discussion on 14 December, the American and British High Commissioners succeeded in persuading M. François-Poncet that it would be 'premature and improper' for the High Commissioners to broach the Deputies' report with Dr. Adenauer before Brussels (Wahnerheide telegram No. 1781 on C 8065/20/18). When later that day the A.H.C. met Dr. Adenauer, 'he earnestly hoped that the Foreign Ministers would not agree a plan and present it to the Federal Government as a *fait accompli*. He begged that the proposal should be put forward in the form of a plan for discussion between the High Commission on the one hand and the Federal Government on the other ... At the Chancellor's urgent request we agreed to insert a phrase in the communiqué issued after our meeting to the effect that we had told him we had reason to believe that the results of the Brussels conference would form the

subject of exchange of view between ourselves and the Federal Government' (*ibid.*). Most of the discussion at the A.H.C. meeting on 14 December was devoted to the question of Dr. Adenauer's reply to a public letter addressed to him on 1 December by Herr O. Grotewohl, Minister-President of the German Democratic Republic. In this letter Dr. Adenauer was invited to begin discussions for the formation of an all-German Constituent Council as a first stage towards the reunification of Germany (cf. No. 78). This invitation was effectively rejected by Dr. Adenauer in a broadcast reply of 15 January in which he set pre-conditions for negotiation e.g. guarantees for free elections.

No. 136

Memorandum by the Secretary of State for Foreign Affairs[1]

C.P. (50) 311 [CAB 129/43]

Secret   FOREIGN OFFICE, *12 December 1950*

German Participation in the Defence of Western Europe

I circulate to my colleagues herewith (Annex 'A') a summary, prepared in the Foreign Office, of the points contained in the reports of the North Atlantic Council Deputies and the North Atlantic Military Committee,[2] relating to the conditions of a German contribution to the integrated Atlantic force. The reports themselves are long and still subject to minor revision, and I do not think the Cabinet need read them at this stage.

2. The two reports, when finally approved and put together at a joint meeting of the Deputies and the Military Committee, will come before the North Atlantic Defence Committee and the North Atlantic Council for final approval in the name of the Governments concerned. These two Ministerial Committees have been called to meet in Brussels on Monday next, 18th December, and I need the authority of the Cabinet for the line I should adopt in regard to them.

3. If the Atlantic Council approves the substance of these reports, the way will be clear for the following next steps:

(*a*) a request to the High Commissioners of the three Occupying Powers in Western Germany 'to discuss with the German Federal

[1] Mr. Bevin gave instructions for the preparation of this Cabinet paper at an Office meeting on 11 December with Sir I. Kirkpatrick (on recall from Wahnerheide), Sir W. Strang, Sir D. Gainer, Lord Henderson, Sir P. Dixon and Mr. Mallet. Questions raised by Sir P. Dixon in his minute of 9 December (see No. 133.i) were then discussed. Sir I. Kirkpatrick 'emphasised that if the Spofford Plan were put to the German Federal Government at the present time they would certainly reject it. He saw no prospect of securing German agreement to a contribution to Western defence until the Supreme Commander for Europe had been appointed and some progress had been made with the establishment of the integrated force' (C 8026/27/18). At Mr. Bevin's request Sir I. Kirkpatrick wrote a note of what he had said: attached as Annex B and calendared at i below.

[2] These reports, summarized at Annex A, are printed in *F.R.U.S. 1950*, vol. iii, pp. 531–47.

Government the question of German participation in the defence of Western Europe' along the lines set forth in the two reports;

(b) the calling by the French Government of 'a conference of the countries (including the German Federal Republic) which may wish to participate in a European Army'.

Extent to which His Majesty's Government are committed

4. His Majesty's Government are committed, vis-à-vis the other North Atlantic Treaty Governments, to the principle of a German contribution to Western defence. This commitment was accepted when I was in New York in September last (C.M. (50) 59th Conclusions, Minute 1).[3] Our acceptance of this principle at that time was based on the understanding that it formed a necessary part of a broad plan in which the Americans would nominate a Supreme Commander for the integrated Atlantic force and undertake to send substantial reinforcements to Europe during 1951. Unfortunately, this broad plan could not be put into effect immediately owing to French unwillingness to accept even the principle of a German contribution except under restrictive conditions and in combination with their own ideas for a European Army. During the months that ensued while this was under discussion, the situation deteriorated in the following respects:

(a) The Americans began to take the line that they required more than a mere acceptance of the principle and that they could not nominate the Supreme Commander or agree to send reinforcements to the integrated force until they actually had a 'sight' of the German contribution. At one time they said that their plan could not come into operation until a favourable reply had been received from the German Government. Later this became modified, and their present position seems to be that they could nominate General Eisenhower as Supreme Commander as soon as the 'Spofford compromise' (i.e. the substance of the present reports) had been agreed within the North Atlantic Treaty Organisation, but before the approach has been made to the German Federal Government.

(b) The widespread publicity which has been given to these discussions has led to a hardening of German opinion against participation on any terms but those of complete equality.

(c) The events in the Far East have reduced the prospect of early effective American reinforcements in Europe.

For the above reasons it can legitimately be said that the conditions in which we are called upon to accept the present plans for German participation are different from those in which we committed ourselves, in September last, to the principle of a German contribution.

5. As regards the Deputies' plan itself, His Majesty's Government are not formally committed. The United Kingdom Deputy, acting on my

[3] No. 27.

instructions, has given his approval to the Deputies' report but the report is still subject to Ministerial approval, and it is well understood that the Atlantic Council may have comments to make on the substance of the plan and on details. In particular, the United Kingdom Deputy has reserved my position in regard to the timing of the approach to the German Federal Government which would follow acceptance of the plan.

Implications of acceptance of the Plan by the North Atlantic Council

6. The implications of acceptance of this plan by the North Atlantic Council may be considered under three heads: first, its possible effect on Soviet policy; second, the likely reaction of the Germans themselves to the plan; and thirdly, the attitude of the United States Government to the plan, with particular reference to their willingness to appoint a Supreme Commander and to proceed to build up the integrated force.

Possible effect on Soviet policy

7. I have felt bound to consider most seriously what might be the reaction of the Soviet Government to an announcement that the North Atlantic Powers had formally agreed upon a scheme for the rearmament of Germany and were about to approach, or had approached, the German Government to that end. I had to bear in mind that the circumstances in which we would be taking this action are entirely different from those which obtained when we first agreed with the Americans that it was safe to embark on German rearmament. At that time, there had been good hopes that the Korea situation would be rapidly cleared up and Allied resources released, and we were led to expect the arrival of 5½ American divisions in Europe during 1951. We had not at that time had the evidence, which the Far East situation has now given us, of the willingness of the Communist Powers to take greater risks of war, and we had not had the Soviet Note of 20th October[4] stating that the Soviet Government would not reconcile itself to measures 'directed towards the restoration in Western Germany of a German regular army' or their subsequent note of 3rd November[5] inviting us to hold Four-Power discussions on the demilitarisation of Germany. I had to take account also of the opinion of His Majesty's Ambassador in Moscow, who considers that the Russians would regard the re-creation of German armed forces as different in character from and more provocative than any measures taken by the Western Powers themselves to increase their armed strength. I felt bound therefore to consider whether this was indeed a suitable moment in which the [*sic*] take a public and irrevocable decision to rearm Germany.

8. On the other hand it was arguable that the risks involved had always existed, seeing that, even before the reverses in Korea, there was no prospect of an effective force being in existence in Europe in the near future. It could therefore be argued that the risk must in any case be faced and that there would be greater risk in showing any sign of hesitation over

[4] See No. 78, note 2.   [5] See No. 86, note 5.

what was regarded by the Americans as an essential preliminary to the building up of effective Allied defence forces in Europe. The various considerations were put by myself and the Minister of Defence to the Prime Minister in Washington, in case he should feel able, in the course of his talks with President Truman, to express in strict confidence the doubts which I had in mind. He decided that it would be wrong for him to do so in view of the satisfactory declarations which he had received from the President regarding the importance still attached by the United States to the defence of Europe, their intention to nominate General Eisenhower as Supreme Commander as soon as the 'Spofford plan' was approved, and their proposal to send National Guard reinforcements to Europe. Any sign on our part of drawing back would, in his view, have been fatal to the Washington talks and to the renewed Anglo-American partnership which seemed to be developing.

Probable German reaction

9. The second important factor to be considered is what is likely to be the reaction of the German Government to an approach from the High Commissioners for a German contribution on the lines laid down in the reports. My colleagues will observe from Annex 'A' to this paper that the plan provides for two distinct stages in the process of building up a German contribution. During the first stage, described as the 'transitional period', the Germans would be asked to begin recruiting and training their soldiers to form units under certain clearly defined conditions and restrictions. They would be in a position of definite inequality vis-à-vis the other Powers, in that their units would be limited to brigade groups, while the other nations contributed divisions; their possession of heavy armour and operational aircraft would be restricted; there would be controls over officer recruitment and posting; German war production would be controlled; and there would be a N.A.T.O. High Commissioner whose responsibilities, though ostensibly applying to all member countries, would obviously be primarily for control of the German forces. More important from their point of view, the Supreme Commander would be answerable to North Atlantic Treaty Ministerial organs on which Germany is not represented.

10. The second stage would be reached after 'permanent mechanisms, either military or political' are developed which can 'effectively discharge the various responsibilities'; that is to say, after the French have had an opportunity to work out and obtain acceptance of their plan for a European Army. It is the French thesis that, if the German units were contributed as part of a European Army under their scheme, the Germans would be on a basis of equality with the other participating Governments.

11. The German Chancellor made it quite clear that he will not be able to accept the conditions of inequality laid down under the Spofford plan for the 'transitional period', and he has expressed the hope that proposals

on these lines will not be put formally to him.[6] Sir I. Kirkpatrick, whose comments I attach as Annex 'B' [i] to this paper, takes the view that, whatever conditions were offered to the Germans, they would certainly argue for a period of weeks or months before agreeing to make a contribution, having regard to the general unwillingness of the Germans to rearm at all and their natural desire to make the best bargain they can. Whether or not they would be more favourably disposed towards the French scheme for a European Army is hard to say. One thing, however, is clear, namely that it will be a considerable time before an actual start is made on the recruitment and training of German troops. It seems to me clear that the French Government are well aware of this, and there is no reason to suppose that the Soviet Government think differently.

12. It seems to result from this that neither a decision on 18th December to accept the Spofford plan nor even an approach to the German Federal Government thereafter would in fact constitute or appear to constitute the irrevocable moment of action which might be supposed to provoke Soviet counter-action.

Attitude of the Americans

13. We are all agreed that the first objective of our defence policy must be to secure the early appointment of the Supreme Commander and initiation of the plans for creating an integrated Atlantic defence force for Europe with the greatest possible American contribution. Although the prospects in this respect are very much less favourable than they seemed in September, there is still a hope that some American divisions (albeit not experienced in battle) will be available during 1951.[7] The United States Administration have consistently made it plain that Congress would not sanction reinforcement of Europe by American troops unless the force of which they were to form part was sufficient to have a chance of effective action; and that they do not believe that such a force can be built up without German participation. If therefore we were to show hesitation about approaching the Germans at this stage, there is no doubt that there would be a reaction in the United States which might prejudice the first objective of our policy. Indeed, if we were to suggest that our hesitations

---

[6] See No. 135.

[7] When informing the Chiefs of Staff Committee on 14 December of Mr. Attlee's discussions in Washington, Field-Marshal Sir W. Slim said that General Bradley had informed him that 'there were two schools of thought as to whether newly formed National Guard Divisions should be sent to Germany at once. On the one hand it was felt that even though these Divisions were composed of raw recruits, their presence in Germany would have a great effect on European morale. On the other hand, others felt that the presence of untried and untrained American recruits in Germany would have just the opposite effect. He [Slim] personally was strongly in favour of sending these Divisions to Germany as soon as possible, and had told General Bradley so.' Field-Marshal Slim also reported on American intentions as regards the appointment of General Eisenhower as Supreme Commander with General Gruenther as his Chief of Staff over an organisation based at Fontainebleau (Confidential Annex to C.O.S. (50) 206th Meeting on DEFE 4/38).

were based upon fear of the Russian reaction, it cannot be excluded that there might be a tendency for the Americans to reverse their basic policy of putting the defence of Europe first in priority among their objectives.

Alternative courses of action

14. In the light of the above I am now willing to hold that we cannot afford to suggest any basic doubts or hesitations about going through with our plans for a German contribution. On this I think there will be general agreement. There is, however, in my view still room for consideration of the timing of the next steps in the programme, and the alternative courses before us appear to me to be three-fold. I set them out in the following paragraphs with their advantages and disadvantages.

15. The first course is to agree in the North Atlantic Council to an approach being made to the German Federal Government by the three High Commissioners, as recommended by the Deputies, on the basis of the Spofford plan. The advantage of this is that, according to statements made to the Prime Minister in Washington, the Americans would then be prepared immediately to announce the appointment of General Eisenhower as Supreme Commander, without waiting for the German reaction, and we should thus have set in motion the first part of the broad defence plan to which we attach such importance. We should also have shown to the world and to our allies our determination to press forward regardless of possible risks and despite the evident weakness of the Allied position at the present moment. The disadvantages relate partly to the Russians and partly to the Germans, but to a certain extent they cancel one another out. If it is a fact, and I think it is, that the Germans will not look at conditions of this kind, at any rate without many weeks or months of argument, then it will be a long time before any actual recruitment begins in Germany, and since the Russians are presumably no less aware than we are of the delays which are sure to ensue and of the conditions which the Germans are likely to make, the provocative character of the actual approach to the German Government is likely to be a good deal less than might otherwise have been the case. On the other hand, it is undoubtedly unfortunate that the Allied Governments should have to go to the German Government with proposals for a German contribution containing conditions which the Germans are sure to turn down, thereby putting the Germans in a position in which they can bargain with us. It has always been our view, shared moreover by the United States Government, that we should avoid putting the Germans in this position. Against this, however, it is arguable that, when the Germans see the Supreme Commander appointed and an effective integrated force beginning to be built up, they will themselves begin to desire to take a share in the defence effort and might, after a month or so of argument, be more willing than at present to accept conditions palatable to the other Governments.

16. The second course would be to say to the Americans and to the North Atlantic Council that, while we in no way withdraw from the plan

361

itself, we do not consider that the actual approach to the German Federal Government should be made for the moment, but that it should be timed carefully in relation to the possibility of Four Power discussions and to the world-wide situation resulting from the events in the Far East. The dangers of this course are evident. If there had not been so much publicity about the whole matter, it might have been possible, and would I think have been desirable, to take this line. As it is, there would be grave danger of it being misunderstood in America and on the Continent and the whole momentum, such as it is, of the Atlantic Powers towards the building up of effective defences might be lost. Almost certainly the Supreme Commander would not be appointed and there would be a further period of uncertainty, during which the attitude of the Germans would continue to deteriorate. The advantages would be that we should be better able to use the prospect of German rearmament as a bargaining factor in any talks with the Soviet Government and we should presumably avoid such risk of provoking an early attack in Europe as might arise from the alternative course.

17. Between these two alternatives there appears to me to lie a third course which would consist in seeking to secure some delay in the formal approach to the German Federal Government without however putting the Americans off the immediate appointment of a Supreme Commander. It may not be possible to achieve this, and in that event we could fall back to course one, but the basis on which I would make the attempt in discussions with Mr. Acheson and my other colleagues would be as follows:

(a) First, the declaration by Dr. Adenauer to the International News Correspondent on 11th December,[6] when he is quoted as having said: 'I do not wish to interfere with the negotiations between the Atlantic Pact Powers. I only want to prevent the present plan for the incorporation of German combat teams being formally put before the Federal Government. If this should happen, we would find ourselves in the unfortunate position of having to reject it.'
This statement is bound to be considered by the North Atlantic Council and it may well be that Mr. Acheson himself will raise the question of its effect on the timing and the character (i.e. whether formal or informal) of any approach to Dr. Adenauer by the three High Commissioners.
(b) I could point out that as I consistently maintained at the meetings in New York, it would be fatal to go to the Germans cap in hand with a request for their contribution, thereby putting them in a position where they could bargain with us; but that as and when the integrated Atlantic force in Europe began to be built up and show evidence of strength, the Germans would become increasingly anxious to play their part. I might quote my statement at the meeting of the North Atlantic Council at New York on 15th September,[8] when I said:

[8] See No. 29.i.

'We must first be strong ourselves and then we could invite Germany to join us . . . It would be fatal to admit that Europe could not defend itself without German assistance.'

From this I could argue that the one fatal thing would be to give the Germans the impression that all further progress with the Atlantic defence force is dependent upon their acceptance of a German contribution; and that consequently the essential preliminary to any discussions with the Germans is the appointment of General Eisenhower, which in itself would be bound to affect favourably the whole atmosphere of defence preparations in Europe, including Germany.

(c) In the light of these considerations I would urge that, before the proposals were put to the German Federal Government in a formal manner, the High Commissioners should hold informal and private discussions with Dr. Adenauer in order to ascertain his views.[9]

E.B.

ANNEX A TO No. 136

Summary of the conclusions of the North Atlantic Military Committee and the North Atlantic Council Deputies[2]

German participation in the defence of Europe

(1) The defence of Europe, including Western Germany as far as to the East as possible, will require a German contribution.

(2) A European defence force is militarily acceptable, but its achievements should, under no circumstances, delay the contribution of Germany to the defence of Europe.

(3) Note is taken of the French Government's intention to call a conference of the countries (including the German Federal Republic) which may wish to participate in a European Army.

(4) While work proceeds towards the solution of the political aspects of the problem, however, certain steps, upon which there already exists a large measure of agreement, can and must be taken immediately. For this purpose there must be a transitional period to permit:

(i) The essential preliminary work on the military organisation to be initiated immediately;

(ii) The recruitment of German man-power, the formation of combat-worthy German units and the production of material under

---

[9] The Foreign Office brief on this paper for Mr. Bevin at the Cabinet meeting at No. 137, reminded Mr. Bevin that 'after further thought and after discussion with Sir I. Kirkpatrick, he definitely favours the third course' (WU 1195/525). The corresponding Ministry of Defence brief for Mr. Shinwell took the view that 'while recognising that there are political implications with regard to the timing and method of discussing the problem of German rearmament with the Germans, there is no question that from the military point of view the sooner a start is made with the recruitment and training of German units, the better' (CAB 21/1899).

provisional arrangements pending development of a more permanent system; and

(iii) The consideration of the broader political problems to be undertaken concurrently but free from the pressure attendant upon the initiation of military measures.

These provisional arrangements would be progressively superseded or modified as and to the extent that permanent mechanisms, either military or political, were developed which could effectively discharge the various responsibilities.

(5) The Military Committee and the Deputies therefore recommend that the Occupying Powers be invited by the parties to the North Atlantic Treaty to discuss with the German Federal Government the question of German participation in the defence of Western Europe on the following basis:

(i) It would not serve the best interests of Europe, or of Germany, to bring into being a German national army or German General Staff.

(ii) Any system of German participation must be within the N.A.T.O. structure and any German formations must be under the authority of the Supreme Commander.

(iii) The question, whether German formations should be recruited by conscription or on a voluntary basis should be determined by the Occupying Powers, after consultation with the German authorities.

(iv) Subject to the limitations set out below, German units should be treated on a basis of full equality with units of other participating countries with which they are integrated.

(v) The only militarily practicable short term contribution by Germany would be in the form of complete German formations.

(vi) As regards the land forces, the size of such German formations should not, under present conditions, exceed that of Regimental Combat Teams or Brigade Groups. However, when these Regimental Combat Teams or Brigade Groups are formed and trained, the question of the manner in which they should be used must be determined in the light of conditions at the time, due weight being given to the views of the Supreme Commander.[10]

[10] Paragraph 5(vi) corresponds to paragraph 7(a) of the Deputies' report, the wording of which was the subject of some difficulty (see No. 130 and No. 133, note 3). Despite the omission of any reference to 'divisions', to which the French had objected in earlier drafts, the French Deputy was unable to accept the final wording without reference to his government. On 8 December he informed the Deputies of his government's agreement: 'This removed the last reserved point and the report was thus finally approved, though M. Alphand said that his Government's final attitude would depend on their getting satisfaction on the question of the attaching of the German Brigade Groups to Allied Divisions . . . Mr. Spofford also made a few remarks on the subject of paragraph 7(a) and the interpretation to be placed on the words "the manner in which they (i.e. the German Brigade Groups) should be used must be determined, etc". He said that the Americans regarded this as meaning whether or not the Brigade Groups should be combined to form

(vii) German forces should not be developed to the detriment of other Allied forces, nor should they be permitted to develop at a rate or to a degree that would constitute a threat to Allied security. To this end, the number of German land formations should at no time exceed one-fifth of the total number of like Allied land formations allocated to and earmarked for SHAPE.

(viii) Germany should not be allowed to contribute complete heavy armoured formations. This, however, should not preclude the inclusion of the necessary armour to complete the land formations authorised.

(ix) The German contribution should include complete air units for the defence of Western Germany and the support of German ground units. Such air units would be a part of the integrated air forces under the Supreme Commander.

(x) The German contribution in naval forces should be limited to the manning and operating of mine-craft, patrol-craft and harbour defence craft.

(xi) The rotation of individuals from the regular forces to any reserve should be controlled so as to ensure that no unforeseen or undesired expansion of German forces is possible at any time.

(xii) The Occupying Powers should retain supervision of officer recruitment and should rely, in so far as practicable, upon recruitment and training of new officers. Similarly, supervision should be exercised over the training of Non-commissioned Officers.

(xiii) German officers should be commissioned as required for German units, and some should also be gradually integrated into selected posts on the international staff of the Supreme Commander and his major subordinate Commands when German units are assigned. Determination of the extent of the contribution from the German Officer Corps to the integrated staff should await the recommendations of the Supreme Commander.

(xiv) German forces cannot constitute a military threat unless they possess their own sources of essential war material. Therefore, it is considered that there should remain prohibited and limited industries in Germany. Germany should not be permitted to produce heavy military equipment, military aircraft, or naval vessels other than minor defensive craft.

(xv) The manufacture of atomic, biological and chemical weapons, and long range missiles, should not be permitted to Germany.

(xvi) Research and development should be limited to requirements laid down by the Military Committee, and supervision and control should be exercised by the appropriate N.A.T.O. agency.

---

larger units; and not as meaning the actual tactical manner in which the Brigade Groups might be employed in warfare. M. Alphand said that he agreed with this interpretation' (U.K. Deputy tel. No. 22 Saving on WU 1198/688).

(xvii) Subject to the above safeguards German production should contribute to the greatest extent possible to the support of the German contribution in man-power, and to such other phases of the common defence as may be reasonable and within her capabilities. The nature and size of the contribution to be made by the German armament industry should be recommended by the appropriate agencies of N.A.T.O. Until other arrangements are adopted the safeguards on production will continue to be exercised by the occupying authorities. There must, of course, be close co-operation between them and the Defence Production Board of the N.A.T.O.

(xviii) Detailed plans for the raising and preliminary training of German forces should be made by the occupying authorities in concert with the Supreme Commander and the appropriate German authorities.

(xix) The administration of the German defence effort should be entrusted to a German agency, or agencies. Such agency, or agencies, should be of a civilian character and should remain subject to some system of Allied control, even should the regime of Occupation be modified. During the initial period control will continue to be exercised by the Occupying Powers. A final determination of the form and functions of the German agency must be made in conjunction with the German authorities.

(xx) Any German administration established for this purpose should be capable of fulfilling its functions effectively and rapidly. Its functions should not be such as to permit the development of a Defence Ministry. To ensure against the possible rebirth of a German General Staff, the functions appropriate to the plans, operations and intelligence sections of military staffs, above the level of authorised tactical units, should only be discharged by international staffs under the Supreme Commander and should not be permitted in any German agency.

(xxi) The enforcement of the safeguards set forth above should be the responsibility of the Occupying Powers. The enforcement of those safeguards could be progressively transferred to the appropriate European or N.A.T.O. agency if, and to the extent that this should later be considered advisable.

(6) The Occupying Powers should be invited to keep the other parties to the North Atlantic Treaty informed as fully as possible of the course of the discussions with the German authorities and the steps taken to initiate German participation.

(7) The Deputies should continue to study the proposal for a North Atlantic Treaty Organisation High Commissioner, with responsibilities with regard to both the German and other national contributions to the integrated force.

(8) The appointment of a Supreme Commander at the earliest possible date is a matter of the greatest importance.

i *Annex B to No. 136:* Break-down of different sections of German public and political parties who oppose German rearmament and their reasons [CAB 129/43].

No. 137

Extract from the Conclusions of a Meeting of the Cabinet held at 10 Downing Street on Thursday, 14 December 1950, at 10 a.m.[1]

C.M. (50) 86th Conclusions [CAB 128/18]

Secret

Germany: Rearmament

(Previous Reference: C.M. (50) 84th Conclusions, Minute 4)[2]

4. The Cabinet considered a memorandum by the Foreign Secretary (C.P. (50) 311)[3] on the latest developments in the discussions regarding Germany's participation in the defence of western Europe.

The Foreign Secretary recalled the various stages through which these discussions had passed. When the United States Government had first put forward their proposal that German military units should be included in the integrated force for the defence of western Europe, this had formed part of a comprehensive plan including the appointment of an American as Supreme Commander, the stationing of a substantial force of United States troops in Europe in time of peace and the conception of partnership in sharing the economic burden of North Atlantic defence. It was in consideration of these other aspects of the plan that he had felt able to recommend the Cabinet to accept the principle of Germany's participation in the integrated force. Since then, however, much time had been lost in the discussion of the alternative French plan for the creation of a European army; and during that time reverses in Korea had postponed the date by which fully effective American forces could arrive in Europe. We were therefore in a very much weaker position to run such risks as might be involved in embarking upon the process of rearming Germany. He had therefore felt considerable anxiety about the proposal to go forward at once with the compromise plan for German rearmament

[1] *Present* at this meeting were Mr. Attlee (*in the Chair*); Mr. Morrison; Mr. Bevin; Mr. Gaitskell; Mr. Dalton; Viscount Addison; Viscount Jowitt; Mr. Chuter Ede; Mr. Shinwell; Mr. Isaacs; Mr. Williams; Mr. Tomlinson; Mr. Wilson; Mr. Griffiths; Mr. McNeil; Mr. Gordon Walker. *Also present* for item 4 were Admiral of the Fleet Lord Fraser of North Cape; Field-Marshal Sir W. Slim; Marshal of the R.A.F. Sir J. Slessor. *Secretariat:* Sir N. Brook; Air Marshal Sir W. Elliot; Mr. Johnston.

[2] At this meeting on 11 December, Mr. Bevin informed the Cabinet of the British reservations to the Deputies (see No. 133) and of the decision to convene a meeting of the N.A.C. in Brussels (CAB 128/18).

[3] No. 136.

which had been evolved by the Council of Deputies and the Military Committee of the North Atlantic Council. He had held personal consultations with His Majesty's Ambassador in Moscow and with the United Kingdom High Commissioner in Germany. As a result he was satisfied that, if the German Government were pressed to say at once whether they were willing to contribute to European defence on the basis outlined in Annex A to C.P. (50) 311,[3] they would make an unfavourable response. In that event, if a meeting of the Council of Foreign Ministers were to be held, he would be in a weak bargaining position there. Moreover, if the Germans firmly declined to participate in the defence of western Europe, he had no assurance that the United States would go forward with their original proposal to station a substantial force in Europe.

The Foreign Secretary said that in these circumstances he would prefer to proceed somewhat cautiously with the plan evolved by the Council of Deputies and the Military Committee. If that plan were endorsed at the forthcoming meeting of the North Atlantic Council on 18th December, he would propose that the German Government should at this stage be informed merely that the plan had been adopted but should not be asked either to accept or to reject it. Secondly, he would press the United States Government to proceed at once with the appointment of a Supreme Commander and the creation of an integrated force for the defence of western Europe. In that event, if a meeting of the Council of Foreign Ministers were arranged, the western Powers would be able to discuss the demilitarisation of Germany without having taken any irrevocable step towards the rearming of western Germany. While he would not go back on his acceptance of the principle of German participation in the defence of western Europe, he would urge that discretion should be used in timing the implementation of that principle. This course would have the additional advantage that it would not be necessary to solicit German help in the defence of western Europe. It would create a place for Germany in the scheme of European defence; and informal efforts could then be made to ensure that, when the time was ripe, the Germans would themselves offer to take their place in the scheme.

The Minister of Defence said that he was in broad agreement with the views expressed by the Foreign Secretary. The Cabinet must face the fact that there was little military strength in western Europe to resist any Russian aggression. Europe could not be defended without American support; and our defence policy must therefore continue to be kept in close alignment with that of the United States Government. It was also his view that, as far ahead as could be foreseen, western Europe would require some contribution from Germany if she was to be able to resist a Russian aggression. He therefore considered that we should stand firm on the principle that Germany should participate in the defence of western Europe. But it did not follow that this principle must, or could, be implemented forthwith. He considered that at the forthcoming meeting of the North Atlantic Council we should support the compromise plan put forward by the Council of Deputies and the Military Committee. But, if that plan were then accepted, the next step would be to consider how it could best be presented to the Germans. He himself thought that it would be better to take time to persuade the Germans to offer to participate under that scheme, rather than seek to impose the plan upon them. He therefore favoured the tactical approach suggested by the Foreign Secretary.

Discussion showed that the Cabinet were in agreement with the Foreign Secretary's views. The following were the main points made in the discussion:

(a) The United Kingdom Government should stand firm on the principle of German participation in the defence of western Europe. The Cabinet recognised that an effective German contribution was essential to the successful defence of western Europe.

(b) At the same time it was important to avoid offering any unnecessary provocation to the Russians, who were genuinely apprehensive about the resurgence of German militarism. The form and timing of German rearmament must therefore be considered very carefully and any precipitate action must be avoided.

(c) Public opinion in western Germany must also be brought round to accept the idea of German rearmament. From Annex B of C.P. (50) 311 it appeared that there was at present strong opposition to this in the trade unions and in the Social Democratic Party; and appropriate steps should be taken to secure a change of opinion in those quarters. Time would be needed for this.

(d) There would be difficulty at present in finding military equipment for German forces. The other European Powers should have the first claim on such equipment as was available.

(e) All possible measures should be taken to increase the military strength of France. The Cabinet were informed that some progress was being made. The main obstacles were French commitments in Indo-China, where more than half of the French regular army were engaged; and the short period of compulsory military service, which made it difficult to build up a sufficient cadre of non-commissioned officers.

Further efforts might also be made to allay French apprehensions of German militarism. Could not the French be persuaded that the North Atlantic Treaty guaranteed their defence against any aggressor, whether German or Russian? That assurance had been accepted by the other European Powers.

(f) There was some reason to believe that the approach suggested by the Foreign Secretary might be welcomed by the military advisers of the United States Government, who appeared reluctant to take any step which would give the impression of soliciting German help in the defence of Europe.

The Cabinet:

(1) Reaffirmed their acceptance of the principle that Germany should be enabled to contribute to the defence of western Europe; and authorised the Foreign Secretary to accept, at the forthcoming meeting of the North Atlantic Council in Brussels, the plan for applying that principle which had been evolved by the Council of Deputies and the Military Committee.

(2) Approved the suggestions made by the Foreign Secretary in the discussion regarding the tactics for putting that plan into operation by stages, adjusted to the progress made in building up an integrated force for the defence of western Europe under an American Supreme Commander.

(3) Authorised the Secretary of State for Commonwealth Relations to inform other Commonwealth Governments of the attitude which the United Kingdom Government were proposing to adopt towards this question at the forthcoming meeting of the North Atlantic Council.

No. 138

Sir O. Harvey (Paris) to Mr. Bevin
(Received 15 December, 8.35 p.m.)

No. 372 Telegraphic [C 8079/65/18]

Priority. Secret   PARIS, 15 December 1950, 6.55 p.m.

Repeated to Moscow and Saving to Washington, Wahnerheide, Vienna, The Hague, Brussels, Luxembourg.

Your telegram No. 1360[1] – Russian proposal for a meeting of the C.F.M.

At the meeting with the French and Americans today it proved impossible to reach agreement. United States representative stood firm on latest text of paragraph 6 of the draft reply which was unacceptable to the French as well as to us. The discussion which I am summarising in a Saving telegram[2] showed that there is a difference not simply in wording but in approach, the Americans being determined not to commit

---

[1] This telegram of 15 December conveyed instructions for British agreement to a tripartite draft reply, prepared by officials in Paris (see No. 110, note 3) as amended by the Cabinet at their meeting on 14 December (C.M. (50) 86th Conclusions, minute 3, on CAB 128/18). In the draft reply it was suggested that quadripartite talks at an official level should be held as a preliminary to the C.F.M. proposed by the Soviet government in their note of 3 November (see No. 86, note 5). The Cabinet objected to American wording in paragraph 6 and gave instructions for a reversion to one of two earlier wordings, so that the drawing up of an agenda by officials was not made dependent on their finding a mutually acceptable basis for ministerial discussion (wordings compared in minute on C 8280/65/18).

[2] Not printed from C 8134/65/18.

themselves to a C.F.M. meeting until satisfactory Russian attitude is revealed at the official talks whereas we and the French are not prepared to make a Ministerial meeting conditional upon the successful outcome of the official talks.

2. We agreed to suggest that

(a) The three Foreign Ministers should attempt to resolve this difference themselves, when they meet in Brussels next week perhaps at a special meeting on Monday morning;

(b) In the event of press enquiries about the delay in despatching the reply to the Russians, the answer should be that advantage was being taken of the meeting of three Foreign Ministers early next week to submit to them for final approval the terms of the draft reply to the Soviet Note.[3]

Foreign Office please pass to Moscow as my telegram No. 6.

[3] On 15 December the Soviet government addressed a further note to the British government (text on C 8102/65/18) in which it was alleged that the proposal to include German forces in an integrated N.A.T.O. force not only contravened the Potsdam agreement but also the Anglo-Soviet treaty of 26 May 1942 (*B.F.S.P.*, vol. 144, pp. 1038–41). A corresponding note was addressed to the French government (printed in *Documents on International Affairs 1949–50* – R.I.I.A. 1953 – pp. 179–82) in respect of the Franco-Soviet treaty of 10 December 1944 (*B.F.S.P.*, vol. 149, pp. 632–5). British and French officials immediately began concerting draft replies which it was agreed should be kept separate from the reply to the Soviet note of 3 November.

No. 139

Mr. Bevin to Sir O. Franks (Washington)

No. 1605 [WU 1071/217]

Top secret   FOREIGN OFFICE, *15 December 1950*

Sir,

The United States Chargé d'Affaires called on me to-day in order to give me an indication of the line which Mr. Acheson expected to take at the forthcoming meeting of the North Atlantic Council in Brussels, together with an indication of American thinking generally on future policy in regard to Germany. Mr. Holmes was accompanied by Mr. Achilles, assistant to Mr. Spofford, and Sir P. Dixon was also present.

2. Mr. Holmes began by saying that Mr. Acheson intended to expound to the North Atlantic Council the increased defence efforts which the United States proposed to make and to urge the European countries that they should also increase their efforts. The United States Government were planning greatly to increase their expenditure on defence in the forthcoming fiscal year and were struck by the fact that the European countries, Great Britain apart, had done very little to fulfil their share of the high priority production programme. Mr. Acheson would probably

state the readiness of the United States to speed up delivery of end-item assistance[1] to N.A.T.O. countries which were prepared to increase their own defence measures. Mr. Acheson thought that it would be helpful if I could follow him at the Brussels meeting by urging the need for a speeding up of defence efforts all round.

3. I told Mr. Holmes that I would immediately examine with my colleagues the proposal which he had outlined in regard to end-item assistance and consider whether I could say anything at Brussels on the lines suggested. Mr. Achilles undertook to let me have in writing an outline of Mr. Acheson's proposal, which has since been received and is attached as an Annex.[2]

4. I proceeded to give Mr. Holmes an outline of the manner in which, after discussion with my colleagues in the Cabinet, I thought that the questions of German rearmament and a German contribution to Western defence should be handled at the forthcoming meeting in Brussels. His Majesty's Government accepted the 'Spofford Plan' as approved by the Deputies. We thought, however, that if the German Government were formally asked to say at once whether they were willing to accept this plan they would make an unfavourable response. Furthermore, if I was right in anticipating this unfavourable response from the Germans, the Russians would be able to exploit this attitude on the part of the Germans to our disadvantage at a meeting of the Council of Foreign Ministers. I therefore thought that, after the Atlantic Council had approved the 'Spofford Plan', the three High Commissioners should inform the German Government at this stage merely that the Plan had been adopted, but should not ask them either to accept or reject it. Meanwhile, the Council, I hoped, would be able to agree on the immediate appointment of the Supreme Commander and the creation of the integrated force for the defence of Western Europe. If matters were handled in this way, I thought that we should be in a strong position. We should be building up our strength in Europe, while not courting a collision with the Russians or a rebuff from the Germans.[3]

5. Mr. Holmes replied that Mr. Acheson apeared to be thinking along much the same lines. It was clear that it would be a mistake at this stage to make any formal offer to the Germans.

6. Mr. Holmes went on to say that Mr. Acheson's conception of the

[1] See No. 79, paragraph 28.

[2] Not printed. For the substance of Mr. Acheson's proposed statement, see the second paragraph of Mr. Attlee's statement in No. 143.

[3] The substance of this paragraph formed the basis of a personal message from Mr. Bevin to Mr. Acheson despatched at 1.45 p.m. on 15 December (F.O. telegram to Washington No. 5632 on WU 1198/682). On the following day Sir O. Harvey was instructed to convey a similar message to M. Schuman 'as an indication of the way my mind is working and say that I shall want to discuss the manner of the approach to the Germans with him and Acheson. You may add that we shall also have to clear up the outstanding point in the draft reply to the Soviet note of November 3rd' (F.O. telegram to Paris No. 1371 on C 8144/65/18 – text of message on C 8165/27/18).

approach to the Germans was the following. The 'Spofford Plan' should be introduced by the three High Commissioners to the German Federal Government much in the way that I had suggested. The High Commissioners should, however, go on to press the German Federal Government to conclude the agreement on the 'Schuman Plan' and should also encourage them to accept the French invitation to Paris and approach the French idea of a European Army in a constructive manner.

7. I told Mr. Holmes that I saw little difficulty in His Majesty's Government joining with the French and United States Governments in encouraging the Germans to conclude the agreement on the 'Schuman Plan', provided that it was well understood that His Majesty's Government could not participate in the Plan, but could only be associated with it. I would think over the further proposal that we should give the Germans positive encouragement to fall in with the French idea of a European Army. We had withdrawn our opposition to this idea, but did not feel any great enthusiasm for it. I thought that once the Supreme Commander was appointed, the whole position should become easier. In reply to a question, Mr. Holmes asserted that it was certainly not the intention of the United States Government to delay the appointment of the Supreme Commander until the proposed Paris Conference had shown whether the Plan for a European Army could be brought to fruition. It was Mr. Acheson's hope that it would be possible to announce the appointment of the Supreme Commander at the end of the Brussels Conference, or immediately afterwards.

8. Mr. Holmes finally raised the question of the relations between the Western Powers and the German Federal Government. Mr. Acheson was coming to the conclusion that it would be necessary to place our relations with the German Federal Government on a new basis, replacing the present system of controls by a new contractual agreement which while still reserving supreme authority to the Occupying Powers would leave the German Federal Government virtually free to conduct its own affairs.

9. I said that I had been giving some thought to this problem, but had not yet come to any firm conclusion. We must be careful of speaking of 'equal status' for the Germans, since this would not be acceptable to the French. On the other hand, merely to relax further controls might not meet the situation in Germany. It might be possible to work out some method by which the progress of German rearmament was linked to the relaxation of the remaining controls, thus enabling Germany to 'work her passage' according to her performance and ability to play her part in Western Europe. I should see no objection to a study of these problems being undertaken by the three High Commissioners, assisted by experts from the three Governments.

10. Mr. Holmes was asked whether it was Mr. Acheson's intention that the three High Commissioners, when communicating the 'Spofford Plan' to the German Federal Government, should speak to them on the lines which he had outlined above. We thought the question needed a great

deal of thinking out before we were in a position to go to the Germans with definite proposals. Mr. Holmes seemed confident that all Mr. Acheson had in mind was an exchange of views on this question with myself and M. Schuman in the course of our meeting in Brussels.[4]

11. I am sending copies of this despatch to His Majesty's Representatives at Paris and Wahnerheide.

I am, &c.,
ERNEST BEVIN

CALENDAR TO No. 139

i *16–20 Dec. 1950   U.S. proposals on German controls* summarized in Washington tel. No. 3437 and confirmed in tel. No. 3438: objective is to bring Germany into equal partnership by: reducing controls to a hard permanent core of atomic, chemical and biological warfare controls; asking F.R.G. for evidence of cooperation by joining Schuman Plan and European Army; replacing occupation statutes by series of undertakings and contractual arrangements under 8 heads (*a*) human rights (*b*) N.A.T.O. – Germany to be full partner (*c*) revision of P.L.I. agreement (*d*) claims (*e*) bilateral agreements e.g. for E.C.A. and broadcasting (*f*) termination of occupation statute (*g*) special arrangements for Berlin (*h*) Eastern frontier of Germany. Acheson to suggest at Brussels that whole question be considered by I.G.G. between Jan.–Feb. 1951. British response includes Bevin's concern that U.S. should not raise future of Germany in N.A.T.O. at N.A.C. meeting. I.G.G. timetable considered too tight. Acheson warned by Bevin on 18 Dec. that as regards special arrangements for Berlin 'it might be dangerous for us to abandon the quadripartite concept in Western Germany and at the same time insist on maintaining it in Berlin' [C 8207/20/18; WU 1198/719, 729].

[4] American proposals on German controls, of which the Foreign Office had been receiving reports since 12 December (e.g. C 8137, 8139, 8227/20/18), were communicated to the Foreign Office on 16 December: see calendar i. Meanwhile the Foreign Office's own thinking about the future of the Occupation was examined in a memorandum by Mr. Mallet of 14 December. Mr. Mallet traced the mounting pressure since November from Dr. Adenauer for political equality and suggested 'that we neither can nor should attempt to resist or to try still further to reduce existing controls without entirely scrapping them.' However, he warned that the working out of a new arrangement to replace the Occupation regime would be 'a long and arduous matter' (C 8227/20/18): see further No. 140, note 2.

No. 140

Brief by Mr. Stevens for Mr. Bevin

[*CJ 5085/91/182*]

FOREIGN OFFICE, *16 December 1950*

Germany: Prohibited and Limited Industries

It is suggested that you might raise the question of the Prohibited and Limited Industries Agreement with M. Schuman in Brussels in the following very general terms:

You have learned with some dismay that the French Government is unwilling to proceed with a revision of German industrial controls until complete agreement has been reached on German rearmament.[1] In your view the P.L.I. Agreement needs to be revised in order to take account of changed circumstances quite apart from any question of German rearmament. These circumstances are:

    (i) The need to associate Germany politically with the West.

    (ii) The fact that we are now thinking less of security against Germany and more of security against the U.S.S.R.

    (iii) The needs of the German economy.

    (iv) The needs of Western defence quite apart from German rearmament.

If the revision of the P.L.I. Agreement has to await agreement on German rearmament this may involve many months delay. In the interval we are likely to be faced with a serious political agitation in Germany on the lines of that on reparations in 1949. The Western Powers may also find that as a result of the restrictions they are unable

---

[1] I.G.G. negotiations towards a revision of the P.L.I. agreement (see No. 55, note 10) were halted on 1 December when M. Massigli informed the Study Group that M. Schuman had agreed at New York to a review of the P.L.I. agreement only on the understanding that no revision would be put into force until agreement was reached on German rearmament. Given the hardening German attitude towards rearmament, the French government was unwilling to surrender a major bargaining lever in the shape of the revision of the P.L.I. agreement until Germany's place in Western defence had been decided by the Western Allies and accepted by the Federal government. The French delegation therefore proposed to suspend the I.G.G. negotiations pending agreement on defence. This position was maintained in two further I.G.G. meetings ending on 14 December with the French Ambassador regretting 'that there appeared to be an unbridgeable gap between the position of his Government and that of the United Kingdom and United States Governments' (F.O. telegram to Wahnerheide No. 1215 Saving on CJ 4599/91/182). Mr. Bevin was informed of Foreign Office concern at these developments in a brief by Sir D. Gainer on 14 December. Sir D. Gainer ascribed the French attitude to (*a*) M. Schuman's genuine, but erroneous, conviction that industrial controls and rearmament had been linked at New York; (*b*) French unwillingness to relax controls until the Federal government had accepted the Schuman Plan; (*c*) recent deterioration in Franco-German relations; (*d*) French concern not to prejudice the proposed Four-Power Meeting.

to place orders in Germany for essential non-warlike stores, thus hampering the progress of Western defence.

You could then appeal to M. Schuman to have the matter reconsidered by the French Cabinet in the light of the views which you have expressed with a view to securing the agreement of the French Government that a revision of the P.L.I. Agreement which would not include permission to make heavy armaments should be completed early in the New Year and put into effect as soon as possible.

If M. Schuman says that the Germans have not yet implemented the New York decisions, you could say that you had no intention of suggesting that the revision of the P.L.I. Agreement should take effect before the New York decisions were implemented.

I have ascertained that if you decide to raise the matter in the general terms suggested above, Mr. Acheson will give you full support.[2]

R.B. STEVENS

[2] This brief was counter-signed by Sir D. Gainer on 16 December and discussed that day at an Office meeting with Mr. Bevin together with Mr. Mallet's paper on the future of the Occupation (see No. 139, note 4). With regard to constitutional questions, Mr. Bevin maintained that 'we must not be rushed into hasty or premature decisions. At the same time we must not allow a complete stalemate to develop in our relations with Germany'. It was agreed that German participation in western defence would have a bearing on the constitutional issues but that the two questions should not be too tightly linked. Recommendations from the A.H.C. were considered a necessary preliminary to any constitutional changes. Mr. Bevin agreed that 'the approach should be different from that adopted in the past when the three Occupation Powers had worked out their plans and then presented them to the Federal Government. The new arrangements should be worked out by the Occupation Powers in discussions with the Federal Government . . . The Secretary of State also agreed that if progress were to be made on the above lines in the constitutional field corresponding advances should be made in regard to industrial controls. He accordingly agreed to raise the question of the Prohibited and Limited Industries with Monsieur Schuman and Mr. Acheson in Brussels on the general lines suggested in the attached minute by M. Stevens' (minute of meeting by Mr. Allen on C 8228/20/18).

No. 141

Brief by Sir P. Dixon for Mr. Bevin

[*WU 1071/240*]

BRUSSELS, *17 December 1950*

Brussels Meeting

We are likely to find a very difficult atmosphere in Brussels. The predominant feeling among the European countries, or at least France and Italy, will be fear of Russia; the predominant desire of the United States will be to push on with the rearmament of Germany, and this attitude will add to the anxieties of the Europeans.

The Russians are adroitly exploiting this situation. In addition to their usual propaganda offensive they have developed a diplomatic offensive. This started with the note of the 29th October[1] in reply to the Western Powers' representations about the East German police and with the note of the 3rd November[2] suggesting a meeting of the Council of Foreign Ministers to discuss the fulfilment of the Potsdam Agreement on the demilitarisation of Germany. It culminated in the notes to Great Britain and France, delivered just before the Brussels meeting, alleging that German rearmament is incompatible not only with the Potsdam Agreement but also with the Anglo-Soviet and Franco-Soviet Treaties.[3]

In addition the Russians are believed . . .[4] to be offering inducements to the French in return for French opposition to German rearmament, and we know that the Italian Government have been frightened into believing that a Russian attack on Europe is a serious possibility.[5] Finally the German Federal Chancellor has been brought to believe that the potential effect upon German opinion of Grotewohl's offer to meet him to discuss the unification of Germany must be considered very seriously.[6]

The Russians are supporting this diplomatic barrage in Europe by action, to judge by their attitude at New York, designed to keep open and widen the dispute between China and the U.S.A.

In this situation I think that our first and primary task in Brussels is to rally European morale. Our second task is to persuade the United States to take account of the state of feeling in Europe.

Our objectives might be as follows:

(1) By giving a lead ourselves on increased and accelerated defence measures, urge the European countries to redouble their own defence measures as proposed by the United States. At the same time the U.S. must reassure the European countries by the immediate establishment of the integrated force and the appointment of the Supreme Commander.

[1] See No. 78, note 2, for this note, transmitted on 20 October.
[2] See No. 86, note 5.   [3] See No. 138, note 3.
[4] A confidential reference is here omitted.
[5] On 15 December the Italian Ambassador in London informed Sir W. Strang that 'he had just received a telegram from Count Sforza saying that there was a strong impression that Russia might act immediately in the event of a decision about the rearmament of Germany. Count Sforza did not know how serious this indication was, but as he was meeting his Cabinet tomorrow he would like to know what we thought about it in London'. Sir W. Strang assured the Ambassador that this matter had been considered in London, Washington and Paris and that 'While therefore not entirely disregarding the possibility of Russian reaction, we did not propose to be deterred from proceeding with the plans which had been drawn up by the North Atlantic Deputies and Military Committee . . . Our view was that the decision in principle to organize a German contribution should stand, but that its working out would be a matter for consideration . . . the Ambassador said he thought that this indication of our views would be helpful to Count Sforza' (WU 1195/522). On 16 December the Italian government issued a statement reaffirming its support for German participation in an integrated force provided that steps towards this did not 'afford any suspicion or possible opening for trouble-making elements' (WT 1023/22).
[6] See No. 135, note 2 and No. 135.i.

But such appeals will be unavailing unless the Europeans can be assured that the Russians will not be provoked into acting before we are ready.

(2) The despatch of the reply by the three Western Powers to the Soviet note would be reassuring to European morale. We should aim at getting this reply agreed and despatched by the end of the Brussels Conference, though time must be allowed for it to be shown in advance to the German, Austrian and Benelux Governments.

The effect would be to show that we are ready to discuss a settlement; but on past Soviet form we cannot be expected to relax our efforts to defend ourselves.

(3) We should not rush German rearmament. The United States seem now to be at one with us on this. But they are heading off too fast and too rigidly on a new tack. They now realise that the political evolution of Germany must be speeded up if the Germans are to be persuaded to rearm. We would, I think, say that the political evolution must develop first, and rearmament come later. The Americans want the two processes to go along hand in hand, and to go fast. If they push this too hard at Brussels, the only result will be to jeopardize what agreement has been reached since New York and to start another period of deadlock with the French, and perhaps others.

I think therefore that Mr. Acheson should be persuaded at least to omit all reference to a date-line for the proposed study of a new relationship between the Occupying Powers and Germany, and also to omit any reference to Germany's ultimate membership of N.A.T.O.

(4) Finally we may be pressed to adopt a more positively encouraging line towards ideas of integration in Europe. We ought not at the present stage to commit ourselves to pressing the Germans to join in the French plan for a European Army as a condition of any further relaxation of occupation controls. But we shall probably find it wise to associate ourselves with some encouraging public statement about the French proposal to call a conference and to agree to be represented at it by observers.

A programme at Brussels on these lines ought to achieve our triple object of

(1) Putting flesh on our skeleton defences
(2) Keeping an area of negotiation open with the Russians
(3) Providing for an unprovocative evolution of Germany towards further participation in the benefits and responsibilities of the Western world.

No. 142

Foreign Office[1] to Sir J. Le Rougetel (Brussels)[2]

No. 455 Telegraphic [C 8102/65/18]

Immediate. Secret   FOREIGN OFFICE, 18 December 1950, 3.16 p.m.

Repeated Saving to Moscow, Washington, Berlin, Wahnerheide.

Following for Secretary of State.

Soviet Note of December 15th on German Rearmament[3]

Following is general background appreciation.

2. The Soviet Government is employing every device of propaganda and diplomacy to prevent German participation in the defence of Western Europe. It did the same in an attempt to forestall the establishment of a West German Federal Government and also early in 1949 in order to prevent Norway and Denmark acceding to the North Atlantic Pact. On the latter occasion, in a note dated 31st March,[4] it condemned the forthcoming signature of the Pact as a breach of the Charter and as contrary to the Anglo-Soviet and Franco-Soviet Treaties and to the Yalta and Potsdam agreements: but it did not go beyond words.

3. It does not follow that, because the Soviet Government took no positive action on that occasion, they will not do so now. We have always recognised that the Soviet Government would intensely dislike any step towards the rearmament of Western Germany, which would touch vital Soviet interests even more closely than did the signing of the North Atlantic Pact. The declaration of a state of emergency in the United States[5] may well increase their alarm. The present world situation, with Western democracies preoccupied with affairs in the Far East, must moreover seem to be exceptionally favourable, if they are contemplating military action.

4. If we proceed as we must with our plans for rearming Western Germany, there are three possible courses open to the Soviet Union. They are, in order of probability:

(a) a propaganda and diplomatic campaign to prevent our carrying out our plans, followed in the event of failure by a formal protest for the record;

[1] Mr. Bevin left London for Brussels on Sunday, 17 December in order to attend meetings of the N.A.C. (18–19 December), Tripartite meeting with Mr. Acheson and M. Schuman (19 December) and Brussels Treaty Consultative Council (20 December). Mr. Bevin was joined in Brussels by Mr. Shinwell for the N.A. Defence Committee meeting on 18 December and joint N.A.C./Defence Committee meetings on the afternoon of 18 December and morning of 19 December. Mr. Bevin returned to London on 21 December.

[2] H.M. Ambassador at Brussels.   [3] See No. 138, note 3,

[4] Printed in *Documents on International Affairs 1949–1950* (R.I.I.A., 1953), pp. 38–42.

[5] Announced by President Truman on 15 December (*ibid.*, pp. 83–90) and proclaimed on the following day.

(*b*) various measures short of war, including the reimposition of the Berlin blockade, denunciation of the Anglo-Soviet and Franco-Soviet Treaties, and possibly withdrawal from United Nations.

(*c*) military measures against Western Germany.

5. As regards (*c*), recent intelligence appreciations agree that the re-arming of Germany is one of the developments which might provoke the Soviet Government to start a preventive war. But they also agree that the Russians probably do not want a general war yet. It is difficult to see what military action they could undertake in Europe which would not bring about such a war.

6. For all the practical value that it may have, we could accept the denunciation of the Anglo-Soviet Treaty with equanimity. It is out-dated and serves no practical purpose. But its denunciation, if combined with a Soviet withdrawal from United Nations, would amount to the virtual severing of all links between Soviet Union and the free world except for formal diplomatic representation and such economic exchanges as seemed worth while to either party.

7. We are clearly at a dangerous stage in our attempt to build up a situation of strength in Europe and it would be rash to discount the possibility that the Russians might go to war to prevent our embarking on the rearmament of Western Germany. But the balance of probability is that their immediate object is to sow dissension in the Western camp and to intimidate us, and particularly the French, into postponing a final decision at least until there have been Four Power discussions. At such discussions the Russians might conceivably be prepared to offer consider-able concessions, including the dissolution of the Bereitschaften, in return for our abandonment of our own plans for rearming Western Germany. If we refused, the Russians would then proclaim that they had taken every possible step to prevent our rearming Germany. This would strengthen their propaganda position, if they then decided to take positive action.[6]

[6] When discussing the Soviet notes with Sir W. Strang on 18 December, M. Massigli 'asked whether German rearmament was not for the Russians what the 38th parallel was for the Chinese.' In reply Sir W. Strang observed that 'Korea was not an area which was regarded as in itself so important by the Western Powers as to make a world war inevitable', whereas 'the Russians knew quite well that any move in Europe either by the Bereitschaften or by the Satellites or by themselves would, in present circumstances, be almost bound to lead to war. On the whole, therefore, we thought that they would be prudent, at any rate until their economy was in a better state to stand a war and until their air defences had been perfected. The danger, however, was that the margin for manoeuvre had been greatly narrowed.' For this reason Sir W. Strang explained, both British and French wanted to send 'a less uncompromising reply' to the Russian proposal for Four-Power talks. 'We did not really think, any more than did the Americans, that Four-Power talks were likely to succeed. But so long as one was talking, one was talking . . . In the same way our line at New York about the Far East was to give time for discussion and to put off decisive or provocative acts. This was not appeasement, but common prudence. Diplomacy still had a beneficent part to play in the world' (WF 1023/35).

8. Draft reply to Soviet note is being prepared and will be telegraphed to you as soon as possible.[7]

[7] A draft reply was telegraphed to Brussels that evening for discussion between Mr. Bevin and M. Schuman. In the event this did not take place. The British delegation were, however, given a copy of the French draft reply. A text of the British reply, sent on 5 January 1951 (C 8276/65/18), is printed in *Documents on International Affairs 1951* (R.I.I.A., 1954), pp. 321–3: *ibid.*, pp. 323–331 for further Anglo-Soviet exchanges.

No. 143

Extract from the Conclusions of a Meeting of the Cabinet held at 10 Downing Street on Monday, 18 December 1950, at 11 a.m.[1]

C.M. (50) 87th Conclusions [CAB 128/18]

Secret

Defence: Acceleration of Defence Preparations

(Previous Reference: C.M. (50) 85th Conclusions, Minute 3)[2]

1. *The Prime Minister* recalled that when, on 12th December, he had made his report to the Cabinet on his talks with President Truman he had said that he had undertaken to consider the President's request that this country should increase its defence effort. Since his return from Washington he had been considering this matter in the light of the continuing gravity of the international situation and, after discussion with the Foreign Secretary and the Minister of Defence, he had come to the conclusion that some acceleration in the pace of defence preparations was now unavoidable. The war planning of Departments generally was still based on the assumption that there would be no major war before 1957, though some of the Departments had adjusted some of their preparations to take account of the earlier date of 1954 to which the Medium Term

[1] *Present* at this meeting were Mr. Attlee (*in the Chair*); Mr. Morrison; Mr. Gaitskell; Mr. Dalton; Viscount Addison; Viscount Jowitt; Mr. Chuter Ede; Mr. Isaacs; Mr. Bevan; Mr. Williams; Mr. Tomlinson; Mr. Wilson; Mr. Griffiths; Mr. McNeil; Mr. Gordon Walker. *Also present* for item 1 was Mr. Davies. *Secretariat*: Sir N. Brook, Mr. Johnston, Mr. Morland.

[2] At this meeting on 12 December Mr. Attlee gave the Cabinet a report on his visit to Washington. He explained why he had no alternative but to support the Spofford Plan (see Nos. 131 and 133) and said that as regards the supply of raw materials 'the President and his advisers had been very forthcoming' (CAB 128/18). Mr. Attlee referred to American pressure at Washington for an increased defence effort from the United Kingdom (see Nos. 132, 134) and warned that the Americans were likely to return to the subject. Preparations for a Cabinet paper on the acceleration of defence were overtaken by the news relayed by Mr. Holmes (No. 139) that Mr. Acheson intended to call on European powers for a greater defence effort at Brussels. With a view to obtaining instructions for Mr. Bevin to make a quick and positive response at Brussels, Sir N. Brook suggested to Mr. Attlee in a minute on 16 December that he should raise the matter orally at the next Cabinet meeting. Mr. Attlee's statement below was based on this minute (WU 1071/243) and on speaking notes provided the next day by Sir N. Brook (CAB 21/2248).

Defence Plan of the North Atlantic Treaty Organisation was related.[3] The United States were now accelerating their own preparations on the basis that major war might occur in 1952 or even 1951. These different planning dates gave rise to a measure of confusion and the position ought to be rationalised: this process would necessarily involve some acceleration of defence preparations. If Departments were told to plan on the basis that a major war was inevitable within the next two or three years very large expenditure would be involved (*e.g.*, on civil defence), and he believed that a satisfactory hypothesis could be framed on the basis that the aim was to strengthen the active defences of this country for the purpose of preventing a major war. Some increase in defence expenditure over the next two years appeared, however, to be unavoidable. The existing programme would have to be accelerated in some respects, and there would be need for quicker progress with the completion of paper plans. The Chiefs of Staff were examining as a matter of urgency the measures which would be required: they were likely to recommend the calling up of reserves in batches for special training, increased production of weapons and equipment, and the completion of plans for the expansion of war production in the early stages of a war. Specific proposals would be put before the Cabinet as soon as possible after Christmas.

Meanwhile, it had been learned that, at the meeting of the North Atlantic Council on 19th December, the United States Secretary of State intended to make a statement calling on European Governments to increase their defence effort. He would announce that the United States Government aimed to complete their share of the Medium Term Defence Plan in two years instead of three, and that the United States aid towards European military effort would be continued in 1952 at the same rate as in 1951 ($5,000 million). He would estimate that Europe's contribution to the accelerated Medium Term Defence Plan should be between $15,000 and $18,000 million in the period to 30th June, 1953, and on this basis he would ask European countries to double their pre-Korean rate of defence expenditure. In his talks in Washington, the Prime Minister had persuaded the Americans to accept Anglo-American partnership as the mainspring of Atlantic defence. Much of the advantage we had gained

[3] In a draft report on defence preparedness of 15 December, overtaken by the present action in Cabinet, the Chiefs of Staff considered that while 'there is still reason to believe that Russia is unlikely deliberately to embark on a war during the next two or three years . . . Nevertheless, the state of international tension resulting from Chinese intervention in Korea, and the unbalancing effect of this on American opinion, together with the possibility of a sharp Russian reaction to the proposal to re-arm Western Germany, all these have increased the danger that world war may break out in 1951. A further factor is the impression that may be gaining ground behind the Iron Curtain that the Western allies do not intend in any event to use the atom bomb . . . the risk of war has undoubtedly increased over the last few weeks to the extent that all possible steps, short of general mobilisation, should be taken to increase our defence preparedness' (C.O.S. 1690/15/12/50 on DEFE 7/663).

would be lost if we were now to be treated as merely one of the European countries which were being urged by America to make a larger contribution to the common defence effort. We should align ourselves with the Americans in urging the others to do more.[4] One could not ignore the risk, however remote it might seem, that the United States might lose interest in the defence of Europe, if her allies in the North Atlantic Treaty Organisation failed to play their proper part.

The Prime Minister accordingly proposed that the Foreign Secretary should express general agreement with all that the United States Secretary of State was to say about the urgency of building up the military strength of the West: that he should also emphasise the substantial contributions which the United Kingdom Government had already made: but that he should be authorised to go on to say that the United Kingdom Government, in view of the disturbed and dangerous international situation, had decided to increase and accelerate their defence preparations still further, with the sole object of assisting the Atlantic community and the other nations of the free world to resist aggression and to secure their own safety and freedom, and were now considering the form and direction which this additional effort should take.

The Prime Minister said that it was not his intention that, if his proposal were accepted, the United Kingdom Government should at this stage give any new figure for their enlarged defence programme: indeed, they should resist any United States pressure to specify a figure. They should not follow the procedure adopted in the summer when, in response to a United States request, they had stated a figure of defence expenditure before working out a definite programme. They should now revert to the more normal procedure of considering first what further measures were required to meet the needs of the situation, how far they were physically possible, and then calculating their cost.

In discussion the following points were made:

(a) The other Western European countries had made a disappointing response to earlier proposals for increased defence preparations, and it was certainly desirable that there should be a greater measure of equality of sacrifice within the North Atlantic community. But the fact

[4] The above passage from 'In his talks . . .' was based on Sir N. Brook's minute of 16 December (see note 2) in which he referred to the danger of slipping 'back into the European "queue" . . . We must try hard to preserve the position that we are seconding the Americans by example as well as exhortation in the pressure which must now be brought to bear upon the others to do more. There is reason to believe that the Americans would like us to align ourselves with them in this way at the Brussels meeting, and have no desire to see us drop back into the European "queue". From what was said by the United States Minister in London when he informed us of Mr. Acheson's intentions, it is a fair assumption that we were given this advance indication of what Mr. Acheson is proposing to say in the hope that we would follow with something on the same lines.' Sir N. Brook went on to emphasise the importance of Mr. Bevin making an immediate positive response since otherwise 'it will be difficult for him to give the impression that the United States and the United Kingdom are jointly calling upon the others to match their contributions' (WU 1071/243).

remained that, since the invasion of Korea, there had been a steady deterioration in the international situation, and some acceleration of our defence preparations was required as a measure of self-preservation. It might be true that the Soviet Government did not at present desire a major war, but there could be no certainty on this point; and there was, in any event, a serious risk that the Soviet Government might plunge into adventures which would set in train a succession of consequences leading to a major war.

(b) At the same time the Western democracies must endeavour to strike a balance between, on the one hand, reasonably adequate defence preparations and, on the other, the maintenance of stable economies and a reasonable standard of living. The Soviet Government would be well satisfied if defence preparations in the West were pushed to a point which brought economic chaos and mass unemployment. While the United States Congress and Administration had shown themselves prepared to devote great resources to building up the defence of the West, they might have to be reminded, in present circumstances, of the continued need to maintain the economic viability of Western Europe as an essential foundation for military strength.

(c) The defence contribution so far made by continental Powers in Western Europe had been disappointing. At the same time it had to be born in mind that about 90 per cent. of the defence production of the North Atlantic Treaty Powers was in the United Kingdom, North America and France; and the contributions of some of the smaller Powers, while important on general grounds, could not greatly affect the issue from the material point of view. It would be helpful if the main contributors to Atlantic defence could reach a common appraisal of what was required, and what could be done, over the next two or three years to build up the defences of Western Europe.

(d) Differing views were expressed about the stage at which Western Germany should be invited to co-operate in the defence of the West. On the one hand, it was pointed out that, without the assistance of land forces drawn from Western Germany, there was no prospect of securing forces which could contain the vast Soviet land and air forces. On the other hand, attention was drawn to the risk that Russia might in present circumstances treat the rearmament of Germany as a *casus belli*, and that the rearmament of Germany might consolidate Soviet power in the satellite countries which feared Germany and had suffered recently from German occupation. There was, however, general agreement that, in view of the present attitude of the Federal Government and people of Western Germany and the caution which the Russian note of remonstrance[5] would induce in the French Government, the question of German rearmament was not an immediate one and could be handled on the lines which the Cabinet

[5] See No. 138, note 3.

had approved at their meeting on 14th December (C.M. (50) 86th Conclusions Minute 3[4]).[6]

(*e*) Some disquiet was expressed about the language which the United States Secretary of State was intending to use about the United States contribution to an acceleration of Western rearmament. This departed from the conception of a common partnership and pooling of resources, and reverted to the earlier idea of United States aid towards accelerated defence programmes. While it was understandable, from the point of view of difficulties in Congress, that the United States Government should wish to relate the amount of United States aid to the increase in defence efforts in Europe, this approach would not be helpful to European Governments in dealing with their own Parliaments and in countering Communist propaganda. It was, in any event, important that this form of approach should not be adopted in connection with the United States contribution towards this country's defence programme. Public opinion in this country had greeted with relief the termination of Marshall Aid, and would not welcome a new form of dependence upon American aid.

(*f*) While no new figure of defence expenditure should be put forward at the Brussels meeting, Ministers should consider in the next few weeks the exact extent of the increase and acceleration of defence preparations which were regarded as desirable and practicable.

(*g*) In view of the extent to which this country had increased its defence preparations before the aggression of Korea, we could not accept any United States suggestion that all North Atlantic countries should agree to double their pre-Korean expenditure on defence.

(*h*) It was already clear that the implementation of the existing defence programme would involve the introduction of a number of controls designed to ensure that the necessary resources were available for rearmament and to counter inflation. To the extent to which the defence programme was further increased and accelerated more controls and a wider use of emergency powers would be required. Thus, if the proposed call-up of reservists was not to interfere with production, some form of deferment and of control of labour would probably be required. These implications of an enlarged defence programme would be brought before the Cabinet, when a fresh programme had been drawn up, after discussion with the Chiefs of Staff and the Central Economic Planning Staff. An effort should be made at some stage to secure acceptance of some degree of equality of sacrifice by the civilian population of North America and Europe.

(*i*) It was suggested that Ministers should be given a clearer picture of the content of the rearmament programme and the extent to which it was to be increased and accelerated by the measures now proposed. Ministers should have more precise and readily available information

---

[6] See No. 137.

showing what was being done by this country and how it was related to the strategic position in Europe.

(*j*) The Foreign Secretary was aware of the need to ensure that adequate raw materials were made available for the increased defence programme, and he would be discussing this aspect of the matter with the United States Secretary of State. He would also ask for United States co-operation in preventing increases in world prices, which would mean that less effective results were secured from any given expenditure on defence.

The Cabinet:

(1) Agreed that at the meeting of the North Atlantic Council on the following day the Foreign Secretary should say that the United Kingdom Government had already decided to increase and accelerate their defence preparations still further and were considering what form and direction this increased effort should take.

(2) Instructed the Secretary of the Cabinet to inform the Foreign Secretary of the views expressed in the Cabinet's discussion.[7]

(3) Invited the Chiefs of Staff to consider in detail in what directions defence preparations could most profitably be accelerated.[8]

[7] Telegrams Nos. 460–1 and 465 to Brussels were accordingly despatched that evening (WU 1071/224, and F.O. 800/456).

[8] The implications of the Cabinet decisions above were discussed by the Chiefs of Staff that afternoon and action set in train for the necessary reports (DEFE 7/663).

No. 144

Sir J. Le Rougetel (Brussels) to Foreign Office
(Received 19 December, 7 a.m.)

No. 313 Telegraphic [*WU 1071/220*]

Immediate. Secret   BRUSSELS, *19 December 1950, 4.44 a.m.*

Repeated to Washington and Saving to Paris, Brussels, Wahnerheide.

Following from Secretary of State.
North Atlantic Council.
Council held its first meeting this afternoon [18 December]. Following is summary of its discussions.

2. Items on the agenda were:

   (I) German participation in defence of Western Europe;
   (II) Creation of an integrated force.

3. Council approved, almost without discussion, joint report of Military Committee and deputies on German participation.[1] Rather to my

[1] See No. 136, note 2.

surprise, no one raised the question of the manner and timing of an approach to the German Federal Government, although I gave the other Ministers an opportunity to do so by saying that it would be useful for the three Occupying Powers to know the views of the other North Atlantic Treaty Organisation (N.A.T.O.) countries on this point.

4. The Council approved the proposals for the immediate establishment of the integrated force and the appointment of a Supreme Commander. It also passed a resolution inviting the United States Government to designate a United States officer as Supreme Commander. Mr. Acheson said he hoped the United States would be able to do this before the meeting of the Council tomorrow morning and suggested that the Council might wish to propose a name. The Council took the hint and unanimously proposed General Eisenhower.

5. Full record of discussion follows by Saving telegram.[2]

6. Please pass to Ministry of Defence.

Foreign Office please pass to Washington as my telegram No. 22 and Saving to Paris and Wahnerheide as my telegrams Nos. 53 and 20 respectively.

[2] See No. 145.i.

No. 145

Sir J. Le Rougetel (Brussels) to Foreign Office
(Received 19 December, 4.40 p.m.)

No. 316 Telegraphic [*WU 1071/225*]

Immediate. Secret   BRUSSELS, *19 December 1950, 3.53 p.m.*

Repeated to Washington and Paris.

Following from Secretary of State.

Your telegrams Nos. 460, 461 and 465:[1] increased defence effort.

Discussion of this question at this morning's meeting of the Atlantic Council went off satisfactorily.

2. Mr. Acheson did not in the event appeal to other powers to double their defence expenditure; nor did he suggest that there should be any direct relation between increased European effort and increased American aid. He confined himself to a general appeal for increased forces and production. For my part I was able to take the lead in responding to United States appeal and delivered the declaration authorised in your telegram 460 which was well received.[2] I also said something to safeguard

[1] See No. 143, note 7.
[2] The declaration transmitted in telegram No. 460 to Brussels read: 'I am authorised by His Majesty's Government to say that, in view of the disturbed and dangerous international situation, the United Kingdom Government have decided to increase and accelerate their

our position on raw material and our unwillingness to fix figures of defence expenditure and consider afterwards how the amounts should be spent.[3]

3. Mr. Acheson made three points in his statement.

(a) The need to place at once all available forces under the command of the Supreme Commander. He said that before the day was out all United States Forces in Europe would have been put under General Eisenhower (whose appointment had just been confirmed by the Council)[4] and he appealed to other countries to take similar action.

(b) The need to increase forces and especially those under the Supreme Commander. He was authorised by the President to say that the United States would increase its forces in Europe.

(c) The need to increase production of war material. A vast increase in United States raw production was planned and a new appropriation of more than 40 billion dollars had been asked for. Mr. Charles Wilson, a former President of General Electric, had been appointed to direct the new production effort of the United States and Mr. Acheson urged North Atlantic Treaty Organisation (N.A.T.O.) countries to consider both individually and collectively similar appointments in the field of defence production.

4. Apart from reading the declaration authorised in your telegram No.

defence preparations still further with the sole object of assisting the Atlantic Community and the other nations of the free world to resist aggression and to secure their own freedom and safety. The United Kingdom Government are now considering the form and direction which this additional effort should take.'

[3] When Mr. Bevin informed Mr. Acheson in private conversation on 18 December that he was expecting Cabinet authority to support an American appeal for an increased defence effort, he warned that 'anything His Majesty's Government could do would, however, be dependent on satisfactory arrangements with regard to raw materials' (F.O. 800/517). Anglo-American differences over the size of the proposed Central Group for Raw Materials were aggravated at Brussels by complaints from Dr. Stikker at the N.A.C. meeting on 19 December (reported separately in Brussels telegram No. 326 on UR 1030/28) that bilateral decisions had been taken in Washington on a question on which other European powers should have been consulted. Reassurances from Mr. Acheson suggested some Anglo-American misunderstanding as to whether an Organisation had been agreed in principle at Washington or not. When acknowledging this misunderstanding to Mr. Bevin after the meeting, Mr. Acheson suggested that the matter should be cleared up between President Truman and Mr. Attlee, who were then in communication over the size of the Central Group. This group was eventually formed on a tripartite basis in February 1951 and enlarged the following month to include Australia, Brazil, Canada, India, Italy, O.E.E.C. and its American equivalent.

[4] At the beginning of this meeting Mr. Acheson read a letter from President Truman announcing the appointment of General Eisenhower as Supreme Commander. It was agreed that all N.A.T. Foreign and Defence Ministers would sign a resolution accepting this appointment and that each Minister of Defence would later send to the Chairman written confirmation on behalf of their respective governments. British acceptance of this appointment, cleared with H.M. The King and Mr. Attlee (correspondence on DEFE 7/685), was conveyed in writing by Mr. Shinwell on 1 January after an examination of the constitutional position (F.O. 371/96522: WU 11915).

460,[2] I concentrated my remarks largely on the question of increased production. I said that His Majesty's Government were ready to make a supreme effort. We owed it to the men we were going to provide for the integrated force, to see that they were fully and properly equipped. Two things were required—greater volume and greater speed. How successful our increased production effort was going to be would depend on how quickly we could solve the various associated problems such as raw materials. The essential thing was to get down to work and not let our whole effort be endangered by theoretical arguments. We did not want to commit ourselves to a definite figure for defence expenditure and then have to manipulate our production programme and our forces to fit into it. We intended to get on with our present programme and to increase it, to build up and develop our contribution to the integrated force and then to look at the financial and economic implications.[5]

5. Full record of meeting follows by saving telegram.[6]

CALENDARS TO No. 145

i *18–20 Dec. 1950 Brussels meetings (a) N.A. Defence Committee* on 18 Dec. (Brussels tel. 314): agree to establish Defence Production Board; discuss reorganisation of N.A.T.O. and appointment Supreme Commander [WU 1198/722]; (*b*) *N.A.C. meetings* 18–19 Dec. (Brussels tels. 61–2 and 66 Saving) with Resolution on Supreme Commander and Communiqué (Brussels tels. 60 and 63 Saving) [WU 1071/226–9, 232]; (*c*) *Brussels Treaty Consultative Council* meet on 20 Dec. and consider the implications for Western Union Defence of the establishment of N.A.T. integrated force [WU 1077/3].

ii *Dec. 1950 (a) Proposed Reorganisation of N.A.T.O.* Canadian proposals for the re-organisation of N.A.T.O., tabled in the Deputies in early December, are examined in F.O. memo. circulated to Cabinet Defence Committee (D.O. (50) 102 on 18 Dec. Mr. Bevin agrees that Defence and Finance Ministers should join N.A.C. (even though practical difficulties of arranging meetings for 36

---

[5] In the Foreign Office Miss J.C. Petrie of Western Organisations Department commented: 'The last paragraph of this telegram reflects an important change in our attitude towards the finance of defence . . . We are at last moving away—as we had anyway expected we would have to if the high cost of our interim target under the Medium-Term Defence Plan were to be fully covered—from the fixed "ceiling price" for defence (our original £3,600 millions). But this time we are going to put the requirement horse before the financial cart—i.e. work out larger programmes and see later how we pay for them . . . The results of our latest departure from the maximum £3,600 millions programme is that we—like the Americans—can no longer say, in financial terms, what we anticipate that our defence programme will be' (WU 1071/225). When explaining this to Mr. Acheson at the end of the tripartite talks on 19 December, Mr. Bevin stated: 'I recognised that this approach was somewhat different to that of Mr. Harriman and others in Washington, but it was the final result that mattered, and I hoped that the United States Administration would not embarrass us by pressing us to adopt a different method. We were most anxious to avoid a repetition of some of the arguments which had taken place with regard to E.R.P. 2. Mr. Acheson said that he quite understood our position' (F.O. telegram to Washington No. 5733 on UR 1050/3).
[6] See calendar *ib*.

rather than 12 Ministers). Also agrees closer coordination of production, supply and financial bodies by the Deputies with overall aim of strengthening role of N.A.C. and Deputies in N.A.T.O. However objects to proposed subordination of Standing Group and Military Committee to Deputies. Defence Committee agree with Mr. Bevin on 21 Dec. D.O. (50) 102 becomes guideline for U.K. Deputy in further discussions by the Deputies on Canadian proposals: new version of which is considered in F.O. on 9 Jan. 1951. [CAB 131/9, 8: WU 11915/14] (*b*) *Proposed Reorganisation of Brussels Treaty Organisation* Progress towards rationalisation of Brussels Treaty Organisations with those of N.A.T. explained in U.K. military delegation note of 14 Dec. [WU 11915/16].

No. 146

Record of a Tripartite Meeting held at the Ministry of Foreign Affairs, Brussels, on 19 December 1950, at 8.45 p.m.

[C 8281/65/18]

Top secret

Present:
United States Mr. Acheson, Mr. Bohlen.
France M. Schuman, M. Parodi.
United Kingdom Mr. Bevin, Sir P. Dixon.

Soviet Proposal for a Council of Foreign Ministers

(At the end of the full Tripartite Meeting,[1] Mr. Bevin had stated the British position in regard to the Soviet proposal for a Council of Foreign Ministers, and in particular had drawn attention to our desire that the reply to the Soviet Note[2] should be worded in such a way as to enable the proposed preliminary 4-Power discussions between officials to result in a meeting of the 4 Ministers. Mr. Acheson had expressed the view that the subject was too delicate for discussion in an open meeting, and it had accordingly been agreed that the three Ministers should meet in restricted session, with one adviser each.)

Mr. Acheson said that he wished to explain the way in which he viewed the Soviet move for a meeting of the Council of Foreign Ministers. The Soviet Government were trying to do two things at the same time. On the one hand, they were attempting to eliminate Western influence from Asia and the Far East. This campaign was directed against the position of all of us—the American position in the Philippines; the British position in Malaya; and the French position in Indo-China. (*Mr. Bevin* interposed that India was also threatened.) At the same time, the Soviet Government were attempting to bring to nothing the defensive arrangements of the Western Powers. That was the object which they had in mind when they

[1] See No. 147.i.
[2] See No. 86, note 5.

denounced the Western Powers as having broken the Potsdam Agreement.

Mr. Acheson went on to say that if the Russians were successful in forcing us into a position where our occupation troops had to leave Germany, there would be no place in Europe where our forces could be stationed, and the whole defensive effort of the West would be frustrated. The Russians were clearly aiming at bringing about a situation where public opinion in Germany and elsewhere would render our position in Germany untenable. The Russian aim, in fact, was to render null and void the decisions which had just been taken to set up an integrated force for the defence of Europe with a German contribution.

Mr. Acheson admitted that public opinion must be considered. But we must not embark on a course of action which might end in mortally damaging our position, simply on account of the feelings of a few thousand people. It was against this background that the Russian proposal for a meeting of the Council of Foreign Ministers must be considered. In Mr. Acheson's view it would be extremely dangerous for us to plunge straight into a meeting of Ministers. It was essential, in his view, that there should be a preliminary meeting which would give us the opportunity of exploring Russian intentions and would leave us with the possibility of manoeuvre. It was probable that such a meeting would not reveal much of Russian intentions. But it should help us to manoeuvre the Russians into a position which would not be disadvantageous to us when it came to a meeting of Ministers. For example, the question of the Far East could be raised in the preliminary meeting and the Russians could be asked whether they were prepared to put a stop to their aggressive actions in that part of the world. If it became clear that the Russians had no intention of doing this, it would be to our advantage to establish the fact before we went into a meeting of Ministers. It might well be impossible to avoid holding a meeting of Ministers, but at least let us hold it in as favourable conditions to ourselves as possible.

M. Schuman asked whether he was right in thinking that Mr. Acheson wanted more time for the preparation of the ground and for this reason favoured a preliminary meeting.

Mr. Acheson replied that that was one of his reasons. His main reason, however, was that it would be a mistake for us to reply to the Russians in such a way that the preliminary meeting would result in committing us to a meeting of the Ministers before we had explored Russian intentions and manoeuvred the Russians into a bad position when it came to the meeting of Ministers.

M. Schuman commented that if, for example, at the preliminary meeting the Russians proposed, as a condition of holding a meeting of Ministers, that the Atlantic Council decisions of to-day should be abrogated, clearly it would not be possible for the preliminary meeting to agree that a meeting of the Council of Foreign Ministers should be held.

Mr. Acheson assented.

The Secretary of State suggested that we might announce that if the preliminary meeting failed, the Foreign Ministers of the 3 Western Powers would meet to consider the situation. Public opinion in England would be very much perturbed if a breakdown with the Russians resulted from a meeting of officials. There was a strong feeling, shared by people of all parties, that the responsibility of talking to the Russians should be shouldered by Ministers. People had not forgotten that in 1939 we had sent a Foreign Office official to Moscow.[3] It was now generally regarded as a mistake not to have sent a member of the Government. Grave political difficulties would be caused at home if the Government appeared to be evading a chance of discussions with the Soviet Government.

Mr. Acheson and *M. Schuman* demurred to the suggestion that we should announce that a meeting of the 3 Western Ministers would be held to consider the situation in the event of a failure on the part of the preliminary 4-Power meeting to agree on the holding of a meeting of Ministers. This would look like anticipating failure.

At this stage *Mr. Acheson* read out a redraft of the first part of paragraph 6 of the proposed reply to the Russians,[4] which ran as follows:

'H.M. Government are prepared to designate a representative who, together with representatives of the French, United States and Soviet Governments, would examine the problems referred to in the preceding paragraph with a view to finding a mutually acceptable basis for a meeting of the Foreign Ministers of the four countries and recommending to their Governments a suitable agenda.'

M. Schuman said that he could accept this redraft.

Sir P. Dixon pointed out that, whereas the first agreed draft prepared by the Ambassadors' meeting in Paris had spoken of the Governments designating 'an official', the re-draft spoke of 'a representative'. He enquired whether there was any significance in this change.

Mr. Acheson stated that he had in mind to appoint Mr. Jessup, who would not be an official in our sense of the word. He would be the highest qualified negotiator outside the Cabinet. He thought it important from the point of public opinion to appoint some such person in order to demonstrate that a sincere attempt was being made to find a mutually acceptable basis.

The Secretary of State said that in the light of Mr. Acheson's explanations he could accept the redraft.

The Ministers therefore *agreed* that the Note as amended should be despatched.

[3] In June 1939 Mr. W. Strang, then head of F.O. Central department, was sent to Moscow to assist with negotiations for an Anglo-Franco-Soviet mutual assistance pact. The course of these negotiations, which reached stalemate in August shortly before the conclusion of the Nazi-Soviet pact on 23 August, is documented in *D.B.F.P.*, Third Series, Volume VI: see also Lord Strang, *Home and Abroad* (London, 1956), pp. 156–198.

[4] See No. 138, note 1.

It was agreed that officials should determine the procedure and timing, which would allow for prior notification to the Austrian, German, and Benelux Governments, and would provide for publication the day after delivery of the Note in Moscow.[5]

[5] The agreed draft (text at No. 147.i) was communicated accordingly to the German Federal, Austrian and Benelux governments on 20 December. Separate identic notes from the British, American and French governments were addressed to the Soviet government on 22 December (British text printed in *D.G.O.*, pp. 542–4) and published the next day. Sir D. Kelly reported that when he delivered the British note to the Soviet First Deputy Minister for Foreign Affairs, 'Mr. Gromyko seemed, if anything, more tense and buttoned-up than usual. He read the note in my presence and then asked if I had any comments; I replied that the note was self-explanatory; and he said that Soviet Government would be informed. 2. French and United States interviews were equally brief and formal' (Moscow telegram No. 1175 on C 8260/65/18). As the next step the Foreign Office began to consider the timing of a Council of Foreign Ministers. In a memorandum on the subject of 21 December Mr. Gilchrist pointed out that as a result of decisions at Brussels 'we are now committed to the difficult policy of hoeing two rows at once—negotiating with the Federal Republic about rearming the Germans and with Moscow about disarming them ... *Fundamentally, however, we see no hope of reaching an acceptable solution with the Russians* ... Since this is the case there appears to be every advantage in having the Council of Foreign Ministers as early as possible, and so generate a new head of steam which will enable us to proceed with that degree of our own and of German re-armament which military opinion declares to be essential'. Mr. Gilchrist thought it possible that the Soviet government would now start delaying tactics and that it was therefore important to rally the Americans for an early tripartite meeting to agree future action (C 8259/20/18).

No. 147

Sir J. Le Rougetel (Brussels) to Foreign Office
(Received 20 December, 3.15 p.m.)[1]

No. 323 Telegraphic [C 8197/20/18]

Priority. Secret   BRUSSELS, *20 December 1950, 2.42 p.m.*

Repeated Saving to Paris, Wahnerheide, Washington, Brussels.

The Foreign Ministers of the three Occupying Powers met on the afternoon of the 19th December to discuss German affairs. The three High Commissioners were present.

2. The Ministers agreed that the decisions of the North Atlantic Council on German participation in European defence should be explained orally to the German Federal Chancellor by the High Commissioners with an indication that they were ready to discuss the matter with him further but without handing him any document and without conveying the impression that he was expected to take hasty decisions.

[1] The text contained in this telegram was also despatched by bag as Brussels telegram No. 64 Saving on 19 December and received by the Foreign Office on 21 December (C 8347/20/18).

3. The Ministers also agreed upon a directive requesting the Allied High Commission to examine the problems involved in the development of a new relationship between the Occupying Powers and Germany with a view to the elaboration for consideration by Governments of a general outline of arrangements to be made with the Federal Republic of Germany which would reflect changes in the present occupation régime by reason of Germany's participation in Western defence. The High Commissioners were asked to recommend the aspects of these problems which should be dealt with by the Intergovernmental Study Group which should reconvene in London during January to consider these matters and to complete the work assigned to it by the Foreign Ministers in September.

4. It was agreed that failure of German Federal Government to implement New York decisions need not preclude discussion of further changes with the German Federal Republic but that these should not be brought into force until the New York decisions had been implemented.[2]

5. It was agreed that the question of revision of the Prohibited and Limited Industries Agreement was covered by the concluding phrase of paragraph 3 above.[3]

6. A brief communiqué was issued after the meeting stating that the three Ministers had authorised their respective High Commissioners in discussions with the German Federal Government further to explore the problem of associating Germany in the common defence effort on the basis of the North Atlantic Treaty proposals, as well as any changes in the present occupation arrangements which might logically attend a German defence contribution.[4]

[2] In particular the A.H.C. was concerned to secure the assurances on external debts and the equitable apportionment of raw materials requested on 23 October (see No. 60, note 13) before implementing the first revisions of the Occupation Statute, already worked out with the I.G.G. (November drafts on C 7683–4/20/18). When pressed on this by the A.H.C. on 14 December, Dr. Adenauer had declared himself willing to give the required assurances but anticipated difficulties with the Bundestag.

[3] The delay over the revision of the P.L.I. agreement (see No. 140, note 1) was raised by Mr. Bevin at the end of discussion on Germany. Mr. Bevin asked M. Schuman to agree that the negotiations should be resumed. M. Schuman said that the matter was covered by the instruction to the I.G.G. just agreed. 'Mr. Acheson supported this view and I agreed that the matter might be left there. The position therefore is that the French Government have agreed that the revision of the Prohibited and Limited Industries Agreement is among the questions the study of which is to be completed by the Intergovernmental Study Group when it reconvenes in London in the course of next month' (Brussels telegram No. 72 Saving). Also on the I.G.G. agenda for January was the resumption of work on Foreign Interests, Claims and Restitution as explained in the interim I.G.G. report of 16 December (not printed from C 8322/3780/18). This report recorded that the only completed work related to the revision of the Tripartite Controls Agreement and Charter. Mr. Bevin commented: 'Our decision at Brussels should speed this up now.'

[4] This communiqué was published in *The Times* on 20 December, p. 6. For the text and full record of discussion at the tripartite meeting, see calendar i below. This meeting was followed by the private tripartite meeting recorded in No. 146. At the end of the session that evening Mr. Bevin said to Mr. Acheson that 'he hoped that Mr. Acheson did not mind

i *19 Dec. 1950 Tripartite Meeting on Germany.* A.H.C. explain why approach to Dr. Adenauer on defence should not be too rigid e.g. his internal difficulties—Bundestag and growing public support for neutralisation. Ministers agree to move slowly towards contractual agreements. French represent necessity of obtaining quadripartite agreement to changes in Occupation. This challenged by Mr. Acheson, but not pursued. Annexed documents include communiqué and reply to Soviet govt. on C.F.M. [ZP 6/2 of 1951].

ii *21 Dec. 1950 A.H.C. Meeting with Dr. Adenauer* (Wahnerheide tels. 1819–1822). Dr. Adenauer informed by A.H.C. of Brussels decisions on Germany. German conditions for participation in defence are (*a*) Allied commitment to defend F.R.G.—this fulfilled by recent decisions (*b*) equality of rights in military sphere—German military experts will study this. Concern from Dr. Adenauer at Allied insistence on maintenance of A.H.C. as supreme authority. Formula for communiqué eventually agreed whereby 'the allied governments are prepared to place their relationship with the German Federal Republic to an increasing degree on a contractual basis. Conversations to this end will begin shortly.' Mr. Bevin minutes telegrams as 'unsatisfactory' and requests note of position. This note of 1 Jan. sets out the next steps: Allied-German military discussions opening at the Petersberg on 9 Jan.; similar joint study on occupation controls; Paris conference on European Army; reconvening of I.G.G. to continue work on P.L.I., claims, interests and foreign restitution [C 8326, 8347/20/18; C 10110/5].

iii *22 Dec. 1950f. Future policy towards Germany.* F.O. views 'far from crystallised' but outline of Mr. Bevin's thinking prepared for French govt. in response to enquiries from M. Parodi (Paris tel. 561 Saving). U.K. relationship with F.R.G. 'must always be considered in the light of our relations with Russia'. Ultimate aim of policy, as explained in F.O. tel. to Paris No. 16 Saving of 3 Jan., is 'full and equal partnership' for F.R.G. with the west. A.H.C. to retain only minimum supervisory or emergency powers. Supreme Authority would then 'in practice be shadowy and difficult to reassert'. Case for relinquishing it altogether is considered. French alarm at this leads to assurances that no question of abandoning supreme authority until contractual agreements reached: tels. to and from Paris Nos. 58 and 11 Saving [C 8247/20/18; C 10110/9].

him (Mr. Bevin) sending him personal messages through Sir O. Franks, setting out his views on important matters of foreign policy. Mr. Acheson replied that on the contrary he warmly welcomed these messages which were often very helpful in dealing with the President. He said that the President attached considerable importance to the views expressed by Mr. Bevin' (AU 1053/38).

No. 148

Note by Sir P. Dixon

[*WU 1195/1 of 1951*]

Secret   FOREIGN OFFICE, *21 December 1950*

Brussels Meeting

The series of meetings held at Brussels on December 18th, 19th and 20th—North Atlantic Council,[1] Tripartite Meeting[2] and Meeting of the Brussels Treaty Consultative Council[3]—was surprisingly successful from our point of view. We can, I think, feel that we attained our double objective of putting flesh on the bare bones of defence, while not unduly provoking the Russians into aggesssive action and leaving an area of negotiation open between West and East.

Our chief objective was to persuade the Americans to appoint the Supreme Commander and establish the integrated force for the defence of Europe. This was successfully achieved. The choice of General Eisenhower is eminently satisfactory. He has already struck a steadying note in a public statement.[4]

Our second main objective was to ensure that the question of German re-armament would not be rushed. We wanted to do this partly because we were convinced that shock tactics would not be successful with the Germans and partly because we wanted to avoid producing any unnecessarily sharp Soviet reaction. We also wanted the Americans to appoint the Supreme Commander without awaiting the outcome of the discussions with the German Federal Republic about their contribution to European defence. The agreements reached between the three Foreign Ministers in the discussions held immediately after the end of the North Atlantic Council meeting were extremely successful: an agreement was reached without much difficulty to enable the three High Commissioners to pursue the question with the Federal Chancellor. The essence of the agreed approach was that a decision by Germany to defend herself and enter into Western defence arrangements would logically carry with it an evolution in the relationship between the three Occupying Powers and Germany; and that progress on the part of Germany in defence matters would entitle her to corresponding advances in freedom and equality.

Thirdly, we set out with the twin objectives of avoiding decisions on Germany which might provoke a violent Russian reaction and of leaving open the possibility of negotiation with the Russians. Agreement was reached between the three Foreign Ministers on terms of a reply to the Russian proposal for a meeting of the Council of Foreign Ministers, and this fact was announced at the same time as the announcement regarding Germany was made. Mr. Acheson gave his colleagues to understand that

[1] See Nos. 144–5.   [2] See Nos. 146–7.
[3] See No. 145.i(*c*).   [4] See *The Times* of 20 December, p. 6.

396

the United States did not exclude a meeting of the Council of Foreign Ministers, though they thought it essential that preliminary discussions should take place in order to explore Soviet intentions and to ensure that a meeting of Foreign Ministers, if it was held, was held in conditions favourable to the Western Powers.

One other successful feature of the meetings may be mentioned. The meeting of the Brussels Treaty Consultative Council, held after the Atlantic Council and Tripartite meetings, undoubtedly enhanced the leadership of Great Britain in this inner European group. The confidential explanation, which the Secretary of State gave, of the manner in which it had been decided to handle the German question was received by the Foreign Ministers of Holland, Belgium and Luxembourg with satisfaction and with protestations of the confidence which they reposed in Mr. Bevin.

On the debit side it would only be right to draw attention to a disquieting factor which may become important. It is not possible to be precise, but I sensed in Mr. Acheson an attitude which might be described as an attitude of deflation. This may have been a subjective impression, for Mr. Acheson showed unmistakeable signs of being under strain.[5] But it does seem to me likely that the American frame of mind is disillusioned and resentful at the failure of the 'New York packet'. The force of events has compelled them to recognise that they cannot expect to produce a re-armed Germany by a wave of the wand and to realise that it must be a gradual process. It would not be a very long step to a state of mind which would either despair of Europe or decide to act quickly before the supposed American superiority in atomic weapons was narrowed.

One further difficulty ahead, though at present it is latent, is the prospect of ideas for integration dominating the evolution of relationships between Germany and France. If the French are successful in persuading the Germans to attend the Conference, which they wish to summon early in the new year for the discussion of the proposed European Army, we shall have to take up position, at least to the extent of deciding to be represented at the Conference as observers.[6]

PIERSON DIXON

[5] This impression was endorsed by M. Parodi, who, when discussing the Brussels talks with Sir O. Harvey on 22 December, referred to Mr. Acheson seeming 'not unnaturally perhaps, somewhat preoccupied' (Paris telegram No. 561 Saving, for which see No. 147.iii). This may have been a reference to the Republican motion of no confidence in Mr. Acheson approved on 15 December and rejected by President Truman on 19 December.

[6] Mr. Mallet and Sir W. Strang, to whom this note was addressed, both minuted on 22 December in favour of sending an observer. On receipt of a formal invitation from the French government of 25 January 1951 to attend a European Army conference in Paris in February, the British government declined to attend as a full participating member but nominated Sir O. Harvey to attend as an observer. On 22 December Mr. Bevin approved a suggestion from Sir W. Strang that Sir P. Dixon's note might form the basis of a report to the Cabinet on the Brussels meetings provided that the reference to Mr. Acheson's deflation was omitted. A paper was accordingly circulated on 1 January as C.P. (51) 1 which concluded 'Finally, from the purely United Kingdom point of view, we were able to reassert our leadership in Europe' (CAB 129/44).

No. 149

Sir I. Kirkpatrick (Wahnerheide) to Mr. Bevin
(Received 22 December, 12.50 p.m.)

No. 1823 Telegraphic [C 8237/20/18]

Priority. Secret   WAHNERHEIDE, 22 December 1950, 11. 45 a.m.

Repeated to Paris and Saving to Washington.

My telegram No. 1818.[1]

Our conversation with the Chancellor gave a good insight into the German mind. It confirmed our previous assessment of the position here and we can draw the following conclusions.

1. The Germans are in a nervous, suspicious and almost hysterical temper. They expect us to woo them and behave like a woman scorned if we do not approach them as suitors.

2. In these circumstances when the German experts get to grips with our military proposals we may expect them to drive a hard bargain on every detail. The Chancellor has not yet apprehended that under our proposals Germany will have no representation on the Council of Ministers. This is likely to be a sticking point.

3. On the political side the Germans will continue to press for the abandonment of the basis of the occupation as a primary condition of participation. With the passage of time their insistence will become greater and they will be less willing to accept a provisional half way house. Even on the details (occupation costs, etc.) we may expect long arguments and great difficulty.[2]

4. All this will take much time and we shall constantly be threatened with a rupture of negotiations or an explosion of public wrath. The forebearance of the High Commissioners will be put to a severe test.

5. When, if ever, we succeed in squaring the Chancellor and his minions, it will be necessary to square the Bundestag. It is too early to make any prediction on our prospects but we may assume that the opposition will fume and rage whilst the Chancellor's parties, if they endorse his policy will do so without enthusiasm.

---

[1] This telegram commented on the A.H.C. meeting with Dr. Adenauer on 21 December (No. 147.ii): 'The final result of the meeting was not unsatisfactory . . . It is already clear that the principal obstacle to progress will be the fact that we are unable to promise the Chancellor the surrender of the High Commission's supreme authority' (C 8233/20/18).

[2] Little progress was made on 21 December towards securing the required assurances on debts and raw materials (see No. 147, note 2). The A.H.C. declined to accept a letter of assurance from Dr. Adenauer to the effect that his government accepted responsibility for its debts without ratification by the Bundestag. Renewed negotiation in the New Year led to the issue of the required assurances on 6 March 1951 (D.G.O., pp. 545–9). On the same day the revisions of the Charter of the Allied High Commission for Germany and the Occupation Statute were signed (B.F.S.P., vol. 158, pp. 494–8, 804–6).

6. In short we have a long row to hoe.

Foreign Office please pass to Paris and Washington as my telegram No. 244 Saving and No. 573 respectively.

APPENDIX

Memorandum on the North Atlantic Treaty Organisation and the Brussels Treaty Organisation[1]

P.M.M. (51) 4 [CAB 133/90]

Secret

LONDON, 1 January 1951

The North Atlantic Treaty Organisation is assuming so much importance in present circumstances that Prime Ministers may find it useful to have some account of its organisation and scope. For nearly all practical purposes it may be said to have absorbed most of the functions of the organisms created under the Brussels Treaty, though a note on these is attached at the end of this memorandum.

2. The object of the North Atlantic Treaty was to create collective responsibility for defence among the independent States forming a defined geographical area. The twelve Signatories between them comprise most of the Western European and North Atlantic community and the intention is to make this region of the world secure against any aggressor. The scope of the Treaty is, therefore, limited. It does not come into force if there is aggression in the Far East, but an attack upon the metropolitan territories of any of the Signatories would be a *casus foederis*. There is, however, a provision that the Signatories will consult whenever, in the opinion of one of them, the territorial integrity, political independence or security of any one country is threatened.

3. Defence, nevertheless, is a world-wide subject. Countries like the United Kingdom which have close associations with other nations, or possess colonies, throughout the world cannot confine consideration of defence to Western Europe and the North Atlantic Area only. We recognise that the N.A.T.O. and the work done by it are of the closest interest to the other countries of the Commonwealth.

4. It is, moreover, evident that productive discussions on defence between twelve countries cannot be carried on without admitting consideration of far-reaching political and economic factors. Effective plans for the defence of the West can only be made as a result of close political and economic co-operation. It is the continuous preoccupation of the United Kingdom to maintain the correct balance between its Treaty commitments, especially N.A.T., and its obligations as a member of the Commonwealth.

5. The following paragraphs, which set out in broad outline the organisation of the North Atlantic Treaty and its functions, are intended to form a background to discussions on the relationship between the Commonwealth as a whole and N.A.T.O. It should be remembered that N.A.T.O. is in its infancy and that it grows and changes rapidly. Some of the developments in view are recorded also in the following paragraphs:

Political Authority

6. The supreme political authority in N.A.T.O. as it at present exists is the North Atlantic Council. This Council consists of the Foreign Ministers of all the twelve Signatory Powers and meets at irregular intervals in different capitals. In

[1] This paper was prepared by the Atlantic (Official) Committee for circulation as a background information note to the Commonwealth Prime Ministers meeting in London from 4–12 January 1951.

order to carry out the work and pursue decisions between meetings of the Council, the Foreign Ministers have appointed permanent Deputies. These Deputies are known as the Council Deputies. They are permanently located in London, and the American Deputy, Mr. Spofford, is their permanent Chairman.

7. In addition to the North Atlantic Council, there are two other Ministerial bodies:

(a) The North Atlantic Defence Committee, consisting of the twelve Defence Ministers. This Committee has no regular time-table of meetings and no permanent Chairman. It has in fact met five times since its creation. While it can take decisions on purely defence matters, it is obliged to refer to the North Atlantic Council matters where wide interests are involved.

(b) The Defence Finance and Economic Committee, consisting of the twelve Ministers responsible for finance and economic affairs. This Committee also has no regular time-table of meetings and no permanent Chairman and has, in fact, met twice. Like the Defence Committee, it has to submit matters of major importance to the North Atlantic Council for decisions.

8. The Council Deputies now have before them proposals, sponsored by the Canadian authorities, for simplifying the system of Ministerial Committees, so that the authority of Government can be obtained without the necessity of referring, at least in some cases, to three separate Ministerial bodies. The Canadian proposals, in effect, recommend that there should be only one Ministerial body, which would always carry the authority of Governments. The Ministers attending meetings of this body would vary according to the subject under discussion, and it might on some occasions be necessary for two, or even three, Ministers from each country to attend a meeting. It might equally, in the gravest matters, be desirable that Prime Ministers themselves should attend meetings.

Higher Military Authority

9. At meetings of the Council and of the Defence Committee held in Brussels on 18th and 19th December, 1950, approval was given to proposals for the creation of an integrated force for the defence of Western Europe under a Supreme Commander, Europe, and for certain consequential changes in the North Atlantic Treaty Military Organisation. The Military Committee (acting under the direction of the Defence Committee and consisting of the Chiefs of Staff of the Twelve Powers), and the Standing Group (composed of representatives of the Chiefs of Staff of the United Kingdom, United States and France with its permanent head-quarters in Washington), were preserved in their present form. It was agreed, however, that the most satisfactory way of establishing a military authority capable of providing rapid decisions on strategic matters without the necessity of repeated meetings of the Military Committee in different parts of the world would be to set up a permanent Military Representatives Committee composed of one national representative of each member of the Military Committee. This Military Representatives Committee would be located in Washington and the Standing Group would act as its steering and executive agency. These new arrangements, which have now been approved subject to further consideration of some of the details, would enable those North Atlantic countries which are not members of the Standing Group to make their views heard more effectively than in the past.

10. The real driving force on the military side of the North Atlantic Treaty Organisation remains the Standing Group. The Standing Group has its own Secretariat and inter-service staff working for it and the high level representation provided by the three countries concerned make it an effective instrument for the strategic planning of the North Atlantic Treaty area.

11. Arrangements have been made in Washington for associating Greece and Turkey, who are not signatories of the Treaty, with the strategic planning being done by the Standing Group, in so far as that planning must take account of the situation in the Eastern Mediterranean.

Command Arrangements

12. The most important decision which was reached at the Brussels meeting of the North Atlantic Treaty Council was to approve the establishment of the integrated force in Europe under a Supreme Headquarters, Atlantic Powers in Europe (S.H.A.P.E.). Approval was also given to the appointment of a United States officer as Supreme Commander, Europe, and President Truman's nomination of General of the Army Dwight D. Eisenhower, for the post was welcomed whole-heartedly by the Council.

13. The new organisation, S.H.A.P.E., will receive its directives direct from the Standing Group which will be responsible for higher strategic direction within the North Atlantic Treaty area.

14. The establishment of a Command Organisation which covers the whole of the European area of the North Atlantic Treaty will result in the disappearance of the three European Regional Planning Groups which at present exist to cover Northern Europe, Western Europe and Southern Europe and the Western Mediterranean. S.H.A.P.E. and such subordinate Regional Commands as may be established under it will gradually take over the functions of the various Regional Planning Groups. Provision is also made for the appointment as soon as possible of the Supreme Allied Commander, Atlantic, and for an Atlantic Command Organisation to take over the functions at present exercised by the North Atlantic Ocean Regional Planning Group.

15. So far as the establishment of the integrated force is concerned, the first step is for the various North Atlantic countries to allocate the appropriate units of their national forces to operate immediately under the control of the Supreme Commander. The various North Atlantic countries are beginning to make preliminary arrangements to this end.

16. Great strides have been made in building up the North Atlantic military organisation, but it must be made clear that it has limited responsibilities which are confined to the area covered by the North Atlantic Treaty. It cannot have a global responsibility.

Production Authority

17. Under the direction of the Defence Committee, there existed until the Brussels meetings a North Atlantic Military Production and Supply Board, with a permanent working staff situated in London. The object of this Board was to fulfil military requirements for equipment for the Signatory Powers. Following the meeting of the Defence Committee in Brussels, a Defence Production Board, consisting of representatives of all the Signatory Powers, and under this Board a unified international staff working under a Director has been set up. This Defence Production Board will report to the Council Deputies, but its conclusions

and recommendations will continue to be made known to the Defence Committee, so long as that remains a separate Ministerial Committee.

Finance and Economic Authority

18. Under the direction of the Defence Finance and Economic Committee there is a permanent working staff in London, with the task of maintaining close liaison with the military and production organisations and providing guidance on relevant economic or financial factors to meet the requirements of defence programmes. In practice, a good deal of the work which might have been done by this permanent working staff has now passed into the hands of Working Groups of economic experts. In particular, there is a Working Group engaged on an exercise which is designed to estimate the total cost of defence of the N.A.T.O. countries, including that of the defence of the N.A.T.O. area, and to analyse the economic impact of the resulting defence programmes upon the national income and balance of payments of the member countries.

19. It is probable that the immense amount of detailed and technical work which falls to be done in this exercise, and similar studies which will follow it, will entail the strengthening of the economic and financial staffs at present available for N.A.T.O. work. The exact steps required have not yet been decided. There is obviously a relationship between the economic work required in N.A.T.O. and that being done in O.E.E.C. and the exact division of responsibility remains to be settled.

Authority for Shipping

20. Under the direction of the North Atlantic Council itself there is a North Atlantic Planning Board for Ocean Shipping. This Board will develop plans for merchant shipping on a world-wide basis and is free to invite countries not signatory to the Treaty to participate in its work. While it was felt to be convenient that the Board should be constituted within N.A.T.O., it was recognised that shipping is a subject which cannot be effectively planned in a single limited area of the world. In particular, Australia, New Zealand and South Africa have agreed to co-operate in the work of the Board whenever the interests of these countries are affected.

Secretariat

21. The North Atlantic Council and Council Deputies maintain a small Secretariat permanently in London. The Defence Committee, Military Committee and Standing Group have their own Secretariat in Washington, and there are separate Secretariats for the Defence Finance and Economic Committee and the Military Production and Supply Board.

22. As plans develop for a greater unification and simplification of the whole machine, there will, no doubt, be a requirement for a unified secretariat for all parts of N.A.T.O., except for the military machine, which will continue to operate in Washington. The size and composition of this unified secretariat are still under discussion, and will depend largely upon the amount of financial and economic work which falls to be done in N.A.T.O.

Brussels Treaty Organisation

23. The Brussels Treaty, which was the forerunner of the North Atlantic Treaty and which largely set the pattern for the North Atlantic Treaty

Organisation has, on the military side, been practically absorbed into it. There remains, nevertheless, a particular political affiliation between the five signatories of the Brussels Treaty, and for that reason the Consultative Council, composed of the five Foreign Ministers, continues to meet from time to time and maintains in London a permanent Commission composed of the Ambassadors of France, Netherlands, Belgium and Luxembourg, and a United Kingdom official of ambassadorial rank.

24. Meanwhile, the Command Organisation at Fontainebleau, set up by the Brussels Treaty Defence Ministers, will continue to exercise responsibility for the defence of Western Europe until superseded by the more comprehensive North Atlantic Command Organisation mentioned in paragraphs 12–16.

25. The functions of the Supply Board and Finance and Economic Committee, established under the Brussels Treaty, are gradually being absorbed by N.A.T.O. There is, however, a certain amount of continuing work to be done by these bodies.

Index of Main Subjects and Persons

This straightforward index to document numbers is designed to be used in conjunction with the Chapter Summaries. Subjects are principally indexed under main subject headings. Entries for persons are usually limited to a reference to the descriptive footnote. In the case of leading personalities, e.g. Mr. Bevin, items of special interest have been included.

Acheson, D. 1
bargaining with F.R.G. 21, 41
Berlin security 26.ii
Bevin 9–11, 50, 52, 147
C.F.M. 78, 86, 97, 146, 148
covert army 50
European integration 120, 127, 129, 130, 132
finance of defence 9, 11, 13, 22, 41, 49, 145
Franks 49
German Army 50
equality 120
Occupation 26.i, 62, 120, 139
I.G.G. 26.i, 62
loan to U.K. 49
Marshall mistake 52
Pleven plan 66, 80, 82, 84, 127
political difficulties 46, 148
Soviet reactions 10, 21
U.K. partner 132

Achilles, T.C. 109

Adenauer, K. 3
assurances 45, 60, 147, 149
Bereitschaften 3
Brussels 147.ii, 149
C.F.M. 97, 103.i
equality 60, 103, 111, 135, 139
Generals 73.i, 96
Grotewohl 135.i, 141
Kingsbury Smith 135
military units 3, 33, 45, 48, 60, 111, 135
New York 15, 45

Occupation 45, 103.ii, 111, 120.i, 147
Pleven plan 81, 96, 103.i
police force 3, 8, 45, 48
security guarantee 3, 45
Spofford plan 135–6

Allied High Commission (A.H.C.) 3
Adenauer 45, 60, 103.ii, 120.i, 135–6, 147.ii, 149
bargaining with F.R.G. 60
Berlin 40, 113
German defence 3, 16, 48, 51, 60, 70, 113
negotiations 8, 26, 35, 37, 42–3, 55, 60, 136, 139, 147.ii, 148–9
Occupation 6, 15, 62, 147.i
public opinion 16
New York 15–6, 26.ii, 45, 62

Alexander, Viscount 27

Allen, W.D. 3

Alphand, H. 9
concessions 107, 109

Aron, R. 71

Asia
defence role 100.i
trade restrictions 11.i

Atlantic Confederate Force 101, 106–7, 109, 114–7

Atlantic Official Committee (A.O.C.) 85
N.A.T.O. reorgn. 85
Pleven plan 107

Atomic bomb
  Attlee/Truman 121, 127
  Germany 37, 106, 136
  international control 122
  Soviet Union 126, 143
  United States 148

Attlee, C.R. (*see also* Washington confs.) 1, 6
  Berlin 40
  Bevin 18, 20, 23, 30, 39, 128, 131
  counter-plan 116–8
  criticism of French 40, 76, 101, 102
  East/West trade 26.ii, 39
  European integration 131–2
  finance of defence 49, 53, 79, 104, 121,
    134, 143
  H. of C. 6
  M.C. 30 report 116
  N.A.T.O. 85
  Occupation costs 61
  Pleven 121
  Pleven plan 85, 101, 118, 121, 131–2
  police force 40
  Soviet Union 121
  Supreme Commander 118, 121, 132
  unified force 2
  U.K. defence programme 102, 132,
    134, 143
  U.S. partnership 131, 143

Australia *see* Commonwealth

Austria 78, 86, 110.i, 121, 141, 146

Barclay, R.E. 1
  Bevin 39

Bech, J. 42

Belgium
  Brussels treaty 83, 85
  defence programme 1, 2, 83
  France 83, 94
  German rearmament 29.i, 32, 35.i, 44,
    83
  Socialist pressure 94
  Pleven plan 83, 90, 92, 96, 98, 101,
    114, 117
  U.K. forces 2

Benelux
  consultation 10, 15–16, 26, 44, 141,
    146

Bereitschaften 2, 3
  German generals 73.i

  Notes 78
  Soviet intentions 2–3, 8, 12, 26.ii, 40.i,
    73.i, 126, 128, 142
  strength 3, 8, 40.i

Berlin (*see also* Bereitschaften; German
  military units & police forces)
  Allied garrison 3, 26.ii, 40.i, 55, 113
  Commandants 40
  indefensible 40.i
  police force 3, 3.i, 8, 26.ii, 40, 60, 113
  N.Y. decisions 26.ii, 40, 55, 113
  security 26.ii, 113.i
  supplies 3.iv, 55
  unified command 113

Bevan, A. 27
  defence budget 108

Bevin, E. 1
  absences 6, 53, 142
  Acheson 9–11, 50, 52, 147
  Atlanticism 1.ii, 11, 14, 33, 41, 50, 73,
    84–5, 110, 114–5
  Attlee 18, 20, 23, 30, 39, 128, 131
  bargaining with F.R.G. 5, 10, 15, 21,
    28–9, 56, 59, 136–7
  Berlin 40, 113
  bipartisan policy 20, 29.i, 41, 114
  caution 30, 56, 125–6, 128–30, 133,
    136–7, 139, 147
  C.F.M. 78, 86, 97, 110–11, 121–2, 137,
    139, 146
  Commonwealth 1.ii, 11, 14, 100, 110,
    114
  covert army 58, 60
  counter-plan 115–8
  criticism of French 1.ii, 83, 99, 101
  equipment 14, 17
  European Army 14, 50
    integration 120, 127
    weakness 1.ii, 114, 121
  finance of defence 1, 11, 14, 29.i, 79,
    83, 145
  German Army 2–3, 20, 76
    debts 5, 55, 62
    industrial contribution 33, 61
    military units 2, 3, 10, 18, 20, 28, 56
    Occupation 5, 55, 61, 139, 140,
      147.iii
    police force 2–3, 8, 10, 15, 21, 29.i,
      113

German reliability 1.ii
   visit 101
health 39
'historic moment' 34, 41
India 146
Marshall Aid 79
Marshall formula 68
Mollet 99
N.A.C. adjournment 34
N.A.T. reorgn. 2, 83, 85, 100.i, 145.ii
N.Y. statements 14–5, 29.i, 35, 41, 73
N.Y. review 39, 55–6, 58
period of silence 65, 67, 77
Pleven plan 80, 83, 85, 90, 92, 115–8
pressure on French 58–9, 65, 67, 75,
   77
Soviet Union 3, 10, 15, 17, 20, 34, 41,
   78, 83, 125–6, 128, 133, 136–7, 139
steel scrap 1, 5
'ugly drift' 46
U.K. economy 22

Bidault, G. 57, 75

Blankenhorn, H. 45

Bohlen, C.E. 66
Pleven plan 66, 81

Bonnet, H. 72
Pleven plan 82

Bradley, Gen. O. 73
Pleven plan 82, 98

Bridges, Sir E. 11

British Joint Services Mission 2.i, 66

Brook, Sir N. 23

Bruce, D. 2
European integration 109
in Washn. 59, 93
Pleven plan 93, 109
regrets tactics 57, 93

Brussels Conference Dec. 1950
N.A.T. & Tripartite meetings 144–7
achievements 148
agenda 136, 139, 144
C.F.M. 142, 146
finance of defence 143, 145
N.A.T.O. reorgn. 145.i–ii
Occupation 139, 140, 147, 147.i–iii
origins 90, 91.i, 92, 95, 133, 137
P.L.I. 140, 147

raw materials 143, 145
Soviet pressure 141
Supreme Commander 144–5
U.K. defence effort 139, 143, 145
unified force 144
Western defence 139, 143–5

Brussels Treaty (*see also* N.A.T.O.
   reorgn.) 2, Appendix
Belgium 83, 85
C. in C. committee 2, 48, 85
Consultative Council 85, 95, 145.i, 148
France 96
Germany 38
N.A.T.O. 38, 83
Permanent Commission 38
U.K. guarantee 106.i

Byroade, H.A. 5

Cabinet
Atlantic Confederate Force 118
bargaining with F.R.G. 27–8, 136–7
Brussels 136–7
budget differences 108
C.F.M. 78, 97, 121–2, 136, 138
defence effort 102, 143
East–West trade 11.i
finance of defence 11, 79, 102, 104,
   143
German industrial contribution 4.i, 27,
   92
military units 2, 18–19, 27, 39, 56,
   58, 68, 77, 137, 143
Occupation 4, 4.i, 55, 58, 61
police 2, 4.i, 19, 27, 56, 58
meetings 2, 4.i, 18–9, 27, 58, 77–8, 92,
   97, 102, 104, 137, 143
New York 27, 55–6, 58
Pleven plan 92, 118–9
Soviet danger 143
Spofford plan 118–9, 136–7
unified force 2, 58

Canada (*see also* Commonwealth)
Attlee 121
European defence 14, 58
German rearmament 29.i, 34, 35.i
loan to U.K. 49, 53
N.A.T.O. reorgn. 37, 85, 145.ii
pressure on French 94
Spofford plan 119.i
unified force 47.i

407

Central Economic Planning Staff (C.E.P.S.) 49.i

Chiefs of Staff (C.O.S.) 3
Atlantic Confederate Force 115–7
Bereitschaften 40.i
Berlin 40.i
defence effort 143
defence strategy 73–4
European integration 127
M.C. 30 report 115–116
military units 67, 74
modify U.S. plan 101, 106
Montgomery 7.i
N.A.T.O. reorgn. 7.i
Pleven plan 82, 106.i, 115–8
police 3.i, 12, 44
safeguards 67, 70, 74, 106.i
Soviet danger 125–6, 128
Standing Group 37
Supreme Commander 7.i, 33, 82
unified force 7, 44, 74
U.S. Chiefs of Staff 72–3, 82, 131, 136
Washn. meetings 68, 72, 82

China
C.F.M. 122
Formosa 39
Korea 120, 122, 126, 128, 143
Soviet Union 110
trade 11.i

Churchill, W.S. 20
European Army 20
United States 24

Chuter Ede, J. 27

Clauson, Sir G. 112

COJA telegrams 29

C.O.M.I.S.C.O. 50, 77

Commanders-in-Chief Committee 2, 48

Committee of Seven (N.A.T.) 9, 17

Commonwealth
European defence 1.ii, 8, 11, 14, 137
finance 11, 79, 100, 104
N.A.T.O. 92, 100.i, 118, 124.i
raw materials 17, 124.i
Soviet Union 146
U.K. commitment 79, 110, 118, 121
U.K. war debt 49

Compton, E.G. 112

Council of Europe 2
Bevin 85
Churchill 20
European army 2, 20, 50
Germany 55, 103
meetings 90, 96
'mere façade' 34
Pleven plan 96, 117
Portugal 91
Schuman 96, 111, 117

Council of Foreign Ministers (C.F.M.) *see* Soviet proposal for etc.

Cripps, Sir S. 69

Crouy-Chanel, E. de 71

Dalton, H. 4

Davies, E. 36
pressure on French 46, 50

Defence Committee (Cabinet) 2
Atlantic Confederate Force 118
Berlin 3.i, 113
demolitions 3.i
finance of defence 79, 101
German military units 3.i, 67, 101
police 3.i
N.A.T.O. reorgn. 3.ii
New York 68
safeguards 70, 74, 101
Spofford/Pleven plans 107, 118
U.K. forces in Europe 68
Washington 101

Defence Committee (N.A.T.) (*see also* Brussels and Washington confs.) 2
medium term plan 17
Meetings: The Hague (Mar.) 17
Washington (Oct.) 17, 85, 91, 98, 101
Brussels (Dec.) 145.i
rôle 35, 47.ii, 85, 91.i

Defence Financial and Economic Committee (N.A.T.) 2, Appendix

Defence Production Board 112

Denmark 29.i, 34, 35.i, 41, 47.i
Pleven plan 91, 98

Deputies (N.A.T.) 1, Appendix
German military units 34–35
High Priority Defence programme 1, 53

Medium term plan 17
New York 17, 35
Pleven/U.S. plans 91.i, 96, 98, 101, 107
Spofford plan 130, 133, 136
Supreme Commander 127
unified force 17, 34–35

Dixon, Sir P. 2, 85
C.F.M. 110.i, 141
counter-plans 107.i, 111
German equality 111
Occupation 141
Pleven plan 115, 117
Soviet pressure 126, 141
Spofford bargain 129

Dobell, Wing-Commander F.O.S. 101

Douglas, L.W. 1

East–West trade 11.i, 26.ii, 39, 91.i, 131.i

**Economic Cooperation Administration
(E.C.A.)** 11, 79, 139.i

Economic Policy Committee (E.P.C.) 124

Economic Steering Committee 112

Eden, R.A. 20

Eisenhower, D.D. 85
Supreme Commander 131–2, 136,
144–5

Elliot, Air Marshal Sir W. 7
deadlock 37, 44, 73

End Item Assistance 53, 79, 139

Equipment see Military Production etc.

Erhard, L. 45

European Army see Pleven plan; Council of
Europe

**European Coal and Steel Community
(E.C.S.C.)** see Schuman plan

European defence lines (see also U.S. forces
in Europe)
Acheson 9, 41, 50
Bevin 30, 41, 58, 76, 136
C.O.S. 3.i, 40.i, 74
eastern 9, 10, 27, 30, 41–2, 50, 58, 73
indefensible 3, 9, 10, 12, 18, 28, 36–7,
41, 50, 58, 70, 73–4, 136
Kirkpatrick 70, 73
Moch 63
Montgomery 36

Netherlands 10
Rhine-Ijssel 10, 29.i, 30, 36–7, 73–4
U.S. commitment 24–5, 27, 29, 30, 41,
50, 56, 58, 73

European defence programmes
acceleration 132, 134, 139, 143, 145
Belgium 1, 2, 83
France 1, 2, 63, 68, 71, 73, 76, 79, 83,
134
Netherlands 1, 2, 83
Soviet reaction 143
U.K. 1, 11, 49, 53, 69, 79, 101–2, 104

European Integration 131, 141
Acheson 120, 127
Germany 4, 5, 15, 41, 83, 101, 105,
115, 140
McCloy 109
Pleven 99
Pleven plan 120
Truman 127
U.K. 110, 115, 117, 129, 141, 148
U.S. letter 120, 127, 129, 132–3

European Payments Union (E.P.U.) 112

**European Recovery Programme
(E.R.P.)** 11, 49, 53, 79, 145

Fergusson, Sir D. 112

Finance of Defence (see also German
Industrial etc; Military Production etc;
Raw Materials) 79
Acheson 9, 11, 13, 22, 41, 49, 145
Attlee 49, 53, 79, 104, 121, 134, 143
Bevan 108
Bevin 1, 11, 14, 22, 29.i, 33, 76, 145
Cabinet differences 108, 143
Commonwealth 11, 79.i, 100, 104
defence preparedness 14, 101, 143
discussions bilateral 1, 9, 11, 14, 22, 49,
53, 79
Deputies 1, 53, 69
tripartite 11, 22, 49, 53, 79
equitable distribution 11, 22, 33, 49,
53, 69, 79, 108, 143
European queue 49, 143
France 22, 41, 54, 58, 71, 76, 79
Franks 11, 49, 53, 134
Gaitskell 53, 69, 79, 104, 124
Germany 61, 103, 112

Finance of Defence *contd.*
  Indo China 54, 79
  interim aid 11, 53, 79, 79.i (text), 100,
    102, 104, 108
  loan waiver 49, 53
  military aid prog. 1, 2, 9, 11, 79
  Nitze plan 11, 53, 79, 79.i (text), 104
  package-deal 20, 27, 29, 29.i, 37, 41
  Schuman 13, 22
  S.E.A. 53.i
  sterling balances 49, 53, 79
  U.K. 1, 11, 11.i, 49, 53, 79, 102, 104,
    108, 112, 124, 132, 134, 139, 143, 145

Finletter, T.K. 46

Fontainebleau 2

Formosa 39

France
  Anglo-French relations 65, 71
  bargaining with F.R.G. 37
  Bereitschaften 2
  defence programme 1, 41, 63, 65, 68,
    71, 73, 76, 79, 137
  electoral reform 25
  Germany 6, 41, 46, 83
    fear of 46, 73, 83–4, 86, 89, 105–6
    N.A.T.O. 84, 114–5, 117, 121
  govt. 25, 46.i, 57, 63, 75, 93, 95, 98
  Indo China 75, 79, 137, 146
  Königsberg 63, 65, 106
  military aid 41, 54, 58, 71, 76, 79, 83,
    137
  National Assembly 25, 42, 46, 75
  Soviet pressure 110.i, 141
  U.S. relations 110.i

French Common Fund 9
  Acheson 9, 13, 41
  Bevin 11, 14, 83
  Gaitskell 9.i, 53
  Pleven plan 89
  stimulates U.S. plan 41, 121
  sub-committee 9, 11
  Treasury 9.i

François-Poncet, A. 3
  Adenauer 45, 96

Franks, Sir O. 1
  Acheson 49
  finance of defence 11, 49, 134

Fraser, Lord 3

Gainer, Sir D. 24.i
  Berlin 40
  C.F.M. 86
  German equality 86, 103.ii
    Occupation 62
    police force 24.i, 40, 60
    rearmament 60, 67, 103, 105

Gaitskell, H.T.N. 27, 69
  finance of defence 53, 69, 79, 104, 124
  Marshall Aid 79
  Washn. visit 53, 53.i, 69

Ganeval, Gen. 60

de Gaulle, Gen. C. 121

George VI, H.M. King 39

German Army & General Staff (*see also*
  Safeguards)
  Acheson 50
  Bevin 2–3, 20, 76
  British public opinion 1.ii, 3, 10
  Cabinet 27
  C.O.S. 3.i, 54.ii, 74
  Deputies' report 136
  France 6, 81, 84.i, 89, 91, 101
  Germany 101, 103
  Henderson 105
  Kirkpatrick 70
  N.A.C. resolution 47
  public opinion 1.ii, 3, 10
  S.P.D. 3.iii
  Soviet Union 78, 126, 128, 136
  Strang 24
  U.S. 2, 29, 33, 50, 72.i

German auxiliary forces 3, 4, 6, 8, 10, 48
  Civil Labour Organisation 6, 43, 56,
    60, 68, 103
  Civil Mixed Watchmen's Service 6
  C.O.S. 7, 12
  labour units (Dienstgruppen) 32, 35.i,
    41–3, 48, 68
  N.Y. decisions 43, 48, 56, 60, 68
  Schumacher 103
  Schuman 6, 21, 32

German industrial contribution
  Acheson 9
  Bevin 3.iv, 8, 33
  Cabinet 4, 4.i, 11.i, 27, 92
  controls 1.iii, 4.i

Deputies report   136
export competition   27, 41, 54.i, 61, 92,
   112
France   6, 21, 32, 41–2
N.Y. decisions   43, 48, 55, 136
official study   92, 112
P.L.I. agreement   55, 61, 67, 140
raw materials   26.ii, 41–3
restrictions   9, 33, 43, 54.ii, 67, 70, 74
Schuman plan   140
shipbuilding   4, 55
size   112.iii
steel level   4, 6, 43, 55
steel scrap   1, 5, 112
supplies   61, 112
U.K. proposals   3.iv, 4, 8
U.S. views   9

German military units (*see also* Safeguards;
   Unified force)
U.S. plan   2, 33, 72.i
as package   29, 29.i, 33 (text), 37, 41,
   43, 56
tightened   98, 101
agreement   131, 136 (text), 144

Acheson   9, 13, 18, 21, 25, 28–9, 41, 50
Adenauer   3, 45, 48
A.H.C.   16, 35, 42, 45, 60, 147.ii, 149
air/navy   37, 43, 45, 54, 54.ii, 59, 60, 70,
   74, 130, 136
alternatives   48
Anglo-French relations   65, 71
atomic factor   37, 106, 126, 143
Belgium   32, 83
Bevin agrees   18, 20, 28
   cautious   15, 30, 56, 125–6, 128–30,
      133, 136–7, 139, 147
   hesitates   124–6, 128, 130, 136–7
   overruled   131, 136
   reservations   2, 3, 10, 56, 133
Bidault   57
Brussels   144–5
Cabinet   18–19, 21, 23, 27, 39
'cannon fodder'   135
command structure   74, 136
C.O.S.   3.i, 7, 67, 74, 101, 106, 106.i,
   125, 128
cost   3, 25, 60
criticism of U.S. tactics   57, 62, 65, 71,
   93–4

deadlock   73, 98
Deputies   42, 130, 133, 136
effect of Pleven plan   88–91
European integration   99, 109
European Socialists   50, 94, 99
French Cabinet   21, 28, 30, 36, 41, 54,
   57, 64, 71, 75–6, 99, 101
   complaints   65, 71
   concessions   109, 115
   constitution   46.i, 75, 95, 98
   military   93
   Socialists   65, 71, 94
German attitude   3, 16, 27, 32, 35, 37,
   45, 48, 64, 96, 101, 103, 111
   bargaining   5, 10, 15–6, 21, 28, 32,
      37, 41, 55–6, 60, 74, 136, 149
   conditions   103.ii, 111
   cooperation   3, 27, 45, 48, 60, 111,
      126, 132
   equality   67, 74, 103, 105, 111,
      147.ii, 149
   hardening   45, 59, 103, 119, 120.i,
      135–6
   military   73.i, 96
   timing of approach   35, 111, 128,
      135–7, 144, 147
Healey   50
Italy   32, 141
J.P.S.   67
Kelly   125, 128
Kirkpatrick   48, 51, 67, 70, 119
Labour Party   50, 77
legality   25, 27, 29, 32, 38, 121
Marshall formula   42, 52, 59, 68
M.C. 30 report   106, 115–6, 130, 136
McCloy   12, 119
Moch   41, 46, 56, 63, 73, 91
modifications   98.i, 101, 106, 106.i
Morrison   128
N.A.C. resolution   47, 68
N.A.T.O. High Commissioner   114–5,
   119, 123, 129–30
Netherlands   29.i, 32, 35.i, 73
N.Y. decisions   42–4, 56
Pentagon   2.i, 5, 93
Pleven   88, 99, 121
pressure on French   46, 50, 58–9, 64–5,
   67–8, 75, 89, 94–5, 98–9, 101
proportion   51, 58–9, 67, 70, 74
rearmament committee   63, 65, 68

German military units *contd.*

recruitment   25, 70, 74, 109, 115, 118, 121, 136

Schumacher   3.iii, 26, 45.ii, 48, 103

Schuman   32, 37, 56, 64, 88, 99, 121

secrecy   21, 27–8, 67, 70

Shinwell   42, 63, 68

size   33, 37, 51, 54.ii, 58–9, 67, 99, 116, 130, 136

source of weakness   63

Soviet reactions   3, 10, 19, 24.i, 32, 36–7, 55–6, 125–6, 133, 136–7, 141–3, 146

timescale   12, 28–9, 32, 35, 42, 58–9, 74, 81, 121, 136

U.K. silence   65, 67, 77

U.S. change   12, 42, 52, 73

German police forces (*see also* Berlin)

proposed   2, 3, 3.i, 8

modified   16, 55, 68

N.Y. decisions   16, 26.ii, 42, 43, 56, 68, 113

Acheson   10, 16

Adenauer   3, 45, 60

A.H.C.   16, 45, 60

Allied-German committee   48, 60

Attlee   40

Bevin   3, 10, 15, 21, 29.i, 56, 58, 113

Cabinet   3.i, 4.i, 19, 27–8, 58

Commonwealth   8

C.O.S.   3, 7, 44

cost   4

covert army   7, 12, 45.ii, 46.i, 48, 50, 58, 60, 113

French support   2, 3, 6, 16, 32, 63

frontier police   3–4, 6

implementation   48, 55, 60, 113

inadequacy   44, 51, 59

J.P.S.   44, 60

Kirkpatrick   48, 60

Land/Federal control   6, 16, 43–4, 48, 68

Länder police   3, 43

Marshall formula   42–3, 68

McCloy   3, 45

militarily unsound   44

Moch   63

Soviet reaction   78

S.P.D.   3.iii, 58

State Dept.   5

weapons   7, 40, 43, 113

Germany, Federal Republic (F.R.G.) (*see also* A.H.C.; Berlin; German industrial contribution, military units, Occupation, police force; Soviet proposal for C.F.M.)

air defence   37, 43, 45, 54.ii, 59, 60, 70

Allied forces   3–4, 12, 16, 78, 105

Ambassadors   4–5, 26, 55

atomic bomb   37, 106

Basic Law   4

Benelux   10, 15–6, 26, 44

Council of Europe   55, 105

Dalton   4

debts/claims   4, 5, 26.ii, 45, 55, 60, 62, 147, 149

demolitions   3.i, 3.iv, 4, 15

displaced persons   4, 26.i

economic recovery   112.iv

E.P.U.   112

equality   3.iii, 4, 15, 26, 32, 37, 41, 55, 67, 80, 86, 103, 105, 111, 147.ii

foreign ministry   4–6, 15, 26, 55

Generals   73.i, 96

guerilla warfare   43

Law 27.   45

morale   3, 8, 15, 21, 26, 32–3, 37, 55, 86, 126

N.A.T.O.   1.iii, 37, 73.i, 84, 91.i, 111, 114, 121, 139.i, 149

neutralisation   32, 147.i

New York   15, 26, 45, 55, 62

peace treaty   55, 78

Petersberg protocol (1949)   4

P.L.I. Agreement   4, 5, 15, 26.ii, 55, 61, 112, 140, 147

raw materials   26.ii, 41–2, 53, 60, 147, 149

refugees   4, 26.i

reunification   3, 38, 45, 55, 78, 135, 141

Schuman plan   41, 55

security guarantee   3, 26.ii, 45, 55, 147.ii

sovereignty   105, 147.iii

Soviet alliance   74, 105, 135

status   4, 55

termination war   4, 26.i, 45, 55, 60, 103

United States   38, 83

Warsaw statement (1948)   78

Western integration   4, 5, 15, 33, 41, 83, 101, 103, 105

Germany, Occupation
  Acheson 26.i, 120, 139
  A.H.C. 26, 60, 62, 103.ii, 147
  Bevin 5, 15, 62, 120, 139, 140
  Brussels decisions 147
  Cabinet 4, 55, 58
  contractual proposals 45.i, 103.ii, 111,
    120.i
  costs 4, 61, 103, 149
  European integration 120, 139.i, 140–1
  France 6, 26, 62
  future 70, 74, 103, 105, 111, 120, 139,
    147, 147.i–iii, 149
  I.G.G. 4, 5, 26, 60, 62, 139.i, 147
  Kirkpatrick 6, 60, 62, 70
  legal aspects 111.i
  linked to defence 4, 15, 26, 58, 62, 120,
    139–41
  McCloy 60, 62
  N.Y. decisions 26, 26.i–ii, 45.i, 55, 60,
    62
  Soviet zone 2, 55, 126, 135, 141
  Statute 4, 5, 26.i, 45.i, 55, 58, 60, 62,
    103, 147.i, 149
  U.S. 120, 139, 141
Gilchrist, A. 40
Gordon Walker, P.C. 8, 100.i
Gough, C.E.F. 17
Greece
  'hands off' 110.i
  N.A.T.O. 26, 91.i
Griffiths, J. 27
Gromyko, A.A. 146
Grotewohl, O. 135
Gruenther, Gen. A. 136
Guderian, Gen. H. 71

Hall, R.L. 69
Hall, Viscount 101
Harriman, W.A. 11
  defence effort 134
Harrison, G.W. 122
Harvey, Sir O. 3
  Pleven plan 80, 81
  pressure on French 54

Hays, Gen. T.T. 60
Hayter, W. 71, 75
Healey, D.W. 50
Heinemann, Dr. 64
Henderson, A. 101
Henderson, Lord 27
  German equality 105
  visit to F.R.G. 45.ii
High Priority Defence Programme 1, 9,
  11, 13, 22
Higher direction of Cold War
  (Liaison) 100.i, 124, 131
Holmes, J. 2
House of Commons
  C.F.M. 97, 110, 122
  defence debate 6.i, 18, 20, 23
  German rearmament 8, 71.i
  Pleven/Spofford plans 119
  raw materials 124
Hoyer Millar, Sir F. 1

Iceland 35.i, 73, 119.i
I.G.G. 4
  Acheson 26.i, 62
  A.H.C. 62
  Bevin 5
  McCloy 62
  N.Y. decisions 26.ii, 55
  P.L.I. 55, 113, 140, 147
  report 4, 26, 55, 62
  resumption 60, 62, 139.i, 140, 147
  State Dept 5
Ince, Sir G. 112
India *see* Commonwealth
Iraqi-Syrian resolution 110, 122
Iron Curtain 110.i, 122.i
Isaacs, G.A. 27
Italy
  German rearmament 29.i, 32, 35.i, 47.i
  Pleven plan 96, 114, 119.i
  Soviet pressure 141
  Supreme Commander 98
Jebb, Sir G. 9
Jessup, P.C. 39
Johnson, L. 31

413

Johnston, A. 27
Joint Planning Staff (J.P.S.)
    counter-plans   101, 106–7
    N.A.T.O. High Commissioner   114.i
    police force   44, 60
    safeguards   67, 105–6
Jowitt, Viscount   58

Kelly, Sir D.   78
    C.F.M.   78
    Soviet danger   125–6, 128, 136
Kirkpatrick, Sir I.   3
    counter plans   101
    German morale   3, 103
    military units   48, 51, 70
    N.A.T. High Commissioner   130
    Occupation   6, 60, 62, 70
    police force   3.i, 48, 60
    safeguards   67, 70
    Western defence   70, 73
Königsberg   63, 65, 106
Korean crisis
    Anglo-American relations   39
    atomic bomb   121
    China   120, 122, 126, 128, 143
    European tension   86, 120, 143
    German morale   3, 55, 83
    German rearmament   6, 7, 12, 120–1
    New York   13, 26, 39
    Soviet Union   78, 79
    U.K. economy   49, 79, 143
    U.N. forces   124
    United States   6, 38, 73, 120, 142
    U.S. forces in Europe   1, 6, 9, 17, 73,
        126, 128, 136

Labouisse, H.R.   104
Lange, H.   42
Larock, V.   94
Lattre de Tassigny, Gen. de   73
Laukhuff, P.   62
Law 27.   45
Le Rougetel, Sir J.   142
Lend Lease   49
London Conference of Foreign Ministers
    (May 1950)   10
    Benelux consultation   10

Germany   55, 70
    U.S. troops in Europe   30, 58, 83
Lovett, R.   66
Luxembourg   29.i, 35.i
    Pleven plan   98, 101

MacArthur, Gen D.   20
Makins, Sir R.   30, 85
Mallaby, G.   76
Mallet, W.I.   4
    German equality   105, 111, 139
Margerie, R. de   71
Marshall Aid   11, 79
Marshall, Gen. G.C.   31
    8/10 points   42, 68
    mistake   42, 52
    Pleven plan   87, 98
Marten, F.W.   79
Massigli, R.   2
    C.F.M.   78, 110
    German rearmament   3, 38, 54
    Korea   6, 38
    N.A.T.O. High Commissioner   123
Matthews, H.F.   98.i
Mayer, R.   93
M.C. 30 report   106, 115–6, 130, 136
McCloy, J.J.   3
    bargaining with F.R.G.   60
    Berlin   113
    European integration   109, 130, 132
    Occupation   60, 62
    Pleven plan   88
    police force   3, 45
    Spofford plan   109
McNeil, H.   27
Medium Term Plan   11, 17, 74
    cost   79, 102, 143
    F.R.G.   67
    inadequacy   41–2, 74
    resolutions   17, 29, 35, 91.i, 102
    U.K. contribution   79, 104
    United States   49, 143
Military Committee (N.A.T.)   2, Appendix
    European defence   102, 115–6
    M.C. 30 report   106, 115–6, 130

Pleven/U.S. plans   91.i, 98, 101
Washn. meeting   66, 72, 85, 91.i, 101

Military Production, Supplies &
Equipment
Acheson   9, 17, 21, 29.i, 33, 41, 145
Belgium   83
Bevin   14, 17, 145
Committee of 7   17
France   79
German production   74, 92, 112.i
Moch   41
M.P.S.B.   2, 33, 37, 41, 72.i, 74,
   Appendix
Schuman   13, 32
Shinwell   42, 102
supplies   14, 92, 112

Military Security Board   60, 70, 74

Moch, J.   1
financial talks in Washn.   54, 58, 63
French divisions   46, 63, 65
intransigence   46, 56, 63, 65, 73, 87, 91,
   94, 95, 98, 99, 101
Königsberg   63
less rigid   94, 96
main statements   41–2, 46, 63, 91
Marshall   87.i
Marshall formula   42, 52
New York   31, 36, 41–2, 46, 52, 56
personality   31
Pleven plan   91
Shinwell   54, 63

Mollet, G.   84, 99

Molotov   78

Monnet, J.   84
McCloy   88

Montgomery, Field-Marshal Sir B.   2
Attlee   36
future of   7.i, 85
rearmament   36

Morland, O.C.   27

Morrison, H.S.   27
rearmament   128

Mutual Defence Assistance Programme
(M.D.A.P.)   1, 9, 49

National Service   1, 2, 14, 30, 42, 83–4,
   137

Netherlands (*see also* Benelux)
German rearmament   32, 35.i, 73, 92,
   109, 114
N.A.T.O. High Commissioner   114–5,
   119, 123, 129–30
Pleven plan   92, 116
Rhine defence line   10, 29.i, 30, 76
Socialist pressure   50
Standing Group   37

New York Conferences (Sept. 1950)   2, 6
adjournments   21, 26, 34–5, 47
Benelux   26, 42, 44
Bevin–Acheson   9–11, 28, 50, 52
Bevin–Schuman   28, 31
communiqués   21, 26, 26.ii, 34–5, 47
defence decisions   26.ii, 42–4, 47, 56, 68
Defence Ministers   31, 41–4
Deputies   34–5
Foreign Ministers   13–18, 25–26.ii, 31,
   41–4
N.A.C.   17, 29, 29.i, 32, 34, 35, 35.i, 47.i
Occupation decisions   26, 26.i–ii, 45.i,
   55, 62
progress   37, 39, 46, 62
records   13, 26
resolutions   17, 29, 34–35.i, 43, 44, 47,
   67

New Zealand *see* Commonwealth

Nichols, Sir P.   50

Niemöller, Pastor   64

Nitze, P.   11

Nitze Plan   11, 53, 79, 79.i (text), 79.ii, 104

Noble, Sir A.   39

North Atlantic Council (N.A.C.)   1 *see*
New York and Brussels confs.

North Atlantic Treaty   1, 2, Appendix (*see*
also N.A.T.O. reorganisation)
Bevin   35, 41, 73
Commonwealth   92
France   84, 98, 111, 114, 117–8, 121
Germany   1.iii, 37, 73.i, 84, 91.i, 111,
   121, 139.i, 149
Greece   26
Ocean Shipping Board   34
O.E.E.C.   11, 34–5, 83
Portugal   34
Regional Planning groups   2, 33,
   Appendix

North Atlantic Treaty *contd.*
  Schuman 111, 117
  Spain 34
  Turkey 26, 34, 91.i
  two zones 84
N.A.T.O. High Commissioner 114–5,
  119, 123, 129–30
N.A.T.O. Reorganisation Appendix (*see
  also* Supreme Commander; unified
  force)
  Bevin 2, 83, 85, 100.i, 145.ii
  Brussels Treaty 38, 83, 85, 96, 145.i–ii
  Canadian proposals 85, 145.ii
  C.O.S. 3.ii, 7.i
  France 96
  N.A.C. resolution 47
  Shinwell 85
  U.K. proposals 2, 3.ii, 7.i, 85
  Washington 76, 91.i, 101
Norway
  Pleven plan 98, 114

O'Neill, C. 120.i
**Organisation for European Economic
  Cooperation (O.E.E.C.)**
  N.A.T.O. 11, 34–5, 83

Pakenham, Lord 27.i
Pakistan *see* Commonwealth
Paris Conferences
  Germany (Nov '49) 10
  Pleven plan (Feb '51) 84, 91, 109, 127,
    129, 136, 148
  Soviet proposal (Dec '50) 110, 122, 138
Parker, Sir H. 112
Parodi, A. 54
  C.F.M. 97
  French Cabinet 54, 54.i, 57
  Pleven plan 80
Pearson, L.B. 34
Penson, J.H. 5
  N.Y. decisions 62
Perkins, G.W. 49
Petersberg Protocol 4
Petrie, J.C. 145
Petsche, M. 54

Phillips, Morgan 50, 77

Pleven, R. 2
  Attlee 121, 123
  Königsberg 65
  military units 88, 121
  Pleven plan 88, 99, 121, 123
  police force 2
  regrets N.Y. tactics 65, 71
  Supreme Commander 121

Pleven Plan for European Army (*see also*
  Spofford plan) 80.i (text)
  Acheson 66, 80, 82, 84, 90, 92–3, 132
  Adenauer 81, 96, 103, 103.i
  A.O.C. 107
  Attlee 101, 118, 121, 123, 131–2
  Belgium 83, 92, 98, 114, 117–8
  Bevin 80, 83, 85, 90, 92, 114–6, 118–9
  Bohlen 66, 81
  Bruce 93
  'cancer' 115, 119
  Canada 91.i
  C.O.S. 82, 106.i, 116–8
  counter-plans 101, 106–107.i, 109,
    114, 115 (text), 116–8
  Denmark 91, 98, 119.i
  Deputies/M.C. 91.i, 96, 98, 101, 107,
    115–6, 130, 136
  elaborated 87.i, 88, 99, 107
  European integration 99, 120, 127,
    129, 141, 148
  finance 89
  French Cabinet 80, 88, 99
    isolation 95–6, 98
    military 93
  German equality 80, 88, 96, 103, 120
    Occupation 103.ii, 120, 139, 141
    preference 94, 96, 120.i
    resentment 81, 88, 96, 98, 103
  Germany & N.A.T.O. 84, 114, 121
  Harvey 80–1
  Iceland 119.i
  Italy 96, 98, 114, 119.i
  Kirkpatrick 101
  level of unit 81, 84, 87.i, 88, 95–6
  Luxembourg 98, 117, 119.i
  Marshall 87, 98
  Massigli 84.i
  McCloy 88
  'mere façade' 118

'miasmic cloud' 87
Moch 87.i, 91
Monnet 84, 96
motives 64, 66, 81–2, 84, 84.i, 87–9, 92–3
N.A.C./Defence Cttee. 90, 91, 91.i, 98, 109
Netherlands 92, 98, 114–6, 118–9, 123
Norway 98, 114, 118, 119.i
Paris conf. 84, 109, 127, 129, 136, 148
Pleven 88, 99, 121, 123
Portugal 91, 98, 119.i
Schuman 64, 88, 90, 96, 117, 121, 124
Schuman plan 80–1, 84, 88, 96, 139
Shinwell 87, 91
Spofford bargain 132
U.K. Observer 148
   participation 80–1, 88, 114–5
   reaction 81–2, 84–5, 87, 89, 92, 98, 116–9, 131–2, 139
   rejection 92, 118–9
U.S. 109, 120, 127, 129, 132
viability 84, 88, 91–2, 96, 107.i, 109, 115–8, 119.i

Plowden, Sir E. 112

Poncet *see* François-Poncet

Portugal
German rearmament 29.i, 41
Spain/N.A.T.O. 34

Potsdam Conference (1945) 24, 78

Prague Conference (Oct. '50) 78 (*see also* Soviet proposal for C.F.M.)

Price, C.R. 7

Prohibited and Limited Industries (P.L.I.)
Agreement 4
Bevin 5
Brussels 147
I.G.G. negotiations 55, 113, 140, 147
New York 26.ii, 45.i, 55

Public Opinion
European 32, 37
France 13, 19, 21, 36, 42, 54.i, 65, 78, 83, 98, 110.i
Germany 18–9, 21, 37, 48, 55, 103, 120, 146
U.K. 1.ii, 14–15, 83, 110, 122, 146
U.S. 13, 146

Queuille, H. 36

Rasmussen, G. 44
Raw Materials
Bevin 17, 114
Central Group 124, 131, 145
Commonwealth 11, 49, 124.i
E.P.C. 124
German assurances 26.ii, 45, 60, 147, 149
Moch 41–2
N.A.C. resolution 17, 35
Schuman 17
U.S. stock piling 49, 104, 124
Washn. discussions 53.i, 128, 131, 143

Regional Planning Groups *see* N.A.T.

Reinstein, J.J. 62

Reorganisation of N.A.T.O. *see* N.A.T.O. reorgn.

Rhine defence line *see* **European defence lines**

Rickett, D.H.F. 23

Rowan, Sir L. 11

Rowlands, Sir A. 112

Russia Committee 73

Safeguards
agreed 136
compared 67.i
France 89, 105, 109
German attitude 48, 67
Kirkpatrick 67, 70, 74
Deputies' report 106, 115, 130, 133, 136
U.K./C.O.S. 54.ii, 67, 74, 106–7
U.S. 33, 67–8, 72.i

Sandys, D. 20

Schumacher, Dr. K. 3.iii, 6
C.F.M. 103
German rearmament 3.iii, 26, 45.ii, 48
N.Y. decisions 45.ii
Pleven plan 81, 96, 103
Spofford plan 135

Schuman, R. 2
Attlee 121, 123
bargaining with F.R.G. 16, 21, 32, 64

Schuman, R. *contd.*
Bevin 6, 28, 31, 32, 110, 121
European integration 41, 111, 120,
  127, 129, 132–3
finance 13, 22
German industrial contribution 21, 32
  labour units 21, 32, 35.i
  military units 21, 25
  Occupation 6, 41
  police 2, 6, 16, 28, 46
Germany & N.A.T.O. 121
international legion 21, 27
Metz speech 64, 73
Moch 31, 64–5, 99
N.A.T.O. temporary 111, 117
Pleven plan 88, 90, 96, 99, 117, 121
raw materials 17
Schuman plan 41, 64
secrecy 28
timing 6, 13, 21, 32, 35, 41, 64
unperturbed 35, 64
U.S. forces in Europe 13

Schuman Plan
German equality 55
  hesitations 41
    Occupation 139, 140
Pleven plan 80–1, 84, 88, 96, 114
progress 80, 88
U.K. 64, 80, 139

Schwerin, Count G. von, 71, 73.i, 96

Security Guarantee for F.R.G. 3, 16, 26.ii,
  45, 55

Seeckt, H. von, 6

Sforza, Count C. 32
Soviet pressure 141

S.H.A.E.F. 9

S.H.A.P.E. 116

Shawcross, Sir H. 58, 97

Shinwell, E. 27
Atlantic Confederate Force 118
finance 42, 102
French attitude 58, 95, 101, 118
German military units 42, 68
H. of C. 8, 23
Moch 46, 63, 73
N.A.T.O. reorgn. 85
Pleven plan 87, 91, 95, 118

rearmament cttee. 63, 65, 68
Soviet danger 125–6
U.K. defence effort 102, 104

Shuckburgh, C.A.E. 12

Slessor, Sir J. 3

Slim, Field-Marshal Sir W. 3, 12

Snyder, J.W. 1

South East Asia 110.i

Soviet Proposal for C.F.M. on
  Germany 78, 86, 146
Acheson 78, 86, 97, 146, 148
Adenauer 97, 103.i
agenda 97, 110, 110.i, 121–2
Allied differences 138
Allied replies 97, 110, 146, 148
alternatives 122
atomic energy 122
Austria 78, 86, 110.i, 121, 141, 146
Benelux 141, 146
Bevin 78, 86, 97, 110, 118, 121–2,
  136–9, 146
Brussels conf. 141, 146, 148
'burial procedure' 110
Cabinet 78, 97, 121–2, 136–8
France 78, 84.i, 86, 97, 110, 121, 141
German rearmament 86, 110
Germany 78, 86, 97, 120.i, 122, 141,
  146
Kelly 78, 86
motives 78, 86, 141–2, 146, 148
'olive branch' 86
Paris officials 110, 121–2, 128, 138
Prague communiqué 78
public opinion 110, 122, 146
Schumacher 103.i
Schuman 97, 110, 121, 146
Soviet Notes 78, 86, 138

Soviet Union (*see also* German military
  units; Soviet proposal for C.F.M.)
Far East 146
France 46, 78, 99, 121, 141
Germany 74, 105, 141, 146
military strength 46
non-aggression pact 122
peace campaign 78
percentage agreement (1944) 122.ii
U.S. forces in Europe 83

Spofford, C.M. 1

Spofford Plan   109, 109.i (text)
  Adenauer   135–6
  agreed   133, 136, 144
  Cabinet   118–9, 136–7
  Deputies   109, 119.i, 128, 130, 133, 136
  European integration   109, 127, 129–32
  France   119, 120–1, 123, 130–3
  German opposition   135–7
  H. of C. (29 Nov.)   119
  implementation   136, 137, 139, 144–5, 147.ii
  McCloy   109
  Netherlands   109
  origins   98.i
  timing   128, 133, 133.i, 135–6, 139, 144
  U.K.   115–6, 119, 133, 136–7

Stalin, J.V.   97

Standing Group (N.A.T.)   2
  authority   33, 37, 47, 47.ii, 100.i
  M.C. 30 report   106, 115–6
  N.A.C. resolution   47

Starkenborgh, Dr.   109

Steel, C.E.   15, 119

Sterling Balances   11, 49, 53, 79, 100

Stevens, R.B.   61

Stikker, D.   10
  Benelux consultation   10, 26
  Council of Europe   34
  German rearmament   32, 35.i, 73, 114
  N.A.T.O. High Commissioner   114–5, 119, 123
  O.E.E.C./N.A.T.O.   34–5
  Rhine defence line   10, 29.i

Stimson, H.   72

Strachey, J.   101

Strang, Sir W.   6, 7
  cold war   122.ii
  C.F.M.   142
  German Army   24, 126
  German equality   111
  Moscow mission   146
  Pleven plan   84, 123
  Soviet danger   126, 142
  U.S. tactics   94

Strauss, G.R.   101
  raw materials   124

Strong, Gen. K.   73.i

Study Group see I.G.G.

Supreme Commander   2, 131, 144–5
  Acheson   9, 28, 120, 145
  Adenauer   135
  Attlee   118, 121
  authority   33, 37, 47, 47.ii
  command structure   33, 37, 47, 47.ii
  C.O.S.   33, 82, 136
  delay   17, 28, 98
  Denmark   34, 47.i
  Eisenhower   85, 131–2, 136, 144–5
  France   6, 98, 121
  Italy   98
  Montgomery   85
  Norway   34, 47.i
  Portugal   34, 47.i
  pressed by U.K.   119–21, 127, 132, 137, 139
  significance   73
  timing   17, 33, 47, 85
  Truman   120, 131–2, 145

Syrian-Iraqi resolution   110

Tedder, Lord   2.i

Todt Organisation   41

Tomlinson, G.   27

Truman, H.S.   1
  atomic bomb   121, 127
  European integration   127
  Supreme Commander   120, 131–2, 145
  U.K. partner   131
  U.S. forces in Europe   1, 9, 14, 17, 18, 120, 131–2

Turkey
  N.A.T.O.   26, 34, 91.i

Unified Force (see also German military units; N.A.T.O. reorgn.; Supreme Commander; Spofford plan)
  proposed by U.S.   2, 33
  agreed   144

  Acheson   9, 21, 29, 41
  Attlee   2, 85
  Benelux   37
  Bevin   2, 33, 41, 56, 58, 83, 85
  Cabinet   2, 27, 58, 137
  command structure   29, 33, 37, 44, 47

Unified Force *contd.*
C.O.S. 7, 44, 74
Defence Committee 47
Denmark 34, 35.i, 41
Deputies 34–5
French Cabinet 41, 73
Marshall formula 42–3
Moch 63
N.A.C. resolution 17, 29, 44, 47 (text)
N.Y. decisions 44, 47, 56
Norway 34, 35.i, 41
origins 2.i, 41, 121
package with German units 29, 29.i,
33, 37, 41, 50, 56
Pentagon 2.i
Pleven plan 91, 98, 101
Portugal 34, 35.i, 41
progress 41, 44
Standing Group 44, 47

United Kingdom
bipartisan policy 20, 41, 114
Commonwealth 79, 100, 110
economic strength 11.i, 22, 49, 53, 79,
104, 112, 134
forces in Europe 1, 2, 41, 68
Labour Party 50, 94
national service 1, 2, 14, 30, 42
sterling balances 49
U.S. partner 49, 79, 131–2, 137, 143

United Nations
China 39
General Assembly 2
Iraqi-Syrian resolution 110, 122

United States of America
defence strategy 25, 29–30, 56, 58, 73
elections 46
European integration 120, 127, 129–
30
German alliance 38, 83
German Ambassadors 4, 55
loan to U.K. 49, 53
state of emergency 142
stockpiling 49, 104, 124
unreliability 24, 38, 143

U.S. aid for defence *see* Finance of
defence

U.S. forces in Europe
Acheson 9, 13, 25, 33, 50, 131–2, 145

Bevin 1, 10, 14, 56, 83
implementation 118, 126, 131–2, 136
Korea 6, 9, 17, 120, 126, 128
Moch 42
numbers 1, 68, 132
package 18–20, 23, 25, 27, 29, 29.i, 33,
37, 41, 50, 56, 71
preferable to financial aid 104
Schuman 13, 56
Soviet reaction 83
Truman 1, 131–2, 145
U.S. commitment 2, 27, 33, 42, 50, 71,
73, 143

Vyshinsky, A. 98

Wansbrough-Jones, Lt.-Gen. 60

Warsaw Conference (1948) 78

Washington Conferences 1950
Oct. *Defence Ministers*
agenda 76, 85, 87
arrangements 44, 46
briefing 68, 76, 85
C.O.S. 68, 72, 82
Defence Committee 91, 91.i
East–West trade 91.i
finance of defence 76, 79
Marshall-Shinwell 87
Marshall-Moch 87.i
M.T.P. 85, 91.i, 102
Military Committee 66, 72, 85, 91.i
N.A.T.O. reorgn. 76, 85, 91.i
Personal reps. 64, 66, 70, 72, 80, 82
Pleven plan 85, 91
review 98, 101
Standing Group 85
Turkey 91.i
unified force resolution 64, 67–8, 70,
72.i (text), 91
U.S. silence 98
Dec. *Attlee/Truman* 121
atomic bomb 121, 127
East–West trade 131.i
European integration 127, 129, 131–2
Far East 121, 127
France 121
liaison 124, 131
meetings 127, 131–2, 134
military talks 131

Ottawa 121, 133
raw materials 124, 128, 131, 143, 145
Spofford plan 121, 131–3, 143
U.K. defence effort 124, 131.i, 132,
 134
U.S. partnership 131–2, 143
Watson, J.H.A. 94
Western Union *see* Brussels Treaty
Whiteley, W. 92
Wilford, K.M. 128
Wilgress, D. 85
Williams, T. 27
Wilson, J.H. 27
Wilson-Smith, Sir H. 49
Woods, Sir J. 112

World Peace Congress 122

Yalta Conference 1945 57
Young, G.P. 46.i
 French govt. 46.i, 75
Younger, K. 6
 Massigli 36
Yugoslavia
 economic aid 26.ii

Zeeland, P. van 32, 83
 Brussels treaty 83, 85
 German rearmament 32, 83
 O.E.E.C. 83
 Pleven plan 83, 90, 92

Printed in the United Kingdom for Her Majesty's Stationery Office
Dd291404 3/89 C11 56-1065 10170